Kierkegaard, Søren	
Leibniz, Gottfried	
Leucippus	
Locke, John	1632–1704
Lucretius	ca. 96–55 B.C.
Marx, Karl	1818–1883
Merleau-Ponty, Maurice	1908–1961
Mill, John Stuart	1806–1873
Montaigne, Michel de	1533–1592
Newton, Sir Isaac	1642–1727
Nietzsche, Friedrich	1844–1900
Pascal, Blaise	1623–1662
Peirce, Charles S.	1839–1914
Plato	ca. 428–ca. 348 B.C.
Protagoras	ca. 490–421 B.C.
Pyrrho	ca. 361–ca. 270 B.C.
Pythagoras active	ca. 525–500 B.C.
Quine, W. V. O.	1908–
Rawls, John	1921–
Rorty, Richard	1931–
Rousseau, J. J.	1712–1778
Russell, Bertrand	1872–1970
Ryle, Gilbert	1900–1976
Sartre, Jean-Paul	1905–1980
Schopenhauer, Arthur	1788–1860
Sextus Empiricus	ca. 200
Socrates	ca. 470–399 B.C.
Spinoza, Baruch	1632–1677
Thales	624–546 B.C.
Whitehead, Alfred North	1861–1947
Wittgenstein, Ludwig	1889–1951
Zeno	b. ca. 489 B.C.

Socrates to Sartre and Beyond

A History of Philosophy

SEVENTH EDITION

Samuel Enoch Stumpf
Late, of Vanderbilt University

James Fieser
University of Tennessee

Boston   Burr Ridge, IL   Dubuque, IA   Madison, WI   New York   San Francisco   St. Louis
Bangkok   Bogotá   Caracas   Kuala Lumpur   Lisbon   London   Madrid   Mexico City
Milan   Montreal   New Delhi   Santiago   Seoul   Singapore   Sydney   Taipei   Toronto

McGraw-Hill Higher Education

A Division of The **McGraw-Hill** Companies

SOCRATES TO SARTRE AND BEYOND
Published by McGraw-Hill, a business unit of The McGraw-Hill Companies, Inc., 1221 Avenue of the Americas, New York, NY, 10020. Copyright © 2003, 1999, 1993, 1988, 1982, 1975, and 1966, by The McGraw-Hill Companies, Inc. All rights reserved. No part of this publication may be reproduced or distributed in any form or by any means, or stored in a database or retrieval system, without the prior written consent of The McGraw-Hill Companies, Inc., including, but not limited to, in any network or other electronic storage or transmission, or broadcast for distance learning. Some ancillaries, including electronic and print components, may not be available to customers outside the United States.

This book is printed on acid-free paper.

3 4 5 6 7 8 9 0 FGR/FGR 0 9 8 7 6 5 4 3

ISBN 0-07-256078-9

Publisher: *Kenneth King*
Sponsoring editor: *Jon-David Hague*
Marketing manager: *Greg Brueck*
Senior project manager: *Jean Hamilton*
Lead production supervisor: *Lori Koetters*
Senior designer: *Matthew Baldwin/Laurie Entringer*
Cover design: *Matthew Baldwin*
Cover image: *Georgio DiChirico,* The Great Machine, © Super Stock/ARS
Typeface: *10/12 Palatino*
Compositor: *Shepherd Incorporated*
Printer: *Quebecor World Fairfield, Inc.*

Library of Congress Cataloging-in-Publication Data

Stumpf, Samuel Enoch, 1918–1998
 Socrates to Sartre and Beyond: a history of philosophy / Samuel Enoch Stumpf.—7th ed.
   p. cm.
 Includes bibliographical references and index.
 ISBN 0-07-256078-9 (alk. paper)
  1. Philosophy—History. I. Title
 B72 .S79 2003
 190—dc21

                                                                    2002070957

http://www.mhhe.com

About the Authors

SAMUEL ENOCH STUMPF received his Ph.D. from the University of Chicago. He was a Ford Fellow at Harvard University and a Rockefeller Fellow at Oxford University. For 15 years he was chairman of the Philosophy Department at Vanderbilt University, served a term as president of Cornell College of Iowa, and returned to Vanderbilt as Professor of the Philosophy of Law in the School of Law and as Research Professor of Medical Philosophy in the School of Medicine. He participated in various national organizations and lectured widely in the fields of philosophy, medical ethics, and jurisprudence and was Emeritus Professor of Philosophy and Law at Vanderbilt University. Professor Stumpf died in 1998.

JAMES FIESER received his Ph.D. from Purdue University and is Associate Professor of Philosophy at the University of Tennessee at Martin. He is author of *Moral Philosophy through the Ages* (2001) and coauthor, with Norman Lillegard, of *A Historical Introduction to Philosophy* (2002). He is editor of *Metaethics, Normative Ethics, and Applied Ethics* (2000), the ten-volume *Early Responses to Hume* (1999–2003), the five-volume *Scottish Common Sense Philosophy* (2000), and coeditor of *Scriptures of the World's Religions* with John Powers. Dr. Fieser is the founder and general editor of the *Internet Encyclopedia of Philosophy*.

Contents

Part Three
EARLY MODERN PHILOSOPHY

Part Four
LATE MODERN AND 19TH CENTURY PHILOSOPHY

Part Five
20TH CENTURY AND CONTEMPORARY PHILOSOPHY

Preface

The history of philosophy is in many ways like an epic novel. There are revered ancestors who, through great suffering, establish traditions for the betterment of their descendents. There are black sheep of the family who stir up trouble, embarrass their brothers and sisters, and sometimes even invite the wrath of political authorities. There are bitter feuds between families that last generations, often with no clear victor ever emerging. As the saga passes from one era to another, there is some feeling of progress. Old-fashioned ways are discarded and replaced with new—although sometimes faddish—ones. Thus, the history of philosophy is an adventure of ideas, to use the words of one great philosopher. This book attempts to describe a major thread of that drama.

Changes in the Seventh Edition

- The most visible change in this seventh edition is the reorganization of several chapters.
- Shorter chapters have been combined into longer ones of similar length.
- Chapters covering 19th- and 20th-century philosophy have been arranged more chronologically, and a largely new chapter on recent philosophy appears at the close.
- Except for a short discussion of Rousseau, all of the figures covered in the previous edition appear here as well.
- The style of the book is revised throughout, with the interests of newer readers in mind.
- Some sections are completely rewritten and others stated more concisely, all with the goal of greater clarity.

James Fieser

PART ONE

The Ancient Greek Philosophy

CHAPTER 1

Socrates' Predecessors

*H*uman beings have lived on this planet for hundreds of thousands of years. We, of course, cannot know all the experiences and thoughts of the earliest people. Still, it is reasonable to suppose that people then, as now, were driven by a desire to explain the world. Perhaps our earliest ancestors thought about how the world was formed, whether they were unique among the animals, and whether there was a world beyond the earthly one surrounding them. They may have also wondered whether there was a uniform standard of moral behavior or social order that applied to the various tribes they encountered. Whatever they may have thought about these subjects, their opinions are now irretrievably lost through time. It is only through the introduction of writing—a comparatively recent invention—that we know the precise speculations of any of our ancestors. When we look at the earliest writings from around the globe, we find that various regions had their own speculative traditions—such as those of East Asia, the Indian subcontinent, the Middle East, and Africa. This book is an account of one such tradition, namely that which developed within Europe and was later exported to the Americas and elsewhere around the world. This tradition is often called "Western," designating its origin within the western part of the Eurasian landmass.

The story of Western philosophy begins in a series of Greek islands and colonies during the sixth century BCE (that is, *Before the Common Era*). Some original thinkers were driven by very specific puzzles, most notably, "what are things really like?" and "how can we explain the process of change in things?" The solutions they gave to these puzzles were shortly thereafter dubbed "philosophy"—the love of wisdom. What underlies these speculations was the gradual recognition that things are not exactly what they seem to be. Appearance often differs from reality. There are brute facts of birth, death, growth, and decay—coming into being and passing away. These facts raised sweeping questions of how things and people come into existence, can be different at different times, and pass out of existence only to be followed by other things and persons. Many of the answers given to these questions by the earliest philosophers are not as important as the fact that they focused upon these *specific* questions. They approached these problems with a fresh and new point of view that was in stark contrast to the more mythical approach taken by the great poets of the time.

The birthplace of Greek philosophy was the seaport town of Miletus, located across the Aegean Sea from Athens, on the western shores of Ionia in Asia Minor. Because of their location, the first Greek philosophers are called either Milesians or Ionians. By the time the Milesian philosophers began their systematic work, roughly around 585 BCE, Miletus had been a crossroads for both seaborne commerce and for cosmopolitan ideas. The wealth of the city allowed for leisure time, without which the life of art and philosophy could not develop. Further, the broad-mindedness and inquisitiveness of its people created a congenial atmosphere for philosophical intellectual activity. Earlier, Ionia had produced Homer (*c.* 700 BCE), author of the *Iliad* and *Odyssey*. In these timeless classics of epic poetry, Homer describes the scene of Mount Olympus, where the gods pursued lives very similar to that of their human counterparts on earth. This poetic view of the world also depicted ways in which the gods intruded into people's affairs. In particular, the Homeric gods would punish people for their lack of moderation and especially for their pride or insubordination, which the Greeks called *hubris*. It is not that Homer's gods were exceptionally moral beings. Instead, they were merely *stronger* than us and demanded obedience.

Although Homer depicts the gods with largely human features, he occasionally hints at a rigorous order in nature. Specifically, he suggests that there is a power called "fate," to which even the gods are subject, and to which everyone and everything must be subordinate. Nevertheless, Homer's poetic imagination is dominated so thoroughly by human terms that his world is peopled everywhere with human types. Also, his conception of nature is that of capricious wills at work instead of the reign of physical natural laws. It was Hesiod (*c.* 700 BCE), writing around the same time as Homer, who altered this concept of the gods and fate. He thus removed from the gods all capriciousness and instead ascribed to them a moral consistency. Although Hesiod retains the notion that the gods control nature, he balances this personal element in the nature of things with an emphasis upon the impersonal operation of the moral law of the universe. The moral order, in Hesiod's view, is still the product of Zeus' commands. However, contrary to Homer, these commands are neither capricious nor calculated to gratify the gods, but are instead fashioned for the good of people. For Hesiod the universe is a moral order, and from this idea it is a short step to say, without *any* reference to the gods, that there is an impersonal force controlling the structure of the universe and regulating its process of changes.

This was the short step taken by three great Milesian philosophers, namely Thales (*c.* 585 BCE), Anaximander (*c.* 610–*c.* 546 BCE), and Anaximenes (6th. century BCE). Whereas Hesiod still thought in terms of traditional mythology with human-like gods, philosophy among the Milesians began as an act of independent thought. To ask, as they did, "What are things really like?" and "How can we explain the process of change in things?" substantially departs from the poetry of Homer and Hesiod and a movement toward a more scientific way of thinking. In point of fact, at this stage of history science and philosophy were the same thing, and only later did various specific disciplines separate themselves from the field of philosophy. Medicine was the first to do so. Thus, we can rightly call the Milesians primitive scientists, as well as the first Greek philosophers. The important thing to keep in mind, though, is that Greek philosophy from the start was an *intellectual* activity. It was not a matter only of seeing or believing, but of *thinking*, and philosophy meant thinking about basic questions with an attitude of genuine and free inquiry.

WHAT IS PERMANENT IN EXISTENCE?

Thales

We do not know as much as we would like about Thales of Miletus, and what we do know is rather anecdotal in nature. He left no writings. All that is available are fragmentary references to him made by later writers who recorded memorable incidents in his career. He was a contemporary of Greek king Croesus and statesman Solon, and the years of his life are set between 624 and 546 BCE. During a military campaign against Persia, he apparently solved the difficult logistical problem of enabling the Lydian king's army to cross the wide Halys river. His solution was to dig a channel that diverted part of the flow, thereby making two narrower rivers over which bridges could be built. While traveling in Egypt, Thales worked out a way of measuring the height of the pyramids. His solution here was to use the simple procedure of measuring a pyramid's shadow at that time of day when his own shadow was equal in length to his own height. It may have been during these Egyptian travels, too, that he became acquainted with the kinds of knowledge that enabled him to predict the eclipse of the sun on May 28, 585 BCE. In a practical vein, while in Miletus, he constructed an instrument for measuring the distance of ships sighted at sea. And, as an aid to navigation, he urged sailors to use the constellation Little Bear as the surest guide for determining the direction of the north.

It was probably inevitable that tradition would attach questionable tales to such an extraordinary person as Thales. For example, Plato (427–347 BCE) writes about "the jest which the clever witty Thracian handmaid is said to have made about Thales, when he fell into a well as he was looking up at the stars. She said that he was so eager to know what was going on in heaven that he could not see what was before his feet." Plato adds that "this is a jest which is equally applicable to all philosophers." Aristotle (384–322 BCE) describes another episode:

> There is . . . the story which is told of Thales of Miletus. It is a story about a scheme for making money, which is fathered on Thales owing to his reputation for wisdom. . . . He was reproached for his poverty, which was supposed to show the uselessness of philosophy. But observing from his knowledge of meteorology (as the story goes) that there was likely to be a heavy crop of olives

[during the next summer], and having a small sum at his command, he paid down earnest-money, early in the year, for the hire of all the olive-presses in Miletus and Chios. And he managed, in the absence of any higher offer, to secure them at a low rate. When the season came, and there was a sudden and simultaneous demand for a number of presses, he let out the stock he had collected at any rate he chose to fix; and making a considerable fortune, he succeeded in proving that it is easy for philosophers to become rich if they so desire, though it is not the business which they are really about.

But Thales is famous not for his general wisdom or his practical shrewdness, but because he opened up a new area of thought for which he has rightly earned the title of the first philosopher of Western civilization.

Thales' novel inquiry concerns the nature of things. What is everything made of, or what kind of "stuff" goes into the composition of things? With these questions Thales was trying to account for the fact that there are many different kinds of things, such as earth, clouds, and oceans. From time to time some of these things change into something else, and yet they still resemble each other in certain ways. Thales' unique contribution to thought was his notion that, in spite of the differences between various things, there is nevertheless a basic similarity between them all. *The many* are related to each other by *the One.* He assumed that some single element, some "stuff," a stuff which contained its own principle of action or change, lay at the foundation of all physical reality. To him this One, or this stuff, is *water.*

Although there is no record of how Thales came to the conclusion that water is the cause of all things, Aristotle writes that he might have derived it from observation of simple events, "perhaps from seeing that the nutriment of all things is moist, and that heat is generated from the moist and kept alive by it." Aristotle continues, that Thales "got his notion from this fact and from the fact that the seeds of all things have a moist nature, and water is the origin of the nature of moist things." Other phenomena such as evaporation or freezing also suggest that water takes on different forms. But the accuracy of Thales' analysis of the composition of things is far less important than the fact that he raised the question concerning the nature of the world. His question set the stage for a new kind of inquiry, one that could be debated on its merits and could either be confirmed or refuted by further analysis. Admittedly, Thales also said that "all things are full of gods." But this notion apparently had no theological significance for him. Thus, when he tried to explain the power in things, such as magnetic powers in stones, he shifted the discussion from a mythological base to one of scientific inquiry. From his starting point, others were to follow with alternative solutions, but always with his problem before them.

Anaximander

Anaximander was a younger contemporary and a pupil of Thales. He agreed with his teacher that there is some single basic stuff out of which everything comes. Unlike Thales, however, Anaximander said that this basic stuff is neither water nor any other specific element. Water and all other definite things, he argued, are only specific variations or offshoots of something that is more primary. It may well be, he thought, that we might find water or moisture in various forms everywhere. Water is only one specific thing among many other elements, and all these specific things need some more elementary stuff to account for their origin. The primary substance out of which all these specific things come, Anaximander argued, is an *indefinite* or *boundless* realm. Thus, on the one hand, we find specific and determinate things in the world, like a rock or a puddle of water; yet, on the other hand, we find the origin of these things, which he calls the *indeterminate boundless.* Whereas actual things are specific, their source is indeterminate, and whereas things are finite, the original stuff is infinite or boundless.

Besides offering a new idea about the original substance of things, Anaximander advanced the enterprise of philosophy by attempting some explanation for his new idea. Thales had not dealt in any detail with the problem of explaining how the primary stuff became the many different things we see in the world. Anaximander, though, addressed this question precisely. Although his explanation may seem strange, it represents an advance in knowledge. Specifically, it deals with known facts from which hypotheses can be formulated, instead of explaining natural phenomena in mythical and nondebatable terms. His explanation is this. The indeterminate boundless is the unoriginated and indestructible primary substance of things, yet, he believes, it also has eternal motion. As a consequence of this motion, the various specific elements come into being as they "separated off" from the original substance. Thus "there was an eternal motion in which the heavens came to be." First *warm* and *cold* were separated off, and from these two came *moist;* then from these came *earth* and *air.*

Turning to the origin of human life, Anaximander said that all life comes from the sea and that, in the course of time, living things came out of the sea to dry land. He suggested that people evolved from creatures of a different kind. This, he argued, follows from the fact that other creatures are quickly self-supporting, whereas humans alone need prolonged nursing and that, therefore, we would not have survived if this had been our original form. Commenting on Anaximander's account of the origin of human beings, Plutarch writes that the Syrians

> actually revere the fish as being of similar race and nurturing. In this they philosophize more suitably than Anaximander. For he declares, not that fishes and men came into being in the same parents, but that originally men came into being inside fishes. Having been nurtured there—like sharks—and having become adequate to look after themselves, they then came forth and took to the land.

Returning again to the vast cosmic scene, Anaximander thought that there were many worlds and many systems of universes existing all at the same time. All of them die out and there is a constant alternation between their creation and destruction. This cyclical process, he believed, was a matter of rigorous necessity. Opposite forces in nature conflict and cause an "injustice"—

poetically speaking—which requires their ultimate destruction. The only sentence that survives from Anaximander's writings makes this point, again somewhat poetically: "From what source things arise, to that they return of necessity when they are destroyed; for they suffer punishment and make reparation to one another for their injustice according to the order of time."

Anaximenes

The third and last of the Milesian philosophers was Anaximenes (about 585–528 BCE), who was a young associate of Anaximander. He considered Anaximander's answer to the question concerning the composition of natural things, but was dissatisfied with it. The notion of the *boundless* as being the source of all things was simply too vague and intangible. He could understand why Anaximander chose this solution over Thales' notion that water is the cause of all things. The boundless could at least help explain the "infinite" background to the wide variety of finite and specific things. Still, the indeterminate boundless had no specific meaning for Anaximenes, and he, therefore, chose to focus upon a definite substance the way Thales did. Yet, at the same time, tried to incorporate the advance achieved by Anaximander.

Attempting to mediate between the two views of his predecessors, Anaximenes designated *air* as the primary substance from which all things come. Like Thales' notion of water, air is a definite substance, and we can readily see it at the root of all things. For example, although air is invisible, we live only as long as we can breathe, and "just as our soul, being air, holds us together, so do breath and air encompass the whole world." Like Anaximander's view of the boundless in continued motion, air is spread everywhere—although unlike the boundless, it is a specific and tangible material substance that can be identified. Moreover, the air's motion is a far more specific process than Anaximander's "separating off." To explain how air is the origin of all things, Anaximenes argued that things are what they are by virtue of how condensed or expanded the air is that makes up those things. In making this point he introduced the important new idea that differences in *quality* are caused by differences in *quantity*. The expansion and contraction of air represent quantitative changes, and these changes occurring in a single substance account for the variety of different things that we see in the world around us. Expansion of air causes warming and, at the extreme, fire, whereas contraction, or condensation, causes cooling and the transformation of air into solids by way of a gradual transition where, as Anaximenes says, "air that is condensed forms winds . . . if this process goes further, it gives water, still further earth, and the greatest condensation of all is found in stones."

Although these Milesian philosophers proceeded with scientific concerns and temperaments, they did not form their hypotheses the way modern scientists would, nor did they devise any experiments to test their theories. Their ideas have a dogmatic quality—an attitude of positive assertion, rather than the tentativeness of true hypotheses. But we must remember that the critical questions concerning the nature and limits of human knowledge had not yet been raised. Nor did the Milesians refer in any way to the problem of the relation between spirit and body. Their reduction of all reality to a material origin certainly raises this question, but only later did philosophers recognize this as a problem. Whatever may be the usefulness of their specific ideas about *water*, the *boundless*, and *air* as the primary substance of things, the real significance of the Milesians is, again, that they for the first time raised the question about the ultimate nature of things and made the first halting but direct inquiry into what nature really consists of.

THE MATHEMATICAL BASIS OF ALL THINGS

Pythagoras

Across a span of water from Miletus, located in the Aegean Sea, was the small island of Samos, which was the birthplace of a truly extraordinary and wise man, Pythagoras (*c.* 570–*c.* 497 BCE). From the various scraps of information we have about him and those who were his followers, an incomplete but still fascinating picture of his new philosophic reflections emerges. Apparently dissatisfied with conditions not only on Samos but generally in Ionia during the tyrannical rule of the rich Polycrates, Pythagoras migrated to southern Italy and settled there in the prosperous Greek city of Crotone. His active philosophical life there is usually dated from about 525 to 500 BCE. Aristotle tells us that the Pythagoreans "devoted themselves to mathematics, they were the first to advance this study, and having been brought up in it they thought its principles were the principles of all things." In contrast to the Milesians, the Pythagoreans said that things *consist of numbers.* Although this account of things sounds quite strange, the difficulty of this theory is greatly overcome when we consider why Pythagoras became interested in numbers and what his conception of numbers was.

Pythagoras became interested in mathematics for what appear to be religious reasons. His originality consists partly in his conviction that the study of mathematics is the best purifier of the soul. He is in fact the founder both of a religious sect and a school of mathematics. What gave rise to the Pythagorean sect was people's yearning for a deeply spiritual religion that could provide the means for purifying the soul and for guaranteeing its immortality. The Homeric gods were not gods in the theological sense, since they were as immoral as human beings. As such they could be neither the objects of worship nor the source of any spiritual power to overcome the pervading sense of moral uncleanliness and the anxiety that people had over the shortness of life and the finality of death. The religion of Dionysus had earlier stepped into this area of human concern, and was widespread during the seventh and sixth centuries BCE. The worship of Dionysus satisfied to some extent those yearnings for cleansing and immortality. Organized into small, secret, and mystical societies, the devotees would worship Dionysus under various animal forms. Working themselves into a frenzy of wild dances and song, they would drink the blood of these animals, which they had torn apart in a state of intoxication.

They would finally drop in complete exhaustion, convinced that at the height of their frenzy, the spirit of Dionysus had entered their bodies, purifying them and conferring his own immortality upon their souls.

The Pythagoreans were also clearly concerned with the mystical problems of purification and immortality. It was for this reason that they turned to science and mathematics, the study of which they considered the best purge for the soul. In scientific and mathematical thought they saw a type of life that was purer than any other kind. Thought and reflection represent a clear contrast to the life of vocational trade and competition for various honors. Pythagoras distinguished three different kinds of lives, and by implication the three divisions of the soul. There are, he said, three different kinds of people who go to the Olympian games. The lowest class is made up of those who go there to buy and sell, to make a profit. Next are those who go there to compete, to gain honors. Best of all, he thought, are those who come as spectators, who reflect upon and analyze what is happening. Of these three, the spectator illustrates the activity of philosophers who are liberated from daily life and its imperfections. To "look on" is one of the meanings of the Greek word "theory." Pythagoreans considered theoretical thinking, or pure science and pure mathematics, to be a purifier of the soul. Mathematical thought could liberate people from thinking about particular things and, instead, lead their thought to the permanent and ordered world of numbers. The final mystical triumph of the Pythagorean is liberation from "the wheel of birth," from the migration of the soul to animal and other forms in the constant progress of death and birth. In this way the spectator achieves a unity with god and shares his immortality.

To connect this religious concern with the philosophical aspects of the Pythagoreans, we should first of all mention their interest in music. They considered music highly therapeutic for certain nervous disorders. There was, they believed, some relation between the harmonies of music and the harmony of a person's interior life. But their true discovery in the field of music was that the musical intervals between the notes could be expressed numerically. They discovered that the length of the strings of a musical instrument is proportionate to the actual interval of the sounds they produce. Pluck a violin string, for example, and you will get a specific note. Divide that string in half, and you will get a pitch one octave higher, the ratio here being 2:1. All the other intervals could similarly be expressed in numerical ratios. Thus, for the Pythagoreans, music was a remarkable example of the pervasive relevance of numbers in all things. This led Aristotle to say that "they saw that the attributes and the ratios of the musical scales were expressible in numbers; all other things seemed in their whole nature to be modeled after numbers, and numbers seemed to be the first things in the whole of nature, and the whole heaven to be a musical scale and a number."

Pythagoreans had a special practice of counting and writing numbers, and this may have facilitated their view that all things *are* numbers. Apparently they built numbers out of individual units, using pebbles to count. The number *one* was therefore a single pebble and all other numbers were created by the addition of pebbles, somewhat like our present practice of representing numbers on dice by the use of dots. But the significant point is that the Pythagoreans discovered a relation between arithmetic and geometry. A single pebble represents *one* as a single point. But *two* is made up of two pebbles or two points, and these two points make a line. Three points, as in the corners of a triangle, create a plane or area and four points can represent a solid. This suggested to Pythagoreans a close relationship between number and magnitude, and Pythagoras is credited with what we now call the Pythagorean Theorem: the square of the hypotenuse is equal to the squares of the other two sides of a right-angled triangle. This correlation between numbers and magnitude provided immense consolation to those who sought evidence of a principle of structure and order in the universe. It is understandable how an interesting but possibly apocryphal story could have arisen. A Pythagorean named Hippasus, so the story goes, was drowned in the Hellespont for letting out the secret that this principle does not hold true in the case of the isosceles right-angled triangle. That is, in such cases, the relation between its hypotenuse and its sides cannot be expressed by any numerical ratio, only by an irrational number.

The importance of the relation between number and magnitude was that numbers, for the Pythagoreans, meant certain figures, such as a triangle, square, rectangle, and so forth. The individual points were "boundary stones" which marked out "fields." Moreover, the Pythagoreans differentiated these "triangular numbers," "square numbers," "rectangular numbers," and "spherical numbers" as being odd and even, thereby giving them a new way of treating the phenomenon of the conflict of opposites. In all these forms, numbers were, therefore, far more than abstractions: they were specific kinds of entities. To say, then, as the Pythagoreans did, that all things *are* numbers meant for them that there is a numerical basis for all things which possess shape and size. In this way they moved from arithmetic to geometry and then to the structure of reality. All things had numbers, and their odd and even values explained opposites in things, such as one and many, square and oblong, straight and curved, rest and motion. Even light and dark are numerical opposites, as are male and female, good and evil.

This way of understanding numbers led the Pythagoreans to formulate their most important philosophical notion, namely the concept of *form*. The Milesians had conceived the idea of a primary *matter* or stuff out of which everything was constituted, but they had no coherent concept of how specific things are differentiated from this single matter. They all spoke of an unlimited stuff, whether it was water, air, or the indeterminate boundless, by which they all meant some primary *matter*. The Pythagoreans now came forth with the conception of *form*. For them, form meant *limit*, and limit is understandable especially in numerical terms. The concept of limit, they believed, was best exemplified in music and medicine. For in both of these arts the central fact is harmony, and harmony is achieved by taking into account proportions and limits. In music there is a numerical ratio by which different notes must be separated in order to achieve concordant intervals. Harmony is the form that the limiting structure of numerical ratio imposes upon the unlimited possibilities for sounds possessed by the strings of a musical instrument. In medicine the Pythagoreans saw the same principle at work. Health is the harmony or balance or proper ratio of certain opposites, such as hot and cold, wet and dry, and the volumetric balance of various specific elements later known as biochemicals. Indeed, the Pythagoreans looked upon the body as they would a musical instrument. Health, they said, is achieved when the body is "in tune" and that disease is a consequence of undue tensions or the loss of proper tuning of the strings. In the literature of early medicine, the concept of number was frequently used in connection with health and disease, particularly when number was translated to mean "figure." The *true* number, or figure, therefore, refers to the proper balance of all the elements and functions of the body. Number, then, represents the application of *limit* (form) to the *unlimited* (matter), and the Pythagoreans referred to music and medicine only as vivid illustrations of their larger concept, namely, that all things *are* numbers.

The brilliance of Pythagoras and his followers is measured to some extent by the great influence they had upon later philosophers and particularly upon Plato. There is much in Plato that first came to light in the teachings of Pythagoras, including the importance of the soul and its threefold division, and the importance of mathematics as related to the concept of form and the Forms.

Model of the Acropolis
(Royal Ontario Museum)

ATTEMPTS TO EXPLAIN CHANGE

Heraclitus

Earlier philosophers attempted to describe the ultimate constituents of the world around us. Heraclitus (*c.*540–*c.*480 BC), nobleman from Ephesus, shifted attention to a new problem, namely, the problem of *change*. His chief idea was that "all things are in flux," and he expressed this concept of constant change by saying that "you cannot step twice into the same river." The river changes because "fresh waters are ever flowing in upon you." This concept of *flux*, Heraclitus thought, must apply not only to rivers but to all things, including the human soul. Rivers and people exhibit the fascinating fact of becoming different and yet remaining the same. We return to the "same" river although fresh waters have flowed into it, and the adult is still the same person as the child. Things change and thereby take on many different forms, but, nevertheless, they contain something which continues to be the same throughout all the flux of change. There must be, Heraclitus argued, some basic *unity* between these many forms and the single continuing element, between the many and the one. He made his case with such imaginative skill that much of what he had to say found an important place in the later philosophies of Plato and the Stoics; in more recent centuries, he was deeply admired by Hegel and Nietzsche.

Flux and Fire   To describe change as unity in diversity, Heraclitus assumed that there must be *something* which changes, and he argued that this something is *fire*. But he did not simply substitute the element of fire for Thales' water or Anaximenes' air. What led Heraclitus to fasten upon fire as the basic element in things was that fire behaves in such a way as to suggest how the process of change operates. Fire is simultaneously a deficiency and a surplus; it must constantly be fed and it constantly gives off something either in the form of heat, smoke, or ashes. Fire is a process of transformation, then, whereby what is fed into it is transformed into something else. For Heraclitus it was not enough simply to point to some basic element, such as water, as the basic nature of reality; this would not answer the question of how this basic stuff could change into different forms. When, therefore, Heraclitus fastened upon fire as the basic reality, he not only identified the *something* which changes, but thought he had discovered the principle of change itself. To say that everything is in flux meant for Heraclitus that the world *is* an "ever-living Fire" whose constant movement is assured by "measures of it kindling and measures going out." These "measures" meant for Heraclitus a kind of balance between what kindles and what goes out of the fire. He describes this balance in terms of financial exchange, saying that "all things are an exchange for Fire, and Fire for all things, similar to wares for gold and gold for wares." With this explanation of exchange, Heraclitus maintained that nothing is really ever lost in the nature of things. If gold is exchanged for wares, both the gold and the wares still continue to exist, although they are now in different hands. Similarly, all things continue to exist, although they exchange their form from time to time.

There is a stability in the universe because of the orderly and balanced process of change or flux. The same "measure" comes out as goes in, just as if reality were a huge fire that inhaled and exhaled equal amounts, thereby preserving an even inventory in the world. This inventory represents the widest array of things, and all of them are simply different forms of fire. Flux and change consist of the movements of fire, movements which Heraclitus called the "upward and downward paths." The downward path of fire explains the coming into being of the things that we experience. So, when fire is condensed it becomes moist, and this moisture under conditions of increased pressure becomes water; water, in turn, when congealed becomes earth. On the upward path this process is reversed, and the earth is transformed into liquid; from this water come the various forms of life. Nothing is ever lost in this process of transformation because, as Heraclitus says, "fire lives the death of earth, and air the death of fire; water lives the death of air, earth that of water." With this description of the constant transformation of things in fire, Heraclitus thought he had explained the rudiments of the unity between the *one* basic stuff and the *many* diverse things in the world. But there was another significant idea that Heraclitus added to his concept of Fire, namely, the idea of *reason* as the universal law.

Reason as the Universal Law   The process of change is not a haphazard movement but the product of God's universal Reason (*logos*). This idea of *Reason* came from Heraclitus' religious conviction that the most real thing of all is the soul, and the soul's most distinctive and important attribute is wisdom or thought. But when he speaks about God and the soul, he does not have in mind separate personal entities. For him there is only one basic reality, namely, Fire, and it is this material substance, Fire, which Heraclitus calls the One, or God. Inevitably, Heraclitus was a *pantheist*—a term meaning that God is identical with the totality of things in the universe. For Heraclitus, all things are Fire/God. Since Fire/God is in everything, even the human soul is a part of Fire/God. As wisdom is Fire/God's most important attribute, wisdom or thought is people's chief activity. But inanimate things also contain the principle of reason, since they are also permeated with the fiery element. Because Fire/God *is* Reason and since Fire/God is the One, permeating all things, Heraclitus believed that Fire/God is the universal Reason. And, as such, Fire/God unifies all things and commands them to move and change in accordance with thought and rational principles. These rational principles constitute the essence of *law*—the universal law immanent in all things. All people share this universal law to the degree that they possess Fire/God in their own natures and thereby possess the capacity for thought.

Logically, this account of our rational nature would mean that all of our thoughts are God's thoughts, since there is a unity between the One and the many, between God and human beings. We all must share in a common stock of knowledge since we all have a similar relation to God. Even stones partake in that part of God's Reason which makes them all equally behave according to the "law" of gravity. But people notoriously disagree and behave quite inconsistently. Recognizing this fact about human disagreement, Heraclitus said that "those awake have one ordered universe in common, but in sleep everyone turns away to one of his own." "Sleep," for Heraclitus, must mean to be thoughtless or even ignorant. Unfortunately, he does not explain how it is possible for people to be thoughtless if their souls and minds are part of God. In spite of it's limitations, though, Heraclitus's theory had a profound impact on succeeding thinkers. This is particularly so concerning his conviction that there is a common universe available to all thoughtful people, and that all people participate in God's universal Reason or universal law. In later centuries, it was this concept that provided the basis for the Stoics' idea of cosmopolitanism—the idea that all people are equally citizens of the world precisely because they all share in the One, in God's Reason. According to the Stoics, we all contain in ourselves some portion of the Fire, that is, sparks of the divine. It was this concept, too, which formed the foundation for the classic theory of *natural law*. With some variations, the natural law passed from Heraclitus, to the Stoics, to medieval theologians, and eventually became a dynamic force in the American Revolution. Even today natural law is a vital component of legal theory.

The Conflict of Opposites   Although human beings can know the eternal wisdom that directs all things, we do not pay attention to this wisdom. We therefore "prove to be uncomprehending" of the reasons for the way things happen to them. We are distressed by meaningless disorders in the world, overwhelmed by the presence of good and evil, and we long for the peace that means the end of strife. Heraclitus offers us little comfort here, since, for him, strife is the very essence of change itself. The conflict of opposites that we see in the world is not a calamity, but is simply the permanent condition of all things. According to Heraclitus, if we could visualize the whole process of change, we would see that "war is common and justice is strife and that all things happen by strife and necessity." From this perspective, he says, "what is in opposition is in concert, and from what differs comes the most beautiful harmony." Even death is no longer a calamity, for "after death things await people which they do not expect or imagine." Throughout his treatment of the problem of strife and disorder, Heraclitus emphasizes again and again that the many find their unity in the One. Thus, what appear to be disjointed events and contradictory forces are in reality intimately harmonized. For this reason he says that people "do not know how what is at variance agrees with itself. It is an attunement of opposite tensions, like that of the bow and the lyre." Fire itself exhibits this tension of opposites and indeed depends upon it. Fire *is* its many tensions of opposites. In the One, the many find their unity. Thus, in the One "the way up and the way down is the same," "good and ill are one," and "it is the same thing in us that is quick and dead, awake and asleep, young and old." This solution of the conflict of opposites rests upon Heraclitus' major assumption that nothing is ever lost, but merely changes its form.

Following the direction of Reason, the eternal Fire moves with a measured pace, and all change requires opposite and diverse things. Still, "to God all things are fair and good and right, but people hold some things wrong and some right." Heraclitus did not come to this conclusion because he believed that there was a personal God who judged that all things are good. Instead, Heraclitus thought that "it is wise to agree that all things are one," that the One takes shape and appears in many forms.

Parmenides

A younger contemporary of Heraclitus, Parmenides was born about 510 BCE and lived most of his life in Elea, a colony founded by refugee Greek refugees in the southwest of Italy. He flourished there in more than one capacity, giving the people of Elea laws and establishing a new school of philosophy whose followers became known as Eleatics. Dissatisfied with the philosophical views of his predecessors, Parmenides offered the quite startling theory that the entire universe consists of one thing, which never changes, has no parts, and can never be destroyed. He calls this single thing the *One*. Granted, it may *appear* as though things might change in the world, such as when a large oak tree grows from a tiny acorn. It may also *appear* as though there are many different things in the world, such as rocks, trees, houses, and people. According to Parmenides, though, all such change and diversity is an illusion. In spite of appearances, there is only one single, unchanging, and eternal thing that exists. Why would Parmenides offer a theory that is so contrary to appearances? The answer is that he was more persuaded by logical reasoning than what he saw with his eyes.

The logic of Parmenides' theory begins with the simple statement that *something is, or something is not.* For example, cows exist, but unicorns do not exist. On further consideration, though, Parmenides realizes that we can only assert the first part of the above statement, that *something is.* The reason is that we can only conceptualize and speak about things that exist, but are unable to do this with things that don't exist. Can any of us form a mental picture of the non-existent? Thus, according to Parmenides, we must reject any contention that implies that *something is not.* Parmenides then unpacks several implications from this observation. First, he argues that nothing ever changes. Heraclitus, we have seen, held that *everything* is in constant change; Parmenides holds the exact opposite view. We typically observe that things change by coming into existence, and then going out of existence. A large oak tree, for example, comes into existence when it emerges from a tiny acorn; the tree then goes out of existence when it dies and decomposes. Although this is how things appear to our eyes, Parmenides argues that this alleged process of change is logically flawed. We first say that the tree *is not*, then *it is*, then once again it *is not.* Here we begin and end with the impossible contention that *something is not.* Logically speaking, then, we are forced to reject this alleged process of change, and chalk it up to one big illusion. Thus, nothing ever changes.

Parmenides argues similarly that the world consists of one indivisible thing. Again, we typically observe that the world contains many different things. Suppose, for example, that I see a cat sitting on a carpet. My common perception of this is that the cat and the carpet are different things, and not simply one undifferentiated mass of stuff. But this common view of physical differentiation is also logically flawed. I am in essence saying that, beneath the cat's feet the cat *is not*, but from its feet through its head the cat *is*, and above the cat's head the cat *is not*. Thus, when I demarcate the physical borders of the cat, I begin and end with the impossible contention that *something is not*. I must then reject the alleged fact of physical differentiation and once again chalk it up to one big illusion. In short, only one indivisible thing exists.

Using similar logic, Parmenides argues that the One must be motionless: if it moved, then it would not exist where it was before, which involves illogically asserting that *something is not*. Also, Parmenides argues that the One must be a perfect sphere. If it were irregular in any way—such as a bowling ball with three holes drilled in it—this would involve a region within the ball where nothing existed. This too would wrongly assert that *something is not*.

Even if we grant the logical force of Parmenides' arguments, it is not easy for us to cast off our commonsense view that the world exhibits change and multiplicity. Everywhere we see things in flux, and to us this represents genuine change. But Parmenides rejected these commonsense notions and insisted on a distinction between appearance and reality. Change and multiplicity, he said, involve a confusion between appearance and reality. What lies behind this distinction between appearance and reality is Parmenides' equally important distinction between opinion and truth. Appearance cannot produce more than opinion, whereas reality is the basis of truth. Commonsense tells us that things appear to be in flux and, therefore, in a continuous process of change. However, Parmenides says that this opinion based on sensation must yield to the activity of reason. Reason, in turn, is able to discern the truth about things, and tells us that if there is a single substance of which everything consists, then there can be no movement or change. To some extent, Thales made a similar point when he said that everything derives from water. Thales thus implies that the appearance of things does not give us the true constitution or stuff of reality. But Parmenides explicitly emphasized these distinctions, which became of such decisive importance in Plato's philosophy. Plato took Parmenides' basic idea of the unchangeability of being and developed from this his distinction between the intelligible world of truth and the visible world of opinion.

At the age of 65, Parmenides went to Athens accompanied by his chief pupil Zeno, and there is the tradition that on this visit he conversed with the young Socrates. Parmenides' radical views about change and multiplicity inevitably incited critical challenges and ridicule. It was left to Zeno to defend his master's position against his attackers.

Zeno

Born in Elea about 489 BCE, Zeno was over 40 years old when he visited Athens with Parmenides. In defending Parmenides, Zeno's main strategy was to show that the so-called commonsense view of the world led to conclusions even more ridiculous than Parmenides' view. The Pythagoreans, for example, rejected the basic assumption Parmenides had accepted; namely, the assumption that reality is One. Instead, they believed in a plurality of things—that there exist a quantity of separate and distinct things—and that, therefore, motion and change are real. Their argument seemed to accord more closely with commonsense and the testimony of the senses. But the Eleatic approach that Zeno followed required a distinction between appearance and reality. To philosophize, according to Parmenides and Zeno, we must not only look at the world but must also think about it in order to understand it.

Zeno felt strongly that our senses give us no clue about reality but only about appearances. Accordingly, our senses do not give us reliable knowledge but only opinion. He demonstrates this using an example of a millet seed. If we take a millet seed and drop it to the ground, it will not make a sound. But if we take a half-bushel of millet seeds and let them fall to the ground, there will be a sound. From this difference, Zeno concluded that our senses have deceived us. For, either there is a sound when the single seed falls or there is not a sound when the many seeds fall. So, to get at the truth of things it is more reliable to go by way of thought than by way of sensation.

Zeno's Four Paradoxes   In answering Parmenides' critics Zeno fashioned his arguments in the form of paradoxes. The commonsense view of the world makes two principal assumptions: (1) changes occur throughout time, and (2) a diversity of objects are spread throughout space. Following Parmenides, Zeno, of course, rejects both of these assumptions. However, in arguing against the commonsense view of things, Zeno provisionally grants the above two assumptions, and then notes paradoxes that follow from them. The consequences are in fact so absurd that the commonsense view of the world no longer seems so commonsensical. By contrast, then, Parmenides' view of the One seems to be the more reasonable account of the world. Zeno presents four principal paradoxes.

1. *The racecourse.* According to this paradox of motion, a runner crosses a series of units of distance from the beginning to the end of the racecourse. But, Zeno asks, just what takes place in this example? Is there really any motion? In order to go across the racecourse, the runner, according to the Pythagorean hypothesis, would have to cross an infinite number of points, and would have to do this in a finite number of moments. But the critical question is, how can one cross an infinite number of points in a finite amount of time? The runner cannot reach the end of the course until first reaching the dividing line at the halfway point; but the distance from the beginning to the halfway point can also be divided in half, and the runner must first reach that point, the one-quarter mark, before reaching the halfway point. Likewise, the distance between the beginning and the one-quarter point is divisible, and this process of division must go on to infinitude since there is always a remainder and every such unit is divisible. If, then, the runner cannot reach any point without first reaching its previous midpoint, and if there are an infinite number of points, it

is impossible to cross this infinite number of points in a finite amount of time. For this reason, Zeno concludes that motion does not exist.

2. *Achilles and the tortoise.* This paradox is similar to the racecourse illustration. Imagine a race between the swift Achilles and a slow tortoise. Because he is a sport, Achilles gives the tortoise a head start, and is thus in pursuit of the tortoise. Zeno argues that Achilles cannot ever overtake the tortoise because he must always reach the point that the tortoise has passed. The distance between Achilles and the tortoise will always be divisible and, as in the case of the racecourse, no point can be reached before the previous point has been reached. The effect is that there can be no motion at all, and Achilles, on these assumptions, could never overtake the tortoise. What Zeno thought he had demonstrated here was, again, that although the Pythagoreans claimed the reality of motion, their theory of the plurality of the world made it impossible to think of the idea of motion in a coherent way.

3. *The arrow.* Does an arrow move when the archer shoots it at the target? Here again the Pythagoreans, who had argued for the reality of space and therefore of its divisibility, would have to say that the moving arrow must at every moment occupy a particular position in space. But if an arrow occupies a position in space equal to its length, this is precisely what is meant when we say that the arrow is at rest. Since the arrow must always occupy such a position in space equal to its length, the arrow must always be at rest. Moreover, any quantity, as we saw in the example of the racecourse, is infinitely divisible. Hence, the space occupied by the arrow is infinite and as such it must coincide with everything else, in which case everything must be One instead of many. Motion, therefore, is an illusion.

4. *The relativity of motion.* Imagine three passenger cars of equal length on tracks parallel to each other, each car having eight windows on a side. One car is stationary, and the other two are moving in opposite directions at the same speed. In Figure 1, car *A* is stationary, and cars *B* and *C* are moving in opposite directions at the same speed until they reach the positions shown in Figure 2. In order to reach the positions in Figure 2, the front of car *B* would go past four of car *A*'s windows while the front of car *C* would go past all eight of car *B*'s windows. Each window represents a unit of distance, and each such unit is passed in an equal unit of time. Now, car *B* went past only four of *A*'s windows while car *C* went past eight of *B*'s windows. Since each window represents the same unit of time, it would have to follow that four units of time are equal to eight units of time or that four units of distance equal eight units of distance, which is absurd. Whatever may be the inner complications of this argument, Zeno's chief point was that motion has no clear definition, and it is a relative concept.

In all of these arguments, Zeno was simply counterattacking the adversaries of Parmenides, taking seriously their assumption of a pluralistic world—a world where, for example, a line or time is divisible. By pushing these assumptions to their logical conclusions, Zeno attempted to demonstrate that the notion of a pluralistic world lands one into insoluble absurdities and paradoxes. He, therefore, reiterated Parmenides' thesis that change and

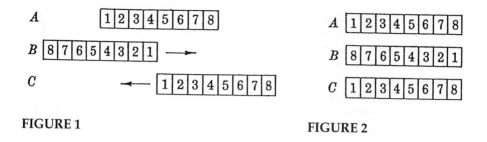

FIGURE 1   **FIGURE 2**

motion are illusions and that there is only one being, continuous, material, and motionless. In spite of Zeno's valiant efforts, the commonsense view of the world persisted, which prompted succeeding philosophers to take a different approach to the problem of change and constancy.

Empedocles

Empedocles was an impressive figure in his native Agrigentum, Sicily, where he lived probably from 490 to 430 BCE. His interests and activities ranged from politics and medicine to religion and philosophy. Legend has it that, wishing to be remembered as a godlike figure, he ended his life by leaping into the crater of Mt. Etna, hoping thereby to leave no trace of his body so that the people would think that he had gone up to heaven. He wrote his philosophy in the form of poetry, of which only a small portion has survived. From it we see not an original or new philosophy but, rather, a new way of putting together what his predecessors had already said. Empedocles believed that the arguments both for and against motion and change had some merit. Instead of taking either side, however, he ingeniously combined both points of view in what was the first attempt at combining the major philosophical contributions of his predecessors. He thereby discovered a consistent way of saying that there is change and at the same time affirming that reality is fundamentally changeless.

Empedocles agreed with Parmenides that being is uncreated and indestructible, and that it simply *is*. He writes that "from what in no wise exists, it is impossible for anything to come into being; and for being to perish completely is incapable of fulfillment and unthinkable; for it will always be there, wherever any one may place it on any occasion." But, unlike Parmenides, he did not agree that existence consists simply of the One. To accept the notion of the One requires us to deny the reality of motion, but to Empedocles the phenomenon of motion was both too obvious and compelling to deny. He therefore rejected the idea of the One. But, agreeing with Parmenides that being is uncreated and indestructible, Empedocles argued that being is not One but many. It is *the many* which are changeless and eternal.

According to Empedocles, the objects that we see and experience do in fact come into being and are also destroyed. But such change and motion are possible because objects are composed of many material particles. Thus, although *objects* can change, as Heraclitus said, the *particles* of which they are composed are changeless, as Parmenides said about the One. But of what did these particles consist? Empedocles held that these particles are four eternal material elements, namely, earth, air, fire and water. He developed this idea by reinterpreting the philosophies of Thales and Anaximenes, who emphasized the primary elements of water and air respectively. Following Greek tradition, which emphasized the four primary elements of earth, air, fire and water, Empedocles expanded on Thales' and Anaximenes' theories. These four elements, he believed, are changeless and eternal, and can never be transformed into something else. What explains the changes in objects that we see around us is the *mixture* of the four elements, but not their transformation. He writes, there is "only a mingling and interchange of what has been mingled." Earth, air, fire, and water, though they are unchangeable particles, mingle together to form objects and thereby make possible what in common experience we see as change.

Empedocles' account of earth, air, fire, and water constitutes only the first part of his theory. The second part is an account of the specific forces that animate the process of change. The Ionians assumed that the stuff of nature simply transformed itself into various objects. Only Anaximenes had made any detailed attempt to analyze the process of change with his theory of condensed and expanded air. By contrast, Empedocles assumed that there are in nature two forces, which he called *Love* and *Hate* (alternatively, Harmony and Discord). These are the forces that cause the four elements to intermingle and later to separate. The force of Love causes elements to attract each other and built up into some particular form or person. The force of Hate causes the decomposition of things. The four elements, then, mix together or separate from each other depending on how much Love or Hate are present. In fact, Empedocles believes that there are cycles within nature that manifest Love and Strife in differing degrees at different times. Expressing this never-ending cycle in his poetic style, Empedocles writes that

> this process is clearly to be seen throughout the mass of mortal limbs: sometimes through love all the limbs which the body has as its lot come together into one, in the prime of flourishing life. At another time again, sundered by evil feuds, they wander severally by the breakers of the shore of life. Likewise too with shrub plants and fish in their watery dwelling, and beasts with mountain lairs and diver birds that travel on wings.

There are four stages to the cycle. In the first stage, Love is present, and Hate is completely absent. Here the four elements are fully mingled together and are held in Harmony by the governing principle of Love. In the second stage, the force of Hate, lurking nearby, starts to invade things, but there is still more Love present than Hate. In the third stage Hate begins to predominate, and the particles fall into Discord and begin to separate. In the final stage only Hate is present, and all particles of earth, air, fire and water separate into their own four groups. There the elements are ready to begin again a new cycle as the force of Love returns to attract the elements into harmonious combinations. This process continues without end.

Anaxagoras

Anaxagoras (500–428 BCE) was from Clazomenae, a coastal town in what is now Turkey. He later moved to Athens, where he was in the company of the statesman Pericles. His major philosophical contribution was the concept of *mind* (*nous*), which he distinguished from matter. Anaxagoras agreed with Empedocles that all coming into and going out of being consists merely in the mixture and separation of already existing substances. But he rejected Empedocles' ambiguous and somewhat mythical notions of Love and Hate, by which various objects supposedly form. For Anaxagoras, the world and all its objects are well-ordered and intricate structures; there must, then, be some being with knowledge and power that organizes the material world in this fashion. Such a rational principle is what Anaxagoras proposed in his concept of *Mind*, or *nous*.

According to Anaxagoras, the nature of reality is best understood as consisting of *Mind* and *matter*. Before Mind has influenced the shape and behavior of matter, matter exists, as a mixture of various kinds of material substances, all uncreated and imperishable. Even when this original mass of matter is divided into actual objects, each part contains portions of every other elemental "thing" (*spermata*, seeds). Snow, for example, contains the opposites of black and white and is called white only because white predominates in it. In a sense, then, each part contains what is in the whole of reality, since each has a special "portion" of everything in it.

According to Anaxagoras, *separation* is the process by which this matter formed into various things, and such separation occurs through the power of Mind. Specifically, Mind produced a rotary motion, causing a vortex which spread out so as to encompass more and more of the original mass of matter. This forces a "separation" of various substances. This rotary motion originally caused a separation of matter into two major divisions, one mass that contained the warm, light, rare, and dry, and a second mass that contained the cold, dark, dense, and moist. This process of separation is continuous, and there is constant progress in the process of separation. Particular objects are always combinations of substances in which some particular substance predominates. For example, water predominates with the elemental stuff moistness, but nevertheless has all other elemental things present. Describing this process in one of the preserved fragments of his last book, Anaxagoras says that

> Mind set in order all things that were to be and are now and that will be, and this revolution in which now revolve the stars and the sun and the moon and the air and the aether which are separated off. . . . The revolution itself caused the separating off, and the dense is separated off from the rare, the warm from the cold, the bright from the dark, and the dry from the moist. And there are many portions of many things.

Emphasizing the continued mixture of things, he says that "no thing is altogether separated off from anything else except Mind." Forces set in motion in the vortex account for the appearance of the thick and moist at the center and the thin and warm at the circumference, that is, of the earth and the atmosphere. The forces of rotation also caused red-hot masses of stones to be torn away from the earth and to be thrown into the ether, and this is the origin of the stars. The earth, originally mud, was dried by the sun and fertilized by germs contained in the air. Everything, even now, is animated by Mind, including life in plants and sense perception in human beings. Mind is everywhere, or as Anaxagoras says, Mind is "there where everything else is, in the surrounding mass."

Although Anaxagoras considered Mind the moving or controlling force in the cosmos and in human bodies, his account of the actual role of Mind was limited. For one thing, the Mind was not the *creator* of matter, since he held that matter is eternal. Moreover, he did not see in Mind the source of any purpose to the natural world. Mind's role in the origin of particular things appears to be a mechanical explanation, principally in through the process of "separation". Things are the products of material causes, and Mind appears to have no distinctive role apart from starting motion.

Aristotle, who later distinguished between different kinds of causes, offered a mixed evaluation of Anaxagoras' views. He contrasts Anaxagoras with his predecessors, who attributed the origin of things to spontaneity and chance. According to Aristotle, when Anaxagoras said that "reason was present—as in animals, so throughout nature—as the cause of order and of all arrangement, he seemed like a sober man in contrast with the random talk of his predecessors." But, adds Aristotle, Anaxagoras made use of his concept of Mind only "to a small extent." His criticism was that "Anaxagoras uses reason as a divine machine for making the world, and when he is at a loss to tell from what cause something necessarily is, then he drags reason in, but in all other cases ascribes events to anything rather than reason." Anaxagoras seemed to provide only an explanation of how matter acquired its rotary motion, leaving the rest of the order of nature to be a product of that motion.

Still, what Anaxagoras had to say about reason was of great consequence in the history of philosophy because he thereby introduced a mental principle into the nature of things. He differentiated Mind and matter. While he may not have described Mind as completely immaterial, he did nevertheless distinguish Mind from the matter it had to work with. He stated that Mind, unlike matter, "is mixed with nothing, but is alone, itself by itself." What makes Mind different from matter was that it is "the finest of all things and the purest, and it has all knowledge about everything and the greatest power." Thus, while matter is composite, Mind is simple. But Anaxagoras did not distinguish two different worlds—that of Mind and that of matter—but saw these two as always interrelated. Thus he writes that Mind is "there where everything else is." Although he had not worked out all the possibilities of his concept of Mind, this concept was nevertheless destined to have enormous influence in later Greek philosophy.

THE ATOMISTS

Leucippus and Democritus formulated a theory about the nature of things that bears an astonishing resemblance to some contemporary scientific views. However, it is difficult now to disentangle the individual contribution Leucippus and Democritus each made to this atomistic theory. Their writings are lost for the most part, but we at least know that Leucippus was the founder of the atomist school and that Democritus supplied much of the detailed elaboration of it. Leucippus was a contemporary of Empedocles (490–430 BCE), but we know little else of his life beyond that. Democritus, born in Abdera, Thrace, is reputed to have lived 100 years, from 460 to 360 BCE. Through his immense learning and painstaking attempt to state with clarity his abstract theory of atomism, Democritus inevitably overshadowed Leucippus. It is to Leucippus, though, that we must credit the central contention of Atomism, namely, that everything is made up of atoms moving in empty space.

Atoms and the Void

According to Aristotle, the philosophy of atomism originated as an attempt to overcome the logical consequences of the Eleatic denial of space. Parmenides denied that there could be many independent things because everywhere there was *being,* in which case the total reality would be One. Specifically, he denied the existence of nonbeing or the void (empty space), because to say that there *is* the void is to say that the void *is something.* It is impossible, he thought, to say that there *is* nothing. Leucippus formulated his new theory precisely to reject this treatment of space or the void.

Leucippus affirmed the reality of space and thereby prepared the way for a coherent theory of motion and change. What had complicated Parmenides' concept of space was his thought that whatever exists must be *material,* and so space, if it existed, must also be material. Leucippus, on the other hand, thought it possible to affirm that space exists without having to say at the same time that it is material. Thus, he described space as something like a receptacle that could be empty in some places and full in others. As a receptacle, space, or the void, could be the place where objects move, and Leucippus apparently saw no reason for denying this characteristic of space. Without this concept of space, it would have been impossible for Leucippus and Democritus to develop their view that all things consist of atoms.

According to Leucippus and Democritus, the nature of things consists of an infinite number of particles or units called atoms. Leucippus and Democritus ascribed to these atoms the two chief characteristics that Parmenides had ascribed to the One, namely, indestructibility and eternity. Whereas Parmenides had said reality consists of a single One, the atomists now said that there are an infinite number of atoms, each one being completely solid in itself. These Atoms contain no empty spaces and therefore are completely hard and indivisible. They exist in space and differ from each other in shape and size, and because of their small size, they are invisible. Since these atoms are eternal, they did not have to be created. Nature consists, therefore, of two things only: namely, *space,* which is a vacuum, and *atoms.* The atoms move about in space, and their motion leads them to form the objects we experience.

The atomists did not think it was necessary to account for how atoms first began moving in space. The original motion of these atoms, they thought, was similar to the motion of dust particles as they dart off in all directions in a sun-beam, even when there is no wind to impel them. Democritus said that there is no absolute "up" or "down," and, since he did not ascribe weight to atoms, he thought that atoms could move in any direction. Things as we know them have their origin in the motion of the atoms. Moving in space, the atoms origi-nally were single individual units. Inevitably, though, they began to collide with each other. In cases where their shapes were such as to permit them to in-terlock, they began to form clusters, or what Anaxagoras had called *vortices*. In this the atomists resembled the Pythagoreans, who said that all things are numbers. Things, like numbers, are made up of combinable units; for the atomists, things are simply combinations of various kinds of atoms. Mathe-matical figures and physical figures are, therefore, similar.

In the beginning, then, there were atoms in space. Each atom is like the Parmenidean One, but though they are indestructible, they are in constant mo-tion. The atomists described earth, air, fire and water as different clusters of changeless atoms—the product of the movement of originally single atoms. These four elements were not the primeval roots of all other things, as earlier philosophers believed, but were themselves the product of the absolutely orig-inal stuff, the atoms.

The atomists produced a mechanical conception of the nature of things. For them, everything was the product of the collision of atoms moving in space. Their theory had no place in it for the element of *purpose* or *design*, and their materialistic reduction of all reality to atoms left no place for a creator or designer. They saw no need to account either for the origin of the atoms or for the original motion impelling the atoms. For, the question of origins could al-ways be asked, even about God; to ascribe eternal existence to the material atoms seemed as satisfactory as any other solution.

The theory of atomism envisioned by Leucippus and Democritus had a long and influential history. So formidable was this atomistic theory that, al-though it went into a decline during the Middle Ages, it was revived during the Renaissance and provided science with its working model for centuries to come. Isaac Newton (1642–1727) still thought in atomistic terms when he wrote his famous *Principia Mathematica*. In this work he deduced the motion of the planets, the comets, the moon, and the sea; he wrote in 1686,

> I wish we could devise the rest of the phenomena of Nature by the same kind of reasoning from mechanical principles, for I am induced by many reasons to suspect that they may all depend upon certain forces by which the particles of bodies, by some causes hitherto unknown, are either mutually impelled to-wards one another and cohere in regular figures, or are repelled and recede from one another.

Although Newton assumed God had set things in motion, his physical analy-sis of nature was restricted to the mechanical principles of matter moving in space. After Newton, atomism held sway until the quantum theory and Ein-stein gave contemporary science a new conception of matter, which denied the attribute of indestructibility to the atoms.

Theory of Knowledge and Ethics

Besides describing the structure of nature, Democritus was concerned with two other philosophical problems: the problem of knowledge and the problem of human conduct. Being a thorough materialist, Democritus held that *thought* can be explained in the same way that any other phenomenon can, namely, as the movement of atoms. He distinguished between two different kinds of perception, one of the senses and one of the understanding, both of these being physical processes. When our eyes see something, this something is an "effluence" or the shedding of atoms by the object, forming an "image." These atomic images of things enter the eyes, and other organs of sense, and make an impact upon the soul, which is itself made up of atoms.

Democritus further distinguishes between two ways of knowing things: "there are two forms of knowledge, the trueborn and the bastard. To the bastard belong all these: sight, hearing, smell, taste, touch. The trueborn is quite apart from these." What distinguishes these two types of thought is that, whereas "trueborn" knowledge depends only on the object, "bastard" knowledge is affected by the particular conditions of the body of the person involved. For example, two people can agree that what they have tasted is an apple (trueborn). However, they can still disagree about the apple's taste (bastard knowledge), one saying the apple is sweet and the other saying it is bitter. So, according to Democritus, "by the senses we know in truth nothing sure, but only something that changes according to the disposition of the body and of the things that enter into it or resist it." Still, Democritus had to say that both sensation and thought are the same type of mechanical process.

Concerning ethics, Democritus developed a very ambitious set of rules for human behavior. In general, he maintained that the most desirable goal of life is cheerfulness, and we best achieve this through moderation in all things along with the cultivation of culture. With the emergence of ethics as its primary concern, philosophy reached one of its major watersheds, closing out the first era where the principal question had been about the natural physical order. Now people would ask more searching questions about how they should behave.

CHAPTER 2

The Sophists and Socrates

The first Greek philosophers focused on nature; the Sophists and Socrates shifted the concerns of philosophy to the study of human beings. Instead of asking large cosmic questions about the ultimate principle of things, they instead asked questions that more directly related to moral behavior. This transition from predominantly scientific concerns to basic ethical questions is explained in part by the failure of the pre-Socratic philosophers to arrive at any uniform conception of the cosmos. They proposed inconsistent interpretations of nature, and there appeared to be no way of reconciling them. Heraclitus said that nature consists of a plurality of substances and that everything is in a process of constant change. Parmenides took the opposite view, arguing that reality is a single, static substance—the One—and that motion and change are illusions cast upon our senses by the appearances of things. Philosophy might have stopped at this point if these contradictory cosmologies simply produced an intellectual fatigue through the sheer difficulty of deciphering the secrets of nature. As it was, the controversy over the ultimate principle of things had generated an attitude of skepticism about the ability of human reason to discover the truth about nature. But this skepticism provided the impulse for a new direction for philosophy. For skepticism itself became the subject of serious concern.

Instead of debating alternative theories of nature, philosophers now addressed the problem of human knowledge, asking whether it was possible to discover any universal truth. This question was further aggravated by cultural differences between various races and societies. Consequently, the question about truth became deeply entwined with the problem of goodness. Could there be a universal concept of goodness if people were incapable of knowing any universal truth? The principal parties to this new debate were the Sophists and Socrates.

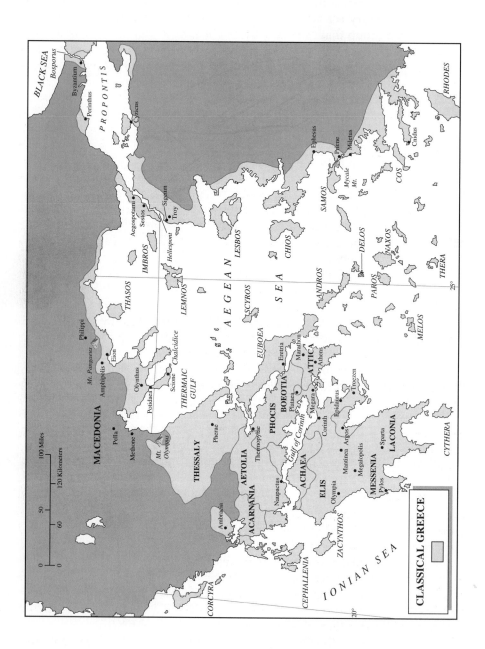

CLASSICAL GREECE

BLACK SEA
Bosporus
Byzantium
Perinthus
PROPONTIS
Cyzicus

Ephesus
Priene
Miletus
Mycale Mt.
Cnidus
COS
RHODES

Sigeum
Aegospotami
Sestos
Troy
Hellespont
IMBROS
THASOS
LESBOS
SAMOS
CHIOS
LEMNOS
AEGEAN
SEA
SCYROS
ANDROS
DELOS
NAXOS
PAROS
THERA
MELOS
CYTHERA

Philippi
Mt. Pangaeus
Amphipolis
Eion
Olynthus
Scione
Potidaea
Chalcidice
THERMAIC
GULF

MACEDONIA
Pella
Methone
Mt. Olympus
THESSALY
Pherae
EUBOEA
Eretria
Marathon
ATTICA
Athens
BOEOTIA
Plataea
Megara
Troezen
Epidaurus
PHOCIS
Thermopylae
Corinth
Gulf of Corinth
Argos
Mantinea
AETOLIA
Naupactus
ACHAEA
ELIS
Olympia
MESSENIA
Pylos
Megalopolis
Sparta
LACONIA
ACARNANIA
Ambracia
ZACYNTHOS
CEPHALLENIA
CORCYRA
IONIAN SEA

25°
20°

100 Miles
120 Kilometers
50
60
0

30

THE SOPHISTS

The three most outstanding Sophists who emerged in Athens some time during the fifth century BCE were Protagoras, Gorgias, and Thrasymachus. They were part of a group that came to Athens either as traveling teachers or, as in the case of Hippias of Elis, as ambassadors. They specifically called themselves Sophists, or "intellectuals." Coming as they did from different cultures— Protagoras from Abdera in Thrace, Gorgias, from Leontini in southern Sicily, and Thrasymachus from Chalcedon—they took a fresh look at Athenian thought and customs and asked searching questions about them. In particular, they forced Athenians to consider whether their ideas and customs were founded upon truth or simply upon conventional ways of behaving. Was the Athenian distinction between Greeks and barbarians, as well as that between masters and slaves, based upon evidence or simply upon prejudice? Not only had the Sophists lived in different countries with their different customs, but they had also gathered a wide fund of information based upon their observation of a multitude of cultural facts. Their encyclopedic knowledge of different cultures made them skeptical about the possibility of attaining any absolute truth by which society might order its life. They forced thoughtful Athenians to consider whether Hellenic culture was based upon artificial rules (*nomos*) or upon nature (*physis*). They had them question whether their religious and moral codes were *conventional* and therefore changeable, or *natural* and therefore permanent. In a decisive way, the Sophists set the stage for a more deliberate and careful consideration of human nature, specifically how knowledge is acquired and how humans might order their behavior.

The Sophists were primarily practical people, and especially competent in grammar, writing, and public discourse. These skills made them uniquely qualified to address a special social need within Athenian society. Under the leadership of Athenian statesman Pericles (490–429 BCE), the old aristocracy of Athens had been replaced by democracy. This, in turn, intensified political life by drawing free citizens into political discussion and making them eligible for leadership roles. But the older aristocratic educational system—based mainly on family tradition—did not prepare people for the new conditions of democratic life. There was no disciplined and theoretical training in the areas of religion, grammar, and the careful interpretation of the poets. The Sophists moved into this cultural vacuum, and their practical interest in teaching filled an urgent need. They became popular lecturers and were the chief source of new education. What made them particularly sought after was that they professed, above all, to teach the art of *rhetoric*, that is, persuasive speech. The power of persuasion was a political necessity in the democratic Athens for anyone who hoped to rise to the level of leadership. The Sophists possessed the exact skills to facilitate this need.

The reputation of the Sophists was at first very favorable. They provided an immense service by training people to present their ideas clearly and forcefully. In a public assembly, it would be disastrous to permit debate among unskilled speakers who could neither present their own ideas effectively nor discover the errors in their opponents' arguments. But rhetoric became somewhat like a knife, in that it could be employed for good or ill use—to cut bread or to kill. On the one hand, those who possessed the power of persuasion could use that power to psychologically impel listeners to adopt a good idea. On the other hand, though, persuasive speakers could put over morally questionable ideas in which they had special interests. The inherent skepticism of the Sophists greatly facilitated a shift from the commendable use of rhetoric to its regrettable use. In time, the Sophists' skepticism and relativism made them suspect. No one could criticize them for training lawyers to argue either side of a case—a technique called *antilogic.* Surely people deserve to have their defense presented with as much skill as the prosecutor uses against them. As long as the art of persuasion was linked to the pursuit of truth there could be no quarrel with the Sophists. But since they looked upon truth as a relative matter, they were eventually accused of teaching the young citizens how to make a bad case look good or to make the unjust cause appear to be just. Furthermore, they developed the reputation of taking young people from good families and leading them in a critical and destructive analysis of their traditional religious and ethical views. To add further to their ill repute, they departed from the earlier image of the philosopher as a disinterested thinker who engaged in philosophy with no concern for financial gain. The Sophists, by contrast, charged fees for their teaching, and they sought out the rich who were able to pay these fees. Socrates had studied under the Sophists, but because of his poverty could only afford their "shorter courses." This practice of charging fees for their teaching prompted Plato to disparage them as "shopkeepers with spiritual wares."

Protagoras

Among the Sophists who came to Athens, Protagoras of Abdera (*c.* 490–*c.* 420 BCE) was the oldest and, in many ways, the most influential. He is best known for his statement that "man is the measure of all things, of the things that are, that they are, and of the things that are not, that they are not." That is, a person is the ultimate standard of all judgments that he or she makes. This means that whatever knowledge I might achieve about anything would be limited to my human capacities. Protagoras dismissed any discussion of theology, saying that "About the gods, I am not able to know whether they exist or do not exist, nor what they are like in form; for the factors preventing knowledge are many: the obscurity of the subject, and the shortness of human life." Knowledge, Protagoras said, is limited to our various perceptions, and these perceptions will differ with each person. If two people observe the same object, their sensations would be different, because each would occupy a different position in relation to it. Similarly, the same breeze blowing on two people would feel cool to one, while it would be warm to the other. Whether the breeze is or is not cold cannot be answered in a simple way. It is in fact cold for one person and warm for the other. To say that a person is the measure of all things is, therefore, to say that our knowledge is measured by what we perceive. If something within us makes us perceive things differently, there is then no standard for testing whether one person's perception is right and another person's is wrong. Protagoras thought that the objects we perceive by our various senses must possess all of the properties that different people perceive as belonging to them. For this reason, it is impossible to discover what is the "true" nature of anything; a thing has as many characteristics as there are people perceiving it. Thus, there is no way to distinguish between the *appearance* of a thing and its *reality*. On this theory of knowledge, it would be impossible to attain any absolute scientific knowledge since there are built-in differences in each observer, which lead each of us to see things differently. Protagoras concluded, therefore, that knowledge is relative to each person.

When he turned to the subject of ethics, Protagoras held that moral judgments are relative. He was willing to admit that the idea of law reflects a general desire in each culture to establish a moral order among all people. But he denied that there was any uniform law of nature pertaining to human behavior that all people everywhere could discover. He distinguished between nature and custom and said that laws and moral rules are based, not upon nature, but upon custom. Each society has its own laws and its own moral rules, and there is no way of judging some to be right and others wrong. But Protagoras did not carry this moral relativism to the extreme view that every individual can decide what is moral for him or herself. Instead, he took the conservative position that the state makes the laws, and everyone should accept these laws because they are as good as any that can be made. Other communities might have different laws, and individuals within a state might think of different laws, but in neither case are these better laws: they are only different. In the interest of a peaceful and orderly society, then, people should respect and uphold the customs, laws, and moral rules that their tradition has carefully nurtured. In matters of religion, Protagoras took a similar view: just because we cannot with certainty know the existence and nature of the gods, this should not prevent us from participating in the worship of the gods. The interesting outcome of Protagoras' relativism was his conservative conclusion that the young should be educated to accept and support the tradition of their society, not because this tradition is true but because it makes possible a stable society. Still, there is no question that Protagoras' relativism seriously dislodged confidence in the possibility of discovering true knowledge. This brought upon his skepticism the heavy criticism of Socrates and Plato.

Gorgias   skeptic

Gorgias (late 5th century BCE) came to Athens from Sicily as ambassador from his native city of Leontini in 427 BCE. He took such a radical view regarding truth that he eventually gave up philosophy and turned instead to the practice and teaching of rhetoric. His extreme view differed from Protagoras' since, while Protagoras said that everything is true relative to the spectator, Gorgias denied that there is any truth at all. With hair-splitting keenness, and employing the type of reasoning used by the Eleatic philosophers Parmenides and Zeno,

Gorgias propounded the extraordinary notions (1) that nothing exists, (2) that if anything exists it is incomprehensible, and (3) that even if it is comprehensible, it cannot be communicated. Taking this third notion, for example, he argued that we communicate with words, but words are only symbols or signs, and no symbol can ever be the same as the thing it symbolizes. For this reason, knowledge can never be communicated. By this type of reasoning, Gorgias thought he could prove all three of his propositions, or at least that his reasoning was as coherent as any used by those who disagreed with him. He was convinced, consequently, that there could be no reliable knowledge, and certainly no truth.

Abandoning philosophy, Gorgias turned to rhetoric and tried to perfect it as the art of persuasion. In this connection, tradition relates that he developed the technique of deception, making use of psychology and of the powers of suggestion. Having earlier concluded that there is no truth, he was willing to employ the art of persuasion for whatever practical ends he chose.

Thrasymachus

In the *Republic,* Thrasymachus (late 5th century BCE) is portrayed as the Sophist who asserted that injustice is to be preferred to the life of justice. He did not look upon injustice as a defect of character. On the contrary, Thrasymachus considered the unjust person as positively superior in character and intelligence. Indeed, he said that "injustice pays," not only at the meager level of the pick-pocket (although there is profit in that too), but especially for those who carry injustice to perfection and make themselves masters of whole cities and nations. Justice, he said, is pursued by simpletons and leads to weakness. Thrasymachus held that people should aggressively pursue their own interests in a virtually unlimited form of self-assertion. He regarded justice as being the interest of the stronger and believed that "might is right." Laws, he said, are made by the ruling party for its own interest. These laws define what is right. In all countries alike, the notion of "right" means the same thing, since "right" is simply the interest of the party established in power. So, Thrasymachus says, "the sound conclusion is that what is 'right' is the same everywhere: the interest of the stronger party."

Here, then, is the reduction of morality to power. This is an inevitable consequence of the Sophists' skepticism, which led them to a relativistic attitude toward truth and ethics. It was Socrates' chief concern to unravel the logical inconsistencies of the Sophists, to rebuild some notion of truth, and to establish some firm foundation for moral judgments.

SOCRATES

Many Athenians mistook Socrates for a Sophist. The fact is that Socrates was one of the Sophists' keenest critics. That Socrates should have been identified with them was due in part to his relentless analysis of any and every subject—a technique also employed by the Sophists. Nevertheless, there was a fundamental difference between the Sophists and Socrates. The Sophists split hairs to show that equally good arguments could be advanced on either side of any issue. They were skeptics who doubted that there could be any certain or reliable knowledge. Moreover, they concluded that since all knowledge is relative, moral standards are also relative. Socrates, on the other hand, had a different motivation for his constant argumentation. He was committed to the pursuit of truth and considered it his mission to seek out the basis for stable and certain knowledge. He was also attempting to discover the foundation of the good life. As he pursued his mission, Socrates devised a method for arriving at truth; he linked *knowing* and *doing,* so that to know the good is to do the good. In that sense, "knowledge is virtue." Unlike the Sophists, then, Socrates engaged in argumentation, not for ends destructive of truth or to develop pragmatic skills among lawyers and politicians, but to achieve substantive concepts of truth and goodness.

Socrates' Life

Seldom has there been a time and place so rich in genius as the Athens into which Socrates was born in 470 BCE. By this time, the playwright Aeschylus had written some of his great dramatic works. The playwrights Euripides and Sophocles were young boys who were to later produce great tragedies that Socrates may very well have attended. Pericles, who was to usher in a great age of democracy and the flowering of art, was still a young man. Socrates could have seen the Parthenon and the statues of Phidias started and completed during his lifetime. By this time, too, Persia had been defeated, and Athens had advanced toward becoming a naval power with control over much of the Aegean Sea. Athens had reached a level of unprecedented power and splendor. Although Socrates grew up in a golden age, his declining years were to see Athens defeated in war and his own life brought to an end in prison. In 399 BCE, at the age of 71, he drank hemlock poison in compliance with the death sentence issued by the court that tried him.

Socrates wrote nothing. Most of what we know about him has been preserved by three of his famous younger contemporaries, Aristophanes, Xenophon, and, most importantly, Plato. From these sources Socrates emerges as an intense genius who, along with extraordinary rational rigor, possessed a personal warmth and a fondness for humor. He was a robust man with great powers of physical endurance. In his playful comedy, *The Clouds,* Aristophanes depicts Socrates as a strutting waterfowl, poking fun at his habit of rolling his eyes and referring impishly to his "pupils" and "thinking shop." From Xenophon comes the portrait of a loyal soldier who has a passion for discussing the requirements of morality and who inevitably attracted the younger people to seek out his advice. Plato confirms this general portrait and in addition pictures Socrates as a man with a deep sense of mission and absolute moral purity. In the *Symposium,* Plato relates how Alcibiades, a fair youth, expected to win the amorous affections of Socrates, contriving in

Socrates
(New York Public Library Picture Collection)

various ways to be alone with him. But, Alcibiades says, "nothing of the sort occurred at all: he would merely converse with me in his usual manner, and when he had spent the day with me he would leave me and go his way." In military campaigns, Socrates could go without food longer than anyone else. Others wrapped themselves up with "prodigious care" against the bitter cold of winter, using "felt and little fleeces" over their shoes. But Socrates, Alcibiades says, "walked out in that weather, clad in just such a coat as he was always wont to wear, and he made his way more easily over the ice unshod than the rest of us did in our shoes."

Socrates was capable of intense and sustained concentration. On one occasion during a military campaign, he stood in deep contemplation for a day and night, "till dawn came and the sun rose; then walked away after offering a prayer to the sun." He had frequently received messages or warnings from a mysterious "voice," or what he called his *daimon*. Although this "supernatural" sign invaded his thoughts from early childhood, it suggests more than anything else Socrates' sensitivity as a "visionary," particularly his sensitivity to the moral qualities of human actions that make life worth living. He must have been familiar with the natural science of the earlier Greek philosophers, although he does say in Plato's *Apology* that "the simple truth is, O Athenians, that I have nothing to do with physical speculations." For him, such speculations gave way to the more urgent questions about human nature, truth, and goodness. The decisive event that confirmed his mission as a moral philosopher was the reply of the Delphic Oracle. As the story goes, one day a young religious zealot named Chaerophon went to the temple of Apollo near Delphi and asked whether there was any living person who was wiser than Socrates; the priestess replied that there was not. Socrates interpreted this reply to mean that he was the wisest because he realized and admitted his own ignorance. In this attitude, Socrates set out on his quest for abiding truth and wisdom.

Socrates as a Philosopher

Because Socrates left no writings of his own, there is today some disagreement over what philosophical ideas can be properly attributed to him. Our most extensive sources of his thought are the *Dialogues* of Plato, in which he is the leading character. But the persistent question is whether Plato is here reporting what Socrates had actually taught or expressing his own ideas through the figure of Socrates. There are those who argue that the Socrates found in Plato's dialogues is the historically correct Socrates. This would mean that Socrates must get all the credit for the novel philosophical activity these dialogues contain. On this view, Plato would get credit only for the literary form he devised for preserving, elaborating, and lending precision and color to Socrates' thought. On the other hand, Aristotle distinguished between the philosophical contributions made by Socrates and Plato. To Socrates Aristotle gave the credit for "inductive arguments and universal definitions," and to Plato he ascribed the development of the theory of Forms—the notion that universal archetypes exist independently of the particular things that embody them. In essence, the argument is over whether Socrates or Plato developed the theory of Forms. Since Aristotle was himself particularly interested in this subject, and, having discussed it at length with Plato in the Academy, it seems reasonable to suppose that his distinction between Socrates' and Plato's ideas is accurate. At the same time, some of the early dialogues appear to represent Socrates' own thought, as in the case of the *Apology* and the *Euthyphro*. The most plausible solution to the problem, therefore, would be to accept portions of both views. Thus we can agree that much of the earlier dialogues are portrayals of Socrates' philosophic activity, whereas the later dialogues especially represent Plato's own philosophic development, including his formulation of the metaphysical theory of the Forms. On this basis, we should see Socrates as an original philosopher who developed a new method of intellectual inquiry.

If Socrates was to be successful in overcoming the relativism and skepticism of the Sophists, he had to discover some immovable foundation upon which to build the edifice of knowledge. Socrates discovered this foundation within people, and not in the facts of the world outside. The interior life, said Socrates, is the seat of a unique activity—the activity of knowing, which leads to the practical activity of doing. To describe this activity, Socrates developed the conception of the soul, or *psyche*. For him the soul was not any particular faculty, nor was it any special kind of substance. Instead, it was the capacity for intelligence and character; it was a person's conscious personality. Socrates further described what he meant by the soul as "that within us in virtue of which we are pronounced wise or foolish, good or bad." By describing it in these terms, Socrates identified the soul with the normal powers of intelligence and character instead of as some ghostly substance. The soul was the structure of personality. However difficult it may have been for Socrates to describe exactly what the soul is, he was sure that the activity of the soul is to *know* and to influence or even direct and govern a person's daily conduct. Although for Socrates the soul was not a *thing,* he could say that our greatest concern should be the proper care of our souls so as to "make the soul as good as possible." We take best care of our souls when we understand the difference between fact and fancy, and thereby build our thought upon a knowledge of what human life is really like. Having attained such knowledge, those who have the proper care of their soul in mind will conduct their behavior in accordance with their knowledge of true moral values. In a nutshell, Socrates was primarily concerned with *the good life,* and not with mere contemplation.

For Socrates, the key point in this conception of the soul concerns our conscious awareness of what some words mean. To know that some things contradict others—for example, that justice cannot mean harming others—is a typical example of what the soul can discover just by using its abilities to know. We thus do violence to our human nature when we act in defiance of this knowledge, such as if we harm someone while fully aware that such behavior is contrary to our knowledge of justice. Socrates was certain that people could attain sure and reliable knowledge, and that only such knowledge could be the proper basis of morality. His first major task was, therefore, to clarify for himself and his followers just *how* one attains reliable knowledge.

Socrates' Theory of Knowledge: Intellectual Midwifery

Socrates was convinced that the surest way to attain reliable knowledge was through the practice of disciplined conversation, with this conversation acting as an intellectual midwife. This method, which he called *dialectic,* was a deceptively simple technique. It would always begin with a discussion of the most obvious aspects of any problem. He believed that through the process of dialogue, where all parties to the conversation were forced to clarify their ideas, the final outcome of the conversation would be a clear statement of what was meant. Although the technique appeared simple, it was not long before anyone upon whom Socrates employed it could feel its intense rigor, as well as the discomfort of Socrates' irony. In the earliest dialogues in which this method is displayed, Socrates pretends to be ignorant about a subject and then tries to draw out from the other people their fullest possible knowledge about it. He considered this method of dialectic a kind of intellectual midwifery. His assumption was that by progressively correcting incomplete or inaccurate notions, we could coax the truth out of anyone. He would often expose contradictions lurking beneath the other person's views—a technique called *elenchus*—and thereby force the person to abandon his or her misdirected opinion. If the human mind was incapable of knowing something, Socrates would want to demonstrate that too. Accordingly, he believed that no unexamined *idea* is worth having any more than the unexamined *life* is worth living. Some dialogues therefore end inconclusively, since Socrates was concerned not with imposing a set of dogmatic ideas upon his listeners but with leading them through an orderly process of thought.

We find a good example of Socrates' method in his dialogue *Euthyphro.* The scene is in front of the Hall of King Archon, where Socrates is waiting in the hope of discovering who has brought suit against him for *impiety,* which was a capital offense. Young Euthyphro arrives upon the scene and explains that he plans to bring charges of impiety against his own father. With devastating irony, Socrates expresses relief at his good fortune in meeting him, for Euthyphro is making the identical charge against his father that has been made against Socrates. Sarcastically, Socrates says to Euthyphro that "not every one could rightly do what you are doing; only a man who is well advanced in wisdom." Only someone who knew exactly what impiety meant would charge anyone with such a serious offense. And to bring such a charge against one's *father* would only corroborate the assumption that the accuser knew what he was talking about. Socrates professes ignorance of the meaning of impiety and asks Euthyphro to explain what it means, since he has charged his father with this offense.

Euthyphro answers Socrates by defining piety as "prosecuting the wrongdoer" and impiety as not prosecuting him. To this Socrates replies that "I did not ask you to tell me one or two of all the many pious actions that there are; I want to know what is the *concept* of piety which makes all pious actions pious." Since his first definition was unsatisfactory, Euthyphro tries again, this time saying that "what is pleasing to the gods is pious." But Socrates points out that the gods quarrel among each other, which shows that the gods disagree among themselves about what is better and worse. The same act, then, can be pleasing to some gods and not pleasing to others. So, Euthyphro's second definition is also inadequate. Trying to repair the damage, Euthyphro offers a new definition, saying that "piety is what *all* the gods love, and impiety is what they *all* hate." But, asks Socrates, "do the gods love an act because it is pious, or is it pious because the gods love it?" In short, what is the *essence* of piety? Trying again, Euthyphro says that piety is "that part of justice which has to do with the attention which is due to the gods." Again, Socrates presses for a clearer definition by asking what kind of attention is due to the gods. By this time, Euthyphro is hopelessly adrift, and Socrates says to him that "it cannot be that you would ever have undertaken to prosecute your aged father . . . unless you had known exactly what is piety and impiety." And when Socrates presses him once more for a clearer definition, Euthyphro answers, "Another time . . . Socrates. I am in a hurry now, and it is time for me to be off."

The dialogue ends inconclusively as far as the subject of piety is concerned. Nevertheless, it is a vivid example of Socrates' method of dialectic and a portrayal of his conception of the philosophical life. More specifically, it illustrates Socrates' unique concern with *definition* as the instrument of clear thought.

Definition   Nowhere is Socrates' approach to knowledge more clearly displayed than in his preoccupation with the process of definition. For him, a definition is a clear and fixed concept. Although particular events or things varied in some respects or passed away, Socrates was impressed with the fact that something about them was the same, that never varied and never passed away. This was their definition, or their essential nature. It was this permanent meaning that Socrates wanted Euthyphro to give him when he asked for that "concept of Piety which makes all pious acts pious." In a similar way, Socrates sought after the concept of *Justice* by which acts become just, and the concept of *Beauty* by which particular things are said to be beautiful, and the concept of *Goodness* by which we recognize human acts to be good. For example, no particular thing is perfectly beautiful; it is beautiful, though, only because it partakes of the larger concept of Beauty. Moreover, when a beautiful thing passes away, the concept of Beauty remains. Socrates was struck by our ability to think about general ideas and not only about particular things.

He argued that in some way we think of two different kinds of objects whenever we think about anything. A beautiful flower is at once *this particular flower* and at the same time a single example or partaker of the general or *universal meaning of Beauty*. Definition, for Socrates, involves a process by which our minds can distinguish or sort out these two objects of thought, namely, the particular (this beautiful flower) and the general or universal (the concept of Beauty of which this flower partakes so as to make it a beautiful flower). If Socrates asked, "What is a beautiful flower?" or "What is a pious act?" he would not be satisfied with your pointing to this flower or this act. For, although Beauty is in some way connected with a given thing, that thing does not either equal or exhaust the concept of Beauty. Moreover, although various beautiful things differ from each other, whether they are flowers or people, they are each called beautiful because, in spite of their differences, they share in common that element by which they are called beautiful. Only by the rigorous process of definition can we finally grasp the distinction between a particular thing (this beautiful flower) and the general fixed notion (Beauty or beautiful). The process of definition, as Socrates worked it out, was a process for arriving at clear and fixed concepts.

Through this technique of definition, Socrates showed that true knowledge is more than simply an inspection of facts. Knowledge has to do with our ability to discover in facts the abiding elements that remain after the facts disappear. Beauty remains after the rose fades. To the mind an imperfect triangle suggests *the* Triangle; imperfect circles are seen as approximations to the perfect Circle, the definition of which produces the clear and fixed notion of Circle. Facts can produce a variety of notions, for no two flowers are the same. By the same token, no two people or no two cultures are the same. If we limited our knowledge simply to uninterpreted facts, we would conclude that everything is different, and there are no universal likenesses. The Sophists did just this, and, from the facts they had collected about other cultures, they argued that all notions of justice and goodness are relative. But Socrates would not accept this conclusion. To him the factual differences between people—for example, the differences in their height, strength, and mental ability—did not obscure the equally certain fact that they were all people. By his process of definition, he cut through the obvious factual differences about particular people and discovered what makes each person a person, in spite of the differences. His clear concept of *humanness* provided him with a firm basis for thinking about people. Similarly, though cultures differ, though their actual laws and moral rules differ, still, said Socrates, the notions of Law, Justice, and Goodness can be defined as rigorously as the notion of human being. Instead of leading to intellectual skepticism and moral relativism, Socrates believes that the variety of facts around us could yield clear and fixed concepts, so long as we employ the technique of analysis and definition.

Behind the world of facts, then, Socrates believed there was an order in things that we could discover. This led him to introduce into philosophy a way of looking at everything in the universe, namely a *teleological* conception of things—the view that things have a function or purpose and tend toward good. To say, for example, that a person has a definable nature is also to say that a special activity is appropriate to his or her nature. If people are rational beings, acting rationally is the behavior appropriate to human nature. From this it is a short step to saying that people *ought* to act rationally. By discovering the essential nature of everything, Socrates believed that he could thereby also discover the intelligible order in everything. In this view, things not only have their own specific natures and functions, but these functions have some additional purpose in the whole scheme of things. There are many kinds of things in the universe, not because of some haphazard mixture, but because each thing does one thing best, and things acting together make up the orderly universe. Clearly, Socrates could distinguish between two levels of knowledge, one based upon the *inspection* of facts and the other based upon the *interpretation* of facts. Alternatively, one is based upon particular things and the other is based upon general or universal concepts.

The fact that universal concepts, such as Beauty, Straight, Triangle, and Human Being, are always used in discourse certainly suggests that there is some basis in reality for their use. The big question soon to arise was whether these universal concepts refer to some *existing reality* in the same way that particular words do. If the word *John* refers to a person existing in a particular place, does the concept *Human Being* also refer to some reality someplace? Whether Socrates dealt with this problem of the metaphysical status of universals depends upon whether we consider Plato or Socrates to be the author of the theory of the Forms. Plato certainly taught that these conceptual Forms, whatever they are, are the most real things there are and that they have a separate existence from the particular things we see, which partake of these Forms. Aristotle rejected this theory of the separate existence of Forms, arguing that in some way universal forms exist only in the actual things we experience. He showed, too, that Socrates had not "separated off" these Forms from things. If Socrates was not the author of the theory of Forms, found in the Platonic dialogues, he was, nevertheless, the one who had fashioned the notion of an intelligible order lying behind the visible world.

Socrates' Moral Thought

For Socrates, knowledge and virtue were the same thing. If virtue has to do with "making the soul as good as possible," it is first necessary to know what makes the soul good. Therefore, goodness and knowledge are closely related. But Socrates said more about morality than simply this. He in fact identified goodness and knowledge, saying that to know the good is to do the good, that knowledge is virtue. By identifying knowledge and virtue, Socrates meant also to say that vice, or evil, is the absence of knowledge. Just as knowledge is virtue, so, too, vice is ignorance. The outcome of this line of reasoning was Socrates' conviction that no one ever indulged in vice or committed an evil act knowingly. Wrongdoing, he said, is always involuntary, being the product of ignorance.

To equate virtue with knowledge and vice with ignorance may seem to contradict our most elementary human experiences. Commonsense tells us that we frequently indulge in acts that we know to be wrong, so that wrongdoing for us is a deliberate and voluntary act. Socrates would have readily agreed that we commit acts that can be called evil. He denied, however, that people deliberately did evil acts because they knew them to be evil. When people commit evil acts, said Socrates, they always do them thinking that they are good in some way.

When he equated virtue and knowledge, Socrates had in mind a particular conception of virtue. For him, virtue meant fulfilling one's function. As a rational being, a person's function is to behave rationally. At the same time, every human being has the inescapable desire for happiness or the well-being of his or her soul. This inner well-being, this "making the soul as good as possible," can be achieved only by certain appropriate types of behavior. Because we have a desire for happiness, we choose our acts with the hope that they will bring us happiness. Which acts, or what behavior, will produce happiness? Socrates knew that some forms of behavior *appear* to produce happiness, but in *reality* do not. For this reason, we frequently choose acts that may in themselves be questionable but that we nevertheless think will bring us happiness. Thieves may know that stealing as such is wrong, but they steal in the hope that it will bring them happiness. Similarly, we pursue power, physical pleasure, and property, which are the symbols of success and happiness, confusing these with the true ground of happiness.

The equating of vice with ignorance is not so contrary to common sense after all, since the ignorance Socrates speaks of refers to an act's ability to produce happiness, not to the act itself. It is ignorance about one's soul, about what it takes to "make the soul as good as possible." Wrongdoing is, therefore, a consequence of an inaccurate estimate of types of behavior. It is the inaccurate expectation that certain kinds of things or pleasures will produce happiness. Wrongdoing, then, is the product of ignorance simply because it is done with the hope that it will do what it cannot do. Ignorance consists in failing to see that certain behavior cannot produce happiness. It takes a true knowledge of human nature to know what is required to be happy. It also takes a true knowledge of things and types of behavior to know whether they can fulfill the human requirements for happiness. And it requires knowledge to be able to distinguish between what *appears* to give happiness and what *really* does.

To say, then, that vice is ignorance and is involuntary is to say that no one ever deliberately chooses to damage, disfigure, or destroy his or her human nature. Even when we choose pain, we do so with the expectation that this pain will lead to virtue and to the fulfillment of our human nature—a nature that seeks its own well-being. We always think we are acting rightly. But whether our actions are right depends upon whether they harmonize with true human nature, and this is a matter of true knowledge. Moreover, because Socrates believed that the fundamental structure of human nature is constant, he also believed that virtuous behavior is also constant. This was the basis for his great triumph over the Sophists' skepticism and relativism. Socrates set the direction that moral philosophy would take throughout the history of Western civilization. His thought was modified by Plato, Aristotle, and the Christian theologians, but it remained the dominant intellectual and moral tradition around which other variations developed.

Socrates' Trial and Death

Convinced that the care of the human soul should be our greatest concern, Socrates spent most of his time examining his own life as well as the life and thought of other Athenians. While Athens was a secure and powerful democracy under Pericles, Socrates could pursue his mission as a "gadfly" without serious opposition. He relentlessly looked for the stable and constant moral order underlying people's irregular behavior. This quest proved alternately irritating and amusing and gave him the reputation as an intellectual who dealt in paradoxes. Worse still, people believed that he thought too freely about sensitive issues that, according to many Athenians, shouldn't be questioned. Nevertheless, as long as Athens was in a position of economic and military strength, Socrates could question things as he pleased, without penalty. But, as Athens' social climate moved towards a condition of crisis and defeat, Socrates was no longer immune from penalty. His efforts to develop dialectical skill among young people from leading families had raised suspicions about Socrates earlier—particularly the skill of raising searching questions about customs in moral, religious, and political behavior. But his actions were not considered a clear and present danger until Athens was at war with Sparta.

A series of events connected with this war eventually led to the trial and sentence of Socrates. One event was the traitorous actions of Alcibiades, whom the Athenians knew was Socrates' pupil. Alcibiades actually went to Sparta and gave valuable advice to the Spartans in their war with Athens. Inevitably many Athenians concluded that Socrates must in some way be responsible for what Alcibiades did. In addition, Socrates found himself in serious disagreement with the Committee of the Senate of Five Hundred, of which he was a member. The issue before them was the case of eight military commanders who were charged with negligence at a naval battle off the islands of Arginusae. The Athenians won this battle in the end but at the staggering cost of 25 ships and 4,000 men. It was decided that the eight generals involved in this expensive campaign should be brought to trial. However, instead of determining the guilt of each general one by one, the Committee was instructed to take a single vote concerning the guilt of the whole group of eight generals. At first the Committee resisted this move, holding it to be a violation of the regular constitutional procedures. But when the prosecutors threatened to add the names of the Committee members to the list of generals, only Socrates stood his ground, and the rest of the Committee capitulated. The generals were then found guilty, and the six of them who were in custody were immediately put to death. These events occurred in 406 BCE. In 404 BCE, with the fall of Athens, Socrates once again found himself in opposition to a formidable group. Under pressure from the Spartan victor, a Commission of Thirty was set up in order to fashion legislation for the new government of Athens. Instead, this group became a violent oligarchy, arbitrarily executing former supporters of Pericles' democratic order and taking property for themselves. Within a year, this oligarchy had been removed by force and a democratic order restored. But unfortunately for Socrates, some of the members of the revolutionary oligarchy had been his close friends, particularly Critias and Charmides. This was another occasion of guilt by association, as in the case of Alcibiades, where Socrates was put in the position of being a teacher of traitors. By this time, irritation had developed into distrust, and in around 399 BCE, Socrates was brought to trial on the charge, as Diogenes Laertius recorded it,

"(1) of not worshipping the gods whom the State worships, but introducing new and unfamiliar religious practices; (2) and, further, of corrupting the young. The prosecutor demands the death penalty."

Socrates could have gone into voluntary exile upon hearing the charges against him. Instead, he remained in Athens and defended himself before a court whose jury numbered about five hundred. His defense, as recorded in Plato's *Apology*, is a brilliant proof of his intellectual activities. It is also a powerful exposure of his accusers' motives and the inadequacy of the grounds for their charges. He emphasized his lifelong devotion to Athens, including references to his military service and his actions in upholding constitutional procedures in the trial of the generals. His defense is a model of forceful argument, resting wholly upon a recitation of facts and upon the requirements of rational discourse. When he was found guilty, he was given the opportunity to suggest his own sentence. Being convinced not only of his innocence but of the great value his type of life and teachings had been to Athens, he proposed that Athens should reward him by giving him what he deserved. Comparing himself to someone "who has won victory at the Olympic games with his horse or chariots," Socrates said, "such a man only makes you seem happy, but I make you really happy." Therefore, he said, his reward should be "public maintenance in the prytaneum," an honor bestowed upon eminent Athenians, generals, Olympian winners, and other outstanding people. Affronted by his arrogance, the jury sentenced him to death.

To the end, his friends tried to make possible his escape, but Socrates would have none of it. Just as he refused to play on the emotions of the jury by calling attention to his wife and young children, so now he was not impressed by the plea of his student, Crito, that he should think of his children. How could he undo all he had taught others and unmake his conviction that he must never play fast and loose with the truth? Socrates was convinced that to escape would be to defy and thereby injure Athens and its procedures of law. That would be to strike at the wrong target. The laws were not responsible for his trial and sentence; it was his misguided accusers, Anytus and Meletus, who were at fault. Accordingly, he confirmed his respect for the laws and the procedures by complying with the court's sentence.

Describing Socrates' last moments after he drank the poisonous potion, Plato writes in his *Phaedo* that "Socrates felt himself, and said that when it came to his heart, he should be gone. He was already growing cold . . . and spoke for the last time. Crito, he said, I owe a cock to Asclepius; do not forget to pay it. . . . Such was the end . . . of our friend, a man, I think, who was, of all the men of his time, the best, the wisest and the most just."

CHAPTER 3

Plato

*P*lato's comprehensive treatment of knowledge was so powerful that his philosophy became one of the most influential strands in the history of Western thought. Unlike his predecessors, who focused upon single main problems, Plato brought together all the major concerns of human thought into a coherent organization of knowledge. The earliest Greek philosophers, the Milesians, were concerned chiefly with the constitution of physical nature, not with the foundations of morality. Similarly, the Eleatic philosophers Parmenides and Zeno were interested chiefly in arguing that reality consists of a changeless, single reality, the One. Heraclitus and the Pythagoreans, on the other hand, described reality as always changing, full of flux, and consisting of a multitude of different things. Socrates and the Sophists showed less interest in physical nature and, instead, steered philosophy into the arena of morality. Plato's great influence stems from the manner in which he brought all these diverse philosophical concerns into a unified system of thought.

PLATO'S LIFE

Plato was born in Athens in 428/27 BCE, one year after the death of Pericles and when Socrates was about 42 years old. Athenian culture was flourishing, and as Plato's family was one of the most distinguished in Athens, his early training included the rich ingredients of that culture in the arts, politics, and philosophy. His father traced his lineage to the old kings of Athens and before them to the god Poseidon. His mother, Perictione, was the sister of Charmides and the cousin of Critias, both of whom were leading personalities in the short-lived oligarchy which followed the fall of Athens in the Peloponnesian War. When his father died, early in Plato's childhood, his mother married Pyrilampes, who had been a close friend of Pericles. Such close ties with eminent public figures had long distinguished Plato's family. This is especially so on his mother's side, where an early relative had been a friend of the great

Plato conversing with a student
(Corbis-Bettmann)

giver of law, Solon, and another distant member of the family was the archon, or the highest magistrate, in 644 BCE.

In such a family atmosphere, Plato learned much about public life and developed at an early age a sense of responsibility for public political service. But Plato's attitude toward Athenian democracy was also influenced by what he saw during the last stages of the Peloponnesian War. He saw the inability of this democracy to produce great leaders and saw also the way it treated one of its greatest citizens, Socrates. Plato was present at Socrates' trial and was willing to guarantee payment of his fine. The collapse of Athens and the execution of his master, Socrates, could well have led Plato to despair of democracy and to begin formulating a new conception of political leadership in which authority and knowledge are appropriately combined. Plato concluded that as in the case of a ship, where the pilot's authority rests upon knowledge of navigation, so also the ship of state should be piloted by someone who has adequate knowledge. He developed this theme at length in his *Republic*.

Around 387 BCE, when he was about 40 years old, Plato founded the Academy at Athens. This was, in a sense, the first university to emerge in the history of Western Europe, and for 20 years, Plato administered its affairs as its director. The chief aim of the Academy was to pursue scientific knowledge through original research. Although Plato was particularly concerned with educating future leaders, he was convinced that their education must consist of rigorous intellectual activity, by which he meant scientific study, including mathematics, astronomy, and harmonics. The scientific emphasis at the Academy was in sharp contrast to the activities of Plato's contemporary Isocrates, who took a more practical approach to training young people for public life. Isocrates had little use for science, holding that pure research had no practical value or humanistic interest. But Plato put mathematics into the center of his curriculum, arguing that the best preparation for those who will wield political power is the disinterested pursuit of truth or scientific knowledge. A brilliant group of scholars associated with the Academy made significant advances over the mathematical knowledge of the older Pythagoreans, and this activity caused the famous mathematician Eudoxus to bring his own school from Cyzicus to unite with Plato's Academy in Athens.

The execution of Socrates deeply disillusioned Plato about politics, thus diverting him personally from an active life of public service. Plato nevertheless continued to teach that rigorous knowledge must be the proper training of the ruler. He gained a wide reputation for this view and was invited to Syracuse, a place he traveled to at least three times, to give instruction to a young tyrant, Dionysius II. His efforts did not meet with success since his student's education was started too late and his character was too weak. Plato continued to write in his ripe years, and while still active in the Academy, died in 348/47 BCE at the age of 80.

Plato lectured at the Academy without the use of notes. Because his lectures were never written, they were thus never published, although notes by his students were circulated. Aristotle, for example, who entered the Academy in 367 BCE when he was 18 years old, took notes of Plato's lectures. Nevertheless, Plato did compose more than 20 philosophical dialogues, with the longest one occupying around 200 pages. Scholars debate about the exact chronology of these dialogues, but they are now commonly placed in three groups. The first of these is a group of early writings, usually called Socratic dialogues because of their preoccupation with ethics. These consist of the *Apology, Crito, Charmides, Laches, Euthyphro, Euthydemus, Cratylus, Protagoras,* and *Gorgias*. The second, or middle group in which the theory of Forms and metaphysical theories are expounded include the *Meno, Symposium, Phaedo, Republic,* and *Phaedrus.* Later in life, Plato wrote some more technical dialogues which often display an attitude of deepening religious conviction; these include the *Theaetetus, Parmenides, Sophist, Statesman, Philebus, Timaeus,* and the *Laws.* There is no one work to which we can go to find a schematic arrangement of Plato's thought. Different dialogues address different issues, and many of his treatments shifted over time. Nevertheless, dominant themes emerge from the various dialogues, to which we will now turn.

THEORY OF KNOWLEDGE

The foundation of Plato's philosophy is his account of knowledge. The Sophists, we have seen, had skeptical views regarding our ability to acquire knowledge. Human knowledge, they believed, was grounded in social customs and the perceptions of individual people. Such "knowledge" fluctuated from one culture or person to another. Plato, though, staunchly rejected this view. He was convinced that there are unchanging and universal truths, which human reason is capable of grasping. In his dialog, *The Republic,* he picturesquely makes his case with the Allegory of the Cave and the metaphor of the Divided Line.

The Cave

Plato asks us to imagine some people living in a large cave where from childhood they have been chained by their legs and necks so that they cannot move. Because they cannot even turn their heads, they can only see what is in front of them. Behind them is an elevation that rises abruptly from the level where the prisoners are seated. On this elevation there are other persons walking back and forth carrying artificial objects, including the figures of animals and human beings made out of wood and stone and various other materials. Behind these walking persons is a fire, and further back still is the entrance to the cave. The chained prisoners can look only forward against the wall at the end of the cave and can see neither each other nor the moving persons nor the fire behind them. All that the prisoners can ever see are the shadows on the wall in front of them, which are projected as people walk in front of the fire. They never see the objects or the people carrying them, nor are they aware that the shadows are shadows of other things. When they see a shadow and hear someone's voice echo from the wall, they assume that the sound is coming from the shadow, since they are not aware of the existence of anything else. The prisoners, then, recognize as reality only the shadows formed on the wall.

What would happen, asks Plato, if one of these prisoners were released from his chains, were forced to stand up, turn around, and walk with eyes lifted up toward the light of the fire? All of his movements would be exceedingly painful. Suppose he was forced to look at the objects being carried and the shadows of which he had become accustomed to seeing on the wall. Would he not find these actual objects less pleasing to his eyes, and less meaningful, than the shadows? And would not his eyes ache if he looked straight at the light from the fire itself? At this point he would undoubtedly try to escape from his liberator and turn back to the things he could see with clarity, being convinced that the shadows were clearer than the objects he was forced to look at in the firelight.

Suppose this prisoner could not turn back, but was instead dragged forcibly up the steep and rough passage to the mouth of the cave and released only after he had been brought out into the sunlight. The impact of the radiance of the sun upon his eyes would be so painful that he would be unable to see any of the things that he was now told were real. It would take some time before his eyes became accustomed to the world outside the cave. He would first of all recognize some shadows and would feel at home with them. If it was the shadow of a person, he would have seen that shape before as it appeared on the wall of the cave. Next, he would see the reflections of people and things in the water, and this would represent a major advance in his knowledge. For what he once knew only as a solid dark blur would now be seen in more precise detail of line and color. A flower makes a shadow that gives very little, if any, indication of what a flower really looks like. But its image as reflected in the water provides our eyes with a clearer vision of each petal and its various colors. In time, he would see the flower itself. As he lifted his eyes skyward, he would find it easier at first to look at the heavenly bodies at night, looking at the moon and the stars instead of at the sun in daytime. Finally, he would look right at the sun in its natural positions in the sky and not at its reflection from or through anything else.

This extraordinary experience would gradually lead this liberated prisoner to conclude that the sun is what makes things visible. It is the sun, too, that accounts for the seasons of the year, and for that reason the sun is the cause of life in the Spring. Now he would understand what he and his fellow prisoners saw on the wall—how shadows and reflections differ from things as they really are in the visible world, and that without the sun there would be no visible world. How would such a person feel about his previous life in the cave? He would recall what he and his fellow prisoners there took to be wisdom. He would recall how they would giving prizes to the one who had the sharpest eye for the passing shadows and the best memory for the order in which they followed each other. Would the released prisoner still think such prizes were worth having, and would he envy the people who received honors in the cave? Instead of envy he would have only sorrow and pity for them.

If he went back to his former seat in the cave, he would at first have great difficulty, for going suddenly from daylight into the cave would fill his eyes with darkness. He could not, under these circumstances, compete very effectively with the other prisoners in making out the shadows on the wall. While his eyesight was still dim and unsteady, those who had their permanent residence in the darkness could win every round of competition with him. They would at first find this situation very amusing and would taunt him by saying that his sight was perfectly all right before he went up out of the cave and that now he has returned with his sight ruined. Their conclusion would be that it is not worth trying to go up out of the cave. Indeed, Plato says, "if they could lay hands on the person who was trying to set them free and lead them up, they would kill him."

This allegory suggests that most of us dwell in the darkness of the cave. People have oriented their thoughts around the blurred world of shadows. It is the function of *education* to lead people out of the cave into the world of light. Education is not simply a matter of putting knowledge into a person's soul that does not possess it, any more than vision is putting sight into blind eyes. Knowledge is like vision in that it requires an organ capable of receiving it. The prisoner had to turn his whole body around so that his eyes could see the light instead of the darkness. Similarly, it is necessary for us to turn completely away from the deceptive world of change and appetite that causes a kind of intellectual blindness. Education, then, is a matter of *conversion*—a complete turning around from the world of appearance to the world of reality. "The conversion of the soul," says Plato, is "not to put the power of sight in the soul's eye, which already has it, but to insure that, instead of looking in the wrong direction, it is turned the way it ought to be." But looking in the right direction does not come easily. Even the "noblest natures" do not always want to look that way, and so Plato says that the rulers must "bring compulsion to bear" upon them to ascend upward from darkness to light. Similarly, when those who have been liberated from the cave achieve the highest knowledge, they must not be allowed to remain in the higher world of contemplation. Instead, they must come back down into the cave and take part in the life and labors of the prisoners.

Plato rejected the skepticism of the Sophists by arguing that there are these two worlds, the dark world of the cave and the bright world of light. For Plato, knowledge was not only possible, but it was virtually infallible. What makes knowledge infallible is that it is based upon what is most real. The dramatic contrast between the shadows, reflections, and the actual objects parallels the different degrees to which human beings could be enlightened. The Sophists were skeptical about the possibility of true knowledge because they were impressed by the variety change that we experience, which is relative to each person. Plato recognized that, if all we could know were the shadows, then indeed we could never have reliable knowledge. For these shadows would always change in size and shape depending upon the, to us, unknown motions of the real objects. However, Plato was convinced that we could discover the real objects behind all the multitude of shadows, and thereby attain true knowledge.

The Divided Line

In his metaphor of the Divided Line, Plato provides more detail about the levels of knowledge that we can obtain. In the process of discovering true knowledge, we move through four stages of development. At each stage, there is a parallel between the kind of object presented to our minds and the kind of thought this object makes possible. These objects and their parallel types of thought can be diagramed as follows:

Objects	y	Modes of Thought	
[The Good] Intelligible World	The Good [Forms]	Knowledge	⎫ ⎬ Knowledge *Reality* *permanence*
	Mathematical Objects	Thinking	⎭
[The Sun] Visible World	Things	Belief	⎫ ⎬ Opinion *World of change*
	Images	Imaging	⎭
	x		

Plato's Divided Line

The vertical line from x to y is a continuous one, suggesting that there is some degree of knowledge at every point. But as the line passes through the lowest forms of reality to the highest, there is a parallel progression from the lowest degree of truth to the highest. The line is divided, first of all, into two unequal parts. The upper and larger part represents the intelligible world and the smaller, lower part the visible world. This unequal division symbolizes the lower degree of reality and truth found in the visible world as compared with the greater reality and truth in the intelligible world. Each of these parts is then subdivided in the same proportion as the whole line, producing four parts, each one representing a clearer and more certain type of thought than the one below. Recalling the allegory of the Cave, we can think of this line as beginning in the dark and shadowy world at x and moving up to the bright light at y. Going from x to y represents a continuous process of our intellectual enlightenment. The objects presented to us at each level are not four different kinds of real objects: rather, they represent four different ways of looking at the same object.

Imagining   The most superficial form of mental activity is found at the lowest level of the line. Here we confront images, or the least amount of reality. The word *imagining* could, of course, mean the activity of penetrating beyond the mere appearances of things to their deeper reality. But here Plato means by *imagining* simply the sense experience of appearances wherein we take these appearances as true reality. An obvious example is a shadow, which can be mistaken for something real. Actually, the shadow *is* something real; it is a real shadow. But what makes imagining the lowest form of knowing is that at this stage we do not know that it *is* a shadow or an image that it has confronted. If a person knew that it was a shadow, she would not be in the state of imagining or illusion. The prisoners in the cave were trapped in the deepest ignorance because they were unaware that they were seeing shadows.

Besides shadows, there are other kinds of images that Plato considered deceptive. These are the images fashioned by the artist and the poet. The artist presents images that are at least two steps removed from true reality. Suppose an artist paints a portrait of Socrates. Socrates represents a specific or concrete version of the ideal human. Moreover, the portrait represents only the artist's own view of Socrates. The three levels of reality here are, then, (1) the Form of Humanness, (2) the embodiment of this Form in Socrates, and (3) the image of Socrates as represented on canvas. Plato's criticism of art is that it produces images that, in turn, stimulate illusory ideas in the observer. Again, it is when the image is taken as a perfect version of something real that illusion is produced. For the most part, we know that an artist puts on canvas his or her own way of seeing a subject. Still, artistic images do shape thoughts, and if people restrict their understanding of things to these images with all their distortions and exaggerations, they will certainly lack an understanding of things as they really are.

What concerned Plato most were the images fashioned by the art of using words. Poetry and rhetoric were for him the most serious sources of illusion. Words have the power of creating images before our minds, and the poet and rhetorician have great skill in using words to create such images. Plato was particularly critical of the Sophists, whose influence came from this very skill in the use of words. They could make either side of an argument *seem* as good as the other.

Belief   The next stage after imagining is belief. It may strike us as strange that Plato should use the word *believing* instead of *knowing* to describe the state of mind induced by seeing actual objects. We tend to feel a strong sense of certainty when we observe visible and tangible things. Still, for Plato, seeing constitutes only believing, because visible objects depend upon their context for many of their characteristics. There is a degree of certainty that seeing gives us, but this is not absolute certainty. If the water of the Mediterranean looks blue from the shore but turns out to be clear when taken from the sea, our certainty about its color or composition is at least open to question. If may seem a certainty that all bodies have weight because we see them fall. But this testimony of our vision must also be adjusted to the fact of the weightlessness of bodies in space at certain altitudes. Plato therefore says that believing, even if it is based upon seeing, is still in the stage of opinion. The state of mind produced by visible objects is clearly on a level higher than imagining, because it is based upon a higher form of reality. But although actual things possess greater reality than their shadows, they do not by themselves give us all the knowledge that we want to have about them. Whether it be color, weight, or some other quality, we experience these properties of things under particular circumstances. For this reason, our knowledge about them is limited to these particular circumstances. But we are unsatisfied with this kind of knowledge, knowing that its certainty could very well be shaken if the circumstances were altered. True scientists, therefore, do not want to confine their understanding to these particular cases, but look for principles behind the behavior of things.

Thinking   When we move from believing to thinking, we move from the visible world to the intelligible world, and from the realm of opinion to the realm of knowledge. The state of mind that Plato calls *thinking* is particularly characteristic of the scientist. Scientists deal with visible things but not simply with their vision of them. For the scientist, visible things are symbols of a reality that can be thought but not seen. Plato illustrates this kind of mental activity in reference to the mathematician. Mathematicians engage in the act of "abstraction," of drawing out from the visible thing what that thing symbolizes. When mathematicians see the diagram of a triangle, they think about *triangularity* or triangle-in-itself. They distinguish between the *visible* and the *intelligible* triangle. By using visible symbols, science provides a bridge from the visible to the intelligible world. Science forces us to think, because scientists are always searching for laws or principles. Although scientists may look at a particular object—a triangle or a brain—they go beyond this particular triangle or brain and think about *the* Triangle or *the* Brain. Science requires that we "let go" our senses and rely instead upon our intellects. Our minds know that two and two equal four no matter two of what. It knows also that the angles of an equilateral triangle are all equal, regardless of the size of the triangle. Thinking, therefore, represents the ability of our minds to abstract from a visible object that property which is the same in all objects in that class even though each such actual object will have other variable properties. We can, in short, think the Form "Humanness" whether we observe small, large, dark, light, young, or old persons.

Thinking is characterized not only by its treatment of visible objects as symbols, but also by reasoning from hypotheses. By an *hypothesis* Plato meant a truth which is taken as self-evident but which depends upon some higher truth: "You know," says Plato, "how students of subjects like geometry and arithmetic begin by postulating odd and even numbers, or the various figures and the three kinds of angle. . . . These data they take as known, and having adopted them as assumptions, they do not feel called upon to give any account of them to themselves or to anyone else but treat them as self-evident." Using hypotheses, or "starting from these assumptions, they go on until they arrive, by a series of consistent steps, at all the conclusions they set out to investigate." For Plato, then, an hypothesis did not mean what it means to us, namely, a temporary truth. Rather, he meant by it a firm truth but one that is related to a larger context. The special sciences and mathematics treat their subjects as if they were independent truths. All Plato wants to say here is that if we could view all things as they really are, we should discover that all things are related or connected. Thinking or reasoning from hypotheses does give us knowledge of the truth, but it does still bear this limitation, that it isolates some truths from others, thereby leaving our minds still to ask *why* a certain truth is true.

Perfect Intelligence   We are never satisfied as long as we must still ask for a fuller explanation of things. But to have perfect knowledge would require that we should grasp the relation of everything to everything else—that we should see the unity of the whole of reality. With perfect intelligence we are completely released from sensible objects. At this level, we deal directly with the *Forms.* The Forms are those intelligible objects, such as Triangle and "Human," that have been abstracted from the actual objects. We are grasp these pure

Forms without any interference from even the symbolic character of visible objects. Here, also, we no longer use hypotheses, which represent only limited and isolated truths. We approach this highest level of knowledge to the extent that we are able to move beyond the restrictions of hypotheses toward the unity of all Forms. It is through our intellectual capacity of *dialectic* that we move toward its highest goal, which invoves the ability to see at once the relation of all divisions of knowledge to each other. Perfect intelligence therefore means the unified view of reality and this, for Plato, implies the unity of knowledge.

Plato concludes his discussion of the Divided Line with the summary statement, "now you may take, as corresponding to the four sections, these four states of mind: *intelligence* for the highest, *thinking* for the second, *belief* for the third and for the last *imagining.* These you may arrange as the terms in a proportion, assigning to each a degree of clearness and certainty, corresponding to the measure in which their objects possess truth and reality." The highest degree of reality, he argued, consists of the *Forms,* as compared with shadows, reflections, and even the visible objects. Just what he meant by the Forms we must now explore in greater detail.

Theory of Forms

Plato's theory of the *Forms* is his most significant philosophical contribution. In a nutshell, the *Forms* are those changeless, eternal, and nonmaterial essences or patterns of which the actual visible objects we see are only poor copies. There is the Form of *the* Triangle, and all the triangles we see are mere copies of that Form. There are at least five questions that we might ask about the Forms. And although they cannot be answered with precision, the replies to them that are found in his various dialogues will provide us with Plato's general theory of the Forms.

What Are the Forms?   We have already suggested Plato's answer to this question by saying that Forms are eternal patterns of which the objects that we see are only copies. A beautiful person is a copy of Beauty. We can say about a person that she is beautiful because we know the Form of Beauty and recognize that a person shares more or less in this Form. In his *Symposium,* Plato states that we normally apprehend beauty first of all in a particular object or person. But having discovered beauty in this limited form, we soon "perceive that the beauty of one form is akin to another," and so we move from the beauty of a particular body to the recognition that beauty "in every form is one and the same." The effect of this discovery that all types of beauty have some similarity is to loosen our attachment to the beautiful object and to move from the beautiful physical object to the concept of Beauty. When a person discovers this general quality of Beauty, Plato says, "he will abate his violent love of the one, which he will . . . deem a small thing and will become a lover of all beautiful forms; in the next stage he will consider that the beauty of the mind is more honorable than the beauty of outward form." Then, "drawing towards and contemplating the vast sea of beauty, he will create many fair and noble thoughts and notions in boundless love of wisdom; until on that shore he grows and waxes strong, and at last the vision is revealed to him of a single science, which is the science of beauty everywhere." That is, beautiful things in their multiplicity point toward a Beauty from which everything else derives its Beauty. But this Beauty is not merely a concept: Beauty has objective reality. Beauty is a Form. Things *become* beautiful: but Beauty always *is.* Accordingly, Beauty has a separate existence from those changing things that move in and out of Beauty.

In the *Republic,* Plato shows that the true philosopher wants to know the essential nature of things. When he asks what is justice or beauty, he does not want examples of just and beautiful things. He wants to know what makes these things just and beautiful. The difference between opinion and knowledge is just this, that those who are at the level of opinion can recognize a just act but cannot tell you why it is just. They do not know the essence of Justice, which the particular act shares. Knowledge does not involve simply the passing facts and appearances—that is, the realm of *becoming.* Knowledge seeks what truly *is:* its concern is with *Being.* What really is, what has Being, is the essential nature of things. These *essences* are eternal Forms, such as Beauty and Goodness, which make it possible for us to judge things as beautiful or good.

There are many other forms besides those of Beauty and Goodness. At one point, Plato speaks of the Form of Bed, of which the beds we see are mere copies. But this raises the question whether there are as many Forms as there are essences or essential natures. Although Plato is not sure that there are Forms of dog, water, and other things, he shows in the *Parmenides* that there are "certainly not" Forms of mud and dirt. Clearly, if there were Forms behind all classifications of things, there would have to be a duplicate world. These difficulties increase as we try to specify how many and which Forms there are. Nevertheless, what Plato means by the Forms is clear enough, for he considers them to be the essential archetypes of things, having an eternal existence, apprehended by our minds and not our senses.

Where Do the Forms Exist?   If the Forms are truly real, it would seem that they must be some place. But how can the Forms, which are immaterial, have a location? We could hardly say that they are located in space. Plato's clearest suggestion on this problem is that the Forms are "separate" from concrete things, and they exist "apart from" the things we see. To be "separate" or "apart from" must mean simply that the Forms have an independent existence; they persist even though particular things perish. Forms have no dimension, but the question of their location comes up as a consequence of our language, which implies that Forms, being something, must be some place in space. It may be that nothing more can be said about their location than the fact that the Forms have an independent existence. But there are three additional ways in which Plato emphasizes this. For one thing, Plato argues that, before our souls were united with our bodies, our souls preexisted in a spiritual realm; and, in that state, our souls were acquainted with the Forms. Secondly, Plato argues that, in the process of creation, the God used the Forms in fashioning particular things; this suggests that the Forms had an existence prior to their embodiment in things. Thirdly, these Forms seem to have originally existed in the "mind of God" or in the supreme principle of rationality. In our treatment of Plato's metaphor of the Divided Line, we showed how Plato traced the journey of the mind from the lowest level of images to the highest level, where the Form of the Good contained the perfect vision of *reality*.

Just as the sun in the allegory of the Cave was at once the source of light and life, so also, said Plato, the Form of the Good is "the universal author of all things beautiful and right, parent of light and of the lord of light in this world, and the source of truth and reason in the other." Whether the Forms truly exist in the mind of God is a question, but that the Forms are the agency through which the principle of reason operates in the universe seems to be just what Plato means.

What Is the Relation of Forms to Things?   A Form can be related to a thing in three ways (which may, actually, just be three ways of saying the same thing). First, the Form is the *cause* of the essence of a thing. Next, a thing may be said to *participate* in a Form. And, finally, a thing may be said to imitate or *copy* a Form. In each case, Plato implies that although the Form is separate from the thing—that the Form of Humanness is different from Socrates—still, every concrete or actual thing in some way owes its existence to a Form. It in some degree participates in the perfect model of the class of which it is a member, and is in some measure an imitation or copy of the Form. Later on, Aristotle argued that form and matter are inseparable and that the only real good or beauty was found in actual things. But Plato would only allow participation and imitation as the explanation of the relation between things and their Forms. He accentuated this view by saying that it was the Forms through which order was brought into the chaos, indicating the separate reality of form and matter. Aristotle's criticism of Plato's view was formidable, since there seems to be no coherent way of accounting for the existence of the Forms apart from actual things. Still, Plato would ask him what makes it possible to form a judgment about the imperfection of something if our minds do not have access to anything more than the imperfect thing.

What Is the Relation of Forms to Each Other?   Plato says that "we can have discourse only through the weaving together of Forms." Thinking and discussion proceed for the most part on a level above particular things. We speak in terms of the essences or universals that things illustrate; thus we speak of queens, dogs, and carpenters. These are definitions of things and as such are universals or Forms. To be sure, we also refer to specific things in our experiences, such as dark and beautiful and person, but our language reveals our practice of connecting Forms with Forms. There is the Form Animal, and within that there are also subclasses of Forms, such as Human and Horse. Forms are, therefore, related to each other as genus and species. In this way Forms tend to interlock even while retaining their own unity. The Form

Animal seems to be present also in the Form Horse, so that one Form partakes of the other. There is therefore a hierarchy of Forms representing the structure of reality, of which the visible world is only a reflection. The "lower" we come in this hierarchy of Forms, the closer we come to visible things and therefore the *less* universal is our knowledge, as when we speak of "red apples." Conversely, the higher we go, or the more abstract the Form, as when we speak of Apple in general, the broader our knowledge. The discourse of science is the most abstract, and it is so precisely because it has achieved such independence from particular cases and particular things. For Plato, it possesses the highest form of knowledge. The botanist who has proceeded in knowledge from *this rose* to Rose and to Flower has achieved the kind of abstraction or independence from particulars of which Plato was here thinking. This does not mean, however, that Plato thought that all Forms could be related to each other. He only meant to say that every significant statement involves the use of some Forms and that knowledge consists of understanding the relations of the appropriate Forms to each other.

How Do We Know the Forms?   Plato mentions at least three different ways in which our minds discover the Forms. First there is *recollection*. Before our souls were united with the body, the soul was acquainted with the Forms. People now recollect what their souls knew in their prior state of existence. Visible things remind them of the essences previously known. Education is actually a process of reminiscence. Second, people arrive at the knowledge of Forms through the activity of *dialectic*, which is the power of abstracting the essence of things and discovering the relations of all divisions of knowledge to each other. And third, there is the power of *desire*, Love (*eros*), which leads people step by step, as Plato described in the *Symposium*, from the beautiful object to the beautiful thought and then to the very essence of Beauty itself.

Although the theory of the Forms solves many problems regarding human knowledge, it also leaves many questions unanswered. Plato's language gives the impression that there are two distinct worlds, but the relationship between these worlds is not easily conceived. Nor is the relation between Forms and their corresponding objects as clear as we would wish. Still, his argument is highly suggestive, particularly as he tries to account for our ability to make judgments of value. To say a thing is better or worse implies some standard, which obviously is not there as such in the thing being evaluated. The theory of the Forms also makes possible scientific knowledge, for clearly the scientist has "let go" of actual visible particulars and deals with essences or universals, that is, with "laws." The scientist formulates "laws," and these laws tell us something about *all* things, not only the immediate and particular things. Although this whole theory of the Forms rests upon Plato's metaphysical views—that ultimate reality is nonmaterial—it goes a long way toward explaining the more simple fact of how it is possible for us to have ordinary conversation. Any discourse between human beings, it seems, illustrates our independence from particular things. Conversation, Plato would say, is the clue that leads us to the Forms, for conversation involves more than seeing.

Our eyes can see only the particular thing, but our thinking animates conversation and departs from specific things as our thoughts "see" the universal Form. There is, in the end, a stubborn lure in Plato's theory, even though it ends inconclusively.

MORAL PHILOSOPHY

There is a natural progression from Plato's theory of Forms to his ethical theory. If we can be deceived by appearances in the natural physical world, we can be equally deceived by appearances in the moral realm. There is a special kind of knowledge that helps us to distinguish between shadows, reflections, and real objects in the visible world. This is also the kind of knowledge that we need to discriminate between the shadows and reflections of the genuinely good life. Plato believed that there could be no science of physics if our knowledge were limited to visible things. Similarly, there could be no knowledge of a universal Form of Good if we were limited to the experiences we have of particular cultures. The well-known skepticism of the Sophists illustrated to both Socrates and Plato this connection between knowledge and morality. Believing that all knowledge is relative, the Sophists denied that people discover any stable and universal moral standards. The Sophists' skepticism led them to some inevitable conclusions regarding morality. First, they held that moral rules are fashioned deliberately by each community and have relevance and authority only for the people in that place. Second, the Sophists believed that moral rules are unnatural and that people obey them only because of the pressure of public opinion. If their acts could be done in private, they argued, even the "good" among us would not follow the rules of morality. Third, they argued that the essence of justice is power, or that "might is right." Fourth, that in answer to the basic question "what is the good life?" the Sophists felt that it is the life of pleasure. Against this formidable teaching of the Sophists, Plato put forward the Socratic notion that "knowledge is virtue". Elaborating on Socrates' view of morality, Plato emphasized (1) the concept of the *soul* and (2) the concept of *virtue* as function.

The Concept of the Soul

In the *Republic*, Plato describes the soul as having three parts, which he calls *reason, spirit,* and *appetite.* He based this three-part conception of the soul on the common experience of internal confusion and conflict that all humans share. When he analyzed the nature of this conflict, he discovered that there are three different kinds of activity going on in a person. First, there is an awareness of a goal or a value, and this is the act of reason. Second, there is the drive toward action—the spirit—which is neutral at first but responds to the direction of reason. Last, there is the desire for the things of the body, the appetites. What made him ascribe these activities to the soul was his assumption that the soul is the principle of life and movement. The body by itself is inanimate, and, therefore, when it acts or moves, it must be moved by the principle of life, the soul. Our reason could suggest a goal for behavior only to be overcome by sensual appetite, and the power of the spirit could be pulled in either direction by these sensual desires. Plato illustrated this human condition in the *Phaedrus,* where he portrays the charioteer driving two horses. One horse, Plato says, is good, and "needs no touch of the whip, but is guided by word and admonition only." The other is bad, and is "the mate of insolence and pride . . . hardly yielding to whip and spur." Though the charioteer has a clear vision of where to go and the good horse is on course, the bad horse "plunges and runs away, giving all manner of trouble to his companion and the charioteer."

Plato vividly illustrates the breakdown of order with the spectacle of horses moving in opposite directions and the charioteer standing helpless as his commands go unheeded. The charioteer, by being what he is—namely, the one who holds the reins—has the duty, the right, and the function to guide and control the horses. In the same way, the rational part of the soul has the right to rule the spirited and appetitive parts. To be sure, the charioteer cannot get anywhere without the two horses, and for this reason these three are linked together and must work together to achieve their goals. The rational part of the soul has this same sort of relation to its other parts, for the powers of appetite and spirit are indispensable to life itself. Reason works upon spirit and appetite, and these two also move and affect the reason. But the relation of reason to spirit and appetite is determined by what reason is: namely, a goal-seeking and measuring faculty. Of course, the passions also engage in goal seeking, for they constantly seek the goal of pleasure. Pleasure is a legitimate goal of life. However, the passions are simply drives toward the things that give pleasure. As such, the passions cannot distinguish between objects that provide higher or longer-lasting pleasure and those that only appear to provide these pleasures.

It is the function of the rational part of the soul to seek the true goal of human life, and it does this by evaluating things according to their true nature. The passions or appetites might lead us into a world of fantasy and deceive us into believing that certain kinds of pleasures will bring us happiness. It is, then, the unique role of reason to penetrate the world of fantasy and to discover the true world and thereby direct the passions to objects of love that are capable of producing true pleasure and true happiness. When we confuse appearance with reality, we become unhappy and experience a general disorder of the human soul. This confusion occurs chiefly when our passions override our reason. This is why Plato argued, as Socrates had before him, that moral evil is the result of *ignorance.* There can be order between the charioteer and the horses only if the charioteer is in control. Similarly, our human souls can achieve order and peace only if our rational part is in control of our spirit and appetites.

Throughout his account of the moral experience of human beings, Plato alternates between an optimistic view of our capacity for virtue and a rather negative opinion about whether we will fulfill our potentiality for virtue. This double attitude rests upon Plato's theory of moral evil. We have already seen Socrates' view that evil or vice is caused by ignorance—that is, by false knowledge. False knowledge occurs when our passions influence our reason to think that what appears to bring happiness will do so, although in reality it cannot. When my appetites thus overcome my reason, the unity of my soul is adversely affected. While there is still a unity, this new unity of my soul is inverted, since now my reason is subordinated to my appetites and has thereby lost its rightful place. What makes it possible for this disordered unity to occur, or what makes false knowledge possible? In short, what is the cause of moral evil?

The Cause of Evil: Ignorance or Forgetfulness

We discover the cause of evil in the very nature of the soul and in the relation of the soul to the body. Before it enters the body, Plato says, the soul has a prior existence. As we have seen, the soul has two main parts, the rational and the irrational. This irrational part in turn is made up of two sections, the spirit and the appetites. Each of the two original parts has a different origin. The rational part of the soul is created by the Demiurge out of the same receptacle as the World Soul; by contrast, the irrational part is created by the celestial gods, who also form the body. Thus, even before it enters the body, the soul is composed of two different kinds of ingredients. In the soul's prior existence, the rational part has a clear vision of the Forms and of truth. At the same time, though, the spirit and appetites, by their very nature, already have a tendency to descend. If we ask why the soul descends into a body, Plato says that it is simply the tendency of the irrational part—the part of the soul that is not perfect—to be unruly and to pull the soul toward the earth. Plato says that "when perfect and fully winged she [the soul] soars upward . . . whereas the imperfect soul, losing her wings and drooping in her flight at last settles on the solid ground—there, finding a home, she receives an earthly frame . . . and this composition of soul and body is called a living and mortal creation." Thus, the soul "falls," and that is how it comes to be in a body. But the point is that the soul has an unruly and evil nature in its irrational parts even before it enters the body. In one sense, then, the cause of evil is present even in the soul's preexistent state. It is in "heaven" that the soul alternates between seeing the Forms or the truth and "forgetting" this vision, whereupon its decline sets in. Evil, in this view, is not a positive thing but is rather a characteristic of the soul wherein the soul is "capable" of forgetfulness. It is those souls only that do forget the truth that in turn descend, being dragged down by the attraction for earthly things. The soul, then, is perfect in nature, but one aspect of its nature is this possibility to lapse into disorder, for the soul also contains the principle of imperfection as do other parts of creation. Upon its entrance into the body, however, the difficulties of the soul are greatly increased.

Plato believed that the body stimulated the irrational part of the soul to overcome the rulership of reason. The soul's entrance into the body, therefore, is a further cause of disorder or the breakdown of the harmony between the various parts of the soul. For one thing, when the soul leaves the realm of the Forms and enters the body, it moves from the realm of the One to the realm of the many. Now the soul is adrift in the bewildering sea of the multiplicity of things and subject to all sorts of errors because of the deceptive nature of these things. In addition, the body stimulates such activities in the irrational part of the soul as the indiscriminate search for pleasure, exaggerating such appetites as hunger, thirst, and the desire to create offspring. This in turn can become lust. In the body the soul experiences sensation, desire, pleasure, and pain, as well as fear and anger. There is love, too, for a wide range of objects. This varies from the simplest morsel that can satisfy some taste to a love of truth or beauty that is pure and eternal. All this suggests that the body acts as a sluggish encumbrance to the soul, and that the spirit and appetites of the soul are peculiarly susceptible to the workings of the body. In this way, then, our bodies disturb the harmony of our souls. For our bodies expose our souls to stimuli that deflects our reason from true knowledge or that prevents our reason from recalling the truth we once knew.

In the world of people, error is perpetuated whenever a society has the wrong values, causing individuals to accept as their own these wrong values. Every society inevitably acts as a teacher of its members, and for this reason society's values will become the values of individuals. Moreover, societies tend to perpetuate the evils and errors committed by earlier generations. Plato underscored this notion and suggested that, in addition to such a social transmission of evil, human souls would reappear through a transmigration and bring into a new body their earlier errors and judgments of value. It is the body, in the last analysis, that accounts for ignorance, rashness, and lust. For the body disturbs that clear working of the reason, spirit, and appetites by exposing the soul to a cascade of sensations.

Looking back upon Plato's account of the human moral condition, we have seen that he begins with a conception of the soul as existing independently of the body. In this state, the soul enjoys a basic harmony between its rational and irrational parts—a harmony wherein the reason controls the spirit and appetites through its knowledge of the truth. But since the irrational part of the soul has the possibility of imperfection, it expresses this possibility by being attracted through its appetites to the lower regions, dragging with it the spirit and reason. Upon entering the body, the original harmony of the parts of the soul is further disrupted, former knowledge is forgotten, and the inertia of the body obstructs the recovery of this knowledge.

Recovering Lost Morality

For Plato, morality consists in the recovery of our lost inner harmony. It means reversing the process by which our reason has been overcome by our appetites and the stimuli of our body. People always think that whatever they do will in some way give them pleasure and happiness. No one, Plato says, ever knowingly chooses an act that will be harmful to oneself. We may do "wrong" acts, such as murder or lying, and even admit the wrongness of these and other acts. But we always assume that some benefit will come from them. This is false knowledge—a kind of ignorance—which people must overcome in order to be moral. To say, then, that "knowledge is virtue" means that false knowledge must be replaced with an accurate appraisal of things or acts and their values.

Before we can go from false to true knowledge, we must somehow become aware that we are in a state of ignorance. It is as if we must be awakened from a "sleep of ignorance." We can be awakened by something that is happening within us or by something external to us or by someone else. Similarly, with regard to knowledge and particularly moral knowledge, human awakening works in these two ways. Assuming, as Plato does, that knowledge is lodged deeply in the mind's memory, this latent knowledge will from time to time come to the surface of consciousness. What the soul once knew is raised to present awareness by the process of *recollection.* Recollection begins first of all when our minds experience difficulties with the seeming contradictions of sense experience. As we try to make sense out of the multiplicity of things, we begin to go "beyond" the things themselves to ideas, and this action of our minds is set in motion by our experience of a problem that needs to be solved. Besides this internal source of awakening, Plato argues that this is also accomplished through a teacher. In his allegory of the Cave, Plato depicted how people moved from darkness to light, from ignorance to knowledge. But in this allegory he portrays the attitude of self-satisfaction among the prisoners; they do not know that they are prisoners, that they are chained by false knowledge and dwell in the darkness of ignorance. Their awakening must come through some teacher. As Plato says, "their release from the chains and the healing of their unwisdom" is brought about by their being "forced suddenly to stand up, turn . . . and walk with eyes lifted to the light." That is, someone must break off the prisoner's chains and turn him around. Then, having been forcibly released, he can be led step by step out of the cave. Socrates, with the power of his irony and the persistence of his dialectic method, was one of history's most effective awakeners of people from their sleep of ignorance. But besides awakening us, or breaking off our chains, the effective teacher must turn the prisoner around so that he will shift his gaze from shadows to the real world.

Virtue as Fulfillment of Function

Throughout his discussions of morality, Plato viewed the good life as the life of inner harmony, of well-being, and of happiness. He frequently compared the good life to the efficient functioning of things. A knife is good, he said, when it cuts efficiently, that is, when it fulfills its function. We say of physicians that they are good when they fulfill the function of doctoring. Musicians are similarly good when they fulfill the function of their respective art. Plato then asks, "Has the soul a function that can be performed by nothing else?" Living, said Plato, is likewise an art, and the soul's unique function is the art of living. Comparing the art of music with the art of living, Plato saw a close parallel, for in both cases the art consists of recognizing and obeying the requirements of limit and measure. When musicians tune their instruments, they know that each string should be tightened just so much, no more and no less, for each string has its specific pitch. The musicians' art consists, therefore, in acknowledging the limit beyond which a string should not be tightened and, in playing their instruments, observing the "measure" between intervals. In a similar way, sculptors must be ruled by a vivid awareness of measure and limit, for as they work with their mallets and chisels, they must regulate the force of each stroke by the form they want to accomplish. Their strokes will be heavy as they begin to clear away the larger sections of marble. But as they work around the head of the statue they must have a clear vision of the limits beyond which their chisels must not go, and their strokes must be gentle as they fashion the delicate features of the face.

Similarly, the art of living requires a knowledge of limits and of measure. The soul has various functions, but these functions must operate within the limits set by knowledge or intelligence. Because the soul has various parts, each part will have a special function. Since virtue is the fulfillment of function, there will be as many virtues as there are functions. Corresponding to the three parts of the soul are three virtues, which are achieved when those parts are respectively fulfilling their functions. The appetites need to be kept within limits and in their measure, avoiding excesses so that they do not usurp the position of the other parts of the soul. This moderation in pleasures and desires leads to the virtue of *temperance.* The energy of will, which issues from the spirited part of the soul, also needs to be kept within limits, avoiding rash or headlong action and becoming instead a trustworthy power in aggressive and defensive behavior. By doing this we achieve the virtue of *courage.* Reason achieves the virtue of *wisdom* when it remains undisturbed by the onrush of appetites and continues to see the true ideals in spite of the constant changes experienced in daily life. Between these three virtues there are interconnections, for temperance is the rational control of the appetites, and courage is the rational ordering of the spirit. At the same time, each part of the soul has its own function, and when each is in fact fulfilling its special function, a fourth virtue, *justice,* is attained, for justice means giving to each its own due. Justice, then, is the general virtue, which reflects a person's attainment of well-being and inner harmony, which, in turn, is achieved only when every part of the soul is fulfilling its proper function.

POLITICAL PHILOSOPHY

In Plato's thought, political theory is closely connected with moral philosophy. In the *Republic,* he says that different classes of the state are like different parts of an individual's soul. Likewise, the different types of states, with their characteristic virtues and vices, are analogous to different types of people, with their virtues and vices. In both cases, we should analyze the health of the state or person in terms of whether the classes or parts are performing their functions well and have the proper relationships to one another. Indeed, Plato held that the state is like a giant person. As justice is the general virtue of the moral person, so also it is justice that characterizes the good society. In the *Republic* Plato argues that the best way to understand the just person is to analyze the nature of the state. "We should begin," he says, "by inquiring what justice means in a state. Then we can go on to look for its counterpart on a smaller scale in the individual."

The State as a Giant Person

For Plato, the state grows out of the nature of the individual, so that the individual comes logically prior to the state. The state, said Plato, is a natural institution—natural because it reflects the structure of human nature. The origin of the state is a reflection of people's economic needs, for, Plato says, "a state comes into existence because no individual is self-sufficing; we all have many needs." Our many needs require many skills, and no one possesses all the skills needed to produce food, shelter, and clothing, as well as the various arts. Therefore, there must be a division of labor, for "more things will be produced and the work more easily and better done, when every person is set free from all other occupations to do, at the right time, the one thing for which he is naturally fitted." Our needs are not limited to our physical requirements, for our goal is not simply survival but a life higher than an animal's. Still, the healthy state soon becomes affected by a wide range of desires and becomes "swollen up with a whole multitude of callings not ministering to any bare necessity." Now there will be "hunters and fishermen . . . artists in sculpture, painting and music; poets with their attendant train of professional reciters, actors, dancers, producers; and makers of all sorts of household gear, including everything for women's adornment. And we shall want more servants . . . lady's maids, barbers, cooks and confectioners."

This desire for more things will soon exhaust the resources of the community and before long, Plato says, "we shall have to cut off a slice of our neighbor's territory . . . and they will want a slice of ours." At this rate, neighbors will inevitably be at war. Wars have their "origin in desires which are the most fruitful source of evils both to individuals and states." With the inevitability of war, it will now be necessary to have "a whole army to go out to battle with any invader, in defence of all this property and of the citizens." Thus emerge the guardians of the state, who, at first, represent the vigorous and powerful people who will repel the invader and preserve internal order. Now there are two distinct classes of people, those who fill all the crafts—farmers, artisans, and traders—and those who guard the community. From this latter class are then chosen the most highly trained guardians, who will become the rulers of the state and will represent a third and elite class.

The relation between the individual and the state now becomes plain: the three classes in the state are an extension of the three parts of the soul. The craftspeople or artisans represent as a class the lowest part of the soul, namely, the appetites. The guardians embody the spirited element of the soul. And the highest class, the rulers, represent the rational element. So far, this analysis seems quite plausible, since it does not strain our imaginations to see the connection (1) between the individual's appetites and the class of workers who satisfy these appetites, (2) between the spirited element in people and the large-scale version of this dynamic force in the military establishment, and (3) between the rational element and the unique function of leadership in the ruler. But Plato was aware that it would not be simple to convince people to accept this system of classes in the state, particularly if they found themselves in a class that might not be the one they would choose if they had the chance.

The assignment of all people to their respective classes would come only after extensive training, where only those capable of doing so would progress to the higher levels. Although theoretically people would have the opportunity to reach the highest level, they would in fact stop at the level of their natural aptitudes. To make all of them satisfied with their lot, Plato thought it would be necessary to employ a "convenient fiction . . . a single bold flight of invention." He writes, "I shall try to convince, first the Rulers and the soldiers, and then the whole community, that all that nurture and education which we gave them was only something they seemed to experience as it were in a dream. In reality they were the whole time down inside the earth, being molded . . . and fashioned . . . and at last when they were complete, the earth sent them up from her womb into the light of day."

This "noble lie" would also say that the god who fashioned all people "mixed gold in the composition" of those who were to rule and "put silver in the guardians, and iron and brass in the farmers and craftspeople." This would imply that by nature some would be rulers and others craftspeople, and that this would provide the basis for a perfectly stratified society. But whereas later societies in Europe assumed that children born into such a stratified society would stay at the level at which they were born, Plato recognized that children would not always have the same quality as their parents. He said, therefore, that among the injunctions laid by heaven upon the rulers "there is none that needs to be so carefully watched as the mixture of metals in the souls of children. If a child of their own is born with an alloy of iron or brass, they must, without the smallest pity, assign him the station proper to his nature and thrust him out among the farmers and craftspeople." Similarly, if a child with gold or silver is born to craftspeople, "they will promote him according to his value." Most important of all, Plato thought that everyone should agree on who is to be the ruler and agree also on the reason why the ruler should be obeyed.

The Philosopher-King

Plato believed that competence should be the qualification for authority. The ruler of the state should be the one who has the peculiar abilities to fulfill that function. Disorder in the state is caused by the same circumstances that produce disorder in the individual, namely, the attempt on the part of the lower elements to usurp the role of the higher faculties. In both the individual and the state the uncontrolled drives of the appetites and spirited action lead to internal anarchy. At both levels, the rational element must be in control. Who should be the captain of a ship—should it be a most "popular" person, or the one who knows the art of navigation? Who should rule the state—should it be someone whose training is in war or commerce? The ruler, said Plato, should be the one who has been fully educated and has come to understand the difference between the visible world and the intelligible world—between the realm of opinion and the realm of knowledge, between appearance and reality. In short, the philosopher-king is one whose education has led him up step by step through the ascending degrees of knowledge of the Divided Line until at last he has a knowledge of the Good, that synoptic vision of the interrelation of all truths to each other.

To reach this point, the philosopher-king will have progressed through many stages of education. By the time he is 18 years old, he will have had training in literature, music, and elementary mathematics. His literature would be censored, for Plato accused certain poets of outright falsehood and of impious accounts of the behavior of the gods. Music also would be prescribed so that seductive music would be replaced by a more wholesome variety. For the next few years there would be extensive physical and military training, and at age 20 a few would be selected to pursue an advanced course in mathematics. At age 30, a five-year course in dialectic and moral philosophy would begin. The next 15 years would be spent gathering practical experience through public service. Finally, at age 50, the ablest people would reach the highest level of knowledge, the vision of the Good, and would then be ready for the task of governing the state.

The Virtues in the State

Whether justice could ever be achieved in a state would depend, Plato thought, upon whether the philosophic element in society could attain dominance. He wrote that "I was forced to say in praise of the correct philosophy that it affords a vantage-point from which we can discern in all cases what is just for communities and for individuals." He also believed that "the human race will not be free of evils until either the stock of those who rightly and truly follow philosophy acquire political authority, or the class who have power in the cities be led by some dispensation of providence to become real philosophers." But justice, as we have already seen, is a general virtue. It means that all parts are fulfilling their special functions and are achieving their respective virtues. Justice in the state will be attained only if the three classes fulfill their functions.

As the craftspeople embody the element of the appetites, they will also reflect the virtue of temperance. Temperance is not limited to the craftspeople but applies to all the classes, since, when it is achieved it shows the willingness of the lower to be ruled by the higher. Still, temperance applies in a special way to the craftspeople insofar as they are the lowest and must be subordinate to the two higher levels.

The guardians, who defend the state, manifest the virtue of courage. To assure the state that these guardians will always fulfill their function, special training and provision are made for them. Unlike the craftspeople who marry and own property, the guardians will have both property and wives in common. Plato considered these arrangements essential if the guardians were to attain true courage, for courage means knowing what to fear and what not to fear. The only real object of fear for the guardian should be fear of moral evil. He must never fear poverty or privation, and for this reason his type of life should be isolated from possessions. Although wives will be held in common, this did not imply a form of sexism. On the contrary, Plato believed that men and women were equal in respect to certain things, saying, for example, that "a man and a woman have the same nature if both have a talent for medicine." This being the case, they should both be assigned to the same task whenever they possess the appropriate talent. For this reason, Plato believed that women could be guardians as well as men.

In order to preserve the unity of the members of the class of guardians, the permanent individual family would be abolished, and the whole class would become a single family. Plato's reasoning here was that the guardians must be free not only from the temptation to acquire property, but free also from the temptation to prefer the advantages of one's family to those of the state. Moreover, he thought it was foolish to take such pains in breeding racing dogs and horses and at the same time rely upon pure chance in producing the guardians and rulers of the state. For this reason, sexual relations would be strictly controlled and would be limited to the special marriage festivals. These festivals would occur at stated times, and the partners, under the illusion that they had been paired by drawing lots, would, instead, be brought together through the careful manipulation of the rulers to ensure the highest eugenic possibilities. Plato does say that "young men who performed well in war and other duties, should be given, among other rewards and privileges, more liberal opportunities to sleep with a wife," but only for the practical purpose, that "with good excuse, as many as possible of the children may be begotten of such fathers." As soon as children are born to the guardians, they will be taken in charge by officers appointed for that purpose and will be reared in a nursery school in a special part of the city. Under these circumstances, Plato thought, the guardians would be most likely to fulfill their true function of defending the state without being deflected by other concerns, and would thereby achieve their appropriate virtue of courage.

Justice in the state is therefore the same as justice in the individual. It is the product of people staying in their place and doing their special task. Justice is the harmony of the virtues of temperance, courage, and wisdom. Since the state is made up of individuals, it will also be necessary for each of these virtues to be attained by each person. For example, even craftspeople must have the virtue of wisdom, not only to keep their appetites in check but also to know that they rightly belong where they are and must obey the rules. Similarly, as we have seen, the guardians must have sufficient wisdom in order to know what to fear and what not to fear so that they can develop genuine courage. Most important of all, the ruler must come as close as possible to a knowledge of the Good, for the well-being of the state depends upon the ruler's knowledge and character.

The Decline of the Ideal State

Plato argued that, if the state is a giant person, then a state will reflect the kind of people a community has become. What he had in mind was that although human nature is fixed, in that all people possess a tripartite soul, the kind of people they become will depend upon the degree of internal harmony they achieve. The state will therefore reflect these variations in human character. For this reason, Plato argued that "constitutions cannot come out of stocks and stones; they must result from the preponderance of certain characters which draw the rest of the community in their wake. So if there are five forms of government, there must be five kinds of mental constitution among individuals." And these five forms of government are *aristocracy, timocracy, plutocracy, democracy,* and *despotism.*

Plato considered the transition from aristocracy to despotism as a step-by-step decline in the quality of the state corresponding to a gradual deterioration of the moral character of the rulers and the citizens. His ideal state was aristocracy, in which the rational element embodied in the philosopher-king was supreme and where people's reason controlled their appetites. Plato emphasized that, although this was only an ideal, it was nevertheless a very significant target to aim at. He was deeply disenchanted with politics, particularly because of the way Athens had executed Socrates and had failed to produce consistently good leaders. "As I gazed upon the whirlpool of public life," he said, "[I] saw clearly in regard to all States now existing that without exception their system of government is bad." Still, the norm for a state is *aristocracy,* since in that form we find the proper subordination of all classes.

Even if this ideal were achieved, however, there would be a possibility for change, since nothing is permanent, and aristocracy would decline first of all into a *timocracy.* This represents a degeneration, for timocracy represents the love of honor, and insofar as ambitious members of the ruling class love their own honor more than the common good, the spirited part of their soul has usurped the role of reason. Although this is only a small break in the structure of the soul, it does begin a process whereby the irrational part assumes a progressively larger role. It is a short step from love of honor to the desire for wealth, which means allowing the appetites to rule.

Even under a timocracy there would be the beginning of a system of private property, and this desire for riches paves the way for a system of government called *plutocracy,* where power resides in the hands of people whose main concern is wealth. And, Plato says, "as the rich rise in social esteem, the virtuous sink." What is serious about plutocracy, according to Plato, is that it breaks the unity of the state into two contending classes, the rich and the poor. Moreover, plutocrats are consumers of goods, and when they have used up their money, they become dangerous because they want more of what they have become accustomed to. The plutocrat is like the person who seeks constant pleasure. But the very nature of pleasure is that it is momentary and must therefore be repeated. There can never be a time of perfect satisfaction; the seeker of pleasure can never be satisfied any more than a leaky pail can be filled. Still, the plutocrat knows how to distinguish three sorts of appetites: (1) the necessary, (2) the unnecessary, and (3) the lawless; and so is torn between many desires. "His better desires will usually keep the upper hand over the worse," and so the plutocrat, Plato says, "presents a more decent appearance than many."

Democracy is a further degeneration, Plato said, for its principles of equality and freedom reflect the degenerate human characters whose whole range of appetites are all pursued with equal freedom. To be sure, Plato's concept of democracy, and his criticism of it, were based upon his firsthand experience with the special form that democracy took in the small city-state of Athens. Here democracy was direct in that all citizens had the right to participate in the government. The Athenian Assembly consisted, theoretically at least, of all citizens over 18 years of age. Thus, Plato did not have in mind modern liberal and representative democracy. What he saw in his day was rather a type of direct popular government that clearly violated his notion that the rulership of a state should be in the hands of those with the special talent and training for it.

What produced this spirit of equality was the gradual legitimizing of all the appetites under the plutocracy, by the sons of the more restrained father-plutocrats, where the aim of life was to become as rich as possible. And, said Plato, "this insatiable craving would bring about the transition to democracy," for "a society cannot hold wealth in honor and at the same time establish self-control in its citizens." Even the dogs in a democracy exhibit equality and independence by refusing to move out of the way in the streets. It is, however, when the rich and poor find themselves in a contest under plutocracy that the turning point is reached, for "when the poor win, the result is a democracy." Then, "liberty and free speech are rife everywhere; anyone is allowed to do what he likes." Now, "you are not obliged to be in authority . . . or to submit to authority, if you do not like it." All this political equality and freedom stem from a soul whose order has been shattered. It is a soul whose appetites are now all equal and free and act as a "mob" of passions. The life of liberty and equality declares that "one appetite is as good as another and all must have their equal rights."

But the continuous indulgence of the appetites leads us inevitably to the point where a single master passion will finally enslave the soul. We cannot yield to every craving without finally having to yield to the strongest and most persistent passion. At this point we say that we are under the tyranny of our master passion. Likewise, in the state, the passion for money and pleasures leads the masses to plunder the rich. As the rich resist, the masses seek out a strong person who will be their champion. But this person demands and acquires absolute power and makes slaves of the people, and only later do the people realize to what depths of subjugation they have fallen. This is the unjust society, the enlargement of the unjust soul. The natural end of democracy is *despotism*.

VIEW OF THE COSMOS

Although Plato's most consistent and sustained thought centered around moral and political philosophy, he also turned his attention to science. His theory of nature, or physics, is found chiefly in the *Timaeus*—a dialogue which, according to some scholars, Plato wrote when he was about 70 years old. Plato had not deliberately postponed this subject, nor had he chosen to deal with moral matters instead of promoting the advancement of science. On the contrary the science of his day had reached a blind alley, and there seemed to be no fruitful direction to take in this field. Earlier, according to Plato, Socrates had had "a prodigious desire to know that department of philosophy which is called the investigation of nature; to know the causes of things." However, Socrates was disillusioned by the conflicting answers and theories put forward by Anaximander, Anaximenes, Leucippus and Democritus, and others. Plato shared this same disappointment. Moreover, as his own philosophy took shape, some of his theories about reality cast doubt upon the possibility of a strictly accurate scientific knowledge. Physics, he thought, could never be more than "a likely story." It was particularly his theory of the Forms that rendered science as an exact type of knowledge impossible. The real world, he said, is the world of Forms, whereas the visible world is full of change and imperfection. Yet, it is about the visible world of things that science seeks to build its theories. How can we formulate accurate, reliable, and permanent knowledge about a subject matter which is itself imperfect and full of change? At the same time, Plato clearly felt that his theory of the Forms—as well as his notions of morality, evil, and truth—required a view of the cosmos in which all these elements of his thought could be brought together in a coherent way. Recognizing, then, that his account of the material world was only "a likely story," or at best probable knowledge, he nevertheless was convinced that what he had to say about the world was as accurate as the subject matter would allow.

Plato's first thought about the world is that, though it is full of change and imperfection, it nevertheless exhibits order and purpose. He rejected the explanation given by Democritus, who had argued that all things came into being through the accidental collision of atoms. When Plato considered, for example, the orbits of the planets, he observed that they were arranged according to a precise series of geometrical intervals, which, when appropriately calculated, produced the basis for the harmonic scale. Plato made much of the Pythagorean use of mathematics in describing the world. However, instead of saying, as the Pythagoreans did, that things are numbers, he said that things *participate* in numbers and that they are capable of a mathematical explanation. This mathematical characteristic of things suggested to Plato that behind things there must be thought and purpose, and not merely chance and subsequent mechanism. The cosmos must therefore be the work of *intelligence*, since it is the mind that orders all things. Humanity and the world bear a likeness to each other, for both contain first an intelligible and eternal element, and second a sensible and perishing element. This dualism is expressed in people by the union of soul and body. Similarly, the world is a soul in which things as we know them are arranged.

Although Plato said that *mind* orders everything, he did not develop a theory of creation. The theory of creation holds that things are created out of nothing. But Plato's explanation of the origin of the visible world bypasses this theory of creation. Granted, Plato does say that "that which becomes must necessarily become through the agency of some cause." However, this agent, which he calls the divine Craftsman or Demiurge, does not bring new things into being but rather confronts and orders what already exists in chaotic form. We have, then, a picture of the Craftsman with the material upon which he will work. Thus, in explaining the generation of things as we know them in the visible world, Plato assumes the existence of all the ingredients of things, namely, that out of which things are made, the Demiurge who is the Craftsman, and the Forms or *patterns* after which things are made.

Plato departed from the materialists who thought that all things came from some original kind of matter, whether in the form of earth, air, fire, or water. Plato did not accept the notion that matter was the basic reality. Matter itself, Plato said, must be explained in more refined terms as the composition not of some finer forms of matter but of something other than matter. What we call matter, whether in the form of earth or water, is a reflection of a Form, and these Forms are expressed through a medium. Things are generated out of what Plato calls the *receptacle,* which he considered the "nurse of all becoming." The receptacle is a "matrix," or a medium that has no structure but that is capable of receiving the imposition of structure by the Demiurge. Another word Plato uses for the *receptacle* is *space,* which, he says, "is everlasting, not admitting destruction; providing a situation for all things that come into being, but itself apprehended without the senses by a sort of bastard reasoning, and hardly an object of belief." There is no explanation of the origin of the receptacle, for in Plato's thought it is underived, as are the Forms and the Demiurge. The receptacle is where things appear and perish.

To an unreflective person, earth and water may appear to be solid and permanent kinds of matter. But Plato said that they are constantly changing and therefore do not hold still long enough "to be described as 'this' or 'that' or by any phrase that exhibits them as having permanent being." What the senses consider "matter" or "substance" when they apprehended the elements of earth and water are only *qualities.* These qualities, then, appear through the medium of the receptacle "in which all of them are always coming to be, making their appearance and vanishing out of it." Material objects are composed of nonmaterial compounds. Here Plato is again influenced by the Pythagorean perspective when he argues that solid objects of matter are described and defined in geometric terms according to their surfaces. Any surface, he said, can be resolved by triangles, and, in turn, any triangle can be divided into right triangles. These shapes, these triangular surfaces, are irreducible and must therefore be the ingredients of the compound known as matter. The simplest solid, for example, would be a pyramid that consists of four triangular surfaces. Similarly, a cube could be made of six square surfaces, where each square surface is composed of two half squares, that is, two triangles. What we normally call "solid" never contains anything more than "surfaces," so that we can say that "body" or "molecules" are geometric figures. Indeed, the whole universe could be thought of in terms of its geometrical diagram—and could be defined simply as what is happening in space, or as space reflecting various forms. What Plato wanted particularly to establish was the notion that matter is only the appearance of something more basic.

If various kinds of triangles represent the basic constituents of all things, how can we account for the variations in things as well as their stability? What, in short, makes it possible to have the kind of world and universe that we know? Here again Plato was forced to assume that all things must be ordered by mind, that the cosmos is the activity of the World Soul in the receptacle. The world of things is the world of *phenomena*, which is the Greek word for appearances. What is presented to our perception is the multitude of appearances, which, when analyzed, are found to consist of geometric surfaces. These surfaces, again, are primary and irreducible and are found as "raw material" in the receptacle and require some organizing agency to arrange them into triangles and then into phenomena. All this activity is achieved by the World Soul. The World Soul is eternal, though at times Plato appears to say that it is the creation of the Demiurge. Although the World Soul is eternal, the world of appearance is full of change, just as in humans the soul represents the eternal element whereas the body contains the principle of change. The world of matter and body changes because it is composite and always tends to return to its basic constituents, "going into" and "going out of" space. But insofar as the World Soul is eternal, there is, in spite of all the change in the world of our experience, an element of stability and permanence, a structure, a discernible universe.

There is evil in the world, Plato says, because there are obstacles in the way of the Demiurge. The world is not perfectly good even though the Demiurge sought to make it as much like its pattern as possible. Although the Demiurge represents divine reason and the agency that fashioned the order of the universe, "the generation of this cosmos," Plato say Plato, "was a mixed result of the combination of Necessity and Reason." Necessity in this context signifies unwillingness to change and, when applied to the "raw material" of the *receptacle,* it shows a recalcitrance as though impervious to the ordering of *mind.* In this sense, *necessity* is one of the conditions of evil in the world, for evil is the breakdown of purpose, and purpose is characteristic of mind. Whatever, then, frustrates the working of mind contributes to the absence of order, which is the meaning of evil. This suggests that in human life, too, the circumstance of a recalcitrant body and lower parts of the soul produces evil insofar as mind is not in control. Necessity is expressed in various types, such as inertia and irreversibility, and reason, even God's reason, must cope with these obstacles while trying to order the world according to a definite purpose.

Finally, there is the question about *time.* According to Plato, time comes to be only after phenomena are produced. Not until there are things as we know them, as imperfect and changing, can there be time. Until then, by definition, whatever is, is eternal. The very meaning of time is change, and therefore in the absence of change there could be no time. Whereas the Forms are timeless, the various copies of them in the receptacle constantly "go in" and "go out," and this going in and out is the process of change, which is the cause of time. Still, time represents the double presence in the cosmos of time and eternity; since the cosmos is ordered by mind, it contains the element of eternity, and since the cosmos consists of temporary combinations of surfaces, it contains the element of change and time. And since change is not capricious but regular, the very process of change exhibits the presence of eternal mind. This regularity of change, as exhibited, for example, by the regular change or motion of the stars and planets, makes possible the measurement of change and makes it possible to "tell time."

Plato's "likely story" about the cosmos consisted, then, of an account of how the Demiurge fashioned things out of the receptacle, using the Forms as patterns. The World Soul is produced by the Demiurge and is the energizing activity in the receptacle, producing what to us appears to be substance or solid matter—though in reality is only qualities caused by the arrangement of geometric surfaces. Evil and time are, in this account, the product of imperfection and change. The world as we know it depends upon an agency and "raw material" that are not found in the physical world as we know it, this agency being mind, and the raw material being explained chiefly in terms of mathematics.

At this point we would wish to engage in a sustained and critical appraisal of Plato's vast system of philosophy. But in a sense, the history of philosophy represents just such a large-scale dialogue, where thinkers arise to agree and disagree with what he taught. So powerful was the mold into which he had cast the enterprise of philosophy that for centuries to come his views dominated the intellectual scene. Indeed, Alfred North Whitehead once remarked that "the safest general characterization of the European philosophical tradition is that it consists of a series of footnotes to Plato." Many of these footnotes, it might be added, were written by Plato's prodigious successor, Aristotle, to whom we now turn.

CHAPTER 4

Aristotle

ARISTOTLE'S LIFE

Aristotle was born in 384 BCE in the small town of Stagira on the northeast coast of Thrace. His father was the physician to the king of Macedonia. It could be that Aristotle's great interest in biology and science in general was nurtured in his early childhood. When he was 17 years old, Aristotle went to Athens to enroll in Plato's Academy, where he spent the next 20 years as a pupil and a member. At the Academy, Aristotle had the reputation of being the "reader" and "the mind of the school." He was profoundly influenced by Plato's thought and personality even though eventually he was to break away from Plato's philosophy in order to formulate his own version of certain philosophical problems. Still, while at the Academy, he wrote many dialogues in a Platonic style, which his contemporaries praised for the "golden stream" of their eloquence. In his *Eudemus,* he even reaffirmed, the very notion so central to Plato's thought, the theory of the Forms, which he later criticized so severely.

There is no way now to reconstruct with exactness just when Aristotle's thought diverged from Plato's. Plato's own thought, it must be remembered, was in the process of change while Aristotle was at the Academy. Indeed, scholars believe that Aristotle studied with Plato during Plato's "later" period, a time when Plato's interests had shifted toward mathematics, method, and natural science. During this time, also, specialists in various sciences, such as medicine, anthropology, and archeology, came to the Academy. This meant that Aristotle was exposed to a vast array of empirical facts, which, because of his outlook, he found useful for research and for his way of formulating scientific concepts. It may be, therefore, that the intellectual atmosphere of the Academy marked by some of Plato's latest dominant concerns and the availability of collected data in special fields provided Aristotle with a direction in philosophy that was congenial to his scientific disposition.

The direction Aristotle took did eventually cause him to depart from some of Plato's theories, though the degree of difference between Plato and Aristotle is still a matter of careful interpretation. But even when they were together at the Academy, certain temperamental differences must have been apparent. Aristotle, for example, was less interested in mathematics than Plato and more interested in empirical data. Moreover, as time went on, Aristotle's gaze seemed to be more firmly fixed upon the concrete processes of nature, so that he considered his abstract scientific notions to have their real habitat in this living nature. By contrast, Plato separated the world of thought from the world of flux and things, ascribing true reality to the Forms, which, he thought, had an existence separate from the things in nature. We can say, therefore, that Aristotle oriented his thought to the dynamic realm of *becoming,* whereas Plato's thought was fixed more upon the static realm of timeless *Being.* Whatever differences there were between these two great minds, the fact is that Aristotle did not break with Plato personally, as he remained at the Academy until Plato's death. Moreover, throughout Aristotle's later major treatises, we find unmistakable influences of Plato's thought in spite of Aristotle's unique interpretations and style. But his distinctly "Platonist" period came to an end upon Plato's death. The direction of the Academy had then passed into the hands of Plato's nephew Speusippos, whose excessive emphasis upon mathematics was uncongenial to Aristotle. For this and other reasons Aristotle withdrew from the Academy and left Athens.

It was in 348/47 BCE that Aristotle left the Academy and accepted the invitation of Hermeias to come to Assos, near Troy. Hermeias had formerly been a student at the Academy and was now the ruler of Assos. Being somewhat of a philosopher-king, he gathered a small group of thinkers into his court, and here Aristotle was able for the next three years to write, teach, and carry on research. While at Hermeias' court, he married this ruler's niece and adopted daughter, Pythias, who bore him a daughter. Later, when they had returned to Athens, his wife died, and Aristotle then entered into a relationship with a woman named Herpyllis, which was never legalized. Nevertheless, it was a happy, permanent, and affectionate union from which there came a son, Nicomachus, after whom the *Nicomachean Ethics* was named. After his three years in Asso, Aristotle moved to the neighboring island of Lesbos, settling there for the time being in Mitylene, where he taught and continued his investigations in biology, studying especially the many forms of marine life. Here he also became known as an advocate of a united Greece, urging that such a union would be more successful than independent city-states in resisting the might of Persia. Then, in 343/42 BCE, Philip of Macedon invited Aristotle to become the tutor of his son Alexander, who was then 13 years old. As a tutor to a future ruler, Aristotle's interests included politics, and it is possible that it was here that he conceived the idea of collecting and comparing various constitutions, a project he later carried out by collecting digests of the constitutions of 158 Greek city-states. When Alexander ascended the throne after his father Philip's death, Aristotle's duties as tutor came to an end, and after a brief stay in his hometown of Stagira, he returned to Athens.

Upon his return to Athens in 335/34 BCE, Aristotle began the most productive period of his life. Under the protection of the Macedonian statesman Antipater, Aristotle founded his own school. His school was known as the

Aristotle
(Scala/Art Resource, NY)

Lyceum, named after the groves where Socrates was known to have gone to think and which were the sacred precincts of Apollo Lyceus. Here Aristotle and his pupils walked in the Peripatos, a tree-covered walk, and discussed philosophy, for which reason his school was called *peripatetic*—meaning "walking about". Besides these peripatetic discussions, there were also lectures, some technical for small audiences and others of a more popular nature for larger audiences. Tradition maintains that Aristotle also formed the first great library by collecting hundreds of manuscripts, maps, and specimens, which he used as illustrations during his lectures. Moreover, his school developed certain formal procedures whereby its leadership would alternate among members. Aristotle formulated the rules for these procedures, as he also did for the special common meal and symposium once a month. At these occasions a member was selected to defend a philosophical position against the critical objections of the other members. For 12 or 13 years Aristotle remained as the head of the Lyceum teaching and lecturing. Above all, though, while there he formulated his main ideas about the classification of the sciences, fashioned a bold new science of logic, and wrote his advanced ideas in every major area of philosophy and science, exhibiting an extraordinary command of universal knowledge.

When Alexander died in 323 BCE, a wave of anti-Macedonian feeling arose, making Aristotle's position in Athens very precarious because of his close connections with Macedonia. As Socrates before him, Aristotle was charged with "impiety," but, as he is reported to have said, "lest the Athenians should sin twice against philosophy," he left the Lyceum and fled to Chalcis, where he died in 322 BCE of a digestive disease of long standing. In his will he expressed sensitive human qualities by providing amply for his relatives, preventing his slaves from being sold and providing that some of his slaves should be emancipated. As with Socrates and Plato, Aristotle's thought was of such decisive force that it was to influence philosophy for centuries to come. From the vast range of his philosophy, we will consider here some aspects of his logic, metaphysics, ethics, politics, and aesthetics.

LOGIC

Aristotle invented formal logic. He also invented the idea of the separate sciences. For him, there was a close connection between logic and science, inasmuch as he considered logic to be the instrument (*organon*) with which to formulate language properly when analyzing what a science involves.

The Categories and the Starting Point of Reasoning

Before we can logically demonstrate or prove something, we must have a clear starting point for our reasoning process. For one thing, we must specify the subject matter that we are discussing—the specific "kind" of thing we are dealing with. To this we must add the properties and causes that are related to that kind of thing. In this connection, Aristotle developed his notion of the *categories,* which explains how we think about things. Whenever we think of a distinct subject matter, we think of a subject and its predicates—that is, of some *substance* and its accidents. We think the word *human* and also connect the word *human* with such predicates as *tall* and *able.* The word *human* is here a substance, and Aristotle says that there are about nine *categories* (that is, predicates) that can be connected with a substance, including *quantity* (e.g., six feet tall), *quality* (e.g., articulate), *relation* (e.g., double), *place* (e.g., at the school), *date* (e.g., last week), *posture* (e.g., standing), *possession* (e.g., clothed), *action* (e.g., serves), and *passivity* (e.g., is served). We can consider *substance* itself as a category, since we say, for example, "he is a human," in which case *human* (a substance) is a *predicate.* These categories represented for Aristotle the classification of concepts that are used in scientific knowledge. They represent the specific ways in which whatever exists does exist or is realized. In our thinking, we arrange things into these categories, classifying such categories into genera, species, and the individual thing. We see the individual as a member of the species and the species as related to the genus. Aristotle did not consider these categories or these classifications as artificial creations of the mind. He thought that they were actually in existence outside the mind and in things. Things, he thought, fell into various classifications by their very nature, and we think of them as members of a species or genus because they *are*. Thinking, as Aristotle saw it, was connected with the way things are, and this underlies the close relation between logic and metaphysics. Thinking is always about some specific individual thing, namely, a substance. But a thing never simply exists; it exists some*how* and has a reason *why*.

There are always predicates (categories) related to subjects (substances). Some predicates are intrinsic to a thing. Such predicates or categories belong to a thing simply because it is what it is. We think of a horse as having certain predicates *because* it is a horse; it has these predicates in common with all other horses. It also has other predicates, not so intrinsic but rather "accidental," such as color, place, size, and other determinations affecting its relation to other material objects. What Aristotle wants to underscore is that there is a sequence that leads to "science." This sequence is, first of all, the *existence* of things and their processes; secondly, our *thinking* about things and their behavior; and, finally, the transformation of our thought about things into *words*. Language is the instrument for formulating scientific thought. Logic, then, is the analysis of language, the process of reasoning, and the way language and reasoning are related to reality.

The Syllogism

Aristotle develops a system of logic, based on the *syllogism*, which he defines as a "discourse in which certain things being stated, something other than what is stated follows of necessity from their being so." The classic example of a syllogism is this:

Major premise. All humans are mortal.

Minor premise. Socrates is a human.

Conclusion. Therefore, Socrates is mortal.

The first two statements are premises, which serve as evidence for the third statement, which is the conclusion. How, then, can we be sure that a conclusion follows from its premises? The answer rests in the basic structure of valid syllogistic arguments, and Aristotle devised a set of rules that determine when conclusions were rightly inferred from their premises. Up until the 19th century, philosophers believed that Aristotle account of the syllogism constituted everything there was to say about the subject of logic. It is only in more recent decades that alternative systems of logic have been offered, which supercede Aristotle's account.

Although Aristotle's theory of the syllogism is an effective tool for determining valid relationships between premises and conclusions, his aim was to provide an instrument for scientific demonstration. For this reason, again, he emphasized the relation between logic and metaphysics—between our way of knowing and what things are and how they behave. That is, he thought that words and propositions are linked together because the things which language mirrors are also linked together. Accordingly, Aristotle recognized that it is entirely possible to employ the syllogism consistently without necessarily arriving at science or truth. This would happen if the premises did not rest upon true assumptions—that is, if they did not reflect reality. Aristotle distinguished between three kinds of reasoning, each of which might use the instrument of the syllogism, but with different results. These are, first, *dialectical* reasoning, which is reasoning from "opinions that are generally accepted"; second, *eristic* or contentious reasoning, which begins with opinions that seem to be generally accepted but are really not; and, third, what Aristotle calls *demonstrative* reasoning, where the premises from which reasoning starts are true and primary.

Thus, the value of syllogistic reasoning depended for Aristotle upon the accuracy of the premises. If true scientific knowledge is to be achieved, it is necessary that the premises we use be more than opinion or even probable truth. Demonstrative reasoning moves backward, as it were, from conclusions to those premises that constitute the necessary beginnings of the conclusion. When we say "all humans are mortal," we in effect move back to those causes and properties in animals that constitute their mortality. We then link humans with these properties by including them in the class of animals. Demonstrative reasoning must therefore lay hold of reliable premises, or what Aristotle calls *first principles* (*archai*)—that is, accurately defined properties of any thing, class, or distinctive area of subject matter. Valid reasoning therefore presupposes the discovery of true first principles from which conclusions can be drawn.

How do we arrive at these first principles? Aristotle answers that we learn these from observation and induction. When we observe certain facts many times, "the universal that is there," he says, "becomes plain." Whenever we observe any particular "that," our memories store it away. After observing many similar "thats," we generate from all these particular "thats" a general term with a general meaning. We discover the universal within the particulars by the process of induction, which is a process that results in the discovery of additional meanings in the particular "thats" observed.

If we then ask the additional question whether and how we can know that the first principles, are true, Aristotle says we know they are true simply because our minds, working with certain facts, recognize and "see" their truth. These first principles are not in turn demonstrated. If it were necessary to demonstrate every premise, this would involve an infinite regress, since each prior premise would also have to be proved, in which case the enterprise of knowledge could never get started. Aristotle, referring again to first principles, says that "not all knowledge is demonstrative: on the contrary, knowledge of the immediate premises is independent of demonstration." Scientific knowledge, he said, rests upon knowledge that is not itself subject to the same proof as scientific conclusions. So, "besides scientific knowledge there is its originative source which enables us to *recognize* the definitions."

Here Aristotle uses the word *recognize* to explain how we know certain truths; this is in contrast to Plato's use of the word *recollect* or *remember*. To "recognize" a truth is to have a direct intuitive grasp of it, as when we know that two and two equal four. It may be that the occasion for "recognizing" this truth of arithmetic was the act of adding particular things such as bricks or stones. Still, from these specific factual cases we "see" or "recognize" the truth that certain things belong to a species or genus and that certain relations exist between them, such as two and two equal four. Thus, Aristotle argued that science rests upon primary premises, which we arrive at by intellectual intuition (*nous*). Once these primary premises and definitions of the essential natures of things are in hand, it is then possible for us to engage in demonstrative reasoning.

METAPHYSICS

In his work entitled *Metaphysics* Aristotle develops what he called the science of *first philosophy*. The term "metaphysics" has a somewhat cloudy origin, but in this context it seems at least in part to signify the position of this work among Aristotle's other writings, namely, that it is *beyond*, or it comes *after*, his work on physics. Throughout his *Metaphysics,* he deals with a type of knowledge that he thought could be most rightly called *wisdom.* This work begins with the statement that "All men by nature desire to know." This innate desire, Aristotle says, is not only a desire to know in order to do or make something. In addition to these pragmatic motives, there is in us a desire to know certain kinds of things simply for the sake of knowing. An indication of this, Aristotle says, is "the delight we take in our senses; for even apart from their usefulness they are loved for themselves" inasmuch as our seeing "makes us know and brings to light many differences between things."

There are different levels of knowledge. Some people know only what they experience through their senses, as, for example, when they know that fire is hot. But, Aristotle says, we do not regard what we know through the senses as wisdom. Instead, wisdom is similar to the knowledge possessed by scientists. They begin by looking at something, then repeat these sense experiences, and finally go beyond sense experience by thinking about the *causes* of the objects of their experiences. There are as many sciences as there are definable areas of investigation, and Aristotle deals with many of them, including physics, ethics, politics, and aesthetics. In addition to the specific sciences, though, there is another science, *first philosophy*, or what we now call *metaphysics*, which goes beyond the subject matter of the other sciences and is concerned with the knowledge of true reality.

The Problem of Metaphysics Defined

The various sciences seek to find the first principles and causes of specific kinds of things, such as material bodies, the human body, the state, a poem, and so on. Unlike these sciences, which ask "What is such-and-such a thing like and why?" metaphysics asks a far more general question—a question that each science must ultimately take into account, namely, "What does it mean to be anything whatsoever?" What, in short, does it mean *to be?* It was precisely this question that concerned Aristotle in his *Metaphysics,* making metaphysics for him "the science of any existent, as existent." The problem of metaphysics as he saw it was therefore the study of Being and its "principles" and "causes."

Aristotle's metaphysics was to a considerable extent an outgrowth of his views on logic and his interest in biology. From the viewpoint of his logic, "to be" meant for him to be *something* that could be accurately defined and that could therefore become the subject of discourse. From the point of view of his interest in biology, he was inclined to think of "to be" as something implicated in a dynamic process. "To be," as Aristotle saw the matter, always meant to be *something.* Hence, all existence is individual and has a specific nature. All the categories (or predicates) that Aristotle dealt with in his logical works— categories such as *quality, relation, posture, place,* and so on—presuppose some subject to which these predicates can apply. This subject to which all the categories apply Aristotle called *substance (ousia).* To be, then, is to be a particular kind of substance. Also, "to be" means to be a substance as the product of a dynamic process. In this way, metaphysics is concerned with *Being* (i.e., existing substances) and its *causes* (i.e., the processes by which substances come into being).

Substance as the Primary Essence of Things

Aristotle believed that the way we know a thing provides a major clue as to what we mean by substance. Having in mind again the categories or predicates, Aristotle says that we know a thing better when we know *what it is* than when we know the color, size, or posture it has. We separate a thing from all its qualities and we focus upon what a thing really is, upon its *essential nature.* To this end, Aristotle distinguishes between *essential* and *accidental* properties of things. For example, to say that a person has red hair is to describe something accidental, since to be a human it is not necessary or essential that one have red hair—or even any hair for that matter. But it is essential to my being human that I am mortal. We similarly recognize that all humans are *human* in spite of their different sizes, colors, or ages. *Something* about each concretely different person makes him or her a person in spite of the unique characteristics that make him or her *this particular* person. At this point, Aristotle would readily agree that these special characteristics (categories, predicates) also exist and have some kind of being. But the being of these characteristics is not the central object of metaphysical inquiry.

The central concern of metaphysics is the study of substance, that is, the essential nature of a thing. In this view, substance means "that which is not asserted of a subject but of which everything else is asserted." Substance is what we know as basic about something, *after* which we can say other things about *it.* Whenever we define something, we get at its essence *before* we can say anything about it, as when we speak of a large table or a healthy person. Here we understand table and person in their "essence"—in what makes them a table or a person—before we understand them as large or healthy. It is true that we can know only specific and determinate things—actual individual tables or persons. At the same time, the essence, or substance, of a table or a person has its existence peculiarly separate from its categories or its qualities. This does not mean that a substance is ever in fact found existing separately from its qualities. Still, Aristotle believes that we can know the essence of a thing such as "tableness" as separated from its particular qualities of round, small, and brown. Thus, he believes, there must be some universal essence that is found wherever we see a table. And this essence or substance must be independent of its particular qualities inasmuch as the essence is the same even though in the case of each actual table the qualities are different. Aristotle's point is that a thing is more than the sum of its particular qualities. There is something "beneath" *(sub stance)* all the qualities; thus, any specific thing is a combination of qualities, on the one hand, and a substratum to which the qualities apply, on the other. With these distinctions in mind, Aristotle was led, as was Plato before him, to consider just how this essence, or universal, was related to the particular thing. What, in short, makes a substance a substance; is it *matter* as a substratum or is it *form?*

Matter and Form

Although Aristotle distinguished between *matter* and *form,* he nevertheless said that, in nature, we never find matter without form or form without matter. Everything that exists is some concrete individual thing, and every *thing* is a unity of matter and form. Substance, therefore, is always a composite of form and matter. Plato, we will recall, argued that Forms, such as Human or Table, had a separate existence. Particular things, such as the table in front of me, obtain their nature by *participating* in the Forms, such as the Form Tableness. Aristotle rejected Plato's explanation of the universal Forms, criticizing specifically the contention that the Forms existed separately from individual things. Of course, Aristotle did agree that there are universals, and that universals such as Human and Table are more than merely subjective notions. Indeed, Aristotle recognized that without the theory of universals, there could be no scientific knowledge, for then there would be no way of saying something about all members of a particular class.

What makes scientific knowledge effective is that it discovers classes of objects (for example, a certain form of human disease), so that whenever an individual falls into this class, we can also assume that other facts are relevant. These classes, then, are not merely mental fictions but do in fact have objective reality. But, Aristotle said, we simply find their reality in the individual things themselves. What purpose, he asked, could be served by assuming that the universal Forms existed separately? If anything, this would complicate matters, since everything would have to be replicated in the world of Forms— not only individual things but also their relationships. Moreover, Aristotle was not convinced that Plato's theory of the Forms could help us know things any better: "they help in no wise toward the knowledge of other things." Since presumably the Forms are motionless, Aristotle concluded that they could not help us understand things as we know them, which are full of motion. Nor could they, being immaterial, explain objects of which we have sense impressions. Again, how could the immaterial Forms be related to any particular thing? It is not a satisfactory explanation to say, as Plato did, that things *participate* in the Forms: "to say that they are patterns and that other things share in them, is to use empty words and poetical metaphors."

When we use the words *matter* and *form* to describe any specific thing, we seem to have in mind the distinction between what something is made of and what it is made into. This, again, inclines us to assume that matter— what things are made of—exists in some primary and unformed state until it is made into a thing. But, again, Aristotle argues that we shall not find anywhere such a thing as "primary matter," that is, matter without form. Consider the sculptor who is about to make a statue of Venus out of marble. He or she will never find marble without some form. It will always be this marble or that, a square piece or an irregular one. But he or she will always work with a piece in which form and matter are already combined. That the sculptor will give it a different form is another question. The question here is, how does one thing become another thing? What, in short, is the nature of *change?*

The Process of Change: The Four Causes

In the world around us we see things constantly changing. Change is one of the basic facts of our experience. For Aristotle, the word *change* means many things, including motion, growth, decay, generation, and corruption. Some of these changes are *natural,* whereas others are the products of *human art.* Things are always taking on new form; new life is born and statues are made. Because change always involves taking on new form, we can ask several questions about the process of change. Of anything, Aristotle says, we can ask four questions, namely (1) what is it? (2) what is it made of? (3) by what is it made? and (4) for what end is it made? The four responses to these questions represent Aristotle's four *causes.* Although the word *cause* refers in modern use primarily to an event prior to an effect, for Aristotle it meant an *explanation.* His four causes therefore represent a broad pattern or framework for the total explanation of anything or everything. Taking an object of art, for example, the four causes might be (1) a statue (2) of marble (3) by a sculptor (4) for a decoration. Distinguished from objects produced by human art, there are also things that are caused *by nature.* Although nature does not, according to Aristotle, have "purposes" in the sense of "the reason for," it does always and everywhere have "ends" in the sense of having built-in ways of behaving. For this reason, seeds sprout and roots go down (not up!) and plants grow. In this process of change, plants move toward their "end," that is, their distinctive function or way of being. In nature change will involve these same four elements. Aristotle's *four causes* are therefore (1) the *formal* cause, which determines *what* a thing is, (2) the *material* cause, or that out of which it is made, (3) the *efficient* cause, by what a thing is made, and (4) the *final* cause, the "end" for which it is made.

Aristotle looked at life through the eyes of a biologist. For him, nature is *life*. All things are in motion—in the process of becoming and dying away. The process of reproduction was for Aristotle a clear example of the power inherent in all living things to initiate change and to reproduce their kind. Summarizing his causes, Aristotle said that "all things that come to be come to be by some agency and from something, and come to be something." From this biological viewpoint, Aristotle elaborated the notion that form and matter never exist separately. In nature, generation of new life involves first of all an individual who already possesses the specific form which the offspring will have (the male parent). After that there must be the matter capable of being the vehicle for this form (this matter being contributed by the female parent). Finally, from this comes a new individual with the same specific form. In this example, Aristotle shows that change does not involve bringing together formless matter with matterless form. On the contrary, change occurs always in and to something that is already a combination of form and matter and that is on its way to becoming something new or different.

Potentiality and Actuality

All things, said Aristotle, are involved in processes of change. Each thing possesses a power to become what its form has set as its end. There is in all things a dynamic power of striving toward their "end." Some of this striving is toward external objects, as when a person builds a house. But there is also the striving to achieve ends that pertain to a person's internal nature, as when we fulfill our nature as a human being by the act of thinking. This notion of a self-contained end led Aristotle to consider the distinction between *potentiality* and *actuality*. He uses this distinction to explain the processes of change and development. If the *end* of an acorn is to be a tree, in some way the acorn is only potentially a tree but not actually so at this time. A fundamental type of change, then, is the change from potentiality to actuality. But the chief significance of this distinction is that Aristotle argues for the priority of actuality over potentiality. That is, although something actual emerges from the potential, there could be no movement from potential to actual if there were not first of all something actual. A child is potentially an adult, but before there could be a child with that potentiality, there had to be an actual adult.

As all things in nature are similar to the relation of a child to an adult, or an acorn to a tree, Aristotle was led to see in nature different levels of being. If everything were involved in change—in generation and corruption—everything would partake of potentiality. But, as we have seen, for there to be something potential, there must already be something actual. To explain the existence of the world of potential things, Aristotle thought it was necessary to assume the existence of some actuality at a level above potential or perishing things. This led to the notion of a Being that is pure actuality, without any potentiality, at the highest level of being. Since change is a kind of motion, Aristotle saw the visible world as one composed of things in motion. But motion, a type of change, involves potentiality. Things are potentially in motion but must be moved by something that is actually in motion.

The Unmoved Mover

For Aristotle, the Unmoved Mover is the ultimate cause of all change in the natural world. However, this notion is not the same thing as a *first* mover, as though motion could be traced back to a *time* when motion began. Nor did he consider the Unmoved Mover as a *creator* in the sense of later theology. From his previous distinction between potentiality and actuality, Aristotle concluded that the only way to explain how motion or change can occur is to assume that something actual is *logically* prior to whatever is potential. The fact of change implies the existence of something actual, something *purely* actual without any mixture of potentiality. This *Mover* is not, according to Aristotle, an *efficient* cause in the sense of a mighty force exerting its power or expressing a *will*. Such acts would imply potentiality, as when we say that God "willed" to create the world. This would mean that *before* God created the world, he was potentially capable or intended to create it.

Aristotle did not think of the Unmoved Mover as a Being that *thinks* or establishes *purposes* for the world. In a sense, the Unmoved Mover does not know anything. This is because it is not a *kind* of being as much as it is a *way* of explaining the fact of motion. All of nature is full of things that strive toward fulfilling their particular purposes. Each thing aims at perfecting its possibilities and its *end,* that is, at becoming the perfect tree, the perfectly good person, and so on. The aggregate of all these strivings constitutes the large-scale processes of the world order. All of reality, then, is in the process of change, moving from its potentialities and possibilities to the ultimate perfection of these potentialities. To explain this comprehensive or general motion, Aristotle referred to the Unmoved Mover as the "reason for" or the "principle of" motion. For this reason, the Unmoved Mover stood for the actual, and—because there is here no potentiality—the *eternal* principle of motion. Since this explanation of motion implies an eternal activity, then, there was never a "time" when there was not a world of things in process. For this reason, too, Aristotle denied that there was a "creation" in time.

Although there are passages in Aristotle that have a distinctly religious and theistic flavor, the dominant direction of his thought on this matter is less religious than it is scientific. Still, to speak of an Unmoved Mover involved Aristotle in certain metaphorical language. In explaining how an Unmoved Mover can "cause" motion, he compared it to a beloved who "moves" the lover just by being the object of love, by the power of attraction and not by force. In a more technical way, Aristotle considered the Unmoved Mover as the *form* and the world as the substance. From the point of view of his four causes, Aristotle considered the Mover as the *final* cause, in the way that the *form* of the adult is in the child, directing the motion of change toward a *final* end—one that is fixed or appropriate. By being a final cause, the Unmoved Mover thereby becomes an *efficient* cause of the world. Through the power of attraction, it inspires things to strive toward their natural ends. Although Aristotle's Unmoved Mover was largely an unconscious principle of motion and immanent form of the world, centuries later—especially at the hands of Aquinas in the 13th century—this notion was transformed into the philosophical description of the God of Christianity.

THE PLACE OF HUMANS: PHYSICS, BIOLOGY, AND PSYCHOLOGY

In the hierarchical nature of things, Aristotle placed people in a spot distinct from inanimate things and animals. In the order of nature there are, first of all, simple bodies, plants, and animals. Unlike artificially created objects, such as chairs and tables, natural objects are such that "Each of them has *within* itself a principle of motion and of rest." This internal motion is the decisive aspect of things, for through this motion Aristotle explains the whole process of generation and corruption.

Physics

Limiting our concern only to the question of how things come to be in the natural world, Aristotle begins with the notion of *prime matter.* We have already said that Aristotle rejected the position that either pure forms or pure matter could exist separately. There is no *primary matter* existing by itself anywhere. By *prime matter* Aristotle meant the substratum in things that is capable of changing, of becoming other substances or things, of assuming novel forms. The processes of nature, then, involve the continuous transformation of matter from one form to another. When the sculptor makes a statue, his material, let us say marble, already has some form, and he will then transform it. In this same sense, Aristotle says that there are certain materials out of which *nature* makes things and he calls these *simple bodies,* namely air, fire, earth, and water. In one way or another, he says, all things are analyzable down to these. Still, when these bodies combine with one another, they form novel substances. Unlike the statue, however, the genesis of these new forms is a product of nature itself, since these bodies have within themselves a "principle of motion and rest." For this reason, fire tends to rise and become air, water to fall and become earth, the solid to become liquid, and the wet to become dry. In any case, to say that things *change* is to say that these basic simple bodies are constantly being transformed into things through their internal principle of motion and by the motion of other things.

Biology

What gives life to certain kinds of bodies? Aristotle accounts for the transition from inorganic to organic bodies by considering the nature of the *soul.* All bodies, he says, are a combination of the primary elements, but some have life and others do not. By life Aristotle means "self-nutrition and growth (with its correlative decay)." Matter as such is not the principle of life, since material substance is only potentially alive. Matter is always potentiality, whereas form is actuality. A body, then, that is actually alive has its life from the source of actuality, namely *form.* The soul, then, is the form of an organized body. Neither can exist without the other, nor are they identical, and, Aristotle says, "that is why we can wholly dismiss as unnecessary the question whether the soul and body are one: it is as meaningless as to ask whether the wax and the shape given to it by the stamp are one." The soul, as Aristotle defines it, is "the first grade of actuality of a natural organized body." When a body is "organized," its parts have set motions to perform, Thus, in a living plant, "the leaf serves to shelter the pericarp, the pericarp to shelter the fruit, while the roots of plants are analogous to the mouth of animals . . . serving for the absorption of food." The soul is "the definitive formula of a thing's essence." The soul exists when there is a particular kind of body, namely, "one having *in itself* the power of setting itself in movement and arresting itself." Soul and body are not two separate things but are rather the matter (body) and form (soul) of a single unity. And, "from this it indubitably follows that the soul is inseparable from its body." Without the body, the soul could not exist, any more than there could be vision without an eye.

Aristotle distinguished between three types of soul in order to show the three different ways a body can be organized. He called these the *vegetative, sensitive,* and *rational* souls. They represent various capacities of a body for activity, the first being simply the act of living, the second both living and sensing, and the third a body that includes living, sensing, and thinking.

Psychology

We find the sensitive soul at the animal level. Its chief characteristic lies in its power to absorb qualities and *forms* of things without taking in their *matter.* This is in contrast to the lower nutritive soul, which takes in the *matter* (e.g., food) but has no capacity to absorb its *form.* The basic sense is tactile, or touch, and is capable of absorbing what all bodies have in common. For the other senses, Aristotle says that "each sense has one kind of object which it discerns, and never errs in reporting that what is before it is color or sound." Again, the sensitive soul absorbs only the form and not the matter, "in the way in which a piece of wax takes on the impress of a signet ring without the iron or gold . . . in a similar way the sense is affected by what is colored or flavored or sounding, but it is indifferent to what in each case the *substance* is."

Aristotle used the notion of *potentiality* to explain how the sensitive soul senses things. The sense organs must be capable of sensing many different forms. They must therefore be potentially capable of adjusting to any quality. The eye, for example, must be composed of material that potentially can become blue and that in fact does become blue when a certain kind of object is sensed. This neutral material of the eye must potentially possess all colors and shapes. Our various other senses have similar potentialities with respect to other qualities. Moreover, the five senses have a way of combining their information into a unified whole, reflecting the single object or world from which these "sensibles" come. The qualities we sense can continue even after we are no longer directly perceiving an object, and this Aristotle explains in terms of *memory* and also *imagination*. Much of what we remember retains its associations with other things, suggesting that neither sensation nor memory is a random act but rather tends to reproduce what in fact exists in the real world. From the power of memory and imagination comes finally the higher form of soul, the human or the rational soul.

Human Rationality   The human soul combines in itself all the lower forms of soul—the vegetative, nutritive, and sensitive—and has in addition to these the *rational soul*. The rational soul has the capacity of scientific thought. Our *reason* is capable of distinguishing between different kinds of things, which is the capacity of analysis, and it also understands the relationships of things to each other. Besides scientific thought, the rational soul has the capacity of *deliberation*. Here we not only discover what truth is in the nature of things, but we discover the guides for human behavior.

Again, for Aristotle, the soul is the definitive form of the body. Without the body, the soul could neither be nor exercise its functions. Aristotle says that the body and soul together form one substance. This is in sharp contrast to Plato's explanation of the body as the prison house of the soul. Because he separated soul and body, Plato could speak of the preexistence of the soul. He could also describe knowledge or learning as the process of recollection of what the soul knew in its previous state. Moreover, Plato could also speak of the immortality of the individual soul. Aristotle, on the other hand, tied soul and body so closely together that with the death of the body, the soul, its organizing principle, also dies.

The rational soul of people, like the sensitive soul, is characterized by potentiality. Just as the eye is capable of seeing a red object but will only see it when it actually confronts a red object, so, also, our rational soul is capable of understanding the true nature of things. But reason has its knowledge only potentially; it must reason out its conclusions. Human thought, in short, is a possibility and not a continuous actuality, for if it is *possible* for the human mind to attain knowledge, it is also possible for it *not* to attain knowledge. Human thought is therefore intermittent between *actually* and *potentially* knowing. Truth is never continuously present in the human intellect.

The continuity of truth is implied by the continuity of the world. What the human mind has as potential knowledge must therefore be perfect and continuous knowledge in some mind. Aristotle spoke of the Unmoved Mover as the soul (*nous*) of the world and its intelligible principle. In his *De Anima* he speaks of the Active Intellect, saying that "*Nous* does not at one time function and at another not." Here he appears to compare the individual human intellect, which knows only intermittently, with the Active Intellect, which is in some sense independent of particular people and is eternal. If this intellect is indeed purely active, it possesses no potentiality. And this is what Aristotle had described as the Unmoved Mover. The distinctive activity of the Unmoved Mover is pure act, which is an exercise of the mind in complete harmony with the truth about the whole of reality. The whole system of Forms taken as the intelligible structure of all things must therefore constitute the continuous knowledge of the Unmoved Mover, the Active Intellect. This Intellect is immortal, and to the extent that our passive and potential intellects know any truth, they have in them what the Active Intellect always knows. What is immortal when we die is what belongs to the Active Intellect, but as this is not a part of *us*, our own individual souls perish with the matter for which it was the form. Only what is pure act is eternal, and our substance, being an admixture of potentiality, does not survive.

ETHICS

Aristotle's theory of mortality centers around his belief that people, as everything else in nature, have a distinctive end to achieve and a function to fulfill. He begins his *Nicomachean Ethics* by saying that "Every art and every inquiry, and similarly every action and pursuit, is thought to aim at some good." If this is so, the question for ethics is, "What is the *good* at which human behavior aims?" Plato had answered this question by saying that people aim at a knowledge of the Form of the Good. For him this supreme principle of Good is separate from the world of experience and from individuals; we arrive at it by ascending from the visible world to the intelligible world. For Aristotle, on the other hand, the principle of good and right was imbedded within each person. Moreover, this principle could be discovered by studying the human nature and could be attained through actual behavior in daily life. Aristotle warns his readers, however, not to expect more precision in a discussion of ethics than "the subject-matter will admit." Still, just because this subject is susceptible of "variation and error" does not mean that ideas of right and wrong "exist conventionally only, and not in the nature of things." With this in mind, Aristotle set out to discover the basis of morality in the structure of human nature.

Types of "Ends"

Aristotle sets the framework for his ethical theory with a preliminary illustration. Having said that all action aims toward an end, he now wants to distinguish between two major kinds of ends, which can be called *instrumental* ends (acts that are done as *means* for other ends) and *intrinsic* ends (acts that are done for their own sake). These two types of ends are illustrated, for example, in activities connected with war. When we consider step by step what is involved in the total activity of a war, we find, Aristotle says, that there is a series of special kinds of acts. There is, for one thing, the art of the bridle maker. When the bridle is finished, its maker has achieved his end as a bridle maker. But the bridle is a means for the horseman to guide his horse in battle. Also, a carpenter builds a barrack, and when it is completed, he has fulfilled his function as a carpenter. The barracks also fulfill their function when they provide safe shelter for the soldiers. But the ends here achieved by the carpenter and the building are not intrinsic ends in themselves but are only instrumental in housing soldiers until they move on to their next stage of action. Similarly, the function of the builder of ships is fulfilled when the ship is successfully launched, but again this end is in turn a means for transporting the soldiers to the field of battle. The doctor fulfills his function to the extent that he keeps the soldiers in good health. But the "end" of health in this case becomes a "means" for effective fighting. The officer aims at victory in battle, but victory is the means to peace. Peace itself, though sometimes taken mistakenly as the final end of war, is the means for creating the conditions under which people can fulfill their function as human beings. When we discover what people aim at, not as carpenters, doctors, or generals, but as *humans,* we will then arrive at action *for its own sake,* and for which all other activity is only a means, and this, Aristotle says, "must be the Good of Humanity."

How should we understand the word *good*? As Plato before him, Aristotle tied the word *good* to the special function of a thing. A hammer is good if it does what hammers are expected to do. A carpenter is good if he or she fulfills his or her function as a builder. This would be true of all the crafts and professions. But here Aristotle distinguishes between a person's craft or profession and a person's activity as a human. For example, Aristotle felt that being a good doctor did not mean the same thing as being a good person. I could be a good doctor without being a good person, and vice versa. There are two different functions here, the function of doctoring and the function of acting as a person. To discover the good at which a person should aim, Aristotle said we must discover the distinctive function of human nature. The good person, according to Aristotle, is the person who is fulfilling his or her function as a human being.

The Function of Human Beings

Aristotle asks, "Are we then to suppose that while carpenter and cobbler have certain works and courses of action, people as Human Beings have none, but are left by Nature without a work?" Or, if "the eye, hand, foot and in general each of the parts evidently has a function, may we lay it down that humans similarly have a function apart from all these?" Surely, people too have a distinctive type of activity, but what is it? Here Aristotle analyzes human nature in order to discover its unique activity, saying, first of all, that our human end "is not mere life," because that plainly is shared even by vegetables, and, Aristotle says, "we want what is peculiar to [human beings]." Next there is the life of sensation, "but this again manifestly is common to horses, oxen and every animal." There remains then "an active life of the element that has a rational principle." He contends further that, "if the function of people is an activity of soul which follows or implies a rational principle . . . then the human good turns out to be activity of soul in accordance with virtue."

Since a person's function as a human being means the proper functioning of the soul, Aristotle sought to describe the nature of the soul. The human soul is the form of the human body. As such, the soul refers to the total person. Accordingly, Aristotle said that the soul has two parts, the irrational and the rational. The irrational part is composed of two subparts. First, as with plants, there is a vegetative component that gives us the capacity to take in nutrition and sustain our biological lives. Second, as with animals, there is an appetitive component that gives us the capacity to experience desires, which in turn prompts us to move around to fulfill those desires. Both of these irrational parts of soul tend to oppose and resist the rational part. The conflict between the rational and irrational elements in human beings is what raises the problems and subject matter of morality.

Morality involves action. Thus Aristotle says that "as at the Olympic games it is not the finest and strongest people who are crowned, but they who enter the lists, for out of these the prize-men are selected; so too in life, of the honorable and good, it is they who act who rightly win the prizes." The particular kind of action implied here is the rational control and guidance of the irrational parts of the soul. Moreover, the good person is not the one who does a good deed here or there, now and then. Instead, it is the person whose whole life is good, "for as it is not one swallow or one fine day that makes a spring, so it is not one day or a short time that makes a person happy."

Happiness as the End

Human action should aim at its proper end. Everywhere people aim at pleasure, wealth, and honor. Although these ends have some type of value, they are not the chief good for which people should aim. To be an ultimate end, an act must be *self-sufficient* and *final,* "that which is always desirable in itself and never for the sake of something else," and it must be *attainable by people.* Aristotle is certain that all people will agree that *happiness* is the end that alone meets all the requirements for the ultimate end of human action. Indeed, we choose pleasure, wealth, and honor only because we think that "through their instrumentality we shall be happy." Happiness, it turns out, is another word or name for *good,* for like good, happiness is the fulfillment of our distinctive function. As Aristotle says, "Happiness . . . is a working of the soul in the way of excellence or virtue."

How does the soul attain happiness? The general rule of morality is "to act in accordance with Right Reason." What this means is that the rational part of the soul should control the irrational part. It is obvious that the irrational part requires guidance when we consider what it consists of and what its mechanism is. When looking at our appetites, we discover first that they are affected or influenced by things outside of the self, such as objects and people. Also, there are two basic ways in which the appetitive part of the soul reacts to these external factors—these ways being *love* (or the *concupiscent* passions) and *hate* (or the *irascible* passions). Love leads us to desire things and persons, whereas hate leads us to avoid or destroy them. It becomes quickly apparent that these passions for love and hate could easily "go wild" when taken by themselves. In themselves they do not contain any principle of measure or selection. What should a person desire? How much? Under what circumstances? How should we relate ourselves to things, wealth, honor, and other persons?

We do not automatically act the right way in these matters. As Aristotle says, "none of the moral virtues arises in us by nature; for nothing that exists by nature can form a habit contrary to its nature." Morality has to do with developing habits, the habits of right thinking, right choice, and right behavior.

Virtue as the Golden Mean

Human passions are capable of a wide range of action, all the way from too little to too much. Consider our appetites for food. On the one hand we can become dominated by an excessive desire to eat. On the other hand we can have a deficiency in our appetite for food to the point of starvation. The proper course of action—that is, the *virtuous* course—is a middle ground or *mean* between excess and deficiency. We should seek out this middle ground with all of our passions, such as those of fear, confidence, lust, anger, compassion, pleasure, and pain. When we fail to achieve this middle ground, we expose ourselves to vices of excess or vices of deficiency. We control our passions through the rational power of the soul, and thereby form virtuous habits that lead us to spontaneously follow the middle course. The virtue of *courage*, for example, is the mean between two vices: cowardice (a deficiency) and rashness (an excess). Virtue, then, is a state of being, "a state apt to exercise deliberate choice, being in the relative mean, determined by reason, and as the person of practical wisdom would determine." Therefore, virtue is a habit of choosing in accordance with a mean.

The mean is not the same for every person, nor is there a mean for every act. Each mean is relative to each person to the degree that our personal circumstances vary. In the case of eating, the mean will obviously be different for an adult athlete and toddler. But for each person, there is nevertheless a proportionate or relative mean, which is the virtue of *temperance*. This stands between two extreme vices, namely, gluttony (excess) and starvation (deficiency). Similarly, when we give money, *liberality* is the virtuous mean between the vices of prodigality and stinginess. There is no fixed amount of money that constitutes the virtue of liberality; instead, the dollar figure is relative to our assets. Although a large number of virtues stand between two extreme vices, there are other actions that have no mean at all. Their very nature already implies badness, such as spite, envy, adultery, theft, and murder. These are bad in themselves and not in their excesses or deficiencies. We are thus always wrong in doing them.

Moral virtue, then, consists of cultivating habits which will spontaneously incline us to take the middle course of action—or simply avoid bad conduct in the case of actions like theft and murder. Plato had listed four main virtues (later called "cardinal" virtues), which Aristotle also endorses, namely, courage, temperance, justice, and wisdom. In addition to these, Aristotle also discusses the virtues of magnificence, liberality, friendship, and self-respect.

Deliberation and Choice

There are two kinds of reasoning within the rational soul. The first is theoretical, giving us knowledge of fixed principles or philosophical wisdom. The other is practical, giving us a rational guide to our moral action under the particular circumstances in which we find ourselves, and this is practical wisdom. What is important about the role of reason is that without this rational element, we would not have any moral capacity. Again, Aristotle stressed that although we have natural capacity for *right* behavior, we do not act rightly *by nature.* Our life consists of an unfixed number of possibilities. Goodness is in us all *potentially.* An oak will grow out of an acorn with almost mechanical certainty. With people, though, we must move from what is potential in us to its actuality by knowing what we must do, deliberating about it, and then choosing in fact to do it. Unlike Plato and Socrates, who thought that to know the good was sufficient to do the good, Aristotle saw that there must be deliberate choice in addition to knowledge. Thus, Aristotle said that "the origin of moral action—its efficient, not its final cause—is choice, and (the origin) of choice is desire and reasoning with a view to an end."

There is an important connection between free choice and human responsibility. Suppose, for example, that you have a brain tumor that triggers within you an irresistible impulse to be violent. If your violent conduct is truly beyond your control, then you cannot be held morally responsible for your conduct. Aristotle—and many other moral philosophers—accordingly held that people are responsible for their conduct and, consequently, moral behavior is voluntary. But not all our actions are voluntary. There are some exceptions, though, for Aristotle said that "praise and blame arise upon such as are voluntary, while for the involuntary allowance is made, and sometimes compassion is excited." The principal distinction for Aristotle between voluntary and involuntary acts is this. *Involuntary* acts are those for which a person is not responsible because they are: (1) done out of ignorance of particular circumstances, (2) done as a result of external compulsion, or (3) done to avoid a greater evil. *Voluntary* acts are those for which a person is responsible because none of these three extenuating circumstances take place.

Contemplation

Human nature consists for Aristotle not simply in rationality but in the full range covered by the vegetative, appetitive, and the rational souls. Virtue does not imply the negation or rejection of any of these natural capacities. The moral person employs all of his or her capacities, *physical* and *mental.* Corresponding to these two broad divisions in human nature there are two functions of reason, the moral and intellectual, and each has its own virtues. We have already seen Aristotle's account of *moral virtues,* namely, the habits that help us follow the middle ground in response to the desires of our appetitive nature. The intellectual virtues, by contrast, focus on our intellectual rather than bodily nature; chief among these is philosophical wisdom (*sophia*), which includes scientific knowledge and the ability to grasp first principles.

Aristotle concludes his principal work on ethics with a discussion of philosophical wisdom and the act of contemplating intellectual truths. If happiness is the product of our acting according to our distinctive nature, it is reasonable to assume that we are most happy when acting according to our *highest* nature, which is contemplation. This activity is the best, Aristotle says, "since not only is reason the best thing in us, but the objects of reason are the best of knowable objects." Moreover, contemplation "is most continuous, since we can contemplate truth more continuously than we can *do* anything." Finally, "we think happiness has pleasure mingled with it, but the activity of philosophical wisdom is admittedly the pleasantest of virtuous activities."

POLITICS

In his *Politics,* as in his *Ethics,* Aristotle stresses the element of purpose. Just like human beings, the state is naturally endowed with a distinctive function. Combining these two ideas, Aristotle says that "it is evident that the State is a creature of nature, and that human beings are by nature political animals." Human nature and the state are so closely related that "he who is unable to live in society, or who has no need because he is sufficient for himself, must be either a beast or a god." Not only does human nature incline us to live in a state, but the state, as every other community, "is established with a view to some good" and exists for some end. The family exists primarily to preserve life. The state comes into existence in the first instance to preserve life for families and villages, which in the long run cannot survive on their own. But beyond this economic end, the function of the state is to ensure the supreme good of people, namely, our moral and intellectual life.

Unlike Plato, Aristotle did not create a blueprint for an ideal state. Even though Aristotle viewed the state as the agency for enabling people to achieve their ultimate goals as human beings, he nevertheless realized that any theory of the state must take note of several practical issues. For example, we must determine "what kind of government is adapted to particular states" even though the best of these is often unattainable. Also, we must determine "how a state may be constituted under any given condition" and how it may be preserved. For Aristotle, "political writers, although they have excellent ideas, are often impractical." For these reasons, he had little patience with Plato's most radical ideas. He ridicules Plato's arrangement for the abolition of the family for the guardian class and providing a public nursery for their children. With this kind of arrangement, according to Aristotle, "there is no reason why the so-called father should care about the son, or the son about the father, or brothers about one another." The communal ownership of property would likewise destroy certain basic human pleasures as well as create inefficiency and endless disputes.

Types of States

Aristotle was willing to recognize that, under appropriate circumstances, a community could organize itself into at least three different kinds of government. The basic difference among them is primarily the number of rulers each has. A government can have as its rulers *one*, a *few*, or *many*. But each of these forms of government can have a true or a perverted form. When a government is functioning rightly, it governs for the common good of all the people. A government is perverted when its rulers govern for their own private gain or interests. The true forms of each type of government, according to Aristotle, are *monarchy* (one), *aristocracy* (few), and *polity* (many). The perverted forms are tyranny (one), oligarchy (few), and democracy (many). His own preference was aristocracy, chiefly because there are not enough people of exceptional excellence, in spite of our best efforts. In an aristocracy, there is the rule of a group of people whose degree of excellence, achievement, and ownership of property makes them responsible, able, and capable of command.

Differences and Inequalities

Because he relied so heavily upon anecdotal observation of things, it was inevitable that Aristotle would make some mistakes. Nowhere is this truer than with his view of slavery. Observing that slaves invariably were strong and large, he concluded that slavery was a product of nature. "It is clear," Aristotle said, "that some men are by nature free, and others slaves, and that for these slavery is both expedient and right." To be sure, Aristotle took great care to distinguish between those who became slaves by nature, a type of slavery that he accepted, and those who became slaves by military conquest, a type he rejected. Aristotle rejected slavery by conquest on the highly defensible grounds that to overpower people does not mean that we are superior to them in nature. Moreover, the use of force may or may not be justified, in which case enslavement could very well be the product and extension of an unjust act. At the same time, speaking of the "proper treatment of slaves," he proposed that "it is advantageous that liberty should be always held out to them as the reward of their services." The fact is that in his own last will and testament, Aristotle provided for the emancipation of some of his slaves.

Aristotle also believed in the inequality of citizenship. He held that the basic qualification for citizenship was a person's ability to share in ruling and being ruled in turn. A citizen had the right and the obligation to participate in the administration of justice. Since citizens would therefore have to sit in the assembly and in the law courts, they would have to have both ample time as well as an appropriate temperament and character. For this reason, Aristotle did not believe that laborers should be citizens, as they had neither the time nor the appropriate mental development, nor could they benefit from the experience of sharing in the political process.

Good Government and Revolution

Over and over again Aristotle made the point that the state exists for the sake of everyone's moral and intellectual fulfillment. "A state," he says, "exists for the sake of a good life, and not for the sake of life only"; similarly, "the state is the union of families and villages in a perfect and self-sufficing life, by which we mean a happy and honorable life." Finally, he said, "our conclusion . . . is that political society exists for the sake of noble actions, and not mere companionship." Still, whether a state produces the good life depends upon how its rulers behave. We have already seen that Aristotle distinguishes between perverted forms of government and true forms, and that the good rulers seek to achieve the good of all, whereas the perverted rulers seek their own private gain.

Whatever form government has, it will rest upon some conception of justice and proportionate equality. But these conceptions of justice can bring disagreement and ultimately revolution. Democracy, as Aristotle knew it, arises out of the assumption that those who are equal in any respect are equal in all respects: "because people are equally free, they claim to be absolutely equal." On the other hand, Aristotle said *oligarchy* is based upon the notion that "those who are unequal in one respect are in all respects unequal." Hence, "being unequal . . . in property, they suppose themselves to be unequal absolutely." For these reasons, whenever the democrats or oligarchs are in the minority and the philosophy of the incumbent government "does not accord with their preconceived ideas, [they] stir up revolution. . . . Here then . . . are opened up the very springs and fountains of revolution."

Aristotle concludes that "the universal and chief cause of this revolutionary feeling [is] the desire of equality, when men think they are equal to others who have more than themselves." He did not overlook other causes such as "insolence and avarice" as well as fear and contempt. Knowing these causes of revolution, Aristotle said that each form of government could take appropriate precautions against it. For example, a king must avoid despotic acts, an aristocracy should avoid the rule by a few rich men for the benefit of the wealthy class, and a polity should provide more time for its abler members to share in the government. Most importantly, Aristotle urged that "there is nothing which should be more jealously maintained than the spirit of obedience to law." In the end, people will always criticize the state unless their conditions of living within it are such that they can achieve happiness in the form of what they consider the good life.

PHILOSOPHY OF ART

Aristotle had a far more sympathetic interest in art than did Plato. For Plato, as for Aristotle, art was essentially a matter of imitating nature. What made Plato so contemptuous of some forms of art was his notion that a work of art is at least three steps removed from truth. The true reality of human beings, let us say, is the eternal Form of Humanity. A poor copy of this Form would be any particular person—Socrates, for example. A statue or portrait of Socrates would then be a copy of a copy. Plato was particularly concerned with the cognitive aspect of art, feeling that it had the effect of distorting knowledge because it was removed several steps from reality. Aristotle, on the other hand, believing that the universal Forms exist only in particular things, felt that artists are dealing directly with the universal when they study things and translate them into art forms. For this reason Aristotle affirmed the cognitive value of art, saying that since art does imitate nature, it therefore communicates information about nature.

In his *Poetics,* he stresses the cognitive aspect of poetry by contrasting poetry with history. Unlike the historian, who is concerned only with particular persons and events, the poet deals with basic human nature, and therefore universal experience. The true difference between them is that history relates what has happened, whereas poetry considers what may happen. "Poetry, therefore, is a more philosophical and a higher thing than history: for poetry tends to express the universal, history the particular." By universality, Aristotle means "how a person of a certain type will on occasion speak or act, according to the law of probability or necessity," and it is "this universality at which poetry aims."

In addition to its cognitive value, art has in Aristotle's view considerable psychological significance. For one thing, art reflects a deep facet of human nature by which people are differentiated from animals, this being their implanted instinct for imitation. Indeed, from earliest childhood learning takes place through imitation. In addition to this instinct, there is also the pleasure that people feel upon confronting art. Thus, "the reason people enjoy seeing a likeness is, that in contemplating it they find themselves learning or inferring, and saying perhaps, 'Ah, that is he.'"

Aristotle gave detailed analyses of *epic, tragic,* and *comic* poetry, showing what each consists of and what its function is. However, it was his remarks about tragedy that became most famous in subsequent thought. He particularly emphasized the emotional aspect of tragedy, centering upon the notion of *catharsis*—a purging of unpleasant emotions. "A tragedy," Aristotle says,

> is the imitation of an action that is serious and also, as having magnitude, complete in itself; in language with pleasurable accessories, each kind brought in separately in the parts of the work; in a dramatic, not a narrative form; with incidents arousing pity and fear, *wherewith to accomplish its catharsis of such emotions.*

Does the term *catharsis* imply that through tragedy we "get rid of" our feelings? Or, does it mean that we are given an occasion to express or give vent to our deepest emotions in a vicarious way? In either case, what Aristotle seems to be saying is that the artistic representation of deep and great suffering arouses in the audience genuine terror and pity, thereby purging and in a sense purifying the audience member's spirit. Thus, Aristotle says that "tragedy is an imitation of an action . . . through pity and fear effecting the proper purgation of these emotions."

Hellenistic and Medieval Philosophy

CHAPTER 5

Classical Philosophy after Aristotle

*A*fter Aristotle completed his great speculative system, philosophy moved toward a new emphasis. Four groups of philosophers helped to shape this new direction, namely, the Epicureans, the Stoics, the Skeptics, and the Neoplatonists. They were, of course, greatly influenced by their predecessors. Thus, we find that Epicurus relied upon Democritus for his atomic theory of nature; the Stoics made use of Heraclitus' notion of a fiery substance permeating all things; the Skeptics built a method of inquiry upon the Socratic form of doubt; and Plotinus drew heavily upon Plato. What made their philosophy different, however, was not so much its subject matter as its direction and its emphasis. Its emphasis was practical, and its direction was individually centered. Philosophy became more practical by emphasizing the art of living. To be sure, each of these new movements of thought did involve speculative descriptions of the structure of the universe. But instead of working out blueprints for the ideal society and fitting individuals into large social and political organizations, as Plato and Aristotle did, these new philosophers led people to think primarily about themselves and how they as individuals in the larger scheme of nature could achieve the most satisfactory personal life.

These new directions in philosophy were brought about to a great extent by the historical conditions of the times. After the Peloponnesian War and with the fall of Athens, Greek civilization declined. With the breakdown of the small Greek city-state, individual citizens lost the sense of their own importance and their ability to control or perfect their social and political destiny. As they were absorbed into the growing Roman Empire, people increasingly felt this loss of personal control over their lives within the community. When Greece became a mere province of Rome, people lost interest in pursuing the speculative questions concerning the ideal society. What was needed was a practical philosophy to give life direction under changing conditions. And at a time when events overwhelmed people, it seemed idle to try to change history. But if history was beyond humanity's control, at least a person's own life could be managed with some success. Philosophy, therefore, shifted to this

103

practical emphasis in a direction of increasing concern for the more immediate world of the individual.

The Epicureans turned in the direction of an ideal for living through what they called *ataraxia,* or tranquility of soul. The Stoics sought to control their re-actions to inevitable events. The Skeptics sought to preserve personal freedom by refraining from any basic commitment to ideals whose truth was doubtful. Finally, Plotinus promised salvation in a mystical union with God. They looked to philosophy for a source of meaning for human existence, and it is no wonder that their philosophy, particularly Stoicism, was later to compete with religion for allegiance. They sought to discover ways in which individual peo-ple could successfully achieve happiness or contentment in a world that was not altogether friendly and filled with many pitfalls.

EPICUREANISM

Epicurus was born about five or six years after Plato's death, when Aristotle was 42 years old. Born in 342 or 341 BCE on the island of Samos in the Aegean Sea, he was exposed in his teens to the writings of Democritus, whose ideas about nature had a permanent influence upon his own philosophy. When the Athenians were driven out of Samos, Epicurus went to Asia Minor, where he became a teacher in several schools. About the year 306 BCE, he moved to Athens and here founded his own school. The meeting place of his school was his own garden. In time this ranked with Plato's Academy, Aristotle's Lyceum, and Zeno's Stoa as one of the influential schools of ancient times. Here Epicurus attracted a close group of friends, who were attached to him by deep affection and reverence, and to each other by the love of cultivated con-versation. In spite of the loss of the bulk of his prolific writings, there emerged from this school a definite approach to philosophy, which survived Epicurus' death in 270 BCE. The lasting impact of his teaching is shown by its continuous appearance in Athens and its spread to Rome, where the poet Lucretius (98–55 BCE) embodied the major thoughts of Epicurus in his memorable poem *On the Nature of Things (De Rerum Natura),* which survives to our day.

Epicurus was a practical philosopher. He thought that ideas should have as much effect upon the control of life as medicine has upon the health of the body. Indeed, he considered philosophy as the medicine of the soul. He did not deal at length with the intricate aspects of questions such as "what is the world made of?" The picture of the world as consisting of atoms, or bits of matter, which had been developed by Democritus, seemed to Epicurus a rea-sonable answer. If that is what the world consists of, thought Epicurus, what consequences follow from that for human behavior?

To Epicurus, the chief aim of human life is pleasure. But it is ironic that his name should be linked even today with the indulgent glutton, for nothing could be further from the teaching of Epicurus than the notion that pleasure consists in the triple formula of eat, drink, and be merry. Instead, he took great pains to distinguish between various types of pleasures. For example, some

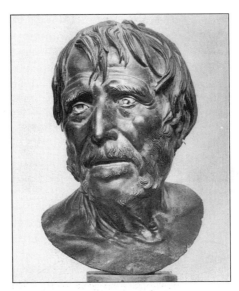

Lucretius
(*MuseoNazionale Romano*)

are intense but last only a short while, and others are not so intense but last longer. Also, some pleasures have a painful aftermath, and others give a sense of calm and repose. He tried to refine the principle of pleasure as the basis of conduct.

Physics and Ethics

What made Epicurus turn to the pleasure principle was the "science" or physics inherited from Democritus. This science had the effect of eliminating the notion that God has created everything and that human behavior should be based upon obedience to principles whose source is God. Building upon this "atomic theory," Epicurus concluded that everything that exists must be made up of eternal atoms—small, indestructible bits of hard matter. Apart from these clusters of atoms, nothing else exists. This would mean that if God or gods exist, they too must be material beings. Most importantly, God is not the source or the creator of anything but is himself the result of a purposeless and random event.

The origin of everything is explained by the notion that there is no beginning to the atoms. Atoms have always existed in space. As raindrops, they were at one time separately falling in space, and since they encountered no resistance, they always remained the same distance apart from each other. During this vertical drop, thought Epicurus, one atom instead of falling perfectly straight had developed a slight easing to one side—that is, a lateral "swerve." In time, this atom moved into the path of an oncoming atom, and the resulting impact forced both of these atoms into the paths of other atoms, thereby setting in motion a whole series of collisions until all the atoms had formed into clusters. These clusters or arrangements of atoms are the things we see even now, including rocks, flowers, animals, human beings, in short, the world. Since there were an infinite number of atoms, there must now be an infinite number of worlds. In any case, human beings are not part of a created or purposeful order caused or ruled by God but rather the accidental product of the collision of atoms.

God and Death

With this explanation of the origin of human beings—and for that matter of all beings including "divine beings"—Epicurus thought that he had liberated people from the fear of God and from the fear of death. We no longer have to fear God because God did not control nature or human destiny and was, therefore, unable to intrude into people's lives. As for death, Epicurus said that this need not bother anyone, because only a living person has sensation either of pain or pleasure. After death, there is no sensation, since the atoms that make up our bodies and our minds come apart. Thus, there is no longer this particular body or mind but only a number of distinct atoms that return, as it were, to the primeval inventory of matter to continue the cycle of new formations. Only matter exists, and in human life all we know is this body and this present moment of experience. The composition of human nature includes atoms of different sizes and shapes. The larger atoms make up our bodies, and the smaller, smoother, and swifter atoms account for sensation and thinking. No other principle is needed to explain a person's nature, no God and, therefore, no afterlife. Liberation from the fear of God and of death sets the stage for a way of life completely under a person's own control.

This was a new direction in moral philosophy, for it focused upon the individual and his immediate desires for bodily and mental pleasures instead of upon abstract principles of right conduct or considerations of God's commands. Just as his physical theory made the individual atom the final basis of all existence, so also Epicurus singled out the individual person as the arena of the moral enterprise.

The Pleasure Principle

Epicurus portrayed the origin of all things in a mechanical way and placed humans into the nature of things as just another small mechanism whose nature leads us to seek pleasure. Nevertheless, Epicurus reserved for people both the power and the duty to regulate the traffic of our desires. Even though Epicurus had liberated people from the fear of God's providence, he had no intention, thereby, of opening the floodgates of passion and indulgence. He was certain that pleasure was the standard of goodness, but he was equally certain that not every kind of pleasure had the same value.

If we asked Epicurus how he knew that pleasure was the standard of *goodness*, he would answer simply that all people have an immediate feeling of the difference between pleasure and pain and of the desirability of pleasure. He writes, "we recognize pleasure as the first good innate in us, and from pleasure we begin every act of choice and avoidance, and to pleasure we return again." Feeling, Epicurus said, is as immediate a test of goodness or badness as sensation is the test of truth. To our senses, pain is always bad and pleasure always good, just as seeing tells us whether something is in front of us or not.

Still, in order to guide people to the happiest life, Epicurus emphasized the distinction between various kinds of pleasures. It is clear that some desires are both natural and necessary, as in the case of food. Others are natural but not necessary, as in the case of some types of sexual pleasure. Still others are neither natural nor necessary, as, for example, any type of luxury or popularity. It was because he could make these clear distinctions that he concluded that

> when . . . we maintain that pleasure is the end, we do not mean the pleasures of profligates and those that consist of sensuality, as is supposed by some who are either ignorant or disagree with us or do not understand, but freedom from pain in the body and from trouble in the mind. For it is not continuous drinkings and revelings, nor the satisfaction of lusts, nor the enjoyment of fish and other luxuries of the wealthy table, which produce a pleasant life, but sober reasoning, searching out the motives for all choice and avoidance, and banishing mere opinions, to which are due the greatest disturbance of the spirit.

Epicurus did not mean to denounce the pleasures of the body. Instead, he meant only to emphasize that too great a concern with these pleasures was both unnatural and the surest way to unhappiness and pain. Certain kinds of bodily pleasures could never be fully satisfied. Further, if such pleasures required continuous indulgence it followed that people pursuing such pleasures would by definition always be unsatisfied and would, therefore, constantly suffer some pain. If, for example, they wanted more money, or more public acclaim, or more exotic foods, or a higher position, they would always be dissatisfied with their present situation and would suffer some internal pain. The wise person, on the other hand, is able to determine what is the minimum his or her nature requires, and is able easily and quickly to satisfy these needs. When these needs are satisfied, a person's constitution is in balance. The wise person's diet of bread and water is far more likely to bring happiness than the gourmet's surplus of fancy foods, for the wise person has learned not only to consume little but, also—and this is the clue—to *need* little.

The ultimate pleasure human nature seeks is *repose,* by which Epicurus means the absence of bodily pain and the gentle relaxation of the mind. This sense of repose can be most successfully achieved by scaling down our desires, overcoming useless fears, and, above all, turning to the pleasures of the mind, which have the highest degree of permanence. In a sense these pleasures of the mind are physical pleasures inasmuch as they have the effect of preventing overindulgence in matters of the flesh and, therefore, preventing their ensuing pain.

Individual Pleasure versus Social Duty

In the end, Epicurus fashioned a self-centered moral philosophy, for his concern was not primarily with human society but with individual pleasure. Even the life of the philosopher is looked upon as a means to avoid pain and not as an influence for creating a good society. Just as Epicurus sought to detach himself from the tyranny of exotic foods, so also did he seek to detach himself from entanglements with other people and particularly with poor people, whose needs and problems are many. For him, we do not find the good life through our service to our fellow human beings, but in the pleasant, decent company of intellectually fascinating friends. The only function of civil society that Epicurus would recognize was to deter those who might inflict pain upon individuals. His theory of physics, which rules out all purpose and any realm of rational order, left him without a firm idea of justice. There was, for Epicurus, no higher value than the absence of pain and the control of desires by the mind. We shall see that for centuries to come this moral philosophy fashioned by Epicurus challenged and in turn was challenged by alternative concepts of the moral life.

STOICISM

Stoicism as a school of philosophy includes some of the most distinguished intellectuals of antiquity. Founded by Zeno of Citium (334–262 BCE), who assembled his school on the Stoa (Greek for *porch,* hence the term *stoic*), this philosophical movement attracted Cleanthes (303–233 BCE) and Aristo in Athens. Later it found such advocates in Rome as Cicero (106–43 BCE), Epictetus (60–117 CE), Seneca (4 BCE?–65 CE), and the Emperor Marcus Aurelius (121–180 CE). This influence helped to fix the overwhelming emphasis of Stoic philosophy upon ethics, although the Stoics addressed themselves to all three divisions of philosophy formulated by Aristotle's Lyceum, namely, logic, physics, and ethics.

Wisdom and Control versus Pleasure

In their moral philosophy, the Stoics aimed at happiness, but unlike the Epicureans they did not expect to find it in pleasure. Instead, the Stoics sought happiness through wisdom, a wisdom by which to control what lay within human ability and to accept with dignified resignation what had to be. Zeno was inspired as a youth by the ethical teachings and the life of Socrates, who had faced death with serenity and courage. This example of superb control over the emotions in the face of the supreme threat to one's existence—the threat of death—provided the Stoics with an authentic model after which to pattern their lives. Centuries later the Stoic Epictetus said that "I cannot escape death, but cannot I escape the dread of it?" Developing this same theme in a more general way, he wrote, "Do not demand that events should happen as you wish; but wish them to happen as they do

Stoa—the corridor where Zeno delivered his lectures. His new school of philosophy, named Stoicism after this meeting place, was founded here.
(American School of Classical Studies at Athens/Agora Excavations)

happen, and you will go on well." We cannot control all events, but we can control our attitude toward what happens. It is useless to fear future events, for they will happen in any case. But it is possible by an act of will to control our fear. We should not, therefore, fear events—in a real sense we have "nothing to fear but fear itself."

There is an elegant simplicity to this moral philosophy, and yet it was a philosophy for an intellectual elite. The conclusion was simple enough, to control our attitudes, but how did the Stoics arrive at this conclusion in a philosophical way? They did it by creating a mental picture of what the world must be like and how human beings fit into this world. The world, they said, is an orderly arrangement where people and physical things behave according to principles of *purpose.* They saw throughout all of nature the operation of *reason* and *law.* The Stoics relied upon a special idea of God to explain this view of the world, for they thought of God as a rational substance existing not in some single location but in all of nature, in all things. It was this kind of God—a pervading substantial form of *reason* that controls and orders the whole structure of nature—that the Stoics said determines the course of events. Herein lay the basis for moral philosophy, but the direction in which Stoic thought moved on these matters was set by their theory of knowledge.

Stoic Theory of Knowledge

The Stoics explained in great detail how we are able to achieve knowledge. They did not entirely succeed in their account, but their theory of knowledge was nevertheless important for at least two reasons. First, it laid the foundation for their materialistic theory of nature, and, secondly, it provided the basis for their conception of truth or certainty.

Both of these consequences of the Stoic theory of knowledge stem from their account of the origin of ideas. Words, they said, express thoughts, and thoughts are originated by the impact of some object upon the mind. The mind is blank at birth and builds up its store of ideas as it is exposed to objects. These objects make impressions upon our minds through the channel of the senses. A tree, for example, impresses its image upon our minds through the sense of vision in the same way that a seal leaves its imprint in wax. Repeated exposure to the world of things increases the number of impressions, develops our memory, and enables us to form more general conceptions beyond the objects immediately before us.

Epictetus—a Stoic philosopher
(New York Public Library Picture Collection)

The real problem the Stoics faced was how to explain this last point, that is, how to account for our general ideas such as goodness and beauty. They had to show how our thinking is related to our sensations. It is one thing to prove that our idea of a tree comes from our vision of trees. But how can we account for general ideas—ideas that refer to things beyond our senses? The Stoics replied that all thought is in some way related to the senses, even thoughts that represent judgments and inferences. A judgment or an inference that something is good or true is the product of the mechanical process of impressions. Our thinking in all its forms starts with impressions, and some of our thinking is based upon impressions that start from within us, as in the case of feelings. Feelings can, therefore, give us knowledge; they are the source of "irresistible perceptions," which, in turn, are the ground of our sense of certainty. As the Skeptics later pointed out, this explanation could not stand up to all the critical questions we could raise against it. But, through this theory, the Stoics not only found in it a basis for truth; they had also imposed a most distinctive slant upon their general philosophy. For to argue as they did that all thought derives from the impact of objects on the senses is to affirm that nothing real exists except things that possess some material form. Stoic logic had cast Stoic philosophy into a materialistic mold.

Matter as the Basis of All Reality

This materialism provided Stoicism with an ingenious conception of the physical world and the human nature. The broad picture the Stoics drew of physical nature followed from their position that all that is real is material. Everything in the whole universe is, therefore, some form of matter. But the world is not just a pile of inert or passive matter—it is a dynamic, changing, structured, and ordered arrangement. Besides inert matter, there is force or power, which represents the active shaping and ordering element in nature. This active power or force is not different from matter but is rather a different form of matter. It is a constantly moving, subtle thing, like an air current or breath. The Stoics said it was fire, and this fire spread to all things, providing them with vitality. This material fire had the attribute of rationality, and since this was the highest form of being, the Stoics understood this rational force to be God.

Good in Everything

The pivotal idea of Stoicism was the notion that God is in everything. When we say that God is in everything—as fire, or force, or logos, or rationality—we imply that all of nature is filled with the principle of reason. In a detailed manner the Stoics spoke of the permeability of matter, by which they meant that different types of matter are mixed up together. The material substance of God, they said, was mixed with what would otherwise be motionless matter. Matter behaves the way it does because of the presence in it of the principle of reason. *Natural law* is the continued behavior of matter in accordance with this principle; it is the law or principle of a thing's nature. Thus, for the Stoics, nature has its origin in God—the warm, fiery matrix of all things—and all things immediately receive the impress of God's structuring reason. Because things continue to behave as they were arranged to behave, we can see how the Stoics developed their notions of fate and providence.

Fate and Providence

To the Stoics, *providence* meant that events occur the way they do because all things and people are under the control of the Logos, or God. The order of the whole world is based upon the unity of all its parts, and what unifies the whole structure of matter is the fiery substance that permeates everything. Nothing "rattles" in the universe, for nothing is loose. Ultimately, the Stoics fashioned their moral philosophy against this background of a totally controlled material universe.

Human Nature

The Stoics knew that to build a moral philosophy it is necessary to have a clear view of what human nature is like. They shaped their view of human nature by simply transferring to the study of human beings the very same ideas they had used in describing nature at large. Just as the world is a material order permeated by the fiery substance called reason or God, so also a person is a material being who is permeated by this very same fiery substance. The Stoics are famous for the saying that people contain a spark of the divine within them. By this expression they meant that, in a real sense, a person contains part of the substance of God. God is the soul of the world, and each person's soul is part of God. This spark of the divine is a very fine and pure material substance that permeates a person's body, causing it to move and to be capable of all sensations. This pure material soul is transmitted by parents to children in a physical way. The Stoics thought that the soul was centered in the heart and that it circulated through specifically the bloodstream. What the soul added to the body was the delicate mechanism of the five senses as well as the powers of speech and reproduction. But since God is the rational Logos, the human soul is also rooted in reason and consequently human personality finds its unique expression in its rationality. For the Stoics, however, human rationality did not mean simply that people are able to think or to reason about things. Instead, human rationality means that a person's nature participates in the rational structure and order of the whole of nature. Human rationality represents our awareness of the actual order of things and our place in this order. It involves our awareness that all things obey law. To relate human behavior to this order of law was the chief concern of Stoic moral philosophy.

Ethics and the Human Drama

According to Epictetus, moral philosophy rested upon a simple insight, wherein each person is an actor in a drama. What Epictetus meant when he used this image was that an actor does not choose a role, but, on the contrary, it is the author or director of the drama who selects people to play the various roles. In the drama of the world, it is God, or the principle of reason, who determines what each person shall be and how he or she will be situated in history. Human wisdom, said the Stoics, consists in recognizing what our role in this drama is and then performing the part well. Some people have "bit parts," while others are cast into leading roles. "If it is [God's] pleasure that you should act a poor person, see that you act it well; or a handicapped person, or a ruler, or a private citizen. For it is your business to act well the given part." The actor develops a great indifference to those things over which he or she has no control, as, for example, the shape and form of the scenery as well as who the other players will be. The actor especially has no control over the story or its plot. But there is one thing that actors can control, and that is their attitudes and emotions. We can sulk because of a bit part, or be consumed with jealousy because someone else is chosen to be the hero, or feel terribly insulted because the makeup artist has provided a particularly ugly nose. But neither sulking nor jealousy nor feeling insulted can in any way alter the fact that we have bit parts, are not heroes, and must wear an ugly nose. These feelings can only rob the actors of happiness. If we can remain free from these feelings, or develop what the Stoics called *apathy*, we will achieve a serenity and happiness that are the mark of a wise person. The wise person is the one who knows what his or her role is.

The Problem of Freedom

There is, however, a persistent problem in Stoic moral philosophy, and this concerns the nature of human freedom. We can easily understand the Stoic notion that nature is fixed and ordered by God's reason, especially when we think of this grand scheme as a cosmic drama. It may be true that actors do not choose their roles. But what is the difference between choosing your *role* in the drama, on the one hand, or choosing your *attitude* on the other? If you are not free to choose one, how can you be free to choose the other? It could very well be that God not only chose you to be a poor person, but also cast you as a particularly disgruntled poor person. Do attitudes float around freely and wait to be chosen by the passing parade of people, or are they as much a part of a person as eye color?

The Stoics stuck doggedly to their notion that attitudes are under the control of a person's choice, and that by an act of will we can decide how we shall react to events. But they never provided a satisfactory explanation for the fact that providence rules everything while at the same time providence does not rule our attitudes. The closest they came to an explanation was to imply that whereas everything in the whole universe behaves according to divine law, it is the special feature of human beings that they behave according to their knowledge of the law. For example, water evaporates from the heat of the sun and later condenses and returns in the form of rain. But one drop never says to the other, "here we go again," as if to register disgust at being uprooted from the blue sea. People undergo a similar process of change when we begin to age and face death. However, in addition to the mechanical process of aging, we know what is happening to us. No amount of additional knowledge will change the fact that people are mortal. Nevertheless, the Stoics built their whole moral philosophy on the conviction that if we know the rigorous law and understand our role as inevitable, we will not strain against the inevitable but will move cheerfully with the pace of history. Happiness is not a product of choice; it is rather a quality of existence, which follows from agreeing to what has to be. Freedom, therefore, is not the power to alter our destiny but rather the absence of emotional disturbance.

Cosmopolitanism and Justice

The Stoics also developed a strong notion of cosmopolitanism—the idea that all people are citizens of the same human community. To look at the world process as a drama is to admit that everyone had a role in it. The Stoics viewed human relations as having the greatest significance, for human beings were the bearers of a divine spark. What relates people to each other is the fact that each person shares a common element. It is as though the Logos is a main telephone line and all people are on a conference call, thereby connecting God to all people and all people to each other. Or, as Cicero put it:

> since reason exists both in people and God, the first common possession of human beings and God is reason. But those who have reason in common must also have right reason in common. And since right reason is Law, we must believe that people have Law also in common with the Gods. Further, those who share Law must also share Justice, and those who share these are to be regarded as members of the same commonwealth.

Universal brotherhood and the theory of a universal natural law of justice were among the most impressive contributions made to the Western thought by the Stoics. They injected basic themes into the stream of thought that was to have a decisive impact in the centuries to come, particularly in Medieval philosophy.

Although Stoicism shared many of the characteristics of Epicurean philosophy, it made some radical innovations. With the Epicureans, the Stoics put their chief emphasis upon the practical concerns of ethics, regarded self-control as the center of ethics, viewed all of nature in materialistic terms, and sought happiness as the end. The most significant variation injected by the Stoics was that they viewed the world not as the product of chance but as the product of an ordering mind, or reason. This view involved the Stoics in a highly optimistic attitude regarding the possibilities of human wisdom. Yet it was against this claim to wisdom—a claim that we can know so much about the detailed operation of the world—that there developed the critical philosophy of the Skeptics.

SKEPTICISM

Today we refer to skeptics as those whose basic attitude is that of doubt. But the old Greek word, *skeptikoi,* from which *skeptics* is derived, meant something rather different, namely, *seekers* or *inquirers.* The Skeptics certainly were doubters too. They doubted that Plato and Aristotle had succeeded in discovering the truth about the world, and they had these same doubts about the Epicureans and Stoics. But for all their doubt, they were nevertheless seekers after a method for achieving a tranquil life. Pyrrho of Elis (361–270 BCE) was the founder of a specific school of skepticism that had an especially profound impact on philosophy many centuries later. His particular approach is known after him as *Pyrrhonism*. At the same time that Pyrrho was attracting followers, a rival school of skepticism emerged within Plato's Academy, particularly through the leadership of Arcesilaus (ca. 316–241 BCE), who was head of the Academy a generation or so after Plato. Known as *Academics*, they rejected Plato's metaphysics, and revived Socrates' technique of dialectic argument, which they used as a tool for suspending judgment. Pyrrho wrote nothing and the principal views of the Academics survive mainly through second-hand histories and discussions. The principal surviving text of ancient Greek skepticism is by Sextus Empiricus (ca. 200 CE), a follower of the Pyrrhonian tradition. In the opening sections of his *Outlines of Pyrrhonism*, Sextus offers an illuminating account of the meaning and purposes of the viewpoint of Skepticism.

What gave rise to Skepticism? Sextus says that Skepticism originated in the hope of attaining mental peace or calmness. People have been disturbed, he says, by the contradiction in things and plagued by doubt as to which alternative they should believe. One philosopher tells us one thing, and another tells us something quite the opposite. Accordingly the Skeptics thought that if they could by investigation determine truth from falsehood they could then attain mental tranquility. The Skeptics were struck, however, by the different conceptions of truth that different philosophers had proposed. They also noticed that people who searched for truth could be placed into three groups: those who think they have discovered the truth (and these the Skeptics called *dogmatists*), those who confess they have not found it and also assert that it cannot be found (and this they also considered a dogmatic position) , and finally those who persevere in the search for it. Unlike the first two, Sextus says, "the Skeptics keep on searching." Skepticism is not a denial of the possibility of finding truth, nor is it a denial of the basic facts of human experience. It is rather a continuous process of inquiry in which every explanation of experience is tested by a counter-experience. The fundamental principle of Skepticism, Sextus says, is that to every proposition an equal proposition is opposed. It is in consequence of this principle, he says, that "we end by ceasing to dogmatize."

The Skeptics were greatly impressed by the fact that the same "appearances" result in a wide variety of explanations from those who experience them. They discovered also, Sextus says, that arguments opposed to each other seem to have equal force. That is, opposing arguments seem to have an equal probability of alternative explanations. Accordingly, the Skeptics were led to suspend judgment and to refrain from denying or affirming anything. From this suspension of judgment they hoped to achieve an undisturbed and calm mental state.

Clearly, the Skeptics did not give up the enterprise of vigorous thought and debate. Nor did they deny the evident facts about life, that people become thirsty and hungry and that they are in peril when they come near a precipice. It was very clear to the Skeptics that people must be careful about their behavior. They had no doubt that they lived in a "real" world. They only wondered whether this world had been accurately described. No one, Sextus says, will dispute that objects have this or that appearance; the question is whether "the object is in reality such as it appears to be." Therefore, even though the Skeptics refused to live dogmatically, they did not deny the evident facts about experience. "We pay due regard to appearances," says Sextus. Daily life seemed to the Skeptics to require careful recognition of four items, which Sextus calls (1) the guidance of nature, (2) the constraint of the feelings, (3) the tradition of laws and customs, and (4) the instruction of the arts. Each of these contributes to successful and peaceful living, and not one of them requires any dogmatic interpretation or evaluation, only acceptance. Thus, it is by Nature's guidance that we are naturally capable of sensation and thought. Also, it is by the force of our feelings that hunger drives us to food and thirst to drink. And it is the tradition of laws and customs that constrains us in everyday life to accept piety as good and impiety as evil. Finally, Sextus says, it is by virtue of the instruction in the arts that we engage in those arts in which we choose to participate.

There can be no doubt, therefore, that the Skeptics were far from denying the evident facts of sense perception. Indeed, Sextus says that those who say that the Skeptics deny appearances "seem to me to be unacquainted with the statements of our School." They did not question appearances but only "the account given of appearances." As an example, Sextus says that honey appears to be sweet, and "this we grant, for we perceive sweetness through the senses" But the real question is whether it is really, in essence, sweet. Thus, the arguments of the Skeptics about appearances are expounded not with the intention of denying the reality of appearance but in order to point out the rashness of the "Dogmatists." The moral Sextus drew from this treatment of the objects of sense was that if human reason can be so easily deceived by appearances, "if reason is such a trickster as to all but snatch away the appearances from under our very eyes," should we not be particularly wary of following reason in the case of nonevident matters and thus avoid rashness?

Nonevident matters had a central place in the great philosophical systems of Plato, Aristotle, and the Stoics. Here the Skeptics found elaborate theories, especially about the nature of physical things. But how can any theory of physics—an inquiry that deals with nonevident matters—give us reliable truth? The Skeptics had a double attitude toward the study of physics. On the one hand, they refused to theorize about physics as if to find "firm and confident opinions on any of the things in physical theory about which firm theories are held." Nevertheless, they did touch on physics "in order to have for every argument an equal argument to oppose it, and for the sake of mental tranquility." Their approaches to matters of ethics and logic were similar. In each case their pursuit of mental tranquility was not a negative approach, or a refusal to think, but rather an active approach. Their method of "the suspension of judgment" involved the activity of "setting things in opposition." As Sextus says, "we oppose appearances to appearances, or thoughts to thoughts, or appearances to thoughts."

Sextus, then, distinguished between two types of inquiry, namely, those dealing with evident matters and those dealing with nonevident matters. Evident matters, such as whether it is night or day, raise no serious problems of knowledge. In this category, too, are evident requirements for social and personal tranquility, for we know that customs and laws bind society together. But nonevident matters, as, for example, whether the stuff of nature is made of atoms or some fiery substance, do raise intellectual controversies. Whenever we go beyond the sphere of what is evident in human experience, our quest for knowledge should proceed under the influence of creative doubt. Thus, if we ask how we know what the universe is like, the Skeptics would answer that we do not yet know. It may be, they said, that people can attain the truth; it may also be that they are in error. But we cannot decide whether they have the truth or are in error because we do not yet have a reliable criterion for determining the truth in nonevident matters.

The Senses Are Deceptive

Sextus argued that if our knowledge comes from experience or sense impressions then there is all the more reason to doubt the adequacy of all knowledge. For the fact is that our senses give us different information about the same object at different times and under different circumstances. From a distance, a square building looks round. A landscape looks different at different times of the day. To some people honey is bitter. Painted scenery at a theater gives the impression of real doors and windows when only lines exist on a flat surface. That we do have impressions is certain, as, for example, when we "see" a bent oar in the water. But what we can never be certain about is whether in fact the oar is bent. Although we can take the oar out of the water and discover the error of perception, not every perception affords such an easy test for its accuracy and truth. Most of our knowledge is based upon perceptions for which we have no criterion of truth. The Skeptic's conclusion is that we cannot be certain that our knowledge of the nature of things is true or not true.

Moral Rules Raise Doubts

Moral conceptions as well as physical objects are subject to doubt. People in different communities have different ideas of what is good and right. Customs and laws differ with each community and in the same community at different times. The Stoics said that there is a universal reason in which all people share, leading to a general consensus of all people regarding human rights. The Skeptics challenged both the theory and the fact, saying that there was no proof that all people have the capacity to agree upon the truth of universal moral principles. Further, they argued, there is no evidence that people in fact exhibit this universal agreement. The fact is that people disagree. Moreover, those who disagree can all make equally strong cases for their own points of view. On matters of morality there is no absolute knowledge; there is only opinion. The Stoics had argued that on certain matters the test for truth was "irresistible perception." The Skeptics responded by saying that the sad fact is that however strongly an opinion is held, it is, after all, still only an opinion, and we can with as much evidence support an opposite opinion. When people take a dogmatic stand, their conclusions always seem to them to be irresistible, but this is no guaranty that their conceptions are true.

The outcome of this skeptical attitude toward our knowledge of the nature of things and our knowledge of moral truth is that we have a right to doubt the validity of such knowledge. Since we lack sure knowledge, it is best to withhold judgment about the true nature of morality. But ethics is a matter about which it is difficult for people to withhold judgment. When we face a problem of behavior, we want to know what is the right thing to do, and this requires knowledge of the right. Critics of Skepticism, then, would argue that the Skeptics had made ethics impossible and had removed from people any guide for human behavior.

Morality Possible without Intellectual Certainty

The Skeptics argued, however, that it was not necessary to have knowledge in order to behave sensibly. It is enough, they said, to have reasonable assurance, or what they called *probability*. There could never be absolute certainty, but if there was a strong probability that our ideas would lead us to a life of happiness and peacefulness, we are justified in following these ideas. We are able from daily experience to distinguish between notions that are not clear and those that have a high degree of clarity. When notions of right have a high degree of clarity, they create in us a strong belief that they are right, and this is all we need to lead us to action. For this reason customs, the laws of the land, and our basic appetites are for the most part reliable guides. But even here the Skeptic wants to retain a certain amount of caution, so that we will not mistake appearance for reality and that above all we will avoid fanaticism and dogmatism. Although we are able to act enthusiastically even without a criterion of truth, our psychological safety requires that we leave open the channels of inquiry. The only safe attitude to take is one of doubt about the absolute truth of any idea, including moral convictions. And the person who can maintain a sense of imperturbability under this attitude of doubt has the best chance of achieving the happy life.

If we ask whether the Skeptics had a "system," Sextus answers "No," if by a *system* we mean "an adherence to a number of dogmas which are dependent both on one another and on appearances" and where we take *dogma* to mean "assent to a non-evident proposition." But if by a *system* we mean "a procedure which, in accordance with appearance, follows a certain line of reasoning . . . indicating how it is possible to seem to live rightly," then the Skeptic did have a system. For, as Sextus says, "we follow a line of reasoning which . . . points us to a life conformable to the customs of our country and its laws and institutions, and to our own instinctive feeling."

PLOTINUS

At the culmination of classical philosophy stands the influential figure of Plotinus (ca. 204–270 CE). He lived at a time when there was no single compelling philosophical theory that could satisfy the special concerns of his age. The great variety of religious cults attested to the desperate attempt by people in the second and third centuries of the Roman world to lay hold of an explanation of life and its destiny. It was an age of syncretism, when ideas were taken from several sources and put together as philosophies and religions. The cult of Isis combined Greek and Egyptian ideas of the gods; the Romans developed the Imperial Cult and worshiped their emperors, living and dead; devotees of the Mithraic cult worshiped the sun; and there was the Phrygian worship of the Great Mother of the Gods. Christianity was still considered a cult, even though some Christian thinkers already emerged, such as Justin Martyr (100–165), Clement of Alexandria (ca. 150–220), Tertullian (ca. 160–230), and Origen (185–254), who sought to give the Christian faith a systematic character and an intellectual defense. Origen tried to provide a Platonic and Stoic framework for Christianity. Earlier, Clement of Alexandria also tried to join Christian thought with philosophic ideas. But Christian theology would not achieve its full strength until Augustine had formulated his mixture of Christian and Platonic thought. The decisive bridge between classical philosophy and Augustine was the writings of Plotinus. But Plotinus nowhere mentions Christianity; his original contribution consisted of a fresh version of Plato's philosophy, and for this reason is known as Neoplatonism.

Plotinus was born in Egypt about 204 CE. He was the pupil of Ammonius Saccas in Alexandria. Alexandria was at this time an intellectual crossroads of the ancient world, and here Plotinus developed a wide grasp of classical philosophy, including the ideas of Pythagoras, Plato, Aristotle, Epicurus, and the Stoics. Out of all these strands he selected Platonism as the surest source of truth and indeed criticized the others by using his version of Plato's thoughts as his standard. At age 40, he went from Alexandria to Rome, where the atmosphere was charged by considerable chaos in morality and religion and by social and political unrest. At Rome he opened his own school, to which he attracted some of that city's elite, including the emperor and his wife. For a while he planned to develop a city based upon the theories of Plato's *Republic* to be called Platonopolis, but this plan was never realized. He wrote 54 treatises with no particular order and in a style less eloquent than his speech. These treatises were assembled after Plotinus' death by his ablest pupil, Porphyry, who arranged them into six sets of nines, or, as they are now called, *Enneads*. Plotinus was a brilliant lecturer and at the same time a man of spiritual idealism. Indeed, it was his moral and spiritual force combined with his intellectual rigor that influenced not only his contemporaries but especially Augustine. Later, Augustine said that Plotinus would have to change "only a few words" to become a Christian. In any case, the thought of Plotinus became a major strand in most of medieval philosophy.

What made Plotinus' philosophy distinctive was that he combined a speculative description of reality with a religious theory of salvation. He not only described the world, but also gave an account of its source, of our place in it, and of how we overcome our moral and spiritual difficulties in it. In short, Plotinus developed a theory about God as the source of all things and as that to which people must return. In formulating his thought, Plotinus successively analyzed and rejected as inadequate the views of the Stoics, Epicureans, Pythagoreans, and Aristotelians. Among his objections to these schools of thought was his conviction that they did not understand the true nature of the soul. The Stoics described the soul as a material body—a physical "breath." But Plotinus argued that neither the Stoics nor Epicureans, both materialists, understood the essential independence of the soul from the material body. Likewise, the Pythagoreans, who had said that the soul is the "harmony" of the body, would have to admit that when the body is not in harmony, it has no soul. Finally, Plotinus rejected Aristotle's notion that the soul is the form of the body and as such cannot exist without a body. For Plotinus, if part of the body loses its form, this would mean that to that extent the soul would also be deformed. This would make the body primary, whereas, Plotinus said, it is the soul that is primary and gives life to the body as a whole. Everything for Plotinus turned upon the accurate understanding of a person's essential nature.

To understand human nature, Plotinus pursued the line of thought Plato had set forth in his vivid myths and allegories. He was struck by Plato's comprehensive treatment of reality. There was Plato's account of the Demiurge fashioning matter into the world. There was also Plato's theory that the Form of the Good is like the rays of light emanating from the sun. Next there was Plato's notion that the soul has an existence before it enters the body, is a prisoner in the body, and struggles to escape from this captivity and return to its source. Finally, there was Plato's conviction that we find true reality in the spiritual world, and not in the material world. Plotinus took these basic ideas, emphasizing particularly the central Platonic theme that only the spirit is true reality, and reformulated Plato's ideas into a new kind of Platonism.

God as the One

The material world, with its multiplicity of things, cannot be the true reality, Plotinus thought, because it is always changing. The true changeless reality is God, about whom nothing specifically descriptive can be said except that he absolutely transcends or lies beyond everything in the world. For this reason God is not material, is not finite, and is not divisible. He has no specific form—either as matter, soul, or mind—each of which undergoes change. He cannot be confined to any idea or ideas of the intellect and for this reason cannot be expressed in any human language. He is accessible to none of the senses and can only be reached in a mystical ecstasy that is independent of any rational or sense experience. For this reason, Plotinus spoke of God as the One, signifying thereby that in God there is absolutely no complexity, and that, indeed, God is Absolute Unity. The One signifies, moreover, that God does not change. He is indivisible, has no variety, is un-created, and is in every way unalterable.

Plotinus held that the One cannot be the sum of particular things because it is precisely these things whose finite existence requires explanation and a source. Thus, the One "cannot be any existing thing, but is prior to all exis-tents." There are no positive attributes that we can ascribe to the One because all our ideas of attributes are derived from finite physical things. It is not pos-sible therefore to say that God is this and not that since this procedure would fasten upon God certain limits. To say, then, that God is One is to affirm that God *is* and that God transcends the world. It is to say that he is simple, with-out any duality, potentiality, or material limitation, and that he transcends all distinctions. In a sense, God cannot engage in any self-conscious activity since this would imply complexity through thinking *particular* thoughts *before* and *after*, thus implying change. God in no way resembles a human. He is indeed simply One, Absolute Unity.

The Metaphor of Emanation

If God is One, he cannot create, for creation is an act, and activity implies change. Then how can we account for the many things of the world? Striving to maintain a consistent view of the Unity of God, Plotinus explained the ori-gin of things by saying that they come from God, not through a free act of cre-ation but through necessity. To express what he meant by "necessity," Ploti-nus used several metaphors, especially the metaphor of *emanation*. Things emanate—they flow from God—the way that light emanates from the sun, or the way that water flows from a spring that has no source outside itself. The sun is never exhausted, and it does not *do* anything: it just *is*. And being what it is, the sun necessarily emanates light. In this way, God is the source of everything, and everything manifests God. But nothing is equal to God, any more than the rays of light are equal in any way to the sun. All of these emanations fall in a spectrum between pure being (i.e., God himself), and com-plete non-existence. Thus, Plotinus does not appear to be a strict Pantheist—the view that God is identical with nature as a whole. Although the entire universe consists of God and his emanations, there is nevertheless a hierarchical arrangement in nature. Just as the light closest to the sun is the brightest, so also the highest form of being is the first emanation. Plotinus described this first emanation from the One as *mind (nous)*. It is most like the One but is not absolute and can therefore be said to have a specific attribute or character. This *nous* is *thought* or *universal intelligence* and signifies the underlying ration-ality of the world. It is the nature of rationality to have no spatial or temporal boundaries. But rationality does imply multiplicity in that thinking contains the ideas of all particular things.

The World Soul   Just as light emanates from the sun in ever-diminishing intensity, so also is there a decline in the degrees of perfection as emana-tions are further from God. Moreover, each succeeding emanation is the cause of the next-lower emanation, as if there were a principle at work requiring that every nature bring into being that which is immediately subordinate to it. In this way, the *nous* is in turn the source of the next emanation, which Plotinus calls the Soul. The Soul of the World has two aspects: looking upward, as it were, toward *nous* or pure rationality, the Soul strives to contemplate the eternal ideas of all things. Looking downward, it further emanates one thing at a time and provides the life principle to all of nature. It thus bridges the gap between the ideas of things (in *nous*) and the realm of the natural world. The activity of the Soul accounts for the phenomenon of *time,* since now there is the emergence of things. The relations of things to each other results in events, and events come *after* one another, and this relationship of events is what we mean by time. To be sure, the One, the *nous,* and the World Soul are all coeternal and are thus outside of time. Below the World Soul lies the realm of nature and of particular things, which reflects through time the changing eternal ideas.

The Human Soul　The human soul is an emanation from the World Soul. Like the World Soul, it also has two aspects. Again, looking upward, the human soul shares in the *nous* or universal reason. Looking downward, the human soul becomes connected with, but is not identical with, the body. Here Plotinus reaffirmed Plato's theory of the preexistence of the human soul, believing also that the union of the soul with the body is a product of a "fall." Moreover, after death the human soul survives the body, and conceivably enters a sequence of transmigrations from one body to another. Being spiritual and therefore truly real, the human soul will not be annihilated but will join all other souls again in the World Soul. While in the body, it is the human soul that provides the power of rationality, sensitivity, and vitality.

The World of Matter　At the lowest level in the hierarchy of being, that is, at the farthest remove from the One, is matter. There is a principle at work in emanation, which requires that the higher grades of being overflow in accordance with the next realm of possibilities. After ideas and souls, then, there is the world of material objects. It exhibits a mechanical order whose operation or movement is the work of reason, subjecting all objects to the laws or rules of cause and effect. Once again, the material world displays a higher and lower aspect. The higher component is its susceptibility to the laws of motion. However, the lower, its bare material nature, is a dark world of gross matter that moves aimlessly with sluggish discord toward collision and extinction. Plotinus compared matter to the dimmest and farthest reach of light—the most extreme limit of light—which is darkness itself. Darkness, clearly, is the very opposite of light; similarly, matter is the opposite of spirit and is therefore the opposite of the One. Again, insofar as matter exists in conjunction with the soul, either the individual or the World Soul, to this extent matter is not complete darkness. But just as light tends to emanate finally to the point of utter darkness, so also matter stands at the boundary line of nothingness, where it tends to disappear into non-being.

What Causes Evil?   Through the theory of emanation, Plotinus argued that God necessarily overflows in order to share his perfection as much as possible. Since God could not reduplicate himself perfectly, he did so in the only possible way, namely, by representing all the possible degrees of perfection by means of the emanations. To represent *all* degrees of perfection, it was necessary to have not only the *nous* but also the lowest level of being, namely, matter. However, within this lowest level we find various evils: pain, the continuing warfare of the passions, and, finally, death and sorrow. How could the Perfect One, from whom everything ultimately emanates, permit this kind of imperfection to exist among human beings? Plotinus explained the problem of evil in various ways. For one thing, he said that evil in its own way occupies a place in the hierarchy of perfection, since without evil something would be lacking in the scheme of things. Evil is like the dark shadings of a portrait, which greatly enhance the beauty of the image. Moreover, all events occur with rigorous necessity, as the Stoics had argued earlier. Thus, the good person does not look upon them as evil, and the bad person can consider this to be just punishment. But Plotinus finds the best explanation of evil in his account of matter.

For Plotinus, matter is the necessary and final reach of the emanation from the One. The very nature of emanation as we have seen is that the higher levels necessarily move toward the lower. The One generates the *nous*, and, finally, the individual soul generates a material body. Brute matter, however, continues the process of emanation, as if moving farther and farther from the One, the way the light grows dimmer and dimmer the farther it moves from the sun. There is, then, a tendency for matter to move beyond—or separate itself from—the activity of the soul and to engage in motion that is not rationally directed. Again, as matter faces upward, it encounters the soul or the principle of rationality. For objects in nature this accounts for the orderliness of their movements. For individual people it means that the body responds to the activity of the soul at the levels of rationality, sensitivity, appetite, and vitality. But the natural tendency of matter is to face downward because of the downward momentum of emanation. Because of its downward thrust, matter encounters darkness itself and at this point matter is separated from rationality.

The clue to the problem of moral evil, then, is that the soul is now united with a material body. And in spite of the rational character of the soul, it must contend with the body, whose material nature disposes it to move downward and away from rational control. When the body reaches the level below rationality, it becomes subject to an indefinite number of possible ways of acting. It is the job of the passions to move the body to respond to all kinds of appetites. Evil, then, is the discrepancy between the soul's right intentions and its actual behavior. It is an imperfection in the soul-body arrangement, and much of the cause for this imperfection is ascribed to the final irrational movement of the material body.

Matter, or body, is the principle of evil in the sense that matter is at the fringe of emanation, where the absence of rationality results in formlessness and the least degree of perfection. But since matter comes from God in the sense that everything emanates from the One, it could be said that God is the source of evil. Still, evil, for Plotinus, is not a positive destructive force; it is not a "devil" or rival god contending with the good God. Nor, as some Zoroastrian philosophers thought, is it a contest between the coequal forces of light and darkness. Evil, for Plotinus, is simply the absence of something; it is the lack of perfection and the lack of form for the material body, which is not itself essentially evil. A person's moral struggle is therefore a struggle not against some outside force but against the tendency to be undone within, to become disordered, to lose control of the passions. Evil, again, is no *thing,* but rather the absence of order. The body *as such* is not evil. Evil is the formlessness of matter as darkness is the absence of light. Throughout his analysis, Plotinus tries simultaneously to argue that the soul is responsible for its acts and that all events are determined. Just how these two views can be reconciled is not exactly clear. At the same time, much of Plotinus' appeal came from the promise of salvation, which he thought his philosophy could provide.

Salvation

Plotinus moved from his philosophical analysis of emanation to the religious and mystical plan of salvation. The mystery cults of his day offered a swift fulfillment of a person's desire to unite with God. By contrast, Plotinus described the soul's ascent to unity with God as a difficult and painful task. This ascent required that a person develop successively the moral and intellectual virtues. Since the body and the physical world were not considered evil per se, it was not necessary to reject them altogether. Plotinus' key insight was that the physical things of the world must not distract the soul from its higher aims. We should renounce the world as a means of facilitating the soul's ascent to intellectual activity, as in philosophy and science. We must discipline ourselves in rigorous and correct thinking. Such thinking lifts us out of our individuality, and with a broad knowledge of things, we tend to relate the self to the whole arrangement of the world. All the steps up this ladder of knowledge lead toward the final union of the self with the One in a state of ecstasy, where there is no longer any consciousness of the self's separation from God. This ecstasy is the final result of right conduct, correct thinking, and the proper disposition of the affections.

Plotinus felt that achieving this union could require many incarnations of each soul. Finally the soul is refined and purified in its love, and, as Plato said in his *Symposium,* is capable of the fullest self-surrender. At this point the process of emanation is fully reversed, and the self merges once again with the One. For many, Plotinus' Neoplatonism had all the power of a religion and represented a strong alternative to Christianity. Although its intricate intellectual scheme prevented it from becoming widely popular, Neoplatonism made a considerable impact upon the emerging Christian theology of this era. Augustine saw in the *Enneads* of Plotinus a strikingly new explanation of evil and of salvation through orderly love. Through Augustine, Neoplatonism became a decisive element in the intellectual expression of the Christian faith during the Middle Ages.

CHAPTER 6

Augustine

AUGUSTINE'S LIFE

A ugustine was intensely concerned with his personal destiny and this provided the driving force for his philosophical activity. From his early youth, he suffered from a deep moral turmoil, which sparked within him a lifelong quest for wisdom and spiritual peace. He was born in Tagaste in the African province of Numidia in 354 CE. Although his father was not Christian, his mother, Monica, was a devout believer in the new faith. At the age of 16, Augustine began the study of rhetoric in Carthage, a port city given to immoral ways. Though his mother instilled in him the traditions of Christian thought and behavior, he threw off this religious faith and morality, taking at this time a mistress by whom he had a son and with whom he lived for a decade. At the same time, his thirst for knowledge impelled him to rigorous study, and he became a successful student of rhetoric.

A series of personal experiences led him to his unique approach to philosophy. He was 19 years old when he read the *Hortensius* of Cicero, which was an exhortation to achieve philosophical wisdom. These words of Cicero kindled his passion for learning, but he was left with the problem of where to find intellectual certainty. His Christian ideas seemed unsatisfactory to him. He was particularly perplexed by the ever-present problem of moral evil. How can we explain the existence of evil in human experience? The Christians said that God is the creator of all things and also that God is good. How, then, is it possible for evil to arise out of a world that a perfectly good God had created? Because Augustine could find no answers in the Christianity he learned as a youth, he turned to a group called the Manichaeans. The Manichaeans were sympathetic to much of Christianity but, boasting of their intellectual superiority, rejected the basic monotheism of the Old Testament and with it the view that the Creator and Redeemer of humanity are one and the same. Instead, the Manichaeans taught a theory of dualism, according to which there were two basic principles in the universe: the principle of light or goodness, on the one hand, and the principle of darkness or evil, on the other. They held these two principles to be equally eternal, but eternally in conflict with each other. This conflict, they believed, is reflected in human life in the conflict between the soul, composed of light, and the body, composed of darkness. At first this theory of dualism seemed to provide the perfect answer to the problem of evil: it overcame the contradiction between the presence of evil in a world created by a good God. Augustine could now attribute his sensual desires to the external power of darkness.

Although this dualism seemed to solve the contradiction of evil in a God-created world, it raised new problems. For one thing, how could we explain why there are two conflicting principles in nature? If no convincing reason could be given, is intellectual certitude possible? Far more serious was his awareness that it did not help to solve his moral turmoil to say that it was all engendered by some external force. The presence of fierce passion was no less unsettling just because the "blame" for it had been shifted to something outside of himself. What had originally attracted him to the Manichaeans was their boast that they could provide him with truth that could be discussed and made plain, not requiring, as the Christians did, "faith before reason." He therefore broke with the Manichaeans, feeling that "those philosophers whom they call Academics [i.e., Skeptics] were wiser than the rest in thinking that we ought to doubt everything, and that no truth can be comprehended by human beings." He was now attracted to Skepticism, though at the same time he retained some belief in God. He maintained a materialistic view of things and on this account doubted the existence of immaterial substances and the immortality of the soul.

Hoping for a more effective career in rhetoric, Augustine left Africa for Rome and shortly thereafter moved to Milan, where he became municipal professor of rhetoric in 384. Here he was profoundly influenced by Ambrose, who was then Bishop of Milan. From Ambrose Augustine derived not so much the techniques of rhetoric, but somewhat unexpectedly a greater appreciation of Christianity. While in Milan, Augustine took another mistress, having left his first one in Africa. It was here also that Augustine came upon certain forms of Platonism, especially the Neoplatonism found in the *Enneads* of Plotinus. There was much in Neoplatonism that caught his attention. First there was the Neoplatonist view that the immaterial world is totally separate from the material one. Second there was the view that people possess a spiritual sense that enables them to know God and the immaterial world. Third, from Plotinus Augustine derived the conception that evil is not a positive reality but is rather a matter of privation—that is, the absence of good. Above all, Neoplatonism overcame Augustine's former skepticism, materialism, and dualism. Through Platonic thought he was able to understand that not all activity is physical, and that there is a spiritual as well as a physical reality. He could now see the unity of the world without having to assume the existence of two principles behind soul and body. He thus followed Plotinus' picture of reality as a single graduated system in which matter is simply on a lower level.

Intellectually, Neoplatonism provided what Augustine had been looking for, but it left his moral problem still unsolved. What he needed now was moral strength to match his intellectual insight. This he found in Ambrose's sermons.

Neoplatonism had finally made Christianity reasonable to him, and now he was also able to exercise the act of faith and thereby derive the power of the spirit without feeling that he was lapsing into some form of superstition. His dramatic conversion occurred in 386, when he gave "real assent" to the prospect of abandoning his profession of rhetoric and giving his life totally to the pursuit of philosophy, which, for him, also meant the knowledge of God. He now conceived of Platonism and Christianity as virtually one. Seeing in Neoplatonism the philosophical expression of Christianity, he states that "I am confident that among the Platonists I shall find what is not opposed to the teachings of our religion." He therefore set out on what he called "my whole plan" of achieving wisdom, saying that "from this moment forward, it is my resolve never to depart from the authority of Christ, for I find none that is stronger." Still, he emphasized that "I must follow after this with the greatest subtlety of reason."

For Augustine, true philosophy was inconceivable without a joining of faith and reason. To him, wisdom was Christian wisdom. Reason without revelation was certainly possible, since he came to believe that there is no such thing as a purely natural person without some ultimate spiritual destiny. Consequently, to understand the concrete condition of human existence, we must consider ourselves from the point of view of the Christian faith, and this in turn requires that the whole world be considered from the vantage point of faith. There could be, for Augustine, no distinction between theology and philosophy. Indeed, he believed that we cannot properly philosophize until our human wills are transformed, that clear thinking is possible only under the influence of God's grace. In this way, Augustine set the dominant direction and style of Christian wisdom of the Middle Ages.

It is therefore not possible to discuss Augustine's philosophy without at the same time considering his theological viewpoint. Indeed, Augustine wrote no purely philosophical works in the contemporary sense of that term. He was an incredibly prolific writer, and as he became a noted leader in the Catholic church, he was continually involved in writing as a defender of the faith and an opponent of heresy. In 396 he became bishop of Hippo, the seaport near his native town of Tagaste. Among his many opponents was Pelagius, with whom he entered into a celebrated controversy. Pelagius taught that all people possess the natural ability to achieve a righteous life, thereby denying the notion of original sin—the view that human nature is inherently corrupt. According to Augustine, Pelagius misunderstood human nature by assuming that our human wills are capable of achieving salvation on their own, which thereby minimizes the function of God's grace.

This controversy illuminates Augustine's manner of thought perfectly, since it shows again his insistence that all knowledge upon all subjects must take into account the revealed truth of Scripture along with the insights of philosophy. Since all knowledge is aimed at helping people understand God, this religious dimension clearly had a priority in his reflections. As Aquinas said about him later, "Whenever Augustine, who was imbued with the theories of the Platonists, found in their writings anything consistent with the faith, he adopted it; and whatever he found contrary to the faith, he amended." Still, it was Platonism that rescued Augustine from skepticism, made the Christian faith reasonable to him, and set off one of the great literary achievements in theology and philosophy. As if to symbolize his tempestuous life, Augustine died in 430 at the age of 75 in the posture of reciting the Penitential Psalms as the Vandals besieged Hippo.

HUMAN KNOWLEDGE

Overcoming Skepticism

For a time, Augustine took the Skeptics seriously—specifically the skepticism of the Academy—and he agreed with them that "no truth can be comprehended by human beings." But after his conversion, his problem was no longer *whether* people can attain certainty, but rather *how* they can attain it. Augustine therefore sought to answer the Skeptics, and he did this first of all by showing that human reason does indeed have certainty about various things. Specifically, human reason is absolutely certain of the principle of contradiction. We know that a thing cannot both be and not be at the same time. Using this principle, we can be certain, for example, that there is either one world or many worlds; that if there are many, their number is either finite or infinite. What we know here is simply that both alternatives cannot be true. This is not yet any substantive knowledge, but it meant for Augustine that we are not hopelessly lost in uncertainty. Not only do we know that both alternatives cannot be true simultaneously, we know also that this is always, eternally, the case. In addition, he said that even the Skeptics would have to admit that the act of doubting is itself a form of certainty, for a person who doubts is certain that he doubts. Here, then, is another certainty—the certainty that I exist. For if I doubt, I must exist. Whatever else I can have doubts about, I cannot doubt that I doubt. The Skeptics argued that a person could be asleep and only dreaming that he sees things or is aware of himself. But to Augustine this was not a formidable argument, for in reply he said "whether he be asleep or awake he lives." Any conscious person is certain that he exists, that he is alive, and that he can think. "For we are," says Augustine, "and we know we are, and we love our being and our knowledge of it. . . . These truths stand without fear in the face of the arguments of the Academics." In the 17th century, Descartes formulated a similar argument in his classic statement, "I think, therefore I am" and then proceeded to use it as a foundation for his system of philosophy. Augustine, however, was content merely to refute the Skeptic's basic position. Instead of proving the existence of external objects as Descartes did, Augustine assumed the existence of these objects and referred to them chiefly to describe how we achieve knowledge in relation to things.

Knowledge and Sensation

When we sense objects, we derive some knowledge from the act of sensation. But according to Augustine, such sensory information is at the lowest level of knowing. Still, the senses do give us a kind of knowledge. What puts sensory

St. Augustine
(Alinari/Art Resource, NY)

knowledge at the lowest level is that it gives us the least amount of certainty. There are two reasons for this lack of certainty: first, the objects of sense are always changing, and, second, the organs of sense change. Thus, sensation varies both from time to time and from person to person. Something can taste sweet to one person and bitter to another, warm to one and cold to another. Still, Augustine believed that the senses are always accurate as such. It is unjust, he said, to expect or demand more from the senses than they can provide. For example, there is nothing wrong with our senses when the oar in the water appears bent to us. On the contrary, there would be something wrong if the oar appeared straight, since under these circumstances the oar ought to seem bent. The problem arises when we have to make a judgment about the actual condition of the oar. We would be deceived if we assented to the notion that the oar was in fact bent. To avoid this error, Augustine says, "do not give assent to more than the fact of appearance, and you will not be deceived." In this way, Augustine affirmed the reliability of the senses while also recognizing their limitations. Just how the senses give us knowledge Augustine explained by analyzing the nature or mechanics of sensation.

What happens when we sense an object? To answer this question Augustine relied upon his Platonic interpretation of human nature. A person is a union of body and soul. He even suggested that the body is the prison of the soul. But when he described how the soul attains knowledge, he departed from the Platonic theory of recollection. Knowledge is not an act of remembering. It is an act of the soul itself. When we see an object, the soul (mind) fashions out of its own substance an image of the object. Since the soul is spiritual and not material, the object cannot make a physical "impression" upon the mind the way a signet ring leaves its mark in wax. Accordingly, it is the mind itself that produces the image. Moreover, when we sense an object, we not only sense an image but also make a judgment. We look at a person and say that she is beautiful. In this act of judgment I not only see the person with my senses, but also compare her with a standard to which my mind has access in some realm other than that in which I sense the person. Similarly, when I see seven children and three children I know that they can be added to make 10 children. As other things in nature are mutable, these 10 children, being mortal, will eventually pass away. But we are able to separate the numbers from the children and discover that seven and three do not depend upon the children or any other things and it is necessarily true that they make 10 when added together.

Sensation, then, gives us some knowledge, but its chief characteristic is that it necessarily points beyond its objects. From the sensation of an oar we are moved to think about straightness and bentness; from the sensation of a specific beautiful person we think about beauty in general; and from the sensation of children we think about the eternal truths of mathematics. With each of these inferences the issue of our human nature is once again raised, since the explanation of the mechanics of sensation leads to a distinction between body and soul. Sensation involves the body insofar as some physical organ is required to sense things. However, unlike animals, people not only sense things; we have some rational knowledge of them and make rational judgments about them. When rational people make such judgments, they are no longer dependent solely upon the senses but have directed their minds to other objects, such as Beauty and the truths of mathematics. A careful analysis shows therefore that the act of human sensation involves at least four elements, namely (1) the object sensed, (2) the bodily organ upon which sensation depends, (3) the activity of the mind in formulating an image of the object, and (4) the immaterial object, e.g., Beauty, which the mind uses in making a judgment about the sensed object. What emerges from this analysis is that there are two different kinds of objects that human beings encounter, namely, the objects of bodily sensation and the objects of the mind. With the physical eye people see things, and with the mind we apprehend eternal truths. These different objects account for the different degrees of intellectual certainty. We will have less reliable knowledge when we direct our mutable sense organs toward changing physical objects. By contrast, knowledge will be more reliable when we contemplate eternal truths independently of the senses. Sensation is only the beginning of a path of knowledge that ultimately leads to an activity within people, and not to things outside of us. Knowledge moves from the level of sensed things to the higher level of general truth. The highest level of knowledge is for Augustine the knowledge of God. Sensation plays its part in attaining this knowledge in that it directs our minds upward. Hence, Augustine says that we move toward God "from the exterior to the interior, and from the inferior to the superior."

The Theory of Illumination

In his account of the relation between sensation and knowledge, Augustine was left with the problem of how our minds could make judgments involving eternal and necessary truths. What makes it possible for us to know that seven and three—which at first we see in relation to things—always and necessarily make 10? Why, as a matter of fact, is there a problem here? The problem exists because so far in his account of human knowledge, all the elements involved are mutable or imperfect, hence finite and not eternal. The sensed objects are mutable, and the bodily organs of sense are also subject to change. The mind itself is a creature and is therefore finite and not perfect. How, then, can these elements be deployed in a way that rises above their own imperfection and mutability and discovers eternal truths about which we have no doubts? Such eternal truths confront us with the coercive power of certitude, and are so superior to what our minds could produce on their own that we must adjust or conform to them. Plato answered this question with his theory that knowledge is recollection, whereby the soul remembers what it once knew before it entered the body. Aristotle, on the other hand, argued that the eternal universal ideas were abstracted by the intellect from particular things. Augustine accepted neither one of these solutions. He did, though, follow another of Plato's insights, namely the analogy between (a) the sun in the visible world and (b) the Form of the Good in the intelligible world.

   Augustine was not so much concerned with the *origin* of our ideas as with our *awareness of the certitude* of some of our ideas. Rejecting recollection and some form of innate ideas, he came closer to the notion of abstraction. Actually, Augustine says that people are constructed in such a way that when the eyes of our bodies see an object, we can form an image of it provided the object is bathed in light. Similarly, our minds are capable of "seeing" eternal objects provided that they too are bathed in their own appropriate light. As Augustine says, we ought to believe "that the nature of the intellectual mind was so made that, by being naturally subject to intelligible realities, according to the arrangement of the Creator, it sees these truths [such as mathematical truths] in a certain incorporeal light of a unique kind, just as the eyes of the body sees the things all around it in this corporeal light." The human mind, in short, requires illumination if it is to "see" eternal and necessary truths. We can no more "see" the intelligible objects or truths of the intellect without some illumination than we can see the things in the world without the light of the sun.

Augustine states his theory of *illumination* in succinct form when he says that "there is present in [us] . . . the light of eternal reason, in which light the immutable truths are seen." Just what he means by this theory is not altogether clear. What is clear is that for Augustine the illumination comes from God just as light is shed about by the sun. If we take this analogy seriously, the divine light must illuminate something that is already there. By the light of the sun we can see the trees and houses. If the divine light performs the same kind of function, this light must also illuminate something—our ideas. This light is not so much the source of our ideas as it is the condition under which we recognize the quality of truth and eternity in our ideas. In short, divine illumination is not a process by which the content of ideas is infused into our minds; it is, rather, the illumination of our judgment whereby we are able to discern that certain ideas contain necessary and eternal truths. God, the source of this light, is perfect and eternal, and the human intellect operates under the influence of God's eternal ideas. We could not say that our human minds know God. But it does mean that divine illumination allows us to overcome the limitations of knowledge caused by the mutability of physical objects and the finitude of our minds. With this theory, then, Augustine solved to his satisfaction the problem of how the human intellect is able to go beyond sense objects and make judgments about necessary and eternal truths.

GOD

Augustine was not interested in mere theoretical speculations about the existence of God. His philosophical reflections about God were the product of his intense personal pursuit of wisdom and spiritual peace. His deep involvement in sensual pleasures gave him dramatic evidence that the soul cannot find its peace among the bodily pleasures or sensation. Similarly, in his quest for certainty of knowledge, he discovered that the world of things was full of change and impermanence. His mind, too, he discovered, was imperfect, since it was capable of error. At the same time, he had the experience of knowing certain truths that were eternal. He was able to compare the experience of contemplating truth with the experience of having pleasure and sensations. Of these two experiences he found that the mental activities could provide more lasting and profound peace. He considered the technical question of how it was that his finite human mind was capable of attaining knowledge beyond the capacity of his mind. He concluded that this knowledge could not have come from finite things outside of him; nor could it be produced fully by his own mind. Since the knowledge available to him was eternal and could not come from his limited or finite mind, he was led to believe that immutable truth must have its source in God. What led to this conclusion was the similarity between the characteristics of some of his knowledge and the attributes of God, namely, that both are eternal and true. The existence of some eternal truths meant for Augustine the existence of *the* Eternal Truth, which God is. In this way, Augustine moved through various levels of personal experience and spiritual quest to what amounted to a "proof" of the existence of God.

Since God is truth, God in some sense is within us, but since God is eternal, he also transcends us. But what else can a person say by way of describing God? Actually, like Plotinus, Augustine found it easier to say what God is not than to define what he is. Still, to say that God is superior to finite things was a major step. Taking the scriptural name for God given to Moses, namely, "I Am That I Am," Augustine transposed this to mean that God is *being itself.* As such God is the highest being. This is not the same thing as the beingless One of Plotinus. Instead, it is the "something than which nothing more excellent or more sublime exists"—a phrase that centuries later influenced Anselm to formulate his famous ontological argument. As the highest being, God is perfect being, which means that he is self-existent, immutable, and eternal being. As perfect, he is also "simple," in that whatever plural attributes are assigned to him turn out to be identical. His knowledge, wisdom, goodness, and power are all one and constitute his essence. Further, Augustine reasoned that the world of everyday things reflects the being and activity of God. Although the things we see are mutable in that they gradually cease to be, nevertheless insofar as they exist they have a definite form, and this form is eternal and is a reflection of God. Indeed, Augustine sees God as the source of all being insofar as things possess any being at all.

But unlike the things of the world, God, as Augustine says, "is . . . in no interval or extension of place" and similarly "is in no interval or extension of time." In short, Augustine described God as pure or highest being, suggesting thereby that in God there is no change either from nonbeing to being or from being to nonbeing. God *is;* "I Am That I Am." Again, the principal force of this line of thought is its relevance in solving Augustine's spiritual problem—although Augustine was convinced that this reasoning had sufficient philosophical rigor. As the source of being and truth and the one eternal reality, God now becomes for Augustine the legitimate object both of thought and affection. From God there comes both enlightenment for the mind and strength for the will. Moreover, all other knowledge is possible because God is the standard for truth. His essence is to exist, and to exist is to act, and to act is to know. Being both eternal and all-knowing, God always knew all the possible ways in which he could be reflected in creation. For this reason, the various forms in which the world is shaped were always in God as exemplars. All things therefore are finite reflections of God's eternal thought. If God's thought is "eternal," difficulties arise in our language when it is said that God "foresees" what will happen. What is important to Augustine, however, is that the world and God are intimately related, and that the world reflects God's eternal thought, even though God is not identical with the world but is instead beyond it. Because there is this relation between God and the world, to know one is to know something of the other. This is why Augustine was so convinced that the person who knew most about God could understand most deeply the true nature of the world and especially the human nature and human destiny.

THE CREATED WORLD

Augustine concluded that God is the most appropriate object of thought and affection, and that the physical world could not provide us with true knowledge or spiritual peace. In spite of his emphasis on the spiritual realm, Augustine nevertheless paid considerable attention to the material world. After all, we must live in the physical world, and we need to understand this world in order to relate ourselves appropriately to it. From what he already said about the nature of knowledge and about God, we can see that Augustine believed that the world is the creation of God. In his *Confessions* Augustine says that, wherever we look, all things say "We did not make ourselves, but He that lives forever made us." That is, finite things demand that there should be some permanent being to explain how they could come into existence. Just how God is related to the world was explained by Augustine in his unique theory of creation.

Creation from Nothing

Augustine's distinctive theory was that God created all things *ex nihilo,* out of nothing. This was in contrast to Plato's account of the world which was not "created" but came about when the Demiurge combined the Forms and the receptacle, which always existed independently. Augustine also departed from the Neoplatonic theory of Plotinus, which explained the world as an emanation from God. Plotinus said that there was a *natural necessity* in God to overflow, since the Good must necessarily diffuse itself. Moreover, Plotinus's theory held that there is a continuity between God and the world insofar as the world is merely an extension of God. Against all these notions, Augustine stressed that the world is the product of God's free act, whereby he brings into being, out of nothing, all the things that make up the world. All things, then, owe their existence to God. There is, however, a sharp distinction between God and the things he created. Whereas Plotinus saw the world as the overflowing and therefore continuation of God, Augustine speaks of God as bringing into being what did not exist before. He could not have created the world out of an existing matter because matter, even in a primary form, would already be something. To speak of a formless matter is really to refer to nothing. Actually, according to Augustine, everything, including matter, is the product of God's creative act. Even if there were some formless matter that was capable of being formed, this would also have its origin in God and would have to be created by him out of nothing. Matter is essentially good in nature since God creates matter, and God cannot create anything evil. The essential goodness of matter play an important role in Augustine's theory of morality, as we shall see.

The Seminal Principles

Augustine was struck by the fact that the various species in nature never produce new species. Horses produce horses, and flowers produce flowers; at the human level, human parents produce more human children. What fascinated Augustine about all of this was its relevance to the general question of *causality*. Although in a sense parents are the cause of children and older flowers the cause of new flowers, still, none of these things is able to introduce new forms into nature. In the created order, existing things are able only to animate existing forms into completed beings. Augustine drew from this fact (for which he admittedly did not have decisive empirical information) the conclusion that the causality behind the formation of all things is God's intelligence. There is no original causal power in things capable of fashioning new forms. How then do things, animals, and people produce anything? Augustine's answer was that in the act of creation, God had implanted seminal principles (*rationes seminales*) into matter, thereby setting into nature the potentiality for all species to emerge. These seminal principles are the germs of things; they are invisible and have causal power. Thus, all species bear the invisible and potential power to become what they are not yet at the present time. When species begin to exist, their seminal principle—that is, their potentiality—is fulfilled. Actual seeds then transmit the continuation of the fixed species from potentiality to actuality. Originally, God, in a single act of complete creation, furnished the germinating principles of all species.

With this theory, Augustine explained the origin of species, locating their cause in the mind of God, whence came the seminal principles. By this theory of seminal principles, Augustine thought he also solved a problem in the Bible, where it says in the book Genesis that God created the world in six days. It seemed inconsistent with Augustine's view of God that God should have to create things step by step. There was some question, too, about what is meant here by "six days," especially since the sun was not "created" until the fourth day. The theory of seminal principles enabled Augustine to say that God created all things at once, meaning by this that he implanted the seminal principles of all species simultaneously. But, since these germs are principles of potentiality, they are the bearers of things that are to be, but that have not yet "flowered." Accordingly, though all species were created at once, they did not all simultaneously exist in a fully formed state. They each fulfilled their potentiality in a sequence of points in time.

MORAL PHILOSOPHY

Every philosophical notion developed by Augustine pointed in one way or another to the problem of the human moral condition. For him, therefore, moral theory was not some special or isolated subject. Everything culminates in morality, which clarifies the sure road to happiness, which is the ultimate goal of human behavior. In fashioning his ideas about morality, then, Augustine brought to bear his major insights about the nature of human knowledge, the nature of God, and the theory of creation. From the vantage point of these ideas, he focused upon human moral constitution.

Our human moral quest is the outcome of a specific and concrete condition. The condition is that we are made in such a way that we seek happiness. Although the ancient Greeks also considered happiness as the culmination of the good life, Augustine's theory provided a novel estimate of what constitutes true happiness and just how it is to be achieved. Other philosophers also held that happiness is our aim in life, such as Aristotle who said that happiness is achieved when people fulfill their natural functions through a well-balanced life. Augustine, though, held that true happiness requires that we go beyond the natural to the supernatural. He expressed this view both in religious and philosophical language. In his *Confessions* he wrote, "Oh God You have created us for Yourself so that our hearts are restless until they find their rest in You." In more philosophical language he makes this same point by saying that human nature is so made that "it cannot itself be the good by which it is made happy." There is, in short, no purely "natural" person. The reason there is no purely natural person, Augustine says, is that nature did not produce people. God did. Consequently, human nature always bears the mark of its creation, which means, among other things, that there are some permanent relations between people and God. It is not by accident that we *seek* happiness, but rather is a consequence of our incompleteness and finitude. It is no accident that we can find happiness only in God since we were made by God to find happiness only in God. Augustine elaborates this aspect of human nature through the theory of love.

The Role of Love

According to Augustine, we inevitably love. To love is to go beyond ourselves and to fasten our affection upon an object of love. It is again our incompleteness that prompts us to love. There is a wide range of objects that people can choose to love, reflecting the variety of ways in which people are incomplete. A person can love (1) physical objects, (2) other persons, or even (3) oneself. All of these things will provide us with some measure of satisfaction and happiness. Further, in some sense, all of these things are legitimate objects of love since nothing is evil in itself—as we've seen, evil is not a positive thing but the absence of something. Our moral problem consists not so much in loving or even in the objects of our love. The real issue is the *manner* in which we attach ourselves to these objects of love and our *expectations* regarding the outcome of this love. Everyone expects to achieve happiness and fulfillment from love, yet we are miserable, unhappy, and restless. Why? Augustine lays the blame upon "disordered" love, that is, the fact that we love specific things more than we should, and at the same time fail to devote our ultimate love to God.

Evil and Disordered Love   Augustine believed that we have different human needs that prompt different acts of love. There is in fact some sort of correlation between various human needs and the objects that can satisfy them. Love is the act that harmonizes these needs and their objects. In addition to the worldly needs that prompt our love of objects, other people and ourselves, we also have a spiritual need that should prompt our love of God. Augustine formulates this point in somewhat quantitative terms. Each object of love can give only so much satisfaction and no more. Each of the person's needs likewise has a measurable quantity. Clearly, satisfaction and happiness require that an object of love contain a sufficient amount of whatever it takes to fulfill or satisfy the particular need. Thus, we love food and we consume a quantity commensurate with our hunger. But our needs are not all physical in that primary sense. We love objects of art too for the aesthetic satisfaction that they give. At a higher level we have the need for love between persons. Indeed, this level of affection provides quantitatively and qualitatively more in the way of pleasure and happiness than love of mere physical things can. From this it becomes clear that certain human needs cannot be met by an interchange of objects. For example, our deep need for human companionship cannot be met any other way than by a relationship with another person. Things can't be a substitute for a person because things do not contain within themselves the unique ingredients of a human personality.

Accordingly, although each thing is a legitimate object of love, we must not expect more from it than its unique nature can provide. But this is particularly the case with our spiritual need. People were made, said Augustine, to love God, and God is infinite. In some way, then, we were made so that only God, the infinite, can give us ultimate satisfaction or happiness. "When," says Augustine, "the will which is the intermediate good, cleaves to the immutable good . . . people find therein the blessed life" for "to live well is nothing else but to love God." To love God, then, is the indispensable requirement for happiness, because only God, who is infinite, can satisfy that peculiar need in us that is precisely the need for the infinite. If objects are not interchangeable—if for example, things cannot substitute for a person—neither can any finite thing or person substitute for God. Yet, we all confidently expect that we can achieve true happiness by confining our love to objects, other people, and ourselves. While these are all legitimate objects of love in a limited way, our love of them is disordered when we love these for the sake of ultimate happiness. Disordered love consists in expecting more from an object of love than it is capable of providing, and this produces all forms of pathology in human behavior. Normal self-love becomes pride, and pride is the cardinal sin that affects all aspects of our conduct. The essence of pride is the assumption of self-sufficiency.

Yet the permanent fact about human nature is precisely that we are not self-sufficient, neither physically, emotionally, nor spiritually. Our pride, which turns us away from God, leads us to many forms of overindulgence, since we try to satisfy an infinite need with finite entities. We therefore love things more than we should in relation to what they can do for themselves. Our love for another person can become virtually destructive of the other person, since we try again to derive from that relationship more than it can possibly give. Appetites flourish, passion multiplies, and there is a desperate attempt to achieve peace by satisfying all desires. We become seriously disfigured and then exhibit envy, greed, jealousy, trickery, panic, and a pervading restlessness. It does not take long for disordered love to produce a disordered person, and disordered people produce a disordered community. No attempt to reconstruct an orderly or peaceful community or household is possible without reconstructing each human being. The rigorous and persistent fact is that personal reconstruction and salvation is possible only by reordering love, that is, by loving the proper things properly. Indeed, Augustine argued that we can love a person properly only if we love God first, for then we will not expect to derive from human love what can be derived only from our love of God. Similarly, we can love ourselves properly only as we subordinate ourselves to God, for there is no other way to overcome the destructive consequences of pride than by eliminating pride itself.

Free Will as the Cause of Evil

Augustine did not agree with Plato that the cause of evil is simply ignorance. There are indeed some circumstances in which we do not know the ultimate good, and thus are not aware of God. Still, Augustine says that "even the ungodly" have the capacity to "blame and rightly praise things in the conduct of people." The overriding fact is that in daily conduct we understand praise and blame only because we already understand that we have an obligation to do what is praiseworthy and to abstain from what is blameworthy. Under these circumstances, our predicament is not that we are ignorant but that we stand in the presence of alternatives. We must choose to turn toward God or away from God. We are, in short, free. Whichever way we choose, it is with the hope of finding happiness. We are capable of directing our affections exclusively toward finite things, other people, or ourselves, and thereby away from God. Augustine says that "this turning away and this turning to are not forced but voluntary acts."

According to Augustine, evil, or sin, is a product of the will. It is not, as Plato said, ignorance, nor, as the Manichaeans said, the work of the principle of darkness permeating the body. In spite of the fact of original sin, we still possess freedom of the will. This freedom (*liberum*) of the will is not, however, the same as spiritual freedom (*libertas*), for true spiritual liberty is no longer possible in its fullness in this life. We now use free will to choose wrongly. But, Augustine argues, even when we choose rightly, we do not possess the spiritual power to do the good we have chosen. We must have the help of God's grace. Whereas evil is caused by an act of free will, virtue, on the other hand, is the product not of our will but of God's grace. The moral law tells us what we must do, but in the end it really shows us what we can't do on our own. Hence, Augustine concludes that "the law was . . . given that grace might be sought; grace was given that the law might be fulfilled."

JUSTICE

For Augustine, public or political life is under the same rule of the moral law as is a person's individual or personal life. There is a single source of truth for both realms, and this truth he considered "entire, inviolate and not subject to changes in human life." All people recognize this truth and know it as natural law or natural justice. Augustine considered natural law as our intellectual sharing in God's truth, that is, God's *eternal law*. Augustine's notion of *eternal law* was already anticipated by the Stoics when they spoke of the diffusion of the principle of reason throughout all of nature. As such, they ascribed to this reason the role and power of ruling everything. Their theory was that *nous*, the principle of reason, constituted the laws of nature. Whereas the Stoics, then, considered the laws of nature to be the working of the *impersonal* force of rational principles in the universe, Augustine interpreted the eternal law as the reason and will of a personal God. He writes that "eternal law is the divine reason and the will of God which commands the maintenance (observance) of the natural order of things and which forbids the disturbance of it." Since *eternal law* is God's reason commanding orderliness, our intellectual grasp of the eternal principles is called *natural law*. When a political state makes a law, Augustine said, such temporal laws must be in accord with the principle of natural law, which in turn is derived from the eternal law.

Augustine's chief argument regarding law and justice was that the political state is not autonomous, and that, in making laws, the state does not merely express its power to legislate. Thus, the state must also follow the requirements of justice. Justice is a standard, moreover, which precedes the state and is eternal. What made Augustine's argument unique was his novel interpretation of the meaning of justice. He accepted Plato's formula that "justice is a virtue distributing to every one his due." But, he asked, what is "due" to anyone? He rejected the notion that justice is a matter of custom which differs in each society. For him, we discover justice in the structure of human nature with its relation to God. Hence, he said that justice is "the habit of the soul which imparts to every person the dignity due him. . . . Its origin proceeds from nature . . . and this notion of justice . . . is not the product of personal opinion, but something implanted by a certain innate power." To require the state to follow such a standard was obviously to place heavy moral limitations upon political power. Indeed, Augustine argued that if the laws of the state were out of harmony with natural law and justice, they would not have the character of laws, nor would there be a state.

By relating justice to the moral law, Augustine argued that justice is not limited merely to the relations between people. The primary relationship in justice is between a person and God: "if people do not serve God what justice can be thought to be in them?" Moreover, collective justice is impossible apart from this individual justice, for "if this justice is not found in one person, no more then can it be found in a whole multitude of such like people. Therefore, among such there is not that consent of law which makes a multitude of people just." To serve God is to love God, but this means also to love our fellow human. All of ethics, then, is based upon our love for God and love for other people. Love is the basis of justice.

Augustine believed that, according to God's law, religion was in a position of superiority over political institutions. Nevertheless, he did concede to the state the right to use coercive force. Indeed, the state is the product of the sinful condition of human nature and therefore exists as a necessary agency of control. Even so, Augustine would never concede that the principle of force was higher than the principle of love. For he says that

> a society cannot be ideally founded unless upon the basis and by the hand of faith and strong concord, where the object of love is the universal good which in its highest and truest character is God Himself and where people love one another with complete sincerity in Him, and the ground of their love for one another is the love of Him from whose eyes they cannot conceal the spirit of love.

The earthly state has an important function, even though its force cannot match the creative power of love. Specifically, the state's action can at least mitigate some evils: "When the power to do harm is taken from the bad people, they will carry themselves in a more controlled manner."

HISTORY AND THE TWO CITIES

Augustine made the love of God the central principle of morality. He also accounted for evil by his theory of disordered love. From this he concluded that the human race can be divided between those who love God, on the one hand, and those who love themselves and the world, on the other. Since there are two basically different kinds of love, there are, then, two opposing societies. Those who love God Augustine called the *City of God,* and those who love self and the world he called the *City of the World.*

Augustine did not consider these two cities to be identical with the church and state, respectively. Having stressed that the decisive element in the formation of a society is the dominant love of its members, he pointed out that those who love the world are found both in the state and in the church. It does not follow therefore that the church contains the whole society called the City of God. Similarly, there are in the state those who love God. These two cities therefore cut across both church and state and have an independence of them in an invisible way. Hence, wherever those people are who love God, there will be the City of God, and wherever there are those who love the world, there will be the City of the World.

History

Within the conflict between the two cities, Augustine saw the clue to a philosophy of history. What he meant by a *philosophy* of history was that history has a meaning. The early Greek historians saw no pattern in human events other than, perhaps, the fact that kingdoms rise and fall and that there are cycles of repetition. Aristotle, we will recall, argued that history is hardly capable of teaching people any important knowledge about human nature. Unlike drama, according to Aristotle, history deals with individual people, nations, and events, whereas drama deals with universal conditions and problems. But Augustine thought that the greatest drama of all is human history. This is in large part because the author of history is God. History begins with creation, is interspersed with important events, such as the fall of humanity and the incarnation of God. History is now involved in a tension between the City of God and the City of the World. Nothing happens without reference to God's ultimate providence. Augustine thought that this was particularly so with the political events of his own day.

When the barbarian Goths sacked Rome in 410, many non-Christians laid the blame upon the Christians, saying that their excessive emphasis upon loving and serving God had the effect of diluting patriotism and weakening the defenses of the state. To answer such charges and many others, Augustine wrote his book *The City of God* in 413. In it he argued that the fall of Rome was due not to the subversive activities of the Christians but, on the contrary, to the rampant vice throughout the Empire, which the Christian faith and love of God could have prevented. The fall of Rome was for Augustine just another example of God's purposeful intrusion into history, whereby he sought to establish the City of God and restrain the City of the World. Augustine believed that we all can find relevance in the drama of history, since our human destinies are inevitably linked with the two cities and with the activity of God. There is an all-embracing destiny for human beings and the world, and it will be achieved in God's good time and when the love of God reigns. With these views, Augustine took what he considered otherwise random people and events and supplied them with a comprehensive meaning, a "philosophy of history."

CHAPTER 7

Philosophy in the Early Middle Ages

*T*he fall of the Roman Empire in 476 ushered in a period of intellectual darkness. The barbarians who destroyed the political might of Rome also shattered the institutions of culture in Western Europe. Learning almost came to a halt. Virtually the whole body of ancient literature was lost. For the next five or six centuries, philosophy was kept alive by Christian scholars who became the channels through which the works of the ancient Greeks were transmitted to the West. Three early and influential thinkers were Boethius, Pseudo-Dionysius, and John Scotus Erigena.

In the ninth century, king Charlemagne of the Holy Roman Empire aggressively attempted to revive classical learning. And with the appearance of Erigena's large-scale and systematic work *The Division of Nature,* one might have expected philosophy to emerge from this intellectually suppressed period and flourish once again throughout Western Europe. This early promise of continued revival was delayed, however, by several historical events. After Charlemagne's death, the Empire was decentralized into feudal divisions. The papacy entered a period of moral and spiritual weakness, and the monasteries exerted no effective leadership in their special province of education and learning. The invasions by the Mongols, Saracens, and Norsemen added to these forces, making for cultural darkness. For almost a hundred years, during most of the 900s, very little philosophical activity was carried on. But philosophy did revive in the next century, and from about 1000 to 1200 it focused on the issues of universals, proofs for God's existence, and the relation between faith and reason. In the discussion of these problems, several sources of philosophy were stimulated, joining together Greek, Christian, Jewish, and Muslim thought.

BOETHIUS

One of the most prominent philosophic figures in the early Middle Ages was Anicius Manlius Severinus Boethius (ca. 480–524), of Rome and Pavia, Italy. He grew up in the kingdom of Theodoric as a Christian. At an early age he was sent

Boethius visited in prison by Philosophia—10th-century
manuscript illumination
(The Granger Collection New York)

to Athens, where he mastered the Greek language and encountered Aristotelianism, Neoplatonism, and Stoicism. Later, in 510, he was elevated to the
position of consul in the court of Theodoric and was eventually showered with
honors. In spite of his fame and his impressive political status, he was suspected
of high treason, stripped of his honors, subjected to a long imprisonment, and,
in 524, finally executed. Boethius became the most important channel through
which Greek thought, especially some of Aristotle's works, was transmitted to
the West in the early Middle Ages. Being an accomplished student of the Greek
language, Boethius originally intended to translate the works of Plato and Aristotle into Latin and to show how their apparent differences could be harmonized. Although he did not accomplish this ambitious project, he nevertheless
did leave a considerable legacy of philosophical writings, consisting of translations of some of Aristotle's works and commentaries on these works and others

by Porphyry and Cicero. In addition to these he wrote theological works and treatises on each of the four liberal arts, namely arithmetic, geometry, astronomy, and music. To these four disciplines he gave the name *quadrivium* to distinguish them from the other three liberal arts, the *trivium,* consisting of grammar, logic, and rhetoric. In his original treatises, Boethius drew upon a wide variety of authors, showing his familiarity with Plato, Aristotle, the Stoics, Plotinus, Augustine, and others, though clearly under the dominant influence of Aristotle. His works achieved the status of classics and were later used by the leading philosophers, including Thomas Aquinas, as authoritative guides for interpreting ancient authors and basic philosophical problems.

The Consolation of Philosophy

During his imprisonment, in Pavia, Boethius wrote his famous work, *The Consolation of Philosophy,* which was widely circulated in the Middle Ages and had such lasting influence that Chaucer translated it and patterned some of his *Canterbury Tales* on its contents. The work is a dialogue between himself and a personification of philosophy, ranged over the subjects of God, fortune, freedom, and evil. In the early pages of this book Boethius offers an allegorical description of philosophy, which can still be seen carved on the facades of many cathedrals in Europe. What led him to see philosophy in these allegorical terms was his attempt to overcome his melancholy by writing poetry as he languished in prison. At this point he was struck by a new vision of philosophy, which he set down with considerable imaginative force. Philosophy came to him as a noble woman with eyes of such keenness as to suggest that philosophy has powers higher than human nature. She gives the impression of having no specific age, indicating that philosophy is perennial. On her robe appear the Greek letters phi (Φ), symbolizing practical philosophy, and theta (θ), symbolizing theoretical philosophy, and a ladder between them shows the ascent on the steps to wisdom. Boethius is consoled by philosophy when he discovers from it that no earthly goods and pleasures can give him true happiness, that one must turn to the Supreme Good to whom philosophy leads. But in addition to this allegorical interpretation, Boethius formulated a more technical definition of philosophy, calling it the "love of wisdom." The word *wisdom* carried the whole freight of his definition. To Boethius *wisdom* meant a reality, something that exists in itself. Wisdom is the living thought that causes all things. In loving wisdom, we love the thought and cause of all things. In the end, the love of wisdom is the love of God. In his *Consolation* he makes no mention of Christianity but rather formulates a natural theology based upon what unaided human reason can provide.

The Problem of Universals

The problem of universals, by no means a new one, struck medieval thinkers as fundamental, because in their judgment the enterprise of thought rested to a great extent upon its solution. The central issue in this problem is how to relate the objects of human thought and the objects that exist outside the mind. Objects outside the mind are individual and many, whereas objects in the mind are single or universal. For example, in normal discourse we use words such as *tree* or *person*, but such words refer to the actual and particular trees and people that we observe with our senses. To *see* a tree is one thing; to *think* it is another. We see particulars but we think universals. When we see a particular thing, we place it into either a species or a genus. We never see *tree* or *person*, only "this oak" or "John." *Tree* stands in our language for all the actual trees—oak, elm, and so on—whereas *person* includes John, Jane, and every other specific person. What, then, is the relation between these general words and these specific trees and people? Is the word "tree" *only* a word, or does it refer to something that exists someplace? If the word *tree* refers to something in this specific oak that belongs to all trees, the word refers to something universal. The universal, then, is a general term, but the objects that exist outside of our minds are single or particular and specific. If the universal is merely an idea in our minds, what is the connection between the way we think, on the one hand, and the actual particular objects outside our minds, on the other? How does my mind go about forming a universal concept? Is there anything *outside* my mind corresponding to the universal idea *in* my mind?

Boethius translated Porphyry's *Introduction to Aristotle's Categories.* There he found a discussion of the problem of universals in terms of certain questions raised by Porphyry. These questions centered on the relation between generic and specific notions. What, in short, is the relation between genera and specific objects? Porphyry raised these three questions: (1) Do genera really exist in nature, or are they merely constructions of our minds? (2) If they are realities, are they material or immaterial? (3) Do they exist apart from sensible things or somehow in them? While Porphyry did not answer his own questions, Boethius formulated a solution chiefly in terms of Aristotle's approach to the problem.

Boethius was aware of the immense difficulty of the problem. If the issue is to discover whether human thought conforms to realities outside our minds, we can quickly discover some ideas in our minds for which there is no corresponding external object. We can think of a centaur, but such a combination of human and horse does not exist. Or, again, we can think of a line, the way a geometer does. But we do not find this kind of line existing as such anywhere. What is the difference between the idea of the centaur and of the line? One can say about the concept of the centaur that it is *false*, whereas the concept of the line is *true*. What Boethius wants to illustrate here is that there are two fundamentally different ways in which we form concepts, namely, by *composition* (putting together horse and human) and *abstraction* (drawing from a particular object some of its predicates). He wanted to say that universal ideas, such as genera, are abstracted by the mind from actual individual things and are, therefore, *true* ideas.

Saying that universals are abstracted from individuals led Boethius to conclude that genera exist *in* the individual things and that they become universals when we *think* of them. In this way, universals are simultaneously in the object and in our minds—*subsisting* in the thing and *thought about* in our minds. Such universals include not only genera, to which Boethius limited his analysis, but also other qualities such as *just, good, beautiful.* What makes two trees both trees is that, as objects, they resemble each other because they contain a universal foundation to their being. At the same time, we can *think* of them both as trees because our minds discover the same universal element in both of them. This, then, was Boethius' way of answering the first question, namely, whether universals exist in nature or only in our minds. For him, they exist both in things and in our minds. To the second question—whether universals are material or immaterial—he could now say that they exist both concretely in things and immaterially or abstractly in our minds. Similarly, his reply to the third question—whether universals exist apart from individual objects or are realized in them—was that they exist both in things and apart from them in our minds.

PSEUDO-DIONYSIUS

Around 500 BCE, a collection of Neoplatonic writings circulated in Western Europe, which were attributed to a first century disciple of the Apostle Paul named Dionysius the Areopagite. However, since these writings embody ideas developed by a much later thinker, Proclus (ca. 410–485), scholars now believe that they were probably written in Syria close to 500, and that the author used a pseudonym. Accordingly, these works are now associated with the name "Pseudo-Dionysius." The treatises of Pseudo-Dionysius attempt to relate Christian thought systematically with Neoplatonic philosophy. These works consist of *The Divine Names, The Celestial Hierarchy, The Ecclesiastical Hierarchy, The Mystical Theology,* and also 10 letters. They were all translated into Latin frequently, and several commentaries were written on them. The influence of Pseudo-Dionysius was very great throughout the Middle Ages. Philosophers and theologians concerned with quite different problems made considerable use of his writings. The mystics drew heavily upon his elaborate theory of the hierarchy of beings, since it afforded a rich source for describing the ascent of the soul to God. Aquinas used his theories in accounting for the great chain of being and the analogical relation between human beings and God. Above all, he was one of the most powerful sources of Neoplatonism, influencing philosophical thought regarding the origin of the world, the knowledge of God, and the nature of evil.

Pseudo-Dionysius gave an account of the relation of the world to God in which he combined the Neoplatonic theory of *emanation* and the Christian doctrine of *creation.* He wanted to avoid the pantheism latent in the Neoplatonic theory that says that all things are emanations from God. At the same time he wanted to establish that whatever exists comes from God, though he apparently had no clear conception of God's creative act as an act of free will. Nevertheless, Dionysius argued that the world is the object of God's providence. God has placed between himself and human beings a virtual ladder or hierarchy of beings called heavenly spirits. From the lowest level of being to the highest, where God is at the peak, there are various degrees of being. Dionysius indeed came close to pantheism and monism because of this continuous scale or chain of being, which he sometimes described as a shaft of light. Still, he countered this with a pluralistic view of things. God is the goal of all created things. He attracts all things to himself by his goodness and the love he inspires.

Dionysius held that we can come to a knowledge of God in two ways: a *positive* way and a *negative* way. When we take the positive way, we ascribe to God all the perfect attributes discovered by a study of creatures. In this way we can give the *divine* such *names* as goodness, light, being, unity, wisdom, and life. Dionysius said that these names belong in their perfection to God and only in a derivative sense to human beings, depending upon the degree to which the creature participates in these perfections. Dionysius thought that these attributes existed in God in a very literal sense, since surely God *is* goodness, life, wisdom, and so on. By contrast, humans *have* these to a lesser degree. Still, God and human beings are more alike than God and a stone, since we cannot say about a stone that it is good, wise, and alive.

Although we do gain knowledge of God through this positive way, Dionysius held that the *negative* way was more important. Dionysius was aware that people unavoidably develop anthropomorphic conceptions of God, and for this reason he undertook to remove from God all the attributes of creatures. It was obvious to him that what characterized God was precisely that he did not have the attributes of finite creatures. Step by step he removed from the conception of God all the things we say about creatures. In the negative way, we consider God's nature by denying of God whatever seems least compatible with him, such as "drunkenness and fury." Then, by a process of "remotion," we remove various categories of attributes from our conception of God. Since all we know is the world of creatures, the negative process of "remotion" leads us not to a clear conception of God but only to a "darkness of unknowing". The only positive aspect of this approach is that we are assured of knowing what God is *not* like. Because God is no object, he is beyond the knowable. This view had a great influence on later mystics, who believed that as people ascended closer to God, the ordinary forms of human knowledge were annihilated by the blindness caused by the excess of God's light.

In Neoplatonic terms, Dionysius denied the positive existence of *evil.* If evil was something positive and had some substantial being, we would be forced to trace it back to God as its cause, since all being is from God. For Dionysius, existence and goodness are identical terms, for whatever is, is good, and if something is good, it obviously must first exist. In God goodness and being are one, and therefore whatever comes from God is therefore good. The corollary of this, though, is not necessarily true, namely, that evil is synonymous with nonbeing. Still, the absence of being amounts to evil because it means the absence of good. Evil people are good in all the ways in which they possess positive being but are evil in whatever respect they are lacking some form of being, particularly in the operation of their wills. Ugliness and disease in physical nature are called evil for the same reason that acts in the province of morality are, namely, because they suffer deficiency in form or the absence of some being. Blindness is the absence of light and not the presence of some evil force.

John Scotus Erigena

Three centuries passed from the time of Boethius and Pseudo-Dionysius before another philosopher of stature appeared in the West. He was a remarkable Irish monk, John Scotus Erigena, who produced the first full-scale philosophical system in the Middle Ages. Born in Ireland in 810, he studied in a monastery and was one of the few scholars of his day who mastered Greek. By any standard, Erigena was an unusually able Greek scholar, and given the philosophical material at his disposal at that time, his systematic writing set him apart as the most impressive thinker of his century.

Erigena left Ireland and appeared in the court of Charles the Bald around 851. His studies at this time were devoted chiefly to Latin authors, especially Augustine and Boethius, on whose *The Consolation of Philosophy* he wrote a commentary. At the request of Charles the Bald, Erigena translated the Greek texts of Pseudo-Dionysius into Latin in 858 and in addition wrote commentaries on these texts. He also translated works by the earlier theologians Maximus the Confessor and Gregory of Nyssa. After this work of translation, Erigena produced his celebrated treatise on *The Division of Nature,* a book written in dialogue form around 864. In this work, Erigena undertook the complicated task of expressing Christian thought and Augustine's philosophical views in terms of the Neoplatonism of Pseudo-Dionysius. Although it became a landmark in medieval thought, it attracted little attention from Erigena's contemporaries. Various later writers appealed to this book to corroborate unorthodox theories, such as pantheism. This led Pope Honorius III to condemn Erigena's *The Division of Nature* on January 25, 1225, and order it to be burned. In spite of this, several manuscript copies have survived down to the present time.

The Division of Nature

The complicated argument of Erigena's *The Division of Nature* revolves around his special understanding of the two key words in the title of his book. First of all, by *nature* Erigena meant "everything there is." In this sense nature includes both God and creatures. Secondly, when he talks about the *division* of nature, he has in mind the ways in which the whole of reality—God and creatures—is divided. In addition, the word *division* has a special meaning. Erigena says that there are two ways of understanding the structure of reality: one is by *division* and the other is by *analysis.* By *division* he means moving from the more universal to the less universal, as when one divides *substance* into *corporeal* and *incorporeal.* In turn, *incorporeal* can be divided into *living* and *inanimate,* and so on. On the other hand, by *analysis* the process of division is reversed, and the elements divided off from substance are worked back into the unity of substance. Underlying Erigena's method of division and analysis was his conviction that our minds work in accordance with metaphysical realities. Our minds are not simply dealing with *concepts* when we "divide" and "analyze"; we are describing how things really exist and behave. If God is the ultimate unity, then things and the world are divisions of this basic unity, and analysis is the process by which things return to God. The laws of thought, according to Erigena, parallel the laws of reality.

With these distinctions in mind, Erigena argued that there is only one true reality and that all other things depend upon it and return to it; this reality is God. Within the total reality of nature, a fourfold division is possible. There is, first, nature that creates and is not created; second, nature that is created and creates; third, nature that is created and does not create; and fourth, nature that neither creates nor is created. Erigena goes into considerable detail elaborating each of these divisions, using Christian, Augustinian, and especially Neoplatonic concepts to formulate his philosophy about them.

Nature that Creates and Is Not Created   By this Erigena meant God, who is the cause of all things but does not himself need to be caused. He brought all creatures into existence out of nothing. Following the distinction made by Pseudo-Dionysius, our knowledge of God is *negative*. This is because none of the attributes we derive from objects in our experience apply in any proper sense to God, who possesses all the perfections in his infinity. To make sure that not even the likely attributes of wisdom and truth are ascribed to God without qualification, Erigena adds the term *super* to them. We thus would say about God that he is super-wisdom and super-truth. None of Aristotle's predicates or categories applies to God, for these predicates assume some form of substance—as, for example, "quantity" implies dimension—but God does not exist in a definable place. Erigena discusses several issues along Augustinian lines, such as God's nature and the notion of creation out of nothing. But as he pursues the subject of the relation between God and creatures, his Neoplatonism seems to become dominant, and it is difficult to avoid the conclusion that for Erigena there is no sharp distinction between God and creatures. "When we hear that God made all things," says Erigena, "we should understand nothing else but that God is in all things." This follows because only God "truly is," and therefore whatever is in anything is God.

Nature that Is Created and Creates   This division refers to the divine Forms, which become the prototypes of all created things. They are the *exemplary causes* of all the created species. To say that they are *created* does not mean, according to Erigena, that they come to be at some point in time. He has in mind a logical and not a chronological sequence. In God there is the full knowledge of everything, including the primordial causes of all things. These primordial causes are the divine Forms and prototypes of things, and they *create* in the sense that all creatures "participate" in them. For example, human wisdom participates in super-wisdom. Though he uses the word *creation* here, his Neoplatonism once again dominates, particularly since creation for Erigena does not occur in time but is an eternal relation between God's Forms and creatures.

Nature that Is Created and Does Not Create   This is the world of things as we experience it. Technically, it refers to the collective external effects of the primordial causes. These effects, whether incorporeal (such as angels or intelligence) or corporeal (such as people and things), are *participations* in the divine Forms. Erigena emphasizes that these things—this full range or hierarchy of beings—contain God as their essence, even though specific things give the impression of being individual. He compares this apparent plurality of things to the many varied reflections of light on the feathers of a peacock. Each color is a real one, but it depends upon the feathers, and therefore, in the end, the color is not an independent reality. In the created world, each individual is real by virtue of its primordial cause, which is in God's mind. But God is, if anything, a unity, and to speak of Forms, prototypes, and archetypes in his mind is to speak metaphorically, since these all constitute a unity. For this reason, the world is also a unity, as the peacock's feathers, and there is also more comprehensive unity between the world and God, since God is in everything. For Erigena, then, the divine *Forms* stand midway between God and creatures, as though they could look "up" toward God and "down" toward these externalized forms. But in the end his Neoplatonism leads him to erase the spaces between the *Forms* and God and creatures, fusing them all into a unity and eventually a pantheism.

Nature that Neither Creates Nor Is Created   This last division refers to God again, this time as the goal or end of the created order. As all things proceed from God, they also all return to God. Using Aristotle's metaphor, Erigena compares God to a beloved who, without moving, attracts the lover. Whatever starts from a principle returns again to this same principle, and in this way the universal cause draws to itself the multitude of things that have risen from it. With this return there is an end to all evil, and people find their union with God.

NEW SOLUTIONS TO THE PROBLEM OF UNIVERSALS

As we've seen, the medieval problem of universals was first formulated by Porphyry and answered by Boethius. It came under discussion almost 500 years later, and precipitated a vigorous debate for centuries to come. Although the issues were formulated in relatively restricted and seemingly unimportant terms, the participants saw serious theological as well as philosophical consequences hinging on the outcome of the debate. At least three major approaches were developed to this problem of universals: exaggerated realism, nominalism, and conceptualism.

Odo and Guillaume: Exaggerated Realism

The problem of universals eventually resolved itself into the simple question of whether a universal is a real *thing* or not. Those who said universals were in fact real things were known as *exaggerated realists*. These people said that genera exist in reality and that individual things *share* in these universals. However, they did not go so far as Plato, who said that the universals were Forms and existed separately from individual things. Rather, the realists said, for example, that *humanity* exists but that it exists in the plurality of human beings.

Why should this form of realism seem such an important matter? We find one answer in the works of Odo of Taurnai, a notable thinker who taught in the Cathedral School of Tours, founded the Abbey of St. Martin, was Bishop of Cambrai, and died in the Monastery at Anchin in 1113. For him realism was the foundation of certain traditional theological doctrines. For example, the doctrine of original sin, according to him, requires the realistic description of human nature. Realism says that there exists a universal substance, which is contained in every member of a species. If we are to understand the condition of human nature accurately, he said, we must realize that in the sin of Adam and Eve, the universal substance of *humanity* was infected so that all subsequent generations have inherited the consequences of their acts. If we deny realism, then what Adam and Eve did would pertain only to themselves, in which case the force of the concept of original sin would be lost.

Another exaggerated realist was Guillaume de Champeaux (1070–1121), who formulated two different views. First, in his *identity* theory, he held that the universal, say *humanity*, is identical in all members, in this case in all people. The *whole* reality of the universal is contained in each person. What differentiates Jane and John is merely certain secondary or accidental modifications of their essence or substance. Abelard (1079–1142) ridiculed this line of reasoning by saying that if each person is the whole human species, then humanity exists in Socrates in Rome and in Plato in Athens. If Socrates is present wherever the human essence is found, and since it is both in Rome and Athens, Socrates must be at the same moment in Rome and in Athens. And this, said Abelard, is not only absurd but leads to pantheism. Guillaume was forced by this and other criticisms to adopt a second theory, that of *indifferentism*, an antirealist view. According to his new view, the individuals of a species are the same thing not through some common essence but because in certain respects they are not different; that is, they are *indifferent.*

Roscellinus: Nominalism

One of the most formidable critics of exaggerated realism was Roscellinus (or Roscelin), who was born in Compiègne and traveled to England, Rome, and Tours. He taught at Taches, Compiègne, and Besançon, and was a teacher of Abelard. His central argument was that only individuals exist in nature. Genera are not real things. A general term such as "humanity" does not refer to anything; it is only a word *(voces)*, or a name *(nomen)*, composed of letters and expressed as a *vocal emission* and therefore only air. For this reason, discussions about universals are about words and not real things. Roscellinus was willing to draw certain obvious conclusions from his argument, particularly that the three persons of the Trinity are three separate beings and that all they have in common is a word but nothing really essential, hence they can be considered three Gods. For these views he was accused by the council at Soissons (1092) of tri-theism, and when he was threatened with excommunication, he denied this doctrine. In spite of this denial, Roscellinus served a decisive function in the history of the problem of universals. Specifically, he rejected exaggerated realism and the attempt to make universals into a thing.

Abelard: Conceptualism or Moderate Realism

Roscellinus seemed to be as extreme in his nominalism as others had been in their realism. Both, though, were exaggerated views. Avoiding both of these extremes was the position developed by Peter Abelard, who was born in Le Pallet in 1079 of a military family. During his tempestuous life, he quarreled with his teachers, had a celebrated romance with Heloïse, was abbott of the monastery in Brittany, was a famous lecturer in Paris, was condemned for his heretical teachings by Innocent II, and finally retired at Cluny, where he died in 1142.

On the problem of universals, Abelard said that universality must be ascribed principally to words. A word is *universal* when it is applied to many individuals. The word *Socrates* is not universal because it applies only to one person, whereas the word *humanity* is universal because it can be applied to all people. The function of a universal term, Abelard says, is to denote individual things in a special way. The question then is, how does it come about that we formulate these universal terms? To this Abelard answers that certain individual things, because of the *way* they exist, cause anyone observing them to *conceive* a likeness in all these individuals. This so-called likeness is not what the realists called an essence or substance. It consists simply in the way things agree in likeness. When we experience an individual, we *see* it but also *think* or *understand* it. Unlike the eye, which requires an object, our minds do not require a physical object since it can form *conceptions*. Thus, our minds are capable of doing two things, namely, forming concepts of individuals, Plato or Socrates, and forming concepts of universals, such as *humanity*. The conception of the individual is clear, whereas the conception of the universal is blurred. We cannot clearly focus on the precise meaning of the universal even though we do in fact know what it means. As conceptions of the mind, universals exist apart from the individual sensible bodies; but as words applied to those individuals they exist only in these bodies. The same word can be applied commonly to several individuals because each individual already exists in such a way as to cause it to be conceived the way others like it are conceived. The universal is therefore abstracted from the individual. The process of abstraction tells us how we understand the universal but not how the universal subsists. We understand things properly insofar as we abstract from them those properties that they truly possess. Abelard concluded, therefore, that the universal is a word and concept representing some reality that supplies the ground for this concept. This ground is the way similar things exist and strike our minds. To this extent, there is an objective ground for the universals, but this ground is not, as the realist held, something *real* in the sense of a *thing*. Nor would Abelard agree with the strict nominalist who would say that the universal is *only* a subjective idea or word for which there is no objective ground. Abelard's theory of universals carried the day, defeating both extremes of realism and nominalism.

ANSELM'S ONTOLOGICAL ARGUMENT

Anselm is famous in the history of thought primarily for his proof for God's existence, which in recent centuries has been titled "the ontological argument." He was born in Piedmont in 1033, entered the Benedictine Order, and eventually became Archbishop of Canterbury, where he died in 1109. For Anselm, there was no clear line between philosophy and theology. Like Augustine before him, he was particularly concerned with providing rational support for the doctrines of Christianity, which he already accepted as a matter of faith. He was convinced that faith and reason lead to the same conclusions. Moreover, Anselm believed that human reason can create a natural theology or metaphysics that is rationally coherent and does not depend upon any authority other than rationality. This did not mean, however, that Anselm denied any connection between natural theology and faith. On the contrary, his view was that natural theology consists of giving a rational version of what is believed. In this he was thoroughly Augustinian, saying that he was not trying to *discover* the truth about God through reason alone, but wanted rather to employ reason in order to *understand* what he was believing. His method therefore was *faith seeking understanding;* "I do not seek to understand in order that I may believe," he said, "but I believe in order that I may understand." He made it particularly clear that his enterprise of proving God's existence could not even begin unless he had already believed in God. Anselm conceded that his human mind could not penetrate into the profundity of God. Nevertheless, from the rational proof of God's existence, Anselm had a limited expectation: "I desire only a little understanding of the truth which my heart believes and loves."

Anselm's Realism

Before he composed the ontological argument, which appears in his book entitled *Proslogion,* he formulated three other arguments in an earlier work called *Monologion.* These three arguments show his overall philosophical orientation, namely, his acceptance of *realism* and his rejection of *nominalism.* His realism comes out in his belief that words are not simply sounds or grammatical conventions but stand for real things outside of our minds. Stated briefly, his three early arguments are these. (1) People seek to enjoy what they consider *good.* Since we can compare things with each other as being *more* or *less* good, these things must share in one and the same goodness. This goodness must be good-in-itself and as such is the supreme good. One could use the same argument as applied to *greatness.* There must therefore be something which is the best and greatest of all. (2) Everything that exists, exists either through something or through nothing. Obviously, it cannot come out of nothing. The only remaining alternative, then, is to say that a thing is caused either by something else or by itself. It cannot be caused by itself because before it is, it is nothing. To say that it is caused by something else could mean that things cause each other, which is also absurd. There must therefore be one thing that alone is

Anselm—French engraving, 1584
(The Granger Collection New York)

from itself and that causes all other things to be, and this is God. (3) There are various *degrees* or *levels* of being, whereby animals have a *higher* being than plants, and people have a higher being than animals. Using a line of reasoning similar to the first argument, Anselm concluded that unless we continued to move up through an infinite number of levels, we must arrive at a *highest* and most perfect being, than which there is none more perfect.

All three of these arguments start from an existing finite thing and move up through a hierarchy until they reach the peak of the scale of Being. Again, Anselm's realism is evident here, as is the influence of Plato and Augustine. He assumes throughout that when a finite thing shares in what our language calls *good, great, cause, being,* these words refer to some existing reality. Finite things therefore share not only in a *word* but in *being,* which somewhere exists in maximum perfection. Like the exaggerated realists Odo and Guillaume, Anselm also felt that the issue of realism had important theological implications— particularly with the doctrine of the Trinity. If we denied that an identical substance exists in several members, then the Trinity would amount to tri-theism, where each member is a totally separate and different being. According to Anselm, "He who does not understand how many men are specifically one only man cannot understand that several persons, each one of which is God, are one only God."

Ontological Argument

Anselm was aware that his above three arguments for God's existence did not have the clarity or power of a mathematical proof. Moreover, his fellow monks wondered whether he could simplify these arguments. Accordingly, after much thought on the matter, Anselm said that he had discovered a single, clear, and virtually flawless argument, which he published in the *Proslogion; or, Faith Seeking Understanding*. The first thing to notice about this proof is that Anselm's thought proceeds from within his mind, rather than starting with the assumption that each proof must begin with some empirical evidence from which the mind can then move logically to God. Anselm followed Augustine's doctrine of divine illumination, which gave him direct access to certain truths. Indeed, before beginning the ontological argument, Anselm asks the reader to "enter the inner chamber of your mind" and to "shut out all things save God and whatever may aid you in seeking God." Clearly, Anselm is assured of the existence of God before he begins, saying again that "unless I believe, I will not understand."

The argument itself moves swiftly. We believe, Anselm says, that God is "that than which nothing greater can be thought"—or, more simply, God is the greatest conceivable being. The question then is, does the greatest conceivable being really exist? There are those who would deny God's existence. Anselm quotes Psalms 14:1, where it says that "The fool has said in his heart: There is no God." What is meant by the word *fool* in this context? It means that a person who denies God's existence is involved in a flat contradiction. For when the fool hears the words "the greatest conceivable being," he understands what he hears, and what he understands can be said to be in his intellect. But it is one thing for something to be in the intellect; it is another to understand that something actually exists. A painter, for example, thinks in advance what he is about to portray. At this point, there is in his intellect an understanding of what he is about to make, though not an understanding that the portrait, which is still to be made, actually exists. But when he has finally painted it, he both has in his understanding and understands as existing the portrait he has finally made. What this proves, according to Anselm, is that something can be in our intellects even before we know it to exist. There is, then, in the fool's intellect an understanding of what is meant by the phrase "the greatest conceivable being," even though the fool does not yet necessarily understand that this being does in fact exist. It is in his intellect because when the fool hears this phrase, he understands it, and whatever we understand is thereby in our understanding. Hence, even the fool knows that there is at least in his intellect a greatest conceivable being.

This brings Anselm to the crux of his argument. We should ask ourselves which of these two conceptions is greater: (a) a "greatest conceivable being" that exists in reality or (b) a "greatest conceivable being" that exists only in our minds? The answer must be (a), since, according to Anselm, for any given being, real existence is greater than imaginary existence. Now, God is defined as "the greatest conceivable being." If God existed only in our minds, then he could be greater; that is, God would be "the greatest possible being that could be greater," and this is a contradiction in terms. Thus, to avoid contradiction, "the greatest conceivable being" must exist in reality. In a concluding prayer, Anselm thanks God "because through your divine illumination I now truly understand that which, through your generous gift, I formerly believed."

Gaunilon's Rebuttal

In the Abbey of Marmontier near Tours, another Benedictine monk, Gaunilon, came to the defense of the "fool." Gaunilon did not want to deny God's existence but only intended to argue that Anselm had not constructed an adequate proof. For one thing, Gaunilon argued that the first part of the "proof" is impossible to achieve. It requires that there be in the understanding an idea of God, that upon hearing this word the fool is expected to have a conception of that than which there is no greater. But, Gaunilon says, the fool cannot form a concept of such a being since there is nothing among other realities he experiences from which this concept can be formed. Indeed, Anselm himself already argued that there is no reality like God. Actually, if the human mind could form such a concept, no "proof" would be necessary, for we would then already connect existence with an aspect of a perfect being. Gaunilon's other major objection is that we often think of things that in fact do not exist. We can, for example, imagine "the greatest conceivable island," but there is no way to prove that such an island exists.

Anselm's Reply to Gaunilon

Anselm gave two replies. First, he said that we, along with the fool, are able to form a concept of "the greatest conceivable being". We do this whenever we compare different degrees of perfection in things and move upward to the maximum perfection, than which there is no more perfect. Secondly, he thought Gaunilon's reference to a perfect island showed that he had missed the point of the argument. The whole concept of a "greatest conceivable island" is conceptually flawed. This is because an "island" is by its very nature finite or limited; thus, it cannot exist in an infinite (or "greatest conceivable") manner. Only the concept of "being" can in fact rise above the limitations of finitude and thereby exist in the "greatest conceivable" manner. It is safe to say that Anselm is victorious on this point: there is no real parallel between inherently finite "islands" and potentially infinite "being". The Ontological Argument, then, survives Gaunilon's critique, and it was left to philosophers of later centuries to offer more convincing criticisms.

FAITH AND REASON IN MUSLIM AND JEWISH THOUGHT

Most of medieval thought is an attempt to reconcile the domains of philosophy and theology—that is, of reason and faith. The leading writers were Christians, who wrote philosophy mixing it with theology. Their religious orientation stemmed from the mainstream of the Christian tradition and was therefore, for the most part, the same for all of them. Their philosophical orientations, however, were quite diverse, since at different times and at different places they were exposed to different philosophers. Even when they relied upon the same philosopher—Aristotle, for example—they were exposed to different interpretations of his writings. Muslim philosophers were important in the Middle Ages since they produced influential commentaries on Aristotle, upon which many Christian writers depended for their understanding of Aristotle. As it turned out, these Muslim interpretations of Aristotle were not only the source of much knowledge about Aristotle but also the cause of serious difficulties in harmonizing the domains of faith and reason.

Under the leadership of Muhammad (570–632) a vast Muslim Empire was established with cultural centers in Persia and Spain, where during the ninth through the 12th centuries significant philosophical activity took place. During these centuries, the Muslim world was far more advanced in its knowledge of Greek philosophy, science, and mathematics than was the Christian world. Moreover, the Muslim world had access to the chief works of Aristotle centuries before Western Europe finally received them. Many texts of the Greek philosophers had been translated into Arabic, from which later Latin translations were made in the West. By 833, philosophy was well established in Baghdad, where a school had been established for translating Greek manuscripts on philosophy and science, and for creative scholarship as well. A distinguished line of thinkers worked here, especially Avicenna (980–1037). The other focal point of Muslim culture was Cordova, Spain, where the other leading Muslim philosopher, Averroës (1126–1198), wrote much of his philosophy. Although Avicenna and Averroës wrote in Arabic and were Muslims, they were not Arabs. Avicenna was a Persian, and Averroës a Spaniard.

Avicenna and Averroës both wrote important commentaries on Aristotle's philosophy, and some Christian writers accepted these interpretations as the authentic views of Aristotle. Because these interpretations showed Aristotle to be at variance with Christian doctrine, some medieval writers, such as Bonaventura, thought it necessary to reject Aristotle to avoid errors. For example, Thomas Aquinas challenged Siger de Brabant, who was the leading exponent of Averroës views at the University of Paris; however, Aquinas had access to other versions of Aristotle. For this reason, Aquinas's debates with Brabant did not focus on the rejection of Aristotle, but instead aimed at interpreting Aristotle in a way that was compatible with Christian doctrine. The significance of Muslim philosophers was therefore twofold in that they were transmitters of Aristotle and other Greek thinkers to the West and were also the authors of interpretations of Aristotle that became the basis of controversy in medieval philosophy.

Avicenna

Avicenna, born in Persia in 980, was a phenomenal scholar. He studied geometry, logic, jurisprudence, the Koran, physics, theology, and medicine, becoming a practicing physician at the age of 16. He was the author of many works, and although his thought centered on Aristotle, he shows some Neoplatonic influences as well as original formulations of problems.

Of particular importance was Avicenna's formulation of the doctrine of creation. Here he combined Aristotelian and Neoplatonic views and arrived at a theory that was hotly debated in the 13th century. Avicenna starts with the assumption that whatever begins to exist (as is the case with everything that we experience) must have a cause. Things that require a cause are called *possible* beings. A cause which is also a *possible* being must be caused by a prior being. This too must have a cause, but there cannot be an infinite series of such causes. There must therefore be a First Cause, whose being is not simply *possible* but is *necessary,* having its existence in itself and not from a cause, and this is God. Aquinas would later make much of this line of reasoning.

God is at the apex of Being, has no beginning, always is in act (i.e., is always expressing his full Being), and therefore has always created. According to Avicenna, then, creation is both necessary and eternal. This conclusion struck Bonaventura in the 13th century as a serious error and in conflict with the Biblical notion of creation. According to Bonaventura, two chief features of creation are that it is a product of God's free will, not of necessity, and that creation occurred at a point in time, not from eternity. Aquinas would agree, however, that philosophically there is no way to decide whether creation occurred in time or from eternity, that this must ultimately be a matter of faith.

If Avicenna's metaphysics caused Christian philosophers difficulties because of his doctrine of creation, his psychology caused even more serious concern. In his psychology, Avicenna wanted particularly to account for human intellectual activity. Central to his theory was the distinction between the *possible* intellect and the *Agent Intellect.* To account for this distinction, Avicenna employed his Neoplatonic view of the gradations of beings, placing people under the lowest level of angelic beings or Intelligences. That is, God creates a single effect, and this effect is called an *Intelligence,* the highest angel, but this Intelligence in turn creates a subordinate Intelligence. There are nine such Intelligences in descending order, each one creating (1) the one below it and (2) the soul of the successive sphere. The ninth Intelligence, then, creates the 10th and final Intelligence, and this is the Agent Intellect. It is the Agent Intellect that creates the four elements of the world and the individual souls of people. The Agent Intellect not only creates the souls or minds of people, it also "radiates forms" to these created minds.

What Avicenna was saying is that since a person's mind has a beginning, it is a *possible* being; therefore, a person has a *possible intellect.* Here Avicenna made a sharp distinction between existence and essence, saying that there are two different things in creatures. That is, because my essence is distinct from my existence, my *essence* is not automatically fulfilled, and it is certainly not given existence by itself. The essence of the human mind is to know, but it does not always know. The intellect is capable of knowing, and its essence is to know; but its knowing is only *possible.* The intellect is actually created without any knowledge but with an essence or possibility for knowledge. The *existence* of knowledge in the human intellect requires two elements, namely,

(1) the bodily senses through which we perceive sensible objects externally and the powers of retaining images of objects in the memory or imagination internally, and (2) the ability to discover the essence or universal in individual things through the power of abstraction. But—and here was Avicenna's unique point—this abstraction is not performed by the human intellect but is the work of the Agent Intellect. The Agent Intellect illuminates our human minds to enable us to *know*, thereby adding existence to our minds' essence. Since the Agent Intellect is the creator of the souls of all people and, in addition, is the active power in human knowledge, there is, then, only one active intellect in all people, in which all people share.

Siger de Brabant taught Avicenna's psychological theory at the University of Paris, and Bonaventura also reacted against this on the ground that it threatened the notion of the discrete individuality of each person. Avicenna did not mean to imply this, for he actually had a doctrine of the immortality of each soul: each returned to its source, the Agent Intellect. Still, Christian writers tended to see in the theory of the Agent Intellect the annihilation of the individual soul. They also criticized that the theory radically separated humans from God, since the Agent Intellect, and not God, confers enlightenment upon the human intellect. Individual people exist only insofar as matter is formed into their bodies, and the soul is the form of the body. But, again, the active part of the intellect is not *theirs*. In these ways, then, Avicenna injected into medieval philosophy some very provocative themes, including (1) the eternity and necessity of creation, (2) the gradations and emanations of a hierarchy of beings, (3) the doctrine of the Agent Intellect who both creates the human soul and illuminates the *possible intellect*, and (4) the distinction between essence and existence as related to possible and necessary being.

Averroës

Like Avicenna before him, Averroës was a prodigious scholar. He was born in 1126 in Cordova, Spain, where he studied philosophy, mathematics, jurisprudence, medicine, and theology. After serving as a judge, as his father had, he became a physician, but spent much of his time writing his famous commentaries, for which reason he became known in the Middle Ages as The Commentator. He spent his last days in Morocco, where he died in 1198 at the age of 72.

Averroës considered Aristotle the greatest of all philosophers, going so far as to say that nature had produced him as the model of human perfection. For this reason, Averroës structured all his work around Aristotle's texts and ideas. At some points he disagreed with Avicenna. For one thing, whereas Avicenna argued that creation is eternal and necessary, Averroës denied altogether the idea of creation, saying that philosophy knows no such doctrine, and that this is merely a teaching of religion. Averroës also rejected the distinction between essence and existence, saying that there is no *real* distinction between them (such as led Avicenna to distinguish between the *possible* and *active intellects*); instead, there is only a *logical* distinction between essence and existence for purposes of analysis. Moreover, Averroës held that the form of a person is the soul, but that the soul is a material and not a spiritual form. As such, the material soul has the same mortality as the body, so that upon death nothing survives. What confers special status to human beings among animals is that, unlike the lower animals, humans are united through knowledge with the Agent Intellect. Avicenna, we've seen, said that each person has a possible intellect and a unique spiritual power, but for all people there is one and the same Agent Intellect. Averroës denied that people have separate *possible* intellects. He therefore explicitly located human knowledge in the universal Agent Intellect and denied the doctrine of immortality. It is no wonder that Christian thinkers thought his teachings impious. But his influence was immense, and Aquinas frequently quotes from his works. Still, Averroës had little respect for theology and went to great lengths to distinguish the domains of philosophy and theology, of faith and reason.

Philosophy and theology each have a function, said Averroës because there are different kinds of people whom they respectively serve. He envisioned three groups of people. (1) The majority of people live by imagination and not by reason. They are kept virtuous through fear communicated by eloquent preachers. By contrast, the philosopher needs no threat, but is motivated by his knowledge. Although religion and philosophy work generally for the same end, they communicate different contents and, in this sense, different truths. These truths do not necessarily contradict each other; they simply are different kinds. Hence, the first group is composed of those who are governed more by dramatic forms of thought than by reason. (2) The second group is of theologians, who differ from the first group only in that while they have the same religious beliefs, they attempt to devise intellectual supports for them as their justification. But, having prejudiced their thinking by resting it upon inflexible assumptions, they cannot arrive at truth even though they have some notion of the power of reason. (3) The third and superior group consists of the philosophers, who constitute a small minority. They are able to appreciate the truth for which religious people and rational theologians are seeking, but they see no reason for trying to see this truth *through* the unavoidably indirect perspective of religion. The philosophers know truth directly. Actually, Averroës thought that religious beliefs had a social function in that they made philosophical truths accessible to minds that were incapable of philosophical thought. He thought, however, that the theologians, as compared with the masses, should have known better than to employ the powers of sophisticated reasoning upon a subject matter, religion, that is by nature a deviation from, though not necessarily contrary to, reason.

Moses Maimonides

In the 12th century, both Jewish and Muslim thought were more advanced than Christian thought. The reason is that at this time Christian philosophers did not have access to the rich apparatus of Greek philosophic concepts. As we have seen, Muslim philosophers had been working with Aristotle's texts since the ninth century. The great Jewish philosopher Maimonides owed his acquaintance with Aristotle to Muslim philosophers. Both Muslim and Jewish philosophers exerted a powerful influence upon the development of 13th-century scholastic philosophy because they had worked out some preliminary solutions to the major philosophical problems and had, moreover, transmitted considerable learning to that century. Maimonides had a special influence upon the succeeding generations of Christian thinkers because he shared with them a common belief in the Old Testament. As such he attempted to harmonize Old Testament thought with Greek philosophy and science; for Thomas Aquinas this served as a model in reconciling Biblical and secular learning.

Moses ben Maimonides was born in 1135 at Cordova and was a contemporary of Averroës, who was also born there. He was forced to leave Spain, and he went first to Morocco and then to Egypt, where he earned his livelihood by practicing medicine. He died in Cairo in 1204 at the age of 69. His principal work was his book entitled *Guide of the Perplexed.* In it he set out to prove that the teachings of Judaism harmonize with philosophical thought and, in addition, that Biblical thought offers certain valid insights that reason alone cannot discover. To accomplish this end, Maimonides drew on an astonishing amount of literature, being dominated, however, by the works of Aristotle.

Apart from expressing many of Aristotle's views, which others had also learned and taught, Maimonides proposed certain distinctive notions, several of which we will list here. *First,* Maimonides believed that there can be no basic conflict between theology, philosophy, and science—between faith and reason. His *Guide of the Perplexed* was addressed principally to those believing Jews who had studied the sciences of the philosophers and had become perplexed by the literal meaning of the religious Law *(Torah)*. Philosophy, he argued, is a distinct form of knowledge from the religious Law. Although the two do not conflict, their range and content are not the same. For this reason, not every religious doctrine will have a rational or philosophical explanation.

Second, the doctrine of the creation of the world is a matter of religious belief. Although Aristotle's philosophy suggests that the world existed from eternity—that there was no creation in time—Maimonides points out that on this matter the philosophical proof is not decisive. That is, philosophically the arguments for and against the doctrine of creation are of equal weight. Aquinas later took this same view, saying, as Maimonides had, that on this matter, the religious view must prevail, since it does not conflict with rational thought.

Third, Maimonides thought that conflicts between faith and reason were produced by two things, namely, the anthropomorphic language of religion and the disorderly way in which problems of faith are approached by the perplexed. We must proceed step by step, moving from mathematics and the natural sciences, to the study of the Law, and then to metaphysics or technical philosophical theology. With this kind of methodical training it becomes easier to understand the allegorical nature of much Biblical language. But to detect the anthropomorphic element in religious language one must be trained in the categories of scientific and philosophical concepts.

Fourth, Maimonides agreed with Avicenna regarding the structure of human nature. Like Avicenna, he accepted the theory of the Agent Intellect as the source of a person's substantive knowledge. Each person has only a *possible* or *passive* intellect, belonging uniquely to him or her. Each person *acquires* an active intellect, which *is* the Agent Intellect, or comes from the Agent Intellect in varying degrees, depending upon each person's degree of merit. Upon death, a person's soul, which is the form of the body, perishes, and the only element that survives is the active intellectual ingredient that came from the Agent Intellect and that now returns to it. If this is a doctrine of immortality, then it is one in which the unique characteristics of each individual has been greatly diminished.

Fifth, Maimonides anticipated three of Aquinas's proofs for the existence of God. Using portions of Aristotle's *Metaphysics* and *Physics,* he proved the existence of a Prime Mover, the existence of a *necessary* Being (relying here also on Avicenna), and the existence of a primary cause. Whether the world was created out of nothing or existed from eternity did not, Maimonides thought, affect the enterprise of natural theology. But having proved the existence of God, Maimonides, unlike Aquinas, rejected the possibility of saying *what* God is like. No positive attributes can be ascribed to God but only negative ones by saying what God is *not* like.

Sixth, the goal of human life is to achieve appropriate human perfection. The philosophers, Maimonides says, have made it clear there are four kinds of perfections that a person can attain. There are, in ascending order, the perfection of possessions, the perfection of the bodily constitution and shape, the perfection of the moral virtues, and, finally, the highest, which is the acquisition of the rational virtues. By rational virtues, Maimonides says, "I refer to the conception of intelligibles, which teach true opinions concerning the divine things. That is in true reality the ultimate end; thus what gives the individual true perfection." This rational account of human perfection had its counterpart also in faith, for Maimonides concluded by saying that "the prophets too have explained the self-same notions—just as the philosophers have interpreted them." Faith and reason are in harmony.

CHAPTER 8

Aquinas and His Late Medieval Successors

The great achievement of Thomas Aquinas (1225–1274) was that he brought together the insights of classical philosophy and Christian theology. Although he drew on classical philosophical themes from Plato and Stoicism, Aquinas's philosophy stands out for its reliance on Aristotle. Aquinas was also aware of the vast scope of thought produced by Christian writers as well as the contributions of Muslim and Jewish philosophers. By the time he began his literary work, a large part of Plato's and Aristotle's writings had become available in Western Europe. Augustine had formulated an earlier blending of philosophy and theology by combining the Christian faith with elements of Plato's thought, which he had discovered in the writings of the Neoplatonist Plotinus. Shortly after Augustine, in the sixth century, Boethius made a portion of Aristotle's works available in Latin for the first time and thereby stimulated philosophical speculation again. From about the seventh to the 13th century, there were several lines of development, leading toward differences and controversies between Platonists and Aristotelians.

This conflict continued after the 13th century as a controversy between Augustinians and Thomists (i.e., followers of Thomas Aquinas), insofar as Augustine and Aquinas built their thoughts around Plato and Aristotle, respectively. In these formative centuries, medieval thinkers wrestled with the problem of relating philosophy and theology, expressing this problem as the relation between faith and reason. There was also the problem of *universals*, which not only reflected the different viewpoints of Plato and Aristotle but also had important ramifications for the Christian faith. On all these matters, Aquinas now exerted a decisive influence by clarifying the precise questions involved, acknowledging alternative solutions offered by different authorities, and answering the major objections to his Aristotelian-Christian solutions. In this way, Aquinas perfected the "scholastic method."

The term *scholasticism* in this context is derived from the intellectual activity carried on in the medieval cathedral *schools,* and its proponents were called *doctores scholastici.* Eventually, scholasticism came to refer to the dominant system of thought developed by the doctors in the schools and to the special method they utilized in teaching philosophy. Scholastic philosophy was an attempt to put together a coherent system of *traditional* thought rather than a pursuit of genuinely novel forms of insight. The content of this system was for the most part a fusion of Christian theology and Greek philosophy—Plato and especially Aristotle. Most distinctive in scholasticism was its *method,* a process relying chiefly upon strict logical deduction, taking on the form of an intricate *system* and expressed in a *dialectical* or disputational form in which theology dominated philosophy. Again, Aquinas perfected what Boethius (480–524)— "the first scholastic"—established as the "scholarly" point of view regarding theological subjects. Boethius urged that "as far as you are able, join faith to reason," and Aquinas raised the conjunction of faith with reason to its highest form. While accepting revealed and traditional theological truths, he simultaneously tried to provide rational argumentation in order to make these revealed truths comprehensible.

AQUINAS'S LIFE

Aquinas was born in 1225 near Naples. His father was a Count of Aquino who had hoped that his son would someday enjoy a high ecclesiastical position. For this reason, Aquinas was placed in the Abbey of Monte Cassino as a boy of five, and for the next nine years he pursued his studies in this Benedictine abbey. At the age of 14, he entered the University of Naples, but while in that city he was fascinated by the life of some Dominican friars at a nearby monastery and decided to enter their order. As the Dominicans were particularly dedicated to teaching, Aquinas had, upon entering their order, resolved to give himself to a religious and also a teaching vocation. Four years later, in 1245, he entered the University of Paris, where he came under the influence of a prodigious scholar whose enormous intellectual achievements had earned him the names "Albert the Great" (Albertus Magnus) and the "Universal Teacher." During his long and intimate association with Albert both at Paris and Cologne, Aquinas's thought was shaped in decisive ways.

Albert recognized the significance of philosophy and science for grounding Christian faith and for developing the capacities of the human mind. While other theologians looked suspiciously at secular learning, Albert concluded that the Christian thinker must master philosophical and scientific learning in all its forms. He had respect for all intellectual activity, and his writings attest to his acquaintance with a vast amount and variety of learning. He knew virtually all the ancient, Christian, Jewish, and Muslim writers. But his mind was encyclopedic rather than creative. Still, it was Albert who had recognized the fundamental difference between philosophy and theology, sharpening more accurately than his predecessors had the boundaries between them. Albert thought that such writers as Anselm and Abelard, for example, had ascribed too much competence to reason, not realizing that from a rigorous point of view much of what they ascribed to reason was in fact a matter of faith. Albert's particular objective was to make Aristotle clearly understandable to all

St. Thomas Aquinas
(Corbis-Bettmann)

of Europe, hoping to put into Latin all of Aristotle's works. He considered Aristotle the greatest of all philosophers, and much of the credit for the dominance of Aristotle's thought in the 13th century must be given to him. It was under these circumstances that his pupil Aquinas would also see in Aristotle the most significant philosophical support for Christian theology.

Unlike Albert, who did not change anything in the philosophers he quoted in his works, Aquinas used Aristotle more creatively, systematically, and with a more specific recognition of the harmony between what Aristotle said and the Christian faith. After an interval of teaching under the auspices of the Papal Court from 1259 to 1268, Aquinas returned once again to Paris and became involved in a celebrated controversy with followers of Averroës. In 1274, Pope Gregory X called him to Lyons to participate in a council, and while on his way there, he died in a monastery between Naples and Rome, at the age of 49.

Aquinas left a huge written legacy, the vastness of which is all the more remarkable when we recall that it was all composed within a 20-year span. Among his principal works are his commentaries on many of Aristotle's writings, careful arguments against the errors of the Greeks and the Averroists, a brilliant early work on essence and existence, a political treatise on rulers, and many other notable works. His most renowned literary achievements, though, are his two major theological works, the *Summa contra Gentiles* and *Summa Theologica*.

Bonaventura and the University of Paris

To understand the issues that drove Aquinas's philosophy, it is important to understand the context of the medieval university in which he wrote. The first universities grew out of what were called "cathedral schools." The University of Paris evolved from the Cathedral School of Notre Dame, its formal rules of organization and procedures being approved officially by the Papal representative in 1215. Originally, like all early universities, Paris consisted of masters and students without any special buildings or other features we now associate with universities, such as libraries and endowments. These were added in the 14th and 15th centuries. But the most important ingredients were there, namely, masters and students with a passion for learning. Being originally church institutions, universities shared a common theological position. This meant, too, that of the four faculties—theology, law, medicine, and arts—the theological faculty enjoyed undisputed supremacy.

Besides its theological orientation, the University of Paris was receptive to universal knowledge. This accounts for the gradual acceptance and triumph of Aristotle's philosophy at Paris. It is easily apparent, however, that the invasion of Aristotelianism would raise problems of orthodoxy. There was, however, not only the concern over the impact of Aristotle's philosophy upon Christian thought, but also serious questions over whether Aristotle was faithfully and accurately interpreted by Muslim philosophers. In addition, whereas Augustine and Platonism triumphed at Oxford, this type of thought, although not dominant in Paris, was nevertheless strongly represented there at this time by Bonaventura, a contemporary of Aquinas. Bonaventura was critical of Aristotle, holding that by denying the Platonic theory of Forms, Aristotle's thought would produce serious errors if incorporated into theology. For example, to deny the Platonic Forms would mean that God does not possess in himself the Forms of all things and would therefore be ignorant of the concrete and particular world. In turn, this would deny God's providence or his control over the universe. This would also mean that events occur either by chance or through mechanical necessity.

Even more serious was Bonaventura's charge that if God does not think the Forms of the world, he could not have created it. On this point Aquinas was later to have serious difficulties with the church authorities, for in following Aristotle, he could discover no decisive reason for denying that the world always existed instead of being created at a point in time. But, said Bonaventura, if the world always existed, there must have existed an infinite number of human beings, in which case there must be either an infinite number of souls, or, as Averroists argued, there is only one soul or intellect, which all human beings share. If this Averroist argument were accepted, it would annul the theory of personal immortality. This was strongly urged by the leading Averroist of the 13th century, Siger de Brabant, who said that there is only one eternal intellect and that while individual people are born and die, this intellect or soul remains and always finds another human being in which to carry out its functions of organizing the body and the act of knowing. In short, there is only one intellect, which all people have in common.

Against Aristotelian philosophy, which Bonaventura considered dangerous to Christian faith because of all these errors it engendered, he offered the insights of Augustine and Platonism. Still, because Aristotle's thought was so formidable and so systematic, particularly concerning matters of nature and science, its forward march was irresistible, and its triumph virtually inevitable. If most parts of the University were to be oriented to Aristotle's thought, the theologians could not avoid coming to terms with this monumental thinker. If Aristotle was to be accepted, the specific task of the theologians would now be to harmonize his philosophy with Christianity, that is, they would have to "Christianize" Aristotle. This is what Aquinas set out to do, contending at the same time against Bonaventura's Augustinianism and Siger de Brabant's version of Aristotle.

PHILOSOPHY AND THEOLOGY

Aquinas thought and wrote as a Christian. He was primarily a theologian. At the same time, he relied heavily upon the philosophy of Aristotle in writing his theological works. That he brought together philosophy and theology did not mean that he confused these two disciplines. On the contrary, it was his view that philosophy and theology played complementary roles in our quest for truth. Like his teacher Albert the Great, Aquinas went to great pains to delineate the boundaries between faith and reason, indicating what philosophy and theology respectively could and could not provide. The dominant religious orientation of 13th-century thought concerned the importance of our knowledge of God; Aquinas combined the insights of both philosophy and theology to address this issue. What made the correct knowledge of God so essential was that any basic errors on this subject could affect the direction of a person's life—directing one either toward or away from God, who is our ultimate end. Philosophy proceeds from principles discovered by human reason, whereas theology is the rational ordering of principles received from authoritative revelation and held as a matter of faith. Aquinas's philosophy, then, consists for the most part in that portion of his theology that he considered rationally demonstrable—that is, *natural theology* as philosophers of later centuries used this term.

Faith and Reason

Aquinas saw specific differences between philosophy and theology—between reason and faith. For one thing, philosophy begins with the immediate objects of sense experience and reasons upward to more general conceptions. Eventually, as in Aristotle's case, we fasten upon the highest principles or first causes of being, ending in the conception of God. Theology, on the other hand, begins with a faith in God and interprets all things as creatures of God. There is here a basic difference in method, since philosophers draw their conclusions from their rational description of the essences of things. Theologians, by contrast, base their demonstrations upon the authority of revealed knowledge. Again, theology and philosophy do not contradict each other, but not everything that philosophy discusses is significant for a person's religious end. Theology deals with what people need to know for their salvation, and to ensure this knowledge, it was made available through revelation. Some of the truths of revelation could never be discovered by natural reason. Other elements of revealed truth, though, could be known by reason alone but were revealed to ensure that we indeed become acquainted with such truths.

For this reason, there is some overlapping between philosophy and theology. For the most part, however, philosophy and theology are two separate and independent disciplines. Wherever reason is capable of knowing something, faith, strictly speaking, is unnecessary, and what faith uniquely knows through revelation cannot be known by natural reason alone. Both philosophy and theology deal with God, but the philosopher can only infer that God exists and cannot by reflecting upon the objects of sensation understand God's essential nature. There is, nevertheless, a connection between the aims of philosophy and theology since they are both concerned with truth. Aristotle had considered the object of philosophy the study of first principles and causes, the study of being and its causes. This led to a First Mover, which he understood as the ground of truth in the universe. This is the philosophical way of saying what the theologian has set as his object of knowledge, namely, God's being and the truth this reveals about the created world. To discover the chief aspects of Aquinas's philosophy, then, we must take from his vast theological writings those portions of it in which he attempts to demonstrate truths in a purely rational way. His philosophical approach is particularly evident in his attempts to demonstrate the existence of God.

PROOFS OF GOD'S EXISTENCE

Aquinas formulated five *proofs* or ways of demonstrating the existence of God. The proofs are deceptively short, each being only a paragraph in length. Some important assumptions, though, lay behind their brevity. Most importantly, his approach was the opposite of Anselm's Ontological Argument. Anselm began his proof with the *idea* of the greatest conceivable being, from which he inferred the existence of that being. Aquinas, though, said that all knowledge must begin with our experience of sense objects. Instead of beginning with innate ideas of perfection, he rested all five of his proofs upon the ideas derived from ordinary objects that we experience with our senses.

Proofs from Motion, Efficient Cause, and Necessary Being

The first three of his proofs share a similar strategy, which we can see in his initial argument from motion. Everywhere we look we find things in motion, and see that things do not simply start moving by themselves. A baseball, for example, moves through the air when someone throws it. The entire world of physical motion involves similar causal connections in which one thing imparts motion to another. Thus, object A gets its motion from object B, which in turn gets its motion from object C. Aquinas then asks, how far back can we trace this motion? Avicenna argued earlier that it is impossible to trace such causal connections back through time and, ultimately, we must arrive at a first cause, namely, God. Aquinas, though, sees the situation differently. Why, at least in theory, couldn't this causal sequence trace back through time, to infinity past, and never have a starting point? Although this may be a strange contention, there is nothing logically contradictory about it.

Aquinas suggests that we view the causal sequence somewhat differently. Some causal sequences do indeed take place over time, as Avicenna points out, such as when Abraham produces his son Isaac, who later produces his own son Jacob. But in addition to these time-based sequences, there are also *simultaneous* causal sequences, which do not trace back through time. Imagine, for example, if I hold a stick in my hand and use it to move a stone. According to Aquinas, my hand, the stick, and the stone all move at the same time. Aquinas's causal proof, then, proceeds like this. We see motion all around us, such as the motion of the winds. At the very moment that the winds are moving, there are larger physical forces at work that create this motion. In medieval science, the motion of the moon is responsible for the motion of the winds. But the moon itself moves because it too is being simultaneously moved by other celestial motions, such as the planets, the sun, and the stars. According to Aquinas, simultaneous causal sequences of motion cannot go on forever, and we must eventually find a first cause of this motion, which "everyone understands to be God."

The second argument, from efficient causes, similarly focuses on sequences of simultaneous events. We experience various kinds of effects, and in every case we assign an efficient cause to each effect. The efficient cause of the statue is the work of the sculptor. If we took away the activity of the sculptor, we would not have the effect, the statue. But there is an order of efficient causes: the hammer strikes the chisel which in turn strikes the marble. Again, we find this simultaneous sequence of efficient causes in the natural world. But it is impossible to have an infinitely long sequence of simultaneous efficient causes, and so we arrive at a first efficient cause.

The third argument, from necessary being, considers the fact that all of the objects that we see around us exist only as a matter of *possibility*. For example, there was a time when this tree did not exist; it exists now, and finally it will go out of existence. According to Aquinas, possible objects do not contain the explanation of their existence within themselves. Instead, a possible object, such as this tree, exists because of some other thing independent of the tree itself. Thus, possible object A relies for its existence on possible object B, which in turn rests on possible object C. Once again, we cannot have a simultaneously long sequences of possible objects. There must be some necessary being— whose existence is explained by itself—which accounts for possible beings.

Proofs from Perfection and Order

The final two proofs rest on different strategies. Aquinas's fourth proof is from the degrees of perfection that we see in things. In our experience we find that some things are more and some less good, true, and noble. But these and other ways of comparing things are possible only because things resemble in their different ways something that is the maximum. There must be something that is truest, noblest, and best. Similarly, we can say about things that they have more or less being, or a lower or higher form of being, as when we compare a stone with a rational creature. Thus, there must also be "something which is most being." Aquinas then argues that the maximum in any genus is the cause of everything in that genus, as fire, which is the maximum of heat, is the cause of all hot things. From this, Aquinas concludes that "there must also be something which is to all beings the cause of their being, goodness, and every other perfection; and this we call God."

Finally, Aquinas constructs a proof for God based on the order that we see in the world. We see things such as parts of the natural world or parts of the human body, which do not possess intelligence but nevertheless behave in an orderly manner. They act in special and predictable ways to achieve certain ends or functions. But things that lack intelligence, such as an ear or a lung, cannot carry out a function unless it is directed by something that does have intelligence. This is just as an arrow is directed by an archer. Aquinas concludes that "some intelligent being exists by whom all natural things are directed to their ends; and this being we call God."

Assessment of the Proofs

Aquinas's five proofs are a substantial intellectual achievement and are among the most famous arguments in Western philosophy. Nevertheless, his proofs are only as strong as the assumptions upon which they are based. The first three proofs are especially vulnerable in this regard. Today we would reject the entire notion of "simultaneous causal sequences"; to say that A causes B assumes that A occurs before B in time. Also, science has come a long way since the Middle Ages and there is almost nothing in the system of medieval astronomy that we can relate to today. Thus, we must reject Aquinas's conception of simultaneous causes tracing up through the heavens. Another problem with the first three proofs is that, even if successful, they do not lead to the idea of a God who is conscious and personal. These are, however, proofs that Aquinas considered philosophical corroborations of the religious notion of God, and we must remember that they were composed in the context of his theological task. In spite of the problems with the first three proofs, his arguments nevertheless advanced beyond Avicenna's. Also, as philosophers in later centuries refined the causal argument for God, they relied on a modified version of Aquinas's distinction between causal sequences.

The fourth proof is also questionable because of its assumption that fire, for example, is the maximum of heat—a view initially developed by Aristotle. Science today would reject this contention. The final proof—based on natural purposes—is a different case. For centuries following Aquinas, philosophers believed that we could decisively prove God's existence based on the appearance of natural order in the world. In point of fact, they argued, the world exhibits design, and the most reasonable explanation for this is that a cosmic designer produced the natural design around us. The greatest challenge to this argument occurred during the 19th century with the theory of evolution. Darwin and other theorists offered an alternative and thorough explanation for the apparent design that we see in the natural world. At minimum, theologians could no longer argue that a cosmic designer was the only possible explanation of design.

KNOWLEDGE OF GOD'S NATURE

To prove *that* God exists does not tell us positively *what* God is. Traditional theologians commonly state that there is a vast gulf between the powers of human knowledge and the infinitude of God's nature. Aquinas was always aware of this virtually unbridgeable gulf, saying that "the divine reality surpasses all human conceptions of it." But each of the five proofs adds something to the conception of God. As First Mover, God is seen as unchangeable and therefore eternal. As First Cause, God is seen as all powerful to create. To say that God is a necessary rather than a possible being is to say that God is pure actuality. As the ultimate truth and goodness, God is perfection itself. And as the orderer or designer of the universe, God is the supreme intelligence directing things.

The Negative Way *(Via Negativa)*

Although the five proofs give us some information about God, it is more indirect knowledge than it is direct. We know what we do about God only in a negative way by knowing what God is not. The proof shows only that God is *un*moved, and that therefore he must be *un*changeable. This must mean that God is *not* in time, and is therefore eternal. Similarly, to account for motion, it is necessary that there be something that does *not* have potentiality—it is matter in particular that has potentiality—therefore, in God there is nothing material. God is pure act and *im*material. Since there is neither matter nor potentiality in God, he is then *simple, without* any composition. This idea of God's *simplicity* is achieved not by our direct apprehension of it but by way of negation, whereby we *remove* from our conception of God such notions as compositeness and corporeality. Philosophically, God's simplicity means that unlike creatures that possess both potentiality and actuality, God is simply pure act. Whereas a creature *has* its being, God *is* his being. Whereas in creatures existence is one thing and essence another, God's essence is his existence. But even these positive-sounding attributes of God are in the end ways of saying what God is not, saying that God is other than creatures.

Knowledge by Analogy

All human language is inevitably derived from our experience with things in our sensed world. For this reason, as Aquinas realized, the names that we apply to God are the same ones we use when describing human beings and things. These names, such as *wise* or *loving*, certainly cannot mean the same thing when applied to finite people on the one hand and to the infinite God on the other. If, then, these names and words mean different things to us when we use them respectively to describe creatures and God, the critical question is whether we can know anything at all about God from our knowledge about creatures.

Aquinas distinguishes between three possible ways that our human vocabulary might relate to God. The first possible type of relation is *univocal,* in which case words, such as *wise,* used about God and human beings would mean exactly the same things and would imply that God and people are alike in nature. This clearly cannot be the case since God and people are not alike. God is infinite, and human beings are finite. A second possible type of relation is what Aquinas calls *equivocal,* where terms applied to both would mean totally different things for each, implying that God and people are totally unlike. In this case our knowledge of people would give us no knowledge whatsoever about God. Aquinas insists, however, that insofar as we are creatures of God, we must in some degree, even though imperfectly, reflect the nature of God. The third and final possibility is that people and God are neither totally alike nor totally unlike, but that their relationship is *analogical.* It is, in a sense, midway between univocal and equivocal. When a word such as *wise* is used to describe both God and humans, it does not mean that God and humans are wise in exactly the same sense, nor does it mean that they are wise in completely different ways.

uses
anselm); aristotle
augustine,?
plato,?

Analogy for Aquinas is an ontological term—that is, a term about the being or nature of a thing. The notion of "analogy" implies that what is in God is also in human beings. This is more than mere metaphor or simile. To say that there is an analogical relationship between God and us is to say that we resemble God. "Resemble" here means that we are in some degree what God uniquely is. For example, Aquinas says that people have a degree of being. God, on the other hand, *is* Being. What makes the relationship between God and us analogical is, therefore, the fact that we are linked together with God by common attributes. Human nature derives its very existence from God, and this fact accounts for the common elements in both God and people. When we use a word such as *wise,* we refer to (but do not fully comprehend) an attribute perfectly realized in God and only partially realized in human beings. Wisdom is something that exists both in God and us. What makes wisdom different in people is that our minds are located in our physical bodies and are dependent upon our senses. When we think and speak, we do so discursively, saying and thinking a word or an idea at a time. God, being pure act with no material substance, knows all things simultaneously. Analogy would mean, then, that we know what God knows but not everything that God knows and not the way God knows it. Again, what makes this analogical relation possible is that God's creatures bear a likeness to God. Analogy means, then, that we are simultaneously like and unlike God. To know what people are like is to have *some* degree of knowledge about God. For this reason, names and terms that people formulate first of all about human beings have some meaning when applied to God, provided that the meanings in each case are adjusted to reflect the different degrees and types of being which differentiate God from people.

CREATION

Throughout his discussion of the proofs of God's existence and of God's nature, Aquinas assumes the notion of creation. According to the five proofs, the objects of our senses cannot derive their existence from themselves but must have it from the First Mover, First Cause, Necessary Being, Perfect Being, and Orderer of the Universe. However, Aquinas sees specific philosophical problems concerning the theory of creation.

Is the Created Order Eternal?

According to biblical revelation, creation occurred at a point in time. How, though, could philosophical reasoning support this doctrine of faith? Aquinas did not think that it is possible to decide in a philosophical manner whether the world has existed from eternity or whether it was created in time. That it was created must follow from the revealed nature of God. Being pure act and free, God willed to create. Aquinas distinguishes Creation, as a free act, from a *necessary* emanation, as taught by Plotinus. But since God is pure act, he could have acted to create the world from eternity. In short, there is no contradiction in saying that God created and that he created eternally. There might be a more serious question of contradiction if we argued that God created in time, since this could imply potentiality in God—that before he created things he was potentially a creator. Aquinas was somewhat inconclusive on this point, which raised questions about his orthodoxy. But he maintained that Aristotle, who argued that God had created from eternity, could not be refuted, in spite of Bonaventura's attempts to do so. In the end, Aquinas settled the question by accepting the authority of revelation, concluding that philosophically either solution is possible.

Creation out of Nothing

What does it mean to say that God creates out of nothing, or *ex nihilo?* Again, Aquinas thought that if God is the source of all being, then there cannot be any other source of being. There is, in short, no useful comparison between God and an artist at this point. An artist rearranges already existing materials, as when a sculptor fashions a statue. Prior to creation there is only God: God does not act upon any existing material since no such primary matter exists. Only God exists originally, and whatever comes to be derives its existence from God. Everything, then, is a creature of God, because it came ultimately from God, and there are no independent sources of being other than God.

Is This the Best Possible World?

Philosophers often speculate about whether the current world is indeed the best of all possible worlds that God could have created. To answer this question, according to Aquinas, we need to bear two things in mind. First, unlike God, who is infinite, we are finite, and our perfection will therefore be less than God's. Secondly, the universe cannot be any better than or any different from what creatures are capable of by their nature. Throughout this discussion, Aquinas stresses that certain limitations must pervade the universe only because creating certain kinds of beings sets limits on others. The world is the best only in the sense that it contains the best arrangement possible of the kinds of things that have been created.

Evil as Privation

If God is all powerful and good, why does suffering occur? This question is aggravated further when we consider that everything that exists comes from God. Since there is evil in the world, it would appear that evil, too, comes from God. But Aquinas accepted Augustine's solution of the problem of evil, saying that evil is not anything positive. God is not the cause of evil because evil is not a thing. Natural evil—that is, the suffering caused by forces of nature—represents the absence (or privation) in something that is otherwise good in itself. For example, blindness consists of the absence of sight. Similarly, moral evil—that is, the suffering caused by willful human choices—also involves an absence, and is thus not a positive thing. In this sense, absence consists of an inappropriate type of action, although the action as such is not evil. The act of the adulterer, Aquinas says, is evil not in its physical aspects but in that which makes it adultery, namely, the absence of correctness. Still, in the moral realm, there appear to be those who choose to indulge in ways that are obviously wicked. Like Plato, Aquinas argues that people always will their acts with the hope that some good will come out of them, however diabolical the acts may seem. The adulterer never wills his or her act solely as an evil but rather for that aspect of the act that is good and affords pleasure.

The question remains, however, why God should permit defects both in physical nature and in people's moral behavior. Aquinas replies that the perfection of the universe required the existence of various kinds of beings. This includes corruptible as well as incorruptible beings, which consequently provides the possibility for defect and suffering. But having created corruptible things, there will be corruption. In the moral order, the primary fact is that people possess freedom. Without freedom we could not love God; with freedom we possess the capacity to choose for or against God, right, just, and good. Evil is the possibility for wrong choice that accompanies a persons' freedom. God did not will its actual occurrence, even though God willed that people should have freedom. The possibility of evil is the unavoidable corollary of the greater good that comes from our freedom to love and serve God. Aquinas therefore concludes that God is not the cause of evil even though by creating human beings with freedom he permitted the possibility of it. Moral evil, under these circumstances, is the product of the will whereby the essentially good element in the willed act lacks its true end.

The Range of Created Being: The Chain of Being

Aquinas describes the universe as consisting of a full range, or hierarchy, of different things—as if there existed a great *chain of being*. These beings differ in species and in the degree of their being. This full range of beings is needed so that God's perfection can be most adequately represented in the total created order. Because no single creature could ever reflect God's perfection suitably, God created many levels of being, which overlap in such a way that there are no gaps in the structure of being. Thus, below God is the hierarchy of angels. Aquinas calls these *intelligences* and says that they are immaterial. We can know of their existence both through reason and through revelation. Reason requires their existence in order to account for the full continuity of beings from the lowest to the highest without any unaccounted for spaces. Below these angels are human beings, whose nature includes both material and spiritual aspects. Then come animals, plants, and finally the four elements of air, earth, fire, and water. As to revelation, the Bible speaks of these intelligences in various terms, such as principles, powers, and seraphim.

Aquinas points out that there are no gaps between the various levels of beings: they interlock like links in a chain. For example, the lowest species of animals overlap with the highest forms of plants, the highest forms of animals correspond to the lowest form of human nature, and the highest element in people (intelligence) corresponds to what uniquely constitutes angels. What distinguishes the beings on all these levels is their particular composite nature, or the way their form and matter are related. In a person, the soul is the form, and the body is the material substance. Angels have no material substance, and because they do not possess the kind of matter that designates the particular qualities of a specific individual, each angel is its own species. Each angel, then, occupies a separate grade in the hierarchy of being, differing from other angels in the degree or amount of its being. The highest angel is nearest God and the lowest nearest human beings, and below us are the animals, plants, and single elements, all representing the full range of created beings.

MORALITY AND NATURAL LAW

Aquinas built upon Aristotle's theory of ethics. Like Aristotle, he considered ethics a quest for happiness. Moreover, following Aristotle's lead, Aquinas argued that happiness is connected closely with our end or purpose. To achieve happiness we must fulfill our purpose. But whereas Aristotle envisioned a *naturalistic* morality whereby people could achieve virtue and happiness by fulfilling their natural capacities or end, Aquinas added to this his concept of a person's *supernatural* end. As a Christian, Aquinas viewed human nature as having both its source and ultimate end in God. For this reason, human nature does not contain its own standards of fulfillment. It is not enough for us to simply be human and to exercise our natural functions and abilities in order to achieve perfect happiness. Aristotle thought such a naturalistic ethics was possible. Aquinas agreed with most of this claim, adding only that the Aristotelian ethics is incomplete. Aquinas therefore argued that there is a double level to morality corresponding to our natural end and to our supernatural end.

The ingredients of our moral experience are provided by human nature. For one thing, the fact that we have bodies inclines us to certain kinds of acts. Our senses become the vehicle for appetites and passions. Our senses also provide a certain level of knowledge about sensible objects so that we are attracted to some objects, which we perceive as pleasurable and good (concupiscent appetite), and repel some objects, which we perceive as harmful, painful, or bad (irascible appetite). This attraction and rejection are the rudiments of our capacity for love and pleasure, and hate and fear.

In animals these irascible and concupiscent appetites immediately control and direct behavior. In a person, however, the will, in collaboration with the power of reason, consummates the human act. The will is the agency that inclines a person toward the achievement of good. That is, our full range of appetites seeks to be satisfied, and the process of satisfaction requires that we make choices between alternative objects. We must make this choice by our wills under the direction of reason. If we make right choices, then we achieve happiness. But not every choice is a correct one. For this reason, the will by itself cannot always make the right move; the intellect must be the guide. Nor is the intellect the final source of knowledge, for our supernatural end requires God's grace and revealed truth. Still, the will represents our appetite for the good and right, whereas the intellect has the function and capacity for apprehending the general or universal meaning of what is good. The intellect is our highest faculty, and a natural end requires that the intellect, as well as all the other faculties, seek its appropriate object. The appropriate object of the intellect is truth, and truth in its fullness is God. When the intellect directs the will, then, it helps the will to choose the good. The intellect knows, however, that there is a hierarchy of goods, and that some goods are limited and must not be mistaken for our most appropriate and ultimate good. Riches, pleasure, power, and knowledge are all goods and are legitimate objects of the appetites, but they cannot produce our deepest happiness because they do not possess the character of the universal good that our souls seek. The perfect happiness is found not in created things, but in God, who is the supreme good.

Moral constitution consists, then, of sensuality, appetites, the will, and reason. What confers upon a person the attributes of morality is that these elements are the ingredients of *free* acts. If I am moved to act by my appetites in a mechanical or rigorously determined way, then my acts would not be free and could not be considered from a moral point of view. Not only is freedom a prerequisite for an act to be considered *moral;* Aquinas adds that an act is *human* only if it is free. For freedom is possible only where there is knowledge of alternatives and the power of will to make choices. Virtue, or goodness, consists in making the right choices, the mean between extremes. Aquinas agreed with Aristotle that the virtues of the natural person are achieved when the appetites are duly controlled by the will and reason. The dominant or "cardinal" natural virtues are courage, temperance, justice, and prudence. In addition to these particular virtues, our natural end is further realized through our knowledge of the natural law, that is, the moral law.

Natural Law

Morality, as Aquinas viewed it, is not an arbitrary set of rules for behavior. The basis of moral obligation, he thought, is found, first of all, in human nature itself. Built into our nature are various inclinations, such as the preservation of life, the propagation of species, and, because people are rational, the inclination toward the search for truth. The basic moral truth is simply to "do good and avoid evil." As a rational being, then, I am under a basic natural obligation to protect my life and health, in which case suicide and carelessness are wrong. Secondly, the natural inclination to propagate the species forms the basis of the union of wife and husband, and any other basis for this relation would be wrong. And thirdly, because we seek for truth, we can do this best by living in peace in society with all others who are also engaged in this quest. To ensure an ordered society, human laws are fashioned for the direction of the community's behavior. All these activities of preserving life, propagating the species, forming an ordered society under human laws, and pursuing the quest for truth—all these, again, pertain to us at our natural level. The moral law is founded upon human nature, upon the natural inclinations toward specific types of behavior, and upon the reason's ability to discern the right course of conduct. Because human nature has certain fixed features, the rules for behavior that correspond to these features are called *natural law.*

Aristotle already developed much of this theory of natural law. In his *Ethics,* Aristotle distinguished between natural justice and conventional justice. Some forms of behavior, he said, are wrong only after a law has been made to regulate such behavior. It is wrong, for example, to drive a vehicle at certain speeds only because a speed limit has been set, but there is nothing in nature that requires that vehicles travel at that speed. Such a law is therefore not natural but conventional, because before the law was passed, there was nothing wrong with traveling at speeds exceeding the new limit. On the other hand, there are some laws that are derived from nature, so that the behavior they regulate has always been wrong, as in the case of murder. But Aquinas did not limit his treatment of natural law to the simple notion that in some way human reason is able to discover the natural basis for human conduct. Instead, he reasoned that if human existence and nature can be fully understood only when seen in relation to God, then natural law must be described in metaphysical and theological terms, as the Stoics and Augustine had done.

Law, Aquinas says, has to do primarily with reason. Human reason is the standard of our actions because it belongs to reason to direct our whole activity toward our end. Law consists of these rules and measures of human acts and therefore is based upon reason. But Aquinas argues that since God created all things, human nature and the natural law are best understood as the product of God's wisdom or reason. From this standpoint, Aquinas distinguishes between *four* kinds of law.

Eternal Law   This law refers to the fact that "the whole community of the universe is governed by Divine Reason. Because of this, the very notion of the government of things in God the Ruler of the universe, has the nature of a law. And since the Divine Reason's conception of things is not subject to time but is eternal . . . therefore it is that this kind of law must be called eternal."

Natural Law   For Aquinas, natural law consists of that portion of the eternal law that pertains particularly to people. His reasoning is that "all things share somewhat of the eternal law . . . from its being imprinted on them" and from this all things "derive their respective inclinations to their proper acts and ends." This is particularly true of people, because our rational capacity "has a share of the Eternal Reason, whereby it has a natural inclination to its proper act and end." And, Aquinas says, "this participation of the eternal law in the rational creature is called the natural law," and again, "the natural law is nothing else than the rational creature's participation in the eternal law." We have already noted the basic precepts of the natural law as being the preservation of life, propagation and education of offspring, and pursuit of truth and a peaceful society. Thus the natural law consists of broad general principles that reflect God's intentions for people in creation.

Human Law   This refers to the specific statutes of governments. These statutes or human laws are derived from the general precepts of natural law. Just as "we draw conclusions of the various sciences" from "naturally known indemonstrable principles," so also "from the precepts of the natural law . . . human reason needs to proceed to the more particular determination of certain matters." And "these particular determinations, devised by human reason, are called human laws." What was so far-reaching about this conception of human law was that it repudiated the notion that a law was a law only because it was decreed by a sovereign. Aquinas argued that what gives a rule the character of law is its moral dimension, its conformity with the precepts of natural law, and its agreement with the moral law. Taking Augustine's formula, namely, that "that which is not just seems to be no law at all," Aquinas said that "every human law has just so much of the nature of law, as it is derived from the law of nature." But, he adds, "if in any point it deflects from the law of nature, it is no longer a law but a perversion of law." Such laws no longer bind in conscience but are sometimes obeyed to prevent an even greater evil. Aquinas went further than simply denying the character of law to a command of a government that violated the natural moral law; such a command, he said, should not be obeyed. Some laws, he said, "may be unjust through being opposed to the Divine Good: such are the laws of tyrants inducing to idolatry, or to anything else contrary to the Divine Law." He concluded that "laws of this kind must nowise be observed, because . . . *we ought to obey God rather than human beings.*"

Divine Law   The function of law, Aquinas said, is to direct people to their proper end. Since we are ordained to an end of eternal happiness, in addition to our temporal happiness, there must be a kind of law that can direct us to that supernatural end. Here, in particular, Aquinas parted company with Aristotle, for Aristotle knew only about our natural purpose and end, and for this purpose the natural law known by human reason was considered a sufficient guide. But the eternal happiness to which people are ordained, said Aquinas, is "in proportion to a person's natural faculty." Therefore, "it was necessary that besides the natural and the human law, people should be directed to their end by a law given by God." The *divine law*, then, is available to us through revelation and is found in the Scriptures. It is not the product of human reason but is given to us through God's grace to ensure that we all know what we must do to fulfill both our natural and, especially, our supernatural ends. The difference between the natural law and divine law is this: The natural law represents our rational knowledge of the good by which the intellect directs our wills to control our appetites and passions. This, in turn, leads us to fulfill our natural end by achieving the cardinal virtues of justice, temperance, courage, and prudence. The divine law, on the other hand, comes directly from God through revelation and is a gift of God's grace. Through this we are directed to our supernatural ends and obtained the theological virtues of faith, hope, and love. These virtues are infused into human nature by God's grace, and are not the result of our natural abilities. In this way, Aquinas completed and surpassed the naturalistic ethics of Aristotle. He showed how the natural human desire to know God can be assured and how revelation becomes the guide for reason. He also described the manner in which our highest nature is perfected through God's grace.

THE STATE

The state, Aquinas said, is a natural institution. It is derived from human nature. In this view, Aquinas was following the political theory of Aristotle, from whom he took the phrase that "people are by nature social animals." But insofar as Aquinas had a different view of human nature, he was bound to have a somewhat different political philosophy also. The difference lay in the two conceptions of the role or task of the state. Aristotle supposed that the state could provide for all the needs of people because he knew only about our natural human needs. Aquinas, on the other hand, believed that, in addition to our material or natural needs, we also have a supernatural end. The state is not equipped to deal with this more ultimate end. It is the church that directs us to this end. But Aquinas did not simply divide these two realms of human concern, giving one to the state and the other to the church. Instead, he looked upon the state, and explained its origin, in terms of God's creation.

The state, in this view, is willed by God and has its God-given function, which addresses the social component of human nature. For Aquinas, the state is not a product of people's sinfulness, as it was for Augustine. On the contrary, Aquinas says that even "in the condition of innocence people would have lived in society." But even then, "a common life could not exist, unless there were someone in control, to attend to the common good." The state's function is to secure the common good by keeping the peace, organizing the activities of the citizens into harmonious pursuits, providing for the resources to sustain life, and preventing, as far as possible, obstacles to the good life. This last item concerning threats to the good life gives to the state not only a function tied to our ultimate human end; it also accounts for the state's position in relation to the church.

The state is subordinate to the church. To say this did not mean that Aquinas considered the church a super-state. Aquinas saw no contradiction in saying that the state has a sphere in which it has a legitimate function and that at the same time it must subordinate itself to the church. Within its own sphere the state is autonomous. But, insofar as there are aspects of human life that bear upon our supernatural end, the state must not put arbitrary hindrances in the way to frustrate our spiritual life. The church does not challenge the autonomy of the state; it only says that the state is not absolutely autonomous. Within its own sphere, the state is what Aquinas calls a "perfect society," having its own end and the means for achieving it. But the state is like a person; neither the state nor a person has only a natural end. Our human spiritual end cannot be achieved, as Aquinas says, "by human power, but by divine power." Still, because our destiny is connected with spiritual happiness, the state must recognize this aspect of human affairs: in providing for the common good of the citizens, the sovereign must pursue the community's end with a consciousness of our spiritual end. Under these circumstances, the state does not become the church, but it does mean that the sovereign "should order those things which lead to heavenly beatitude and prohibit, as far as possible, their contraries." In this way, Aquinas affirmed the legitimacy of the state and its autonomy in its own sphere. The state should be subordinate to the church only to insure that our ultimate spiritual end be taken into account.

As the state rules the behavior of its citizens through law, the state is in turn limited by the requirements of just laws. Nowhere is Aquinas's rejection of the absolute autonomy of the state so clearly articulated as when he describes the standards for the making of human or positive law. We have already analyzed the different types of law: eternal, natural, human, and divine. The state is particularly the source of human law. Each government is faced with the task of fashioning specific statutes to regulate the behavior of its citizens under the particular circumstances of its own time and place. Lawmaking, however, must not be an arbitrary act but instead must be done under the influence of the natural law, which involves human participation in God's eternal law. Human-made laws must consist of particular rules derived from the general principles of natural law. Any human law that violates the natural law loses its character as law, as a "perversion of law," and loses its binding force in the consciences of humanity. The lawmaker has authority to legislate from God and is responsible to God. If the sovereign decrees an unjust law by violating God's divine law, then, according to Aquinas, such a law "must in no way be observed."

The political sovereign has this authority from God, and the purpose of this authority is to provide for the common good. Authority is never to be used as an end in itself or for selfish ends. Nor must the common good be interpreted in such a way that we lose sight of the individual within the collective whole. The common good must be the good of concrete people. Thus Aquinas says that "the proper effect of law is to lead its subjects to their proper virtue . . . to make those to whom it is given good." The only "true ground" of the lawgiver is the intention to secure "the common good regulated according to divine justice," and thus it follows that "the effect of the law is to make people good." Thus, the phrase *common good* has no meaning for Aquinas except insofar as it results in the good of individuals. At the same time, Aquinas says that "the goodness of any part is considered in comparison with the whole. . . . Since then every person is a part of the state, it is impossible that a person be good unless he be well proportionate to the common good." The entire scheme of society and its laws is characterized by the rational elements in it. Law itself, Aquinas says, is "an ordinance of reason for the common good, made by the ruler who has care of the community, and promulgated." Thus, although the sovereign has authority and power, the laws must not reflect this power in an unrestrained manner, but as domesticated by reason and aimed at the common good.

HUMAN NATURE AND KNOWLEDGE

Human Nature

Aquinas had a distinctive conception of human nature. Human nature, he said, is a physical substance. What made this a unique conception was that Aquinas insisted upon the *unity* of human nature. Plato had talked about the soul as being imprisoned in the body. Similarly, Augustine considered the soul as a spiritual substance. Both Plato and Aristotle agreed that the soul is the form of the body but did not see, as Aquinas did, that the soul of a person is as dependent upon the body as the body is upon the soul. To say, as Aquinas did, that a person is a physical substance underscored the substantial unity of human nature. Human beings *are* a unity of body and soul. Without the soul, the body would have no form. Without the body, the soul would not have its required organs of sense through which to gain its knowledge. As a physical substance, we are a composite of soul and body. The angels are pure intelligence and have no body, but although people, too, are rational creatures, our special attribute is to exist and function as people only when unified as body and soul. Since the soul confers upon us bodily form, it is the soul that gives us life, understanding, and special physical features. The soul accounts also for our human capacity for sensation and the powers of intellect and will. Our highest human capacity is located in the intellect, making us rational animals and conferring upon us the means by which to attain the contemplation of God.

Knowledge

Aquinas followed Aristotle's theory of knowledge. He was especially impressed with Aristotle's answer to those who doubted that our human minds could arrive at certainty on any subject. Some ancient philosophers argued that there could be no certainty since human knowledge is limited to sense perception, and objects in the sensible world are always in flux. Plato agreed with this estimate of sense knowledge, saying that it could give us no certainty. But Plato avoided intellectual pessimism by assuming the existence of a separate world, the intelligible world, contrasting it with the visible world. For Plato, there are Forms that possess eternal being and provide the basis for knowledge. Augustine adapted this Platonic theory of Forms to Christian thought by saying that God possesses these Forms in his mind and that human beings are able to know the truth insofar as these Forms illumine our minds through the divine light. But Aquinas accepted Aristotle's approach, saying that the human mind knows what it does through its confrontation with actual concrete objects. Our minds are able to grasp what is permanent and stable within sensible things. When we sense things or people, we *know* their essence—for example, the essence of tree and human—even though they are in the process of change. These things indeed are in flux, we are not in doubt about what they are. Our intellects, then, *see* the universal *in* the particular things; we *abstract* the universal from the particular. Following Aristotle, he calls this mental capacity the *active intellect.*

Aquinas denied that universals exist apart from particular concrete objects. For example, there is no *humanity* distinct from individual people. There is only the abstracted concept—not an independently existing Form—which our active intellect grasps. For Aquinas, then, we can have no knowledge without sense experience, for nothing can be in the intellect that was not first in the senses (*nihil in intellectu quod prius non fuerit in sensu*).

For the most part, Aquinas was a moderate realist regarding the problem of universals. Following both Avicenna and Abelard, he held that universals exist (1) *outside of things* (*ante rem*) but as such only as the divine concepts in God's mind, (2) *in things* (*in re*) as the concrete individual essence in all members of a species, and (3) *in the mind* (*then post rem*) after abstracting the universal concept from the individual. The problem of universals had one more major treatment in the Middle Ages, and this time it was given a different solution by William of Ockham.

SCOTUS, OCKHAM, AND ECKHART

Aquinas's most important achievement was to fuse theology with philosophy. Over the next century, the most significant reactions to his work were from those who tried to split theology and philosophy apart again. The key figures here are John Duns Scotus (1265–1308), William of Ockham (ca. 1280–1349), and Johannes Eckhart (ca. 1260–1327). These thinkers did not disagree with everything Aquinas taught. Indeed, on many matters they were in general agreement with his ideas. However, they each set out a basic criticism that had the effect of driving a wedge between philosophy and theology—between faith and reason. Against Aquinas's notion of the supremacy of reason, Scotus argued that God's *will* (rather than God's reason) is most supreme; this became known as the theory of *voluntarism*. Against Aquinas's notion that universals have at least some kind of real existence, Ockham argued that universals are only words; this view became known as *terminism* or *nominalism*. And against Aquinas's highly rational and technical articulation of religious concepts, Eckhart felt that religion involves a more direct encounter with God through the spiritual exercise of *mysticism*.

Voluntarism

Why should these three developments have the effect of separating philosophy and theology? The problem becomes clear when we consider some of the implications of voluntarism. Aquinas argued that, with both human beings and God, the will is subordinate to the intellect; reason guides or determines the will. Scotus rejected this view. If God's will was subordinate to his reason, or was limited by eternal truths, then God himself would be limited. In that situation, God could not do whatever he wants since he would be bound or determined by some prior rational standard looming *above* him. So, if God is to be free in any meaningful way, he must have an absolutely free will. Consequently, God's *will* is his dominant faculty, and not his reason. During the

19th century, this position was dubbed *voluntarism* based on the Latin word *voluntas,* or will.

There is an important moral consequence to saying that God's will is primary over his intellect: God's actions and moral commands are acts of will and as such nonrational. God's moral law does not reflect his adherence to the standards of rationality, but rather his unconstrained will. Accordingly, God could have willed any kind of moral rules he chose. Both murder and adultery could, strictly speaking, become good actions if God willed them to be so. To put it bluntly, morality would seem to be the result of an arbitrary choice on God's part. And, if moral standards are arbitrary edicts from God, then it would be equally arbitrary for God to punish us or condemn us to hell for violating these edicts. If God is absolutely free then he can reward or punish any behavior he chooses. For Scotus, then, morality is grounded not in reason but in will. Consequently, morality cannot be a subject of rational and philosophical inquiry, but only a matter of faith and acceptance.

A broader consequence of voluntarism is that there can be no *natural theology* by which human reason discovers any divine rational order to the universe. That is, on this view we could not discover any rational connection between the world of experience and God. Proofs for God's existence are at best only *probable* demonstrations, and the existence of God becomes a matter of faith, not a matter of philosophical discovery. Rational knowledge is thus limited to the empirical world, and religious knowledge in general becomes a product of divine illumination or revelation. In this way, the subject matter of philosophy is split off from that of theology.

The alternative to voluntarism is a position called *intellectualism*—that God's reason is primary over his will, and God's choices are in fact directed by rational standards. Aquinas held this view when saying that we know moral principles through a *natural light,* which we habitually contain in our consciences. On this view, morality is capable of an intellectual discipline insofar as the principles of good can be discovered rationally. And, from a broader perspective, the entire universe created by God in fact reflects God's rational mind and choices. As philosophers, we can view the rational order in creation, and make logically valid inferences about God's existence and nature. For centuries following Scotus, most great theologians and philosophers took some stand on the voluntarism-intellectualism dispute.

Nominalism

Like Scotus, Ockham was a voluntarist, and some of his more radical statements on the subject created problems for him within the Catholic Church hierarchy. Ockham, though, is perhaps best remembered for his theory of *nominalism,* the view that universal terms such as *humanity* are simply *signs* or *names* that designate mental concepts that we form when looking at particular things. The central problem of universals is whether terms such as *humanity* refer to any reality other than particular humans, for example, James and John. Is there a *substance* in addition to these particular humans to which the *univer-*

sal term *humanity* refers? For Ockham, only concrete individual things exist, and when we use universal terms we are simply thinking in an orderly way about particular things. Universal terms such as *humanity* refer equally to James and John, but not because there is some real substance of "human-ness" in which both James and John *share* or *participate*. Rather, it is because the nature that is James is like the nature that is John. Human reason, then, is limited to the world of individual things. Ockham's view was genuinely empirical. Our minds, he said, do not know anything more than individual things and their qualities even though we are able to use universal terms. Such terms are nothing more than names for classes of individual things. Above all, universal terms do not refer to a realm of reality beyond the world of concrete individual things. One of Ockham's arguments for nominalism is based on a principle of simplicity known as Ockham's razor: "what can be explained on fewer principles is explained needlessly by more." In this case, we should not postulate two realms of existence when one will do. The realist actually posits three realms of existence: (1) individual objects, (2) the independently existing attributes that they have in common and (3) our mental concepts of these. On Ockham's account there are only two: (1) individual objects and (2) our verbalized mental concepts about those objects.

How did this view differ from Aquinas's treatment of the problem of universals? For the most part their views harmonize. Aquinas said that universals are found in particular things (*in re*), and are abstracted from things (*post rem*), after our experiences of them. However, Aquinas believed that universals exist in the mind of God (*ante rem*) and thus have a metaphysical status prior to individual things. If universals exist in the mind of God, then two people are alike because they share in this metaphysical reality in God's mind. Also, our human minds, when we think about universals, share in some way in God's thought. This is where Ockham parted company with Aquinas. He rejected the theory of divine ideas for the same reason Scotus had: God's will is supreme over God's reason. People are what they are because God chose to make them that way and not because they reflect an eternal pattern that exists in God's mind.

If our thoughts are restricted to individual things in experience, then our knowledge of these things does not lead to any reality beyond experience. Realists believed that universal terms pointed to something beyond individual things, and they accordingly felt that our use of such terms gave us reliable knowledge about reality beyond the empirical scene. And if we assume further that universals are ideas in God's mind, then we can conclude that philosophical reasoning about individual things could lead to various theological truths. There could thus be a natural theology. But Ockham's strict interpretation of universals had the effect of severing philosophy from metaphysics, making out of philosophy something more like science. Theology and religious truth could not be achieved by philosophy or science. Indeed, his position involves the theory of *double truth:* that one kind of truth is available through science or philosophy, and another kind of truth is received through revelation. The first truth is the product of human reason, and the other is a matter of faith. One kind of truth, moreover, cannot influence the other kind. The ultimate consequence of the double-truth theory was that theological and philosophical truths were not only independent and not derivable from each other but that these different truths could even contradict each other. This was the explicit teaching held by followers of Averroës. For example, they argued that, while it is true in philosophy that there is no personal immortality, such a theory is false for theology. Ockham had not gone that far in separating faith and reason. He had, nevertheless, set the stage for an empirical and scientific way of thinking about the facts of experience. His nominalism had the effect of separating science from metaphysics. The study of natural things became more and more independent of both metaphysical and theological explanations.

Mysticism

Strongly influenced by Neoplatonism, Eckhart offered a mystical approach to theology, which shifted emphasis from reason to feeling. Whereas Aquinas built his demonstrations of God's existence upon our experience of finite things, Eckhart urged people to pass beyond sensory knowledge, which is after all limited to material objects. Though he considered in great detail many traditional theological questions concerning God's nature, creation, and human nature, he was primarily a mystic who wanted to share with others his rich experiences of unity with God. This union, he believed, cannot be reached except by liberating oneself from the objects of the world. But union with God, he believed, is not achieved by human effort. Instead, only through God's grace and illumination is union consummated, and only in the deepest reaches of our souls do we grasp God in his fullness. When this happens, Eckhart says, people become one with God, for "we are transformed totally into God and are converted into him in a similar manner as in the sacrament the bread is converted into the body of Christ." Our mystical union with God is an experience beyond rationality, and Eckhart feels forced to use such terms as *wilderness* or *darkness* to express this mystical union. God, he believes, is both beyond existing beings and beyond knowledge. As such, normal human concepts and categories do not apply to him, and thus we must fall back on metaphorical descriptions of God and our experience of him.

Eckhart's mysticism did not supplant the more rational approach to theology espoused by Aquinas. However, he gave a new voice to the older Neoplatonic views of Pseudo-Dionysius and others, and had a strong impact on the mystical tradition that followed him.

PART THREE

Early Modern Philosophy

Galileo
(Corbis-Bettmann)

CHAPTER 9

Philosophy during the Renaissance

THE CLOSING OF THE MIDDLE AGES

*F*or most philosophers in the Middle Ages, the sky hung low, suggesting a close bond between heaven and earth, and, accordingly, between philosophy and theology. During that time, philosophy was virtually the handmaiden of theology, supplying religious thought with a reasoned account of its various doctrines. Plato and Aristotle had previously been concerned with the question of how the daily affairs of people could and should be related to the permanent structures of reality and to God. But the blending of theology and philosophy in the Middle Ages was an unstable one. For one thing, there were serious questions about the compatibility of Aristotle's nontheistic philosophy and the belief in the personal God of Christianity. Moreover, much of Aristotle's thought was made available at this time through Muslim thinkers, who construed Aristotle in ways that could hardly be accepted by Christians. Aquinas tried to reinterpret and Christianize Aristotle to overcome this incompatibility. Yet, philosophy now found itself to a great extent doing a task that it had not originally set out to do, namely, providing an intellectual and metaphysical foundation for revealed religion. Nor had philosophy been previously restrained by an institution the way it was by the church in the Middle Ages. It is true that even the earliest philosophers were in mortal jeopardy when their teachings threatened the status quo. Socrates, after all, was put to death for just this reason, and Aristotle left Athens to keep his townsfolk from "sinning against philosophy for a second time." Nevertheless, classical philosophy had been more or less free to move wherever the pursuit of truth led it. By confining itself simply to human reasoning, philosophy could dwell upon the subjects of human nature, ethics, the cosmos, God, and political authority. The spirit of medieval philosophy was sharply different in that its starting point was fixed by the doctrines of Christian theology, and the whole cultural atmosphere was affected by the predominance of the church.

191

By the close of the Middle Ages the medieval marriage between religion and philosophy became strained, and during the Renaissance there was a decisive separation between the two. The Renaissance—literally meaning "rebirth"—was a revival of Greek learning that took place during the 15th and 16th centuries. The writings of many philosophers and other great writers of antiquity once again became available. Scholars in the the Middle Ages were often only indirectly acquainted with Greek thinkers such as Plato, who they read about in works by Plotinus and Augustine. However, during the Renaissance Greek manuscripts were brought back from Athens to Rome, and these texts could now be directly accessed. For example, In Florence, Cosimo de' Medici founded an academy where Plato's philosophy was the chief subject of study. This academic influence, reinforced by similar academies in Naples and Rome, further diluted the preeminence of Aristotelian thought and scholastic methodology. Direct access to texts also created a deep fascination for language.

The discovery of ancient Greek and Roman literature had the effect of encouraging a new style of writing, which was less formal than the texts of medieval authors and had its expression increasingly in the vernacular. With the use of the vernacular, literature became more and more the property of the people. Wycliffe's rendering of the Bible into the vernacular would in time set off widespread reverberations in religious thought as the masses acquired direct access to the contents of the Scriptures. The extensive diffusion of culture was most effectively facilitated by Johann Gutenberg's invention of movable type in the mid-15th century, which made books readily available, smaller and easier to handle, and cheaper to buy. Printing presses soon appeared in Paris, London, Madrid, and in Italy at the monastery of Subiaco. The making of books and the use of the vernacular inevitably affected the type of writing philosophy in that the sense of liberation implied in these activities led philosophers to engage more in original formulations rather than in writing commentaries on authoritative thinkers. In time, the modern philosophers would write their treatises in the language of their own people, and thus Locke and Hume would write in English, Voltaire and Rousseau in French, and Kant in German.

As with the revived attention to Plato, interest in Epicureanism, Stoicism, and even skepticism was rekindled. A new breed of philosophy also emerged, namely humanism, which emphasized the study of classical authors and the central role of human reason in discovering truth and structuring the community. Humanist philosophers did not reject religion, but only affirmed that areas of human nature could be fruitfully studied by methods and assumptions not directly derived from religion. Other intellectual changes occurred during the Renaissance that impacted philosophy. Many European countries launched a religious Reformation against the domination of the Roman Catholic church. Scientists investigated the makeup of the physical world from a nonreligious perspective. In this chapter we will explore the philosophical themes of humanism, the Reformation, Skepticism, and the Scientific Revolution.

HUMANISM AND THE ITALIAN RENAISSANCE

The Renaissance began first as an artistic movement within Italy. Art through-out the Middle Ages was filled with religious symbolism and often viewed principally as a tool for teaching Biblical stories and doctrines to illiterate parishioners. Paintings and sculptures were far from being photographic images of their subject matter. Conveying very little sense of reality, early medieval art instead attempted to evoke an other-worldly spiritual quality. Late medieval art slowly moved more toward accurate depictions of the world, incorporating three-dimensional artistic techniques and a study of human anatomy. This facilitated a transition to Renaissance artwork, which exalted nature through the accurate depiction of landscapes and the human form. We see this in the works of two of the most famous Italian artists of the time. Michelangelo (1475–1564), even while serving the church with the genius of his art, gave strong expression to life-like forms. His Sistine Chapel painting of Adam is a striking description of physical beauty and strength. Leonardo da Vinci (1452–1519) looked behind beauty with care to the more minute ingredients of human anatomy, as we see in his Mona Lisa.

Like artwork, Italian Renaissance literature also paid special attention to human nature. A leading figure is the poet and historian Petrarch (1304–1374), who is often credited with founding the humanist movement. His poetical works emphasize the joys and sorrows that we routinely experience as human beings. As a champion of classical learning, his writings in history attempted to breathe life into events of ancient Rome. In other works he attacked the medieval Aristotelian tradition, and instead offered a Stoic perspective of life. His work *On the Remedies of Good and Bad Fortune* emphasizes the importance of moderation and the avoidance of senseless recreational activities, such as watching wrestling.

Pico

Perhaps the most vivid representative of Renaissance humanism is Pico della Mirandola (1463–1494). At an early age Pico was schooled in every imaginable area of classical study—Greek, Muslim, and Christian traditions, and even Jewish mysticism—and his philosophical writings combine all of these elements. His most famous piece is the *Oration on Human Dignity,* a brief speech that he composed in 1486. The philosophical context of this discussion is the classic theory of the "great chain of being." Philosophers from Aristotle on through the Middle Ages believed that there was a natural hierarchy of things in the world. At the very bottom of the chain we find rocks and other nonliving material things. Above that would be plants, and then simple animal forms such as worms and bugs. After that there are small animals like mice, and large animals like horses. Humans are next up on the chain, followed by angels, and then God. The medieval assumption behind this hierarchy is that all things are fixed in their unique places, and, as Aristotle argued, the purpose of a natural thing is defined in relation to where it resides on this scale.

Pico begins his *Oration* asking, What makes humanity so special? A typical answer to this question is that God placed us in a unique spot in the chain of being, just above animals and just below the angels. In this position, we can experience things in the physical world around us, yet at the same time we can grasp the spiritual truths of the eternal heavenly realm. As lofty as this answer sounds, Pico finds it unsatisfactory. Offering an alternative theory, he speculates about God's intentions when creating the world. "He gave animated souls to the celestial spheres. He filled the dregs of the lower world with a variety of animals." God, in fact, filled every conceivable niche in the chain of being with some kind of creature. Then, when it was time to create humans, God saw that every slot was already occupied by some thing. God's solution, then, was to allow people to select their own spot within the great chain. God tells Adam, "You can degenerate into the forms of the lower animals, or climb upward by your soul's reason, to a higher nature which is divine." What, then, makes humanity so special? The answer is that we have a unique ability to choose our own destiny, and, unlike the animals and even angels, we are not confined within any boundaries. Pico's observation is as true as it is insightful. People can in fact neglect their reason and civility and sink to the lowest level of animal existence, as we unfortunately see all to often in criminal behavior. Yet, people can also cultivate the highest levels of moral selflessness, as Gandhi did, or push scientific knowledge to its utmost limits. According to Pico, then, we are not rigidly locked into a predefined conception of human existence, as his medieval predecessors presumed. We should take pride in our ability to choose our human destiny, Pico argued, and make the most of it.

Machiavelli

Niccoló Machiavelli (1469–1527) was not technically speaking a humanist, but was nevertheless a product of the Italian Renaissance. The son of an Italian lawyer, he was a young man in his 20s when the great preacher Savonarola was at the height of his influence in Florence. Savonarola had established a remarkably successful democratic government in that city, but, in spite of his most virtuous efforts, he clashed with religious and political officials, and was ultimately executed. That such an influential man came to such a miserable end taught Machiavelli an early lesson about the relative power of good and evil forces in society. During his own career in government and diplomacy, he gave considerable thought to the rules or principles of effective political behavior, recording his thoughts in two books, *The Discourses* and *The Prince,* both composed in 1513 but published after his death. In *The Discourses,* Machiavelli writes approvingly of the Roman Republic, expressing enthusiasm for self-government and liberty. In *The Prince,* however, his emphasis is upon the need for an absolute monarch. ~~In the preference~~

The clue to Machiavelli's thought lies in the reason for his apparent inconsistency in these two books. By expressing a preference for an absolute monarch in *The Prince,* he did not intend to reject the desirability of self-government about which he spoke so approvingly in *The Discourses.* Rather, he felt that the moral decay in Italy at that time did not allow for the kind of popular government exemplified in the Roman Republic. Machiavelli thought that it was all too obvious that people are evil. He found corruption at every level of political and religious government; even the Popes of his day were of such bad repute that Machiavelli could write that "we Italians then owe to the Church of Rome and to her priests our having become irreligious and bad." A basically corrupt society requires a strong government. He believed that a monarchy—or rule by a single person—was the most preferable form of government since republics are rarely well-ordered.

The lasting fame of *The Prince* rests on its recommendation that rulers should develop the art of deception and do whatever necessary—even abandon traditional moral virtues—for political survival. Only the shrewdest and most crafty individuals, he believed, could endure the precarious art of governing. Basing his thought upon a very close inspection of the actual behavior of his contemporaries, he quickly concluded that to think of political behavior in moral terms would be to expose oneself to all the dangers that clever opponents could create. For this reason he developed an indifference to the claims of morality. Christian morality emphasized humility and lowliness, whereas the morality of ancient Greek and Roman religion emphasized the "grandeur of soul" and "strength of body." His chief criticism against Christian ethics was that it had "made men feeble, and caused them to become an easy prey to evil-minded men." Machiavelli envisioned a double standard of behavior, one for rulers and the other for the people. The masses, he believed, need to follow Christian ethics as a necessary means of securing peace within society. Being concerned only with the social usefulness of religion, and not its truth, Machiavelli put forward a pragmatic view of religion that many political philosophers would adopt for centuries to come.

In contrast to the morality of the masses, rulers, he believed, must have the freedom to adjust their acts to the requirements of each occasion without feeling bound to any objective moral rules. Machiavelli felt that the attitudes of the masses continually shifted, and this inconsistency must be matched by the ruler's shrewdness and swift adaptability. He writes that "People are ungrateful, fickle, false, cowards, covetous and as long as you succeed they are yours entirely," but when the ruler really needs help, "they turn against you." Machiavelli was therefore repelled by any notions that would require the ruler to be domesticated by morality. He recognized no higher law, such as Aquinas had propounded, but urged a thoroughly secular approach to politics. He valued skill in cunning higher than moral conviction; the ruler should choose only those means that could guarantee that the ends be in fact achieved. In the context of unscrupulous and egotistical people, morality must give way to sheer power if the ruler is to succeed. The ruler should be virtuous only if his best interests are served thereby. But even when he abandons traditional morals for the sake of survival, the ruler must "disguise this character well, and to be a great feigner and dissembler." Thus, while it is not necessary for the ruler to have all of the virtues, "it is very necessary to seem to have them."

Even ruthlessness has its place, and Machiavelli provides an example. Caesar Borgia, a tyrant of the Romagna region of northern Italy, risked losing favor with his subjects because of unpopular policies enacted by his subordinate, Ramiro d'Orco. To overcome the damage, Borgia had him executed and left his body in the town square, with "the block and a bloody knife at his side." According to Machiavelli, "the barbarity of this spectacle caused the people to be at once satisfied and dismayed."

There is some question whether *The Prince* was in any sense intended to be a philosophy of politics. Since it grew out of the particular circumstances of Machiavelli's day, one might argue that it was mainly a practical plan of action for existing rulers. Still, there appears to be a more universal message in this work, namely, that the most useful course of action is in fact the right one. So influential were his views that the term "Machiavellianism" quickly became part of political vocabulary—namely, the view that leaders can justifiably use any means, however unscrupulous, to achieve political power.

THE REFORMATION

On October 31, 1517, German priest Martin Luther launched the Protestant Reformation when nailing a document of protest to the door of Wittenberg Castle. Luther was offended at many Roman Catholic policies that emerged during the Middle Ages and became mainstream by the time of the Renaissance. Papal authority, he believed, had gotten out of hand. To raise money, Popes would routinely endorse the sale of certificates that promised the forgiveness of sins, which one could purchase for oneself, on behalf of a loved one who died and went to purgatory. Luther spent years diplomatically protesting against these abuses. When these efforts failed, he led a movement within the German churches to completely sever ties with the Roman Catholic hierarchy. The movement spread to other European countries, and thus a group of "Protestant" Christian churches emerged. The Reformation had a profound impact on philosophy, especially in these Protestant countries. In addition to abandoning Catholic Church authority, many Protestant philosophers also abandoned the entire tradition of medieval thought, replacing it with the revived theories of ancient Greece, and also new philosophies of their own devising.

Luther

Martin Luther (1483–1546) was deeply influenced by two great medieval philosophers, namely Augustine and Ockham. Ockham had rejected Thomas Aquinas' impressive system of natural theology, which traced causal connections in the world around us back to a first cause. Ockham developed instead a strictly empirical and, in a sense, skeptical view regarding knowledge. He argued that "from the fact that one thing is known to exist, it cannot be inferred that another thing exists." To say that some things are caused by other things gives us no warrant to argue that God is the cause of the natural order. Ockham concluded from this that unaided reason cannot discover God. Instead, knowledge of God is a gift of grace and is assured by an act of faith. Luther adopted this position wholeheartedly. In addition to rejecting Aquinas' natural theology, he also condemned the entire metaphysical system of Aristotle, saying of the great philosopher that "God sent him as a plague for our sins."

Luther was similarly inspired by Augustine's conception of sin, which located the human predicament not in ignorance or undeveloped reason but rather in the bondage of the will. It is therefore faith, not reason, that overcomes this predicament. In fact, Luther said, "it is the quality of faith that it wrings the neck of reason." Thus, things that seem impossible to reason are possible to faith. According to Luther, the difficulty with human reason is that, being finite, it tends to reduce everything to its own limited perspective. This is especially true when the natural reason contemplates the nature and capacities of God. Here human reason limits God to strictly human estimates of what God is and can do. Luther was particularly struck by the intellectual difficulties faced by Abraham when God promised that from his barren wife Sarah he would give him offspring. "There is no doubt," said Luther, that "faith and reason mightily fell out in Abraham's heart about this matter, yet at last did faith get the better, and overcame and strangled reason, that all-cruelest and most fatal enemy of God."

Luther's version of the Christian life had the effect of challenging not only the medieval system of scholastic theology but also those optimistic visions of individual and social perfection based upon good works. Luther said "all manner of works, even contemplation, meditation and all that the soul can do, avail nothing." Only one thing is necessary for righteousness, liberty, and the Christian life, and "that one thing is the most holy word of God." If someone asks "what then is this word of God, and how shall it be used, since there are so many words of God?" Luther answers, "the Apostle explains that in Romans 1.17 'The just shall live by faith.' . . . It is clear then that a Christian man has in his faith all that he needs, and needs no works to justify him."

Luther's emphasis upon faith in religious matters had its counterpart in his political thought. Government, according to Luther, is ordained by God. For this reason, government's key function is the "preservation of the peace." Our sinful nature makes us defiant, and this, in turn, requires a strong ruler: "God has subjected them to the sword, so that even though they would do so, they cannot practice their wickedness." For Luther, obedience in the political realm in many ways parallels the function of faith in the religious realm. The individual must obey the ruler in spite of what the ruler commands, since his comments are directed toward the preservation of peace and order. Without the power of the ruler, self-centered people would produce anarchy "and thus the world would be reduced to chaos." What should we do, though, if we fall under the reign of a corrupt and brutal tyrant? Are we entitled to rebel? The answer, for Luther, is no. Life upon earth is not our most important consideration; what counts most is the salvation of our souls. Whatever a ruler or sovereign does "cannot harm the soul but only the body and property." Even to God, "the temporal power is a very small thing," and, so, we too should not be bothered by rulers to the point that we consider disobeying them. For Luther, "to suffer wrong destroys no one's soul, nay, it improves the soul, although it inflicts loss upon the body and property." This is a far cry from the medieval view that Aquinas formulated when he said that we need not obey the human laws of the state if they are perversions of natural law.

Erasmus

Desiderius Erasmus (1466–1536) was an important figure both as a humanist and for the Reformation. He was born in Rotterdam in 1466, the illegitimate son of a priest. Although a foe of scholastic medieval theology, he had no intention of rejecting the Christian faith. Through his humanistic learning, especially in the Greek language, he sought to uncover the pure and simple elements of Christianity that had been overlaid and obscured by the excessive rationalism of scholastic doctrine. His earliest training began in the school of the Brethren of the Common Life, from which he later entered the Augustinian monastery of Steyn. At the monastery, life was miserable for Erasmus since he was unfitted mentally, physically, and temperamentally for a regime that offered little physical comfort and virtually no intellectual freedom. Through good fortune, he was invited by the Bishop of Cambrai to become his Latin secretary. The Bishop sent him to study for a while at the Collège Montaigue in Paris, where again he felt only contempt for scholastic methods of instruction. It was here, nevertheless, that his enthusiasm for classical literature was stimulated. It was here, too, that he began his first book, which would in time become one of his famous volumes, a book of proverbs entitled *Adagiorum Chiliades*. In 1499, Erasmus visited England, where he soon came under the influence of John Colet, a Biblical scholar, and Sir Thomas More. Erasmus thought it strange that Colet should lecture on the Bible without a knowledge of Greek. He therefore set out to become proficient in this language, eventually publishing a widely accepted Greek Testament with a new Latin translation. During a second visit to England in 1511, Erasmus became a member of the academic community of Cambridge, where he was appointed Lady Margaret Professor. He had little respect for his colleagues, whom he called "Cyprian bulls and dung-eaters," nor did he have any good words for the English beer or climate. After a few years he went to Basel, where he made his home until his death in 1536 at the age of 70.

Erasmus made several contributions to the spirit of the Renaissance. His enthusiasm for classical learning was a decisive influence at this time. He realized that the invention of printing now made it possible to popularize the ancient classics by bringing inexpensive editions within the reach of large numbers of intelligent readers. These books opened up new worlds of classical learning that had not been available in the Middle Ages. But Erasmus was not simply an editor, even though his work in making available these classic Greek and Latin editions would have secured his reputation and significance in the history of thought. More important was his contribution to the development of a new style of literary expression. Erasmus loved words and spent much thought in selecting just the right word or phrase to express his insights.

As painters would display genius in their use of colors, Erasmus, long a foe of the incredible lifelessness of scholastic discourse, found deep joy and freedom in fashioning a new and pure literary style marked by the elegance of each phrase.

Erasmus criticized scholastic jargon not only because of its lack of elegance but even more because it obscured the true teachings of the Gospels. It appeared to Erasmus that the ideas of the great classical writers were in basic harmony with the Gospels. In particular, he saw a close similarity between Plato's philosophy and the teachings of Jesus. He sensed a deep incongruity between the simple teachings of Jesus and the opulence and arrogance of the Papal Court. This moved him to write the satirical *Julius Exclusus* in which Pope Julius II is forbidden by St. Peter to enter the heavenly gates. His own earlier experience with life in the monasteries prompted him to write a criticism of the clergy in a book called *Praise of Folly*, which Luther made much use of in his decisive argument with the church. But Erasmus was neither a religious skeptic nor did he become a Lutheran. His was a lover's quarrel with the Catholic Church. He wished to harmonize the church's teachings with the new humanistic learning.

Erasmus' *Praise of Folly* was both an ironic and a serious treatment of various kinds of folly within institutionalized religion and academia. He first lashed out against priests for their intricate calculations regarding the exact duration of a soul's residence in purgatory. He ridiculed the disputations of the theologians as they struggled valiantly with each other over the doctrines of the Incarnation, Trinity, and transubstantiation. His chief complaint was that the whole point of religion had been lost, and that too much emphasis was being put on trivial and irrelevant details, especially in the monasteries where matters of dress and minutiae of discipline deflected men from the central aim of Christianity. Imagining how these priests would stand before the judgment seat seeking to enter heaven by calling attention to all their good works, Erasmus, going beyond good humor to invective, describes a priest who points to "so many bushels of prayers, another brags of not having touched a penny without at least two pairs of gloves on." To all these Jesus answers, "I left you but one precept, of loving one another, which I do not hear anyone plead that he has faithfully discharged." Closely connected with this criticism of monastic life was Erasmus' abiding dislike of the hair-splitting logic of scholastic doctrine. In contrast with these follies of the clergy which he condemned, he praised the so-called follies of simple faith. True religion, he felt, is a matter of the heart and not of the head. This view was central for the Protestant Reformers and was again expressed with great force by Pascal, who wrote that "the heart has reasons which the reason does not know."

While Luther became a passionate Reformer, Erasmus remained only a critic. In his moderate book *Essay on Free Will*, Erasmus expressed the Renaissance view that we have a great capacity for moral improvement. In a response to this book, Luther dismissed him as a "babbler," a "skeptic," or "some other hog from the Epicurean sty." In this debate Erasmus was the great exponent of the spirit of the Renaissance. With unfaltering optimism he continued to believe that education would eventually conquer stupidity and ignorance. His interest in classical literature and philosophy did not lead him to formulate a new scholasticism or to subordinate Christian faith to the philosophy of Plato. Rather, he used his knowledge of the classical languages to discover the real words of the Gospels, saying that "if there is any fresh Greek to be had, I had rather pawn my coat than not get it, especially if it is something Christian, as the Psalms in Greek or the Gospels."

If Erasmus looked back to antiquity for the treasure of the classics, the Reformers, particularly Luther, looked back to the primitive community of Christians for the original spirit of Christianity. In this way the Renaissance and the Reformation both epitomized a revival of the past. Erasmus and Luther could agree on many points in their mutual attacks upon the state of Christianity in the 16th century. However, whereas Erasmus could balance classical humanistic learning with a simplified Christian faith, Luther's exaltation of faith had the effect of throwing serious doubt upon the capacity of human reason to lead humanity to salvation.

SKEPTICISM AND FAITH

One of the most important philosophical developments during the Renaissance was the revival of ancient Greek skepticism, particularly the skeptical tradition of Pyrrho, which was refined and systematized by Sextus Empiricus (*c.* 200 BCE). The writings of Sextus became widely available during the Renaissance, and many readers felt the allure of skeptical tranquility that he advocated. Others were horrified at Sextus's assault on human reason, and felt compelled to attack his views. Thus, much of philosophy in the following centuries involved an intellectual tug-of-war between skeptics and nonskeptics.

Montaigne

In his celebrated *Essays*, Michel de Montaigne (1533–1592) expressed a captivating version of classical skepticism. Within the ancient writings of the skeptics, Montaigne discovered a new way of viewing daily life. The word skepticism has over the centuries come to mean chiefly the attitude of doubt, which is often accompanied with indifference to the drift of life's events. But these were not the chief characteristics of classical skepticism or of Montaigne's thought. Central to classical skepticism was the atmosphere of inquiry coupled with a desire to live a thoroughly exemplary human life. This also was Montaigne's chief concern. He was particularly attracted to a way of life that permitted him constantly to discover new insights and at the same time enjoy all the powers he possessed as a human being. Montaigne wrote that "Pyrrho did not want to make himself into a stone; he wanted to make himself a living man, discoursing and reasoning, enjoying all pleasures and natural commodities, using all of his corporeal and spiritual parts regularly and properly."

Michel de Montaigne
(Corbis-Bettmann)

Montaigne saw himself as "an unpremeditated philosopher"—one who was not confined intellectually to some rigid set of ideas within which his thought and life must be expressed. His desire to live a happy life could not be fulfilled if he committed himself to doctrines about which perfectly reasonable objections could be raised. Many problems, he felt, had no clear solutions. This is the case with questions about the true nature of things, which so preoccupied the pre-Socratics. Montaigne accepted the judgment of the skeptics, who said that there is "no more likelihood that this is true than that that is true." But, again, this formula of skepticism was not intended to deny what common sense tells us is the case. Skepticism was a liberating force for Montaigne, freeing him from the rigid theories of other philosophical systems, and, quite paradoxically, freeing him from the theory of skepticism itself! To be truly skeptical, we must doubt the very doubting process that we are engaged in, and thus avoid being swayed by its own theoretical force. We should never make any permanent commitment to any doctrines but instead assume a perpetual attitude of inquiry. Contentment, said Montaigne, is possible only when we achieve a tranquility of mind. What disturbs this tranquility is the attempt to go beyond our ordinary experiences and penetrate the inner nature of things. The saddest spectacle of all is to find people formulating final answers on questions that are far too subtle and variable for such treatment. The final folly of this attempt is the attitude of fanaticism and dogmatism.

Montaigne knew well the frightful outcome of fanaticism. In his lifetime he saw wars and fierce religious persecution. He wrote of his "neighborhood grown so old in riot" that he wondered whether his society could be held together. "I saw," he wrote, "common and general behavior so ferocious, above all in inhumanity and treachery, that I cannot think of it without blenching in horror." This he blamed upon the fires of fanaticism. The loss of inner peace of mind would in time, he felt, be reflected in social turmoil. He genuinely believed that an attitude of constructive skepticism could prevent such outbursts of cruelty. In the attitude of true skepticism, human energies would be directed toward manageable subjects and purposes. Rather than struggling with riddles about the universe and its destiny, Montaigne would counsel people to start their philosophy of life by reflecting upon matters close at hand.

A good place to begin, said Montaigne, is with one's own personal experiences: "Every man carries within himself the whole condition of humanity." For this reason he was convinced that whatever proved useful to himself might also be useful for someone else. In the true spirit of the Renaissance, Montaigne sought an open and clear form of expression about the most natural and normal actions of men, rejecting the obscurity of technical jargon. "My page," he writes, "makes love and knows what he is doing. But read to him Leo Hebraeus or Ficino where they speak of the actions and thoughts of love, and he can't make head or tail of it." Montaigne complained that "I can't recognize most of my daily doings when they appear in Aristotle. They are decked out or hidden in another cloak for the benefit of schoolmen." What Montaigne thought was needed was to "do as much to make art natural as they do to make nature artificial." The art of life is to recognize what it means to be human, he says, for "there is nothing so handsome as to play the man properly and well. Of all our diseases, the worst is to despise our own being." Nothing disfigures human nature more than a person's attempt to think higher of himself than he should. Whenever this happens, Montaigne says, "I have always observed a singular accord between supercelestial ideas and subterranean behavior." Whenever men "would flee from themselves and escape from being men [they] engage in folly. Instead of transforming themselves into angels, they turn themselves into beasts."

For Montaigne, skepticism did not mean either pessimism as an attitude or a rule for behavior. On the contrary, he saw in skepticism a source for a positive affirmation of all the facets of human life. Although he saw serious limits to the power of technical reason, he glorified the human capacity for critical judgment. To be a human being in the deepest sense, he thought, is to have fully conscious experiences—experiences in which we consciously weigh alternative and control our behavior through an act of judgment. He expressed the insight of classical skepticism with this formula: "I stop—I examine—I take for my guide the ways of the world and the experience of the senses." Our senses give us sufficiently reliable information about ourselves and the physical world, which ensure physical survival and genuine pleasure. The ways of the world also have value almost irrespective of their objective rightness or truth. Political laws and religion are fixed facts about the world, and to deny or reject them is virtually the same as saying that one is in no danger as one stands at the edge of a precipice. As to politics, good judgment requires us to accept the conditions and organization of our respective countries, and by looking around us, we can distinguish between appropriate and inappropriate restrictions upon our life. Skepticism should not lead us to revolutionary or anarchic behavior. Montaigne himself became a true political conservative who believed that social change must not be abrupt. Since there are no absolute truths, there are no specific ends toward which society must be forced to move. Custom acquires therefore a strong claim upon people's political allegiance. In matters of religion also the person of good judgment will respect the authority of tradition, seeing in the stability of the organized religious community the condition for continued inquiry that anarchy would render impossible.

Thus Montaigne sought to remind his generation that wisdom lies in accepting life as it is and realizing how difficult it is to know anything with certainty. He wanted particularly to direct people's attention to the richness of human life that respectful acceptance of human capacities could make possible. In this he was a true representative of the main current of the Renaissance.

Pascal

Blaise Pascal (1623–1662) was another thinker who was strongly influenced by the resurgence of skepticism at the time. Although officially distancing himself from the school of skepticism, he nevertheless believed that human reason was incapable of obtaining the most important of life's truths. Pascal was renown as a mathematician and scientist. He laid the foundations of the infinitesimal calculus and the integral calculus. In 1639, at the age of sixteen, he wrote an essay on conic sections. Shortly thereafter, he invented an adding machine—a kind of mechanical computer. He also tried to prove the truth of Torricelli's experimental discovery of the vacuum.

When Pascal was 31 years old, he underwent a deep religious experience which influenced the rest of his life as a thinker. Although he devoted himself to his deep faith in God, this did not mean that this new dimension in his thinking would lead him to abandon his scientific interests. Rather than considering scientific activities as too worldly and therefore of lesser significance than religion, he saw these two activities as working together, though not always at an equal level. The formula for his new way of thinking is found in his famous statement that "the heart has its reasons which the reason does not understand." It would appear that instead of reason or rigorous thinking, Pascal would substitute the elements of feeling or emotion. Thus, for Pascal, the guide to truth is the heart. He does not give a precise definition of "the heart" but from the various ways in which he uses the term it becomes clear that by the heart Pascal means the power of intuition. He was convinced that certain basic propositions in our thinking cannot be demonstrated; instead, we arrive at these principles through a special insight. Things are true or false according to the context or perspective from which we see them. Hence, "we know the truth not only by reason but also by the heart." It is by the heart that we know the difference between a dream and waking life. Here the term heart refers to "instinctive, immediate, unreasoned apprehension of a truth." In geometry we have an immediate awareness of principles. In ethics we have a spontaneous and direct apprehension of right and wrong. And, in religion, the believer has a loving apprehension of God, which in no way rests on the rational proofs of natural theology.

Whereas other philosophers set out to prove the existence of God by rational arguments, Pascal approached the existence of God by asking us instead to assume the point of view of the gambler. Every gambler, he says, takes a certain risk for an uncertain gain. If there are as many chances on one side as on the other, you are playing for the same odds. And in that case the certainty of what you are risking is equal to the uncertainty of what you may win. In life, what you are wagering or what you are risking is your eternal life and happiness as compared with your finite life and unhappiness. To say that there is an eternal life is a way of affirming the existence of God. But how do we *know* that God exists? We simply do not *know.* The issue, then, is a matter of a wager. There are four possible outcomes to the wager, which have radically different consequences. (1) If God exists, and we believe in him, then our reward will be infinitely great. (2) If God exists, and we do not believe in him, then we will lose out on this reward. (3) If God does not exist, and we believe in him, then we've gained or lost nothing. (4) If God does not exist, and we do not believe in him, then we've gained or lost nothing. By weighing these outcomes, Pascal thinks that we should be psychologically compelled to believe in God, since that promises the greater possibility of reward. Pascal does not feel that we can mathematically calculate our way to a conviction of religious belief. Instead, he feels that our calculation will at least prompt us to begin down the path of faith. We may start by mechanically suppressing our passions, adopting religious virtues and following religious customs. After immersing ourselves in religious traditions, he contends, a genuine faith commitment will naturally grow.

THE SCIENTIFIC REVOLUTION

A scientific revolution began in the Renaissance that had a sweeping and permanent impact on virtually all branches of knowledge. Unlike the medieval thinkers who proceeded for the most part by reading traditional texts, the early modern scientists laid greatest stress upon observation and the formation of hypotheses. The method of observation implied two things. First, traditional explanations of the behavior of nature should be empirically demonstrated, since such explanations could very well be wrong. Second, new information might be available to scientists if they could penetrate beyond the superficial appearances of things. People now began to look at the heavenly bodies with a new attitude, hoping not solely to find the confirmation of Biblical statements about the divine creation, but to discover the principles and laws that describe the movements of bodies. Observation was directed not only upon the stars but also in the opposite direction, toward the minutest constituents of physical substance.

New Discoveries and New Methods

There are two distinct components to the scientific revolution: the new scientific discoveries and new methods of conducting scientific inquiry. As to new discoveries, to enhance the exactness of their observations, scientists invented various scientific instruments. In 1590 the first compound microscope was created. In 1608 the telescope was invented. The principle of the barometer was discovered by Evangelista Torricelli (1608–1647). Otto von Guericke (1602–1686) invented the air pump, which was so important in creating a vacuum for the experiment that proved that all bodies regardless of their weight or size fall at the same rate when there is no air resistance. With the use of instruments and imaginative hypotheses, fresh knowledge began to unfold. Galileo Galilei (1564–1642) discovered the moons around Jupiter, and Anton Leeuwenhoek (1632–1723) discovered spermatozoa, protozoa, and bacteria. Harvey (1578–1657) discovered the circulation of the blood. William Gilbert (1540–1603) wrote a major work on the magnet, and Robert Boyle (1627–1691), the father of chemistry, formulated his famous law concerning the relation of temperature, volume, and pressure of gases.

Among the more dramatic discoveries of the time were new conceptions of astronomy. Medieval astronomers believed that human beings were the focus of God's creative activity, and thus, God placed us quite literally in the center of the universe. Renaissance astronomers shattered this conception. The Polish astronomer Nicolaus Copernicus (1473–1543) formulated a new hypothesis in his *Revolutions of the Heavenly Spheres* (1543), which said that the sun is at the center of the universe and that the earth rotates daily and revolves around the sun annually. Copernicus was a faithful son of the church and had no thought of contradicting any traditional Biblical doctrines. His work expressed rather his irrepressible desire to work out a theory of the heavens that would conform to the available evidence. Tycho Brahe (1546–1601) made additional and corrective observations, and his young associate Johannes Kepler (1571–1630) formulated three important laws of planetary motion in which he added mathematical equations to support mere observation. It was Galileo, though, who provided the greatest theoretical precision to the new astronomy and, in the course of this endeavor, formulated his important laws of acceleration and dynamics.

The second contribution of the scientific revolution involved the development of new scientific methods. Medieval approaches to science were grounded in Aristotle's system of deductive logic. Several Renaissance and early modern scientists proposed alternative systems, often quite different from each other. The scientific methods that we follow today, though, are in many respects the direct descendents of these early theories, particularly that of Francis Bacon (1561–1626), which stresses the importance of observation and inductive reasoning. Scientific methodology made further progress as new fields of mathematics were opened. Copernicus had employed a two-fold method: first, the observation of moving bodies, and, second, the mathematical calculation of the motion of bodies in space.

What Copernicus had begun was then considerably refined by Kepler and particularly by Galileo. Galileo stressed the importance of direct observation, and avoided secondhand information based simply upon tradition and opposing conjectures contained in books. This led to his discovery of the satellites around the planet Jupiter. He writes, "To demonstrate to my opponents the truth of my conclusions, I have been forced to prove them by a variety of experiments." In a letter to Kepler, he reflects on the stubborn attitudes of old-school astronomers of his time: "My dear Kepler, what would you say of the learned here, who, replete with the pertinacity of the asp, have steadfastly refused to cast a glance through the telescope? What shall we make of all this? Shall we laugh or shall we cry?" In addition to his emphasis on observation, Galileo sought to give astronomy the precision of geometry. By using the model of geometry for his reasoning about astronomy, he assumed that he could demonstrate the accuracy of his conclusions if he could, as one does in geometry, produce basic axioms from which to deduce his conclusions. Moreover, he assumed that empirical facts correspond to geometric axioms, or that the axioms that the mind formulates correspond to the actual characteristics of observable moving bodies. To think in terms of geometry is to know how things actually behave. Specifically, Galileo formulated, for the first time, a geometric representation of the motion of bodies and their acceleration.

The mathematical component of scientific inquiry was developed further by Isaac Newton (1642–1727) and Gottfried Wilhelm Leibniz (1646–1716), who independently invented differential and integral calculus. In time, the method of observation and mathematical calculation became the hallmarks of modern science. What most of these thinkers had in common was their belief that human knowledge about the nature of things is available to anyone who used the appropriate method in its pursuit. Instead of looking back to tradition or to the testimony of ancient authorities, individuals can have direct access to the truth about nature, and this truth would most likely be discovered if one took the information received through observation and organized it into a system of axioms.

Modern Atomism

One of the growing assumptions among scientists and philosophers of the time was the view that the universe and all that it contained was composed of material substances. According to this conception, everything behaves in orderly and predictable ways. The heavens above and the smallest particles below all exhibit the same laws of motion, thus implying that everything conforms to a mechanical model. Pushing the issue further, philosophers attempted to explain human thought and behavior in mechanical terms, which earlier moralists described as the product of free will.

As early as the fifth century BCE, Democritus reduced all things in the universe to atoms in motion–that is, to matter. Later, Lucretius (98–55 BCE) showed how deceptive appearances can be. He described how a person standing on one side of a valley might see on the other side something that looked like a white cloud only to find upon going there that the "cloud" was a flock of sheep. Similarly, Galileo stressed the distinction between appearance and reality, where appearance is made up of secondary qualities while reality consists of primary qualities. He believed that we cannot trust appearances as a reliable path to truth. For example, our notion based upon appearances leads us to the erroneous conclusion that the sun moves around the earth. Similarly, a tree or a rock appears to be a single solid thing but in reality is composed of a multitude of atoms. The most accurate knowledge available to us is produced by the mathematical analysis of moving bodies, not only as in astronomy but also closer to hand as in physics.

Having in mind the distinction between primary and secondary qualities, Galileo certainly gave the impression that only those qualities that belong to bodies or matter have true reality. Primary qualities, such as size, position, motion, and density, are truly real because they can be dealt with mathematically. By contrast, secondary qualities, such as color, taste, emotions, and sounds, "reside only in consciousness; if the living creature were removed, all these qualities would be wiped away and annihilated." A human being can be defined as a body with physical organs. But when one is defined as a person, it turns out that most personal characteristics are represented by secondary qualities. This would mean that either these secondary qualities must be explained mathematically—as being aspects of the primary qualities of matter— or that the secondary qualities do not participate at all in the realm of reality. In either case, the unique dignity, value, or special status of human beings in the nature of things is severely diminished.

Newton, accepting the view that nature is composed of "particles and bodies," expressed the wish that all the phenomena of nature could be explained "by the same kind of reasoning derived from mechanical principles, for I am induced by many reasons to suspect that they may all depend upon certain forces by which the particles or bodies . . . are either mutually impelled towards one another and cohere in regular figures, or are repelled and recede from one another." Accordingly, Newton refined the earlier formulations of the laws of motion in his great work *Principia Mathematica* (1687), a work that had enormous influence for generations to come. Although Newton still spoke of God as the one who created the machine of nature, it became increasingly unnecessary to refer to God when explaining the phenomena of nature. The whole drift of the new scientific method was toward a new conception of man, of nature, and of the whole mechanism of human knowledge.

As the universe was now viewed as a system of bodies in motion, so now all other aspects of nature were described as bodies in motion. Human nature and human thought also were soon to be viewed in mechanical terms. If all things consist of bodies in motion, this mechanical behavior, it was thought, must be capable of mathematical description. Thus, again, observation and the use of mathematics emerged in the Renaissance as the ingredients of the new method of scientific thought. With this method, it was assumed that new knowledge could be discovered. It was the view of Renaissance scientists that medieval thinkers had simply worked out explanatory systems for what we already knew, but had provided no method for discovering new information. But the spirit of discovery, dramatized by Columbus' discovery of a new continent and by the discovery of new worlds in the arts, in literature, and in the unused faculties and capacities of humans, was now impelling scientists to open up new worlds in the structure of nature. And it was this new attitude of science that had the most immediate effect upon the development of modern philosophy, especially upon Francis Bacon and Thomas Hobbes, to whom we now turn.

FRANCIS BACON

Francis Bacon assigned himself the task of reforming the philosophy and science of his day. His central criticism was that learning had become stagnant. Science was identified with learning, and learning meant reading ancient texts. The study of medicine, for example, was chiefly literary and was practiced by poets, rhetoricians, and clergymen, whose qualifications to practice was their ability to quote Hippocrates and Galen. Philosophy was still dominated by Plato and Aristotle, whose teachings Bacon denounced as "shadows" and "phantoms." Although Bacon said that "Knowledge is power," he was particularly agitated by the "uselessness" of traditional learning. What made this learning inadequate was that science had become mixed up with "superstition," unguided speculation, and theology. Bacon challenged this approach to science, charging that it had no adequate method for discovering what nature and its workings are really like. The one ancient thinker for whom he did have respect was Democritus, whose materialism he adopted. But the teachings of the schoolmen of the Middle Ages he considered as "degenerate" versions of Aristotle. Instead of deriving substantial evidence from the actual nature of things, they worked upon their own imaginations. They were like spiders that brought forth "cobwebs of learning, admirable for the fineness of thread and work, but of no substance or profit."

Bacon advocated wiping the slate of human knowledge clean and starting over again, using a new method for assembling and explaining facts. He was convinced that he had discovered such a method, which would unlock all the secrets of nature. He was aware of other attempts to correct the inadequacies of traditional learning—particularly attempts by Gilbert, Copernicus, and Galileo to amend Aristotle's physics. But what impressed him most was Galileo's construction and use of telescopes. He considered this event one of the most important in the history of astronomy because it made possible a true advancement of learning. For example, whereas the ancients did not know the composition of the Milky Way, the telescope made it evident that it is a collection of distant stars. Bacon considered the mind as being like a glass or mirror, which had been made rough and uneven both by natural tendencies of passions as well as by the errors of traditional learning. In such a condition, the mind cannot reflect truth accurately. Bacon's method, and his hope, was to make the mind's surface clean and smooth and to supply it with new and adequate instruments so that it could observe and understand the universe accurately. To achieve this, he would have to free science from entrenched and traditional learning. This meant separating scientific truth from revealed truths of theology, and fashioning a new philosophy based upon a new method of observation and a new interpretation of nature.

By birth and breeding, Bacon was destined to live, work, and think in a style befitting one of high social rank. He was born in 1561, the son of Sir Nicholas Bacon, who was then Lord Keeper of the Great Seal. He entered Cambridge at the age of 12 and at the age of 16 was admitted at a relatively senior status to the legal world of Gray's Inn. Through the succeeding years, he was honored by Queen Elizabeth and King James I as a member of Parliament, the House of Lords, and in time became Solicitor-General, Lord Keeper, and finally Lord Chancellor. We can appreciate Bacon's philosophical brilliance all the more when we consider that he was engaged in a full legal and political career. His philosophical works are as significant as they are monumental. The best known of these are his *Advancement of Learning* and *New Organon*. He was aware that his political life had interfered with his primary objectives as a thinker, saying that "I reckoned that I was by no means discharging my duty, when I was neglecting that by which I could of myself benefit man." To add further misery to his last years, shortly after being named Lord Chancellor, he was accused of accepting bribes and was thereupon fined, sentenced to a short imprisonment, and barred from public office forever. The end came when, pursuing his zeal for experimentation, wondering whether the putrefaction of flesh could be halted by freezing, he went out in the cold and stuffed a chicken with snow. Getting badly chilled, he died in a few days in 1626 at the age of 65.

Bacon's principal objective was, as he said, "the total reconstruction of the sciences, arts and all human knowledge," and this he called his "great instauration." But before he could proceed with his creative task, he leveled some fierce criticisms against Oxford, Cambridge, and universities in general, and also against the reigning schools of philosophy, denouncing them for their slavish attachment to the past. He thus gathered up the rising discontent with medieval philosophy and sounded the call for a break with the lingering influence of Aristotle.

Distempers of Learning

Bacon attacked past ways of thinking, calling them "distempers of learning," to which he offered a cure. He named three of these: fantastical learning, contentious learning, and delicate learning. In fantastical learning, people concern themselves with words, emphasizing texts, languages, and style, and "hunt more after words than matter, and more after choiceness of phrase . . . than after the weight of matter." Contentious learning is even worse, he said, because it begins with the fixed positions or points of view taken by earlier thinkers, and these views are used as the starting point in contentious argumentation. Finally, there is delicate learning, wherein earlier authors, who claim more knowledge than can be proved, are accepted by readers as knowing as much as they claim. This accounts for the acceptance of Aristotle, for example, as the dictator of science. These three diseases, he argued, must be cured in order to relieve the mind of the errors they create.

Idols of the Mind

Similarly, the human thinking is corrupted by Idols. Bacon refers to four Idols, which he metaphorically calls the Idols of the Tribe, the Cave, the Market Place, and the Theatre. These Idols, or "false phantoms," are distortions of the mind, like distortions of beams of light reflected from an uneven mirror: "For from the nature of a clear and equal glass, wherein the beams of things should reflect according to their true incidence, it is rather like an enchanted glass, full of superstition and imposture." The only way to correct this wayward type of thought is through observation and experimentation—that is, through the inductive method. These Idols, or "false opinions," "dogmas," "superstitions" and "errors," distort knowledge in different ways.

The Idols of the Tribe are involve our preoccupation with opinions, following from "the false assertion that the sense of man is the measure of things." Here Bacon wanted to make the point that simply looking at things is no guarantee that we shall see them as they really. We all bring our hopes and fears, prejudices, and impatience to things and thereby affect our understanding of them. The Idols of the Cave were taken by Bacon from the Platonic allegory and again suggest the limitations of the untrained mind, which is shut in the cave of its own environment of customs and opinions, reflecting the kinds of books one reads, the ideas one considers significant, and the intellectual authorities to whom one defers.

The third class of Idols is very aptly designated as the Idols of the Market Place, since it stands for the words people use in the commerce of daily life, words that are common coin in daily conversation. In spite of their usefulness, words can weaken knowledge because they are not created with care or precision, but framed so that the common person will understand their use. Even philosophers are diverted by these Idols, for they often give names to things that exist only in their imaginations. In addition, they fashion names for mere abstractions, such as "element" of fire, or the "qualities" of heaviness, rareness, or denseness. Finally, the Idols of the Theatre are the grand systematic dogmas of long philosophic treatises. These represent "worlds of their own creation after an unreal and scenic fashion." Bacon wants to include here not only whole systems, but all principles or axioms in science that "by tradition, credibility and negligence have come to be received."

Inductive Method

Having duly warned his generation that human understanding can be distorted by these Idols, Bacon described a new method for acquiring knowledge. In order to "penetrate into the inner and further recesses of nature," he said, we need to derive our notions from things "in a more sure and guarded way." This way would include ridding ourselves of prejudices and looking at things as they are: "We must lead men to the particulars themselves." To assist our observations we need to correct our errors "not so much by instruments as by experiments. For the subtlety of experiments is far greater than that of sense itself." Bacon's concept of experiment and his method of observation rests on the notion of induction, that is, deriving "laws" from the simple observation of particulars and their series and order. The alternative view, which he harshly criticized, was Aristotle's deductive method. Aristotle's classic example of a deductive argument is this: (1) All men are mortal; (2) Socrates is a man; (3) Therefore, Socrates is mortal. The problem with this approach, according to Bacon, is that the conclusions we draw only perpetuate the errors that are already contained in the premises. Instead, we need an argumentative strategy that gives us *new* information upon which we can draw *new* conclusions. Induction does just this.

Bacon knew the limitations of "induction by simple enumeration," for example, concluding that all horses are black because the first 18 counted were black. The solution, Bacon believed, was to look for the underlying nature or "form," which we find represented in the particulars that we observe. The example he gives of his inductive method involves discovering the nature of heat. The first step is to draw up a list of all the instances in which we encounter heat, such as "the rays of the sun." This list he called the "Table of Essence and Presence." Next, another list must be compiled to include items that resemble those on the first list but that do not have heat, such as "the rays of the moon and of stars" which are not hot to the touch. This second list he called the Table of Deviation. A third, the Table of Comparison, is a further attempt to discover the nature of heat by analyzing the different degrees of heat to be found in different things. "Ignited iron, for instance, is much hotter and more consuming than flame of spirit of wine."

The fourth step is the Process of Exclusion, whereby, setting "induction to work," we try to find some "nature" that is present whenever there is heat and absent when heat is absent. Is light the cause of heat? No, because the moon is bright but is not hot. This process of exclusion was central to Bacon's method of science, and this process he called "the foundation of true induction." He assumed that "the Form of a thing is to be found in each and all the instances, in which the thing itself is to be found." Applying this assumption to the problem of heat, Bacon concluded that "Heat itself, its essence and quiddity, is motion and nothing else." The emphasis on "essence" has an Aristotelian sound, and suggests that Bacon's break with Aristotle was not complete. Nevertheless, this final step does have a modern ring, for Bacon wanted to verify his conclusions by checking them against all the items listed in his tables.

The major weakness in Bacon's method is that he had no grasp of what modern scientists mean by an "hypothesis." Bacon assumed that if we simply looked at enough facts, an hypothesis would suggest itself. However, contemporary scientists know that it is necessary to have an hypothesis before we inspect facts. This hypothesis, then, serves as a guide in the selection of facts relevant to the experiment. Bacon also underestimated the importance of mathematics for science. Nevertheless, he permanently dislodged the grip of scholastic thought and provided the impetus for making philosophy scientific.

THOMAS HOBBES

The life of Thomas Hobbes spans 91 eventful years, from 1588 to 1679. He was born at Westport near Malmesbury, England, the son of a vicar. His education at Oxford stirred in him a fascination for classical literature, whereas his exposure to Aristotelian logic left him bored. In 1608 he left Oxford and had the good fortune of becoming the tutor of the Earl of Devonshire, William Cavendish. This association with the Cavendish family was to influence Hobbes's development significantly, as it afforded him the opportunity to travel widely on the Continent and to meet many leading thinkers and personages of the day. In Italy he met Galileo, and in Paris he formed a lasting friendship with Descartes's admirer, Mersenne, and also Descartes's antagonist, Gassendi. There is some question whether he ever met Descartes in person, but his carefully reasoned objections to the *Meditations* show Hobbes's close familiarity with Descartes's philosophy. In England, Hobbes was much admired by Bacon, who, as Lord Chancellor, enjoyed conversations with him and frequently dictated his thoughts to Hobbes during "delicious walks at Gorambery." Hobbes's early interest in classics led him to translate Thucydides. In his early 40s, his interests shifted to mathematics and analysis with his discovery of Euclid's *Elements*—a book that "made [him] in love with geometry." The next stage of his development, which was to persist for the rest of his life, witnessed the publication of his brilliant philosophical treatises, among which the most renowned is his *Leviathan.*

Influence of Geometry upon Hobbes's Thought

Although the Leviathan is primarily a book on social and political philosophy, Hobbes had not intended to restrict his attention to that subject. Caught up in the rising tide of scientific discovery, he was deeply impressed by the precision of science and above all by the certainty of scientific knowledge. The intellectual atmosphere of the 16th and 17th centuries had been undergoing a radical alteration as one area of inquiry after another yielded to the probing method of science. Hobbes caught the spirit of the times. His initial fascination with mathematics came from his encounter with Euclid. He joined that small but eloquent company of thinkers who saw in geometry the key to the study of nature. With a razor-sharp intellect and a fervor that caused him to exaggerate the possibilities of this method, Hobbes undertook to recast the whole gamut of knowledge in accordance with this single approach. Hobbes assumed that it mattered little what the object of study was. We could gain exact knowledge through the method of observation and deductive reasoning from axioms, formed from observation. He therefore set out an ambitious project, which was to recast the study of physical nature, human nature, and society, using the same method throughout. He published *De Cive* (The Citizen) in 1642, *De Corpore* (Concerning Body) in 1655, and *De Homine* (Concerning Man) in 1658. In the end, it was his political philosophy that made him famous, for it was here that his application of rigorous logic and the scientific method produced startling new results.

As a political philosopher, Hobbes is frequently, though not accurately, called the father of modern totalitarianism. His books *De Cive* and *Leviathan* read like grammars of obedience. He describes the relation between citizen and sovereign in such severe terms that it is no wonder he brought upon himself widespread criticism. Two considerations led Hobbes to formulate his unique theory of political obligation. The first was the political turbulence of his times, which saw Cromwell preparing to lead his people in a savage civil war. This experience of violence, growing out of deep disagreements on political matters, contrasted sharply in Hobbes's mind with the relatively quick agreements people achieved in mathematical and scientific matters. Secondly, Hobbes looked at political philosophy as a variation of the science of physics. He assumed that from a thoroughly materialistic view of human nature, in which human behavior could be explained simply in terms of bodies in motion, he could formulate an accurate political philosophy. He hope that if political theory could be formulated with logical precision, people would be more likely to achieve agreement among themselves and thereby arrive at what Hobbes longed for most of all, namely, peace and order. There is some question whether Hobbes was logically consistent in his systematic political philosophy, and there is even greater question about his assumption that people would become orderly in their relations to each other just because they had been provided a logical plan for harmonious behavior. In any case, his theory of humanity and society took its novel turn mainly because he built it according to a mechanical model, the chief ingredients of which were bodies and motion. And because Hobbes's political theory depends so much upon his unique theory of knowledge and his mathematical model of reality, these aspects of his philosophy need to be considered in some detail as the background to his views on political community.

Bodies in Motion: The Object of Thought

Philosophy, according to Hobbes, is concerned chiefly with the causes and characteristics of bodies. There are three major types of bodies: physical bodies such as stones, the human body, and the body politic. Philosophy is concerned with all three types, inquiring into their causes and characteristics. There is one principal characteristic that all bodies share and which alone makes it possible to understand how they came to be and do what they do, and that characteristic is motion. Motion is a key concept in Hobbes's thought. Equally important is the assumption Hobbes makes that only bodies exist, that knowable reality consists solely of bodies. He will not admit that anything such as spirit or God exists if these terms refer to beings that have no bodies, or are incorporeal. Of God's existence, Hobbes writes that "by the visible things in this world, and their admirable order, a man may conceive there is a cause of them, which men call God: and yet not have an idea or image of him in his mind." Hobbes was willing to concede that God exists but argued that people do not know what God is. Still, it made no sense to Hobbes that there could be something with an incorporeal substance, as the theologians characterized God. Substance, he argued, could be only corporeal, and for this reason God would possess some form of body. But Hobbes did not wish to pursue theological subtleties. He appears to have dealt with God's nature in this connection only to make the broader point that whatever exists is corporeal and that the scope of philosophy is limited to the study of bodies in motion.

Hobbes set out to explain both physical and mental events as nothing more than bodies in motion. "Motion," says Hobbes, "is a continual relinquishing of one place and acquiring of another." Anything that moves is changing its location, and, similarly, whatever is caused to move changes its place. If something is at rest, it will always be at rest unless something moves it. Only a moving body can cause a resting body to move, for "by endeavoring to get into its place by motion [it] suffers it no longer to remain at rest." Similarly, a body in motion tends to stay in motion unless its movement is halted by some other body. This account of motion appears to be restricted to locomotion. For such concepts as inertia, force, impetus, resistance, and endeavor—terms that Hobbes uses to describe motion—all seem to apply to things in space that occupy or change their location. But since Hobbes started with the premise that only bodies exist, it was inevitable that he would have to explain all of reality and all processes in terms of moving bodies. Motion is therefore not only locomotion in the simple sense, but is also what we know as the process of change. Things become different because something in them has been moved by something else, and this refers not only to physical but also to mental change.

Hobbes refers to two kinds of motion that are peculiar to animals or people, namely, vital and voluntary motions. Vital motions begin with the process of birth, continue through life, and include such motions as pulse, nutrition, excretion, the course of the blood, and breathing, "to which motions there needs no help of imagination." On the other hand, voluntary motions, such as going, speaking, and the deliberate movement of our limbs, are first of all movements in our minds, and "because going, speaking and the like voluntary motions, depend always upon a precedent thought of whither, which way, and what; it is evident that the imagination is the first internal beginning of all voluntary motion." Imagination is the cause of voluntary acts, but imagination itself and the human activity we call thought are also explained as being effects of prior causes—as being consequences of prior motions.

Mechanical View of Human Thought

The human mind works in various ways, ranging from perception, imagination, memory, to thinking. All of these types of mental activity are fundamentally the same because they are all motions in our bodies. It was particularly obvious to Hobbes that perception, imagination, and memory are alike. Perception, by which he meant our ability to "sense" things, is our basic mental act, and the others are "derived from that original." The whole structure and process of human thought is explained as bodies in motion, and the variations in mental activity are accounted for by designating the location of each type of mental act along a describable causal chain. Thus, the thought process begins when a body external to us moves and causes a motion inside of us, as when we see a tree, and seeing the tree is perception or sensation. When we look at an object, we see what Hobbes called a phantasm. A phantasm is the image within us caused by an object outside of us. Perception is not the sensation of motion, or the sensation of the exact qualities that an object actually possesses. We see the green tree, but green and tree are two phantasms—a quality and an object—and these represent the ways we experience the motion caused by the body external to us. The initial impact upon us caused by an external object creates not only our immediate sensation but more lasting effects as well, just as on the ocean, though the wind cease, "the waves give not over rolling for a long time after." And "so also it happens in that motion, which is made in the internal parts of man . . . for after the object is removed, or the eye shut, we still retain an image of the thing seen, though more obscure than when we see it." This retention of the image within us after the object is removed is what Hobbes means by imagination. Thus, imagination is simply a lingering—or what Hobbes called a decaying—sensation. When, later, we wish to express this decay and show that the sense is fading, we call this memory, "so that imagination and memory are but one thing, which for divers considerations hath divers names."

It would appear that thinking, as when we have conversations with each other, is something quite different from sensation and memory. In sensation the sequence of images in our mind is determined by what is happening outside of us, whereas in thinking we seem to put ideas together whichever way we wish. But, using his mechanical model, Hobbes explained thinking in exactly the same terms that he used in his account of sensation, so that thinking, for him, is a variation of sensation. Ideas follow each other in thought because they first followed each other in sensation. For, "those motions that immediately succeeded one another in sense, continue also together after sense." Our ideas have a firm relationship to each other for the reason that in any form of continued motion—and thought is such a motion—"one part follows another by cohesion." But the mechanism of thought is not all that perfect, and people are always thinking in ways that do not mirror their past sensations exactly. Hobbes was aware of this, but he tried to explain even the broken sequences as the invasions of more dominant sensations into the stream of imagination and memory. For example, the thought of the civil war might remind him of a personal experience and thereby break the chain of events for which the civil war stood in his memory. He wanted to establish the view that nothing happens in thinking that cannot be accounted for by sensation and memory.

Still, there is a difference between the mind of an animal and the mind of a human being, even though both have sensation and memory. What distinguishes them is that people are able to form signs or names to mark their sensations. With these names we are able to recall their sensations. Moreover, science and philosophy are possible because of the human capacity to formulate words and sentences. Knowledge, then, takes on two different forms, one being knowledge of fact and the other knowledge of consequences. Knowledge of fact is simply memory of past events. Knowledge of consequences is hypothetical or conditional, but still based upon experience. For it affirms that if A is true, B will also be true—or, using Hobbes's illustration"If the figure shown be a circle, then any straight line through the center shall divide it into two equal parts." Scientific knowledge, or philosophy in the broad sense, is possible only because of the human capacity to use words and speech. Although Hobbes spoke of signs and names as word "taken at pleasure to serve for a mark," these words represent our experiences. Words and sentences point to the actual way things behave. Reasoning with words is therefore not the same as playing with words, for once the meaning of words is established, certain consequences follow for their use, mirroring the reality they help our imagination recall.

Thus, for two reasons it is a true proposition to say that a human is a living creature. First, the word "human" already includes the idea of living. Second, the word "human" is a mark for the sensation we have when we see an actual human being. The relation of words to each other is based upon the relations between the events for which the words stand as representations. Reasoning, then, is "nothing but reckoning—that is adding and subtracting, of consequences of general names." And even if the word "human" does not refer to any general or universal reality but only to particular people, Hobbes still maintains that we have reliable knowledge, that although "experience concludes nothing universally," science, based on experience, does "conclude universally." This encapsulates Hobbes's nominalism, which led him to say that universal terms such as "human" are merely words and point to no general reality. This also exhibits his empiricism, which led him to argue that we can know things about all people because of what we know from our experience about some people.

Political Philosophy and Morality

When we turn directly to Hobbes's political philosophy, we find that he employed as much of his theory of motion and his logic—as well as the method of geometry—as this subject would permit. Just as he looked to the concepts of motion and bodies to describe human nature—and particularly to describe human knowledge—so also he now analyzes the structure and nature of the state in terms of moving bodies. Moreover, his account of the state is the most impressive example of his conception of philosophy. For if philosophy is a matter of "reckoning, that is adding and subtracting of consequences of general names," it is preeminently in his political philosophy that he exhibits his skill and rigor with the meanings of words.

What strikes us first about Hobbes's theory of state is that he approaches the subject not from an historical point of view but from the vantage point of logic and analysis. He does not ask, "when did civil societies emerge?" but asks rather, "how do you explain the emergence of society?" He hopes to discover the cause of civil society, and, in harmony with his general method, he sets out to explain the cause of the state by describing the motion of bodies. His thought about political philosophy resembles the method of geometry only in the sense that from axiom-like premises he deduces all the consequences or conclusions of his political theory, and most of these premises cluster around his conception of human nature.

The State of Nature

Hobbes describes people, first of all, as they appear in what he calls "the state of nature," which is the condition of people before there was any state or civil society. In this state of nature all humans are equal and equally have the right to whatever they consider necessary for their survival. Equality here means simply that people are capable of hurting their neighbors and taking what they judge they need for their own protection. Differences in strength can in time be overcome and the weak can destroy the strong. The "right of all to all" which prevails in the state of nature does not mean that one person has a right whereas others have corresponding duties. The word "right" in the bare state of nature is a person's freedom "to do what he would, and against whom he thought fit, and to possess, use and enjoy all that he would, or could get." The driving force in a person is the will to survive, and the psychological attitude pervading all people is fear—the fear of death and particularly the fear of violent death. In the state of nature all people are relentlessly pursuing whatever acts they think will secure their safety. The picture we get of this state of nature is of people moving against each other—bodies in motion—or the anarchic condition Hobbes called "the war of all against all."

Why do people behave this way? Hobbes analyzes human motivation by saying that everyone possesses a twofold drive, namely appetite and aversion. These two drives account for our motions to and from other people or objects, and have the same meanings as the words love and hate. People are attracted to what they think will help them survive, and they hate whatever they judge to be a threat to them. The words good and evil have whatever meaning each individual will give them, and people will call good whatever they love and evil whatever they hate, "there being nothing simply and absolutely so." We are fundamentally egotistical in that we are concerned chiefly about our own survival and we identify goodness with our own appetites. It would appear therefore that in the state of nature there is no obligation for people to respect others or that there is no morality in the traditional sense of goodness and justice. Given this egotistical view of human nature, it would appear also that we did not possess the capacity to create an ordered and peaceful society.

But Hobbes argued that several logical conclusions or consequences can be deduced from our concern for our survival, among these being what Hobbes called natural laws. Even in the state of nature, people know these natural laws, which are logically consistent with our principal concern for our own safety. A natural law, said Hobbes, "is a precept, or general rule, found out by reason," telling what to do and what not to do. If the major premise is that I want to survive, I can logically deduce, even in the state of nature, certain rules of behavior that will help me survive. The first law of nature is therefore that everyone ought to "seek peace and follow it." Now this law that urges me to seek peace is natural because it is a logical extension of my concern for survival. It is obvious that I have a better chance to survive if I help to create the conditions of peace. My desire for survival therefore impels me to seek peace. From this first and fundamental law of nature is derived the second law, which states that "a man be willing, when others are so too, as far-forth as for peace, and defense of himself he shall think it necessary, to lay down his right to all things; and be contented with so much liberty against other men, as he would allow other men against himself." More simply, we should willingly give up our hostile rights toward other people if they are willing to give up their hostile rights toward us.

Obligation in the State of Nature

If we know these and other natural laws even in the state of nature, do we have an obligation to obey them? Hobbes answers that these laws are always binding, in the state of nature as well as in civil society. But he distinguishes between two ways in which these natural laws are applicable in the state of nature, saying that "the laws of nature oblige *in foro interno;* that is to say, they bind to a desire they should take place: but *in foro externo;* that is, to putting them in act, not always." Thus, it isn't as if there were no obligations in the state of nature; it's just that the circumstances for living by these laws in the state of nature are not always present. People have a right to all things in the state of nature not because there is no obligation, but because if a person was modest, tractable, and kept his promises "in such time and place where no man else should do so, [he] should but make himself a prey to others, and procure his own ruin, contrary to the ground of all laws of nature, which tend to nature's preservations." And even when we act to preserve ourselves, we are not free from rational natural laws, for even in the state of nature we ought to act in good faith: "If any man pretend somewhat to tend necessarily to his preservation, which yet he himself does not confidently believe so, he may offend against the laws of nature."

Hobbes was aware that anarchy is the logical outcome of egotistical individuals all deciding how best to survive. It would be a horrible condition in which there is "no arts; no letters; no society; and which is worst of all, continual fear, and danger of violent death; and the life of man solitary, poor, nasty, brutish, and short." We should thus avoid this condition of anarchy to the extent that it is in our power. The chief cause of this war is the conflict of individual and egotistical judgments. By following the dictates of natural law, though, we should seek peace, renounce some of our rights or freedoms, and enter into a social contract. We will thereby create an artificial person—that great leviathan—called a commonwealth, or state.

The Social Contract

The contract by which we avoid the state of nature and enter civil society is an agreement between individuals, "as if every man should say to every man, I authorize and give up my right of governing myself, to this man, or to this assembly of men, on this condition, that you give up your right to him, and authorize all his actions in like manner." Two things stand out clearly in this contract. First, the parties to the contract are individuals who promise each other to hand over their right to govern themselves to the sovereign; it is not a contract between the sovereign and the citizens. The sovereign has absolute power to govern and is in no way subject to the citizens. Secondly, Hobbes clearly states that the sovereign can be either "this man" or "this assembly of men," suggesting that, in theory, at least, his view of sovereignty was not identified with any particular form of government. It may be that he had a preference for a single ruler with absolute power, but he recognized the possible compatibility of his theory of sovereignty with democracy. But whatever form the sovereign would take, it is clear that Hobbes saw the transfer of the right to rule from the people to the sovereign as both absolute and irrevocable.

Hobbes was particularly anxious to demonstrate with logical rigor that sovereign power is indivisible. Having shown that in the state of nature anarchy is the logical consequence of independent individual judgments, he concluded that the only way to overcome such anarchy is to make a single body out of the several bodies of the citizens. The only way to transform multiple wills into a single will is to agree that the sovereign's single will and judgment represent the will and judgment of all the citizens. In effect, this is what the contract says when people agree to hand over their right to govern themselves. The sovereign now acts not only on behalf of the citizens, but as if he embodied the will of the citizens—thereby affirming an identity between the wills of the sovereign and citizens. Resistance against the sovereign by a citizen is therefore illogical on two counts. First, such resistance would amount to resistance to oneself, and, second, to resist is to revert to independent judgment, which is to revert to the state of nature or anarchy. The power of the sovereign must therefore be absolute in order to secure the conditions of order, peace and law.

Civil Law versus Natural Law

Law begins only when there is a sovereign. This is a logical truism, for in the judicial or legal sense, a law is defined as a command of the sovereign. It follows that where there is no sovereign, there is no law. To be sure, Hobbes affirmed that even in the state of nature people have knowledge of the natural law, and in a special sense the natural law is binding even in the state of nature. But only after there is a sovereign can there be a legal order, because only then is there the apparatus of law in which the power of enforcement is central. Without the power to enforce, said Hobbes, covenants are "mere words." Hobbes identifies law with sovereign command, and he makes the additional point that "there can be no unjust law."

Nowhere does Hobbes's severe authoritarianism express itself in more startling form than when he argues that there can be no unjust law. It appears that justice and morality begin with the sovereign, that there are no principles of justice and morality that precede and limit the acts of the sovereign. Hobbes affirmed this in a notable passage: "To the care of the sovereign, belongs the making of good laws. But what is a good law? By good law, I mean not a just law: for no law can be unjust." Hobbes gives two reasons for saying no law can be unjust: first, because justice means obeying the law, and this is why justice comes into being only after a law has been made and cannot itself be the standard for law. Secondly, when a sovereign makes a law, it is as though the people were making the law, and what they agree upon cannot be unjust. Indeed, the third natural law Hobbes speaks of is "that men perform their covenants made," and he says that this is the "fountain of justice." Hence, to keep the contract in which you agreed to obey the sovereign is the essence of Hobbesian justice.

It is evident that Hobbes forces the reader to take each word seriously and "reckon" all the "consequences" that can be deduced from it. If law means the sovereign's command and if justice means obeying the law, there can be no unjust law. But there can be a bad law. For Hobbes was enough of an Aristotelian to recognize that a sovereign has a definite purpose "for which he was trusted with the sovereign power, namely, the procuration of the safety of the people; to which he is obliged by the law of nature, and to render an account thereof to God." But even in such a case, where the sovereign has commanded a "bad" law, the citizens are not the ones to judge it as such, nor does this justify their disobedience. The sovereign has the sole power to judge what is for the safety of the people. If the people disagree with him, they would revert to anarchy. If the sovereign engages in iniquitous acts, this is a matter between the sovereign and God, not between the citizens and the sovereign. And because he feared anarchy and disorder so deeply, Hobbes pushed his logic of obedience to the point of making religion and the church subordinate to the state. To the Christian who felt that the sovereign's command violated the law of God, Hobbes gave no comfort, but insisted that if such a person could not obey the sovereign, he must "go to Christ in martyrdom."

With these bold strokes, Hobbes altered the course of philosophy. He was among the first to apply the methods of science to the study of human nature, providing novel explanations for human knowledge and moral behavior, departing also from the medieval notion of natural law, and arriving in the end at a highly authoritarian concept of sovereignty. Although Hobbes did not win widespread approval in his day, and even though there is much in his philosophy to question and criticize, his enduring influence was assured by the precision of his formulation of the problems of philosophy.

CHAPTER 10

Rationalism on the Continent

*A*lthough philosophy rarely alters its direction with radical suddenness, there are times when its new concerns and emphases clearly separate it from its immediate past. Such was the case with 17th-century continental rationalism, whose founder was René Descartes and whose new plan initiated what is called *modern philosophy*. In a sense, much of what the Continental rationalists set out to do had already been attempted by the medieval philosophers and by Bacon and Hobbes. But Descartes, Spinoza, and Leibniz fashioned a new vision for philosophy. Influenced by the progress and success of science, they attempted to provide philosophy with the exactness of mathematics. They set out to formulate clear rational principles that could be organized into a system of truths from which accurate information about the world could be deduced. They emphasized the rational capacity of the human mind, which they now considered the source of truth both about human nature and the world. Although they did not reject the claims of religion, they did consider philosophical reasoning something independent of supernatural revelation. They saw little value in subjective feeling and enthusiasm as means for discovering truth. Instead, they believed that, by following the appropriate method, we can discover the nature of the universe. This was an optimistic view of human reason, which offset the recent attempts at reviving ancient skepticism, particularly those by Montaigne. The rationalists assumed that what they could think clearly with their minds did in fact exist in the world outside their minds. Descartes and Leibniz even argued that certain ideas are innate in the human mind, and, given the proper occasion, experience would cause these innate truths to become self-evident. The highly optimistic plan of rationalism was not altogether successful, as shown by the differences in the views of the leading proponents. To be sure, all the rationalists ascribed determinism to all physical events, interpreting the natural world after the mechanical model of physics. But Descartes described reality as a dualism consisting of two basic substances—namely thought and extension.

Spinoza proposed a monism, saying that there is only a single substance—namely, Nature. Leibniz was a pluralist, saying that there are different kinds of elemental substances which make up the world.

DESCARTES

Life

René Descartes, usually called the father of modern philosophy, was born in Touraine in 1596. His father, Joachim Descartes, was a councillor of the Parliament of Brittany. From 1604 to 1612 young Descartes studied in the Jesuit college of La Flèche, where his education included mathematics, logic, and philosophy. He was most impressed, during these years, with the certainty and precision of mathematics, as compared with traditional philosophy which invariably produced doubts and disputes. For a time he was a soldier in the army of Maximilian of Bavaria. After traveling widely throughout Europe, he decided, in 1628, to settle down in Holland, and it was here that Descartes wrote his principal philosophical works, including his *Discourse on Method* (1637), *Meditations on First Philosophy* (1641), *Principles of Philosophy* (1644), and *The Passions of the Soul* (1649). He went to Sweden in 1649 at the invitation of Queen Christina, who wanted Descartes to instruct her in his philosophy. As the queen could see him only at five o'clock in the morning, this unaccustomed encounter with the bitter cold at that hour made him easy prey to illness. Within a few months he suffered an attack of fever, and in February, 1650, he died at the age of 54.

Descartes was chiefly concerned with the problem of intellectual certainty. He had been educated, as he says, "at one of the most celebrated schools in Europe," and yet he found himself embarrassed with "many doubts and errors." Looking back on his studies, he saw that ancient literature provided him charming fables that stimulated his mind. However, these could not guide his behavior since these fables portrayed types of human conduct that were simply beyond the power of human beings to perform. He spoke kindly of poetry, saying that the poet gives us knowledge with "imaginative force," even making truth "shine forth the more brightly" than could the philosophers. Still, poetry is a gift of the mind and not the fruit of study; therefore it gives us no method for consciously discovering truth. Though he honored theology, he concluded that its "revealed truths" were quite above human intelligence, and that if we think successfully about them, "it was necessary to have some extraordinary assistance from above, and to be more than a mere man." He did not want to deny these truths, for he apparently remained a pious Catholic to the end. Nevertheless, he did not find in theology a method by which these truths could be arrived at solely through the capacities of human reason. Nor was the philosophy he learned at college any more helpful in this regard, for "no single thing is to be found in it which is not subject of dispute, and in consequence which is not dubious."

Classroom, University of Paris—1600s, in the time of Descartes
(Snark International, Art Resource, NY)

His quest for certainty led Descartes to turn from his books to that "great book of the world" where through travel he met "men of diverse temperaments and conditions" and collected "varied experiences." It was his thought that among men of the world, he would discover more exacting reasoning, since in practical life, as compared with scholarly activity, a mistake in reasoning has harmful consequences. But, he says, he found as much difference of opinion among practical people as among philosophers. From this experience with the book of the world, Descartes decided "to believe nothing too certainly of which I had only been convinced by example and custom." He resolved to continue his search for certainty, and on a memorable night, November 10, 1619, he had three dreams, which unmistakably convinced him that he must construct the system of true knowledge upon the capacities of human reason alone.

Descartes broke with the past and gave philosophy a fresh start. In particular, since his system of truth would have to be derived from his own rational capacities, he would no longer rely on previous philosophers for his ideas, nor would he accept any idea as true only because it was expressed by someone with authority. Neither the authority of Aristotle's great reputation nor the authority of the church could suffice to produce the kind of certainty he sought. Descartes was determined to discover the basis of intellectual certainty in his own reason. He therefore gave philosophy a fresh start by using only those

René Descartes
(Stock Montage, Inc.)

truths he could know through his own powers as the foundation for all other knowledge. He was well aware of his unique place in the history of philosophy, for he writes that "although all the truths which I class among my principles have been known from all time and by all men, there has been no one up to the present, who, so far as I know, has adopted them as the principles of philosophy . . . as the sources from which may be derived a knowledge of all things else which are in the world. This is why it here remains to me to prove that they are such."

His ideal was to arrive at a system of thought whose various principles were not only true but connected in such a clear way that we could move easily from one true principle to another. But in order to achieve such an organically connected set of truths, Descartes felt that he must make these truths "conform to a rational scheme." With such a scheme he could not only organize present knowledge but could "direct our reason in order to discover those truths of which we are ignorant." His first task therefore was to work out his "rational scheme"—that is, his *method.*

Descartes' Method

Descartes' method consists of harnessing the abilities of the mind with a special set of rules. He insisted upon the *necessity* of method, and upon systematic and orderly thinking. He was appalled at scholars who sought aimlessly for truth, and he compared them to people who, "burning with an unintelligent desire to find treasure, continuously roam the streets, seeking to find something that a passerby might have chanced to drop." He continues that "It is very certain that unregulated inquiries and confused reflections of this kind only confound the natural light and blind our mental powers." But by themselves our mental capacities can lead us astray unless they are carefully regulated. Method consists, therefore, in those rules by which our capacities of intuition and deduction are guided in an orderly way.

The Example of Mathematics　Descartes looked at mathematics for the best example of clear and precise thinking. "My method," he writes, "contains everything which gives certainty to the rule of arithmetic." Indeed, Descartes wanted to make all knowledge a sort of "universal mathematics." He was convinced that mathematical certainty is the result of a special way of thinking. If he could discover this way, he would have a method for discovering true knowledge "of whatever lay within the compass of my powers." Mathematics is not itself the method, but merely exhibits the method Descartes was searching for. Geometry and arithmetic, he says, are only "examples" or "the outer covering" and not "the constituents" of his new method. What then is there about mathematics that led Descartes to find in it the basis of his own method?

In mathematics, Descartes discovered something fundamental about mental operations. Specifically, he fastened upon the mind's ability to apprehend directly and clearly certain basic truths. He was not so much concerned with explaining the mechanics of how we form ideas from experience. Instead, he wanted to affirm the fact that our minds are capable of knowing some ideas with absolute clarity and distinctness. Moreover, mathematical reasoning showed how we progress in an orderly way from what we do know to what we don't know. For example, in geometry we begin with concepts of lines and angles and discover from these more complex concepts, such as the degrees of an angle. Why can we not use this same method of reasoning in other fields as well? Descartes was convinced that we could, and he claimed that his method contained "the primary rudiments of human reason" and that with it he could elicit the "truths in every field whatsoever." From his perspective, all the various sciences are merely different ways in which the same abilities of reasoning and the same method are used. In each case it is the orderly use of intuition and deduction.

Intuition and Deduction　Descartes placed the whole edifice of knowledge upon the foundation of intuition and deduction, saying that "these two methods are the most certain routes to knowledge," adding that any other approach should be "rejected as suspect of error and dangerous." In a nutshell,

intuition gives us foundational concepts, and deduction draws more information from our intuitions. Descartes describes intuition as an intellectual activity or vision of such clarity that it leaves no doubt in the mind. The fluctuating
testimony of our senses and the imperfect creations of our imaginations leave
us confused; intuition, though, provides "the conception which an unclouded
and attentive mind gives us so readily and distinctly that we are wholly freed
from doubt about that which we understand." Intuition gives us clear notions
but also some truths about reality, as, for example, that *I think,* that *I exist,* and
that *a sphere has a single surface*—truths that are basic, simple, and irreducible.
Moreover, it is by intuition that we grasp the connection between one truth
and another—such as the formula "if A = B and C = B, then A = C."

Descartes describes deduction as "all necessary inference from facts that
are known with certainty." What makes intuition and deduction similar is that
both involve truth. By intuition we grasp a simple truth completely and immediately, whereas by deduction we arrive at a truth by a process, a "continuous
and uninterrupted action of the mind." By typing deduction so closely with
intuition, Descartes gave a new interpretation of deduction, which up to his
time had been identified with a type of reasoning called the syllogism. Deduction, as Descartes described it, is different from a syllogism. Whereas a syllogism involves the relationship of *concepts* to each other, deduction for
Descartes involves the relation of *truths* to each other. It is one thing to go
from a premise to a conclusion as one does in a syllogism. But, it is another
thing to move from an indubitable fact to a conclusion about that fact, as
Descartes says we must do by deduction. Descartes emphasized this difference between reasoning from a *fact* and from a *premise,* for the central point of
his method was at stake here. Descartes' quarrel with earlier philosophy and
theology was that conclusions were drawn syllogistically from premises that
were either untrue or else based only upon authority. If we start with facts,
though, we are guaranteed the truth of our conclusion through proper deduction. Descartes wanted to rest knowledge upon a starting point that had absolute certainty in the individual's own mind. Knowledge requires the use,
therefore, of intuition and deduction, where "first principles are given by intuition alone while the remote conclusions . . . are furnished only by deduction." This, then, is key component of Descartes' method. Another component
of his method consists of rules to guide intuition and deduction.

Rules of Method   The chief point of Descartes' rules is to provide a clear
and orderly procedure for the operation of the mind. It was his conviction that
"method consists entirely in the order and disposition of the objects toward
which our mental vision must be directed if we would find out any truth." We
must begin with a simple and absolutely clear truth and must move step by
step without losing clarity and certainty along the way. Descartes spent many
years at the task of formulating concrete rules. Of the 21 rules found in his
Rules for the Direction of the Mind, the following are among the most important.
Rule III: When we propose to investigate a subject, "our inquiries should be

directed, not to what others have thought, nor to what we ourselves conjecture, but to what we can clearly and perspicuously behold and with certainty deduce." Rule IV: This is a rule requiring that other rules be adhered to strictly, for "if a man observe them accurately, he shall never assume what is false as true, and will never spend his mental efforts to no purpose." Rule V: We shall comply with the method exactly if we "reduce involved and obscure propositions step by step to those that are simpler, and then starting with the intuitive apprehension of all those that are absolutely simple, attempt to ascend to the knowledge of all others by precisely similar steps." Rule VIII: "If in the matters to be examined we come to a step in the series of which our understanding is not sufficiently well able to have an intuitive cognition, we must stop short there."

In a similar way, Descartes formulated four precepts in his *Discourse on Method,* which he believed were perfectly sufficient, "provided I took the firm and unwavering resolution never in a single instance to fail in observing them." In Descartes' own words, these are the rules:

> The *first* was never to accept anything for true which I did not clearly know to be such; . . . to comprise nothing more in my judgment than what was presented to my mind so clearly and distinctly as to exclude all ground of doubt. The *second,* to divide each of the difficulties under examination into as many parts as possible, and as might be necessary for its adequate solution. The *third,* to conduct my thoughts in such order that by commencing with objects the simplest and easiest to know, I might ascend by little and little, and, as it were, step by step, to the knowledge of the more complex. . . . And the *last,* in every case to make enumerations so complete, and reviews so general, that I might be assured that nothing was omitted.

Compared with Bacon and Hobbes, Descartes' method puts very little emphasis upon sense experience and experiment in achieving knowledge. How is it that we know the essential qualities, for example, of a piece of wax, Descartes asks? At one time a piece of wax is hard, has a certain shape, color, size, and fragrance. But when we bring it close to the fire its fragrance vanishes, its shape and color are lost, and its size increases. What remains in the wax that permits us still to know it is wax? "It cannot," says Descartes, "be anything that I observed by means of the senses, since everything in the field of taste, smell, sight, touch, and hearing is changed, and still the same wax nevertheless remains." It is "nothing but my understanding alone which does conceive it . . . solely an inspection by the mind," which enables me to know the true qualities of the wax. And, Descartes says, "what I have said here about the wax can be applied to all other things external to me." He relies for the most part upon the truths contained in the mind, "deriving them from [no] other source than certain germs of truth which exist naturally in our souls." Descartes assumed that we possess certain innate ideas, in the sense that we are "born with a certain disposition or propensity for contracting them." Because we can know these truths, we can be assured of a reliable foundation for our deductions. Descartes was confident that he could start from the beginning and rethink and rebuild all of philosophy by having recourse solely to his own rational abilities, and directing them in accordance with his rules. He therefore set out to show that we can have certainty of knowledge not only about mathematical concepts but also about the nature of reality.

Methodic Doubt

Descartes used the method of doubt in order to find an absolutely certain starting point for building up our knowledge. Having set out in his *Rules* that we should never accept anything about which we can entertain any doubt, Descartes now tries to doubt everything. He says, "because I wished to give myself entirely to the search after truth, I thought it was necessary for me . . . to reject as absolutely false everything concerning which I could imagine the least ground of doubt." His intention is clear, for he wants to sweep away all his former opinions, "so that they might later on be replaced, either by others which were better, or by the same, when I had made them conform to the uniformity of a rational scheme."

By this method of doubt, Descartes shows how uncertain our knowledge is, even of what seems most obvious to us. What can be clearer than "that I am here, seated by the fire . . . holding this paper in my hands"? But when I am asleep, I dream that I am sitting by the fire, and this makes me realize that "there are no conclusive indications by which waking life can be distinguished from sleep." Nor can I be sure that *things* exist for I cannot tell when I am imagining or really knowing, for "I have learned that [my] senses sometimes mislead me." But surely arithmetic, geometry, or sciences that deal with things must contain some certainty, for "whether I am awake or asleep, two and three together will always make the number five." Here Descartes refers to his longheld belief that there is a God who can do anything. But, he asks, how can he be sure that God "has brought it about that there is no earth, no sky, no extended bodies?" In spite of how evident his impressions are of the world around him, there is a possibility—remote as it may be—that it is all a divinely implanted hallucination. Perhaps God is deceiving him with *everything* he is experiencing!

At this point, Descartes says that "if I am fortunate enough to find a single truth which is certain and indubitable," that will suffice to reverse doubt and establish a philosophy. Like Archimedes, who demanded only an immovable fulcrum to move the earth from its orbit, Descartes searched for his one truth and found it in the very act of doubting. I may doubt that my body exists, or that I am awake, and, in short that all is illusion or false. Nevertheless, one thing remains about which I can have no doubt at all, that *I am*. Descartes makes his point here, in one of the most famous passages in the history of philosophy:

> But I was persuaded that there was nothing in all the world, that there was no heaven, no earth, that there were no minds, nor any bodies: was I not then likewise persuaded that I did not exist? Not at all; of a surety I myself did exist since I persuaded myself of something. But there is some deceiver or other, very powerful and very cunning, who ever employs his ingenuity in deceiving me. Then without doubt I exist also if he deceives me, and let him deceive me as much as he will, he can never cause me to be nothing so long as I think that I am something.

According to Descartes, even if God is deceiving me in every possible way, I know that I exist since, since, in the very mental act of doubting I am affirming my own existence. Descartes expresses this in the phrase, "I think, therefore I am" (*cogito ergo sum,* in Latin).

At first, nothing more is proved by this truth, "I think, therefore I am," than the existence of my thinking self. My doubts still remain about the existence of my own body and about anything else that is other than my thinking. To say "I think, therefore I am" is to affirm *my* existence: "But what then am I? A thing which thinks. What is a thing which thinks? It is a thing which doubts, understands, affirms, denies, wills, refuses and which also imagines and feels." Throughout, Descartes assumes that because thinking is a fact, there must also be a thinker, "a thing which thinks." This "thing" is not the body, for "I knew that I was a substance the whole nature of which is to think, and that for its existence there is no need of any place, nor does it depend on any material thing." This much then seems absolutely certain, namely, that I, an ego, exist, "for it is certain that no thought can exist apart from a thing which thinks." But so far, the thinker is alone, a Robinson Crusoe, enclosed in his ideas.

The Existence of God and External Things

To go beyond the certainty of his own existence as a thinking being, Descartes asks again how we know something to be true. "What," he asks, "is required in a proposition for it to be true and certain?" What is there about the proposition, "I think, therefore I am" that makes it certain? "I came to the conclusion that I might assume as a general rule that the things which we conceive very *clearly* and *distinctly* are all true." In this context *clear* means "that which is present and apparent to an attentive mind," in the same way that objects are clear to our eyes. "Distinctness" refers to "that which is so precise and different from all other objects that it contains within itself nothing but what is clear." The reason, then, that the proposition "I think, therefore I am," is true is simply that it is clear and distinct to my mind. This is the reason, too, that mathematical propositions are true, for they are so clear and distinct that we cannot help accepting them. But to guarantee the truth of our clear and distinct ideas, Descartes had to prove that God exists and that he is not a deceiver who makes us think that false things are true.

Descartes cannot use Aquinas' proofs for the existence of God because those proofs are based upon the very facts which are still subject to Descartes' doubt, namely, facts about the external world such as *motion* and *cause* among physical things. Instead, Descartes must prove God's existence solely in terms of his rational awareness of his own existence and internal thoughts. He therefore begins his proof by examining the various ideas that pass through his mind.

Two things strike him about these ideas, that they are caused, and that according to their content they differ markedly from each other. Ideas are effects, and their causes must be discovered. Some of our ideas seem to be "born with me," some "invented" by me, whereas others "come from without." Our reason tells us that "something cannot be derived from nothing" and also that "the more perfect . . . cannot be a consequence of . . . the less perfect." Our ideas possess different degrees of reality, but "it is manifest by natural light that there must be at least as much reality in the efficient and total cause as in the effect." Some of our ideas, judging by the degree of their reality, could have their origin in myself. But the idea of God contains so much "objective reality" that I wonder whether I could have produced that idea by myself. For "by the name God I understand a substance which is infinite, independent, all-knowing, all-powerful and by which I myself and everything else, if anything else exists, have been created." How can I, a finite substance, produce the idea of an infinite substance? Indeed, how could I know that I am finite unless I could compare myself with the idea of a perfect being? The idea of perfection is so clear and distinct that I am convinced that it could not proceed from my imperfect nature. Even if I were *potentially* perfect, the idea of perfection could not come from that potentiality, for an actual effect must proceed from a being that *actually* exists. Thus, Descartes holds that (1) ideas have causes, (2) the cause must have at least as much reality as the effect, and (3) he is finite and imperfect. From these three points he concludes that his idea of a perfect and infinite Being comes from outside himself—from a perfect Being who exists, from God. In addition, Descartes concludes that God cannot be a deceiver, "since the light of nature teaches us that fraud and deception necessarily proceed from some defect," which could hardly be attributed to a perfect Being.

In addition to this argument from causation, by which he proved the existence of God, Descartes, following Augustine and Anselm, offered his version of the ontological argument. In this argument Descartes sought to demonstrate the existence of God by exploring what the very idea of God implies. He says that if "all which I know clearly and distinctly as pertaining to this object really does belong to it, may I not derive from this an argument demonstrating the existence of God?" How is it possible to move from an analysis of an idea to the certainty that God exists?

Some of our ideas, Descartes says, are so clear and distinct that we immediately perceive what they imply. We cannot, for example, think of a triangle without at once thinking of its lines and angles. Although we cannot think about a triangle without also thinking about its attributes of lines and angles, it does not follow that to think about a triangle implies that it exists. But just as the idea of a triangle implies certain attributes, so also the idea of God implies attributes, and specifically the attribute of existence. The idea of God signifies a perfect Being. But the very idea of perfection implies existence. To speak of a nonexistent perfection is to engage in contradiction. We cannot coherently conceive of a Being who is supremely perfect in all respects and at the same time nonexistent. Just as we cannot think the idea of a triangle without recognizing its attributes, so also we cannot think the idea of God, Descartes says, without recognizing that this idea clearly implies the attributes of existence. Descartes says, "That which we clearly and distinctly understand to belong to the true and immutable nature of anything, its essence or form, can be truly affirmed of that thing. But after we have with sufficient accuracy investigated the nature of God, we clearly and distinctly understand that to exist belongs to his true nature. Therefore we can with truth affirm of God that he exists." Against this line of reasoning, Descartes' critic Gassendi said that perfection does not imply existence, since existence is not a necessary attribute of perfection. To lack existence, he said, implies no impairment of perfection, only the lack of reality. Kant, as we shall see, went into considerably greater detail in his criticism of these attempts to prove the existence of God.

From his own existence, Descartes has proved God's existence. Along the way he has also established the criterion of truth and provided thereby the foundation for mathematical thought and for all rational activity. Now, Descartes takes another look at the physical world, at his own body, and other things, and asks whether he can be certain that they exist. To be a thinking thing does not of itself prove that my body exists, for my thinking self "is entirely and absolutely distinct from my body and can exist without it." How then can I know that my body and other physical things exist?

Descartes answers that we all have the clear and distinct experiences of changing our position and moving about, activities that imply a body, or what he calls "an extended substance." We also receive sense impressions, of sight, sound, and touch, frequently even against our will, and these lead us to believe that they come from bodies other than our own. This overwhelming inclination to believe that these impressions "are conveyed to me by corporeal objects" must come from God; otherwise, he could not "be defended from the accusation of deceit if these ideas were produced by causes other than corporeal objects. Hence we must allow that corporeal objects exist." For Descartes, then, knowledge of the self is prior to knowledge of God, and both the self and God are prior to our knowledge of the external world.

Mind and Body

Descartes has now reversed all his doubts and has satisfied himself absolutely that the self, things, and God exist. He has concluded that there are thinking things and things that are extended, have dimension. Since a person has both a mind and body, Descartes is left with the problem of determining how body and mind are related. The whole drift of Descartes' thought is in the direction of *dualism*—the notion that there are two different kinds of substances in nature. We know a substance by its attribute, and since we clearly and distinctly know two quite different attributes, namely, *thought* and *extension,* there must be two different substances, the spiritual and the corporeal, mind and body. Because Descartes defines a *substance* as "an existent thing which requires nothing but itself to exist," he considers each substance as thoroughly independent of the other. To know something about the mind, therefore, we need make no reference to the body, and similarly, the body can be thoroughly understood without any reference to the mind. One of the consequences of this dualism was that Descartes hereby separated theology and science and assumed that there need be no conflict between them. Science would study physical nature in isolation of any other discipline, since material substance possessed its own sphere of operation and could be understood in terms of its own laws.

If thought and extension are so distinct and separate, how can one account for living things? Descartes reasoned that because living bodies partake of extension, they are part of the material world. Consequently, living bodies operate according to the same mechanical and mathematical laws that govern other things in the material order. Speaking, for example, of animals, Descartes considered them to be automata, saying that "the greatest of all prejudices we have retained from infancy is that of believing that brutes think." We assume animals think, Descartes says, only because we see them act as humans do on occasion, as when dogs do acrobatic tricks. Because humans have two principles of motion, one physical and the other mental, we assume that when animals perform human-like acts, their physical movements are caused by their mental faculties. But Descartes saw no reason for attributing mental abilities to animals, because all of their motions, or actions, can be accounted for by mechanical considerations alone. For, it is "nature which acts in them according to the disposition of their organs, just as a clock, which is only composed of wheels and weights." Thus animals are machines or automata. But what about human beings?

Many activities of the human body, said Descartes, are as mechanical as those of animals. Such physical acts as respiration, circulation of the blood, and digestion are automatic. The workings of the human body could be reduced, he thought, to physics. Every physical event can be adequately accounted for by a consideration of mechanical or efficient causes; there is no need to consider a final cause when describing the physical processes of the body. Moreover, Descartes believed that the total quantity of motion in the universe is constant. This led him to conclude that the movements of the human body could not *originate* in the human mind or soul; the soul, he said, could only affect or alter the direction of the motion in certain elements and parts of the body. Just how the mind could do this was difficult to explain precisely, because thought and extension—mind and body—were for Descartes such different and separate substances. He argued that the soul does not move the various parts of the body directly. Instead, having "its principal seat in the brain," in the pineal gland, comes first of all in contact with the "vital spirits," and through these the soul interacts with the body. Clearly, Descartes tried to give the human body a mechanical explanation and at the same time preserve the possibility of the soul's influence upon human behavior through the activity of the will. Humans, therefore, unlike animals, are capable of several kinds of activities. We can engage in pure thought, our minds can be influenced by physical sensations and perceptions, our bodies can be directed by our minds, and our bodies are moved by purely mechanical forces.

But Descartes' strict dualism made it difficult for him to describe how the mind and body could interact upon each other. If each substance is completely independent, the mind must dwell in the body as a pearl in an oyster, or, to use Descartes' own metaphor, as a pilot in a ship. Scholastic philosophy had described humans as a unity, in which mind is the form and body is the matter, and said that without one there could not be the other. Hobbes had reduced mind to bodies in motion and achieved human unity in that way. But Descartes aggravated the separation of mind and body by his novel definition of "thinking." For he included in the act of thinking some experiences that had traditionally been referred to the body, namely, the whole sphere of sense perceptions, for example, "feeling." When Descartes defines "what I am" as "a thing which thinks," he makes no mention of the body, for everything essential to me is included in "thinking." A thinking thing "is a thing which doubts, understands, affirms, denies, wills, refuses, and which also imagines and *feels.*" Presumably the self could feel heat without a body. But here Descartes cannot, apparently, accept his own dualism. He admits that "nature also teaches me by these sensations of pain, hunger, thirst, etc., that I am not lodged in my body as a pilot in a vessel, but that I am very closely united to it, and, so to speak, so intermingled with it that I seem to compose with it one whole." He even tried to locate the mind in the pineal gland, though even there the technical problem of interaction remains. If there is interaction, there would have to be contact, and so mind would have to be extended. On this problem, his rules of method did not lead him to any clear and distinct conclusion.

SPINOZA

Sspinoza was among the greatest of Jewish philosophers. His originality of mind is suggested by his expulsion from the Synagogue of Amsterdam for his unorthodox views. His refusal to accept the chair of philosophy at Heidelberg was further evidence of his desire to preserve his freedom to pursue his ideas wherever the search for truth might lead him. Though he was content to live in simplicity, to earn a modest living grinding lenses, his fame as a thinker spread abroad and aroused both admiration and condemnation. Baruch Spinoza was born in Amsterdam in 1632 in a family of Portuguese Jews who had fled from persecution in Spain. He was trained in the study of the Old Testament and the Talmud and was familiar with the writings of the Jewish philosopher Maimonides. Having been forced to leave Amsterdam, in 1663 he went to The Hague, where he carried on his literary career, of which his *Ethics* is the crowning work. In 1677 he died of consumption at the age of 45.

Spinoza was influenced by Descartes' rationalism, by his method, and by his choice of the major problems of philosophy. But their similarity of interest and even terminology does not mean that Spinoza was a follower of Descartes. At many points Spinoza brought something new to Continental rationalism, which Descartes had begun.

Method

In common with Descartes, Spinoza thought that we can achieve exact knowledge of reality by following the method of geometry. Descartes had worked out the basic form of this method for philosophy, starting with clear and distinct first principles and attempting from these to deduce the whole content of knowledge. What Spinoza added to Descartes' method was a highly systematic arrangement of principles and axioms. Whereas Descartes' method was

Spinoza
(Stock Montage, Inc.)

simple, Spinoza almost set out literally to write a geometry of philosophy, that
is, a complete set of axioms or theorems (about 250 altogether) that would explain the whole system of reality the way geometry explains the relations and
movement of things. In geometry, conclusions are demonstrated, and Spinoza
believed that our theory of the nature of reality could also be demonstrated.
Hobbes questioned whether Spinoza had accomplished anything by arranging
his vast number of axioms and theorems into a system of knowledge. Hobbes
argued that it is certainly possible to draw consistent conclusions from axioms, but that since these axioms consist of nothing more than arbitrary definitions, they do not tell us about reality. Spinoza would not agree that his definitions were arbitrary, for he believed, as did Descartes, that our rational

faculties are capable of forming ideas that reflect the true nature of things. "Every definition or clear and distinct idea," says Spinoza, "is true." It must follow, therefore, that a complete and systematic arrangement of true ideas will give us a true picture of reality, for "the order and connection of ideas is the same as the order and connection of things."

The order of things also provides the pattern for the order in which the philosopher should arrange his subjects. It is of utmost importance to observe this order carefully if we are to understand the various aspects of nature accurately. If, for example, we say that things depend for their nature upon God, we must first know all that we can about God before we can understand things. For this reason Spinoza could find little value in Francis Bacon's method, which consisted of enumerating observations of visible events and drawing conclusions from these observations by induction. Nor would he use Aquinas' method of accounting for the existence of God by first of all analyzing the nature of our ordinary experience with things and persons. At this point, too, Spinoza rejects Descartes' approach. Descartes started with a clear and distinct idea of his *own* existence and from the formula *I think, therefore I am*, proceeded to deduce the other parts of his philosophy. Because in the true nature of things God is prior to everything else, Spinoza believed that philosophy must formulate ideas about God first. These ideas of God, then, could appropriately affect the conclusions we draw about such matters as human nature, ways of behaving, and the relation between mind and body. And because Spinoza had such novel things to say about God, it was inevitable that he would say novel things also about human nature. Spinoza, therefore, begins his philosophy with the problem of the nature and existence of God.

God: Substance and Attribute

Spinoza offered a strikingly unique conception of God, in which he identified God with the whole cosmos—a view that we now call "pantheism." His famous formula was God or Nature *(Deus sive Natura)*, as if to say that these two words are interchangeable. We might find hints of pantheism in Biblical descriptions of God as he "in whom we live and move and have our being." However, Spinoza stripped the idea of God of earlier meanings by emphasizing not the *relation* between God and humans but a basic *unity* between them. "Whatever is," he said, "is in God, and nothing can exist or be conceived without God." The clue to Spinoza's unique conception of God is found in his definition: "God I understand to be a being absolutely infinite, that is, a substance consisting of infinite attributes, each of which expresses eternal and infinite essence." Spinoza's special thoughts revolve around the ideas of *substance* and its *attributes.*

Through an intricate sequence of arguments, Spinoza arrives at the conclusion that the ultimate nature of reality is a single substance. He defines *substance* as "that which is in itself and is conceived through itself: I mean that the conception of which does not depend on the conception of another thing from which it must be formed." Substance, then, has no eternal cause but has the cause of itself within itself. So far this is only a *conception*, an idea of a self-caused infinite substance. This idea, however, includes not only what this substance is like but also that it exists. The very idea of substance includes its existence, for "existence appertains to substance," and "therefore from its mere definition its existence can be concluded." This resembles Anselm's *ontological* argument and raises the same problems. Still, Spinoza was certain that we can go with assurance from our idea of this perfect substance to its existence, saying that "if anyone says that he has a clear and distinct, that is, a true idea of substance and nevertheless doubts whether such a substance exists, he is like one who says that he has a true idea and yet doubts whether it may not be false." That this substance is one and infinite follows from the previous definition Spinoza has given of substance. There is therefore a single substance with infinite attributes.

An *attribute*, Spinoza says, is "that which an intellect perceives as constituting the essence of substance." If God is defined as a "substance consisting of infinite attributes," it would appear that there would be an infinite number of substances or that God would possess infinite essence. But Spinoza could very well mean here that since an attribute is "that which an intellect perceives," it is possible for the intellect to perceive the single substance in an infinite number of ways. Actually, Spinoza says, we can know only two attributes of substance, namely, thought and extension. Descartes thought that these two attributes showed the existence of two substances, thereby leading him to affirm the dualism of mind and body. Spinoza, though, saw these two attributes as different ways of expressing the activity of a single substance. God is therefore substance perceived as infinite thought and infinite extension. Being infinite, God contains everything.

The World as Modes of God's Attributes

Spinoza does not contrast God and the world as if they were as different and distinct as cause and effect—as though God were the immaterial cause and the world the material effect. He has already established that there is only one substance and that the word *God* is interchangeable with *Nature*. But Spinoza does distinguish between two aspects of Nature, using for this purpose the two expressions *natura naturans* and *natura naturata*. By *natura naturans* Spinoza means substance and its attributes of God, insofar as God is considered to act by the requirements of his own nature. On the other hand, by *natura naturata*, he means "everything which follows from the necessity of the nature of God, or of any one of God's attributes." Further, "by *natura naturata* I understand . . . all the modes of God's attributes in so far as they are considered as things which are in God, and which without God can neither be nor can be conceived." What in earlier language was called the *world*, Spinoza now called the *modes* of God's attributes. The *world* is not distinct from God but *is* God expressed in various modes of thought and extension, of thought and corporeality.

As the *world* consists of the modes of God's attributes, everything in the world acts in accordance with necessity—that is, everything is determined. Thus, the modes in which thought and extension take form in the world are determined by God's substance. As Spinoza says, these modes represent "everything which follows from the necessity of the nature of God." Spinoza gives us a picture of a tight universe where every event unfolds in the only possible way in which it can occur. He writes, "in the nature of things nothing contingent is granted, but all things are determined by the necessity of divine nature for existing and working in a certain way." In a special way God is free, not that he could have created a different kind of world but that though he had to create just what he did, he was not forced to do this by some external cause, only by his own nature. On the other hand, people are not even that free, for we are determined to exist and behave according to God's substance, of whose attributes humanity is a mode. All modes of God's attributes are fixed from eternity, for "things" could not have been produced by God in any other manner or order than that in which they were produced." All the things we experience "are nothing else than modifications of the attributes of God [Nature], or modes by which attributes are expressed in a certain and determined manner." Thus, everything is intimately connected, the infinite substance providing a continuity through all things. Particular things are simply modes or modifications of the attributes of substance, or Nature, or God.

Because everything is eternally as it must be, and because particular events are simply finite modifications of substance, there is no direction toward which things are moving. There is no *end*, no *purpose*, no final cause. From our human vantage point, we try to explain events as either fulfilling or frustrating some purpose of history. Ideas of purpose, Spinoza says, are derived from our tendency to act with an end in view. From this habit we tend to look at the universe as though it too had some goal. But this is a wrong way of looking at the universe and indeed at our own behavior. For neither the universe nor human beings are pursuing purposes; they are only doing what they must. This "truth might have lain hidden from the human race through all eternity, had not mathematics, which does not deal with final causes but with the essences of things, offered to men another standard of truth." And the truth is that all events are a continuous and necessary set of modifications of the eternal substance, which simply *is.* Thus Spinoza reduced the biological to the mathematical.

Knowledge, Mind, and Body

How can Spinoza claim to know the ultimate nature of reality? He distinguishes between three levels of knowledge and describes how we can move from the lowest to the highest. We begin with the things most familiar to us, and says Spinoza, "the more we understand individual things the more we understand God." By refining our knowledge of things, we can move from (1) *imagination,* to (2) *reason,* and finally to (3) *intuition.*

At the level of *imagination,* our ideas are derived from sensation, as when we see another person. Here our ideas are very concrete and specific, and the mind is passive. Though our ideas on this level are specific, they are vague and inadequate, for we know things only as they affect our senses. For example, I know that I *see* a person, but as yet I do not know simply by looking what this person's essential nature is. I can form a general idea, such as *human,* by seeing several people, and the ideas I form from experience are useful for daily life, but they do not give me true knowledge.

The second level of knowledge goes beyond imagination to *reason.* This is scientific knowledge. Everyone can participate in this kind of knowledge because it is made possible by a sharing in the attributes of substance, in God's thought and extension. There is in humanity what is in all things, and since one of these common properties is mind, the human mind shares in the mind that orders things. At this level a person's mind can rise above immediate and particular things and deal with abstract ideas, as it does in mathematics and physics. At this level, knowledge is *adequate* and *true.* If we ask Spinoza how we know that these ideas of reason and science are true, he replies in effect that truth validates itself, for "he who has a true idea knows at the same time that he has a true idea, nor can he doubt concerning the truth of the thing."

The third and highest level of knowledge is *intuition.* Through intuition we can grasp the whole system of nature. At this level we can understand the particular things we encountered on the first level in a new way, for at that first level we saw other bodies in a disconnected way, and now we see them as part of the whole scheme. This kind of knowing "proceeds from an adequate idea of the formal essence of certain attributes of God to the adequate knowledge of the essence of things." When we reach this level we become more and more conscious of God and hence "more perfect and blessed," for through this vision we grasp the whole system of Nature and see our place in it, giving us an intellectual fascination with the full order of Nature, of God.

Descartes was left with the difficult problem of explaining how the mind interacts with the body. This was for him virtually unsolvable because he assumed that mind and body represent two distinct substances. For Spinoza, however, this was no problem at all because he viewed mind and body as attributes of a single substance. There is only one order of Nature, to which both the body and mind belong. Humans constitute a single mode. It is only because we are able to consider humans as a mode of extension that we speak of a body, or, as a mode of thought that we speak of a mind. There can be no separation of mind and body because they are aspects of the same thing. For every body there is a corresponding idea, and, in general, Spinoza says that the mind is the idea of the body, which is his way of describing the relationship of the mind to the body. The structure within which the mind and body operate is the same. Thus, human beings are finite versions of God, for it is a mode of God's attributes of thought and extension. This interpretation of both humans and God set the stage for Spinoza's distinctive theory of ethics.

Ethics

The central feature of Spinoza's account of human behavior is that he treats people as an integral part of Nature. Spinoza says that he looks upon "human actions and desires exactly as if I were dealing with lines, planes, and bodies." His point is that human behavior can be explained just as precisely in terms of causes, effects, and mathematics, as any other natural phenomenon. Although people think they are *free* and are able to make *choices,* they are victims of an illusion, for it is only human ignorance that permits us to think we possess freedom of the will. People like to think that in some special way they stand outside the rigorous forces of cause and effect—that though their wills can cause actions, their wills are themselves not affected by prior causes. But Spinoza argued for the unity of all Nature, with people as an intrinsic part of it. Spinoza therefore develops a naturalistic ethics whereby all human actions, both mental and physical, are said to be determined by prior causes.

All people possess as a part of their nature the drive to continue or persist in their own being, and this drive Spinoza calls *conatus.* When this *conatus* refers to the mind and body, it is called *appetite,* and insofar as appetite is conscious, it is called *desire.* As we become conscious of higher degrees of self-preservation and perfection, we experience pleasure, and with a reduction of such perfection, we experience pain. Our ideas of good and evil are related to our conceptions of pleasure and pain. As Spinoza says, "By good I understand here all kinds of pleasure whatever conduces to it, and more especially that which satisfies our fervent desires, whatever they may be. By bad I understand all kinds of pain, and especially that which frustrates our desires." There is no intrinsic *good* or *bad.* We simply call something *good* if we desire it and *bad* if we dislike it. Goodness and badness reflect a subjective evaluation. But because our desires are determined, so are our judgments.

If all our desires and actions are determined by external forces, how can there be any occasion for morality? Here Spinoza resembles the Stoics, who also argued that all events are determined. The Stoics called for resignation and acquiescence to the drift of events, saying that though we cannot control events, we can control our attitudes. In a similar way, Spinoza tells us that through our knowledge of God we can arrive at "the highest possible mental acquiescence." Morality, therefore, consists of improving our knowledge by moving from the level of confused and inadequate ideas up to the third level of intuition, where we have clear and distinct ideas of the perfect and eternal arrangement of all things in God. Only knowledge can lead us to happiness, for only through knowledge can we be liberated from the bondage of our passions. We are enslaved by passions when our desires are attached to perishable things and when we do not fully understand our emotions. The more we understand our emotions, the less excessive will be our appetites and desires. And "the mind has greater power over the emotions and is less subject hereto, in so far as it understands all things as necessary."

We must study not only our emotions but the whole order of Nature, for it is only from the perspective of eternity that we can really understand our own particular lives, for then we see all events through the idea of God as cause. Spiritual unhealthiness, Spinoza says, can always be traced to our "excessive love for something which is subject to many variations and which we can never be masters of." But we possess by nature the desire for and the capacity for higher degrees of perfection, and we achieve levels of perfection through our intellectual faculties. Passions enslave us only when we lack knowledge. But "from this kind of knowledge necessarily arises the intellectual love of God. From this kind of knowledge arises pleasure accompanied by the idea of God as cause, that is, the love of God; not in so far as we imagine Him as present, but in so far as we understand Him to be eternal; this is what I call the intellectual love of God." This love of God is of course not the love of a divine person. Instead, it is more akin to the mental pleasure we have when we understand a mathematical formula or a scientific operation. That the way to morality described here is "exceeding hard" Spinoza was willing to admit, adding that "all things excellent are as difficult as they are rare."

LEIBNIZ

From his early youth, Leibniz showed unmistakable signs of a brilliant mind. At the age of 13, he was reading difficult scholastic treatises with the same ease that others would be reading novels. He developed the infinitesimal calculus and published his results three years before Sir Isaac Newton had released his manuscript to the printers, the latter claiming to have made the discovery first. He was a man of the world, courting the favor and receiving the patronage of eminent people. He was personally acquainted with Spinoza, whose philosophy impressed him, though he departed from Spinoza's ideas in decisive ways. Leibniz engaged in extensive correspondence with philosophers, theologians, and men of letters. Among his grand projects were attempts to achieve a reconciliation between Protestantism and Catholicism, and an alliance between Christian states, which in his day would have meant a United States of Europe. He became the first president of the Society of the Sciences at Berlin, which was later to become the Prussian Academy.

Gottfried Wilhelm von Leibniz was born at Leipzig in 1646 and entered the university there at the age of 15. At Leipzig he studied philosophy, going next to Jena to study mathematics and then to Altdorf, where he completed the course in jurisprudence and received the doctorate in law at the age of 21. With extraordinary vigor he lived actively in the two worlds of action and thought. He was the author of several significant works. His *New Essays on Human Understanding* examines systematically Locke's *Essay*. His *Essays in Theodicy* deals with the problem of evil. He also wrote shorter philosophical works, including *Discourse on Metaphysics,* the *New System of Nature and the Interaction of Substances,* and the *Monadology.* He was in the service of the House of Hanover, but when George I became King of England, Leibniz was not invited to go with him, possibly because of his quarrel with Newton. His public influence declined, and in 1716, neglected and unnoticed even by the learned society he founded, he died at the age of 70.

Substance

Leibniz was dissatisfied with the way Descartes and Spinoza had described the nature of substance, because he felt they had distorted our understanding of human nature, freedom, and the nature of God. To say, as Descartes did, that there are two independent substances—thought and extension—was to produce the impossible dilemma of trying to explain how those two substances could interact as body and mind either in human beings or in God. Spinoza had tried to solve the dilemma by saying that there is only one substance with two knowable attributes, thought and extension. But to reduce all reality to a single substance was to lose the distinction between the various elements in nature. To be sure, Spinoza spoke of the world as consisting of many modes, in which the attributes of thought and expression appear. Still, Spinoza's monism was a pantheism in which God was everything and everything was part of everything else. To Leibniz, this conception of substance was inadequate because it blurred the distinctions among God, humans, and nature, each of which Leibniz wanted to keep separate. Paradoxically, Leibniz accepted Spinoza's single-substance theory and his mechanical model of the universe. However, he presented such a unique theory of this one substance that he was able to speak of the individuality of persons, the transcendence of God, and the reality of purpose and freedom in the universe.

Extension versus Force   Leibniz challenged the fundamental assumption upon which both Descartes and Spinoza had built their theory of substance, namely, that *extension* implies three-dimensional size and shape. Descartes assumed that *extension* refers to a material substance that is extended in space and is not divisible into something more primary. Spinoza, too, considered extension as an irreducible material attribute of God or Nature. Leibniz disagreed. Observing that the bodies or things we see with our senses are divisible into smaller parts, why can we not assume, asked Leibniz, that all things are compounds or aggregates? "There must be," he said, "simple substances, since there are compound substances, for the compound is only a collection or *aggregatum* of simple substances."

There is nothing new in saying that things must be made of simple substances, for Democritus and Epicurus had argued centuries before that all things consist of small atoms. But Leibniz rejected this notion of atoms, because Democritus had described these atoms as extended bodies, as irreducible bits of matter. Such a particle of matter would have to be considered lifeless or inert and would have to get its motion from something outside itself. Rejecting the idea of matter as primary, Leibniz argued that the truly simple substances are the *monads,* and these are "the true atoms of nature . . . the elements of things." The monads differ from atoms in that atoms were viewed as extended bodies, whereas Leibniz described the monad as being *force* or *energy.* Leibniz therefore said that matter is not the primary ingredient of things. Instead, monads with their element of force constitute the essential substance of things.

Monads   Leibniz wanted to emphasize that substance must contain life or a dynamic force. Whereas Democritus' material atom would have to be acted upon from outside itself in order to move or become a part of a large cluster, Leibniz said that simple substance, the monad, is "capable of action." He added that "*compound* substance is the collection of *monads. Monas* is a Greek word which signifies unity, or that which is one. . . . Simple substances, lives, souls, spirits are unities. Consequently all nature is full of life."

Monads are unextended, they have no shape or size. A monad is a point, not a mathematical or a physical point but a metaphysically existent point. Each monad is independent of other monads, and monads do not have any causal relation to each other. It is difficult to imagine a *point* that has no shape or size, yet Leibniz wanted to say just this in order to differentiate the monad from a material atom. Actually his thinking here resembles the 20th-century notion that physical particles are reducible to energy, or that particles are a special form of energy. Essentially Leibniz was saying that monads are logically prior to any corporeal forms. True substances, then, are monads, and these Leibniz also calls *souls* to emphasize their nonmaterial nature. Each monad is different from the others, and each possesses its own principle of action and its own force. Leibniz says, "there is a certain sufficiency which makes them the source of their internal actions and, so to speak, incorporeal automata." Monads are not only independent and different. They also contain the source of their activity within themselves. Moreover, in order to emphasize that the rest of the universe does not affect their behavior, Leibniz says that the monads are *windowless.* But there must be some relation between all monads which make up the universe—some explanation for their orderly actions. This explanation Leibniz finds in his idea of a *preestablished harmony.*

Preestablished Harmony   Each monad behaves in accordance with its own created purpose. These *windowless* monads, each following its own purpose, form a unity of the ordered universe. Even though each is isolated from the other, their separate purposes form a large-scale harmony. It is as though several clocks all struck the same hour because they keep perfect time. Leibniz compares all these monads to "several different bands of musicians and choirs, playing their parts separately, and so placed that they do not see or even hear one another." Nevertheless, Leibniz continues, they "keep perfectly together, by each following their own notes, in such a way that he who hears them all finds in them a harmony that is wonderful, and much more surprising than if there had been any connection between them." Each monad, then, is a separate world, but all the activities of each monad occur in harmony with the activities of the others. In this way we can say that each monad mirrors the whole universe—but from a unique perspective. If anything "were taken away or supposed different, all things in the world would have been different" from what they are like at present. Such a harmony as this could not be the product of an accidental assortment of monads; instead, they must be the result of God's activity, whereby this harmony is preestablished.

God's Existence

To Leibniz, this fact of a universal harmony of all things provided a "new proof of the existence of God." He had accepted, for the most part, the earlier attempts to prove God's existence. He says of these that "nearly all of the means which have been employed to prove the existence of God are good and might be of service, if we would perfect them." But he was particularly impressed by "this perfect harmony of so many substances which have no communication with each other." This harmony, he believed, pointed to the existence of God with "surprising clearness," because a harmony of many windowless substances "can only come from a common cause." This resembles the argument from design and from a first cause, although Leibniz modified the argument from cause with his principle of *sufficient reason.*

Principle of Sufficient Reason   Leibniz argued that any event can be explained by referring to a prior cause. But that prior cause must itself be explained by a still earlier cause. In theory, then, we might find a continual chain of finite causes, tracing back to infinity. So, when seeking for the ultimate cause of any event, it will not help to single out any individual cause in this infinite chain, since there will always be another preceding it. The solution, according to Leibniz, is to recognize the existence of some cause outside the series of causes. That is, it must be outside the complex organization of the universe itself. This cause must be a substance whose own existence is necessary, whose existence requires no cause or further explanation, a Being "whose essence involves existence, for this is what is meant by a necessary Being." The sufficient reason for the ordinary things we experience in the world of fact lies therefore in a Being outside the series of obvious causes—in a Being whose very nature or essence is a sufficient reason for its own existence, requiring no prior cause, and this being is God.

Evil and the Best of All Possible Worlds   The harmony of the world led Leibniz to argue not only that God had preestablished it but also that in doing this God has created the best of all possible worlds. Whether this is the best or even a good world is open to question because of the disorder and evil in it. Indeed, Schopenhauer thought that this is, if anything, the worst of all possible worlds and that consequently we are not justified in concluding that God exists or that the world with all its evil is the creation of a good God. Leibniz was aware of the fact of evil and disorder but considered it compatible with the notion of a benevolent creator. In his perfect knowledge, God could consider all the possible kinds of worlds he could create, but his choice must be in accord with the moral requirements that the world should contain the greatest possible amount of good. Such a world would not be without imperfection. On the contrary, the world of creation consists of limited and imperfect things, "for God could not give the creature all without making it God; therefore there must needs be . . . limitations also of every kind." The source of evil is not God but rather the very nature of things God creates, for as these things are finite or limited, they are imperfect. Evil, then, is not something substantial but merely the absence of perfection. Evil for Leibniz is privation. This is why Leibniz could say that "God wills *antecedently* the good and *consequently* the best," since the most that God can do, in spite of his goodness, is to create the best possible world. As a final consideration, Leibniz agrees that we cannot rightly appraise evil if we consider only the particular evil thing or event. Some things that in themselves appear to be evil turn out to be the prerequisites for good, as when "sweet things become insipid if we eat nothing else; sharp, tart and even bitter things must be combined with them, so as to stimulate the taste." Again, events in our lives, taken by themselves, lose their true perspective. Leibniz asks, "If you look at a very beautiful picture, having covered up the whole of it except a very small part, what will it present to your sight, however thoroughly you examine it . . . but a confused mass of colors, laid on without selection and without art? Yet if you remove the covering, and look at the whole picture from the right point of view, you will find that what appeared to have been carelessly daubed on the canvas was really done by the painter with very great art."

Freedom   How can there be any freedom in the determined world Leibniz portrays, where God preestablishes an orderly arrangement by infusing specific purposes into the several monads? Each monad is involved in developing its built-purpose, and "every present state of a simple substance is naturally a consequence of its preceding state, in such a way that its present is big with its future." Each person, whose identity centers around a dominant monad, his soul, must represent in this mechanical view an unfolding of a life that has been set from the beginning. Yet, since the basic nature of this person is thought, his development through life consists in overcoming confused thoughts and arriving at true ideas, which lie in all of us in the murky form of potentiality seeking to become actual. When our potentialities become actual, we see things as they really are, and this, Leibniz says, is what it means to be free. For him freedom does not mean volition—the power of choice—but rather self-development. So, although I am determined to act in specific ways, it is my own internal nature that determines my acts and not outside forces. Freedom in this sense means the ability to become what I am destined to be without obstructions. It also means a quality of existence whereby my knowledge has passed from confusion to clarity. I am free to the extent that I know why I do what I do. It was along these lines that Leibniz thought he had succeeded in reconciling his deterministic view of nature with freedom.

Whether Leibniz succeeded in reconciling his world of monads with the notion of freedom is certainly questionable. Although he does at one point speak of freedom in terms of "choice in our will" and say that "free and voluntary means the same thing," still his dominant emphasis appears to be upon determinism—upon the notion of a mechanical-like universe, or a spiritual machine. Actually, Leibniz does not use the mechanical model in describing the universe, for if he did, he would have to say that the various parts of the universe act upon each other the way parts of a clock affect the movements of each other. In a sense, Leibniz's explanation is even more rigorously deterministic than the mechanical model suggests. For his monads are all independent of each other, are not affected by each other, but behave in accordance with their original purpose which they received from the beginning through God's creation. This kind of determinism is more rigorous because it does not depend upon the vagaries of external causation but upon the given and permanently fixed internal nature of each monad.

Knowledge and Nature

This deterministic view of nature is further supported by Leibniz's theory of knowledge. A person, for example, is for Leibniz similar to a "subject" in the grammatical sense. For any true sentence or proposition, the predicate is already contained in the subject. Thus, to know the subject is already to know certain predicates. "All men are mortal" is a true proposition because the predicate *mortal* is already contained in the notion of *men*. Leibniz therefore says that in any true proposition "I find that every predicate, necessary or contingent, past, present, or future, is comprised in the notion of the subject." Similarly, in the nature of things, all substances are, so to speak, subjects, and the things they do are their predicates. Just as grammatical subjects contain their predicates, so also existing substances already contain their future behavior. Thus, Leibniz concludes that "in saying that the individual notion of Adam involves all that will ever happen to him, I mean nothing else but what all philosophers mean when they say that the predicate is in the subject of a true proposition." Leibniz patterned his theory of substance or metaphysics after his theory of knowledge or logic. At the center of his argument is his special treatment of the notion of truth.

Leibniz distinguished between truths of reason and truths of fact. We know truths of reason purely by logic, whereas we know truths of fact by experience. The test of a truth of reason is the law of contradiction, and the test for a truth of fact is the law of sufficient reason. A truth of reason is a necessary truth in that to deny it is to be involved in a contradiction. Truths of fact, on the other hand, are contingent, and their opposite is possible. A truth of reason is a necessary truth because the very meaning of the terms used and the type of human understanding require that certain things be true. For example, that a triangle has three sides is true because to have three sides is what a triangle means. To say that a triangle has four sides is clearly to be involved in a contradiction. That 2 and 2 equals 4, that *A* is *A*, that *A* is not not-*A*, that heat is not cold—all these propositions are true because to deny their truth would be contradictory. Truths of reason are tautologies, because in such propositions the predicate simply repeats what is already contained in the subject. Once the subject is clearly understood, there needs to be no further proof about the truth of the predicate. Truths of reason do not require or affirm that the subject of the proposition exists. It is true, for example, that a triangle has three sides even though one does not refer to any specific existing triangle. Truths of reason tell us what would be true in any case where a subject, in this case triangle, is involved. They deal with the sphere of the possible. It is impossible and contradictory that a triangle should be a square, and therefore cannot be true.

Mathematics is a striking example of the truths of reason, since its propositions are true when they pass the test of the law of contradiction. Thus Leibniz says that "the great foundation of mathematics is the principle of contradiction . . . that is, that a proposition cannot be true and false at the same time." He concludes that "This single principle is sufficient to demonstrate every part of arithmetic and geometry." In short, truths of reason are self-evident truths. They are *analytic* propositions, the predicate of which is contained already in the subject, and to deny the predicate is to be involved in a contradiction.

What about truths of fact? These truths are known through experience. They are not necessary propositions. Their opposites can be considered possible without contradiction, and for this reason their truth is contingent. The statement "Mary exists" is not a truth of reason; its truth is not *a priori*. There is nothing in the subject *Mary* that necessarily implies, or makes it possible for us to deduce, the predicate *exists*. We know the predicate that she exists only *a posteriori*—that is, after an experience. This truth of fact, as is the case with all truths of fact, is based upon the law of sufficient reason, which says that "nothing happens without a reason why it should be so rather than otherwise." As it stands, the proposition "Mary exists" is contingent upon some sufficient reason. In the absence of any sufficient reason, it would be just as true to say that "Mary does not exist." When a sufficient reason is present, other propositions have a basis of truth, so that we say "if *A*, then *B*." This hypothetical character of *A* shows that although there may be a necessary connection between *A* and *B*, it is not absolutely necessary that *A* exist. The existence of *A* is contingent, that is, is *possible*. Whether it will in fact exist depends upon whether there is or will be a sufficient reason for it to exist. For every truth of fact that we entertain, we can see that its opposite is possible, without contradiction.

When we consider all the possibilities that propositions about facts imply, a principle of limitation emerges. Whereas some events can be considered possible, simply as the opposite of others, they cannot be possible once other possibilities have become actual. That is, some possibilities are *compossible* with some events though not with others. Thus Leibniz says that "not all possible species are compossible in the universe, great at it is, and that this holds not only in regard to things that exist contemporaneously but also in regard to the whole series of things."

The universe of facts, as we know it, is only a collection of certain kinds of compossibles, that is, the collection of all the *existent* possibles. There could be other combinations of possibles than the ones our actual universe contains. The relation of the various possibles to each other requires us to understand the sufficient reason that connects each event to another event. Physical science, unlike mathematics, cannot, however, be a deductive discipline. The truths of mathematics are analytic. But in propositions concerning facts, the subject does not contain the predicate. The law of sufficient reason, which governs truths of fact, requires that these truths be verified. But this verification is always partial, since each preceding event in the causal chain of events must also be verified. However, no human being is able to account for the infinite sequence of causes. If the cause of *A* is *B*, it is then necessary to account for the cause of *B* and to go back as far as the beginning. The first fact about the universe is like any other fact; it does not contain, so far as the power of human analysis is capable of discovering, any clearly necessary predicate. To know its truth requires that we discover the sufficient reason for its being what it is.

The final explanation of the world, Leibniz says, is that "the true cause why certain things exist rather than others is to be derived from the free decrees of the divine will." Things are as they are because God willed them to be that way. Having willed some things to be what they are, he limited the number of other possibilities and determined which events can be compossible. God could have willed other universes, and other combinations of possibilities. But having willed this universe, there now exist certain necessary connections between specific events. Although from the perspective of human reason, propositions concerning the world of facts are *synthetic,* or require experience and verification, if we are to know their truth, these propositions are, from God's perspective, *analytic.* Only God can deduce all the predicates of any substance. And only our ignorance prevents us from being able to see in any particular person all the predicates connected with that person. In the end, truths of fact are also analytic, according to Leibniz. A person does already contain his predicates, so that if we really comprehended the complete notion of a person, we could deduce these predicates, as, for example, "the quality of king, which belongs to Alexander the Great."

For Leibniz, then, logic is a key to metaphysics. From the grammar of propositions, he inferred conclusions about the real world. In the end, he argued that all true propositions are analytic. For this reason, substances and persons are for Leibniz equivalent to subjects of an analytic proposition; they really contain, he said, all their predicates. He also applies a *law of continuity* to his notion of substance in order to confirm his theory that each substance unfolds its predicates in an orderly and (from God's perspective) predictable way. The *law of continuity* states that "Nature makes no leaps." Among created things, every possible position is occupied, so that all change is continuous. According to the law of continuity, rest and motion are aspects of each other, merging into each other through infinitesimal changes, "so much so that the rule of rest ought to be considered as a particular case of the rule of motion." The *windowless* monads, then, bear in themselves all their future behavior. And as this is true of each monad, all the combinations and possibilities of events already contained in the world also contain the whole future of the world, and the sufficient reason for this order is "the supreme reason, which does everything in the most perfect way." Although the human mind cannot know all reality as God knows it, still, Leibniz says, we know certain innate ideas, self-evident truths. A child does not know all these truths at once but must wait until maturity and for specific occasions in experience when these ideas are called forth. Such notions are *virtually* innate, since we know them only on specific occasions. Still, this doctrine of innate ideas, along with Leibniz's general treatment of the relation of logic to reality bear the clear marks of the rationalist tradition. He optimistically appraises the capacity of reason to know reality and felt that we could deduce considerable knowledge from innate self-evident truths.

CHAPTER 11

Empiricism in Britain

Although the school of empiricism came upon the scene in an unpretentious way, it was destined to alter the course and concerns of modern philosophy. Whereas Bacon aimed at "the total reconstruction of . . . all human knowledge," Locke, who was the founder of empiricism in Britain, aimed at the more modest objective of "clearing the ground a little, and removing some of the rubbish that lies in the way of knowledge." But in the process of "clearing" and "removing," Locke hit upon a bold and original interpretation of how the mind works and, from this, described the kind and extent of knowledge we can expect from the human mind.

The scope of our knowledge, Locke said, is limited to our experience. This was not a new insight, for others before him had said much the same thing. Both Bacon and Hobbes had urged that knowledge should be built upon observation, and to this extent they could be called *empiricists*. But neither Bacon nor Hobbes raised any critical question about the intellectual capacities of human beings. They both uncovered and rejected types of thought that they considered fruitless and erroneous. However, they accepted without challenge the general view that we can attain certain knowledge, so long as we use the proper method. Similarly, Descartes assumed that there was no problem that human reason could not solve if the correct method was employed. This was the assumption Locke called into critical question—namely, the belief that the human mind has capabilities that enable it to discover the true nature of the universe. David Hume pushed this critical point even further and asked whether any secure knowledge at all is possible. In their separate ways, the British empiricists—Locke, Berkeley, and Hume—challenged not only their English predecessors but also the Continental rationalists, who had launched modern philosophy upon an optimistic view of our rational abililities that the empiricists could not accept.

John Locke
(Stock Montage, Inc.)

LOCKE

John Locke was born in 1632 at Wrington, Somerset, and died 72 years later in 1704. He grew up in a Puritan home, trained in the virtues of hard work and the love of simplicity. After a thorough education in the classics at Westminster School, Locke became a student at Oxford University, where he took the bachelor's and master's degrees and was appointed Senior Student and later Censor of Moral Philosophy. He spent 30 years of his life in the city of Oxford. Though he continued his studies of Aristotle's logic and metaphysics, he was gradually drawn toward the newly developing experimental sciences, being influenced in this direction particularly by Robert Boyle. His scientific interests led him to pursue the study of medicine, and in 1674 he obtained his medical degree and was licensed to practice. As he pondered what direction his career might take, there was added to the considerations of medicine and Oxford Tutor an alternative: political diplomacy. He actually served in various capacities, eventually becoming the personal physician and confidential adviser to the Earl of Shaftesbury, one of the leading politicians of London. But earlier influences—among them his reading of Descartes' works while at Oxford—confirmed his desire to devote his creative abilities to working out a philosophical understanding of certain problems that perplexed his generation. He wrote on such diverse topics as *The Reasonableness of Christianity, An Essay Concerning Toleration,* and the *Consequences of the Lowering of Interest and Raising the Value of Money,* indicating his active participation in the public affairs of his day.

In 1690, when he was 57 years old, Locke published two books which were to make him famous as a philosopher and as a political theorist: *An Essay Concerning Human Understanding* and *Two Treatises on Civil Government.* Although other philosophers before him had written about human knowledge, Locke was the first one to produce a full-length inquiry into the scope and limits of the human mind. Similarly, others had written important works on political theory, but Locke's second of the *Two Treatises* came at a time when it could shape the thoughts of an era and later affect the course of events. The *Two Treatises* and *Essay* show Locke's way of combining his practical and theoretical interests and abilities. The *Two Treatises* were expressly formulated to justify the revolution of 1688. Some of its ideas took such strong hold upon succeeding generations that phrases contained in it, as, for example, that we are "all equal and independent" and possess the natural rights to "life, health, liberty and possessions," worked their way into the Declaration of Independence and affected the shaping of the American Constitution. Regarding his *Essay,* he tells us that it grew out of an experience that occurred about 20 years before this work was published. On that occasion, five or six friends met to discuss a point in philosophy, and before long they were hopelessly snarled, "without coming any nearer a resolution of those doubts which perplexed us." Locke was convinced that the discussion had taken a wrong turn. Before we could address "the principles of morality and revealed religion," we first needed to "examine our own abilities, and see what *objects* our understandings were, or were not, fitted to deal with." From this examination Locke eventually composed his *Essay on Human Understanding,* which became the foundation of empiricism in Britain.

Locke's Theory of Knowledge

Locke set out "to enquire into the origin, certainty, and extent of human knowledge." He assumed that if he could describe what knowledge consists of and how it is obtained, he could determine the limits of knowledge and decide what constitutes intellectual certainty. His conclusion was that knowledge is restricted to *ideas*—not the innate ideas of the rationalists, but ideas that are generated by objects we experience. Without exception, according to Locke, all our ideas come to us through some kind of experience. This means that each person's mind is in the beginning like a blank sheet of paper upon which experience alone can subsequently write knowledge. Before he could elaborate these conclusions, Locke felt that he must lay to rest the persisting theory of innate ideas, the notion that in some way we all come into the world with a standard stock of ideas built into the mind.

No Innate Ideas It is obvious that if Locke is going to say that all ideas come from experience, he must reject the theory of innateness. He points out that "It is an established opinion among some men, that there are in the understanding certain innate principles . . . stamped upon the mind of man, which the soul receives in its very first beginning, and brings into the world with it." Not only does Locke reject this as not true, but he considers this doctrine a dangerous tool in the hands of those who could misuse it. If a skillful ruler could convince people that certain principles are innate, this could "take them off from the use of their own reason and judgment, and put them on believing and taking them upon trust without further explanation." And, "in this posture of blind credulity, they might be more easily governed." But there were those whose interest in the theory of innate ideas was not so malignant.

This was so with Ralph Cudworth (1617–1688)—member of a school of thought called Cambridge Platonism, which, following Plato, maintained that reason was the ultimate criterion of knowledge. Cudworth published his *True Intellectual System of the Universe* in 1678, just at the time when Locke was trying to sort out his thoughts on these problems. Cudworth took the position that the demonstration of God's existence rested upon the premise that certain principles are innate in the human mind. He contended further that the famous empiricist formula that "nothing exists in the intellect which was not first in the senses" leads to atheism. According to Cudworth, if knowledge consists solely of information supplied to the mind by objects external to it, the external world existed before there was knowledge. In that case, knowledge could not have been the cause of the world. Locke disagreed with this view, saying that it was indeed possible to prove the existence of God without recourse to the notion of innate principles. He was particularly concerned to expose the groundless claim for innate ideas in order to keep clear the distinction between prejudice, enthusiasm, and opinion, on the one hand, and knowledge on the other. He therefore set out a series of arguments against this claim to innate ideas.

Those who argued for the theory of innate ideas did so on the grounds that people universally accept the truth of various rational principles. Among these are the principles that "What is, is," which is the principle of identity, and that "It is impossible for the same thing to be, and not to be," which is the principle of noncontradiction. But are these innate? Locke denied that they are, though he does not question their certainty. These principles are certain not because they are innate, but because, once we reflect on the nature of things as they are, our minds will not let us think otherwise. And, even if these principles were accepted by everyone, this would not prove that they were innate, provided that an alternative explanation could be given for this universal consent. Moreover, he argued, there is some question whether there is universal knowledge of these principles. "Seldom," says Locke, are these general principles "mentioned in the huts of Indians, much less are they found in the thoughts of children." If it is argued that such principles can be apprehended only after the mind matures, then why call them *innate?* If they were truly innate, they must always be known, for "No proposition can be said to be in the mind, which it never yet knew which it never yet was conscious of." As Locke saw the matter, the doctrine of innate ideas was superfluous because it contained nothing that he could not explain in terms of his empirical account of the origin of ideas.

Simple and Complex Ideas   Locke assumed that knowledge could be explained by discovering the raw materials out of which it was made. Of these ingredients he spoke this way: "Let us then suppose the mind to be, as we say, white paper, void of all characters, without any ideas:—How comes it to be furnished? . . . Whence has it all the *materials* of reason and knowledge? To this I answer, in one word, from *experience.*" Experience gives us two sources of ideas: sensation and reflection. From the senses we receive into our minds several distinct perceptions and thereby become conversant about objects external to us. This is how we come to have the ideas of yellow, white, heat, cold, soft, hard, bitter, sweet, and all the other sensible qualities. Sensation is the "great source of most of the ideas we have." The other facet of experience is reflection, an activity of the mind that produces ideas by taking notice of previous ideas furnished by the senses. Reflection involves perception, thinking, doubting, believing, reasoning, knowing, willing, and all those activities of the mind that produce ideas as distinct as those we receive from external bodies affecting the senses. All the ideas we have can be traced either to sensation or to reflection, and these ideas, in turn, are either simple or complex.

Simple ideas constitute the chief source of the raw materials out of which our knowledge is made. These ideas are received passively by the mind through the senses. When we look at an object, ideas come into our minds single file. This is so even when an object has several qualities blended together. For example, a white lily has the qualities of whiteness and sweetness without any separation. Our minds receive the ideas of *white* and *sweet* separately because each idea enters through a different sense, namely the sense of sight and the sense of smell. Sometimes different qualities enter by the same sense, as when both the hardness and coldness of ice come through the sense of touch. In this case, our minds sort out the difference between them because there are in fact two different qualities involved. Simple ideas originate first of all, then, in sensation. But some also originate in reflection. Just as the senses are affected by objects, so too are our minds *aware* of the ideas we have received. In relation to the ideas received through the senses, our minds can develop other simple ideas by reasoning and judging. Thus, a simple idea of reflection might be pleasure or pain, or the idea of causal power obtained from observing the effect natural bodies have on one another.

Complex ideas, on the other hand, are not received passively but are rather put together by our minds as a compound of simple ideas. Here the emphasis is upon the activity of our minds, which takes three forms: (1) the mind *joins* ideas, (2) brings ideas together but holds them separate, (3) and *abstracts.*

Thus, my mind joins the ideas of whiteness, hardness, and sweetness to form the complex idea of a lump of sugar. My mind also brings ideas together but holds them separate for the purpose of thinking of relationships, as when we say the grass is greener than the tree. Finally, my mind can separate ideas "from all other ideas that accompany them in their real existence" as when we separate the idea of *man* from John and Peter." In this manner of abstraction, "all its general laws are made."

Primary and Secondary Qualities   To describe in even more detail how we get our ideas, Locke turned his attention to the problem of how ideas are related to the objects that produce them. Do our ideas reproduce exactly the objects we sense? If, for example, we consider a snowball, what is the relation between the ideas that the snowball engenders in our minds and the actual nature of the snowball? We have ideas such as round, moving, hard, white, and cold. To account for these ideas, Locke says that objects have *qualities*, and he defines a quality as "the power [in an object] to produce any idea in our mind." The snowball, then, has qualities that have the power to produce ideas in our minds.

Locke attempts here an important distinction between two different kinds of qualities in order to answer the question of how ideas are related to objects. He terms these qualities *primary* and *secondary*. Primary qualities are those that "really do exist in the bodies themselves." Thus our ideas, caused by primary qualities, resemble exactly those qualities that belong inseparably to the object. The snowball looks round and *is* round, appears to be moving and *is* moving. Secondary qualities, on the other hand, produce ideas in our mind that have no exact counterpart in the object. We have the idea of *cold* when we touch the snowball and the idea of *white* when we see it. But there is no whiteness or coldness in the snowball. What *is* in the snowball is the quality, the power to create in us the ideas of cold and white. Primary qualities, then, refer to solidity, extension, figure, motion or rest, and number—or qualities which belong to the object. Secondary qualities, such as colors, sounds, tastes, and odors, do not belong to or constitute bodies except as powers to produce these ideas to us.

The importance of Locke's distinction between primary and secondary qualities is that through it he sought to distinguish between appearance and reality. Locke did not invent this distinction. Democritus had long ago suggested something similar when he said that colorless atoms are the basic reality and that colors, tastes, and odors are the results of particular organizations of these atoms. Descartes also separated secondary qualities from the basic substance he called *extension*. Locke's distinction reflected his interest in the new physics and the influence of the "judicious Mr. Newton's incomparable book" upon his thought. Newton explained the appearance of *white* as the motions of invisible minute particles. Reality, then, is found not in whiteness, which is only an effect, but in the motion of something, which is the cause. His discussion of primary and secondary qualities assumed throughout that there was *something* that could possess these qualities, and this he called *substance*.

Substance　Locke approached the question of substance from what he regarded as a common-sense point of view. How can we have ideas of qualities without supposing that there is something—some substance—in which these qualities subsist? If we ask what has shape or color, we answer something solid and extended. *Solid* and *extended* are primary qualities, and if we ask in what they subsist, Locke answers *substance.* However inevitable the idea of substance may be to common sense, Locke was unable to describe it with precision. He admitted that "if any one will examine himself concerning his notion of pure substance in general, he will find he has no other idea of it at all, but only a supposition of he knows not what support of such qualities which are capable of producing simple ideas in us." Still, Locke saw in the concept of substance the explanation of sensation, saying that sensation is caused by substance. Similarly, it is substance that contains the powers that give regularity and consistency to our ideas. Finally, it is substance, Locke held, that constitutes the object of sensitive knowledge.

Locke was impelled by the simple logic of the matter: If there is motion, there must be something that moves. Qualities simply cannot float around without something that holds them together. We have ideas of *matter* and of *thinking,* but "we shall never be able to know whether any mere material being thinks or no." But if there is thinking, there must be something that thinks. We also have an idea of God, which, like the idea of substance in general, is not clear and distinct. Yet, "if we examine the idea we have of the incomprehensible supreme being, we shall find that we come by it in the same way, and that the complex ideas we have both of God and separate spirits are made up of the simple ideas that we receive from reflection." The idea of God, as the idea of substance, is inferred from other simple ideas and is the product not of immediate observation but of demonstration. But the idea of substance, being "something we know not what," does raise for Locke the question of just how far our knowledge extends and how much validity it has.

The Degrees of Knowledge　How far our knowledge extends and how much validity it has depends, according to Locke, upon the relations our ideas have to each other. Indeed, Locke finally defines *knowledge* as nothing more than "the perception of the connection of and agreement, or disagreement and repugnancy of any of our ideas." Our ideas enter single file into our minds, but once they are inside they can become related to each other in many ways. Some of the relations our ideas have to each other depend upon the objects we experience. At other times, our imagination can rearrange our simple and complex ideas to suit our fancy. Whether our knowledge is fanciful or valid depends upon our *perception* of the relationships of our ideas to each other. There are three types of perception, namely, *intuitive, demonstrative,* and *sensitive,* and each one leads us to a different degree of knowledge regarding reality.

Intuitive knowledge is immediate, leaves no doubt, and is "the clearest and most certain that human frailty is capable of." Such knowledge "like sunshine forces itself immediately to be perceived as soon as ever the mind turns its view that way." Instantly we know that a circle is not a square or that 6 is not 8 because we can perceive the repugnancy of these ideas to each other. But besides these formal or mathematical truths, intuition can lead us to a knowledge of what exists. From intuition we know that we exist: "Experience then convinces us, that we have intuitive knowledge of our own existence, and an internal infallible perception that we are."

Demonstrative knowledge occurs when our minds try to discover the agreement or disagreement of ideas by calling attention to still other ideas. Ideally, each step of the demonstration must have intuitive certainty. This is particularly the case in mathematics, but again Locke thought that demonstration is a type of perception that leads the mind to a knowledge of some form of existing reality. Thus "man knows, by an intuitive certainty, that bare nothing can no more produce any real being than it can be equal to two right angles." From this starting point Locke argued that since there are in fact existing things that begin and end in time, and since a "nonentity cannot produce any real being, it is an evident demonstration, that from eternity there has been something." Reasoning in a similar way, he concludes that this eternal Being is "most knowing" and "most powerful" and that "it is plain to me we have a more certain knowledge of the existence of God, than of anything our senses have not immediately discovered to us."

Sensitive knowledge is not knowledge in the strict sense of the term; it only "passes under the name of knowledge." Locke did not doubt that things outside of us exist, for, otherwise, where did we get our simple ideas? But sensitive knowledge does not give us certainty, nor does it extend very far. We sense that we see another man and have no doubt that he exists, but when he leaves us, we are no longer sure of his existence. "For if I saw such a collection of simple ideas as is wont to be called *man*, existing together one minute since, and am now alone, I cannot be certain that the same man exists now, since there is no *necessary connection* of his existence a minute since with his existence now." And therefore, "while I am alone, writing this, I have not that knowledge of it which we strictly call knowledge; though the great likelihood of it puts me past doubt." Since experience simply makes us aware of qualities, we have no assurance of the connections between qualities. In particular, sensitive knowledge does not assure us that qualities, which seem to be related are in fact *necessarily* connected. We simply sense things as they are, and as we never sense *substance*, we never know from sensation how things are *really* connected. Nevertheless, sensitive knowledge gives us *some* degree of knowledge but not certainty. Intuitive knowledge gives us certainty that we exist, demonstrative knowledge shows that God exists, and sensitive knowledge assures us that other selves and things exist but only as they are when we experience them.

Locke's Moral and Political Theory

Locke placed our thoughts about morality into the category of demonstrative knowledge. To him morality could have the precision of mathematics. He writes, "I am bold to think that morality is capable of demonstration, as well as mathematics: since the precise real essence of the things moral words stand for can be perfectly known, and so the congruity and incongruity of the things themselves be perfectly discovered." The key word in ethics, namely *good*, is perfectly understandable, for everybody knows what the word *good* stands for: "Things are good or evil only in reference to pleasure or pain. That we call good which is apt to cause or increase pleasure, or diminish pain in us." Certain kinds of behavior will bring us pleasure, whereas other kinds will bring us pain. Morality, then, has to do with choosing or willing the good.

As a further definition of *ethics*, Locke says that "moral good and evil, then, is only the conformity or disagreement of our voluntary actions to some law." He speaks of three kinds of laws, namely, the *law of opinion*, the *civil law*, and the *divine law*. The real issue here is to ask how Locke knows that these laws exist and also how he understands the relation of all three of them to each other. Bearing in mind that he saw no difficulty in demonstrating the existence of God, he now wants to draw further deductions from that demonstrative knowledge. He thus writes,

> the idea of a supreme being infinite in power, goodness and wisdom, whose workmanship we are and on whom we depend, and the idea of ourselves as understanding rational beings, being such as are clear in us, would, I suppose, if duly considered and pursued, afford such foundations of our duty and rules of actions, as might place morality amongst the sciences capable of demonstration: wherein I doubt not but from self-evident principles, by necessary consequences, as incontestable as those in mathematics, the measures of right and wrong might be made out to anyone that will apply himself with the same indifferency and attention as he does to the other of those sciences.

Locke is here suggesting that by the light of nature, that is, by our reason, we can discover the moral rules that conform to God's law. He did not elaborate this plan into a system of ethics, but he did suggest what relation the different kinds of laws should have to each other. The law of opinion represents a community's judgment of what kind of behavior will lead to happiness. Conformity to this law is called *virtue*, though it must be noticed that different communities have different ideas of what virtue consists of. The civil law is set by the commonwealth and enforced by the courts. This law tends to follow the first, for in most societies the courts enforce those laws that embody the opinion of the people. The divine law, which we can know either through their own reason or revelation, is the true rule for human behavior. He writes, "That God has given a rule whereby men should govern themselves, I think there is nobody so brutish as to deny." And "this is the only true touchstone of moral rectitude." In the long run, then, the law of opinion and also the civil law should be made to conform to the divine law, the "touchstone of moral rectitude." The reason there is a discrepancy between these three kinds of laws is that people everywhere tend to choose immediate pleasures instead of choosing those that have more lasting value. However ambiguous this moral theory may seem to us, Locke believed that these moral laws were eternally true, and upon the insights derived from the divine law he built his theory of natural rights.

The State of Nature   In his *Second Treatise of Government,* Locke begins his political theory as Hobbes did, with a treatment of "the state of nature." But he describes this condition in a very different way, even making Hobbes the target of his remarks. For Locke, the state of nature is not the same as Hobbes' "war of all against all." On the contrary, Locke says that "men living together according to reason, without a common superior on earth with authority to judge between them is properly the state of nature." According to Locke's theory of knowledge, men were able even in the state of nature to know the moral law. He said that "reason, which is that law, teaches all mankind who will but consult it, that, being all equal and independent, no one ought to harm another in his life, health, liberty or possessions." This natural moral law is not simply the egotistical law of self-preservation but the positive recognition of each man's value as a person by virtue of his status as a creature of God. This natural law implied natural rights with corresponding duties, and among these rights Locke emphasized particularly the right of private property.

Private Property   For Hobbes, there could be a right to property only after the legal order had been set up. Locke said that the right to private property precedes the civil law, for it is grounded in the natural moral law. The justification of private ownership is labor. Since a man's labor is his own, whatever he transforms from its original condition by his own labor becomes his, for his labor is now mixed with those things. It is by mixing his labor with something that a man takes what was common property and makes it his private property. There is consequently also a limit to that amount of property one can accumulate, namely, "as much as anyone can make use of to any advantage of life before it spoils, so much he may by his labour fix a property in." Locke assumed also that as a matter of natural right a person could inherit property, for "every man is born with . . . a right, before any other man, to inherit with his brethren his father's goods."

Civil Government   If men have natural rights and also know the moral law, why do they desire to leave the state of nature? To this question Locke answered that "the great and chief end of men's uniting into commonwealths and putting themselves under government is the preservation of their property." By the term *property* Locke meant people's "lives, liberty and estates, which I call by the general name, property." It is true that people know the moral law in the state of nature, or rather they are capable of knowing it if they turn their minds to it. But through indifference and neglect they do not always develop a knowledge of it. Moreover, when disputes arise, people tend to decide them in their own favor. It is desirable therefore to have both a set of written laws and also an independent judge to decide disputes. To achieve those ends, people create a political society.

Locke put great emphasis on the inalienable character of human rights, and this led him to argue that political society must rest upon people's *consent,* for "men being . . . by nature all free, equal and independent, no one can be put out of this estate and subjected to the political power of another without his consent." But to what do people consent? They consent to have the laws made and enforced by society, but since "no rational creature can be supposed to change his condition with an intention to be worse," these laws must be framed so as to confirm those rights that people have by nature. They consent also to be bound by the majority, since "it is necessary the body should move that way whither the greater force carries it, which is the consent of the majority." For this reason Locke considered absolute monarchy as "no form of civil government at all." Whether in fact there was a time when we entered a compact is considered by Locke to be of no great consequence, for the important thing is that logically our behavior shows that we have given our consent, and this Locke calls "tacit consent." For if we enjoy the privilege of citizenship, own and exchange property, rely upon the police and the courts, we have in effect assumed also the responsibilities of citizenship and consented to the rule of the majority. The fact that a person stays in his country, for all he could leave and go to another one, confirms his act of consent.

Sovereignty   Locke gives us a different picture of the sovereign power in society from the one we find in Hobbes. Hobbes' sovereign was absolute. Locke agrees that there must be a "supreme power," but he carefully placed this in the hands of the legislature, for all intents the majority of the people. He emphasized the importance of the division of powers chiefly to ensure that those who execute or administer the laws do not also make them, for "they may exempt themselves from obedience to the laws they make, and suit the law, both in its making and execution, to their own private advantage." The executive is therefore "under the law." Even the legislature is not absolute, although it is "supreme," for legislative power is held as a *trust* and is therefore only a fiduciary power. Consequently, "there remains still in the people a supreme power to remove or alter the legislative when they find the legislative act contrary to the trust reposed in them." Locke would never agree that people had irrevocably transferred their rights to the sovereign. The right to rebellion is retained, though rebellion is justified only when the government is *dissolved.* For Locke, government is dissolved not only when it is overthrown by an external enemy, but also when internally there has been an alteration of the legislature. The legislative branch can be altered, for example, if the executive substitutes his law for the legislature's or if he neglects the execution of the official laws; in these cases rebellion against him is justified. Whereas Hobbes placed the sovereign under God's judgment, Locke stated that "the people shall judge."

BERKELEY

George Berkeley was born in Ireland in 1685. At the age of 15 he entered Trinity College, Dublin, where he studied mathematics, logic, languages, and philosophy. He became a Fellow of the College a few years after he took his B.A. degree and was also ordained a clergyman in the Church of England, becom-

George Berkeley with family group in Newport, Rhode Island, during his brief stay
in America
(Yale University Art Gallery, Gift of Isaac Lothrop)

ing a bishop in 1734. Beginning his famous literary career in his early 20s, his
most important philosophical works include, among others, his *Essay towards a
New Theory of Vision* (1709), *A Treatise Concerning the Principles of Human
Knowledge* (1710), and *Three Dialogues between Hylas and Philonous* (1713). He
traveled in France and Italy, and in London became friends with Steele, Addi-
son, and Swift. While in London he sought to interest Parliament in his project
of creating a college in Bermuda, whose purpose would be "the reformation of
manners among the English in our western plantations, and the propagation
of the Gospel among the American savages." With his new bride, he sailed in
1728 for America and for three years stayed in Newport, Rhode Island, making plans for his college. As the money for his college was never raised, Berkeley returned to London, leaving his influence upon American philosophy
through frequent associations with Jonathan Edwards. Shortly thereafter he
returned to Ireland, where for 18 years he was Bishop of Cloyne. At the age of
67, he settled down in Oxford with his wife and family; a year later, in 1753, he
died and was buried in Christ Church Chapel in Oxford.

   It is ironic that Locke's common-sense approach to philosophy should have
influenced Berkeley to formulate a philosophical position that at first seems so
much at variance with common sense. He became the object of severe criticism

and ridicule for denying what seemed most obvious to anyone. Berkeley had set out to deny the existence of matter. Samuel Johnson must have expressed the reaction of many when he kicked a large stone and said about Berkeley, "I refute him thus."

Berkeley's startling and provocative formula was that "to be is to be perceived," *esse est percipi.* Clearly this would mean that if something were not perceived, it would not exist. Berkeley was perfectly aware of the potential nonsense involved in this formula, for he says, "Let it not be said that I take away Existence. I only declare the meaning of the word so far as I comprehend it." Still, to say that the existence of something depends upon its being perceived does raise for us the question whether it exists when it is not being perceived. For Berkeley the whole problem turned on how we interpret or understand the word *exists:* "The table I write on I say exists; that is, I see and feel it: and if I were out of my study I should say it existed; meaning thereby that if I were in my study I might perceive it, or that some other spirit actually does perceive it." Here Berkeley is saying that the word *exists* has no other meaning than the one contained in his formula, for we can know no instance where the term *exists* is used without at the same time assuming that a mind is perceiving something. To those who argued that material things have some kind of *absolute* existence without any relation to their being perceived, Berkeley replied, "that is to me unintelligible." To be sure, he said, "the horse is in the stable, the books in the study as before, even if I am not there. But since we know of no instance of anything's existing without being perceived, the table, horse, and books *exist* even when I do not perceive them because someone does perceive them."

How did Berkeley come upon this novel view? In his *New Theory of Vision* he argued that all our knowledge depends upon actual vision and other sensory experiences. In particular Berkeley argued that we never sense *space* or *magnitude;* we only have different visions or perceptions of things when we see them from different perspectives. Nor do we *see* distance; the distance of objects is *suggested* by our experience. All that we ever see are the qualities of an object that our faculty of vision is capable of sensing. We do not see the *closeness* of an object; we only have a different vision of it when we move toward or away from it. The more Berkeley considered the workings of his own mind and wondered how his ideas were related to objects outside of his mind, the more certain he was that he could never discover any object independent of his ideas. "When we do our utmost to conceive the existence of external bodies," he said, "we are all the while contemplating our own ideas." Nothing seems easier for us than to imagine trees in a park or books in a closet without anyone's looking for them. But what is all this, Berkeley says, except "framing in your mind certain ideas which you call *books* and *trees.* . . . But do not *you* yourself perceive or think of them all the while?" It is impossible, he concluded, ever to think of *anything* except as related to a mind. We never experience something that exists outside of us and separate from us as our ideas of *close* and *far* might suggest. There is nothing *out there* of which we do not have some perception.

It was Locke's philosophy that had raised doubts in Berkeley's mind about the independent existence of things—about the reality of matter. Locke had failed to push his own theory of knowledge to conclusions that to Berkeley seemed inevitable. When Locke spoke of substance as "something we know not what," he was only a short step from saying that it was nothing, which Berkeley did say. Locke's treatment of the relation between ideas and things assumed there is a real difference between primary and secondary qualities—between an object's size and shape on the one hand and its color, taste, and smell on the other. He assumed that whereas color exists only as an idea in the mind, size has to do with an object's substance. And "substance," for Locke, is the reality that exists "behind" or "under" secondary qualities such as color, and is therefore independent of a mind.

Berkeley, however, argued that size, shape, and motion "abstracted from all qualities, are inconceivable." What, for example, is a cherry? It is soft, red, round, sweet, and fragrant. All these qualities are ideas in the mind that the cherry has the power to produce through the senses. And so we feel its softness, see its color, either feel or see its roundness, taste its sweetness, and smell its fragrance. Again, the very existence of all these qualities consists in their being perceived. And, apart from these qualities, there is no sensed reality—in short, nothing else. The cherry, then, consists of all the qualities we perceive; the cherry (and all things) represents a complex of sensations. Suppose that I insist that there are some primary qualities which are not perceived by the senses, such as size and shape. Berkeley argues in response that it is impossible even to conceive of shape or size as independent of perception and therefore independent of secondary qualities. Is it possible, he asks, to separate primary and secondary qualities "even in thought"? He adds, "I might as easily divide a thing from itself. . . . In truth, the object and the sensation are the same thing, and cannot therefore be abstracted from each other." A thing *is*, therefore, the sum of its perceived qualities, and it is for this reason that Berkeley argued that to be is to be perceived. Since substance, or matter, is never perceived or sensed, it cannot be said to exist. If substance does not exist and if only sensed qualities are real, then only thinking or, as Berkeley says, *spiritual* beings exist.

Besides leading Locke's empirical philosophy to what he thought were obvious conclusions, Berkeley was also contending with a complex of problems. In his *Principles of Human Knowledge,* he refers to these as "the chief causes of error and difficulty in the sciences, with the grounds of scepticism, atheism and Irreligion . . . inquired into." It was the notion of *matter* that caused all the difficulties. For if an inert material substance is admitted as really existing, where is there any place for spiritual or immaterial substances in such a universe? Also, would not scientific knowledge, based upon general ideas drawn from the behavior of things, give us a complete philosophy without requiring the idea of God, leading to "the monstrous systems of atheists"? This is not to say that Berkeley arbitrarily denounced the idea of matter because of these theological consequences. Instead, he had additional reasons for pressing his views, which, he was convinced, were intrinsically right.

Matter a Meaningless Term Locke had said that substance, or matter, *supports* or acts as a *substitute* to the qualities we sense. In Berkeley's *First Dialogue between Hylas and Philonus,* Hylas expresses Locke's view: "I find it necessary to suppose a material *substratum,* without which [qualities] cannot be conceived to exist." Philonous replies that the word *substratum* has no clear meaning for him and that he would want to "know any sense, literal or not literal, that you understand in it." But Hylas admits that he cannot assign any definite meaning to the term *substratum,* saying, "I declare I know not what to say." From this the conclusion is drawn that "The *absolute* existence of unthinking things [matter] are words without meaning." This is not to say that sensible things do not possess reality but only that sensible things exist only insofar as they are perceived. This of course implies that only ideas exist, but Berkeley adds that "I hope that to call a thing 'idea' makes it no less real."

Aware that his idealism can be ridiculed, Berkeley writes: "What therefore becomes of the sun, moon, and stars? What must we think of houses, rivers, mountains, trees, stones; nay even of our own bodies? Are all these so many chimeras and illusions of fancy?" By his principles, he says, "we are not deprived of any one thing in nature. Whatever we see, feel, hear, or any wise conceive or understand, remains as secure as ever, and is as real as ever. There is a *rerum natura,* and the distinction between realities and chimeras retains its full force." If this is the case, why say that only *ideas,* instead of *things,* exist? In order, Berkeley says, to eliminate the useless concept of matter: "I do not argue against the existence of any one thing that we can apprehend, either by sense or reflection. . . . The only thing whose existence we deny, is that which philosophers call matter or corporeal substance. And in doing of this, there is no damage done to the rest of mankind, who, I dare say, will never miss it."

Science and Abstract Ideas Since it was the science of his day, particularly physics, that relied so heavily upon the notion of matter, Berkeley had to come to terms with its assumptions and methods. Science had assumed that we can, and must, distinguish between appearance and reality. The sea appears blue but is really not. Berkeley challenged the scientist to show whether there is any other reality than the sensible world. In this analysis Berkeley was pursuing the principle of empiricism and was trying to refine it. Physicists, he said, were obscuring science by including metaphysics in their theories. They used such words as *force, attraction, gravity* and thought they referred to some real physical entity. Even to speak of minute particles, whose motions cause the quality of color, is to engage in a rational and not empirical analysis. What disturbed Berkeley most was that scientists used general or abstract terms as though these terms accurately referred to real entities, particularly to an underlying material substance in nature. Nowhere, Berkeley argues, do we ever come upon such a substance, for substance is an abstract idea. Only sensed qualities really exist, and the notion of substance is a misleading inference drawn from observed qualities: "As several of these [qualities] are observed to accompany each other, they come to be marked by one name, and so to be reputed as one *thing.* Thus, for example, a certain colour, taste, smell, figure and consistence having been observed to go together, are accounted one distinct thing, signified by the name apple; other collections of ideas constitute a stone, a tree, a book and the like sensible things." Similarly, when scientists observe the operations of things, they use such abstract terms as *force* or *gravity* as though these were things or had some real existence in things. But *force* is simply a word describing our sensation of the behavior of things and gives us no more knowledge than our senses and reflections give us.

Berkeley did not mean to destroy science any more than he wanted to deny the existence of the "nature of things." What he did want to do was to clarify what scientific language was all about. Terms such as *force, gravity,* and *causality* refer to nothing more than clusters of ideas which our minds derive from sensation. We experience that heat melts wax, but all we know from this experience is that what we call *melting wax* is always accompanied by what we call *heat*. We have no knowledge of any single thing for which the word *cause* stands. Indeed, the only knowledge we have is of particular experiences. But even though we do not have firsthand knowledge of the causes of all things, we do know the order of things. We experience order, that *A* is followed by *B*, even though we have no experience of *why* this occurs. Science gives us a description of physical behavior, and many mechanical principles can be accurately formulated from our observations that are useful for purposes of prediction. Thus Berkeley would leave science intact, but he would clarify its language so that nobody would think that science was giving us more knowledge than we can derive from the sensible world. And the sensible world shows us neither substance nor causality.

God and the Existence of Things   Since Berkeley did not deny the existence of things or their order in nature, it was necessary for him to explain how things external to our minds exist—even when *we* don't perceive them and how they achieve their order. Thus, elaborating his general thesis that to be is to be perceived, Berkeley says that "When I deny sensible things an existence out of the mind, I do not mean my mind in particular, but all minds. Now it is plain they have an existence exterior to my mind, since I find them by experience to be independent of it. There is therefore some other mind wherein they exist, during the intervals between the time of my perceiving them." And because all human minds are intermittently diverted from things "there is an *omnipresent eternal Mind,* which knows and comprehends all things, and exhibits them to our view in such a manner and according to such rules as he himself has ordained, and are by us termed the *Laws of Nature.*" The existence of things therefore depends upon the existence of God, and God is the cause of the orderliness of things in nature.

Again, Berkeley did not want to deny, for example, that even if he left the room, the candle would still be there, and that when he returned after an interval of time, it would have burned down. But this meant for Berkeley only that experience has a certain regularity that makes it possible for us to predict what our future experiences will be. To say that candles burn even when *I* am not in the room still does not prove that material substance exists independently from a mind. It seemed a matter of common sense to Berkeley to say that I can know about the candle only because I actually experience a perception of it. In a similar way, I know that I exist because I have an awareness of my mental operations.

If, then, I try to describe or interpret reality in terms of my experience, I first come to the conclusion that there are other people like myself who have minds. From this it can be assumed that as I have ideas, other people likewise have ideas. Apart from my finite mind and the finite minds of others, there is a greater Mind analogous to mine, and this is God's Mind. God's ideas constitute the regular order of nature. The ideas that exist in our minds are God's ideas, which He communicates to us, so that the objects or things that we perceive in daily experience are caused not by *matter* or *substance* but by God. It is God, too, who coordinates all experiences of finite minds, assuring regularity and dependability in experience, which, in turn, enables us to think in terms of the "laws of nature." Thus the orderly arrangement of ideas in God's mind is communicated to the finite minds or spirits of people, allowance being made for the differences in competence between the divine and finite minds. The ultimate reality, then, is spiritual (God), and not material, and the continued existence of objects when *we* are not perceiving them is explained by God's continuous perception of them.

To say, as Berkeley does, that people's ideas come from God implies a special interpretation of causation. Again, Berkeley did not deny that we have an insight into causation; he only insisted that our sense data do not disclose to us a unique causal power. We do not, for example, when considering how and why water freezes, discover any power in cold that forces water to become solid. We do, however, understand causal connections through our mental operations. We are, for example, aware of our volition: we can will to move our arm, or, what is more important here, we can produce imaginary ideas in our minds. Our power to produce such ideas suggests that perceived ideas are also caused by a mental power. But whereas imaginary ideas are produced by finite minds, perceived ideas are created and caused to be in us by an infinite mind.

Berkeley was confident that through his treatment of the formula *esse est percipi* he had effectively undermined the position of philosophical materialism and religious skepticism. Locke's empiricism inevitably implied skepticism insofar as he insisted that knowledge is based upon sense experience and that substance, or the reality behind appearances, could never be known. Whether Berkeley's arguments for the reality of God and spiritual beings successfully refuted materialism and skepticism remains a question, for his arguments contained some of the flaws he held against the materialists. His influence was nevertheless significant, but it was his empiricism and not his idealism that had lasting influence. Building upon Locke's empiricism, Berkeley made the decisive point that the human mind reasons only and always about particular sense experiences—that abstract ideas refer to no equivalent reality. Hume, who was to carry empiricism to its fullest expression, spoke of Berkeley as "a great philosopher [who] has disputed the received opinion in this particular, and has asserted that all general ideas are nothing but particular ones. . . . I look upon this to be one of the greatest and most valuable discoveries that has been made of late years in the republic of letters."

David Hume
(Stock Montage, Inc.)

HUME

David Hume took the genuinely empirical elements in the philosophy of Locke and Berkeley, rejected some lingering metaphysics from their thought, and gave empiricism its clearest and most rigorous formulation. Born in Edinburgh in 1711 of Scottish parents, his early interest in literature soon showed to his family that he would not follow their plan for him to become a lawyer. Though he attended the University of Edinburgh, he did not graduate. He was a gentle person with a tough mind who regarded "every object as contemptible except the improvement of my talents in literature," feeling "an insurmountable aversion to everything but the pursuits of philosophy and general learning." He spent the years 1734–1737 in France, under conditions of "rigid frugality," composing his *Treatise of Human Nature*. When this book appeared in 1739, Hume was disappointed in its reception, remarking later that "never literary attempt was more unfortunate," for the book "fell deadborn from the press." His next book, *Essays Moral and Political,* published in 1741–1742, was more successful. Hume then revised key themes in his *Treatise* and published it under the title *An Enquiry Concerning Human Understanding,* by which it is known today. Besides his extensive books on the history of England, Hume wrote three other works that were to enhance his fame, namely, *An Enquiry Concerning the Principles of Morals (1751), Political Discourses (1752),* and the book published after his death, *Dialogues Concerning Natural Religion (1779).*

Hume played a part in public life, going to France in 1763 as secretary to the British ambassador. His books had given him a wide reputation on the Continent, and among his European friends was the philosopher Rousseau. For two years, 1767 to 1769, he was Under-Secretary of State, and in 1769 he returned to Edinburgh, where his house became the center for the most distinguished people of that society. Being now "very opulent," he lived a quiet and contented life among friends and admirers, among them Adam Smith. He died in Edinburgh in 1776.

Hume wanted to build a "science of man," to study human nature by using the methods of physical science. His wide acquaintance with literature had shown him how often conflicting opinions are offered to readers on all subjects. He considered this conflict of opinions the symptom of a serious philosophical problem: How can we know the true nature of things? If artful authors can lead readers to accept conflicting ideas about morality, religion, and the true nature of physical reality, are these ideas equally true, or is there some method by which to discover the reason for this conflict of ideas? Hume shared the optimism of his day, which saw in scientific method the means for solving all the problems of the universe. He believed that such a method could lead us to a clear understanding of human nature and, in particular, the workings of the human mind.

As it turned out, Hume discovered that this optimism about the possibilities of using scientific methods for describing the mechanics of human thought could not be justified. His early faith in reason led, in the end, to skepticism. For as he traced the process by which ideas are formed in the mind, he was startled to discover how limited is the range of human thought. Both Locke and Berkeley had come to this same point, but neither one took his own account of the origin of ideas seriously enough to rest his theory of knowledge wholly upon it. They still had recourse to the "common-sense" beliefs of people, which they were not willing to give up entirely. Although they argued that all our ideas come from experience, they felt confident that experience can give us certainty of knowledge on many subjects. Hume, on the other hand, concluded that if we take seriously the premise that all our ideas come from experience, we must accept the limits of knowledge that this explanation of ideas forces upon us, no matter what our customary beliefs may suggest.

Hume's Theory of Knowledge

The only way, Hume says, to solve the problem of disagreements and speculations regarding "abstruse questions" is to "enquire seriously into the nature of human understanding, and show from an exact analysis of its powers and capacity, that it is by no means fitted for such remote and abstruse subjects." Accordingly, Hume carefully analyzed a series of topics that led him to his skeptical conclusion, beginning with an account of the contents of the mind.

Contents of the Mind   Nothing seems more unbounded, Hume says, than human thought. Although our body is confined to one planet, our mind can roam instantly into the most distant regions of the universe. Nor, it may seem, is the mind bound by the limits of nature or reality, for without difficulty the imagination can conceive the most unnatural and incongruous appearances, such as flying horses and gold mountains. But, though the mind seems to possess this wide freedom, it is, Hume says, "really confined within very narrow limits." In the last analysis, the contents of the mind can all be reduced to the materials given us by the senses and experience, and those materials Hume calls *perceptions*. The perceptions of the mind take two forms, which Hume distinguishes as *impressions* and *ideas*.

Impressions and *ideas* make up the total content of the mind. The original stuff of thought is an *impression*, and an *idea* is merely a copy of an impression. According to Hume, the difference between an impression and an idea is only the degree of their vividness. The original perception is an impression, as when we hear, see, feel, love, hate, desire, or will. These impressions are "lively" and clear when we have them. When we reflect upon these impressions, we have ideas of them, and those ideas are less-lively versions of the original impressions. To feel pain is an impression, whereas the memory of this sensation is an idea. In every particular, impressions and their corresponding ideas are alike, differing only in their degree of vivacity.

Besides merely distinguishing between impressions and ideas, Hume argues that without impressions there can be no ideas. For if an idea is simply a copy of an impression, it follows that for every idea there must be a prior impression. Not every idea, however, reflects an exact corresponding impression, for we have never seen a flying horse or a golden mountain even though we have ideas of them. But Hume explains such ideas as being the product of the mind's "faculty of compounding, transposing, or diminishing the materials afforded us by the senses and experience." When we think of a flying horse, our imagination joins two ideas, wings and horse, which we originally acquired as impressions through our senses. If we have any suspicion that a philosophical term is employed without any meaning or idea, we need, Hume says, "but enquire, *from what impression is that supposed idea derived? And if it be* impossible to assign any, this will serve to confirm our suspicion." Hume subjected even the idea of God to this test and concluded that it arises from reflecting on the operations of our own minds "augmenting without limit" the qualities of goodness and wisdom that we experience among human beings. But if all our ideas follow from impressions, how can we explain what we call *thinking,* or the patterns by which ideas group themselves in our minds?

Association of Ideas   It is not by mere chance that our ideas are related to each other. There must be, Hume says, "some bond of union, some associating quality, by which one idea naturally introduces another." Hume calls it "a gentle force, which commonly prevails . . . pointing out to every one those simple ideas, which are most proper to be united in a complex one." It is not a special faculty of the mind that associates one idea with another, for Hume has no impression of the structural equipment of the mind. But by observing the actual patterns of our thinking and analyzing the groupings of our ideas, Hume thought he had discovered an explanation for the association of ideas.

His explanation was that whenever there are certain qualities in ideas, these ideas are associated with each other. These qualities are three in number: resemblance, contiguity in time or place, and cause and effect. Hume believed that the connections of all ideas to each other could be explained by these qualities and gave the following examples of how they work: "A picture naturally leads our thoughts to the original [*resemblance*]: the mention of one apartment in the building naturally introduces an enquiry . . . concerning the others [*contiguity*]: and if we think of a wound, we can scarcely forebear reflecting on the pain which follows it [*cause and effect*]." There are no operations of the mind that differ in principle from one of these three examples of the association of ideas. But of these, the notion of cause and effect was considered by Hume to be the central element in knowledge. He took the position that the causal principle is the foundation upon which the validity of all knowledge depends. If there is any flaw in the causal principle, we can have no certainty of knowledge.

Causality   Hume's most original and influential ideas deal with the problem of causality. Neither Locke nor Berkeley challenged the basic principle of causality. Although Berkeley did say that we cannot discover efficient causes *in* things, his intention was to look for the cause of phenomena and therefore the predictable order of nature in God's activity.

For Hume, the very idea of causality is suspect, and he approaches the problem by asking the question, "What is the origin of the idea of causality?" Since ideas are copies of impressions, Hume asks what impression gives us the idea of causality. His answer is that there is no impression corresponding to this idea. How then does the idea of causality arise in the mind? It must be, said Hume, that the idea of causality arises in the mind when we experience certain relations between objects. When we speak of cause and effect, we mean to say that A causes B. But what kind of a relation does this show between A and B? Experience furnishes us with two relations: first, there is the relation of *contiguity*, for A and B are always close together; second, there is *priority in time*, for A, the "cause," always precedes B, the "effect." But there is still another relation that the idea of causality suggests to common sense, namely, that between A and B there is a "necessary connection." But neither contiguity nor priority implies "necessary" connection between objects. There is no object, Hume says, that implies the existence of another when we consider objects individually. No amount of observation of oxygen can ever tell us that when mixed with hydrogen it will necessarily give us water. We know this only after we have seen the two together: "It is therefore by *experience* only that we can infer the existence of one object from another." While we do have impressions of contiguity, priority, and constant conjunction, we do *not* have any impression of *necessary connections*. Thus, causality is not a quality in the objects we observe but is rather a "habit of association" in the mind produced by the repetition of instances of A and B.

Insofar as Hume assumed that the causal principle is central to all kinds of knowledge, his attack on this principle undermined the validity of all knowledge. He saw no reason for accepting the principle that *whatever begins to exist must have a cause of existence* as either intuitive or capable of demonstration. In the end, Hume considered thinking or reasoning "a species of sensation," and as such our thinking cannot extend beyond our immediate experiences.

What Exists External to Us?

Hume's extreme empiricism led him to argue that there is no rational justification for saying that bodies or things have a continued and independent existence external to us. Our ordinary experience suggests that things outside of us do exist. But if we take seriously the notion that our ideas are copies of impressions, the philosophical conclusion must be that all we know is impressions. Impressions are internal subjective states and are not clear proof of an external reality. To be sure, we always act as though there is a real external world of things, and Hume was willing to "take for granted in all our reasonings" that things do exist. But he wanted to inquire into the reason why we think there is an external world.

Our senses do not tell us that things exist independent of us, for how do we know that they continue to exist even when we interrupt our sensation of them? And even when we sense something, we are never given a double view of it whereby we can distinguish the thing from our impression of it; we have only the impression. There is no way for the mind to reach beyond impressions or the ideas they make possible: "let us chase our imagination to the heavens, or to the utmost limits of the universe; we never advance a step beyond our selves, nor can we conceive any kind of existence, but those perceptions which have appeared in that narrow compass. This is the universe of imagination, nor have we any idea but what is there produced."

Constancy and Coherence   Our belief that things exist external to us, Hume argues, is the product of our imagination as it deals with two special characteristics of our impressions. From impressions our imagination becomes aware of both *constancy* and *coherence*. There is a constancy in the arrangement of things when, for example, I look out of my window: There are the mountain, the house, and the trees. If I shut my eyes or turn away and then later look at the same view again, the arrangement is still the same, and it is this constancy in the contents of my impressions that leads my imagination to conclude that the mountain, house, and trees exist whether I think of them or not. Similarly, I put a log on the fire before I leave the room, and when I return it is almost in ashes. But even though a great change has taken place in the fire, I am accustomed to finding this kind of change under similar circumstances: "This coherence . . . in their changes is one of the characteristics of external objects." In the case of the mountain, there is a constancy of our impressions, whereas in respect to the fire our impressions have a coherent relation to the processes of change. For these reasons, the imagination leads us to believe that certain things continue to have an independent existence external to us. But this is a *belief* and not a rational proof, for the assumption that our impressions are connected with things is "without any foundation in reasoning." Hume extends this skeptical line of reasoning beyond objects or things to consider the existence of the *self, substance,* and *God.*

The Self   Hume denied that we have any idea of *self.* This may seem paradoxical, that *I* should say that I do not have an idea of myself. Yet here again Hume wants to test what we mean by a self by asking, "from what impression could this idea be derived?" Is there any continuous and identical reality which forms our ideas of the self? Do we have any one impression that is invariably associated with our idea of *self?* "When I enter most intimately into what I call *myself*," says Hume, "I always stumble on some particular perception or other, of heat or cold, love or hatred, pain or pleasure. I never can catch *myself* at any time without a perception and never can observe anything but the perception." Hume denies the existence of a continuous self-identity and says about the rest of humanity that "they are nothing but a bundle or collection of different perceptions." How then do we account for what we think is the self? It is our power of memory that gives the impression of our continuous identity. Hume compares the mind to "a kind of theatre where several perceptions successively make their appearance," but adds that "we have not the most distant notion of the place where these scenes are represented.

Substance   What led Hume to deny the existence of a continuous self that in some way retains its identity through time was his thorough denial of the existence of any form of *substance.* Locke retained the idea of substances as that *something,* which has color or shape, and other qualities, though he spoke of it as "something we know not what." Berkeley denied the existence of substance underlying qualities but retained the idea of spiritual substances. Hume denied that substance in any form exists or has any coherent meaning. If what is meant by the *self* is some form of substance, Hume argued that no such substance can be derived from our impressions of sensation. If the idea of substance is conveyed to us by our senses, Hume asked, "which of them; and after what manner? If it be perceived by the eyes, it must be a colour; if by the ears, a sound; if by the palate, a taste. . . . We have therefore no idea of substance, distinct from that of a collection of particular qualities."

God   It was inevitable that Hume's rigorous premises, that "our ideas reach no further than our experience," would lead him to raise skeptical questions about the existence of God. Most attempts to demonstrate the existence of God rely upon some version of causality. Among these, the argument from *design* has always made a powerful impact on religious believers. Hume is aware of the power of this argument, but he quickly sorts out the elements of the problem, leaving the argument with less than its usual force.

The argument from design begins with the observance of a beautiful order in nature. This order resembles the kind of order the human mind is able to impose upon unthinking materials. From this preliminary observation, we conclude that unthinkable materials do not contain the principle of orderliness within themselves: "Throw several piece of steel together, without shape or form; they will never arrange themselves so as to compose a watch." Order, it is held, requires the activity of a mind, an orderer. Our experience tells us that neither a watch nor a house can come into being without a watchmaker or an architect. From this it is inferred that the natural order bears an analogy to the order fashioned by human effort and that just as the watch requires an ordering cause, so the natural order of the universe requires one. But such an inference, Hume says, "is uncertain; because the subject lies entirely beyond the reach of human experience."

If the whole argument from design rests upon the proposition "that the cause or causes of order in the universe probably bear some remote analogy to human intelligence," then, Hume says, the argument cannot prove as much as it claims. Hume's criticism of the idea of causality has particular force here. We derive the idea of cause from repeated observations of two things. How, then, can we assign a cause to the universe when we have never experienced the universe as related to anything we might consider a cause? The use of analogy does not solve the problem because the analogy between a watch and the universe is not exact. Why not consider the universe the product of a vegetative process instead of a rational designer? And even if the cause of the universe is something like an intelligence, how can moral characteristics be ascribed to such a being? Moreover, if analogies are to be used, which one should be selected? Houses and ships are frequently designed by a group of designers: Should we say there are many gods? Sometimes experimental models are built with no present knowledge of what the finished form will be like: Is the universe a trial model or the final design? By this line of probing, Hume wished to emphasize that the order of the universe is simply an empirical fact and that we cannot infer from it the existence of God. This does not necessarily lead to atheism—although Hume himself seems to have been one. He is simply testing our idea of God the way he had tested our ideas of the *self* and *substance* by his rigorous principle of empiricism. He ends, to be sure, as a skeptic, but finally makes the telling point that "to whatever length any one may push his speculative principles of skepticism, he must act and live and converse like other men. . . . It is impossible for him to persevere in total skepticism, or make it appear in his conduct for a few hours."

Ethics

Hume's skepticism did not prevent him from taking ethics seriously. On the contrary, in the opening passage of the third book of his *Treatise of Human Nature*, Hume writes that "morality is a subject that interests us above all others." His interest in ethics was so strong that he hoped to do for that subject what

Galileo and Newton did for natural science. To that end he says in the first section of his *An Enquiry Concerning the Principles of Morals* that "moral philosophy is in the same condition as . . . astronomy before the time of Copernicus." Older science with its abstract general hypotheses had to give way to a more experimental method. So also the time had come, Hume writes, when philosophers "should attempt a like reformation in all moral disquisitions; and reject every system of ethics, however subtle or ingenious, which is not founded on fact and observation."

For Hume, the central fact about ethics is that moral judgments are formed not by reason alone but through feelings. There is no doubt that reason plays a considerable role in our discussions about ethical decisions. But, Hume says, reason "is not sufficient alone to produce any moral blame or approbation." What limits the role of reason in ethics is that reason makes judgments concerning the truth empirical "matters of fact" and analytical "relations of ideas." Moral assessments are not judgments about the truth and falsehood of anything. Instead, moral assessments are emotional reactions.

Why, for example, do we judge murder to be a crime? Or, to use Hume's words, "where is that matter of fact which we here call *crime?*" Suppose that you describe the action, the exact time at which it occurred, the weapon used, in short, that you assemble all the details about the event. The faculty of reason would still not isolate that fact to which the label of crime is attached. After all, this act cannot always and in all circumstances be considered a crime. The same action might be called self-defense or official execution. The judgment of good or evil is made *after* all the facts are known. The goodness or badness of an act is not a new fact discovered or deduced by reason. Nor is moral assessment similar to mathematical judgment. From a few facts about a triangle or circle, additional facts and relations can be inferred. But goodness, like beauty, is not an additional fact inferred or deduced by reason. "Euclid has fully explained all the qualities of the circle," says Hume, "but has not in any proposition said a word of its beauty. The reason is evident. The beauty is not a quality of the circle. It lies not in any part of the line, whose parts are equally distant from a common center. It is only the effect which that figure produces upon the mind, whose peculiar fabric of structure renders it susceptible to such sentiments."

Hume presses this point by asking us to "see if you can find that matter of fact, or real existence, which you call *vice,*" and he argues that "in whichever way you take it, you find only certain passions, motives, volitions and thoughts. There is no other matter of fact in the case. . . . You can never find it, till you turn your reflection into your own breast and find a sentiment of disapprobation which arises in you toward this action. Here is a matter of fact; but it is the object of feeling, not reason. It lies in yourself, not in the object."

For Hume, moral assessments involve sympathetic feelings of pleasure and pain that we experience when observing the consequences of someone's action. For example, if my neighbor is robbed, I will feel sympathetic pain for her, and this pain constitutes my moral condemnation of the robber's action. If

I see someone help an old woman cross the street, I will feel sympathetic pleasure for the woman, and this pleasure constitutes my moral approval of the person who helped her out. Hume realized that to build a system of ethics upon the faculty of feeling, is to run the risk of reducing ethics to a matter of taste, where moral judgments are subjective and relative. Moreover, to designate feeling or sentiment as the source of praise or blame is to imply that our moral judgments flow from a calculus of our individual self-interest or self-love. Hume rejects these assumptions by affirming that moral sentiments are found in all people, that people praise or blame the same actions and that praise or blame is not derived from a narrow self-love. Hume writes, "a generous, a brave, a noble deed, performed by an adversary, commands our approbation; while in its consequences it may be acknowledged prejudicial to our particular interest." Further, the sympathetic feelings that we experience are not restricted to events that we see before our eyes. Instead, we have an instinctive capacity to "bestow praise on virtuous actions, performed in very distant ages and remote countries; where the utmost subtlety of imagination would not discover any appearance of self-interest, or had any connection of our present happiness and security with events so widely separated from us."

What exactly are the qualities in people that trigger our sympathetic feelings of moral approval? According to Hume, these qualities—or virtues—include "whatever mental action or quality gives to a spectator the pleasing sentiment of approbation; and vice the contrary." These include "discretion, caution, enterprise, industry, economy, good-sense, prudence and discernment." Also, he argues, there is virtually universal agreement, even among the most cynical people of the world, concerning "the merit of temperance, sobriety, patience, constancy, considerateness, presence of mind, quickness of conception and felicity of expression." What is there about these qualities which generates our praise? It is, Hume says, that these qualities are *useful* and *agreeable*. But useful for what? Hume replies, "for somebody's interest, surely. Whose interest then? Not our own only: For our approbation frequently extends farther. It must, therefore, be the interest of those, who are served by the character or action approved of."

Hume's approach here is thoroughly empirical. First, experience tells us that moral assessments involve feelings, and are not judgments of reason. Second, experience tells us that we have sympathetic feelings of pleasure and pain in response to a range of virtuous qualities that people possess. Third, experience tells us that all of these virtuous qualities have two things in common: they are useful or agreeable to those affected by our conduct. Amidst this empirical analysis of moral assessment, we find in Hume a clear criterion of moral judgment: virtuous behavior is that which is useful or agreeable to people who are impacted by this conduct. In Hume's words, "personal merit consists altogether in the possession of mental qualities, useful or agreeable to the person himself, or to others."

Hume's empirical approach to morality had its vocal critics. Morality, many argued, needs to be fixed, permanent, and absolute, and Hume grounds the entire plan of morality in unstable human faculties and emotions. Further, critics argued, we find the role of God completely absent from Hume's account. Thus, his whole approach is both flimsy and atheistic. However, the features about Hume's theory that bothered critics so much were precisely the features that attracted others to it. After reading Hume's moral theory, Jeremy Bentham wrote "I felt as if scales had fallen from my eyes." Bentham himself was in search of a non-religious approach to morality that was based in empirical fact and not in mysterious rational intuitions. Bentham homed in on Hume's contention that we assess actions based on their usefulness—or, as Hume also expressed it, their "utility." This became the basis of the ethical theory of utilitarianism, championed by Bentham and many others throughout the 19th century and on through the present day.

PART FOUR

Late Modern and 19th Century Philosophy

CHAPTER 12

Kant

Immanuel Kant lived all of his 80 years (1724–1804) in the small provincial town of Königsberg in East Prussia. His parents were of modest means, and their religious spirit, nurtured by a sect known as Pietists, was to have a permanent influence upon Kant's thought and personal life. His education began at the local Collegium Fredericianum, whose director was also a Pietist, and in 1740 Kant entered the University of Königsberg. At the university he studied the classics, physics, and philosophy. The German universities were at this time dominated by the philosopher Christian von Wolff (1679–1754), who stimulated philosophical activity by developing a comprehensive system of philosophy along the lines of Leibniz's rationalism and metaphysics. Kant's professor at Königsberg, Martin Kuntzen, had come under the influence of this Wolff–Leibnizian approach to philosophy, and inevitably Kant's university training laid much emphasis upon the power of human reason to move with certainty in the realm of metaphysics. Although Martin Knutzen had thus slanted Kant's early thought toward the tradition of Continental rationalism, it was also Knutzen who stimulated Kant's interest in Newtonian physics, an interest that played a very important part in the development of Kant's original and critical philosophy. Upon completion of his university course, Kant spent about eight years as a family tutor, and in 1755 became a lecturer at the university. In 1770 he was appointed to the chair of philosophy that had been held by Knutzen.

Although Kant's personal life contains no remarkable events, as he did not travel and he developed no notable political or social connections, he was, nevertheless, immensely successful as a lecturer and was an interesting conversationalist and charming host. He is often pictured as an old bachelor whose every activity was scheduled with such precision that neighbors could set their watches when he stepped out of his house each day at half past four to walk up and down his small avenue eight times. Without this discipline, however, he could hardly have produced such a striking succession of famous books as his monumental *Critique of Pure Reason* in 1781, *Prolegomena to Any Future Metaphysics* in 1783, *Principles of the Metaphysics of Morals* in 1785, *Metaphysical First Principles of Natural Science* in 1786, the second edition of the *Critique of Pure Reason* in 1787, the *Critique of Practical Reason* in 1788, the *Critique of Judgment* in 1790, *Religion within the Limits of Pure Reason* in 1793, and the small work *Perpetual Peace* in 1795.

THE SHAPING OF KANT'S PROBLEM

Kant revolutionized modern philosophy. What prompted this revolution in Kant's mind was his profound concern over a problem that the philosophy of his day could not deal with successfully. The elements of his problem are suggested by his famous comment that "two things fill the mind with ever new and increasing admiration and awe . . . the starry heavens above and the moral law within." To him the starry heavens were a reminder that the world, as pictured earlier by Hobbes and Newton, is a system of bodies in motion, where every event has a specific and determinate cause. At the same time, all people experience the sense of moral duty, an experience which implies that humans, unlike some other elements of nature, possess freedom in their behavior. The problem, then, was how to reconcile the two seemingly contradictory interpretations of events—one holding that all events are the product of *necessity* and the other saying that in certain aspects of human behavior there is *freedom.*

As Kant viewed the drift of scientific thought, he saw in it an attempt to include *all* of reality, including human nature in its mechanical model. This would mean that all events, being parts of a unified mechanism, could be explained in terms of cause and effect. Moreover, this scientific approach would eliminate from consideration any elements that could not fit into its method. His method greatly emphasized limiting knowledge to the realm of actual sense experience and to generalizations that could be derived by induction from such experience. Pursuing this method, science would have no need for, nor could it account for, such notions as freedom and God.

Kant was impressed by the obvious success and the constant advance of scientific knowledge. What the success of Newtonian physics did for Kant was to raise some serious questions about the adequacy of the philosophy of his day. The two major traditions of his day were Continental rationalism and British empiricism, and Newtonian physics enjoyed an independence from both of these philosophical systems. Since Continental rationalism had been built upon a mathematical model, this type of philosophizing emphasized the relation of *ideas* to each other and therefore had no clear connection with things as they really are. Rationalism could not produce the kind of knowledge Newtonian physics represented, and for this reason its metaphysical speculations about reality beyond experience were considered dogmatic. Kant was to say with some respect that Christian Wolff, whose Leibnizian metaphysics had influenced Kant's earlier thought, was "the greatest of all dogmatic philosophers." This contrast between rationalism and science raised for Kant the question whether metaphysics can increase our knowledge the way science obviously can. The dogmatic character of metaphysics was made clear particularly by the variety of conclusions to which metaphysicians had come in their systems of thought, as shown by the differences between Descartes, Spinoza, and Leibniz. But the heart of the matter was that the scientists were proceeding successfully in unraveling the nature of reality and were showing less and less concern about such metaphysical notions as freedom and God and the possibility of moral truth.

At the same time, science proceeded independently of the other major philosophical tradition of Kant's day, namely, British empiricism. Hume's most striking philosophical argument was an attack on the traditional notion of causality. Since all our knowledge comes from experience, and we do not experience causality, we cannot therefore infer or predict any future event from our experience of the present. What we call *causality*, said Hume, is simply our habit of associating two events because we experience them together, but this does not justify the conclusion that these events have any necessary connection. Thus, Hume denied inductive inference. And yet, it is precisely upon the notion of causality and inductive inference that science is built. For it assumes that our knowledge of particular events in the present gives us reliable knowledge about an indefinite number of similar events in the future. The logical outcome of Hume's empiricism was that there cannot be any scientific knowledge, and this leads to philosophical skepticism. Kant was left, therefore, with great admiration for science but with serious questions about philosophy because of the dogmatism of rationalism and the skepticism of empiricism.

Although Newtonian physics impressed Kant, science itself raised two major questions for him. The first we have already mentioned, namely, that as the scientific method was applied to the study of all of reality, notions of morality, freedom, and God were threatened by absorption into a mechanical universe. A second problem raised by science for Kant was how to explain, or to justify, scientific knowledge. That is, did the scientist give an adequate explanation of what makes his understanding of nature possible? As it turned out, these two problems were very closely related. As Kant discovered, scientific knowledge is similar to metaphysical knowledge. Thus the justification or explanation of scientific thought on the one hand and metaphysical thought concerning freedom and morality on the other are the same. Kant, therefore, rescued metaphysics without attacking science. Both in science and in metaphysics, our minds start with some given fact, which gives rise to a judgment within our reason. Kant thus says, "the genuine method of metaphysics is fundamentally the same kind which Newton introduced into natural science and which was there so fruitful." With this interpretation of scientific and moral thought, Kant provided a new function and a new life for philosophy. This function is suggested by the title of Kant's major work, the *Critique of Pure Reason,* for now the task of philosophy became the critical appraisal of the capacities of human reason. In pursuing this new critical function, Kant achieved what he called his Copernican revolution in philosophy.

KANT'S CRITICAL PHILOSOPHY
AND HIS COPERNICAN REVOLUTION

The turning point in Kant's intellectual development was his encounter with Hume's empiricism. He tells us that "I openly confess, the suggestion of David Hume was the very thing, which many years ago first interrupted my dogmatic slumber and gave my investigations in the field of speculative philosophy quite a new direction." Hume had argued that all our knowledge is derived from experience and that therefore we cannot have knowledge of any reality beyond our experience. This argument struck at the very foundation of rationalism. Rationalists argued confidently that human reason can derive knowledge about realities beyond experience simply by moving from one idea to another as one does in mathematics. The rationalist proofs for the existence of God were a case in point, and Spinoza's and Leibniz's explanation of the structure of reality was another. Kant eventually turned his back on rationalist metaphysics, calling it "rotten dogmatism," but he did not accept Hume's entire argument, saying that "I was far from following him in the conclusions at which he arrived."

Kant refused to follow Hume all the way, not merely because this would lead to skepticism, but because he felt that although Hume was on the right track, he had not completed the task of explaining how knowledge is acquired. Nor did Kant wish to give up some of the subjects that concerned the rationalist metaphysicians, such as freedom and God, about which it is impossible to be "indifferent," even though he was prepared to say that we cannot have demonstrative knowledge of objects beyond our experience. Kant, therefore, sought to build upon what he thought was significant both in rationalism and empiricism and to reject what could not be defended in these systems. He did not simply combine the insights of his predecessors, but rather embarked upon a genuinely new approach, which he called *critical philosophy.*

The Way of Critical Philosophy

Kant's *critical* philosophy consists of an analysis of the components of human reason, by which he meant "a critical inquiry into the faculty of reason with reference to all the knowledge which it may strive to attain independently of all experience." The way of critical philosophy is, therefore, to ask the question "What and how much can understanding and reason know, apart from all experience?" Earlier metaphysicians engaged in disputes about the nature of the supreme being and other subjects that took them beyond the realm of immediate experience. Kant, though, asked the principal question whether the human reason possessed the powers to undertake such inquiries. From this point of view Kant thought it was foolish for metaphysicians to construct systems of knowledge even before they had determined whether, by pure reason alone, we can apprehend what is not given to us in experience. Critical philosophy for Kant was therefore not the negation of metaphysics but rather a preparation for it. If metaphysics has to do with knowledge as developed by reason alone—that is, prior to experience, or *a priori*—the crucial question is, how is such *a priori* knowledge possible?

Immanuel Kant
(Corbis-Bettmann)

The Nature of *a priori* Knowledge

Kant affirmed that we possess a faculty that is capable of giving us knowledge without an appeal to experience. He agreed with the empiricists that our knowledge starts with experience, but he added that "though our knowledge begins *with* experience, it does not follow that it all arises *out of* experience." This was the point that Hume had missed, for Hume had said that all our knowledge consists of a series of impressions, which we derive through our senses. Yet we clearly possess a kind of knowledge that does not come *out of* experience even though it begins *with* experience. Hume was right that we do not, for example, experience or sense *causality*. But Kant rejected his explanation that *causality* is simply a psychological habit of connecting two events that we call cause and effect. Instead, Kant believed that we have knowledge about causality and that we get this knowledge not from sense experience but directly from the faculty of rational judgment and, therefore, *a priori.*

What, more specifically, is *a priori* knowledge? Kant replies that "if one desires an example from the sciences, one needs only to look at any proposition in mathematics. If one desires an example from the commonest operations of the understanding, the proposition that every change must have a cause can serve one's purposes." What makes a proposition of mathematics, or the proposition that every change must have a cause, *a priori* knowledge? It is, Kant says, that this kind of knowledge cannot be derived from experience. Experience cannot show us that *every* change must have a cause since we have not yet experienced every change. Nor can experience show us that connections between events are *necessary;* the most experience can tell us is "that a thing is so and so, but not that it cannot be otherwise." Experience, then, cannot give us knowledge about *necessary* connections or about the *universality* of propositions. Yet we do in fact have this kind of knowledge about causality and universality, for these are the notions that characterize mathematics and scientific knowledge. We confidently say that all heavy objects will fall in space, or that all instances of 5 added to 7 will equal 12. That there is such *a priori* knowledge is clear, but what concerned Kant was how such knowledge can be accounted for. How, in short, can Hume's skepticism be answered? But it was not simply a question of how *a priori* knowledge is possible, but how "synthetic judgments *a priori*" are possible. To answer this question, Kant had first to discover what constitutes a synthetic judgment *a priori.*

The Synthetic *A Priori*

Kant distinguishes between two kinds of judgments, the *analytic* and the *synthetic*. A *judgment,* he said, is an operation of thought whereby we connect a subject and predicate, where the predicate qualifies in some way the subject. When we say that "The building is tall," we make a judgment, for the mind is able to understand a connection between the subject and the predicate. Subjects and predicates are connected to each other in two different ways, thereby leading us to make two different kinds of judgments.

In *analytic judgments*, the predicate is already contained in the concept of the subject. The judgment that all triangles have three angles is an analytic judgment. Because the predicate is already implicit in the subject of an analytic judgment, such a predicate does not give us any new knowledge about the subject. Again, the judgment that "all bodies are extended" is analytic, for the idea of extension is already contained in the idea of body. An analytic judgment is true only because of the logical relation of subject and predicate. To deny an analytic judgment would involve a logical contradiction.

A *synthetic judgment* differs from the analytic in that its predicate is not contained in the subject. Thus, in a synthetic judgment the predicate adds something new to our concept of the subject. To say that "the apple is red" joins two independent concepts, for the concept apple does not contain the idea of redness. Similarly, for Kant, "all bodies are heavy" is an example of a synthetic judgment, for the idea of heaviness is not contained in the concept of body, that is, the predicate is not contained in the subject.

At this point, Kant makes a further distinction, this time between judgments that are *a priori* and judgments that are *a posteriori*. All analytic judgments are *a priori:* their meaning does not depend upon our experience of any particular cases or events since they are independent of any observations, as in the case of mathematics. As "necessity and strict universality are sure marks of *a priori* knowledge," Kant has no trouble showing that analytic judgments represent *a priori* knowledge. Synthetic judgments, on the other hand, are for the most part *a posteriori*, that is, they occur after an experience of observation. To say, for example, that all boys in school X are six feet tall is a synthetic judgment *a posteriori*, for this proposition regarding their height is contingently and not necessarily true of all the present or future members of that school. This judgment cannot be made without experience with the particular details of this school. Thus, while all analytic judgments are *a priori*, most synthetic judgments are *a posteriori*.

There is, however, still another kind of judgment besides the analytic *a priori* and the synthetic *a posteriori*, and this is the *synthetic a priori*. This is the kind of judgment Kant was most concerned about because he was certain that we make these judgments, yet there was the persistent question how such judgments are possible. The question arises because by definition synthetic judgments are based upon experience, but if that is the case, how can they be called *a priori*, since this implies independence of experience? Still, Kant showed that in mathematics, physics, ethics, and metaphysics, we do make judgments that are not part only *a priori* but also synthetic. For example, the judgment 7 plus 5 equals 12 is certainly *a priori* because it contains the marks of necessity and universality; that is, 7 plus 5 *has* to equal 12, and it *always* has to do so. At the same time, this judgment is synthetic and not analytic because 12 cannot be derived by a mere analysis of the numbers 7 and 5. The act of intuition necessary in order to achieve a synthesis of the concepts 7, 5, and plus.

Kant shows that in propositions of geometry also the predicate is not contained in the subject even though there is a necessary and universal connection between subject and predicate. Thus, propositions of geometry are at once *a priori* and synthetic. For example, Kant says, "that a straight line between two points is the shortest, is a synthetic proposition. For my concept of *straight* contains no notion of quantity, but only of quality. The concept of *shortest* is thus wholly an addition, and it cannot be derived by any analysis from the concept of a straight line. Intuition must, therefore, lend its aid here, by means of which alone is this synthesis possible." In physics, too, we find synthetic *a priori* judgments; Kant says that "natural science contains within itself synthetic *a priori* judgments as principles." The proposition "in all changes of the material world the quantity of matter remains unchanged" is *a priori,* for we make this judgment before we have experienced every change. It is also synthetic, for the idea of permanence is not discoverable in the concept of matter. In metaphysics, we assume that we are extending or increasing our knowledge. If this is so, the propositions of metaphysics, such as the judgment "human beings are free to choose" must be synthetic, for here the predicate adds new knowledge to the concept of the subject. At the same time, this metaphysical judgment is *a priori,* for the predicate *is free* is connected to our idea of all people even before we have experience of all people.

What Kant wanted to show by these illustrations is that it is not only in metaphysics but also in mathematics and physics that we make synthetic *a priori* judgments. If these judgments create difficulties in metaphysics, they create the same ones for mathematics and physics. Kant believed, therefore, that if synthetic *a priori* judgments could be explained or justified in mathematics and physics, they would, thereby, also be justified in metaphysics.

Kant's Copernican Revolution

Kant solved the problem of the synthetic *a priori* judgment by substituting a new hypothesis concerning the relation between the mind and its objects. It was clear to him that if we assume, as Hume did, that the mind, in forming its concepts, must conform to its objects, there could be no solution to the problem. Hume's theory would work for our ideas of things we have actually experienced, but these are *a posteriori* judgments. If I ask, "How do I know that the chair is brown?" my answer is that I can see it; and if my assertion is challenged, I refer to my experience. When I thus refer to my experience, that settles the question, because we all agree that experience gives us a kind of knowledge that conforms to the nature of things. But a synthetic *a priori* judgment cannot be validated by experience; if I say, for example, that every straight line is the shortest way between two points, I certainly cannot say that I have had experience of every possible straight line. What makes it possible for me to make judgments about events before they even occur—judgments that are universally true and can always be verified? If, as Hume believed, the mind is passive and simply receives its information from the objects, it follows that the mind would have information only about that particular object. But the mind makes judgments about all objects, even those that it has not yet experienced, and, in addition, objects do in fact behave in the future according to these judgments we make about them. This scientific knowledge gives us reliable information about the nature of things. But since this knowledge, which is both synthetic and *a priori,* could not be explained on the assumption that the mind conforms to its objects, Kant was forced to try a new hypothesis regarding the relation between the mind and its objects.

According to Kant's new hypothesis, it is the objects that conform to the operations of the mind, and not the other way around. He came to this hypothesis with a spirit of experimentation, consciously following the example of Copernicus, who, "failing of satisfactory progress in explaining the movements of the heavenly bodies on the supposition that they all revolved round the spectator, he tried whether he might not have better success if he made the spectator to revolve and the stars to remain at rest." Seeing an analogy here with his own problem, Kant says that,

> hitherto it has been assumed that all our knowledge must conform to objects. But all our attempts to extend our knowledge of objects by establishing something in regard to them *a priori* by means of concepts, have, on this assumption, ended in failure. We must, therefore, make trial whether we may not have more success in the tasks of metaphysics, if we suppose that objects must conform to our knowledge. . . . If intuition must conform to the constitution of the objects, I do not see how we could know anything of the latter *a priori;* but if the object (as object of the senses) must conform to the constitution of our faculty of intuition, I have no difficulty in conceiving such a possibility.

Kant did not mean to say that the mind creates objects, nor did he mean that the mind possesses innate ideas. His Copernican revolution consisted rather in his saying that the mind brings something to the objects it experiences. With Hume, Kant agreed that our knowledge begins with experience, but unlike Hume, Kant saw the mind as an active agent doing something with the objects it experiences. The mind, Kant says, is structured in such a way that it imposes its way of knowing upon its objects. By its very nature, the mind actively organizes our experiences. That is, thinking involves not only receiving impressions through our senses but also making judgments about what we experience. Just as a person who wears colored glasses sees everything in that color, so every human being, having the faculty of thought, inevitably thinks about things in accordance with the natural structure of the mind.

THE STRUCTURE OF RATIONAL THOUGHT

Kant says that "there are two sources of human knowledge, which perhaps spring from a common but to us unknown root, namely, sensibility and understanding. Through the former objects are *given* to us; through the latter they are *thought.*" Knowledge is, therefore, a cooperative affair between the knower and the thing known. But, although I am able to distinguish the difference between myself as a knower and the thing I know, I can never know that thing as it is in itself, for the moment I know it, I know it as my structured mind permits me to know it. If colored glasses were permanently fixed to my eyes, I should always see things in that color and could never escape the limitations placed on my vision by those glasses. Similarly, my mind always brings certain ways of thinking to things, and this always affects my understanding of them. What does the mind bring to the *given* raw materials of our experience?

The Categories of Thought and the Forms of Intuition

The distinctive activity of the mind is to synthesize and to unify our experience. It achieves this synthesis first by imposing on our various experiences in the "sensible manifold" certain forms of intuition: space and time. We inevitably perceive things as being in *space* and *time.* But space and time are not ideas derived from the things we experience, nor are they concepts. Space and time are encountered immediately in intuition and are, at the same time, *a priori* or, to speak figuratively, lenses through which we always see objects of experience.

In addition to space and time, which deal particularly with the way we sense things, there are certain categories of thought which deal more specifically with the way the mind unifies or synthesizes our experience. The mind achieves this unifying act by making various kinds of judgments as we engage in the act of interpreting the world of sense. The manifold of experience is judged by us through certain fixed forms or concepts, such as *quantity, quality, relation,* and *modality.* When we assert *quantity,* we have in mind one or many; when we make a judgment of *quality,* we make either a positive or a negative statement; when we make a judgment of *relation,* we think of cause and effect, on the one hand, or of the relation of subject and predicate on the other; and when we make a judgment of *modality,* we have in mind that something is either possible or impossible. All these ways of thinking are what constitute the act of synthesis through which the mind strives to make a consistent single world out of the manifold of sense impressions.

The Self and the Unity of Experience

What makes it possible for us to have a unified grasp of the world about us? From his analysis of the way our minds work, Kant's answer is that it is the mind that transforms the raw data given to our senses into a coherent and related set of elements. But this leads Kant to say that the unity of our experience must imply a unity of the self, for unless there was a unity between the several operations of the mind, there could be no knowledge of experience. To have such knowledge involves, in various sequences, sensation, imagination, memory, as well as the capacity of intuitive synthesis. Thus, it must be the same self that at once senses an object, remembers its characteristics, imposes upon it the forms of space and time and the category of cause and effect. All these activities must occur in some single subject. If it were otherwise, there could be no knowledge, for if one subject had only sensations, another only memory, and so on, the sensible manifold could never be unified.

Where and what is this single subject that accomplishes this unifying activity? Kant calls it the "transcendental unity of apperception"—what we should call the *self.* He uses the term *transcendental* to show that we do not experience the self directly even though such a unity, or self, is implied by our actual experience. Thus, the idea of this self is *a priori* as a necessary condition for the experience we do have of having knowledge of a unified world of nature. In the act of unifying all the elements of experience, we are conscious of our own unity, so that our consciousness of a unified world of experience and our own self-consciousness occur simultaneously. Our self-consciousness, however, is affected by the same faculties that affect our perception of external objects. I bring to the knowledge of myself the same apparatus and, therefore, impose upon myself as an object of knowledge the same "lenses" through which I see everything. Just as I do not know things as they are apart from the perspective from which I see them, so also I do not know the nature of this "transcendental unity of apperception" except as I am aware of the knowledge I have of the unity of the field of experience. What I am sure of is that a unified self is implied by any knowledge of experience.

Phenomenal and Noumenal Reality

A major impact of Kant's critical philosophy was his insistence that human knowledge is forever limited in its scope. This limitation takes two forms. In the first place, knowledge is limited to the world of experience. Second, our knowledge is limited by the manner in which our faculties of perception and thinking organize the raw data of experience. Kant did not doubt that the world as it appears to us is not the ultimate reality. He distinguished between *phenomenal* reality, or the world as we experience it, and *noumenal* reality, which is purely intelligible, that is, nonsensual, reality. When we experience a thing, we inevitably perceive it through the "lenses" of our *a priori* categories of thought. But what is a thing like when it is not being perceived? What is a thing-in-itself (*Ding an sich*)? We can obviously never have an experience of a nonsensuous perception. All objects we know are sensed objects. Still, we know that the existence of our world of experience is not produced by the mind. The mind, rather, imposes its ideas upon the manifold of experience, which is derived from the world of things-in-themselves. This means that there is a reality external to us that exists independently of us but that we can know only as it appears to us and is organized by us. The concept of a thing-in-itself does not, then, increase our knowledge but reminds us of the limits of knowledge.

Transcendental Ideas of Pure Reason as Regulative Concepts

Besides the general concept of the noumenal realm, there are three regulative ideas that we tend to think about, ideas that lead us beyond sense experiences but about which we cannot be indifferent because of our inevitable tendency to try to unify all our experience. There are the ideas of the *self*, of the *cosmos*, and of *God*. They are *transcendental* because they correspond to no object in our experience. They are produced not by intuition but by pure reason alone. They are, however, prompted by experience in the sense that we think those ideas in our attempts to achieve a coherent synthesis of all our experience. Kant says that "the first [regulative] idea is the 'I' itself, viewed simply as thinking nature or soul . . . endeavoring to represent all determinations as existing in a single subject, all powers, so far as possible, as derived from a single fundamental power, all change as belonging to the states of one and the same permanent being, and all *appearances* in space as completely different from the actions of thought." In this way our pure reason tries to synthesize the various psychological activities we are aware of into a unity, and it does this by formulating the concept of the *self*.

Similarly, pure reason tries to create a synthesis of the many events in experience by forming the concept of the *world*. Thus, "the second regulative idea of merely speculative reason is the concept of the world in general. . . . The absolute totality of the series of conditions . . . an idea which can never be completely realized in the empirical employment of reason, but which yet serves as a rule that prescribes how we ought to proceed in dealing with such series. . . . The cosmological ideas are nothing but simply regulative principles, and are very far from positing . . . an actual totality of such series."

Kant continues, "The third idea of pure reason, which contains a merely relative supposition of a being that is the sole and sufficient cause of all cosmological series, is the idea of *God*. We have not the slightest ground to assume in an absolute manner the object of this idea. . . . It becomes evident that the idea of such a being, like all speculative ideas, seems only to formulate the command of reason, that all connection in the world be viewed in accordance with the principles of a systematic unity—*as if* all such connection had its source in one single all-embracing being as the supreme and sufficient cause."

Kant's use of these regulative ideas exemplifies his way of mediating between dogmatic rationalism and skeptical empiricism. With the empiricists, Kant agrees that we can have no knowledge of reality beyond experience. The ideas of the self, the cosmos, and God cannot give us any theoretical knowledge of realities corresponding to these ideas. The function of these ideas is simply and solely regulative. As regulative ideas, they give us a reasonable way of dealing with the constantly recurring questions raised by metaphysics. To this extent Kant acknowledged the validity of the subject matter of rationalism. His critical analysis of the scope of human reason, however, led him to discover that earlier rationalists had made the error of treating *transcendental* ideas as though they were ideas about actual beings. Kant emphasizes that "there is a great difference between something given to my reason as an *object absolutely*, or merely as an *object in the idea*. In the former case our concepts are employed to determine the object [transcendent]; in the latter case there is in fact only a scheme for which no object, not even a hypothetical one, is directly given, and which only enables us to represent to ourselves other objects in an indirect manner, namely in their systematic unity, by means of their relation to this idea. Thus, I say, that the concept of a highest intelligence is a mere idea [transcendental]."

The Antinomies and the Limits of Reason

Because regulative ideas do not refer to any objective reality about which we can have knowledge, we must consider these ideas as being the products of our pure reason. As such we cannot bring to these ideas the *a priori* forms of time and space or the category of cause and effect since these are imposed by us only upon the sensible manifold. Science is possible because all people, having the same structure of mind, will always and everywhere order the events of sense experience in the same way. That is, we all bring to the *given* of sense experience the same organizing faculties of understanding. But there can be no science of metaphysics because there is not the same kind of *given* when we consider the ideas of self, cosmos, and God as when we consider "the shortest distance between two points." What is given in metaphysics is the felt need to achieve a synthesis of the wide variety of events in experience at ever-higher levels and of discovering an ever-wider explanation of the realm of phenomenon.

There is a difference for Kant between *a priori* or theoretical scientific knowledge, on the one hand, and speculative metaphysics on the other. The difference is that we can have scientific knowledge of phenomena but cannot have scientific knowledge of the noumenal realm, or the realm that transcends experience. Our attempts to achieve a "science" of metaphysics, Kant says, are doomed to failure. Whenever we try to discuss the self, the cosmos, or God as though they were objects of experience, the inability of the mind ever to do so successfully is showed by what Kant calls the *antinomies* into which we fall. These four antinomies show us that when we discuss the nature of the world beyond experience, we can argue with equal force on opposite sides of various propositions, namely, that (1) the world is limited in time and space, or that it is unlimited; that (2) every composite substance in the world is made up of simple parts, or that no composite thing in the world is made up of simple parts since there nowhere exists in the world anything simple; that (3) besides causality in accordance with the laws of nature there is also another causality, that of freedom, or that there is no freedom since everything in the world takes place solely in accordance with the laws of nature; and, finally, that (4) there exists an absolutely necessary being as part of the world or as its cause, or an absolutely necessary being nowhere exists.

These antinomies reflect the disagreements generated by dogmatic metaphysics. The disagreements occur only because they are based upon "nonsense"—that is, upon attempts to describe a reality about which we have, and can have, no sense experience. Kant did, however, believe that these antinomies have positive value. Specifically, they provide an additional argument for saying that the world of space and time is phenomenal only and that in such a world freedom is a coherent idea. This follows because if the world were a thing-in-itself, it would have to be either finite or infinite in extent and divisibility. But the antinomies show that there can be no demonstrative proof that either alternative is true. Insofar, then, as the world is phenomenal only, we are justified in affirming moral freedom and human responsibility.

As regulative ideas, the concepts of the self, the world, and God have a legitimate function, for they help us to synthesize our experience. Also, to speak of a noumenal realm, or the realm of the thing-in-itself, is to respond to certain given experiences and tendencies of our thought. For this reason we can think of a person in two different ways: as a phenomenon and as a noumenon. As a phenomenon, a person can be studied scientifically as a being in space and time and in the context of cause and effect. At the same time, our experience of moral obligation suggests that a person's noumenal nature, what he is like beyond our sense perception of him, is characterized by freedom. In this context, the concept of freedom, as the idea of the self, or God, is a regulative idea.

There can never be any demonstrative proof either that people are free or that God exists because these concepts refer us beyond sense experience, where the categories of the mind have no data upon which to work.

Proofs of God's Existence

With this critical estimate of the capacities and scope of human reason, it was inevitable that Kant would reject the traditional proofs for the existence of God, namely, the *ontological, cosmological,* and *teleological* proofs. His argument against the *ontological* proof is that it is all a verbal exercise. The essence of this proof is the assertion that since we have the idea of a most perfect being, it would be contradictory to say that such a being does not exist. Such a denial would be contradictory because the concept of a perfect being necessarily includes the predicate of *existence.* A being, that is, that does not exist can hardly be considered a perfect being. But Kant argues that this line of reasoning is "taken from judgments, not from things and their existence," that the idea of God is made to have the predicate of existence by simply fashioning the concept in such a way that existence is made to be included in the idea of a perfect being. This argument nowhere shows why it is necessary to have the subject, *God.* There would be a contraindication if a perfect being did exist and we denied that such a being was omnipotent. But to say that we avoid a contradiction by agreeing that a supreme being is omnipotent does not by itself demonstrate that such a being exists. Moreover, to deny that God exists is not simply to deny a predicate but to abandon the subject and thereby all the predicates that go with it, and "if we reject subject and predicate alike, there is no contradiction; for nothing is then left to be contradicted." Kant concluded, therefore, that "all the trouble and labor bestowed on the famous ontological or Cartesian proof of the existence of a supreme Being from concepts alone is trouble and labor wasted. A man might as well expect to become richer in knowledge by the aid of mere ideas as a merchant to increase his wealth by adding some noughts to his cash account."

Whereas the ontological proof begins with an idea (of a perfect being), the *cosmological* proof "takes its stand on experience." For, it says that "I exist, therefore, an absolutely necessary being exists" on the assumption that if anything exists an absolutely necessary being must also exist. The error of this argument, according to Kant, is that while it begins with experience, it soon moves beyond experience. Within the realm of sense experience it is legitimate to infer a cause for each event, but "the principle of causality has no meaning and no criterion for its application save only in the sensible world." Here is the direct application of Kant's critical method, for he argues that we cannot employ the *a priori* categories of the mind in trying to describe realities beyond sense experience. The cosmological argument cannot, therefore, securely lead us to a first cause of all things, for the most we can infer from our experience of things is a regulative idea of God. Whether there actually is such a being, a ground of all contingent things, raises the same question posed by the ontological argument, namely, whether we can successfully bridge the gap between our idea of a perfect being and demonstrative proof of its existence.

Similarly, the *teleological* argument begins with considerable persuasiveness, for it says that "in the world we everywhere find clear signs of an order in accordance with a determinate purpose. . . . The diverse things could not of themselves have cooperated, by so great a combination of diverse means, to the fulfillment of determinate final purposes, had they not been chosen and designed for these purposes by an ordering rational principle in conformity with underlying ideas." To this argument Kant replies that it may very well be that our experience of order in the universe suggests an orderer, but order in the world does not demonstrate that the material stuff of the world could not exist without an orderer. The most this argument from design can prove, Kant says, "is an *architect* of the world who is always very much hampered by the adaptability of the material in which he works, not a *creator* of the world to whose idea everything is subject." To prove the existence of a creator leads us back to the cosmological argument with its idea of causality. But since we cannot use the category of causality beyond the things in experience, we are left simply with an idea of a first cause or creator, and this takes us back to the ontological argument, with its deficiencies. Kant's conclusion, therefore, is that we cannot use transcendental ideas or theoretical principles, which have no application beyond the field of sense experience, to demonstrate the existence of God.

It follows from Kant's critical remarks about the "proofs," however, that just as we cannot demonstrate God's existence, neither can we demonstrate that God does *not* exist. By pure reason alone we can neither prove nor disprove God's existence. If, therefore, the existence of God cannot be effectively dealt with by the theoretical reason, then some other aspect of reason must be considered as the source of the idea of God. Thus, the idea of God has importance in Kant's philosophy, as do other regulative ideas.

PRACTICAL REASON

Besides the "starry heavens above," it was also the "moral law within" that filled Kant with wonder. He was aware that human beings not only gaze upon a world of things but become participants in a world of action. Reason is, therefore, alternately concerned with theory about things and with practical behavior. But there is "ultimately only one and the same reason which has to be distinguished in its application," says Kant, and of the objectives of reason, "the first is *theoretical,* the second *practical* rational knowledge." It was Kant's way of explaining the scope and powers of pure theoretical reason that made possible his account of the practical reason.

The tendency of scientific thought in Kant's day was to identify reality with what we can know from sense experience, from appearance. If this were a true account of reality, knowledge would consist only of a sensible manifold understood as things strictly related to each other by causality. Reality would then be viewed as a large mechanism whose only activity was the product of prior causes, and people would also be viewed as a part of this mechanical system. If this were the case, Kant says, "I could not . . . without palpable contradiction say of one and the same thing, for instance the human soul, that its will is free and yet is subject to natural necessity, that is, not free." Kant avoided this contradiction by saying that a person's phenomenal self, or the self we can observe, is subject to natural necessity or causality, whereas the noumenal self as a thing-in-itself possesses freedom. It is in a negative way, by limiting the scope of theoretical reason to the sensible manifold, that Kant made way for the positive use of practical reason: insofar as "our Critique limits speculative reason, it is indeed *negative,* but since it thereby removes an obstacle which stands in the way of the employment of practical reason, nay threatens to destroy it, it has in reality a positive and very important use."

Morality becomes possible because even though we cannot know things-in-themselves, or objects in the noumenal realm, "we must yet be in a position at least to *think* them as things-in-themselves; otherwise we should be landed in the absurd conclusion that there can be appearance without anything that appears." But "if our Critique is not in error in teaching that the object [e.g., a human being] is to be taken *in a twofold sense,* namely as appearance and as a thing-in-itself . . . then there is no contradiction in supposing that one and the same will is, in the appearance, that is, in visible acts, necessarily subject to the law of nature, and so far not free, while yet, as belonging to a thing-in-itself, is not subject to that law, and is, therefore *free.*" To be sure, the soul cannot be *known* by speculative reason as being free, "but though I cannot *know,* I can yet *think* freedom." Kant has, therefore, provided the basis for moral and religious discourse. Specifically, he distinguishes between two kinds of reality—the phenomenal and the noumenal; he then limits science to the phenomenal, thereby justifying the use of practical reason in connection with the noumenal world.

The Basis of Moral Knowledge

The task of moral philosophy, according to Kant, is to discover how we are able to arrive at principles of behavior that are binding upon all people. He was sure that we cannot discover these principles simply by studying the actual behavior of people, for although such a study would give us interesting anthropological information about how people *do* behave, it would not tell us how they *ought* to behave. Still, we do make moral judgments when we say, for example, that we ought to tell the truth, and the question is how we arrive at such a rule of behavior. For Kant, the moral judgment that "we ought to tell the truth" is in principle the same as the scientific judgment that "every change must have a cause." What makes them similar is that both of these judgments come from our reason and not from the objects we experience. Just as our theoretical reason brings the category of causality to visible objects and thereby explains the process of change, so also the practical reason brings to any given moral situation the concept of duty, or "ought." Both in science and in moral philosophy we use concepts that go beyond any particular facts we experience at any one time. Experience in both cases is the occasion for triggering the mind to think in universal terms. When we experience a given example of change, our minds bring to this event the category of causality. This makes it possible to explain the relation of cause and effect not only in this case but in all cases of change. Similarly, in the context of human relations, the practical reason is able to determine how we should behave not only at this moment but what should be the principle of our behavior at all times. Like scientific knowledge, moral knowledge is based upon *a priori* judgments. Kant discovered earlier that scientific knowledge is possible because of the *a priori* categories that the mind brings to experience. He now says, similarly, that "the basis of obligation must not be sought in human nature or in the circumstances of the world in which [humanity] is placed, but *a priori* simply in the concepts of reason."

Morality for Kant is, therefore, an aspect of rationality and has to do with our consciousness of rules or "laws" of behavior, which we consider both universal and necessary. The qualities of *universality* and *necessity* are the marks of *a priori* judgments, and this further confirms Kant's view that the principles of behavior are derived by the practical reason *a priori*. Instead of searching for the quality of "goodness" in the effects of our actions, Kant focuses upon the rational aspect of our behavior.

Morality and Rationality

As a rational being, I not only ask the question "What shall I do?" but am also conscious of being under an obligation to act in particular ways, that I "ought" to do something. These rational activities reflect the powers of practical reason, and I can assume that all rational beings are aware of the same problems. When I consider what I must do, therefore, I am also considering what all rational beings must do, for if a moral law or rule is valid for me as a rational being, it must be valid for all rational beings. A major test of a morally good act is, therefore, whether its principle can be applied to all rational beings and applied consistently. Moral philosophy is the quest for these principles that apply to all rational beings and that lead to behavior that we call *good.*

"Good" Defined as the Good Will

Kant says that "Nothing can possibly be conceived in the world, or even out of it, which can be called "good, without qualification, except a good will." He would admit, of course, that other things can be considered good, such as moderation of the passions, "and yet one can hardly call them unreservedly good . . . for without the principles of a good will they may become evil indeed. The cold-bloodedness of a villain not only makes him far more dangerous, but also directly makes him seem more despicable to us than he would have seemed without it." Kant's chief point is that the essence of the morally good act is the principle that a person affirms when he wills an act. "The good will is good not because of what it causes or accomplishes, not because of its usefulness in the attainment of some set purpose, but alone because of the willing, that is to say, it is good of itself."

A rational being strives to do what he *ought* to do, and this Kant distinguishes from an act that a person does either from *inclination* or *self-interest*. We can all compare the differences in these motives, for to act either from inclination or self-interest appears to us to be on a different level morally from acting out of *duty* to the moral law. Kant makes the rather startling statement that the "good will is good not because of what it accomplishes." He says this as a way of emphasizing the dominant role of the will in morality. It is not enough for the effects or consequences of our behavior to *agree with* the moral law; the truly moral act is done *for the sake of the moral law*, "for all these effects—even the promotion of the happiness of others—could have been also brought about by other causes, so that for this there would have been no need of the will of a rational being." The seat of moral worth is in the will, and the good will is one that acts out of a sense of duty; and "an action done from duty must wholly exclude the influence of inclination, and with it every object of the will, so that nothing remains which can determine the will except objectively the *law* and subjective *pure respect* for this practical law."

Duty implies that we are under some kind of obligation—a moral law. And Kant says that as rational beings we are aware of this obligation as it comes to us in the form of an *imperative*. Not all imperatives or commands are connected with morality, for they are not in every case directed to all people and, therefore, they lack the quality of universality that a moral rule requires. There are, for example, *technical* imperatives or rules of skill, which command us to do certain things *if* we want to achieve certain ends. For example, *if* we want to build a bridge across the river, we *must* use materials of certain strength. But we do not absolutely have to build a bridge. We can either build a tunnel or use surface craft to get to the other side. Similarly, there are certain *prudential* imperatives, which say, for example, that if I want to be popular with certain people, I *must* say or do certain things. But again, it is not absolutely necessary that I achieve this popularity. The technical and prudential imperatives are, therefore, *hypothetical* imperatives because they command us only if we decide to enter their sphere of operation.

The Categorical Imperative

Unlike the technical and prudential imperatives, which are hypothetical in nature, the truly moral imperative is *categorical*. This categorical imperative applies to all people and commands "an action as necessary of itself without reference to another end, that is, as objectively necessary." It commands certain conduct immediately, without having any other purpose as a condition. Actually, the categorical imperative commands a law that forms the basis of particular actions. It is *categorical* because it instantly applies to all rational beings, and it is *imperative* because it is the principle on which we *ought to act*. The basic formulation of the categorical imperative is this: "Act only on that maxim whereby you can at the same time will that it should become a universal law." Kant had said that "everything in nature works according to laws. Rational beings alone have the faculty of acting according *to the conception* of laws." Now he wants to show that the categorical imperative is our conception of the law of nature as it pertains to human behavior, and, therefore, he expresses the imperative of duty in an alternate way, namely, "Act as if the maxim of your action were to become a universal law of nature."

It is clear that the categorical imperative does not give us specific rules of conduct, for it appears to be simply an abstract formula. Still, this was precisely what Kant thought moral philosophy should provide us in order to guide our moral behavior. For once we understand the fundamental principle of the moral law, we can then apply it to specific cases. To illustrate how the categorical imperative enables us to discover our moral duties, Kant gives the following example:

> [A man] finds himself forced by necessity to borrow money. He knows that he will not be able to repay it, but sees also that nothing will be lent to him unless he promises stoutly to repay it in a definite time. He desires to make this promise, but he has still so much conscience as to ask himself: Is it not unlawful and inconsistent with duty to get out of a difficulty in this way? Suppose, however, that he resolves to do so, then the maxim of his action would be expressed thus: When I think myself in want of money, I will borrow money and promise to repay it, although I know that I never can do so. Now this principle of self-love or of one's own advantage may perhaps be consistent with my whole future welfare; but the question now is, Is it right? I change then the suggestion of self-love into a universal law, and state the question thus: How would it be if my maxim were a universal law? Then I see at once that it could never hold as a universal law of nature, but would necessarily contradict itself. For supposing it to be a universal law that everyone when he thinks himself in a difficulty should be able to promise whatever he pleases, with the purpose of not keeping his promise, the promise itself would become impossible, as well as the end that one might have in view of it, since no one would consider that anything was promised to him, but would ridicule all such statements as vain pretenses.

If we were still to ask why he must tell the truth, or why he should avoid the contradiction involved in a false promise, Kant answers that there is something about human beings that makes us resist and resent being treated as *things* instead of as *persons*. What makes us human is our rationality, and to be a human, or a rational being, is therefore an end in itself. We become a thing when someone uses us as a means for some other end, as when someone tells us a lie. But however necessary such use of us may seem at times, we nevertheless consider ourselves as being of absolute intrinsic worth as persons. The individual human being as possessing absolute worth becomes the basis for the supreme principle of morality:

> the foundation of this principle is: *rational nature exists as an end in itself.* All men everywhere want to be considered persons instead of things for the same reason that I do, and this affirmation of the absolute worth of the individual leads to a second formulation of the categorical imperative which says: *So act as to treat humanity, whether in your own person or in that of any other, in every case as an end withal, never as a means only.*

There is a third formulation of the categorical imperative, which is already implied in the first two but which Kant wants to make explicit. It is that we should "always so act that the will could regard itself at the same time as making universal law through its own maxim." Here Kant speaks of the *autonomy* of the will, that each person through his own act of will legislates the moral law. He distinguishes autonomy from *heteronomy*, the determination (of a law or action) by someone or something other than the self. Thus a heteronomous will is influenced or even determined by desires or inclination. An autonomous will, on the other hand, is free and independent, and as such is the "supreme principle of morality." Central to the concept of the autonomy of the will is the idea of *freedom*, the crucial regulative idea, which Kant employed to distinguish between the worlds of science and morality—the phenomenal and noumenal worlds. He says that "the *will* is a kind of causality belonging to living beings in so far as they are rational, and *freedom* would be this property of such causality that it can be efficient, independently of foreign causes determining it, just as *physical necessity* is the property that the causality of all irrational being has of being determined to activity by the influence of foreign causes." And again, "I affirm that we must attribute to every rational being which has a will that it has also the idea of freedom and acts entirely under this idea. For in such a being we conceive a reason that is practical, that is, has causality in reference to its objects." The categorical imperative, therefore, speaks of the universality of the moral law, affirms the supreme worth of each rational person, and assigns freedom or autonomy to the will. Our experience of the moral law suggested to Kant some further insights concerning the postulates of freedom, immortality, and God.

The Moral Postulates

Kant did not think it possible to prove or demonstrate that God exists or that the human will is free. Freedom is an idea that it is necessary to assume because of our experience of moral obligation—that is, "because I must, I can." Though we cannot demonstrate that our wills are free, we are intellectually compelled to assume such freedom, for freedom and morality "are so inseparably united that one might define practical freedom as independence of the will of anything but the moral law alone." How could people be responsible or have a duty if they were not able or free to fulfill their duty or respond to the moral command? Freedom must be assumed, and as such it is the first postulate of morality.

A second moral postulate for Kant is *immortality.* The line of reasoning by which Kant was led to postulate immortality begins with his conception of the supreme good, or the *summum bonum.* Although virtue is the supreme good, we as rational beings are fully satisfied only when there is a union between virtue and happiness. Though it does not always happen so, we all assume that virtue ought to produce happiness. Kant had rigorously maintained that the moral law commands us to act not so that we be happy, but so that our actions will be *right.* Still, the full realization of a rational being requires that we think of the supreme good as including both virtue and happiness. But our experience shows that there is no necessary connection between virtue and happiness. If we were to limit human experience to this world, it would then appear impossible to achieve the supreme good in its fullness. Still, the moral law does command us to strive for perfect good, and this implies an indefinite progress toward this ideal, "but this endless progress is possible only on the supposition of the unending duration of the existence and personality of the same rational being, which is called the immortality of the soul."

The moral universe also compels us to postulate the existence of God as the grounds for the necessary connection between virtue and happiness. If we mean by happiness "the state of a rational being in the world with whom in the totality of his experience *everything goes according to his wish and will,*" then happiness implies a harmony between a person's will and physical nature. But a person is not the author of the world, nor is he or she capable of ordering nature so as to effect a necessary connection between virtue and happiness. But we do conclude from our conception of the supreme good that virtue and happiness must go together. Consequently, we must postulate "the existence of a cause of the whole of nature which is distinct from nature and which contains the ground of this connection, namely, of the exact harmony of happiness with morality." And thus "it is morally necessary to assume the existence of God." This is not to say that there cannot be morality without religion, for Kant has already said that a person can recognize his moral duty without the idea of God and that he must obey the law simply out of respect for the law—"for duty's sake." But Kant does say that "through the idea of the supreme good as object and final end of the pure practical reason the moral law leads to religion, that is to the recognition of all duties as divine commands, not as sanctions, that is, as arbitrary commands of an alien will . . . but as essential laws of every free will in itself, which, however, must be looked on as commands of the supreme Being, because it is only from a morally perfect and at the same time all-powerful will . . . that we hope to attain the highest good, which the moral law makes it our duty to take as the object of our endeavor."

Whether Kant succeeded in reaching the objectives he set for his new critical philosophy, his achievement was monumental. It may very well be that his mistakes along the way were more important than most men's successes, but what is beyond question is that although it is not necessary to accept everything Kant said, it is nevertheless difficult to philosophize today without taking his views into account.

AESTHETICS: THE BEAUTIFUL

As we have seen, Kant developed a specific set of rules of morality by which one could determine whether an action can rightly be called "good." These rules apply to all people, so that the test for morally good behavior is a universal or objective standard. Similarly, Kant argued that the human mind can develop reliable scientific knowledge, that nature must be considered uniform throughout, and that scientific laws must be valid or "true" for everyone. However, when he turns to the problems of aesthetics, Kant says that "there can be no rule according to which anyone can be compelled to recognize anything as *beautiful*." There are, Kant says, no reasons or principles which signify that a dress, a house, or a flower is beautiful. Nevertheless, we do say about things that they are beautiful, and we like to think that what *we* call beautiful should also be called beautiful by others. In the end, Kant shows that even though our judgment of the beautiful is based upon our subjective feeling, the beautiful is defined as "that which pleases universally." Just how he moves from our subjective feeling of the beautiful to the conclusion that the beautiful is what pleases universally provides us with some of Kant's key insights into the nature of our aesthetic experience.

The Beautiful as Independent Pleasant Satisfaction

The first step in discovering the nature of our aesthetic judgment is to see it as a matter of subjective taste. When we express the judgment that an object is beautiful, this judgment is subjective because upon experiencing the object, our imagination refers our sensation of the object to us as subjects, to our feeling of pleasure or displeasure. This feeling of pleasure or displeasure denotes nothing in the object but is simply the manner in which the object affects us. Kant's key point here is that the judgment of taste is not a logical matter involving a knowledge of concepts. If I want to say about an object that it is "good," I have to know what kind of thing the object is intended to be. That is, I must have a concept of it. But it is not necessary for me to have a concept of an object to enable me to see beauty in it. For example, "flowers, free patterns, lines aimlessly intertwining—technically termed foliage—have no signification, depend upon no definite concept, and yet please." My judgment of beauty, my taste, is simply *contemplative,* which means that I do not need to know anything more about the object other than how its character affects my feelings of pleasure or displeasure. An aesthetic judgment is not a cognitive judgment; that is, it rests upon neither theoretical nor practical knowledge.

Kant insists that for an aesthetic judgment to be "pure," it must be independent of any special interest; it must be "disinterested." To be disinterested is of course not the same as being uninteresting. It means that the judgment that an object is beautiful is not biased by a prejudice for or against an object. The judgment that a house is beautiful or not must be independent of my prejudice against either large or small houses or of my desire to own such a house. The pure aesthetic judgment affirms that the form of the object is pleasing without reference to any special interest I may have in it. Of course it is possible that I can have an interest in or a desire for an object. But my judgment that it is beautiful is independent of that interest or desire. For this reason, Kant defines the beautiful as follows: "*Taste* is the faculty of estimating an object or a type of representation by means of a delight or aversion *apart from any interest.* The object of such a delight is called *beautiful.*"

The Beautiful as an Object of Universal Delight

If my judgment that an object is beautiful is independent of any private interest or prejudice of mine, then my judgment does not depend upon nor is it influenced by any other interest. My judgment is "free" when, first, I express my view that an object is beautiful, and, second, I am conscious when I do this that I am not depending upon nor influenced by any other interest—whether an appetite, a desire, or a bias. Because no interest peculiar or private to me is influencing my judgment, I have every reason to believe that others, similarly free of their private interests, would arrive at the same judgment of the beautiful. The aesthetic judgment is universal.

Kant is aware that not all uses of the word *taste* refer to universal aesthetic judgments. It is possible to have good taste regarding things about which different people disagree. Someone will say, "canary-wine is agreeable," but a friend will remind him to say "agreeable *to me.*" A violet color may impress someone as soft and lovely; to someone else it appears dull and faded. One person likes the sound of wind instruments, while another likes that of string instruments. On these matters, where something is or is not "agreeable" to us, it is true that "everyone has his own taste." But "agreeable" must not be confused with the beautiful. For if something is agreeable to or even pleases only one person, he must not call it beautiful. As Kant says, many things possess for us charm and agreeableness. But if we put something on a pedestal and call it beautiful, we imply that everyone should make the same judgment, everyone should have the same delight in the object. Those who judge differently can be "blamed" and denied that they have taste. And to this extent, Kant says, "it is not open to men to say: Every one has his own taste. This would be equivalent to saying that there is no such thing at all as taste; that is, no aesthetic judgment capable of making a rightful claim upon the assent of all men."

The ambiguous use of the word *taste* is clarified by distinguishing between the taste of our senses and the taste of reflection or contemplation. It is the taste of the senses—for example the taste of foods and drinks—which is frequently merely private. But taste, which involves a judgment of the beautiful, implies universal agreement. This aesthetic judgment is not based on logic because it does not involve our cognitive faculties; rather, it only involves the feelings of pleasure or displeasure in every subject. The judgment of the beautiful does not rest on any concept, but rather upon feeling. Kant therefore defines the beautiful in yet another way: "The *beautiful* is that which, apart from a concept, pleases universally."

Finality versus Purpose in the Beautiful Object

There are two kinds of beauty: (1) free beauty and (2) beauty which is merely dependent. Free beauty presupposes no concept of what the object should be. By contrast, dependent beauty presupposes a concept of what that object should be, and that concept makes it possible for us to determine whether that object is perfect or not.

A flower is a free beauty of matter. Just by looking at it we can tell whether it is beautiful or not. We need no further knowledge about it. There is no other concept connected with the flower, such as its purpose, that would help us determine whether it is beautiful. The manner in which the flower presents itself to us is final. The flower's form as we see it represents its "finality," and this finality provides the basis for the judgment of its beauty. Surely something is going on in our consciousness and understanding when we make this judgment, but our feeling and not our reasoning powers are in control here. Kant says therefore, that "A judgment is called aesthetic precisely because its determining ground is not a concept but the feeling of that harmony in the play of the mental powers, so far as it can be experienced in feeling." To be sure, botanists can know many things about the flower, but their concepts have no bearing on the judgment whether the flower is beautiful. Similarly, in painting, sculpture, horticulture, and even music, the design is what is essential, so that what pleases by its form is the fundamental prerequisite for taste.

But the beauty of a man, woman, or child, the beauty of a building such as a church or a summerhouse—all these presuppose a concept of the "end" or purpose which defines what each is supposed to be. We can say about each person or building that it is beautiful. But here our judgment of beauty takes into account the concepts of ends or purposes. Moreover, the judgment of beauty becomes dependent upon the fulfillment or lack of fulfillment of the proper end or purpose of the object in question. Here we do not have a pure aesthetic judgment based solely upon feeling. Instead there is an admixture of conceptual knowledge concerning the nature and purpose of a person or the purpose or function of the building. For example, someone might judge that a building excites displeasure because its form (although exquisite) is inappropriate for a church. One person might be judged beautiful because he or she behaves in a moral manner, in which case the judgment of the beautiful becomes confused or at least combined with the judgment of the good—which is a cognitive judgment. If our judgment that a person or building is beautiful depends upon the purpose of human nature or of the building, then our judgment is placed under a restriction and is no longer a free and pure judgment of taste. Accordingly, Kant defines the beautiful in a third way: "Beauty is the form of finality in an object, so far as perceived in it apart from the representation of an end (or purpose)."

Necessity, Common Sense, and the Beautiful

There is something about the beautiful that leads to "a necessary reference on its part to delight (pleasure)." This does not mean, Kant says, that I can know ahead of time "that every one *will in fact feel* this delight in the object that is called beautiful by me." The *necessity* which combines the judgment of the beautiful with delight is neither a theoretical nor a practical necessity. Even though I claim that my aesthetic judgment is universal, I cannot assume that everyone will actually agree with it. Indeed, because I am not even capable of clearly formulating a rule which defines the beautiful in terms of concepts, I am left with my own feeling of beauty which also includes my delight or pleasure. That my delight is referred to in the judgment of beauty does not mean that the element of delight is logically deduced from the concept of beauty. The "necessity" that delight is involved in the experience of the beautiful is, says Kant "a necessity of a special kind." The necessity which is thought in an aesthetic judgment "can only be termed *exemplary*." It is "a necessity of the assent of *all* to a judgment regarded as exemplifying a universal rule incapable of formulation." My judgment, in short, is an example of a universal rule regarding beauty.

If I cannot formulate the principle of beauty in a rational or cognitive form, how is it possible for me to communicate to others the necessary components of the judgment of the beautiful? Two times two necessarily equals four for everyone. How can it be that the judgment of the beautiful also contains the element of necessity? I must have, Kant says, "a subjective principle and one which determines what pleases or displeases, by means of feeling only and not through concepts, but yet with universal validity." For this reason, the judgment of taste depends upon our presupposing the existence of a common sense. Only under such a presupposition of a common sense can I lay down a judgment of taste. This does not mean that everyone will agree with my judgment, but rather that everyone *ought* to agree with it. We can assume, when we communicate that two and two equals four, that others can or even must understand the universal truth of this judgment—even though in this case we are dealing with an objective principle. So also can we assume that there is a common sense in everyone to which we can communicate the subjective judgment of the beautiful. For this reason Kant gives as his fourth definition that "The Beautiful is that which, apart from a concept, is cognized as object of a *necessary* delight."

Kant was himself aware, as he points out in the preface to his *Critique of Judgment*, that "the difficulty of unraveling a problem so involved in its nature may serve as an excuse for a certain amount of hardly avoidable obscurity in its solution." In spite of this confession, Hegel found in Kant's theory of aesthetics "the first rational word concerning beauty."

CHAPTER 13

German Idealism

KANT'S IMPACT ON GERMAN THOUGHT

Following closely upon Kant's *critical* philosophy was the movement of 19th-century German idealism. As a metaphysical theory, idealism in general is the view that the universe is composed solely of mental—or spiritual— things, there is in reality no material stuff. For example, 18th-century British Empiricist George Berkeley held that only spiritual minds exist, and my perception of the so-called physical world is simply a stream of mental perceptions that God feeds into my spiritual mind. The German approach to idealism had Kantian philosophy as its starting point. Kant did not technically deny the existence of the physical world. However, he maintained that the true nature of things-in-themselves is permanently hidden from us. Our minds are structured in such a way that we are forever barred from going beyond the realm of sense experience, that is, the realm of *phenomena.* Further, our interpretation of the world of experience is permanently fixed by the categories that our minds impose upon our experiences. Kant believed that these categories— such as cause and effect, existence and negation, and others—are concepts that our minds possess prior to experience and employ in relation to objects, and this is what makes knowledge possible.

Although we are locked into a view of the world that is limited to our sense experience and mental constructs, Kant still believed that there existed a *noumenal* realm of things-in-themselves, even though we can never access it. For example, we experience only the *appearance* of the red apple—sensory information arranged by our mental abilities of perception. But behind the redness of the apple there must be something to which the color red is related or which can *have* the color red, namely, that apple in itself. For Kant, though, the fact remains that we cannot *know* anything about such things-in-themselves because our mental categories apply only to the phenomenal world.

Johann Gottlieb Fichte (1762–1814) was one of the first German idealists to recognize a glaring contradiction in Kant's argument. How is it possible to say that something exists but that we can know nothing about it? Do we not already know *something* about it when we say that it exists? Further, Kant asserted the existence of things-in-themselves in order to account for our experiences of sensation, saying in effect that the thing-in-itself is the *cause* of any given sensation. But he had clearly argued that the categories of the mind, such as cause and effect, could not be used to give us knowledge about the noumenal world. When Kant says, then, that the thing-in-itself is the cause of our sensations, he thereby contradicts his own rule for limiting the use of the categories to our judgments about the objects of sense experience.

Even to say that the thing-in-itself *exists* is to go beyond the limits that Kant set for knowledge. For, *existence* is simply a category of the mind that helps organize our sense experience in a coherent manner. Indeed, Kant's strongest argument against the earlier metaphysicians was that they wrongly ascribed *existence* to alleged beings and realities beyond sense experience. Now with his doctrine of the thing-in-itself, it seems that Kant has retained just what his critical philosophy was supposed to eliminate. Not only is it impossible, in Kant's theory, to ascribe the category of existence to things-in-themselves, it is also a clear contradiction to say that something can exist if it is unknowable. We can, of course, distinguish between something that is at the moment unknown (but potentially knowable) and something that is permanently unknowable. But to say that something is permanently unknowable is contradictory, because such a statement implies that we already know that something *is*, and to that extent it is knowable. Thus, Kant's conception of the thing-in-itself collapsed.

Fichte put forward the opposite thesis, namely, that whatever is, is knowable. At the same time, Fichte had no intention of reverting to the kind of metaphysics that Kant had rejected. He believed that Kant had achieved genuine progress in philosophy, and Fichte intended to carry forward what Kant had begun. What Fichte tried to do, therefore, was to use Kant's method—stripped of the concept of the unknowable thing-in-itself—and transform Kant's critical idealism into a metaphysical idealism. That is, Fichte took Kant's theory that the mind imposes its categories upon experience and transformed this into the theory that every object and therefore the entire universe is a product of mind.

Other German philosophers also joined in the enterprise of transforming Kant's critical philosophy into a metaphysical idealism, most notably, Georg Wilhelm Friedrich Hegel (1770–1831), Friedrich Wilhelm Joseph von Schelling, (1775–1854), and Arthur Schopenhauer (1788–1860). Each of these philosophers approached this enterprise in his own and somewhat different way. What they did agree on, however, was that there can be no unknowable thing-in-itself as Kant had presumed. Further, Kant believed that things-in-themselves are the ultimate source of our sense experience. Idealists argued instead that our experiential knowledge is the product of mind. In this chapter we will look at the views to two German idealists: Hegel and Schopenhauer.

HEGEL

Life

Hegel's historical significance lies in the fact that he accomplished with extraordinary and systematic thoroughness what Kant so recently said could not be done. Kant argued that metaphysics is impossible, that it is impossible for the human mind to achieve theoretical knowledge about all of reality. Hegel, on the other hand, set forth the general proposition that "what is rational is real and what is real is rational," and from this concluded that everything that is, is knowable. Here was an elaborate metaphysics, which provided a new basis for thinking about the very structure of reality and about its manifestations in morality, law, religion, art, history, and above all thought itself. It might be argued that the eventual decline of Hegelian philosophy was more a matter of abandonment than of studied attack—more like deserting a mansion than capturing a stronghold. But to imply that Hegel's successors merely decided to ignore his elaborate metaphysical system is to misjudge the impact and grip his ideas had upon the generations that followed him. The impact of Hegel's thought can be measured by the fact that most 20th-century philosophy represents ways of revising or rejecting aspects of his absolute idealism.

Georg Wilhelm Friedrich Hegel was born at Stuttgart in 1770 and lived through Germany's most brilliant intellectual period. This was the year when Beethoven was born and when the poet-scientist Goethe, that "complete civilization in himself," was 20 years old. Kant was 46 years old and had not yet written his classic philosophical works. The Englishman Wordsworth was also born in this year, and his poetry in time formed a part of that romanticism that shared some of the attitudes of German idealism. At an early age, Hegel was deeply impressed by ancient Greek writers, coming eventually to believe that Plato and Aristotle were not only the sources of philosophy but even now its life-giving roots. After being a rather ordinary pupil at school in Stuttgart, Hegel enrolled at age 18 in the theological school at the University of Tübingen. Here he became friends with Hölderin and Schelling and was caught up in lively discussions over the issues of the French Revolution. During his five years at Tübingen his interest gradually turned to the relation between philosophy and theology. It was after he left the university that his interest in philosophy finally flowered. He became a family tutor for six years, in Berne and in Frankfurt, and during these years wrote some minor works that nevertheless contained germs of the major problems he eventually made central in his philosophical works.

By this time German idealism had found two influential spokesmen in Fichte and Schelling. In 1801, when Hegel was appointed to the faculty of the University of Jena, he published his first work, on the *Difference between the Philosophical Systems of Fichte and Schelling,* in which he expressed a dislike for Fichte. While he was more sympathetic with Schelling in these early days, it was not long before his independent and original approach to philosophy was

Hegel
(Corbis-Bettmann)

made public in his first major work, *The Phenomenology of Mind,* which, he says, he finished at midnight before the Battle of Jena in 1807. As this battle closed his university, Hegel supported himself and his wife, whom he married in 1811, by becoming rector of the secondary school at Nürnberg, where he remained until 1816. It was here that he wrote his influential *Science of Logic,* which brought him invitations from several universities. In 1816 he joined the faculty at Heidelberg, where in the following year he published his *Encyclopedia of the Philosophical Sciences in Outline,* the work in which Hegel presents the grand structure of his philosophy in its threefold aspect, namely, logic, philosophy of nature, and philosophy of mind. Two years later, Hegel was given the chair of philosophy at the University of Berlin, where he remained until his death from cholera in 1831 at the age of 61. At Berlin Hegel's writing was massive, although most of it was published after his death. His works during this period included his *Philosophy of Right* and his posthumously published lectures on *Philosophy of History, Aesthetics, Philosophy of Religion,* and *History of Philosophy.*

Absolute Mind

As noted, the thrust of German idealism is that mind is ultimately the source and content of knowledge—not physical objects or some mysterious thing-in-itself. As Hegel expressed it, every reality is rational, and the rational is real. But what kind of "mind" actually produces our knowledge? We do experience a world of things external to us, which we recognize as existing independently of us and which we did not create. If all objects of our knowledge are the products of mind, but not *our* minds, it must be assumed that they are the products of an intelligence other than that of a finite individual. Hegel and other idealists concluded that all objects of knowledge, and therefore all objects, and indeed the whole universe, are the products of an absolute subject, an Absolute Mind.

 For Kant the categories of the mind merely make knowledge possible. However, for Hegel the categories have a type of existence that is independent of any individual's mind. Again, for Kant, the categories represented the mental process of an individual and provided for Kant the explanation of the types and limits of human knowledge. The categories, he said, are concepts in the human mind—that the mind brings to experience and by which the mind can understand the world of experience. Hegel, on the other hand, considered the categories not only as mental processes, but as objective realities possessing existence independently of the thinking individual. More specifically, Hegel argued that the existence of the categories is grounded in the Absolute Mind. But, as we shall see, Hegel did not mean to say that there were categories, on the one hand, and things such as chairs and apples on the other. Such a distinction would suggest that ideas and things have separate existences—just as Plato distinguished Forms from things. Hegel, unlike Plato, did not ascribe any independent existence to the categories. Instead, he said that they have *existence* and have their being independently of a person's mind or thought. Hegel wanted to say that the real world is more than the subjective conceptions of people's minds. At the same time, he was saying that reality is rationality, or Thought.

Take, for example, a chair. What is a chair, or what does it consist of? Hegel said that if we take seriously the conclusion that there can be no unknowable thing-in-itself, a chair must consist of the sum of the ideas we can have about it. On this basis a chair must consist of all the universals we find in it when we experience it. We say that the chair is hard, brown, round, and small. These are all universal ideas, and when they are related to each other this way, they are a chair. These universals have their being in the chair; universals or categories never exist singly or independently. Since there is no unknowable aspect of the chair, that is, nothing in addition to the qualities we experience, it follows that the chair *is* what we know about it, and what we know about it is that it consists of a combination of universals or ideas. To say, then, that the categories and universals have objective status means that they have their being independent of the knowing subject. At the same time, as the example of the chair shows, Hegel says that the object of thought consists after all in thought itself. There is, he said, an identity between knowing and being. Knowing and being are simply two sides of the same coin. To be sure, Hegel recognized that there is a subject and an object, a person and the world. But the essence of his idealism consisted in his notion that the object of our consciousness—the *thing* we experience and think about—is itself *thought*. In the end, Hegel arrived at the notion that reality is to be found in the Absolute Idea.

So far, two major points in Hegel's argument have been set forth, namely, (a) that we must reject the notion of an unknowable thing-in-itself and (b) that the nature of reality is thought, rationality, and that ultimate reality is the Absolute Idea. To indicate some of the steps by which Hegel came to this conclusion that reality is Thought, we turn next to a few of the basic elements in his intricate system of philosophy.

The Nature of Reality

Hegel looked upon the world as an organic process. We have already seen that for him the truly real is what he called the Absolute. In theological terms, this Absolute is called God. But Hegel wanted to show that he was not here referring to a Being separate from the world of nature or even from individual people. Whereas Plato made a sharp distinction between appearance and reality, Hegel argued in effect that appearance *is* reality. Nothing, said Hegel, is unrelated. For this reason, whatever we experience as separate things will, upon careful reflection, lead us to other things to which they are related. Eventually the process of dialectical thought will end in the knowledge of the Absolute. Still, the Absolute is not the unity of separate things. Hegel rejected materialism, which held that there are separate, finite particles of hard matter, which, when arranged in different formations, make up the whole nature of things. Nor did Hegel accept the extreme alternative put forward in the ancient world by Parmenides and more recently by Spinoza, namely, that everything is One—a single substance with various types and attributes. Hegel described the Absolute as a dynamic process, as an organism having parts but nevertheless unified into a complex system. The Absolute is therefore not some entity separate from the world but *is* the world when viewed in a special way.

Hegel believed that the inner essence of the Absolute could be reached by human reason because the Absolute is revealed in Nature as well as in the working of the human mind. What connects these three, the Absolute, Nature, and the mind, is Thought itself. A person's way of thinking is, as it were, fixed by the structure of Nature, by the way things actually behave. Things behave as they do, however, because the Absolute is expressing itself through the structure of Nature. Thus, a person thinks about Nature the way the Absolute expresses itself in Nature. Just as the Absolute and also Nature are dynamic processes, so also human thought is a process—a dialectic process.

Logic and the Dialectic Process   Hegel laid great stress upon logic. To be sure, he understood logic to mean virtually the same thing as metaphysics. This was particularly so because he believed that knowing and being coincide. Still, it was Hegel's view that we can know the essence of reality by moving logically step by step and avoiding all self-contradiction along the way. Descartes had advocated a similar method, whereby certainty in knowledge would follow from the movement from one clear idea to the next. Unlike Descartes, however, whose emphasis was upon the relations of ideas to each other, Hegel argued that thought must follow the inner logic of reality itself. That is, since Hegel had identified the rational with the actual, he concluded that logic and logical connections must be discovered *in* the actual and not in some "empty ratiocination." He argued that "since philosophy is the exploration of the rational, it is for that very reason the apprehension of the present and the actual, not the erection of a beyond, supposed to exist, God knows where." Logic, then, is the process by which we deduce, from our experiences of the actual, the categories that describe the Absolute. This process of deduction is at the very heart of Hegel's dialectic philosophy.

Hegel's dialectic process exhibits a *triadic* movement. Usually this triadic structure of the dialectic process is described as a movement from *thesis* to *antithesis* and finally to *synthesis*, after which the synthesis becomes a new thesis, and this process continues until it ends in the Absolute Idea. What Hegel emphasized in his dialectic logic was that thought *moves. Contradiction,* does not bring knowledge to a halt, but acts as a positive moving force in human reasoning.

To illustrate Hegel's dialectic method, we can take the first basic triad of his logic, namely, the triad of *Being, Nothing,* and *Becoming.* Hegel said that the mind must always move from the more general and abstract to the specific and concrete. The most general concept we can form about things is that they are. Although various things have specific and different qualities, they all have one thing in common, namely, their being. Being, then, is the most general concept that the mind can formulate. Also, Being must be logically prior to any specific thing, for things represent determinations or the shaping of what is originally without features. Thus, logic (and reality) begins with the indeterminate, with "the original featurelessness which precedes all definite character and is the very first of all. And this we call Being." Hegel's system begins, therefore, with the concept of Being, and this is the thesis. The question now is, how can thought move from such an abstract concept to any other concept? More important still is the question, how is it possible to *deduce* any other concept from such a universal idea as Being?

It was here that Hegel believed he had discovered something new about the nature of thought. Ever since the time of Aristotle, logicians thought that nothing could be deduced from a category that was not contained in that category. To deduce *B* from *A* requires that in some way *B* already be contained in *A.* Hegel accepted this. But what he rejected in Aristotelian logic was the assumption that nothing could be deduced from a *universal* term. For example, Aristotle argued that everything is a distinct thing and that logic, therefore, provides us only with specific universal terms from which no other universal terms could be deduced. Thus, for example, there is either *blue* or *not-blue;* there is no way to deduce any other color from blue. If blue is blue, you cannot at the same time say that it is something else, a non-blue. This principle of noncontradiction is very important in any formal logic. Still, Hegel believed that it is not true that a universal does not contain another concept. Returning, then, to the concept of Being, Hegel said that we have here an idea which contains none of the particular qualities or characteristics of the many things that have being. The idea of Being has no content, for the moment you give it some content, it would no longer be the concept of pure Being but the concept of something. Unlike Aristotle, however, Hegel believed that from this concept of Being it is possible to deduce another concept. He argued that because pure Being is mere abstraction, it is therefore absolutely negative. That is, since the concept of Being is wholly undefined, it passes into the concept of not-Being. Whenever we try to think of Being without any particular characteristics, the mind moves from Being to not-Being. This, of course, means that in some sense Being and not-Being are the same. Hegel was aware, as he said, that "the proposition that Being and Nothing are the same is so paradoxical to the imagination or understanding, that it is perhaps taken for a joke." Indeed, to understand Being and Nothing as the same, said Hegel, "is one of the hardest things thought expects itself to do." Still, Hegel's point is that Nothing is deduced from Being. At the same time, the concept of Nothing easily leads the mind back to the concept of Being. Of course Hegel is not implying that we can say of particular things that they simultaneously are the same as nothing. His argument is limited to the concept of pure Being, which, he says, contains the idea of Nothing. He has, then, deduced the concept of Nothing from the concept of Being. The antithesis, Nothing, is contained in the thesis, Being. In Hegel's logic, the antithesis is always deduced from the thesis, because it is already contained in the thesis.

The movement of the mind from Being to Nothing produces a third category, namely *Becoming.* The concept of Becoming is formed by the mind when it understands that Being, for the reasons already mentioned, is the same as Nothing. Becoming, Hegel says, is "the unity of Being and Nothing." It is, he says, "*one* idea." Becoming is therefore the *synthesis* of Being and Nothing. If we ask how something can both be and not be, Hegel would answer that it can both be and not be when it becomes.

Throughout his vast and intricate system, Hegel employs this same dialectic method of logic. At each step, he sets forth a thesis from which is deduced its antithesis; this thesis and antithesis then find their unity in a higher synthesis. In the end, Hegel arrives at the concept of the Absolute Idea, which he describes, in accordance with his dialectic method, as Becoming—as a process of self-development. Beginning, then, at the lowest level of knowledge, with the sensation of qualities and characteristics of particular things, Hegel sought to expand the scope of knowledge by discovering the ever-widening interrelationships of all things. In this way our minds move rigorously by way of deduction from one concept to the other, which we find as categories in actuality.

Single facts, for Hegel, are irrational. Only when such single facts are seen as aspects of the whole do they become rational. Thinking is forced to move from one fact to another by the very nature of each concept that facts engender. For example, consider the parts of an engine. By itself, a spark plug has no rational character; what confers rationality upon it is its relation to the other parts of the engine. To discover the essence of the spark plug is, thus, to discover the truth about the other parts and, eventually, the entire engine. The human mind, then, moves dialectically, constantly embracing an ever-increasing scope of reality, discovering the truth of anything only after discovering its relation to the whole—that is, its relation to the *Idea.*

The *Idea* of which Hegel speaks is deduced in his logic by the same method that yielded Becoming out of Being. The category of *subjectivity* is deduced from the fact that a person can have a notion of a thing, make a judgment about it, and be able to reason out logical connections. But from *subjectivity* we can deduce its opposite, namely, *objectivity.* That is, the notion of subjectivity already contains the idea of objectivity. To say that I am a self (subjectivity) implies that there is a not-self (objectivity). Subjectivity consists of thought in its formal sense. Objectivity, on the other hand, is thought that is, as it were, *outside* itself and *in* things. Describing the objective character of a person's notion, Hegel says that it consists of *mechanism, chemism,* and *teleology.* What a subject knows about nature as mechanical laws, for example, objects express in their behavior. The synthesis of the subjective and the objective, Hegel says, is their unity in the Idea. That is, in the Idea, the subjective (formal) and the objective (material) are brought together in unity. The Idea, however, contains its own dialectic, namely, life, cognition, and the Absolute Idea. Thus, the Idea is the category of self-consciousness; it knows itself in its objects. The whole drift of Hegel's logic, therefore, has been to move from the initial concept of Being finally to the notion of the Idea. But this Idea must also be understood as being in a dynamic process, so that the Idea is itself in a continuous process of self-development toward self-perfection.

The Philosophy of Nature   From the Idea we derive the realm of Nature. As Hegel puts it, Nature represents the Idea "outside itself." This expression is somewhat misleading, because it implies that the Idea exists independently of the world. In addition, Hegel ascribes "absolute freedom" to the Idea as it "goes forth freely out of itself as Nature." Recalling, however, Hegel's premise that the real is rational, it must follow here that Nature is simply rationality, or the Idea, in *external* form, somewhat the way a watchmaker's idea is found outside of himself in the watch. But Hegel's view is subtler than the relation of the watchmaker to the watch would suggest. For Hegel does not really refer to two separately existing things, Idea and Nature. Ultimate reality is a single organic and dynamic whole. Hegel's distinction between the logical Idea "behind" all things, on the one hand, and Nature, on the other, is his attempt simply to distinguish between the "inner" and "outer" aspects of the self-same reality. Nature, in short, is the opposite (the antithesis) of the rational Idea (thesis). Our thought moves dialectically from the rational (Idea) to the nonrational (Nature). The concept of Nature leads our thought finally to a synthesis represented by the unity of Idea and Nature in the new concept of Spirit (*Geist*, translated as either Spirit or Mind). What drives our thought from Nature back to Spirit is the dialectic movement within the concept of Nature. Just as logic begins with the most abstract concept, namely, Being, so the philosophy of Nature begins with the most abstract thing, which is, Hegel says, space. Space is empty (just as Being is indeterminate). At one "end" then, Nature touches emptiness. At the other end, it passes over into Spirit. Between space and Spirit is the diversity of particular things, which is what Nature is. Nature exhibits the laws of mechanics, physics, and organics. Each of these aspects of Nature is in turn analyzed by Hegel into its dialectic terms.

Much of what Hegel says about Nature is superceded by the developments of science since his day. But it was not his intention to take over the work of the scientists. He was concerned, rather, to discover through the philosophy of Nature a rational structure and pattern in all of reality. At the same time, he tried to show the difference between *freedom* and *necessity*, saying that Nature is the realm of necessity whereas Spirit is freedom. Nature, Hegel says, "is to be considered as a system of stages, of which one proceeds necessarily from the other." Freedom, on the other hand, is the act of Spirit. There is, then, a dialectic opposition between Spirit and Nature, between freedom and necessity. Indeed, the "career" of reality, the teleological movement of history, represents the gradual and continuous unfolding of the Spirit, of the Idea of freedom.

The Philosophy of Spirit   The third part of Hegel's system, following his logical Idea and his philosophy of Nature, is the philosophy of Spirit or Mind. Here again, Hegel sets forth the elements of his dialectic in which the thesis is subjective spirit, the antithesis is objective spirit, and the synthesis is Absolute Spirit. He goes into considerable detail, piling triad upon triad to illustrate that the Absolute is Spirit and that this Spirit finds its manifestation in the minds of individuals, in the social institutions of family, civil society, and the state, and finally in art, religion, and philosophy. The subjective spirit refers to the inner workings of the human mind, whereas the objective spirit represents the mind in its external embodiment in the social and political institutions. At the apex of knowledge are art, religion, and philosophy, which are the achievement of Absolute Spirit.

Most of what made Hegel's philosophy famous was that portion of his thought that he developed around his concept of objective spirit. Here we come upon the unity of Hegel's thought as he now attempts to connect his moral, social, and political thought with the rest of his system. The whole sphere of human behavior, both individual and collective, is described by him as part of the actual and therefore is essentially rational. Moreover, as part of the actual this objective side of the Spirit is seen as involved in the dialectic process. Human behavior and social and political organisms contain or embody the Spirit, just as Nature is the objective embodiment of the Absolute Idea. For this reason, Hegel looked upon institutions not as human creations, but as the product of the dialectic movement of history, of the objective manifestation of rational reality. Speaking, for example, about his book on the *Philosophy of Right,* Hegel says that "containing as it does the science of the state, [it] is to be nothing other than the endeavor to apprehend and portray the state as something inherently rational. As a work of philosophy, it must be poles apart from an attempt to construct a state as it ought to be." This identification of the actual state with the very grounds of reality is what caused Hegel's political theory to have such a captivating influence among those who wished to think about the state in totalitarian or at least nondemocratic terms. We turn, then, to some of the "moments" in the dialectic process by which Hegel seeks to show the natural movement from the individual's concept of right to the state's authority over society. The basic triadic movement here is from *right* (thesis) to *morality* (antithesis) and then to *social ethics* (synthesis).

Ethics and Politics

The Concept of Right   We must first of all understand human behavior as the actions of individual people. Individuals, Hegel says, are aware of freedom. We express our freedom most concretely by an act of will. Hegel looked upon will and reason as virtually synonymous, saying that "only as thinking intelligence, will is free will." We express freedom chiefly in relation to material things, appropriating them, using them, and exchanging them. "To appropriate," says Hegel, "is at bottom only to manifest the majesty of my will towards things, by demonstrating that they are not self-complete and have no purpose of their own." The basis of the right to property is for Hegel the free

will of the individual in the act of appropriation. Free people, however, are able to "alienate" themselves from property, and this we do through "contract." A contract is the product of two free wills agreeing to exchange property. It also shows the development of a duty, which the terms of the contract now embody. Hegel's central point here is that insofar as individual people act rationally, our free acts conform to the rationality of the universe. Our individual wills harmonize with the universal will. But among free people, the harmony of wills is precarious. Thus, there is always the possibility of the opposite of right; the negation of right is exemplified in violence and fraud. "Wrong" consists in the breakdown of harmony between the individual will and the universal will. The dialectic relation between "right" and "wrong" produces the tension between the way the "wrong" will acts and the way the will should act in order to be universal, that is, rational. This tension or conflict between right and wrong is what gives rise to morality.

Morality, said Hegel, is fundamentally a matter of purpose and intention in the ethical life of humanity. There is more to "goodness," in other words, than merely obeying laws and keeping contracts. Morality has to do with

those deeds for which people can themselves be held responsible. Only those consequences that a person intends and that constitute the purpose of his or her act can affect the goodness or badness of this act. It appears, then, that for Hegel the essence of morality is found internally in a person's intention and purpose. Moral responsibility, then, begins with those acts that can be assigned to a free will—a will that intends the act. But, Hegel argues, this subjective aspect of the act does not exhaust the full scope of morality. After all, human behavior always takes place in a context, especially in a context of other persons, hence other wills. Moral duty or responsibility is therefore broader than the concerns or intentions of the individual. Moral duty derives from the requirement of identifying a person's individual will with the universal will. Although it is perfectly legitimate for people to be concerned with their own happiness and welfare, the principle of rationality requires that we must exercise our own will in such a way that the wills of other people, also acting freely, can achieve their welfare as well. Morality is therefore an element in the dialectic process: the thesis is the abstract right of each individual; the antithesis is morality, for morality represents the duties that the universal will raises as limitations to the individual will. The relation between these two wills is the relation between freedom and duty, subjectivity and objectivity. The dialectic process in this ethical sphere is constantly moving toward a greater harmony between the subjective and objective, and in this regard Hegel described the *good* as "the realization of freedom, the absolute final purpose of the world." But the realization of freedom, for Hegel, had to occur within the limits of duty. In this sense the freest person is the one who most completely fulfills his or her duty. It was inevitable, then, that Hegel should discover the synthesis of the individual's freedom and right on the one hand, and the universal will, on the other, in our concrete human institutions, particularly in the state.

The State   Between the individual and the state there are two dialectic steps, according to Hegel, namely, the *family* and *society*. The family is, as it were, the first stage of the objective will. In marriage, two people give up their individual wills to some degree in order to become one person. Because the family is a single unit, its property becomes a common possession, even though, for legal reasons, the husband might be said to own it. Again, the family, united by a bond of feeling, or love, constitutes the logically first moment of the embodiment of the universal will. At the same time, the family contains its own antithesis, namely, individuals who will eventually grow up, leave the family, and enter into that larger context of similar individuals that is called *civil society*. These individuals now chart out their own lives and have their own purposes. We need to remember at this point that Hegel is here analyzing the dialectic development of the state and is not giving an historical account of its emergence. The state is the synthesis of the family and of civil society. The family, in this analysis, stands for the embodied universal, whereas civil society represents particularity insofar as each individual, unlike the members of a family, sets his or her own goals. These two elements, universality and particularity, cannot exist independently, for they are contained in each other; their unity, therefore, is found in the state, which is the synthesis of universality and particularity. The state is a unity in difference. This does not seem to be a genuine deduction, but Hegel does conclude that the synthesis of the universal and the particular consists in the individual. In this context, the state is conceived as an individual, the true individual, an organic unity of partial individuals.

Hegel did not conceive of the state as an authority imposed from the outside upon the individual. Nor did he consider the state to be the product of the general or majority will. The state, said Hegel, "is absolutely rational—substantial will," and again, "the state is the actuality of the ethical idea." Hegel conferred upon the state the characteristic of a person, saying that the state represents universal self-consciousness. A particular individual, he said, is conscious of himself insofar as he is a part of this larger self. And, Hegel says, "since the state is mind objectified, it is only as one of its members that the individual himself has objectivity, genuine individuality, and an ethical life." A person's spiritual reality is also found in the state, for as Hegel says, a human being's "spiritual reality consists in this, that his own essence—Reason—is objectively present to him, that it has objective immediate existence for him." Recalling that Hegel was not interested in formulating a theory of the *ideal* state, his descriptions of the *actual* state are all the more striking. It was the actual living state about which he said that "the state is the embodiment of rational freedom," and, most striking of all, that "the State is the Divine Idea as it exists on earth."

All these highly exalting descriptions of the state would make it appear that Hegel had advocated the totalitarian state. He did insist, however, that the state preserves individual liberty, by which we are members of civil society. Neither the family nor civil society is destroyed by the state; they continue to exist within the state. The laws of the state and, in general, the legislative and executive arms of the state do not issue arbitrary commands. Laws are universal rules, which have their application in individual cases involving individual people. Moreover, laws must be rational and directed at rational people. The reason for laws is that men, in their ability to make free choices, are capable of choosing ends that harm others. Insofar as their acts harm others, their behavior is irrational. The function of law is therefore to bring rationality into behavior. What makes an act rational is that it at once achieves a person's private good as well as the public good. Only a person who acts rationally can be free, because only rational acts can be permitted in society, because only rational acts avoid social harm. The function of the state is therefore not to compound personal harm or misery by issuing arbitrary and therefore irrational commands, but rather to increase, through its laws, the aggregate of rational behavior. The state is thus an organism that is seeking to develop the Idea of freedom to its maximum, and to achieve objective freedom only as its individual members do. In this way, the laws of the state, rather than being arbitrary, are rational rules of behavior that the individual himself would choose if he were acting rationally. The only limitation upon the individual will that reason allows is the limitation required by the existence of other wills. The sovereign acts in the name of the universal will and reason and not arbitrarily. The state then, "is the Idea of Spirit in the external manifestation of human Will and its Freedom."

When it comes to the relations between states, Hegel emphasizes the autonomy and absolute sovereignty of each state. The relation of one state to another is different for Hegel from the relation of one person to another in civil society. When two people disagree, the state is the higher power that resolves the dispute. But if two states disagree, there is no higher power to resolve the conflict. Each nation, Hegel says, "is mind in its substantive rationality and immediate actuality and is therefore the absolute power on earth." For this reason, "every state is sovereign and autonomous against its neighbors. It is a fundamental proposition of international law that obligations between states ought to be kept." But, Hegel says, "states are . . . in a state of nature in relation to each other," and for this reason there is no universal will binding upon them. The "rights of states are actualized only in their particular wills," insofar as there are no constitutional powers over them. There is no one to judge between states.

It is not clear why Hegel did not carry his dialectic movement to the next level, at which individual states would be united into a community of nations. He was of course aware that Kant had an idea of securing "perpetual peace" by a League of Nations to adjust every dispute. But he said that such an arrangement could not work because it would still be necessary for each state to *will* to obey the international tribunal. But a state will always *will* its own welfare. Indeed, Hegel says," welfare is the highest law governing the relation of one state to another." There can be no moral limitations upon the state, for the state is "the ethical substance." It follows, Hegel says, that "if states disagree and their particular wills cannot be harmonized, the matter can only be settled by war."

World History   In Hegel's view, the history of the world is the history of nations. The dynamic unfolding of history represents the "progress in the consciousness of freedom." This progress is not a matter of mere chance but is rather a rational process. "Reason," says Hegel, "dominates the world and . . . world history is thus a rational process." In a special way, the state is the bearer of reason, and because of this Hegel had said that the state is "the Idea of Spirit" in external form and that the state is "the Divine Idea as it exists on earth." But the dialectic of the historical process consists in the opposition between states. Each state expresses a national spirit and indeed the world spirit in its own collective consciousness. To be sure, only individual minds are capable of consciousness. Still, the minds of a particular people develop a spirit of unity, and for this reason it is possible to speak of a "national spirit." Each national spirit represents a moment in the development of the world spirit, and the interplay between national spirits represents the dialectic in history.

The conflict between nations is inevitable inasmuch as the historical process is the very stuff of reality, and is the gradual working out of the *Idea of Freedom*. Nations are carried along by the wave of history, so that in each epoch a particular nation is "the dominant people in world history for this epoch." A nation cannot choose when it will be great, for "it is only once that it can make its hour strike." At decisive points in history, Hegel says, special world-historical people emerge as agents of the world spirit. These persons lift nations to a new level of development and perfection. Hegel thought that such individuals could hardly be judged in terms of a morality that belonged to the epoch out of which a nation is being led. Instead, the value of such people consists in their creative responsiveness to the unfolding Idea of Freedom.

For Hegel, the time process of history was the logical process of the dialectic. History is moving toward a purposive end, namely, freedom. To illustrate the dialectic of history, Hegel used examples of various nations, which, he thought, showed the three *moments* in the development of freedom. Asians, he thought, knew nothing of freedom except that the potentate alone could do what he wished. Although the ancient Greeks and Romans knew the concept of citizenship, they limited this status only to a few and regarded others as being by nature slaves. It was the *Germanic* nations who, under the influence of Christianity, developed the insight that people are free. Thus, Hegel says that "The East knew and to the present day knows, only that *One* is free; the Greek and Roman world, that *some* are free; the German world knows that *All* are free." The highest freedom, we have seen, occurs, according to Hegel, when the individual acts according to the universal, rational will of the whole society.

Absolute Spirit

Hegel's philosophy has its culmination in our knowledge of the Absolute. In the process of dialectic, knowledge of the Absolute is the synthesis of subjective spirit and objective spirit. Because reality is rationality (Thought, Idea), it followed for Hegel that our knowledge of the Absolute is actually the Absolute knowing itself through the finite spirit of human beings. Just how this moment of self-consciousness of the Absolute occurs in the spirit of people is described by Hegel in a final dialectic.

Our consciousness of the Absolute, Hegel says, is achieved progressively as we move through the three stages from art, to religion, and finally to philosophy. Art provides "a sensuous semblance of the Idea" by providing us with an object of sense. In the object of art, the mind apprehends the Absolute as beauty. The object of art, moreover, is the creation of Spirit and, as such, contains some aspect of the Idea. There is an ever-deepening insight into the Absolute as we move from Asian symbolic art to classical Greek art and finally to romantic Christian art.

Art leads beyond itself to religion. What differentiates religion from art is that religion is an activity of thought, whereas an aesthetic experience is primarily a matter of feeling. Although art can direct consciousness toward the Absolute, religion comes closer to it precisely because the Absolute is Thought. At the same time, religious thought, Hegel said, is pictorial thought. In early religions this pictorial element looms large. "The Greek God," for example, "is the object of naive intuition and sensuous imagination. His shape is therefore the bodily shape of man." At the apex of religion is Christianity, which is the religion of the Spirit.

Hegel regarded Christianity as the pictorial representation of philosophy. He believed that religion and philosophy have basically the same subject matter, that both represent "knowledge of that which is eternal, of what God is, and what flows out of his nature," so that "religion and philosophy come to the same things." Philosophy leaves behind the pictorial forms of religion and rises to the level of pure thought. But philosophy does not offer the knowledge of the Absolute at any particular moment, for such knowledge is the product of the dialectic process. Philosophy itself has a history, a dialectic movement, where the major periods and systems of philosophy are not mere haphazard developments. These systems in the history of philosophy represent the necessary succession of ideas required by the progressive unfolding of the Idea. The history of philosophy is for Hegel, therefore, the development of the Absolute's self-consciousness in the mind of people.

SCHOPENHAUER

A contemporary of Hegel, Schopenhauer refused to acknowledge that Hegel was an appropriate or adequate successor to Kant. So great was Schopenhauer's disrespect for Hegel that he said that "there is no philosophy in the period between Kant and myself; only mere University charlatanism." This criticism aimed at Hegel was in the same vein as Schopenhauer's comment that "out of every page of Hume's there is more to be learned than out of [all] of the philosophical works of Hegel." But Hegel was not the only target of Schopenhauer's withering criticism. He expressed his broader disdain in the judgment that "I should like to see the man who could boast of a more miserable set of contemporaries than mine." What appears as egotism to others was to Schopenhauer simply the recognition by him of his unique gifts just as, he says, a person knows whether he is taller or shorter than the average person. He had no hesitation therefore in saying that "I have lifted the veil of truth higher than any mortal before me."

Schopenhauer's Life

Arthur Schopenhauer was born in Danzig in 1788. Although his family was of Dutch origin, it had for a long time been settled in this German city with its ancient traditions and its Hanseatic commercial connections. His ancestors enjoyed considerable prominence and wealth. When Russia's Peter the Great and Empress Catherine visited Danzig, Arthur's great-grandfather's house was selected as the place where these distinguished visitors would stay. His father was a wealthy merchant and wanted Arthur to follow in his footsteps as a businessman. As a child Arthur accompanied his parents on their many travels, which introduced him to a wide variety of cultures and customs and developed in him a distinctly cosmopolitan point of view. Although he gained much from these travels in France, Italy, England, Belgium, and Germany, his systematic early education was disrupted. But his capacity to learn was so great that he was able to make up his lack of ordinary knowledge very quickly.

His early schooling began in France at age nine; after two years he returned to Germany, where his education focused upon the requirements for a

Schopenhauer
(The Granger Collection, New York)

career as a merchant, with little or no emphasis upon the classics. But soon Schopenhauer showed a strong inclination toward philosophy, a development not at all pleasing to his father, who worried that such a career could only lead to poverty. After more travel and study in England and Switzerland, Schopenhauer returned to Danzig and entered a merchant's office as a clerk. Shortly thereafter his father died, and at age 17 he was on his own without even a close or helpful bond between his mother and himself. He and his mother had opposite temperaments, she being full of optimism and the love of pleasure while he, from an early age, was inclined toward pessimism. This difference between the two made it impossible for them to live in the same house. Later, when his mother moved to Weimar, she wrote to Arthur about the battle of Jena and the occupation of Weimar saying that "I could tell you things that would make your hair stand on end, but I refrain, for I know how you love to brood over human misery in any case."

By the age of 21, Schopenhauer had more than adequately repaired his sketchy earlier education and became enriched with a deep study of the classics, while his considerable aptitude for languages led him comfortably through Greek, Latin, and history, and mathematics was not neglected along the way. He was now ready to set out on a career, and in 1809 he enrolled in the medical school at Göttingen University. But the following year he transferred from medicine to the faculty of philosophy, captivated by Plato "the divine" and "the marvelous Kant." In due course he completed his studies, and for his doctoral dissertation at the University of Jena he wrote a book entitled *On the Fourfold Root of the Principle of Sufficient Reason*, which was published in 1813. The poet Goethe had praise for this book; nevertheless, it attracted virtually no attention from readers and remained unsold.

At Goethe's suggestion, Schopenhauer was encouraged to study the problem of light, which at this time was approached from different points of view by Goethe and Newton. From this study Schopenhauer produced a brief work entitled *On Vision and Colours*, which tended to support Goethe's view.

Schopenhauer's masterpiece is his *The World as Will and Idea*, which he wrote during 1814 and 1818 while living quietly in Dresden and which he published in 1819. Once again, this book aroused little notice and generated the sale of only a few copies. It contains Schopenhauer's complete philosophical system. He was convinced that in this work he had made his most distinctive contribution and was further convinced that he had discovered the solution to many long-standing philosophical problems. As he wrote, "Subject to the limitation of human knowledge, my philosophy is the real solution of the enigma of the world." As if to prepare for shallow criticism or even a brutal disregard of his major book, he wrote, "whoever has accomplished an immortal work will be as little hurt by its reception from the public or the opinions of critics, as a sane man in a madhouse is affected by the upbraidings of the insane."

From Dresden Schopenhauer went to Berlin and began to lecture at the University of Berlin with the hope of winning acceptance or at least recognition of his systematic philosophy. His attempt failed, partly because of the continued indifference toward his view among academics, but also because he overconfidently set the time of his lectures at exactly the hour when the giant Hegel gave his lectures. In 1831 Schopenhauer left Berlin, urged on by a cholera epidemic which included Hegel among its victims. He settled in Frankfurt-am-Main, and wrote other works which further explored and confirmed the fundamental ideas in *The World as Will and Idea*. Among these was *On the Will in Nature* (1836), in which he sought to provide scientific knowledge to support his theory of metaphysics. In 1838 he won a prize given by a scientific society in Norway for his essay on "whether free will could be proved from the evidence of consciousness." A second essay on the source or foundation of morals followed the announcement of a prize competition by the Royal Danish Academy. But even though Schopenhauer was the only one to submit an essay, he did not win this prize. Nevertheless, these two essays were published in 1841 as *The Two Fundamental Problems of Ethics.* In 1851 he published another major book entitled *Parerga and Paralipomena* which was a collection of essays on a variety of subjects. It included "On Women," "On Religion," "On Ethics," "On Aesthetics," "On Suicide," "On the Suffering of the World," and "On the Vanity of Existence." This was the book that first brought him wide popularity.

We find the sources of Schopenhauer's philosophy in his concentrated learning and equally in his pessimistic personal temperament. At an early stage, one of his teachers urged him to concentrate his study of philosophy on Plato and Kant, and we can see the influence of these two seminal philosophers throughout his major work. In addition, Schopenhauer discovered another powerful but unlikely source of insight for his theory of metaphysics, namely, the classic of India the *Upanishads.* This work was brought to his attention by an Asian scholar, Friedrick Mayer, the author of *Brahma, or the Religion of the Hindus.* This strand of Asian philosophy supports Schopenhauer's combination of intellectual and temperamental conclusions that there is no more to experience than appearance. To the questions "is this all?" and "is this life?" the answer is a pessimistic "yes." Schopenhauer's pessimism was certainly a matter of temperament. However, he tried to distinguish between his pessimism, which he considered the product of his mature judgment based upon "an objective recognition of folly," on the one hand, and "malevolence of the wicked," on the other. He called his pessimism "a noble displeasure that arises only out of a better nature revolting against unexpected wickedness." He added that such pessimism as his is not directed at particular individuals only but "it concerns all, and each individual is merely an example." We might even say that Schopenhauer's metaphysical system is not simply another way of dealing with the problems of metaphysics but rather an elaborate metaphysical justification for a pessimistic outlook upon life and reality.

The Principle of Sufficient Reason

As is frequently the case with an original thinker, at an early age Schopenhauer arrived at his major philosophical insights. The foundation for his systematic thought was formulated at age 25 in his doctoral dissertation *On the Fourfold Root of the Principle of Sufficient Reason.* In this work, he sets out to answer to the questions "what can I know?" and "what is the nature of things?" If this sounds grandiose, he intended to give nothing less than a thorough account of the whole scope of reality, and to accomplish this he relied upon the Principle of Sufficient Reason.

In its simplest form, the Principle of Sufficient Reason states that "nothing is without a reason" (or "cause" or "because"). The most obvious application of this principle is found in the field of science, where the behavior and the relationships of physical objects are explained in a manner that is sufficient to satisfy the demands of reason or rationality. But Schopenhauer discovered that there are other variations besides this scientific form of the Principle of Sufficient Reason. This is so, he said, because there are objects other than those with which the scientist deals and these other objects require unique forms of this governing principle.

Altogether, Schopenhauer set forth four basic forms of the Principle of Sufficient Reason corresponding to the four different kinds of ideas which comprise the whole range of human thought. There are four types of objects that give rise to different kinds of ideas.

1. *Physical objects.* These exist and are causally related in space and time, which we know through our ordinary experience of things, and this provides the subject matter of the material sciences, such as, for example, physics. At this point, Schopenhauer closely follows Kant's basic theory that knowledge begins with experience but is not limited, as Hume thought, to what is empirically given or presented to us. Instead, the elements of our experience are organized by our human minds, which brings to our experience a priori categories of space, time, and causality as though these categories are lenses through which we look at objects. In this realm of Phenomena, the Principle of Sufficient Reason explains *becoming* or *change.*

2. *Abstract concepts.* These objects take the form of conclusions that we draw from other concepts, as when we apply the rules of inference or implication. The relationship between concepts and the conclusions they infer or imply is governed by the Principle of Sufficient Reason. This is the realm of logic, and here the Principle of Sufficient Reason is applied to the ways of *knowing.*

3. *Mathematical objects.* Here we encounter, for example, arithmetic and geometry as they are related to space and time. Geometry is grounded in the principle which governs the various positions of the parts of space. Arithmetic, on the other hand, involves the parts of time, for as Schopenhauer says, "on the connection of the parts of time rests all counting." He concludes that "the law according to which the parts of space and time . . . determine one another I call the principle of sufficient reason of *being.*"

4. *The self.* "How can the self be an object?" Schopenhauer says that the self is the subject that wills and that this willing subject is the "object for the knowing subject." This we can call *self-consciousness.* The principle which governs our knowledge of the relation between the self and its acts of will is "the principle of . . . sufficient reason of acting . . . more briefly, the *law of motivation.*"

From these four forms of the Principle of Sufficient Reason he draws the striking conclusion that *necessity* or *determinism* is present everywhere. He stresses the fact of necessity through the whole range of objects, whether they are physical objects, the abstract concepts of logic, mathematical objects, or the self as the object of a knowing subject. Thus we encounter physical necessity, logical necessity, mathematical necessity, and moral necessity. This element of necessity in the very nature of things is what led Schopenhauer to hold that people behave in daily life by necessity. We simply react to the motives produced by our character, leaving aside the question whether we are capable of altering their character. The pervasiveness of necessity produced in Schopenhauer a deep sense of pessimism, which permeates all his writings concerning human existence. His pessimism becomes clearly understandable when we consider his account of the place of human beings in the universe, an account which is the central concern of his major work.

The World as Will and Idea

Schopenhauer's famous book *The World as Will and Idea* opens with the astonishing sentence "The world is my idea." What makes this sentence astonishing is that each word of it, as is the case also with each word in the title of the book, is capable of conveying a strange impression if the word is given its ordinary everyday meaning. What Schopenhauer meant by the "world" and the definition and role he ascribed to "will," as well as the account he gives of our "ideas," gives these words unique meanings and constitutes the major insights of his theory of metaphysics.

The World   For Schopenhauer, the term *world* has the widest possible meaning. It includes human beings, animals, trees, stars, the moon, the earth, planets, and indeed the whole universe. But why call it *my* idea? Why not simply say that the world is "out there." Earlier, British philosopher George Berkeley had formulated the proposition that to be is to be perceived. If something has to be perceived for it to be, what happens to that thing when you are not perceiving it? If you go out of your library, are the books still there? But Schopenhauer insists that anyone who reflects carefully about his experience of the world discovers that "what he knows is not a sun and an earth but only an eye that sees a sun, a hand that feels an earth; that the world which surrounds him is there only as idea." This means, he says, that "all that exists for knowledge, and therefore this whole world, is only object in relation to subject, perception of a perceiver, in a word, idea."

The World as Idea   The English word *idea* does not convey the meaning of the German word *vorstellung* used by Schopenhauer, and the difference between the two meanings helps to explain why the sentence "The world is my idea" strikes us as strange. As used by Schopenhauer, the word *vorstellung* means, literally, anything that is "set in front of" or "placed before," or that is a "presentation." This refers to everything that is placed before or presented to our consciousness or understanding, so that the "world as idea" or "my idea" refers not only to what we *think* about (i.e., ideas in the narrow view) but equally to what we hear, feel, or perceive in various other ways. There is no other object out there besides what we perceive, or, as Schopenhauer says,

"The whole actual, that is active world is determined as such through the understanding and apart from it is nothing." The world presents itself to a person as an object to a subject, and we as subjects know only the world we perceive and thus "the whole world of objects is and remains idea, and therefore wholly and forever determined by the subject."

It may be that no person's idea of the world is perfect, that therefore "my idea" will not be the same as "your idea." But each person can say that "the world is my idea" for the simple reason that I do not know anything about the world other than what I perceive or what is placed before my understanding. Moreover, the "world" surely continues to exist even if I no longer exist. Nevertheless, I do not know a more real world than the one of which I perceive. Perceptions are the basis of knowledge. In addition to perceptions we are able to formulate abstract conceptions. These abstract conceptions, for example, the idea of "tree" and "house," have a very practical function. As Schopenhauer writes, "by means of them the original material of knowledge is more easily handled, surveyed, and arranged." These abstract conceptions are therefore not simply flights of fancy. Indeed, Schopenhauer says, the value of abstract conceptions depends upon whether they rely upon or are "abstracted" from original perceptions, that is, from actual experience, for "conceptions and abstractions which do not ultimately refer to perceptions are like paths in the woods that end without leading out of it." To say, therefore, that "the world is my idea" does not suggest that my idea of the world is an abstract conception unless this conception is, as it is for Schopenhauer, firmly based upon perceptions. Hence the world is my idea because it is an objective or empirical presentation to me as an understanding subject.

The World as Will   Nowhere is it more important to clarify Schopenhauer's language than in his use of the term *will*. Ordinarily, we use the word *will* to signify a conscious and deliberate choice to behave in a certain way. We consider the will as an attribute or faculty possessed by a rational person. There can be no question that the will is influenced by reason. But this account does not prepare us for Schopenhauer's use of the term *will*—a use so novel and significant as to constitute the central theme or essence of his systematic philosophy.

Schopenhauer's concept of the will represents his major disagreement with Kant's theory of the thing-in-itself. Kant had said that we can never know things as they are in themselves. We are always on the outside of things and can never penetrate their inner nature. But Schopenhauer thought he had found a "single narrow door to the truth." There is, he said, a major exception to the notion that we are forever on the outside of things. That exception is our experience or knowledge "which each of us has of his own *willing*." Our bodily action is normally thought to be the product of willing, but for Schopenhauer willing and action are not two different things but rather one and the same thing. "The action of the body," he says, "is nothing but the act of the will objectified . . . it is only a reflection that to will and to act are different." What we know of ourselves within our consciousness is that "we are not merely a *knowing subject*, but, in another aspect, we ourselves also belong to the inner nature that is to be known." He concludes that "we ourselves are the thing in itself." And the thing in itself is *will,* or as Schopenhauer says, "the act of will is . . . the closest and most distinct *manifestation* of the thing in itself." This, then, is that single narrow door to the truth, namely, the discovery that the will is the essence of each person. While we are forever on the outside of everything else, we ourselves belong to the inner nature that can be known. This leads Schopenhauer to conclude that this "way from within [ourselves] stands open for us to that inner nature belonging to things in themselves," so that "in this sense I teach that the inner nature of everything is *will.*" Since "everything" is what constitutes the world, it follows in Schopenhauer's thought that we must view the world as will.

For Schopenhauer, the will does not belong solely to rational people. The will is to be found in everything that is—in animals and even in inanimate things. There is, in fact, only one will, and each thing is a specific manifestation of that will. Schopenhauer attributes the working of will to all of reality, saying that "The will is the agent in all the inner and unconscious bodily functions, the organism being itself nothing but the will. In all natural forces the active impulse is identical with will. In all instances where we find any spontaneous movements or any primal forces, we must regard the innermost essence as will. The will reveals itself as completely in a single oak tree as in a million." There is, then, in the whole of nature a pervasive force, energy, or what Schopenhauer calls "a blind incessant impulse." Moreover, he speaks of will as "endless striving," and this impulse, working "without knowledge" through all nature, is finally "the will to live."

The Ground of Pessimism

Here we come upon the reason for Schopenhauer's pessimism. His concept of the will portrays the whole system of nature as moving in response to the driving force in all things. All things are like puppets "set in motion by internal clockwork." The lowliest being, for example the amoeba, or the highest, that is, a human being, is driven by the same force, the will. The blind will which produces human behavior "is the same which makes the plants grow." Every individual bears the stamp of a "forced condition." Schopenhauer thus rejects the assumption that human beings are superior to animals because animals are controlled only by instincts whereas people are rational beings. The intellect, he says, is itself fashioned by the universal will so that the human intellect is on the same level as the instincts of animals. Moreover, intellect and will in human beings are not to be thought of as two separate faculties. Instead the intellect is for Schopenhauer an attribute of the will; it is secondary or, in a philosophical sense, accidental. He can sustain intellectual effort only for short periods of time. It declines in strength and requires rest, and is, finally, a function of the body. By contrast, the will continues without interruption to sustain and support life. During dreamless sleep the intellect does not function, whereas all the organic functions of the body continue. These organic functions are manifestations of the will. While other thinkers spoke of the freedom of the will, Schopenhauer says "I prove its omnipotence."

The omnipotence of the will in all of nature has pessimistic implications for human beings. As Schopenhauer says, "men are only apparently drawn from in front; really, they are pushed from behind; it is not life that tempts them on, but necessity that drives them forward." The primal drive in all of nature is to produce life. The will to live has no other purpose than to continue the cycle of life. Schopenhauer portrays the realm of nature as a fierce struggle where the will to live inevitably produces constant conflict and destruction. This will to live for one element of nature requires the destruction of other elements or parties. No purpose or aim is violated during this conflict; the underlying drive of the will leaves no alternative outcome. Schopenhauer tells of a report of a place in Java where, for as far as the eye can see, the land is covered with skeletons, which gives the impression of a battlefield. These are skeletons of large turtles, five feet long, three feet wide, and three feet high. They come out of the sea to lay their eggs and are then attacked by wild dogs, who lay them on their backs, strip off their armor, and eat them alive. Now, Schopenhauer says, "all this misery repeats itself thousands and thousands of times, year out, year in. For this, those turtles were born . . . it is thus the will to live objectifies itself."

If we move from the animal world to the human race, Schopenhauer admits that the matter becomes more complicated, "but the fundamental character remains unaltered." Individual human beings do not have any value for nature because "it is not the individual but only the species that nature cares for." Human life turns out to be by no means a gift for enjoyment "but as a task, a drudgery to be performed." Millions of people are united into nations striving for the common good, but thousands fall as a sacrifice for it. "Now senseless delusions, not intriguing politics, incite them to wars with each other. . . . In peace industry and trade are active, inventions work miracles, seas are navigated, delicacies are collected from all ends of the world." But, asks Schopenhauer, what is the aim of all this striving? His answer is "To sustain ephemeral and tormented individuals through a short span of time."

Life, Schopenhauer says, is a bad bargain. The disproportion between human trouble, on the one hand, and reward on the other means that life involves the exertion of all our strength "for something that is of no value." There is nothing to look forward to except "the satisfaction of hunger and the sexual instinct, or in any case a little momentary comfort." His conclusion is that "life is a business, the proceeds of which are very far from covering the cost of it." There can be no true happiness because happiness is simply a temporary cessation of human pain. Pain in turn is caused by desire, and expression of need or want, most of which can never be fulfilled. Finally, human life "is a striving without aim or end." And, "the life of every individual . . . is really always a tragedy, but gone through in detail, it has the character of a comedy."

Is There Any Escape from the "Will"?

How is it possible for a person to escape from the overpowering force of the "will" which pervades everything in nature? Schopenhauer suggests at least two avenues of escape, namely, through ethics and aesthetics. From a moral perspective we can deny passions and desire; from an aesthetic standpoint, we can contemplate artistic beauty. There is, of course, the question of whether the power of the universal will is so strong that any escape from it can only be temporary.

What complicates a person's life and causes pain is the continuous will to live, which expresses itself in the form of endless desires. Desire produces aggressiveness, striving, destruction, and self-centeredness. If there could be some way to reduce the intensity of human desire, a person could achieve at least periodic moments of happiness. To be sure, Schopenhauer always reminds us that "man is at bottom a dreadful wild animal . . . in no way inferior to the tiger or hyena." Still, we are able from time to time to rise to a level of thought and consciousness which is above the realm of things. Problems arise when we desire things and other people, for these objects of desire stimulate our inner will to live at the level of both hunger and procreation. But when these biological functions are satisfied, there still remains the aim of physical survival against violence and conquest. Beyond even this level a person can, Schopenhauer says, understand the difference between the specific individual objects of his desire and certain general or universal objects. That is, we are capable of knowing not only the individuals John and Mary but also universal humanity. This should enable us to move from an intense desire for a person to a sense of sympathy for all humankind. To this extent desire can give way to an ethics of a more disinterested love. At this point, we recognizes that we all share the same nature, and this awareness can produce an ethics of gentleness. Or, as Schopenhauer says, "My true inner being exists in every living creature as immediately as in my own consciousness. It is this confession that breaks forth as pity, on which every unselfish virtue rests, and whose practical expression is every good deed. It is this conviction to which every appeal to gentleness, love and mercy is directed; for these remind us of the respect in which we are all the same being."

In a similar way, aesthetic enjoyment can shift our attention away from those objects which stimulate our aggressive will to live and focus attention instead upon objects of contemplation that are unrelated to passion and desire. When we contemplate a work of art, we become a pure knowing subject—as opposed to a willing subject. What we observe in art, whether in painting or even music, is the general or universal element. We see in a painting of a person not some specific person but a representation of some aspect of humanity which we all share. Here Schopenhauer expresses views very similar to Plato's concept of Forms and shows the strong influence of the philosophy of India. Here, too, Schopenhauer's ethics and aesthetics have a similar function, for they both attempt to raise our consciousness above earthly passion-filled striving to a level beyond the activity of the will where the supreme act is restful contemplation.

In spite of these attempts through ethics and aesthetics to escape from the restricting and directing power of the universal will, Schopenhauer simply does not succeed in discovering a truly free individual will in human beings. His last word on the subject of human behavior is that "our individual actions are . . . in no way free . . . so that every individual . . . can absolutely never do anything other than precisely what he does at that particular moment."

CHAPTER 14

Utilitarianism and Positivism

The views of Kant, Hegel, and Schopenhauer represent one direction that 19th-century philosophy took in response to the earlier debate between rationalists and empiricists, namely, an idealist direction. According to Kant and his German counterparts, traditional rationalism ignored the obvious fact that sense impressions form the content of our ideas. However, traditional empiricism ignored our inherent mental structures that shape our experiences. Kant and German idealists thus emphasized the central role that mind plays in organizing experiences; this role was in fact so central that idealists held that mind was also the *source* of our sense experiences as well as the *shaper* of those experiences. There were, however, other approaches to philosophy during the 19th century that did not take this idealist route. Some philosophers believed that the empiricists largely got the story correct, and the task of philosophy is to refine empirical methodology. In Great Britain, two such leading figures were Jeremy Bentham (1748–1832) and John Stuart Mill (1806–1873). Bentham and Mill both rejected the role of rational intuition in our quest for knowledge and, instead, they refined techniques for sorting and assessing sense experiences. Their most memorable contribution in this regard is in the field of ethics, specifically the theory of utilitariansim. According to this theory, moral actions are those which produce the greatest good for the greatest number of people. In France Auguste Comte (1798–1857) made similar efforts at refining empiricism and founded the approach known as positivism. According to positivism, we should reject any investigation that does not rest on direct observation.

BENTHAM

The moral and political views of Jeremy Bentham and John Stuart Mill dramatically influenced the direction of Western philosophy. Rarely has a way of thinking captured the imagination of generations of people so completely as

Jeremy Bentham
(Corbis-Bettmann)

did their theory of utilitarianism. What attracts people to it is its simplicity and its way of confirming what most of us already believe—that everyone desires pleasure and happiness. From this simple fact, Bentham and Mill argued that moral goodness involves achieving the greatest amount of pleasure—and minimizing the greatest amount of pain—for the greatest number of people.

Such a swift account of moral goodness had not only the merit of simplicity but had, according to Bentham and Mill, the additional virtue of scientific accuracy. Earlier theories of ethics understood moral goodness in terms of commands of God, or the dictates of reason, or the fulfillment of the purpose of human nature, or the duty to obey the categorical imperative. These all raising vexing questions as to just what these commands, dictates, purposes, and imperatives consist of. However, the principle of utility measures every act by a standard that everyone knows, namely, pleasure. To bypass the moral teachings of theology and the classical theories of Plato and Aristotle as well as the recently formulated ethics of Kant, Bentham and Mill followed in the philosophical footsteps of their own countrymen, the British empiricists.

Hobbes already tried to construct a science of human nature and turned his back upon traditional moral thought, emphasizing instead people's selfish concern for their own pleasure. Hume also rejected the intricacies of traditional philosophy and theology and instead built his system of thought around the individual, denying that people can know universal moral laws any more than they can know universal laws of physics. For Hume, the whole enterprise of ethics has to do with our capacity for experiencing sympathy pleasure, a capacity that all people share and by which we "touch a string to which all mankind have an accord." In moral philosophy, Bentham and Mill were, therefore, not innovators, for their predecessors already stated the principle of utilitarianism in its general form. What makes Bentham and Mill stand out as the most famous of the utilitarians is that they, more than others, succeeded in connecting the principle of utility with the many problems of their age. To this end they provided 19th-century England with a philosophical basis not only for moral thought but also for practical reform.

Bentham's Life

Born in Red Lion Street, Houndsditch, London, in 1748, Bentham showed early signs of unusual intellectual abilities. While only four years old, he was already studying Latin grammar, and at eight he was sent off to Westminster School, where, he said later, the instruction "was wretched." He entered Queen's College in Oxford when he was 12 years old. After three years which were not particularly happy ones—as he disapproved of the vice and laziness of his fellow students—he took his B.A. degree in 1763 and entered Lincoln's Inn, in accordance with his father's wish, to prepare for a career in the legal profession. That same year he returned to Oxford for one of the decisive experiences of his intellectual life, for he went to hear the lectures on law given by William Blackstone. What made this such a significant event was that as he listened to these lectures with deep concentration, he says he "immediately detected Blackstone's fallacy respecting natural rights," and this experience crystallized his own theory of law, in which he rejected the theory of "natural rights" as "rhetorical nonsense—nonsense on stilts." He took his M.A. degree in 1766 and again returned to London, but he never developed any affection for the legal profession and decided against being a lawyer. Instead, he was drawn into a vigorous literary career in which he tried to bring order and moral defensibility into what he considered the deplorable state both of the law and the social realities that the law made possible.

Bentham was therefore chiefly a reformer. For the most part, his philosophical orientation was grounded in British empiricism. Locke's enlightened and free thought gave Bentham a powerful weapon against ideas based upon prejudice. Bentham read Hume's *Treatise on Human Nature* with such profit that he said it was "as if scales fell" from his eyes regarding moral philosophy. His first book, *A Fragment on Government*, appeared in 1776 and was an attack upon Blackstone. This *Fragment* was also in sharp contrast to another document that appeared in that year, namely the Declaration of Independence. Bentham thought the Declaration was a confused and absurd jumble of words, which groundlessly presupposed the concept of natural rights. Among his later writings were *A Defense of Usury* (1787), his famous *Introduction to the Principles of Morals and Legislation* (1789), *A Plea for the Constitution* (1803), and *Catechism of Parliamentary Reform* (1809). With these writings and his personal involvement in the social and political problems of his day, Bentham remained a powerful public figure for most of his long life, until his death in 1832 at the age of 84.

The Principle of Utility

Bentham begins his *Introduction to the Principles of Morals and Legislation* with the classic sentence: "Nature has placed mankind under the governance of two sovereign masters, *pain* and *pleasure*. It is for them alone to point out what we ought to do, as well as to determine what we shall do." To be subject to pleasure and pain is a fact we all recognize, and it is also a fact that we desire pleasure and want to avoid pain. He then offers his *principle of utility*, namely, "that principle which approves or disapproves of every action whatsoever, according to the tendency which it appears to have to augment or diminish . . . happiness." Bentham was aware that he had not *proved* that happiness is the basis of "good" and "right," but this was not an oversight. It is rather the very nature of the principle of utility, he says, that one cannot demonstrate its validity: "Is it susceptible to any proof? It should seem not, for that which is used to prove everything else cannot itself be proved; a chain of proofs must have their commencement somewhere. To give such proof is as impossible as it is needless."

But if Bentham could not *prove* the validity of the principle of utility, he felt that he could at least reject so-called "higher" theories. For Bentham, they were either reducible to the principle of utility or else were inferior to this principle because they had no clear meaning or could not be consistently followed. As an example, Bentham takes the social-contract theory and its explanation for our obligation to obey the law. First there is the difficulty of determining whether there ever was such a contract or agreement. Second, even the contract theory itself rests upon the principle of utility, for it really says that the greatest happiness of the greatest number can be achieved only if we obey the law. The case is the same when others say that goodness is determined by our *moral sense*, or *understanding*, or *right reason*, or the *theological* principle of the will of God. All of these, Bentham says, are similar to each other and are reducible to the principle of utility. For example, "The principle of theology refers everything to God's pleasure. But what is God's pleasure? God does not, he confessedly does not now, either speak or write to us. How then are we to know what is his pleasure? By observing what is our own pleasure, and pronouncing it to be his." Only pleasures and pains, therefore, give us the real value of actions. In both private and public life we are in the last analysis all concerned with maximizing happiness.

Sanctions   Just as pleasure and pain give the real values to acts, so do they also constitute the causes of our behavior. Bentham distinguishes four sources from which pleasures and pains can come, and he identifies these as causes of our behavior, calling them *sanctions.* A sanction is what gives binding force to a rule of conduct or to a law, and he terms these four sanctions the *physical,* the *political,* the *moral,* and the *religious* sanctions. He explains these here:

> A man's goods, or his person, are consumed by fire. If this happened to him by what is called an accident, it was a calamity; if by reason of his own imprudence (for instance, from his neglecting to put his candle out), it may be styled a punishment of the *physical* sanction; if it happened to him by the sentence of the political magistrate, a punishment belonging to the *political* sanction; that is, what is commonly called a punishment, if for want of any assistance which his *neighbor* withheld from him out of some dislike to his *moral* character, a punishment of the *moral* sanction; if by an immediate act of *God's* displeasure, manifested on account of some *sin* committed by him . . . a punishment of the *religious* sanction.

In all these areas, then, the cause of behavior, is the threat of pain. In public life, the legislator understands that people feel bound to do certain acts only when such acts have some clear sanction connected with them. This sanction consists of some form of pain if the citizen violates the type of conduct prescribed by the legislator. The legislator's chief concern, therefore, is to decide what forms of behavior will tend to increase the happiness of society and what sanctions will be most likely to bring about such an increase. Bentham's concept of *sanction* thus gave concrete meaning to the word *obligation.* For obligation now meant not some undefined duty but, instead, a prospect of pain if one did not obey a moral or legal rule. Kant argued that the morality of an act depends upon having the right motive and not upon the consequences of the act. Bentham, though, takes the opposite position, saying that morality depends directly upon the consequences. He admits that some motives are more likely than others to increase happiness. But it is still pleasure and not the motive that confers the quality of morality upon the act. Moreover, Bentham took the position that, generally speaking, the law can punish only those who have actually inflicted pain, whatever their motive may be. Bentham believed that moral and legal obligations were similar in this regard since, in both cases, the external consequences of the action were more important than the motives behind them.

The Pleasure–Pain Calculus   Each individual and each legislator is concerned with avoiding pain and achieving pleasure. But pleasures and pains differ from each other and therefore have different values. With an attempt at mathematical precision, Bentham speaks of units—or what he called *lots*–of pleasure or pain. He suggests that before we act, we should calculate the values of these lots. Their value, taken by themselves, will be greater or less depending, Bentham says, upon a pleasure's *intensity, duration, certainty,* and *propinquity* or nearness. When we consider not only the pleasure by itself but what consequences it can lead to, we must calculate other circumstances.

These include a pleasure's *fecundity*, or its chances of being followed by more pleasure, and its *purity*, or the chances that pleasure will be followed by some pain. The *seventh* circumstance is a pleasure's *extent*, that is, the number of persons to whom it *extends* or who are affected by the action.

According to Bentham, we "sum up all the values of all the *pleasures* on the one side, and those of all the pains on the other. The balance, if it be on the side of pleasure, will give the *good* tendency of the act . . . if on the side of pain, the *bad* tendency." This calculus shows that Bentham was interested chiefly in the quantitative aspects of pleasure; thus, all actions are equally good if they produce the same amount of pleasure. Whether we actually do engage in this kind of calculation was a question Bentham anticipated, and he has a reply:

> there are some, perhaps, who . . . may look upon the nicety employed in the adjustment of such rules as so much labor lost: for gross ignorance, they will say, never troubles itself about laws, and passion does not calculate. But the evil of ignorance admits of cure: and . . . when matters of such importance as pain and pleasure are at stake, and these in the highest degree . . . who is there that does not calculate? Men calculate, some with less exactness, indeed, and some with more: but all men calculate.

Law and Punishment

Bentham made an especially impressive use of the principle of utility in connection with law and punishment. Since it is the function of the legislator to discourage some acts and encourage others, how should we classify those that should be discouraged as against those that should be encouraged?

The Object of Law   Bentham's method of legislation was first of all to measure the "mischief of an act," and this mischief consisted in the consequences, the pain or evil inflicted by the act, and acts that produce evil must be discouraged. There are, Bentham says, both primary and secondary evils that concern the legislator. Robbers inflict an evil upon their victims, who lose their money, and this is a case of primary evil. But robbery creates a secondary evil because successful robbery sends the message that theft is easy. This suggestion is evil because it weakens respect for property, and property becomes more insecure. From the point of view of the legislator, the secondary evils are frequently more important than the primary evils. For, taking the example of robbery again, the actual loss to the victim may very well be considerably less than the loss in stability and security in the community as a whole.

The law is concerned with augmenting the total happiness of the community, and it must do this by discouraging those acts that would produce evil consequences. A criminal act is by definition one that is clearly detrimental to the community's happiness. For the most part, the government accomplishes its business of promoting the happiness of society by punishing people who commit offenses that the principle of utility has clearly measured as evil. Bentham felt that governments should only use the principle of utility in deciding

which acts should be considered "offenses." And if they did this, then many il-
legal acts of his time would thereby become only matters of private morals.
Utilitarianism had the effect, then, of requiring a reclassification of behavior to
determine what is and is not appropriate for the government to regulate. In
addition, the principle of utility provided Bentham with a new and simple theory of punishment—a theory that he thought could not only be justified more
readily than the older theories but could achieve the purposes of punishment
far more effectively.

Punishment   "All punishment," Bentham writes, "is in itself evil" because it
inflicts suffering and pain. At the same time, the "object which all laws have in
common, is to augment the total happiness of the community." If we are to
justify punishment from a utilitarian point of view, we must show that the
pain inflicted by punishment must in some way prevent some greater pain.
Punishment must therefore be "useful" in achieving a greater totality of pleasure, and it has no justification if its effect is simply to add still more units or
lots of pain to the community. The principle of utility would clearly call for the
elimination of pure "retribution," or retaliation, since no useful purpose is
served by adding still more pain to the sum total that society suffers. This is
not to say that utilitarianism rejects punishment. It means only that the principle of utility, particularly in the hands of Bentham, called for a reopening of
the question of why society should punish offenders.

  According to Bentham, punishment should not be inflicted in four particular situations. (1) It should not be inflicted when it is *groundless.* This would
be so when, for example, there is an offense that admits of compensation and
where there is virtual certainty that compensation is forthcoming. (2) Punishment should not be inflicted when it is *inefficacious.* This is the case when punishment cannot prevent a mischievous act, such when a law has already been
made but not been announced. Punishment would be inefficacious also where
an infant, an insane person, or a drunkard was involved. (3) It should not be
inflicted when it is *unprofitable* or too *expensive,* "where the mischief it would
produce would be greater than what it prevented." (4) Finally, it should not be
inflicted when it is *needless,* "where the mischief may be prevented, or cease of
itself, without it: that is at a cheaper rate." This is particularly so in cases
"which consist in the disseminating [of] pernicious principles in matters of
duty," since in these cases persuasion is more efficacious than force.

  Whether a given kind of behavior should be left to *private ethics* instead of
becoming the object of *legislation* was a question Bentham answered by simply
applying the principle of utility. The matter should be left to private ethics if it
does more harm than good to involve the whole legislative process and the
apparatus of punishment. He was convinced that attempts to regulate sexual
immorality would be particularly unprofitable, since this would require intricate supervision. This is also the case for offences such as "ingratitude or rude-
ness, where the definition is so vague that the judge could not safely be en-
trusted with the power to punish." Duties that we owe to ourselves could
hardly be the concern of law and punishment, nor must we be coerced to be

benevolent, though we can be liable on certain occasions for failing to help. But the main concern of law must be to encourage those acts that would lead to the greatest happiness of the community. There is, then, a justification for punishment, which is that through punishment the greatest good for the greatest number is most effectively secured.

Besides providing a rationale for punishment, the principle of utility also gives us some clue to what punishment should consist of. Bentham describes the desirable properties of each unit or *lot* of punishment, considering "the proportion between punishments and offenses." To this end he gives the following rules. (1) The punishment must be great enough to outweigh the profit that the offender might get from the offense. (2) The greater the offense, the greater the punishment: where two offenses come in competition, the punishment for the greater offense must be sufficient to induce a person to prefer the less. (3) Punishments should be variable and adaptable to fit the particular circumstances, although each offender should get the same punishment for the same offense. (4) The amount of punishment should never be greater than the minimum required to make it effective. (5) The more uncertain that an offender will be caught, the greater should be the punishment. (6) If an offense is habitual, the punishment must outweigh not only the profit of the immediate offense but of the undiscovered offenses. These rules led Bentham to conclude that punishment should be *variable* to fit the particular case. It should be *equable* so as to inflict equal pain for similar offenses. It should be *commensurable* in order that punishments for different classes of crimes be proportional. It should be *characteristic* so as to impress the imagination of potential offenders. It should be *frugal* so as not to be excessive. It should be *reformatory* in order to correct faulty behavior. It should be *disabling* in order to deter future offenders. It should be *compensatory* to the sufferer. In order not to create new problems, punishment should have *popular* acceptance and be capable of *remittance* for sufficient cause.

Bentham's Radicalism

Bentham quickly discovered elements in the law and the general social structure of England that did not fit the requirements set by the principle of utility. He wanted the legislative process to operate on the principle of utility with practically the same rigor with which the stars obey the principle of gravitation. That is, he wanted to add the notion of systematic action to that of systematic thought. He thus pressed for reforms wherever he found a discrepancy between the actual legal and social order on the one hand and the principle of utility on the other. He traced most of the evils of the legal system to the judges who, he charged, "made the common law. Do you know how they make it? Just as a man makes laws for his dog. When your dog does anything you want to break him of, you wait till he does it and then beat him . . . this is the way judges make laws for you and me." Having exposed one monstrous evil after another, Bentham zealously attempted to reform these evils and, to that end, he became associated with a group of like-minded utilitarians known as "philosophical radicals."

Bentham blamed the aristocratic society of his day for the breakdown of the principle of utility. Why should social evils and evils of the legal system persist even after he demonstrated that certain new types of behavior would produce the "greatest happiness of the greatest number?" The answer, he thought, was that those in power did not want the "greatest happiness of the greatest number." The rulers were more concerned with their own interests. However, from the utilitarian perspective, whenever those in power represent only a class or a small group, their self-interest will be in conflict with the proper end of government. The way to overcome this conflict is to put the government into the hands of the people. If there is an identity between the rulers and the ruled, their interests will be the same, and the greatest happiness of the greatest number will be assured. This identity of interest cannot, by definition, be achieved under a monarchy. The monarch acts in his own interests, or, at best, aims at the happiness of a special class grouped around him. It is in a democracy where the greatest happiness of the greatest number is most apt to be realized, for the rulers are the people, and representatives of the people are chosen precisely because they promise to serve the greatest good. For Bentham, the application of the principle of utility clearly required the rejection of monarchy with all its corollaries. That is, his country would have to do away with the king, house of peers, and the established church. In their place the country would need to construct a democratic order after the model of the United States. Since "all government is in itself one vast evil," its only justification is to apply evil in order to prevent or exclude some greater evil.

JOHN STUART MILL

John Stuart Mill was born in 1806, and between the ages of 3 and 14 he was the object of a rigorous "educational experiment" imposed upon him by his father, James Mill. So intense was this personal tutoring in the classics, languages, and history that he said that "through the training bestowed on me by my father, I started, I may fairly say, with an advantage of a quarter of a century over my contemporaries." But this intense learning, with its emphasis not only upon memorizing but also upon critical and analytical thinking, took its toll upon young Mill, and at the age of 20 he fell into "a dull state of nerves." He attributed his breakdown to the overemphasis upon analysis without a parallel emotional development. He believed that his larger social surrounding underrated expressions of feeling, and he points out that Bentham himself . . . used to say that 'all poetry is misrepresentation.' " But "the habit of analysis has a tendency to wear away the feelings . . . [and] I was thus, as I said to myself, left stranded at the commencement of my voyage, with a well equipped ship and a rudder, but no sail." He eventually turned to such writers as Coleridge, Carlyle, and Wordsworth, who affected his thought so deeply that he could later say that "the cultivation of the feelings became one of the cardinal points in my ethical and philosophical creed." He had a long romance with Harriet Taylor (1807–1858), an acclaimed philosopher in her

John Stuart Mill
(National Portrait Gallery, London)

own right, which began when he was 25 and which later led to their marriage. This further confirmed his high assessment of the role of feeling among human faculties. His literary achievements reflect his attempt to maintain a balance among the wide range of human faculties, starting with the rigorous *System of Logic* (1843) and including *Principles of Political Economy* (1848), the essay *On Liberty* (1859), *Considerations on Representative Government* (1861), the essay *Utilitarianism* (1861), and his *Autobiography* and *Three Essays on Religion*, which were published after he died in 1873 at the age of 67.

Mill was one of the ablest advocates of utilitarianism. His father was closely associated with Bentham's philosophical theory. Later, young Mill wrote in his *Autobiography* that "it was my father's opinions which gave the distinguishing character to the Benthamic or Utilitarian propagandism." His father's ideas flowed into the thought of early 19th-century England through various channels, of which, Mill says, "one was through me, the only mind directly formed by his instructions, and through whom considerable influence was exercised over various young men." John Stuart Mill had not only shared his father's ideas but through him was exposed to the thinking of some of the leading men of the day. He had known and visited the political economist

Ricardo, but "of Mr. Bentham I saw much more, owing to the close intimacy which existed between him and my father." Mill adds that "my father was the earliest Englishman of any great mark, who thoroughly understood, and in the main, adopted, Bentham's general views of ethics, government and law." When young Mill read Bentham's principal work on law and administration, *Introduction to the Principles of Morals and Legislation,* it was "one of the turning points in my mental history." What impressed him most was that Bentham's "greatest happiness principle" rendered unnecessary any attempts to deduce morality and legislation from concepts such as *law of nature, right reason,* the *moral sense,* or *natural rectitude.* As he read Bentham, Mill says that "the feeling rushed upon me, that all previous moralists were superseded, and that here indeed was the commencement of a new era of thought." Upon finishing Bentham's book, he became a different person, for "the 'principle of utility', understood as Bentham understood it . . . gave unity to my conceptions of things. I now had opinions, a creed, a doctrine, a philosophy; in one among the best senses of the word, a religion; the inculcation and diffusion of which could be made the principal outward purpose of a life." When Bentham died, Mill was 26 years old, but already he was developing certain convictions of his own about utilitarianism—convictions which were to distinguish his approach from Bentham's in a significant way.

Mill's Version of Utilitarianism

Mill's purpose in writing his famous essay on *Utilitarianism* was to defend the *principle of utility,* which he learned from his father and Bentham. In the course of his defense, however, he made such important modifications of this theory that his version of utilitarianism turned out to be different from Bentham's in several ways. His definition of utility was perfectly consistent with what Bentham taught: Mill writes that,

> The creed which accepts as the foundation of morals Utility, or the greatest Happiness Principle, holds that actions are right in proportion as they tend to promote happiness, wrong as they tend to produce the reverse of happiness. By 'happiness' is intended pleasure, and the absence of pain; by 'unhappiness,' pain, and the privation of pleasure.

But even though he started with the same general ideas as Bentham did, especially relating *happiness* with *pleasure,* Mill soon took a different approach.

Qualitative versus Quantitative Approach   Bentham said that pleasures differ only in their amount; that is, that different ways of behaving produce different *quantities* of pleasure. He had also said that the game of "pushpin is as good as poetry," by which he meant that the only criterion for goodness is the amount of pleasure an act can produce. It would have to follow on this calculation that all types of behavior that produce the same amount of pleasure would be equally good, whether such behavior be the game of "pushpin" or the enjoyment of poetry. Bentham was so committed to the simple quantitative measurement of pleasure as the chief test of the morality of an act that he even suggested that "there ought to be a moral thermometer." Just as a thermometer measures the different degrees of heat, so also a "moral thermometer" could measure the degrees of happiness or unhappiness. This analogy reveals Bentham's exclusive emphasis upon quantity in his treatment of goodness and pleasure. For just as it is possible to achieve the same degree of heat whether one burns coal, wood, or oil, so also is it possible to achieve equal quantities of pleasure through games, poetry, or other types of behavior. Goodness, for Bentham, is not connected with any particular *kind* of behavior but only with the amounts of pleasure as measured by his "calculus." Inevitably, the utilitarians were accused of being moral relativists who had rejected all moral absolutes in favor of each person's subjective opinion about what is good. Mill sought to defend utilitarianism against these charges, but in the course of his defense he was drawn into the position of altering Bentham's quantitative approach to pleasure by substituting a qualitative approach.

Whereas Bentham said that "pushpin is as good as poetry," Mill says that he would "rather be Socrates dissatisfied than a fool satisfied," or that "it is better to be a human being dissatisfied than a pig satisfied." Pleasures, Mill said, differ from each other in kind and quality, not only in quantity. He took his stand with the ancient Epicureans, who were also attacked for their "degrading" emphasis upon pleasure as the end of all behavior. The Epicureans replied to their accusers that it was in fact they who had a degrading conception of human nature, for *they* assumed that the only pleasures people are capable of are those of which only swine are capable. But this assumption is obviously false, said Mill, because "Human beings have faculties more elevated than the animal appetites, and when once conscious of them, do not regard anything as happiness which does not include their gratification."

Pleasures of the intellect and imagination have a higher value than the pleasures of mere sensation. Though Mill initially developed the notion of higher pleasures as an answer to the critics of utilitarianism, his concern over higher pleasures led to a criticism of the very foundation of Bentham's view of utility. He says that "It would be absurd that . . . the estimation of pleasures should be supposed to depend on quantity alone." For Mill, the mere quantity of pleasure produced by an act was of secondary importance when we have to make a choice between pleasures. Imagine, for example, that a person is acquainted with a specific intellectual pleasure and a specific pleasure of sensation. If she prefers the intellectual pleasure, then this shows its superiority. This is particularly the case even if she knows that the intellectual pleasure is "attended with a greater amount of discontent, and would not resign it for any quantity of the other pleasure which [human] nature is capable of, we are justified in ascribing to the preferred enjoyment a superiority in quality so far outweighing quantity as to render it, in comparison, of small account."

The qualitative aspect of pleasure, Mill thought, was as much an empirical fact as was the quantitative element on which Bentham placed his entire emphasis. Mill departed even further from Bentham by grounding the qualitative difference between pleasures in the structure of human nature, thereby focusing upon certain human faculties whose full use were to be the criterion of true happiness and, therefore, of goodness. In this regard Mill says,

> Few human creatures would consent to be changed into any of the lower animals for a promise of the fullest allowance of a beast's pleasures; no intelligent human being would consent to be a fool, no instructed person would be an ignoramus, no person of feeling and conscience would be selfish and base, even though they should be persuaded that the fool, the dunce, or the rascal is better satisfied with his lot than they are with theirs.

Pleasures, according to Mill, have to be assessed not for their quantity but for their quality. However, Mill's view of qualitative pleasures raises an important problem with the whole notion of the pleasure principle. If we must assess pleasures for their quality, then pleasure itself is no longer the standard of morality. That is, if only the full use of our higher faculties can lead us to true happiness, the standard of goodness in behavior does not have to do with pleasure, but with fulfilling our human faculties. It is not clear whether Mill appreciated the full impact of this problem. Nevertheless, he attempted to go beyond mere quantitative hedonism to a qualitative hedonism, wherein the moral value of life is grounded in the higher pleasures of our higher faculties. Thus, if it is better to be Socrates dissatisfied than a pig satisfied, morality is proportionate to the happiness that we find in being truly human and not in the amount of pleasure we experience. Higher happiness, then, is the aim of all human life, a life "exempt as far as possible from pain, and as rich as possible in enjoyments."

Mill's Departure from Bentham   Mill's version of utilitarianism differs from Bentham's in three key ways. First, by preferring the higher quality of happiness over a mere quantity of pleasure, Mill thereby rejects Bentham's central assumption that pleasures and pains can be calculated or measured. Bentham based his pleasure-pain calculus on simple quantitative considerations, saying that pleasures can be measured as to their duration, intensity, or extent. Mill, though, argued that there is no way to measure either the quantity or quality of pleasures. Whenever we have to make a choice between two pleasures, we can express a preference wisely only if we have experienced both possibilities. Mill asks, "what means are there of determining which is the acutest of two pains, or the intensest of two pleasurable sensations, except the general [feeling] of those who are familiar with both? . . . What is there to decide whether a particular pleasure is worth purchasing at the cost of a particular pain, except the feelings and judgment of the experienced?" Instead of calculating, people simply express a preference, and apart from this attitude of preference, "there is no other tribunal."

A second difference in Mill's theory involves when we should actually consult the utilitarian guideline. Bentham seems to say that for each act we perform, we should consider whether that act produces a greater balance of happiness versus unhappiness. This, though, can become quite tedious, and our lives would grind to a halt when we paused to calculate the outcome of our various actions. According to Mill, though, we rarely need to consider the consequences of our specific actions. Instead, we should go about our lives following general moral rules, such as rules against killing, stealing, and lying. We can trust these rules since, throughout human civilization, people have continually tested these rules to determine whether we facilitate general happiness when we follow them. Only occasionally do we run into problems following these tried and true moral rules. For example, if I am poor and my family is starving, I may want to steal a loaf of bread from the local store. Here I am torn between two moral rules: (1) provide for your family, and (2) do not steal. In this case we resolve the conflict by determining which course of action would bring about the most happiness.

The third difference between Bentham and Mill involves their respective ways of dealing with human selfishness. Bentham simply assumed that we ought to choose those acts that produce for us the greatest quantity of pleasure. He also assumed that we should naturally help other people achieve happiness because in that way we should secure our own. Mill accepted this point but added that we may rely on a variety of social institutions to help broaden our level of concern for others:

> utility would enjoin, first, that laws and social arrangements should place the happiness . . . or the interest of every individual, as nearly as possible in harmony with the interest of the whole; and secondly, that education and opinion, which have so vast a power over human character, should so use that power as to establish in the mind of every individual an indissolvable association between his own happiness and the good of the whole . . . so that a direct impulse to promote the general good may be in every individual one of the habitual motives of action.

Proving and Reinforcing Utilitarianism   Nowhere is Mill's difficulty with the problem of moral obligation and choice more apparent than when he raises the issue of "proving" utilitarianism. But how can we prove that happiness is the true and desirable end of human life and conduct? Mill answers that "the only proof capable of being given that an object is visible, is that people actually see it. The only proof that a sound is audible, is that people hear it; and so of the other sources of our experience. In like manner, I apprehend, the sole evidence it is possible to produce that anything is desirable, is that people do actually desire it." Thus, we can give no reason why general happiness is desirable except that "each person so far as he believes it to be attainable, desires his own happiness."

In addition to the issue of proving utilitarianism, Mill also discusses how we might reinforce this moral conviction as well. He notes that there are both external "sanctions" or motivations and internal ones. External sanctions principally involve other people approving of us when we pursue general happiness and disapproving of us when we instead produce unhappiness. But the most important motivation, according to Mill, is *internal,* and involves a feeling of guilt when we go against the sense of duty towards society as a whole. How do we develop this sense of duty? Mill argues that it forms initially through education, such as through the teachings of our parents, teachers, church, and peer groups. In Mill's words, it is "derived from sympathy, from love and still more from fear; from all forms of religious feeling, from the recollections of childhood and all of our past life; from self-esteem, desire of the esteem of others, and occasionally even self-abasement." If cultivated properly, then, we will all carry with us a strong sense of duty towards others, which will be very difficult for us to resist.

Liberty

Mill was as much concerned with the problems of society as was Bentham. The greatest happiness principle led all utilitarians to consider how the individual and the government should be related. Bentham put his faith in democracy as the great cure for social evils, since in democracies the people being ruled are also the rulers. But Mill did not have the same implicit faith in democracy. Although Mill agreed that democracy is the best form of government, in his essay *On Liberty* he exposes certain dangers inherent in the democracies. Principally, he warned that it is entirely possible for the will of the majority to oppress minorities. In addition, democracies have a kind of tyranny of opinion, which is as dangerous as oppression. Even in a democracy, therefore, it is necessary to set up safeguards against the forces that would deny individual freedom. In this respect, Mill reflected Bentham's desire for reform to eliminate clear social evils. His particular focus is on preserving liberty by setting limits to the actions of government.

Mill argued that "the sole end for which mankind are warranted, individually or collectively, in interfering with the liberty of action of any of their number, is self-protection. That the only purpose for which power can be rightly exercised over any member of a civilized community, against his will, is to prevent harm to others." There is, of course, a legitimate role for government, but there are three conditions under which the government should not interfere with its subjects. First, governments should not interfere when private individuals can do the action better. Second, governments should not interfere when, although the government could possibly do the action better than private individuals, it is desirable for the individuals to do it for their development and education. Third, governments should not interfere when there is danger that too much power will unnecessarily accrue to the government. Mill's argument for liberty was, therefore, an argument for individualism. Let individuals pursue their happiness in their own way. Even in the realm of ideas, we must be free to express our thoughts and beliefs, because truth is most quickly discovered when opportunity is given to refute falsehoods. Mill took the position that "there is the greatest difference between presuming an opinion to be true because, with every opportunity for contesting it, it has not been refuted, and assuming its truth for the purpose of not permitting its refutation." He assumed, however, that it is important that the truth be known. As he considered the ideal goal of human existence, Mill asked "what more or better can be said of any condition of human affairs than that it brings human beings themselves nearer to the best thing they can be? But is it the function of government to make human beings the best thing they can be?" He deeply disliked totalitarian governments even though he lived too soon to see its ugliest manifestations in the 20th century.

The most memorable part of Mill's position is what we now call Mill's Principle of Liberty:

> That the only purpose for which power can be rightfully exercised over any member of a civilized community, against his will, is to prevent harm to others. His own good, either physical or moral, is not a sufficient warrant. . . . The only part of the conduct of any one, for which he is amenable to society, is that which concerns others. In the part which merely concerns himself, his independence is, of right, absolute. Over himself, over his own body and mind, the individual is sovereign.

Mill says here that governments may rightly constrain us when our actions harm other people, but not when our actions only harm ourselves. Thus, we should be at liberty to engage in dangerous activities, even to the point that our own lives are at risk.

COMTE

Comte's Life and Times

Although Auguste Comte is called the founder of *positive philosophy*, he did not discover this theory, for, as John Stuart Mill said, positivism was "the general property of the age." Comte studied in an age and at a place that were characterized by intellectual confusion and social instability. Born at Montpellier in 1798, he was educated at the École Polytechnique and for some years was secretary to the noted socialist Saint-Simon. In his early 20s he published a series of books of which his *Système de Politique Positive* (1824) is the best known. This, as it turned out, was an early sketch of his major work *Cours de Philosophie Positive*, which was written in several volumes between 1830 and 1842. He admitted that there was this contrast between his earlier and later ideas, claiming that he was an Aristotle in the early period of his career—that is, more rational—and a St. Paul in the later—that is, more emotional. Some of his later ideas were somewhat peculiar and even resulted in ridicule. He blamed the severe specialization of university scholars for their refusal to provide him a post for teaching the history of the sciences. Living off voluntary contributions from the friends of positivism, he continued to work in Paris in a little house only a short distance from the place at the Sorbonne where there now stands a statue of him. From this meager setting emerged Comte's other major books, his second *Le système de politique positive* (1851–1854), *Catéchisme positiviste* (1852), and the *Synthèse subjective* (1856). Before he could complete his projected series on ethics, the system of positive industrial organization, and other philosophical works, his career ended in 1857, when he died at the age of 59.

Auguste Comte
(Corbis-Bettmann)

Comte's chief objective was the total reorganization of society. But he was convinced that this practical objective first required the reconstruction or at least reformation of the intellectual orientation of his era. As he saw the situation, the Scientific Revolution, which had been unfolding since the discoveries of Galileo and Newton, had not been sufficiently assimilated in other fields, particularly in social, political, moral, and religious thought. The achievements of science in France had been outstanding, including the work of Ampère and Fresnel in physics, Chevreul and Dumas in chemistry, Magendie in physiology, and Lamarck, Saint-Hilaire, and Cuvier in biology and zoology. What commanded so much respect for their work was that their discoveries could be employed in solving problems of everyday life. This led to new methods in medicine and surgery, and make possible new industrial techniques and transportation. Gaining a sense of authority from its spectacular accomplishments, science challenged other ways of thinking, which could not in their field match these successes. A series of related questions now took on a greater degree of intensity. Such questions included the relation between science and religion, about the freedom of the will, about the value of metaphysics, and about the possibility of discovering objective moral standards.

This was an age, too, when the state of philosophy in France was being influenced by both internal political events and external systems of thought. The major internal event was the French Revolution, which for Saint-Simon as well as for Comte, was a dramatic example of social anarchy. In the aftermath of the Revolution, French thinkers entertained differing theories of society. Some theories were strongly antirevolutionary, contending that the Revolution involved a contest of power whose effect was to destroy the legitimate power and authority both of the government and of the church. The effect could only be the further destruction of the institutions of the family and private property. Other theorists argued that society rests upon the consent of the governed as expressed in a social contract. Added to these internal differences in thought was the gradual importation of philosophies from other countries. These dealt not only with social philosophy, but they also treated the theory of knowledge and metaphysics a way that stimulated an atmosphere of vigorous debate. The French were now reading such varied authors as Kant, Hegel, Fichte, Schelling, Strauss, Feuerbach, and Goethe. Advocates of materialism, idealism, and new metaphysical systems entered the lists, and grandiose theories of human nature, the Absolute, and Progress were put forth.

To overcome both political anarchy and the anarchy of ideas, Comte attempted to reform society and philosophy by developing a science of society, namely, *positivism.* The issue for Comte was how to maintain social unity when theological beliefs were no longer accepted as supports for political authority. Comte believed that a dictatorship of brute force would result when beliefs are no longer held in common and when anarchy of ideas creates anarchy in society. None of the usual arguments against dictatorship seemed satisfactory to Comte. Against those who sought to reinstate the earlier balance of worldly and spiritual powers as they were before the Revolution, Comte answered that it is not possible to reverse the course of historical progress. Against those who advocated the methods of democracy, he argued that their concepts of *equality* and *natural rights—*especially *sovereignty of the people*—were metaphysical abstractions and dogmas. Only the method of positivism, he declared, can guarantee social unity. His task of reorganizing society, therefore, required that he first of all bring about an intellectual reformation, which in turn led him to formulate his classic theory of positivism.

Positivism Defined

Positivism involves both a negative and positive component. On the negative side, it rejects the assumption that nature has some ultimate purpose, and it gives up any attempt to discover either the "essence" or the secret causes of things. On the positive side, it attempts to study facts by observing the constant relations between things and by formulating the laws of science simply as the laws of constant relations among various phenomena. In this spirit, Newton described the phenomena of physics without going beyond useful limits in asking questions about the essential nature of things. Before him Galileo had made great strides in understanding the movements and relations of stars without inquiring into their physical constitution. Fourier discovered mathematical laws of the diffusion of heat without any theoretical assumption concerning the essential nature of heat. The biologist Cuvier worked out some laws concerning the structure of living things without any hypothesis about the nature of life. A consequence of this spirit of research and inquiry was the assumption that knowledge derived from science can also be used in the social realm. This was positivism's great appeal. For on the one hand it promised an effective means for dealing with physical reality, such as the disorders of the body, which concerned medicine. On the other hand, it also concerned the science of society, which concerns the sociologist.

The initial rigor of positivism is suggested by Comte's clear statement that "any proposition which does not admit of being ultimately reduced to a simple enunciation of fact, special or general, can have no real or intelligible sense." Counting himself a positivist and using much of Comte's own language, Mill described the general outlook of positivism in these terms:

> We have no knowledge of anything but Phenomena, and our knowledge of phenomena is relative, not absolute. We know not the essence, nor the real mode of production of any fact but only its relations to other facts in the way of succession or of similitude. These relations are constant; that is, always the same in the same circumstances. The constant resemblances which link phenomena together, and the constant sequences which unite them as antecedent and consequent, are termed their laws. The laws of phenomena are all we know respecting them. Their essential nature, and their ultimate causes, either efficient or final, are unknown and inscrutable to us.

This was the intellectual attitude that Comte and his followers brought to the study of society and religion, saying that in the end every subject must utilize the same approach to truth. Only in that way could we achieve unity in thought as well as social life. To be sure, this method had its own assumptions, the foremost of them being that there is an order in the nature of things whose laws we can discover. Comte also assumed that we can overcome the pitfalls of subjectivity by "transforming the human brain into a perfect mirror of the external order." His optimism for achieving his objectives came from his interpretation of the history of ideas and from his study of the development of the various sciences. These, he believed, clearly pointed to the inevitability and the validity of positivism.

The Law of the Three Stages

The history of ideas, said Comte, shows that there has been a clear movement of thought through three stages, each stage representing a different way of discovering truth. The first stage is *theological,* in which people explain phenomena in reference to divine causal forces. The second is *metaphysical,* which replaces human-centered concepts of divinity with impersonal and abstract forces. The third stage is *positivistic,* or scientific, in that only the constant relations between phenomena are considered and all attempts to explain things by references to beings beyond our experience are given up. He called this evolution from one stage to another the *law of the three stages.* He believed that this law is at work in the history of ideas, in science, and in the political realm. In fact, he argued, the structure of a society reflects the philosophical orientation of an epoch, and any major change in philosophical thought will bring about a change in the political order. For example, in both Greek mythology and traditional Christianity, we find frequent instances of the intervention of the gods or of God. This had its counterpart in political theory in the theory of the divine right of kings. But this theological approach is superseded by metaphysics, which speaks of a *necessary being* as the explanation for the existence of finite things. This concept of necessary being, Comte says, is abstract and impersonal, and although it goes beyond the idea of some capricious being acting upon the physical world, it does not overcome the uselessness of dogmatism. Its counterpart in political thought is the attempt to formulate abstract principles such as *natural rights* or the *sovereignty of the people.* Comte harshly rejected the political structures in both of these stages. The theological stage, he argued, results in slavery and military states. The metaphysical stage involves the assumptions of liberal democracy, and unfounded dogmas such as the equality of all people. Comte believed that these views must give way to the clear scientific fact that people are unequal and have different capacities and must, therefore, have different functions in society. To deal effectively with such questions of political order required a carefully worked out science of society, which Comte did not find already available and which he, therefore, set out to create, calling it *sociology.*

Comte's conception of sociology illustrates his account of the development of knowledge. For in his theory, the movement of thought is from decreasing generality to increasing complexity and from the abstract to the concrete. He notes this particularly with the five major sciences. Mathematics came first; then, in order, came astronomy, physics, chemistry, and biology. In this sequence he saw the movement from generality and simplicity to complexity and concreteness. Specifically, mathematics deals with quantities of a general kind. To quantity, astronomy adds the elements of mass and force and some principles of attraction physics differentiates between types of forces when it deals with gravity, light, and heat. Chemistry makes quantitative and qualitative analyses of materials. Biology then adds the structure of organic and animal life to the material order. A sixth science—sociology—deals with the relations of human beings to each other in society, and as such it is the necessary outcome of the previous stage of science. Comte dramatically describes how mathematics and astronomy came early in the ancient world, whereas physics as a true science had to wait for Isaac Newton in the 17th century. Chemistry then began with Lavoisier, and biology with Bichat. It is now his own task to usher in the science of sociology. For him sociology is the queen of the sciences, the summit of knowledge, for it makes use of all previous information and coordinates it all for the sake of a peaceful and orderly society.

Comte's Sociology and "Religion of Humanity"

Comte stands in contrast with both revolutionary thinkers who called for a radical reconstruction of society and idealists who proposed utopian communities. His approach was to always describe things in reference to science and the actual conditions of history. Two things in particular dominate his sociological theory, namely, what he calls the *static* and the *dynamic* components of social existence. The static component consists of certain stable elements of society, such as the family, private property, language, and religion. Since these are virtually permanent, he does not advocate any revolutionary change in them. At the same time, he does recognize a dynamic component, which he understands as the force of progress. His theory of "the law of the three stages" contains the technical elaboration of this dynamic force. Progress does not involve altering any of the basic social elements. Instead, it involves rather simply understanding how we should utilize these stable structures in an optimum way. The stars and constellations do not change as we move from the theological to the metaphysical and finally to the scientific way of accounting for their behavior. Neither, then, should the structures of society change as far as their basic elements are concerned. The family, for example, must remain, and indeed Comte believes that the family constitutes the fundamental building blocks of society. However, some aspects of the family would change, such as an improved status for women. Similarly, property should be utilized in such a way as to call forth the highest instincts of altruism instead of greed and envy. Comte believes that religion is the key to the whole system, but instead of the worship of a supernatural being, religion should consist of the cult of *humanity*. Positivism also calls for a political organization that utilizes both religious and nonreligious institutions in such a way that these two do not compete but, rather, harmoniously complement each other.

Comte frequently refers to the Middle Ages as a time when the relation between the static and dynamic components of society were most adequately attuned to each other. He in fact uses the medieval community as his model for the new society. He would, of course, reject the theological aspects of this period. But what struck him about it was the intimate relation between religion and society—between a body of thought and the organization of the structures of society in medieval Europe. The family, property, and government—all of these elements had a justification in and derived their motivations from a set of beliefs held in common. The reorganization of 19th-century society would not involve the destruction of old structures and the creation of new ones. Instead, it would bring the permanent elements of society up to date. It would then overcome contemporary anarchy by reestablishing the connection between religion and the institutions of society. This connection between religion and society can only be reestablished through intellectual and technological progress. Much of the anarchy of this period, both intellectual and political, stemmed, as Comte saw it, from the breakdown of theological authority brought on by the rise of science. He believed that it was impossible to reestablish this earlier grip of theology upon modern people. Further, the legacy of the Enlightenment, which was the exaltation of each person's own ideas and opinions, could not lead to any unity.

Only a new religion could create the unity between all people and between their thinking and their ways of living. The Middle Ages had the correct approach to social organization, but, Comte says, they had the wrong intellectual orientation. On the other hand, contemporary Europe seems to him to have the right philosophy in scientific positivism but not an adequate organization. Although science had seriously shaken the hold of theology, it had not yet completely eliminated it. The ensuing debates over the relation between science and religion also raised the specific question of the comparative roles of intellect and feeling. Comte's enormous task, therefore, was to reconceive the whole nature of religion in terms of science. He would have to bind the new religion to the structures of society and unify people's intellects with their feelings. He would thus infuse every person's act with a sense of purpose or direction. Proceeding with this task, Comte said that "Love, then, is our principle; Order our basis; and Progress our end."

What his new society would be like is shown first of all by what he did *not* want it to be. Although the theological stage was now passed, new dogmas created by metaphysics still lingered, and these would have to be rejected. To achieve the new society, every old fiction would have to be given up, whether it is the theistic God or the metaphysical dogma of equality or popular sovereignty. Since the function of the mind now would be to *mirror* the truly real state of things, the contents of the new religion must be drawn from such an objectively real source, and this, Comte says, is *humanity* itself. It is, after all, from humanity that we all draw our material, intellectual, spiritual, and moral resources. But although he did not want to retain past dogmas, he nevertheless built his new *religion of humanity* as though it were a secularized version of Catholicism. Instead of God, Comte substituted humanity, which he called *Grand-Être*, the Supreme Being. He appointed himself as High Priest and instituted a calendar of saints, mostly renowned scientists. He also created a catechism, at the end of which he says, "Humanity definitely occupies the place of God." He adds that "she does not forget the services which the idea of God provisionally rendered." The sacraments become "social" and first include *Baptism*, then *Initiation* at age 14, then *Admission* when at age 21 a person is authorized to serve humanity. *Destination* or choice of career takes place at 28, *Marriage* for men at 28 and for women at 21, and *Retirement* at age 63. Mill regretted Comte's attempt to found a secularized version of the Roman Catholic Church from which all supernatural elements had been removed. Regarding Comte's self-appointed role as High Priest, Mill said that "an irresistible air of ridicule" surrounds Comte's religion and while "others may laugh . . . we could far rather weep at this melancholy decadence of a great intellect."

From the beginning of his systematic thought, Comte undoubtedly considered the goal of his positive science the creation of a "sound philosophy, capable of supplying the foundation of true religion." However, there is equally no doubt that his later writings were influenced by his emotional crisis following his intense love affair with Clotilde de Vaux, his "incomparable angel." Their involvement, which lasted two years, from 1844 to 1846 and ended with her tragic death, had influenced him to recognize the role that affection must play in life. Having in his earlier career emphasized the role of the intellect, he now argued for the supremacy of the affections, claiming that "greater distinctness . . . is given to the truth that the affective element predominates in our nature." In this regard he now states that

> where the moral excellence of true Religion is illustrated, feeling takes the first place. The disastrous revolt of Reason against Feeling will never be terminated till the new Western priesthood can fully satisfy the claims of the modern intellect. But this being done, moral requirements at once reassume the place that belongs to them, since in the construction of a really complete synthesis, Love is naturally the one universal principle.

In light of this supremacy of feeling, it is the function of positive philosophy to fashion "a system which regulates the whole course of our private and public existence, by bringing Feeling, Reason and Activity into permanent harmony." As love is the supreme moral principle, all thought or acts of the intellect must become subordinate to it, thereby making scientists philosophers, and philosophers priests. All of life becomes "a continuous and intense act of worship," and the truly human moral standard is that we should "live for others." The scientists will organize and rule society and the philosopher-priests will exercise their influence over society by the organization of public worship and by controlling education. In this way, Comte tried to achieve a modern version of the medieval separation between religious and political authority. In this way, too, morals would be independent of politics but would nevertheless be a constructive influence upon the political and economic order.

The civil order will also reflect the forces of dynamic progress, particularly as this process shows the movement from a *military* to an *industrial* basis. Comte considered that the military phase of history had much to do with developing the industrial power and organization of the modern state. Specifically, it forced people to bring together otherwise isolated material resources and human labor for the sake of survival. But now the habits of industry and discipline must be used for the sake of peace and internal order and civilization. The central aim of all human effort, Comte argued, must be the amelioration of the order of nature. Science helps us to understand nature so that we can alter it. Our worship of Humanity, the new God, is not solemn inactivity, as religion was previously. Instead, it is a *positive religion,* and "the object of worship is a Being [Humanity] whose nature is relative, modifiable and perfectible." We achieve progress through such worship, and progress is "development of Order under the influence of Love." In place of the theological theory of providence—or divine guidance—Comte stressed human effort. He states that "we must look to our own unremitting activity for the only providence by which the rigor of our destiny can be alleviated."

Comte argued that human providence has four main divisions: women are the *moral providence*, the priesthood the *intellectual providence*, the capitalists the *material providence*, and the workers the *general providence*. "The people," said Comte, "represent the activity of the Supreme Being, as women represent its sympathy, and philosophers its intellect." Of the capitalists, Comte said that they are "the nutritive reservoirs, the social efficiency of which mainly depends on their being concentrated in few hands." He adds that only the influence of moral persuasion can regulate "their foolish and immoral pride." Inevitably, Comte's society would require that each person fulfill a special function by staying in the place most suited to his or her powers. Above all, there must be the supremacy of the intellectual elite, since only specialists can understand the technical problems of administering a complex society. For this reason, Comte thought it was just as senseless to permit the masses to freely inquire about matters of social and political administration as to allow them to voice their opinions about some technical matter in chemistry. These are both fields in which the masses lack proper information, and, therefore, he called for the abolition of the "vagabond liberty of individual minds."

Again, the success of the *religion of humanity* would require the stability of the family and the spirit of altruism and love. Comte would not accept the earlier theological appraisal of the depravity of humanity or the notion that altruism is incompatible with human nature. To Comte, altruistic instincts were a matter of scientific fact. To support this contention he cites Franz Joseph Gall, the founder of phrenology, who argued that there is an "organ" of benevolence in the brain. In addition, women would exert their creative function in the family and would spontaneously consecrate their "rational and imaginative faculties to the service of feeling." For Comte, the very symbol of humanity on the *flag of positivism* was a young mother with her infant son—a final analogy between Christianity and the Religion of Humanity.

The more Comte concerned himself with the creation of a new religion, the further he seemed to depart from the principles of positivism. In the end, he seemed to be indicating the goal toward which society *ought* to be moving instead of describing the course which history *is* in fact taking. Comte's influence was soon eclipsed by the politically more captivating theories of Karl Marx. He is still a leading figure in that impressive line of thinkers that began with Bacon and Hobbes and the empiricists Locke, Berkeley, and Hume, who came before him.

CHAPTER 15

Kierkegaard, Marx, and Nietzsche

Throughout the 19th century the views of Kant, Hegel, and other German idealists had a strong impact not only on philosophy but also on religion, aesthetics, and the new field of psychology. These philosophers devised elaborate systems of thought and introduced complex philosophical vocabulary. While many philosophers embraced their views, three philosophers reacted quite critically to this trend, namely, Søren Kierkegaard (1813–1855), Karl Marx (1818–1883), and Friedrich Nietzsche (1844–1900). Though somewhat obscure figures in their own day, they each had a profound impact on intellectual thought in the following century. Kierkegaard rejected the system-building approach of Hegel and argued instead that the quest for truth involves personal choice, grounded in religious faith. Marx rejected the idealist direction of German philosophy and the entire capitalist economic structure of his time. Instead, he argued that laws governing the material world will eventually replace capitalism with a communist social system. Nietzsche rejected both religious and rational value systems and proposed in its place a morality grounded in individual choice. These three philosophers differ from each other on critical points such as the existence of God. Nevertheless, they share the conviction that 19th-century European culture was terribly dysfunctional. Further, they all argued that we will come to a proper understanding of human existence and society only when we radically break from prevailing cultural attitudes.

KIERKEGAARD

Born in Copenhagen in 1813, Sören Kierkegaard spent his short life in a brilliant literary career, producing an extraordinary number of books before his death in 1855 at the age of 42. Although his writings were soon forgotten after his death, they made an enormous impact upon their rediscovery by some German scholars in the early decades of the 20th century. At the University of

Sören Kierkegaard
(Royal Danish Ministry)

Copenhagen, Kierkegaard was trained in Hegel's philosophy and was not favorably impressed by it. When he heard Schelling's lectures at Berlin, which were critical of Hegel, Kierkegaard agreed with this attack upon Germany's greatest speculative thinker. "If Hegel had written the whole of his Logic and then said . . . that it was merely an experiment in thought," Kierkegaard wrote, "then he could certainly have been the greatest thinker who ever lived. As it is, he is merely comic." What made Hegel comic for Kierkegaard was that this great philosopher tried to capture all of reality in his system of thought and, in the process, lost the most important element, namely, *existence*. Kierkegaard reserved the term *existence* for the individual human being. To exist, he said, implies being a certain kind of individual, an individual who strives, who considers alternatives, who chooses, who decides, and who, above all, makes a commitment. Virtually none of these acts were implied in Hegel's philosophy. Kierkegaard's whole career might well be considered a

Kierkegaard House, second from right corner
(Royal Danish Ministry)

self-conscious revolt against abstract thought and an attempt on his part to live up to Feuerbach's admonition: "Do not wish to be a philosopher in contrast to being a man . . . do not think as a thinker . . . think as a living, real being . . . think in Existence."

Human Existence

To think in terms of existence meant for Kierkegaard to recognize that we face personal choices. For this reason, our thinking ought to deal with our own personal situations and the crucial decisions that we invariably make. Hegel's philosophy falsified people's understanding of reality because it shifted attention away from the concrete individual to the concept of universals. It called upon individuals *to think* instead of *to be*—to think the Absolute Thought instead of being involved in decisions and commitments. Kierkegaard distinguished between the *spectator* and the *actor*, arguing that only the actor is involved in existence. To be sure, we can say that the spectator exists, but the term *existence* does not properly belong to inert or inactive things, whether these are spectators or stones. He illustrated this distinction by comparing two kinds of people in a wagon, one who holds the reins in his hand but is asleep and the other who is fully awake. In the first case, the horse goes along the familiar road without any direction from the sleeping man, whereas in the other case the man is truly a driver. Surely, in one sense we can say that both men exist, but Kierkegaard insists that *existence* must refer to a quality in the individual, namely, his conscious participation in an act. Only the conscious driver exists, and so, too, only a person who is engaged in conscious activity of will and choice can be truly said to exist. Thus, while both the spectator and the actor exist in a sense, only the actor is involved in existence.

Kierkegaard's criticism of rational knowledge was severe. He revolted against the rational emphasis in classic Greek thought, which, he charged, permeated subsequent philosophy and Christian theology. His specific argument was that Greek philosophy was too greatly influenced by a high regard for mathematics. Although he did not want to reject either mathematics or science in their proper uses, he did reject the assumption that the type of thought characteristic of science could be successfully employed when trying to understand human nature. Mathematics and science have no place for the human individual; its value is only for the general and universal. Likewise, Plato's philosophy emphasizes the universal, the Form, the True, the Good. Plato's whole assumption was that if we *knew* the Good we would do it. Kierkegaard thought that such an approach to ethics was a falsification of people's real predicament. Instead, Kierkegaard underscored that even when we have knowledge, we are still in the predicament of having to make a decision. In the long run, the grand formulations of philosophical systems are only prolonged detours that eventually come to nothing unless they lead attention back once again to the individual. Mathematics and science can undoubtedly solve some problems, as can ethics and metaphysics. But over against such universal or general problems stands life—each person's life—which makes demands upon us. At these critical moments abstract thought does not help.

Kierkegaard saw in the biblical story of Abraham the typical human condition: After trying many years for a child, Abraham and his wife Sarah finally produce Isaac, the fulfillment of their life's dreams. God, then, approaches Abraham and tells him to kill his son as a human sacrifice. What kind of knowledge can help Abraham decide whether to obey God? The most poignant moments in life are personal, where we become aware of ourselves as a subject. Rational thought obscures and even denies this subjective element since it only considers our objective characteristics—those characteristics that *all* people have in common. But subjectivity is what makes up each of our unique existences. For this reason, objectivity cannot give the whole truth about our individual selves. That is why rational, mathematical, and scientific thought are incapable of guiding us to a genuine existence.

Truth as Subjectivity

Truth, Kierkegaard said, *is* subjectivity. By this strange notion he meant that there is no prefabricated truth "out there" for people who make choices. As American philosopher William James similarly said, "truth is made" by an act of will. For Kierkegaard, what is "out there" is only "an objective uncertainty." Whatever may have been his criticism of Plato, he did nevertheless find in Socrates' claim to ignorance a good example of this notion of truth. Thus, he says that "the Socratic ignorance which Socrates held fast with the entire passion of his personal experience, was thus an expression of the principle that the eternal truth is related to the Existing individual." This suggests that mental cultivation is not the only important or decisive thing in life. Of more consequence is the development and maturity of our personalities.

In describing the human situation, Kierkegaard distinguished between what we now *are,* and what we *ought* to be. That is, there is a movement from our *essence* to our *existence.* Developing this notion, he draws on the traditional theological notion that our sins separate us from God. Our essential human nature involves a relation to God, and our existential condition is a consequence of our alienation from God. If my sinful actions drive me even further from God, then my alienation and despair are further compounded. Sensing our insecurity and finitude, we try to "do something" to overcome our finitude, and invariably what we do only aggravates our problem by adding guilt and despair to our anxiety. For example, we might try to find some meaning for our lives by losing ourselves in a crowd, whether it is a group of political affiliates or even a congregation in a church. In every case, Kierkegaard says, "a crowd in its very concept is the untruth, by reason of the fact that it renders the individual completely impenitent and irresponsible, or at least weakens his sense of responsibility by reducing it to a fraction." Being in a crowd only dilutes our selves and thereby undoes our nature. The real solution, for Kierkegaard, is to relate ourselves to God, rather than to groups of people. Until we do this, our lives will be full of anxiety. Shifting our orientation toward God, though, is often a tricky process, which Kierkegaard describes in terms of "stages on life's way."

The Aesthetic Stage

Kierkegaard's analysis of the "three stages" stands in sharp contrast to Hegel's theory of the gradual development of a person's self-consciousness. Hegel expounded the dialectic movement of the mind as we move from one stage of intellectual awareness to another through the process of thinking. Kierkegaard, though, describes the movement of the self from one level of existence to another through an act of choice. Hegel's dialectic moves gradually toward a knowledge of the universal, whereas Kierkegaard's dialectic involves the progressive actualization of the individual. Whereas Hegel overcomes the antithesis by a conceptual act, Kierkegaard overcomes it by the act of personal commitment.

The first stage in this dialectic process, Kierkegaard says, is the *aesthetic stage.* At this level, I would behave according to my impulses and emotions. Although I am not simply sensual at this stage, I am for the most part governed by my senses. For this reason, I would know nothing of any universal moral standards. I have no specific religious belief. My chief motivation is a desire to enjoy the widest variety of pleasures of the senses. My life has no principle of limitation except my own taste; I resent anything that would limit my vast freedom of choice. At this stage I can *exist* inasmuch as I deliberately choose to be an aesthetic person. But even though I can achieve some existence at this level, it is a rather poor quality of existence. Even though I may be fully consumed by my aesthetic way of life, I am still aware that my life ought to consist of more than this.

According to Kierkegaard, we must distinguish between our capacity for *spirituality* on the one hand and *sensuousness* on the other. Our spiritual capacity, he believes, builds on the sensuous. To be able to make this distinction about someone else is one thing. However, when we are aware of these two possibilities within ourselves, this triggers a dialectic movement within us. The antithesis of the sensual drive is the lure of the spirit. In experience, this conflict produces anxiety and despair when we discover that we are in fact living in the "cellar" of sensuousness, but that life at this level cannot possibly result in true existence. I am now face to face with an *either-or* decision: either I remain at the aesthetic level with its fatal attractions and inherent limitations, or I move to the next stage. I cannot make this transition by thinking alone, Kierkegaard maintains, but I must instead make a commitment through an act of will.

The Ethical Stage

The second level is the *ethical stage.* Unlike the aesthetic person who has no universal standards but only his or her own taste, the ethical person does recognize and accept rules of conduct that reason formulates. On this level, moral rules give my life the elements of form and consistency. Moreover, as an ethical person I accept the limitations that moral responsibility imposes on my life. Kierkegaard illustrates the contrast between the aesthetic person and the ethical person in their specific attitudes toward sexual behavior. Whereas the aesthetic person gives in to impulses wherever there is an attraction, the ethical person accepts the obligations of marriage as an expression of reason. If Don Juan exemplifies the aesthetic person, it is Socrates who typifies the ethical person or the reign of universal moral law.

As an ethical person, I would have the attitude of moral self-sufficiency. I take firm stands on moral questions and, as Socrates argued, I assume that to know the good is to do the good. For the most part, I consider moral evil to be a product either of ignorance or of weakness of will. But the time comes, Kierkegaard says, when the dialectic process begins to work in the consciousness of the ethical person. I then begin to realize that I am involved in something more profound than an inadequate knowledge of the moral law or insufficient strength of will. I am doing something more serious than merely making mistakes. I ultimately come to realize that I am in fact incapable of fulfilling the moral law, and I even deliberately violate that law. I thus become conscious of my guilt and sin. Guilt, Kierkegaard says, becomes a dialectic antithesis that places before me a new *either-or.* Now I must either remain at the ethical level and try to fulfill the moral law, or I must respond to my new awareness. This specifically involves an awareness of my own finitude and estrangement from God to whom I belong and from whom I must derive my strength. Again, my movement from the ethical to the next stage cannot be achieved by thinking alone, but by an act of commitment—that is, by a leap of faith.

The Religious Stage

When we arrive at the third level—the *religious stage*—the difference between faith and reason is particularly striking. My movement from the aesthetic to the ethical level required an act of choice and commitment. It ushered me into the presence of reason insofar as the moral law is an expression of universal reason. But the movement from the ethical to the religious level is quite different. The leap of faith does not bring me into the presence of a God who I can rationally and objectively describe as the Absolute and Knowable Truth. Instead, I am in the presence of a Subject. Accordingly, I cannot pursue God in an "objective way," or "bring God to light objectively." This, Kierkegaard says, "is in all eternity impossible because God is subject, and therefore exists only for subjectivity in inwardness." At the ethical level, it is possible for me to give my life, as Socrates did, for the moral law that I rationally understand. But when it is a question of my relation to God, I have no rational or objective knowledge about this relationship.

The relationship between God and each individual is a unique and subjective experience. There is no way, prior to the actual relationship, to get any knowledge about it. Any attempt to get objective knowledge about it is entirely an *approximation process.* Only an act of faith can assure me of my personal relation to God. As I discover the inadequacy of my existence at the aesthetic and ethical levels, self-fulfillment in God becomes clear to me. Through despair and guilt I am brought to the decisive moment in life when I confront the final *either-or* of faith. I experience my self-alienation, and thereby become aware that God exists. A paradox of faith arises when I see that God has revealed himself in a finite human being, namely Jesus. It is in fact an extraordinary affront to human reason to say that God, the infinite, is revealed in Jesus, the finite. Kierkegaard writes that this paradox is "to the Jews a stumbling block and to the Greeks foolishness." Nevertheless, for Kierkegaard there is only one way to cross the span between human beings and God, which is an "infinite qualitative distinction between time and eternity." It is not through speculative reason—not even Hegel's. Instead, it is through faith, which is a subjective matter and a consequence of commitment, and this will always involve some risk.

Kierkegaard's philosophy can be summed up in his statement that "Every human being must be assumed in essential possession of what essentially belongs to being a human." This being the case, "the task of the subjective thinker is to transform himself into an instrument that clearly and definitely expresses in existence whatever is essentially human." In short, each person possesses an essential self, which he or she *ought* to actualize. This essential self is fixed by the very fact that human beings must inescapably become related to God. To be sure, we can *exist* at any one of the three stages along life's way. But the experience of despair and guilt creates in us an awareness of qualitative differences in various types of existence. We also become aware that some types of human existence are more authentic than others. But arriving at authentic existence is not an intellectual matter. Instead, it is a matter of faith and commitment, and a continuous process of choice in the presence of varieties of *either-or.*

Karl Marx
(The Granger Collection, New York)

MARX

Marxism provided the official philosophical point of view for at least one-third of the world's population in the second half of the 20th century. When we consider that Marx spent a considerable portion of his adult life in relative obscurity, it is all the more remarkable that his views should have achieved such immense influence for several generations. He rarely spoke in public, and when he did, he displayed none of the attributes of the captivating orator. He was primarily a thinker, thoroughly absorbed in the task of elaborating the intricate details of a theory whose broad outlines he grasped as a young man while still in his 20s. He rarely mingled with the masses whose status occupied the center of his theoretical concern. Although he wrote an enormous amount, his writings were not read extensively during his lifetime. For example, we find no reference to Marx in the social and political writings of his famed contemporary John Stuart Mill. Nor was what Marx said entirely original. We can find much of his economic thought in Ricardo, some of his philosophical assumptions and apparatus in Hegel and Feuerbach, the view that history is shaped by the conflict between social classes in Saint-Simon, and the labor theory of value in Locke. What was original in Marx was that out of all these sources he distilled a unified scheme of thought, which he fashioned into a powerful instrument of social analysis and social revolution.

Marx's Life and Influences

Karl Heinrich Marx was born in Trier, Germany, in 1818, the oldest son of a Jewish lawyer and the descendant of a long line of rabbis. In spite of his Jewish lineage, he was brought up as a Protestant since his father became a Lutheran, for apparently practical reasons rather than religious convictions. The elder Marx had a strong influence on his son's intellectual development through his own rational and humanitarian inclinations. Young Marx was also influenced by Ludwig von Westphalen, a neighbor and a distinguished Prussian government official and his future father-in-law. Westphalen stimulated his interest in literature and a lifelong respect for the Greek poets as well as Dante and Shakespeare. After high school in Trier, Marx went to the University of Bonn in 1835 and began the study of law at the age of 17. A year later he transferred to the University of Berlin, giving up the study of law and pursuing instead the study of philosophy. In 1841, at the age of 23, he received his doctoral degree from the University of Jena, for which he wrote a dissertation entitled *On the Difference between the Democritean and Epicurean Philosophies of Nature.*

At the University of Berlin, the dominant intellectual influence was the philosophy of Hegel, and Marx was deeply impressed by Hegel's idealism and his dynamic view of history. He became a member of a group of young radical Hegelians who saw in Hegel's approach to philosophy the key to a new understanding of human nature, the world, and history. Hegel centered his thought around the notion of *Spirit* or *Mind*. To him, Absolute Spirit or Mind is God. God is the whole of reality. God is identical with all of nature, and therefore God is found also in the configurations of culture and civilization. History consists in the gradual self-realization of God in the sequence of time. What makes Nature knowable is that its essence is Mind, and what produces history is the continuous struggle of Mind to realize itself in perfect form. Thus, God and the world are one. The basic reality is therefore Spirit or Mind. Moreover, Hegel argued, the political dimension of reality, the Idea, is in a continuous process of unfolding from lower to higher degrees of perfection, and this is the process we know as *history*. History is a dialectic process moving in a triadic pattern from *thesis* to *antithesis* and finally to *synthesis*.

Whether Marx ever accepted Hegel's idealism in all its fullness is not certain. But what did strike him with force was Hegel's method of identifying God and Nature or the world. Hegel said that "Spirit [God] is alone reality. It is the inner being of the world, that which essentially is and is *per se."* Whatever there is, and whatever there is to know, exists as the world of nature. Besides the world and its history there is nothing. This rejection of the older theology, which separated God and the world, is what struck Marx as being so novel and significant. Although Hegel did not intend his views to destroy the foundations of religion, a radical young group of Hegelians at the University of Berlin undertook a "higher criticism" of the Gospels. David Strauss wrote a critical *Life of Jesus* in which he argued that much of Jesus' teaching was a purely mythical invention, particularly those portions which referred to another world. Bruno Bauer went even further by denying the historical existence of Jesus. Following the Hegelian method of identifying God and the world, these radical writers shattered the literal interpretation of the language of the Gospels and considered its only value to lie in its pictorial power, not in its truth. The inevitable drift of Hegelianism was to identify God with human beings, since people, among all things in Nature, embodies the element of Spirit or Mind in a unique way. It was then only another step to the position of philosophical atheism, which Hegel himself did not take, but which Marx and others did.

Three components of Hegel's philosophy had a direct impact on Marx. First is the notion that there is only one reality, and this can be discovered as the embodiment of rationality in the world. Second is the recognition that history is a process of development and change from less to more perfect forms in all of reality, including physical nature, social and political life, and human thought. Third is the assumption that the thoughts and behavior of people at any given time and place are caused by the operation in them of an identical spirit or mind, the spirit of the particular time or epoch. Although these were the general themes which Hegelianism seemed to stimulate in Marx's thinking, other influences caused him to reject or reinterpret portions of Hegel's philosophy. For example, shortly after Marx finished his doctoral dissertation, the appearance of Ludwig Feuerbach's writings had a decisive effect upon the young radical Hegelians and especially upon Marx.

Feuerbach took the Hegelian viewpoint to its extreme conclusion and thereby criticized the very foundation of Hegelianism itself. He did this by rejecting Hegel's idealism, substituting instead the view that basic reality is material. In short, Feuerbach revived philosophical materialism, and Marx instantly felt that this explained human thought and behavior much better than Hegel's idealism. Hegel saw the thought and behavior of a particular epoch as the working in all people of an identical spirit. Feuerbach now contended that, on the contrary, the generating influence of people's thoughts was the total sum of the material circumstances of any historical time.

Feuerbach thus rejected Hegel's assumption of the primacy of Spirit, and substituted for it the primacy of the material order. He develops this with particular force in the *Essence of Christianity,* in which he argues that human beings and not God are the basic reality. When we analyze our ideas of God, Feuerbach said, we find no ideas of God beyond our human feelings and wants. All so-called knowledge of God, he said, is only knowledge about people. God, therefore, is humanity. Our various ideas of God simply reflect types of human existence. Thus, God is the product of human thought and not the other way around. In this way, Feuerbach inverted Hegel's idealism, and the resulting materialism struck a fire within Marx and provided him with one of the most decisive and characteristic elements in his own philosophy.

Marx now acknowledged that Feuerbach was the pivotal figure in philosophy. Most importantly, Feuerbach shifted the focal point of historical development from God to human beings. That is, whereas Hegel said that it was Spirit that was progressively realizing itself in history, Feuerbach said that it is really human beings that are struggling to realize themselves. People, and not God, are in some way alienated from themselves, and history has to do with our struggle to overcome self-alienation. Clearly, if this was in fact the human condition, Marx thought, the world should be changed in order to facilitate human self-realization. This is what led Marx to say that hitherto "the philosophers have only *interpreted* the world differently: the point is, however, to *change* it." Marx thus grounded his thought in two major insights, Hegel's dialectic view of history, and Feuerbach's emphasis on the primacy of the material order. Now he was ready to forge these ideas into a full-scale instrument of social analysis and, most importantly, to lay out a vigorous and practical plan of action.

At the age of 25, Marx left Berlin and went to Paris, where he and some friends undertook the publication of the radical periodical *Deutsch-Französiche Jahrbücher.* In Paris, Marx met many radical revolutionaries and utopian thinkers and confronted the ideas of such people as Fourier, Proudhon, Saint-Simon, and Bakunin. Of lasting significance was his meeting with Friedrich Engels, the son of a German textile manufacturer, with whom Marx was to have a long and intimate association. Apart from his progressively deeper involvement in practical social action through his journalism, Marx was greatly preoccupied in Paris with the question of why the French Revolution failed. He wanted to know whether it was possible to discover any reliable laws of history in order to avoid mistakes in the future in revolutionary activity. He read extensively on this subject and discovered several promising answers. He was particularly impressed by Saint-Simon's account of class conflict, which led Marx to focus upon the classes not only as the parties to conflict but also as the bearers of the material and economic realities in which their lives are set. What Marx began to see was that revolutions do not succeed if they consist only in romantic ideas while overlooking the realities of the material order. But it was only a year after Marx arrived in Paris that he was expelled from the city, and for the next three years, from 1845 to 1848, Marx and his family settled in Brussels. Here he helped to organize a German Worker's Union. At a meeting in London in 1847, this group united with similar European organizations and formed an international Communist League. The first secretary was Engels. The League asked Marx to formulate a statement of principles. This appeared in 1848 under the title *Manifesto of the Communist Party.*

From Brussels he returned to Paris briefly to participate in some revolutionary activities, but was again required to leave. This time, in the autumn of 1849, he went to London, where he would spend the rest of his life. England at this time was not ripe for revolutionary activity, since there was no widespread organization of the mass of workers. Marx himself became an isolated figure, prodigiously studying and writing. Each day he went to the reading room of the British Museum, working there from nine in the morning until seven at night with additional hours of work after he returned to his bleak two-room apartment in the cheap Soho district of London. His poverty was deeply humiliating. But he was driven with such single-mindedness to produce his massive books that he could not deviate from this objective to provide his family with more adequate facilities. In addition to his poverty, he was afflicted with a liver ailment and plagued with boils. In this environment his six-year-old son died, and his beautiful wife's health failed. Some financial help came from Engels and from his writing regular articles on European affairs for the *New York Daily Tribune.*

Under these incredible circumstances, Marx produced many notable works, including his first systematic work on economics, which he called the *Critique of Political Economy* (1859). The most important of these is his massive *The Captial (Das Kapital),* whose first volume he published in 1867 and whose second and third volumes were assembled from his manuscripts after his death and published by Engels in 1885 and 1894. Although Marx supplied the theoretical basis for the Communist movement, he participated less and less in the practical activities that he urged. Still, he had a lively hope that the great revolution would come and that his prediction of the downfall of capitalism would become a fact. But in the last decade of his life, as his name became famous around the world, he became less productive. Two years after his wife died and only two months after his eldest daughter's death, Karl Marx died of pleurisy in London on March 14, 1883, at the age of 65.

Marx often protested that he was not a "Marxist," and not every idea or every strategy utilized by world communism can rightly be ascribed to him. There is, nevertheless, a central core of thought, which constitutes the essence of Marxist philosophy and which Marx formulated in the highly charged intellectual atmosphere of the mid-19th-century Europe of which he was a part. This core of Marxist thought consists in the analysis of four basic elements, namely (1) the major epochs of history, (2) the causal power of the material order, (3) the alienation of labor, and (4) the source and role of ideas. We will look at each of these in turn.

The Epochs of History: Marx's Dialectic

Already in his *Communist Manifesto,* Marx formulated his basic theory, which he considered in many ways original. "What I did that was new," he said, "was to prove (1) that the *existence of classes* is only bound up with particular historic phases in the development of production; (2) that the class struggle necessarily leads to the dictatorship of the proletariat; (3) that the dictatorship itself only constitutes the transition to the *abolition of all classes* and to a class-less society." Later, while in London, he worked out his argument in painstaking detail, which he thought provided scientific support for the more general pronouncements in his *Manifesto.* Accordingly, he stated in the preface to *The Capital,* that "it is the ultimate aim of this work to lay bare the economic law of motion of modern society." This law of motion became his theory of dialectical materialism.

The Five Epochs   Marx showed that class struggle is bound up with "particular historic phases." He distinguished five such phases, dividing history into five separate epochs. These he called (1) the primitive communal, (2) slave, (3) feudal, (4) capitalist, and, as a prediction of things to come, (5) the socialist and communist phases. For the most part, this was a conventional division of Western social history into its major periods. But what Marx wanted to do was to discover the "law of motion." These would explain not only *that* history produced these various epochs, but the *reasons why* these particular epochs unfolded as they did. If he could discover history's law of motion, he could not only explain the past but predict the future. He assumed that the behavior of individuals and societies is subject to the same kind of analysis as are the objects of physical and biological science. He considered the commodity and value products of economics as being "of the same order as those [minute elements] dealt with in microscopic anatomy." When analyzing the structure of each historic epoch, he viewed these as the result of conflict between social classes. In time, this conflict itself would have to be analyzed in more detail. Now he looked upon history as the product of conflict and relied heavily upon the Hegelian concept of *dialectic* to explain it.

Marx of course rejected Hegel's idealism but accepted the general theory of the dialectic movement of history, which Hegel proposed. Hegel argued that ideas develop in a dialectic way, through the action and reaction of thought. He described this dialectic process as a movement from *thesis* to *antithesis* and then to *synthesis,* where the synthesis becomes a new thesis and the process goes on and on. In addition, Hegel said that the external social, political, and economic world is simply the embodiment of people's (and God's) ideas. The development or the movement of the external world is the result of the prior development of ideas. Marx, again, considered Hegel's notion of dialectic a most important tool for understanding history. But, through the powerful influence of Feuerbach, Marx supplied a materialistic basis for the dialectic. Accordingly, Marx said that "my dialectic method is not only different from the Hegelian, but is its direct opposite. To Hegel, the process of thinking . . . is the [creator] of the real world." However, with Marx, "the ideal is nothing else than the material world reflected by the human mind, and translated into forms of thought." According to Marx, we are to see history as a movement caused by conflicts in the material order, and for this reason history is a *dialectical materialism.*

Change: Quantitative and Qualitative   History shows that social and economic orders are in a process of change. Marx's dialectical materialism maintains further that material order is primary, since matter is the basis of what is truly real. He rejected the notion that somewhere there are stable, permanent structures of reality or certain "eternal verities." Instead, everything is involved in the dialectic process of change. Nature, he argued, "from the smallest thing to the biggest, from a grain of sand to the sun . . . to man, is in . . . a ceaseless state of movement and change." History is the process of change from one epoch to another in accordance with the rigorous and inexorable laws of historical motion.

For Marx, change is not the same thing as mere growth. A society does not simply mature the way a child becomes an adult. Nor does nature simply move in an eternally uniform and constantly repeated circle. It passes through a real history. Change means the emergence of new structures and novel forms. What causes change is simply alteration in the *quantity* of things, which leads to something *qualitatively* new. For example, as I increase the temperature of water, it not only becomes warmer, but finally reaches the point at which this quantitative change changes it from a liquid into a vapor. Reversing the process, by gradually decreasing the temperature of water, I finally change it from a liquid to solid ice. Similarly, I can make a large pane of glass vibrate, the range of the vibrations increasing as the quantity of force applied to it is increased. But finally, a further addition of force will no longer add to the quantity of vibration but will, instead, cause a qualitative change, the shattering of the glass. Marx thought that history displays this kind of change, by which certain quantitative elements in the economic order finally force a qualitative change in the arrangements of society. This is the process that moved history from the primitive communal to the slave, and in turn to the feudal and capitalist epochs.

Marx's prediction that the capitalist order would fall was based upon this notion that the changes in the quantitative factors in capitalism would inevitably destroy capitalism. He describes development of these epochs with the low-key expression of someone who was describing how water will turn into steam as heat is increased. He writes in *The Capital* that "while there is a progressive diminution in the number of capitalist owners, there is of course a corresponding increase in the mass of poverty, enslavement, degeneration and exploitation, but at the same time a steady intensification of the role of the working class." Then "the centralization of the means of production and the socialization of labor reach a point where they prove incompatible with their capitalist husk. This bursts asunder. The knell of private property sounds. The expropriators are expropriated." This, on the social level, is what Marx describes as the *quantitative leap*, which is "the leap to a new aggregate state . . . where consequently quantity is transformed into quality."

Determinism or Inexorable Law   There is a basic difference between the transformation of water into steam as a laboratory experiment and the movement of society from capitalism to socialism. The difference is that I can *choose* to raise or not to raise the temperature of the water. But there are no such hypothetical qualifications surrounding history. Though I can say *"if* the temperature is raised," *he* cannot say *"if* the social order is thus and so." Marxism holds that there is a fundamental "contradiction within the very essence of things" causing the dialectic movement. Although there are ways of delaying or accelerating this inner movement in the nature of things, there is no way to prevent its ultimate unfolding. All things are related to each other *causally;* nothing floats freely. For this reason there are no isolated events either in physical nature or in human behavior or, therefore, in history. That there is a definite and inexorable process of movement and change at work producing "history" is, for Marx, as certain as the plain fact that nature exists.

There is an important point of distinction that we should make when claiming, as Marx does, that all things behave in accordance with a principle of regularity and predictability. The laws of physics, for example, describe "mechanical determinism." History, on the other hand, displays a law of determinism but not in a strictly mechanical way. The movement of one billiard ball by another is the typical example of the mechanical type of determinism. If we can locate an object in space and measure its distance from another object whose velocity can also be measured, it would then be possible to predict the time of the impact and the subsequent trajectories and rates of motion. This mechanical determinism is hardly applicable to such a complex phenomenon as a social order, which does not have the same kind of location in space and time. But society is nevertheless the result of necessary causation and determinism, and its new forms are capable of prediction just as submicroscopic particles are determined in quantum mechanics, even though there is only "probable" prediction regarding particular particles. Thus, although the specific history of a particular person could not be predicted with any high degree of accuracy, we can plot the future state of a social order. From his analysis of the various epochs of history, Marx thought he discovered the built-in law of change in nature—a kind of inexorable inner logic in events—causing history to move from one epoch to the next with a relentless determinism. From this basis, he predicted that capitalism would inevitably fall and would be transformed by the wave of the future, giving way to the qualitatively different social order of socialism and communism.

The End of History   For Marx, history will end with the emergence of socialism and, finally, communism. Here again, he followed Hegel's theory in an inverted way. For Hegel, the dialectic process comes to an end when the Idea of freedom is perfectly realized. By definition this would mean the end of all conflict and struggle. Marx, though, believed that the dialectic struggle of opposites is in the material order, particularly in the struggle between the classes. When the inner contradictions between the classes are resolved, the principal cause of movement and change would disappear. A classless society would then emerge where all the forces and interests would be in perfect balance, and this equilibrium would be perpetual. For this reason there could be no further development in history, inasmuch as there would no longer be any conflict to impel history on to any future epoch.

Marx's theory of the dialectic development of the five epochs of history rested upon a close relation between the order of material reality, on the one hand, and the order of human thought on the other. He was convinced that the only way to achieve a realistic understanding of history, and therefore to avoid errors in the practical plan of revolutionary activity, was to assess properly the roles of the material order and the order of human thought. Accordingly, Marx made a sharp distinction between the *substructure* and the *superstructure* of society. The *substructure* is the material order, containing the energizing force that moves history, whereas the *superstructure* consists in people's ideas and simply reflects the configurations of the material order.

The Substructure: The Material Order

According to Marx, the material world consists of the sum total of the natural environment, and this included for him all of inorganic nature, the organic world, social life, and human consciousness. Unlike Democritus, who defined matter in terms of irreducible tiny atoms, Marx defines matter as "objective reality existing outside the human mind." Again, unlike Democritus, who considered the atoms as the "bricks of the universe," Marxist materialism does not take this approach of trying to discover a single form of matter in all things. The chief characteristic of Marxist materialism is that it recognizes a wide diversity in the material world without reducing it to any one form of matter. The material order contains everything in the natural world that exists outside of our minds. The notion that any spiritual reality, God, for example, exists outside our minds and as something other than nature is denied. That human beings possess minds means only that organic matter has developed to the point where the cerebral cortex has become the organ capable of the intricate process of reflex action called human thought. Moreover, the human mind has been conditioned by the labor activity of humans as social beings. For this reason, relying upon the Darwinian notion of human evolution, Marxism affirms the primacy of the material order and regards mental activity as a secondary by-product of matter. The earliest forms of life were without mental activity until human ancestors developed the use of their forelimbs, learned to walk erect, and began to use natural objects as tools to procure food and to protect themselves against harm. The big transformation from animal to human being came with the ability to fashion and use tools and to control forces such as fire. This, in turn, made possible a wider variety of food and the further development of the brain. Even now, the complex material order is the basic reality, whereas the mental realm is a derivative from it. In particular, the material order consists of (1) the *factors* of production and (2) the *relations* of production.

The Factors of Production   The basic fact of human life is that in order to live, people must secure food, clothing, and shelter. To have these material things, people must produce them. Wherever we find any society of people, there is always at hand the factors of production, the raw materials, instruments as well as the experienced labor skill, by which things are produced to sustain life. But these factors or forces of production represent chiefly the way people are related to these material things. Of greater importance is the way we are related to each other in the process of production. What Marx wanted to emphasize was that production always takes place as a social act, where people struggle against and utilize nature not as individuals but as groups and societies. For Marx, then, the static analysis of what goes into production was not as important as the dynamic relations of people to each other as a producing society. To be sure, Marx felt that the factors of production affected the relations of production. For example, the scarcity of raw materials could have a considerable effect upon the way people would relate to each other in the process of production. In any case, Marx centered his analysis of the material order upon the way that people engaged in the act of production—upon the *relations of production.*

The Relations of Production   Marx believed that his analysis of the relations of production was the core of his social analysis. It was here that he thought he located the energizing force of the dialectic process. The key to the relations of production was the status of property or its ownership. That is, what determined how men were related to each other in the process of production was their relation to property. Under the slave system, for example, the slave owner owned the means of production, even owning the slave, whom he could purchase or sell. The institution of slavery was a necessary product of the dialectic process, since it arose at a time when advanced forms of tools made possible more stable and sustained agricultural activity and a division of labor. But in the slave epoch, as well as in the subsequent historical epochs, the laborer is "exploited" in that he shares in neither the ownership nor in the fruits of production. The basic struggle between the classes is seen already in the slave system. For the ownership of property divides society between those who have and those who have not. In the feudal system, the feudal lord owns the means of production. The serf rises above the level of the former slaves, has some share in the ownership of tools, but still works for the feudal lord and, Marx says, feels exploited and struggles against his exploiter. In capitalism, the workers are free as compared with the slaves and the serfs, but they do not own the means of production, and in order to survive, they must sell their labor to the capitalist.

The shift from slave to feudal to capitalist relations of production is not the result of rational design but a product of the inner movement and logic of the material order. Specifically, the impelling force to survive leads to the creation of tools, and, in turn, the kinds of tools created affect the way people relate to each other. Thus, whereas certain tools, such as the bow and arrow, permit independent existence, the plough, on the other hand, logically implies a division of labor. Similarly, whereas a spinning wheel can be used in the home or in small shops, heavier machinery requires large factories and a new concentration of workers in a given locality. The process moves in a deterministic way, impelled by basic economic drives whose direction is set by the technological requirements of the moment. The thoughts and behavior of all people are determined by their relations to each other and to the means of production. Although in all periods there is a conflict and struggle between the different classes, the class struggle is particularly violent under capitalism.

There are at least three characteristics of class struggle under capitalism. First, the classes are reduced basically to two, the owners (*bourgeoisie*) and the workers (*proletariat*). Secondly, the relations of those classes to each other rest upon a fundamental contradiction, namely, that although both classes participate in the act of production, the type of distribution of the fruits of production does not correspond to the contribution made by each class. The reason for this discrepancy is that the forces of supply and demand determine the price of labor in the capitalist system, and the large supply of workers tends to send wages down to a subsistence level. But the products created by labor can be sold for more than it costs to hire the labor force. Marx's analysis assumed the labor theory of value, namely, the view that the value of the product is created by the amount of labor put into it. From this point of view, since the product of labor could be sold for more than the cost of labor, the capitalist would then reap the difference, which Marx called *surplus value*. The existence of surplus value constituted the contradiction in the capitalistic system for Marx. For this reason, Marx argued that in the capitalistic system exploitation was not merely an isolated occurrence here or there, now or then. Instead, it existed always and everywhere because of the manner in which the iron law of wages operates. Still, Marx made no moral judgment of this condition, saying that as a matter of fact the worker received what he was worth if the determination of the wage through the supply and demand of labor is the norm. "It is true," he said, "that the daily maintenance of labor power costs only half a day's labor, and that nevertheless the labor power can work for an entire working day, with the result that the value which its use creates during a working day is twice the value of a day's labor power. So much the better for the purchaser, but it is nowise an injustice to the seller [worker]."

In a sense, Marx did not "blame" the capitalist for this arrangement. These are rather the consequences of the material forces of history, which determines the existence of these arrangements. Labor became a coherent group only because large-scale machinery required large factories, and suddenly the multitude of workers who were required to run the machines found themselves living close together. That history produced the capitalist system was one thing, but that it rested upon a contradiction was something else. For this reason, Marx excused the capitalist. However, for scientific reasons he compelled to say that the class conflict caused by this contradiction of surplus value would force the dialectic movement to the next stage of history, namely, socialism and finally communism.

The third characteristic of this class struggle was the prediction that the condition of the workers in capitalism would become progressively more wretched. The poor would become poorer and more numerous while the rich would become richer and fewer, until the masses would take over all the means of production. As a matter of historical fact, Marx could not have been more wrong than he was at this point, since it is precisely the workers whose condition has improved most dramatically in the highly developed capitalistic economies. Still, Marx argued that as long as the means of production remained in the hands of a few, the class struggle would continue inexorably until the contradiction was resolved, ending the dialectic movement. Meanwhile, the workers' lives would be terribly dehumanized by what Marx calls "the alienation of labor."

The Alienation of Labor

While still in his 20s, Marx produced a brief series of manuscripts called the *Economic and Philosophical Manuscripts of 1844,* first published in 1932. The key concept of these manuscripts is that of *alienation,* a theme which moves throughout the whole system of Marx's thought. Although Marx was by no means the first to develop a theory of alienation, his views on this theme were unique because they were based upon his particular economic and philosophical assumptions, which formed the basis of his criticism of capitalism.

If people are alienated—that is, estranged or separated—we must be alienated from something. In Christian theology, people are alienated from God through sin and the fall of Adam. In a legal sense, alienation means selling or giving something away, or as Kant says, "the transference of one's property to someone else is its alienation." In the course of time almost everything became a sellable object. Balzac said ironically that "even the Holy Spirit has its quotation on the Stock Exchange." For Marx there is something crucial within our human nature from which we can be alienated, namely our work.

Marx describes four aspects of alienation. We are alienated (1) from *nature,* (2) from *ourselves,* (3) from our *species-being,* and (4) from *other people.* He begins with the fundamental relation between workers and the product of their labor. Originally, our relation to the product of our labor was quite intimate. We take things from the material world, shape them, and make them our own. Capitalism, though, breaks this relationship by forcing workers to forfeit the products of their labor in exchange for money. In the productive process, a person's labor becomes as much an object as the physical material that is worked upon, since labor is now bought and sold. The more objects I produce, the fewer I can personally possess and therefore the greater is my loss. To the extent that I myself am embodied in my labor, I become alienated from the natural world in which I work. "The worker," says Marx, "puts his life into the object, and his life then belongs no longer to himself but to the object." The object is appropriated and owned by someone else. In this way, the original relation between people and nature is destroyed.

We next become alienated from ourselves by participating in capitalist labor. This comes about because work is *external* to the workers, and not part of our nature. Work is not voluntary but is imposed upon us. We have a feeling of misery instead of well-being. Rather than fulfilling ourselves, we must deny ourselves. We do not freely develop our physical and mental capacities but are instead physically exhausted and mentally debased. As a consequence, we feel like human beings only during our leisure hours. Most important of all, we are alienated from our work because it is not our own work but rather work for someone else. In this sense, workers do not belong to themselves but to someone else, and we have more or less become prostitutes. The result is that a worker "feels himself to be freely active only in his animal functions—eating, drinking and procreating—or at most also in his dwelling and personal adornment—while in his human functions he is reduced to an animal." Although eating, drinking and procreating are genuine human functions, even these become animal functions when separated from our other human functions.

At still another level, people are alienated from their *species*-being—that is, from our truly human nature. The character of any species resides in the type of activity it expresses. The species-character of human beings is "free, conscious activity." By contrast, an animal cannot distinguish itself from its activity. The animal *is* its activity. But, Marx says, a person "makes his life activity itself an object of his will and consciousness." It is true that animals can produce nests and dwellings, as in the case of bees, ants, and beavers. But their production of these things is limited to what is strictly required for themselves or their young. We, on the other hand, produce universally, that is, in a manner that is applicable and understandable to all human beings. Also, whereas animals produce only under the compulsion of specific physical need, we produce our most distinctive products only when we are free from physical need. Animals reproduce only themselves, whereas we can produce a whole world, a world of art, of science and literature. Animals are limited in their activity to the standards of the species to which they belong. We, on the other hand, know how to produce in accordance with the standards of every species. For these reasons, the whole object of our labor is to impose upon the world of nature our species life—our free, spontaneous, and creative activity. In this way we reproduce ourselves in the things we create, not only intellectually in the realm of ideas, but also actively, seeing our own reflection in the physical world that we have created. This unique character of human species-life is lost when our labor is alienated. Just as I am removed from the object of my labor, so also am I stripped of my free and spontaneous activity and creativity. My consciousness is now deflected from creativity and is transferred into simply a means to my individual existence.

This leads to my alienation from other people. The breakdown in my relation to other people is similar to my alienation from the objects of my labor. In an environment of alienated labor we look upon other people from the point of view of workers. We see other workers as objects whose labor is bought and sold, and not as full members of the human species. To say, then, that my species nature is alienated or estranged from me means that I am estranged from other people.

Marx asks, "if the product of labor is alien to me . . . to whom does it belong?" In an earlier age, when temples were built in Egypt and India, ancient people thought that the product belonged to the gods. But, Marx says, the alienated product of labor can belong only to some human being. If it does not belong to the worker, it must belong to a person other than the worker. Thus, as a result of alienated labor workers produce a new relationship between themselves and another person, and this other person is the capitalist. The final product of alienated labor is private property. Private property, in the form of capitalist business, is both a product of alienated labor and also the means by which labor is alienated. In the wage system entailed by private property, labor finds itself not as an end but as the servant of wages. Nor would a forced increase in wages restore to either the workers or to their work their human significance or value. As a statement of eventual liberation, Marx concludes that the freeing of society from private property involves the emancipation of the workers, which in turn will lead to the emancipation of humanity as a whole.

He was convinced that the dialectic process inevitably involves tragic conflicts, wars, and revolutions. He saw in history the deep tension between forces that are incompatible, each exerting its power to overcome the other. The use of revolutionary force could hardly be avoided, but force could not bring into being simply any desired utopian system. Only the relations of production toward which the inner logic of the material order was driving in a determined way could be the objective of revolution. Even when a society is aware of its ultimate direction, this society "can neither clear by bold leaps, nor remove by legal enactments, the obstacles offered by the successive phases of its normal development." What, then, is the function of the revolutionary activities of the working classes? It is, Marx says, to "shorten and lessen the birth-pangs."

With this rigorous view of the nature of the class struggle, Marx clearly assigned to the material substructure the supreme significance in the dialectic process of history. What, then, is the status and role of human thought? Do ideas have power and consequences? For Marx, ideas represent a mere reflection of the basic material reality, and so he described the enterprise of human thought as the *superstructure.*

The Superstructure: The Origin and Role of Ideas

Each epoch, said Marx, has its dominant ideas. People formulate ideas in the areas of religion, morality, and law. Hegel argued that people agreed for the most part in their religious, moral, and legal thought because there was at work in them a universal Spirit, the Idea. Marx, on the contrary, said that the ideas of each epoch grow out of and reflect the actual material conditions of the historical period. For this reason, thinking comes *after* the material order has affected people's minds. In Marx's words, "it is not the consciousness of people that determines their being, but, on the contrary, their social being that determines their consciousness."

The source of ideas is rooted in the material order. Ideas such as justice and goodness and even religious salvation are only various types of rationalizing the existing order. Justice, for the most part, represents the will of the economically dominant class and its desire to "freeze" the relations of production as they are. Marx was impressed during his early years as a law student with the teachings of the jurist Savigny, who defined law as the "spirit" of each epoch. Savigny argued that law is like language and is therefore different for each society. Like Savigny, Marx rejected the notion of a universal and eternal norm of justice. In fact, he argued that if ideas simply reflect the inner order of the relations of production, each successive epoch will have its own set of ideas and its own dominant philosophy.

The conflict of ideas within a society at a given time is due to the dynamic nature of the economic order. The dialectic process, which is a struggle of opposites, has its material aspect but also its ideological side. Since members of a society are related to the dialectic process by belonging to different classes, their interests are different, and therefore their ideas are opposed. Moreover, the greatest error, according to Marx, is to fail to realize that ideas that accurately reflected the material order at an earlier time no longer do so because, in the meantime, the substructure of reality has moved on. Those who hold on to old ideas wrongly believe that some reality still remains that corresponds to the old ideas. Their desire, then, to reverse the order of things to fit these ideas makes them "reactionaries." On the other hand, astute observers can discover the direction in which history is moving and will adjust their thinking and behavior to it. The fact is, Marx says, that the dialectic process involves the disappearance of some things and the birth of new things. That is why one epoch dies and another is born, and there is no way to stop the process. Those who assume the objective reality of eternal principles of justice, goodness, and righteousness do not realize that such notions cannot refer to reality since the material order, which is the only reality, is constantly changing. "The sum total of the productive relations," Marx says, "constitutes the economic structure of society—the real foundation on which rise legal and political superstructure . . . [and which] determines the general character of the social, political and spiritual processes of life."

Because he believed that ideas were chiefly a reflection of the material order, Marx attributed a limited role or function to them. Ideas are particularly useless when they bear no relationship to economic reality. Marx's impatience with reformers, do-gooders, and utopians was intense. He argued that ideas cannot determine the direction of history. Instead, they can only hinder or accelerate the inexorable dialectic. For this reason, Marx thought that his own ideas about capitalism did not constitute a moral condemnation. He did not say that capitalism was either wicked or due to human folly. It was simply caused by the "law of motion of society." In the end, Marx assumed that he was proceeding in his analysis as a scientist, limiting his thought to objective reality, and abstracting from it the laws of motion.

Almost every aspect of Marx's thought raises serious questions. For one thing, he was apparently unaware that at the time he was writing *Das Kapital* the nature of British capitalism was undergoing modifications. His "scientific" style was not adequately supported by empirical observations. Although rejecting traditional metaphysics, he clearly expressed a metaphysical belief in the existence of a predetermined goal for all history. Nevertheless, Marx made a lasting contribution to philosophy, particularly with his conception of alienation.

NIETZSCHE

Friedrich Nietzsche died on August 25, 1900, at the age of 55, leaving a legacy of brilliant writings whose impact and influence were delayed until the 20th century. His life was full of sharp contrasts. The son and grandson of Lutheran ministers, he was nevertheless the herald of the judgment that "God is dead" and undertook a "campaign against morality." He was raised in an environment thoroughly dominated by females, yet his philosophy of the Superperson is anything but nurturing. He called for the fullest expression of human vitality in the name of the Will to Power, yet believed that sublimation and control are the truly human characteristics. His writings rank among the most lucid ever written, although he ended his days in hopeless insanity.

Nietzsche's Life

Named after the reigning King of Prussia, Friedrich Wilhelm Nietzsche was born in Röcken, in the province of Saxony, on October 15, 1844. His father died when he was four years old, and he grew up in a household consisting of his mother, sister, grandmother, and two maiden aunts. At age 14 he was sent to the famed boarding school at Pforta, where for six years he underwent a rigorous education, excelling particularly in the classics, religion, and German literature. It was here that he came under the spell of the ancient Greek thought, discovering it especially in Aeschylus and Plato. In October of 1864 he went to the University of Bonn but stayed only one year as he was unimpressed by the caliber of his fellow students. He decided to follow his excellent teacher of classics and philology, Friedrich Ritschl, who was invited to accept a chair at the University of Leipzig. While at Leipzig he came upon the main work of Schopenhauer, whose atheism and antirationalism deeply influenced Nietzsche for a while and confirmed his own revolt against contemporary European culture, which he came to despise as decadent. It was here also that Nietzsche came under the spell of Wagner's music. "I could not have stood my youth without Wagner's music," Nietzsche said later. "When one wants to rid oneself of an intolerable pressure, one needs hashish. Well, I needed Wagner."

When the University of Basel was looking for someone to fill the chair of philosophy, Nietzsche's name figured prominently. He had not yet completed his doctor's degree, but some of his published papers attracted notice for their exceptional scholarship. On the additional strength of his teacher's enthusias-

Friedrich Nietzsche
(Corbis)

tic recommendation, Nietzsche was appointed a university professor at the age of 24. After the University of Basel confirmed his appointment, the University of Leipzig conferred the doctor's degree upon Nietzsche without examination. In May, 1869, he delivered his inaugural lecture on *Homer and Classical Philology*. During his years at Basel, Nietzsche visited Richard Wagner frequently at his villa on Lake Lucerne. While this friendship was not destined to last, Wagner did exert an influence upon Nietzsche's thought in his first book (1872), *The Birth of Tragedy from the Spirit of Music*. Of longer duration was Nietzsche's friendship with his older colleague, the eminent historian Jacob Burckhardt, with whom he shared a common fascination for ancient Greece and Renaissance Italy. Nietzsche's wretched health and his dislike of his duties at the university led him to resign his professorship in 1879 at the age of 34. For the next decade, he wandered through Italy, Switzerland, and Germany searching for some place where his health might be restored. In spite of his poor health, he wrote several books during the six-year period from 1881–1887, including *The Dawn of Day, Joyful Wisdom*, the famous *Thus Spake Zarathustra, Beyond Good and Evil,* and *A Genealogy of Morals.*

In 1888, when he was 44, Nietzsche felt a brief period of respite from his prolonged cycle of sickness and recovery. During a span of six months he produced five books with incredible speed, namely, *The Case of Wagner, The Twilight of the Idols, Antichrist, Ecce Homo,* and *Nietzsche contra Wagner.* Shortly thereafter, in January 1889, Nietzsche collapsed on a street in Turin. He was taken back to Basel to a clinic. From there he was sent to an asylum in Jena and finally to the care of his mother and sister. For the last 11 years of his life, Nietzsche was irretrievably insane as a result of an infection that affected his brain. He was thus unable to complete his projected major work, the *Revaluation of All Values.* Nietzsche's books have great vivacity of style and are written with a passionate intensity. Even though some of his later works show signs of impending difficulties, scholars generally agree that we should not discount his writings because of his subsequent mental collapse.

"God Is Dead"

Nietzsche wrote philosophy in a manner calculated more to provoke serious thought than to give formal answers to questions. In this regard he resembled Socrates and Plato more than Spinoza, Kant, or Hegel. He produced no formal system because system building, he thought, assumes that we have at hand self-evident truths upon which to build. He also believed that building a system is to lack integrity, since honest thought must challenge precisely these self-evident truths upon which most systems are built. We must engage in dialectic and be willing at times to declare ourselves against our previous opinions. Moreover, most philosophic system builders, he thought, try to solve all problems at once by acting as the "unriddler of the universe." Nietzsche believed that the philosopher must be less pretentious and pay more attention to questions of human values than to abstract systems. Philosophers should also focus on immediate human problems with an attitude of fresh experimentation and a freedom from the dominant values of his culture. Nietzsche took a variety of positions on important problems, and because of this it is easy to interpret his views in contradictory ways. Moreover, he expressed his views on issues with brief aphorisms instead of detailed analyses, leaving the impression of ambiguity and ambivalence. Still, Nietzsche formulated many distinctive views, which emerge from his writings with considerable clarity.

While others saw in 19th-century Europe the symbols of power and security, Nietzsche grasped with prophetic insight the imminent collapse of the traditional supports of the values to which modern people committed themselves. The Prussian army made Germany a great power on the Continent, and the astonishing advances in science further animated the feeling of optimism. Nevertheless, Nietzsche boldly prophesied that power politics and vicious wars were in store for the future. He sensed an approaching period of *nihilism,* the seeds of which had already been sown. He did not base this either on the military power of Germany or the unfolding advances of science. Instead, he was influenced by the incontrovertible fact that belief in the Christian God had drastically declined to the point where he could confidently say that "God is dead."

Although Nietzsche was an atheist, he reflected on the "death" of God with mixed reactions. He was appalled at the consequences that would follow once everyone would become fully aware of all the implications of the death of God. He thought about both the collapse of religious faith and the mounting belief in the Darwinian notion of a relentless evolution of the species. He could see in this combination the destruction of any basic distinction between human and animal. If this is what we are asked to believe, then we should not be surprised when the future brings us colossal wars such as we have never seen before on earth. At the same time, the death of God meant for Nietzsche the opening of a new day—a day when the essentially life-denying ethics of Christianity could be replaced with a life-affirming philosophy. "At last," he said, "the sea, *our* sea, lies open before us. Perhaps there has never been so open a sea." His ambivalent reaction to the nihilistic consequences of the death of God turned Nietzsche to the central question of human values. In his search for a new foundation for values in a day when God could no longer be the goal and sanction of human conduct, Nietzsche believed that aesthetics was the most promising alternative to religion. Only as an aesthetic phenomenon, he said, are human existence and the world eternally justified. The Greeks, he believed, originally discovered the true meaning of human effort. He initially drew his fundamental insights about human nature from the Greek conceptions of Apollo and Dionysus.

The Apollonian versus Dionysian

Nietzsche believed that aesthetic value results from a fusion between two principles, which are respectively represented by the two Greek gods, Apollo and Dionysus. Dionysus symbolized the dynamic stream of life, which knows no restraints or barriers and defies all limitations. Worshipers of Dionysus would lapse into a drunken frenzy and thereby lose their own identity in the larger ocean of life. Apollo, on the other hand, was the symbol of order, restraint, and form. If the Dionysian attitude is best expressed in the feeling of abandonment in some types of music, then the Apollonian form-giving force found its highest expression in Greek sculpture. Thus Dionysus symbolized humanity's unity with life where individuality is absorbed in the larger reality of the life force. Apollo, then, was the symbol of the "principle of individuation"—the power that controls and restrains the dynamic processes of life in order to create a formed work of art or a controlled personal character. From another point of view, the Dionysian represents the negative and destructive dark powers of the soul, which, when unchecked, culminate in "that disgusting mixture of voluptuousness and cruelty" typical of "the most savage beasts of nature." The Apollonian, by contrast, represents the power to deal with the powerful surge of vital energy, to harness destructive powers, and to transmute these into a creative act.

Dionysus, symbol of the power of dynamic passions, whose devotees drank the fruit of the vine and engaged in sensuous and frenzied dance
(Hirmer Fotoarchiv, Munich)

Apollo and His Chariot with the Hours by John Singer Sargent, symbol of restraint, order, and rational control of the powerful passions
(Francis Bartlett Donation of 1912/Courtesy, Museum of Fine Arts, Boston)

Greek tragedy, according to Nietzsche, is a great work of art. It represents the conquest of Dionysus by Apollo. But from this account Nietzsche drew the conclusion that people are not faced with a choice between the Dionysian and the Apollonian. To assume that we even have such a choice to make is to misunderstand the true nature of the human condition. The fact is that human life inevitably includes the dark and surging forces of passion. What Greek tragedy illustrates, according to Nietzsche, is that instead of abandoning oneself to the flood of impulse, instinct, and passion, the awareness of these driving forces becomes the occasion for producing a work of art. This would be so whether in our own character through moderation or in literature or the plastic arts through the imposition of form upon a resisting material. Nietzsche saw the birth of tragedy—that is, the creation of art—as a response of the basically healthy element in a person, the Apollonian, to the challenge of the diseased frenzy of the Dionysian. In this view, art could not occur without the stimulus of the Dionysian. At the same time, if the Dionysian were considered either the only element in human nature or the dominant element, we might very well despair and come finally to a negative attitude toward life. But for Nietzsche, the supreme achievement of human nature occurred in Greek culture where the Dionysian and Apollonian elements were brought together. Nineteenth-century culture denied that the Dionysian element had a rightful place in life. For Nietzsche, though, this only postponed the inevitable explosion of vital forces, which cannot be permanently denied expression. To ask whether life should dominate knowledge or knowledge dominate life is to provoke the question concerning which of these two is the higher and more decisive power. There is no doubt, Nietzsche argued, that life is the higher and dominating power, but raw vital power is finally life-defeating. For this reason, Nietzsche looked to the Greek formula—the fusion of the Dionysian and Apollonian elements—by which human life is transformed into an aesthetic phenomenon. Such a formula, Nietzsche thought, could provide modern culture with a relevant and workable standard of behavior at a time when religious faith was unable to provide a compelling vision of human destiny. What disqualified religious faith, he believed, was the essentially life-denying negativeness of the Christian ethics.

Master Morality versus Slave Morality

Nietzsche rejected the notion that there is a universal and absolute system of morality that everyone must equally obey. People are different, and to conceive of morality in universal terms is to disregard basic differences between individuals. It is unrealistic to assume that there is only one kind of human nature, whose direction can be prescribed by one set of rules. Whenever we propose a universal moral rule, we invariably seek to deny the fullest expression of our elemental vital energies. In this respect, Judaism and Christianity are the worst offenders. Judeo-Christian ethics, he argues, is so contrary to our basic nature that its antinatural morality debilitates humanity and produces only "botched and bungled" lives.

How did human beings ever produce such unnatural systems of ethics? There is, Nietzsche says, a "twofold early history of good and evil," which shows the development of two primary types of morality. These are the *master morality* and the *slave morality*. In the *master morality*, "good" always meant "noble" in the sense of "with a soul of high calibre." "Evil," by contrast, meant "vulgar" or "plebeian." Noble people regard themselves as the creators and determiners of values. They do not look outside of themselves for any approval of their acts. They pass judgment upon themselves. Their morality is one of self-glorification. These noble individuals act out of a feeling of power, which seeks to overflow. It is not out of pity that they help the unfortunate, but rather from an impulse generated by an abundance of power. They honor power in all its forms and take pleasure in subjecting themselves to rigor and toughness. They also have reverence for all that is severe and hard. By contrast, the *slave morality* originates with the lowest elements of society: the abused, the oppressed, the slaves, and those who are uncertain of themselves. For the slave, "good" is the symbol for all those qualities that serve to alleviate the existence of sufferers, such as "sympathy, the kind helping hand, the warm heart, patience, diligence, humility and friendliness." This slave morality, Nietzsche argues, is essentially the morality of utility, since moral goodness involves whatever is beneficial to those who are weak and powerless. With the slave morality, the person who arouses fear is "evil," but with the master morality it is in fact the "good" person who is able to arouse fear.

This revenge took the form of translating the virtues of the noble aristocrat into evils. Nietzsche's great protest against the dominant Western morality was that it exalted the mediocre values of the "herd," which "knows nothing of the fine impulses of great accumulations of strength, as something high, or possibly as the standard of all things." Incredibly, the "herd mentality" in time overcame the master morality by succeeding in making all the noble qualities appear to be vices, and all the weak qualities appear to be virtues. The positive affirmation of life in the master morality was made to seem "evil" and something for which one should have a sense of "guilt." The fact is, Nietzsche says, that

> men with a still natural nature, barbarians in every terrible sense of the word, men of prey, still in possession of unbroken strength of will and desire for power, threw themselves upon weaker, more moral, more peaceful races. . . .
> At the commencement, the noble caste was always the barbarian caste: their superiority did not consist first of all in their physical, but in their psychical power—they were *complete* men.

But the power of the master race was broken by the undermining of its psychological strength. Against the natural impulse to exert aggressive strength, the weak races erected elaborate psychic defenses. New values and new ideals, such as peace and equality, were put forward under the guise of "the fundamental principle of society." This, Nietzsche said, was a not-so-subtle desire on the part of the weak to undermine the power of the strong. The weak have created a negative psychological attitude toward the most natural human drives. This slave morality is, Nietzsche says, "a Will to the *denial* of life, a principle of dissolution and decay." But, he continues, a skillful psychological analysis of the herd's resentment and its desire to exact revenge against the strong will show what must be done. That is, we must "resist all sentimental weakness: life is essentially appropriation, injury, conquest of the strange and weak, suppression, severity, obtrusion of peculiar forms . . . and at the least, putting it mildest, exploitation."

The Will to Power

Exploitation, according to Nietzsche, is not some inherently degenerate human action. Instead, it belongs "to the nature of the living being as a primary function." Exploitation is "a consequence of the intrinsic Will to Power, which is precisely the Will to Life—a *fundamental fact* of all history." The Will to Power is a central drive within human nature to dominate one's environment. This is more than simply the will to survive. It is, rather, an inner impulse to vigorously affirm all of our individual powers. As Nietzsche says, "the strongest and highest Will to Life does not find expression in a miserable struggle for existence, but in a Will to War. A Will to Power, a Will to Overpower!"

European morality denies the central role of the Will to Power—and does so in a dishonest manner. Nietzsche puts the blame for this upon the slavish morality of Christianity. He writes, "I regard Christianity as the most fatal and seductive lie that has ever yet existed—as the greatest and most *impious lie.*" He was appalled that Europe should be subjected to the morality of that small group of wretched outcasts who clustered around Jesus. Imagine, he said, "the *morality of paltry people* as the measure of all things." This he considered "the most repugnant kind of degeneracy that civilization has ever brought into existence." To Nietzsche it was incredible that in the New Testament "the least qualified people . . . have their say in its pages in regard to the greatest problems of existence." Christianity contradicts nature when it requires us to love our enemies, since nature's injunction is to *hate* our enemies. Moreover, Christianity denies the natural origin of morality since it requires us to first love God before we can love anything. By injecting God into our affections, we subvert the immediate and natural moral standard that involves affirming life. By diverting our thinking toward God, we dilute our strongest and most vital energies. Nietzsche admitted that the "spiritual" people of Christianity performed invaluable services to Europe by offering comfort and courage to the suffering. But at what price was Christian charity achieved? The price, Nietzsche writes, was "the deterioration of the European race." It was necessary "to *reverse* all estimates of value—*that* is what they had to do! And to shatter the strong, to spoil great hopes, to cast suspicion on the delight in beauty, to break down everything autonomous, manly, conquering, and imperious." Christianity thus succeeded in inverting "all love of the earthly and of supremacy over the earth into hatred of the earth and earthly things. . . ."

Nietzsche was willing for the weak herd to have their own morality, provided that they did not impose it upon the higher ranks of humanity. Why should people of great creative abilities be reduced to the common level of mediocrity characteristic of the herd? Nietzsche spoke of rising "beyond good and evil," by which he meant rising above the dominant herd morality of his day. He envisioned a new day when, once again, the truly complete person would achieve new levels of creative activity and thereby become a higher type of person—the Superperson (Übermensch). This new person will not reject morality; he or she will reject only the negative morality of the herd. Again, Nietzsche argued that the morality based upon the Will to Power is only an honest version of what the slave morality has carefully disguised. If the Superperson is "cruel," Nietzsche said, we must recognize that, actually, almost everything that we now call "higher culture" is simply a spiritualized intensification of cruelty. "This is my thesis," he said, that "the 'wild beast' has not been slain at all, it lives, it flourishes, it has only been—transfigured." For example, ancient Romans took pleasure in the gladiatorial contests. Christians experience ecstasies of the cross. Spaniards delight at the gory sight of the bullfight. French workers are homesick for a bloody revolution. These are all expressions of cruelty.

From the vantage point of the master morality, the word *cruelty* refers simply to the basic Will to Power, which is a natural expression of strength. People are differentiated into ranks, and it is only quantity of power that determines and distinguishes one's rank. Thus, ideals such as political and social equality are nonsensical. There can be no equality where there are in fact different degrees of power. Equality can only mean the leveling downward of everyone to the mediocrity of the herd. Nietzsche wanted to preserve the natural distinction between two types of people, namely, between that "type which represents ascending life and a type which represents decadence, decomposition, weakness." To be sure, a higher culture will always require mediocre herd, but only to make possible the development and emergence of the Superperson. If the Superperson is to emerge, he or she must go beyond good and evil as conceived by the lower ranks.

Revaluation of All Morals

What does Nietzsche want to put in the place of traditional morality, which he believed was clearly dying? His positive recommendations are not so clear as his critical analysis. However, we can infer much of the content of his new values from his rejection of the slave morality. If the slave morality originated in resentment and revenge, there must again occur a *revaluation* of all values. By *revaluation* Nietzsche did not mean the creation of a new table of moral values. He meant rather to declare war upon the presently accepted values, as Socrates, "applying the knife vivisectionally to the very virtues of the time." Since traditional morality is a perversion of original natural morality, *revaluation* must consist in rejecting traditional morality in the name of honesty and accuracy. Revaluation implies that all the "stronger motives are still extant, but that now they appear under false names and false valuations, and have not yet become conscious of themselves." It is not necessary to legislate new values but only to reverse values once again. Just as "Christianity was a revaluation of all the values of antiquity," so today the dominant morality must be rejected in favor of our original and deepest nature. Thus Nietzsche's plan of *revaluation* was essentially a critical analysis of modern human ideals. He showed that what modern people called "good" was not at all virtuous. Their so-called truth was disguised selfishness and weakness, and their religion was a skillful creation of psychological weapons with which moral pygmies domesticated natural giants. Once the disguise is removed from modern morality, then true values will emerge.

In the final analysis, moral values must be built upon our true human nature and our environment. Unlike Darwin, who laid great stress upon external circumstances when describing the evolution of the species, Nietzsche focused upon the internal power within an individual, which is capable of shaping and creating events—"a power which *uses* and *exploits* the environment." Nietzsche's grand hypothesis was that everywhere and in everything the Will to Power seeks to express itself. "This world," he says, "is the Will to Power—and nothing else." Life itself is a multiplicity of forces, "a lasting form of processes of assertions of force." People's psychological makeup shows that our preoccupation with pleasure and pain reflects a striving toward an increase of power. Pain can be the spur for exerting power to overcome an obstacle, whereas pleasure can involve a feeling of increased power.

The Superperson

Nietzsche's notion of the Will to Power is most clearly represented in the attitudes and behavior of the Superperson. We have already seen that Nietzsche rejected the concept of equality. He also showed that morality must suit each rank. Even after the *revaluation* of all values, the "common herd" will not be intellectually capable of reaching the heights of the "free spirits." In short, there can be no "common good." Great things, Nietzsche says, remain for the great, "everything rare for the rare." The Superperson will be rare, but he is the next stage in human evolution. History is moving not toward some abstract developed "humanity" but toward the emergence of some exceptional people: the *Superperson* is the goal. But the Superperson will not be the product of a mechanical process of evolution. The next stage can be reached only when superior people have the courage to revalue all values and respond with freedom to their internal Will to Power. Human beings need to be surpassed, and it is the Superperson who represents the highest level of development and expression of physical, intellectual, and emotional strength. The Superperson will be the truly free person for whom nothing is forbidden except what obstructs the Will to Power. The Superperson will be the very embodiment of the spontaneous affirmation of life.

Nietzsche did not think that his Superperson would be a tyrant. To be sure, there would be much of the Dionysian element within the Superperson. But these passions would be controlled, thereby harmonizing the animal nature with the intellect, and giving style to his or her behavior. We should not confuse such a Superperson with a totalitarian bully. As a model, Nietzsche had in mind his hero Goethe, as well as "the Roman Caesar with Christ's soul." As Nietzsche's thought matured, his ideal person would have to possess a balanced unity of the Dionysian and Apollonian elements. Earlier, when Wagner and Schopenhauer influenced his thought, Nietzsche criticized Socrates for having caused Western thought to take a wrong turn toward rationality. In later years, he gained a greater appreciation for rationality. Even at the end, though, he believed that rationality must be used in the service of life and that life must not be sacrificed for knowledge. Still, Socrates was important historically precisely because he saved people from self-destruction. The lust for life, he says, would then have led to wars of annihilation. The Dionysian element by itself leads to pessimism and destruction. So it was necessary to harness people's energies, which required the kind of influence that Socrates provided. Although the Apollonian element of rationality risks subverting the vital streams of life, Nietzsche nevertheless believed that we cannot engage in life without some rational form-giving guidance. Socrates became important for Nietzsche precisely because this ancient philosopher was the first to see the proper relation between thought and life. Socrates recognized that thought serves life, while for previous philosophers, life served thought and knowledge. Here, then, was Nietzsche's ideal: the passionate person who has his or her passions under control.

PART FIVE

20th-Century and Contemporary Philosophy

In Praise of Dialectic, René Magritte (1898–1967)
National Gallery of Victoria, Australia

CHAPTER 16

Pragmatism and Process Philosophy

A major theme in 19th-century thought is that the world is continually changing. Hegel believed that human history and everything around us is part of an ever-developing absolute Mind. Darwin argued that all biological life—and even human social institutions—evolve from simple to more complex forms. As philosophy rounded the corner from the 19th to the 20th century, the notion of change remained an important part of intellectual thought. Two philosophical movements in particular focus on change, namely Pragmatism and Process Philosophy. Both approaches deny that there are fixed and unchanging truths; instead we should understand things in terms of changing experiences and metaphysical processes.

Pragmatism emerged at the end of the 19th century as the most original contribution of American thought to the enterprise of philosophy. This movement received its initial theoretical formulation by Charles S. Peirce (1839–1914). It received wide and popular circulation through the brilliant and lucid essays of William James (1842–1910). It was then methodically implemented into the daily affairs of American institutions by John Dewey (1859–1952). The central message of these three philosophers is that there is little value in philosophical theories that do not somehow make a difference in daily life. Pragmatism was more of a method of solving problems than it was a metaphysical system of the world. Process Philosophy, though, did offer a specific vision of the nature of things. Many writers, including some later pragmatists, are associated with process philosophy. The two leading proponents, though, are French philosopher Henri-Louis Bergson (1859–1941) and British philosopher Alfred North Whitehead (1861–1947).

PRAGMATISM

As a movement in philosophy, pragmatism was founded for the purpose of mediating between two divergent tendencies in 19th-century thought. On the one hand, there was the cumulative impact of empiricism, utilitarianism, and science, to which Darwin's theory of evolution gave the most recent and striking claim to authoritative thought about human nature. The drift of this tradition was that human nature and the world were simply parts of a mechanical and biological process. On the other hand, there was a more human-centered tradition, stemming from Descartes' rationalistic philosophy and moving through Kant, Hegel, and other German idealists. Between these two traditions there was an ever-widening gulf. Empirical philosophers and scientists rejected much rationalistic and idealistic philosophy because it lacked objective evidence. From the rational and idealistic points of view, science threatened moral and religious convictions, and a general sense of human purpose.

Pragmatism mediated between these traditions, combining what was most significant in each of them. With the empirical tradition, the pragmatists agreed that we have no conception of the whole of reality. We know things from many perspectives, and we must settle for a multifaceted approach to knowledge. With the rationalists and idealists, they agreed that morality, religion, and human purpose constitute a significant aspect of our experience. Peirce, James, and Dewey each expressed a different aspect of pragmatism. Peirce was initially interested in logic and science, James wrote about psychology and religion, and Dewey was absorbed with the problems of ethics and social thought. They were all contemporaries, they all came from New England, and they were highly skilled academicians.

PEIRCE

Charles Sanders Peirce (pronounced *purse*) was born in Cambridge, Massachusetts, in 1839, where his father was a noted Harvard professor of mathematics. He was educated in mathematics, science, and philosophy both at home under his father's discipline and at Harvard College, where between the ages of 16 and 20 he was a student. After receiving an M.A. in mathematics and chemistry, he worked for three years at the Harvard astronomical observatory and published his photometric researches in 1878. For 30 years, from 1861 to 1891, he was associated with the United States Coastal and Geodetic Survey. He was also for a short period a lecturer in logic at Johns Hopkins University. But Peirce was never a full-time member of a university faculty, presumably because his brilliance was overshadowed by personal eccentricities. Without an academic position, he encountered resistance and indifference from publishers, so that very little of his total literary output appeared during his lifetime, and he received virtually none of the fame to which his abilities entitled him. Decades after his death, his works were collected and organized into several volumes, which stand now as a prodigious achievement of creative thought. In his declining years, Peirce was in financial difficulties, failing health, and virtual social rejection. His loyal friend throughout these difficulties was William James, who not only assisted him, but became the channel through which Peirce's original thoughts about pragmatism found their way into the thought of a whole generation throughout the world.

A Theory of Meaning

At the heart of Peirce's pragmatism is a new explanation of how words acquire their meanings. He coined the word *pragmatism* from the Greek word *pragma* (meaning "act" or "deed") in order to emphasize the fact that words derive their meanings from actions of some sort. Our ideas are clear and distinct only when we are able to translate them into some type of operation. For example, the adjectives *hard* and *heavy* have meaning only because we are able to conceive of some specific effects that are associated with these terms. Thus, *hard* means that which cannot be scratched by many other substances, and *heavy* means that which will fall if we let go of it. Underscoring the decisive role of *effects* in the meanings of words, Peirce argued that there would be absolutely no difference between a hard thing and a soft thing as long as they did not test differently. From such simple examples, Peirce generalized about the nature of meaning and knowledge in general. His basic point was that "our idea of anything *is* our idea of its sensible effects." That is, if words are to have any meaning, we must be able to use the operational formula, which says "if *A* then *B*." This says when specific objects are present, we can expect specific effects to follow. Thus, a word is has no meaning if it refers to an object about which no practical effects can be conceived.

Peirce was highly influenced by the language of science, since it is particularly scientific language that satisfies this pragmatic test for meaning. He was arguing against rationalist theories, which held that validity was based solely upon the consistency between ideas themselves, with no reference to outside things. Earlier empiricists tried to show the shortcomings of rationalism, but Peirce found the assumptions of rationalism still very much alive. Descartes, for example, believed that intellectual certainty consisted in "clear and distinct" ideas, which we grasped by intuition. As such, our minds are purely theoretical instruments that could operate successfully in isolation from environmental circumstances. Against all of these assumptions, Peirce argued that thinking always occurs in a context, not in isolation from it. We do not derive meanings through intuition, but by experience or experiment. Thus, meanings are not individual or private but social and public. Again, if there is no way of testing ideas by their effects or public consequences, such ideas are meaningless. He believed that it was most important to distinguish between meaningful and meaningless contentions, particularly when we are torn between opposing systems of thought.

The Role of Belief

Peirce argued that belief occupies a middle position between thought and action. Beliefs guide our desires and shape our actions. But beliefs are "unfixed" by doubts. It is when the "irritation of doubt" causes a struggle to attain belief that the enterprise of thought begins. Through thought, we try to fix our beliefs so that we have a guide for action. There are several ways in which we can fix our beliefs, according to Peirce. There is the method of *tenacity,* whereby people cling to beliefs, refusing to entertain doubts about them or to consider arguments or evidence for another view. Another method is to invoke *authority,* as when people in authority require the acceptance of certain ideas under threat of punishment. Still another method is that of the metaphysician or philosopher such as Plato, Descartes, or Hegel, who, according to Peirce, settles questions of belief by asking whether an idea was "agreeable to *reason.*" Peirce found himself in disagreement with all of these methods precisely because they could not achieve their intent, namely, to fix or settle belief. What they all lacked was some connection with experience and behavior.

Peirce therefore offered a fourth method, the method of *science,* whose chief virtue was its realistic basis in experience. The above-mentioned methods of *tenacity, authority,* and *reason* all rest upon what we possess within our own minds as a consequence solely of our thinking. The method of science, by contrast, is built on the assumption that there are real things, which are entirely independent of our opinions about them. Moreover, because these real things affect our senses according to regular laws, we can assume that they will affect each observer the same way. Beliefs that are grounded in real things can therefore be verified, and their "fixation" can be a public act rather than a private one. There is in fact no way to agree or disagree with a conclusion arrived at by means of the first three methods. All three attempts refer to nothing whose consequences or real existences can be tested. The method of tenacity is clearly irrational. The method of authority precludes argument. The method of *a priori* reasoning, because it occurs in isolation from facts, permits the affirmation of several different explanations of things, as was the case with the alternative metaphysical systems produced by the Continental rationalists.

The Elements of Method

As a means of resolving conflicts between alternative beliefs, Peirce recommended the scientific method, which he felt combats personal prejudice. For one thing, the method of science requires that we state not only what truth we believe but also how we arrived at it. The procedures followed should be available to anyone who cares to retrace the same steps to test whether the same results will occur. Peirce continually emphasizes this public or community character of the method of science. Second, the method of science is highly self-critical. It subjects its conclusions to severe tests, and wherever shown, the conclusions of a theory are adjusted to fit the new evidence and new insights. This, Peirce says, ought also to be our attitude toward all of our beliefs. Third, Peirce felt that science requires a high degree of cooperation among all members of the scientific community. Such cooperation prevents any individual or group from shaping truth to fit its own interests. Conclusions of science, then, must be conclusions that all scientists can draw. Similarly, in questions of belief and truth, it should be possible for anyone to come to the same conclusions. This method of empirical inquiry means that there must be some practical consequence of any legitimate idea.

William James
(Culver Pictures, Inc.)

JAMES

The rich flavor of William James's writings reflects the equally rich quality and breadth of his life. Born in New York City in 1842, he grew up in a cultured family, which produced not only the outstanding American philosopher, but also his brother Henry James, the gifted novelist. William James studied at Harvard and traveled to universities throughout Europe, acquiring a broad outlook both culturally and intellectually. He received his M.D. degree from the Harvard Medical School in 1869 and was appointed to its faculty in 1872 as an instructor in physiology. From medicine, James moved to psychology and philosophy, producing in 1890 his famous *Principles of Psychology*. He was a member of the Harvard department of philosophy, which included George Santayana and Josiah Royce. Although he did not write any philosophical treatise comparable in scope to his famous book on psychology, he published a great many definitive essays, which singly and as collections in book form were read throughout the world. By the time of his death in 1910 at the age of 68, James fashioned a new approach to philosophy and managed to communicate his pragmatic principles to an unusually wide audience. Starting from the work already done by Peirce, he took a fresh look at pragmatism and developed it along novel lines. Among the important topics to which James turned his attention, we will examine four. These are (1) the pragmatic method, (2) the pragmatic theory of truth, (3) the problem of free will, and (4) the function of the human will in the belief process.

Pragmatism as a Method

James thought that "the whole function of philosophy ought to be to find out what definite difference it will make to you and me, at definite instants of our life, if this world-formula or that word-formula be the true one." He emphasized concrete concerns of life, specifically facts and actions as they affect our lives now and the future. But pragmatism as such contained no substance or content, and no special information about human purpose or destiny. As a philosophy, pragmatism did not have its own creed. It did not, as such, offer a world formula.

"Pragmatism," James writes, "is a method only." Still, as a method, pragmatism assumed that human life has a purpose and that rival theories about human nature and the world need to be tested against this purpose. According to James, there is in fact no single definition of human purpose. Instead, our understanding of human purpose is part of the activity of thinking. Philosophical thinking arises when we want to understand things and the setting in which they live; purpose derives its meaning from a sense of being at home in the universe. James rejected rationalism chiefly because it was dogmatic and presumed to give conclusive answers about the world in terms that frequently left the issues of life untouched. By contrast, pragmatism "has no dogmas and no doctrines save its method." As a method, pragmatism takes its cue from the newly discovered facts of life. We should not accept as final any formulations in science, theology, or philosophy, but instead see them as only approximations. The value of any theory rests in its capacity to solve problems, and not in its internal verbal consistency. Instead of mere consistency, James writes, "you must bring out of each word its practical cash value"—that is we must focus on *results*. When we find a theory that does not make a difference one way or another for practical life, then the theory is meaningless and we should abandon it.

The Pragmatic Theory of Truth

Establishing the meaning of a concept is one thing and establishing its truth is another. For example, it may be meaningful for me to hold to the view that the CIA is watching every move that I make. From a pragmatic standpoint, this contention is meaningful if it produces some kind of consequence—such as various activities among CIA agents, and even some impact on how I conduct my private life. However, this does not mean that the CIA is truly watching me. A test for truth is pickier than a test for mere meaning. Even here, though, pragmatism offers a method. James first rejects standard theories of truth, such as what is now called the *correspondence* theory of truth: an idea is true if it corresponds to reality. This theory assumes that an idea "copies" *reality*, and an idea is therefore true if it copies what is "out there" accurately. According to James, though, on this theory "truth means essentially an inert static relation. When you've got your true idea of anything, there's an end of the matter. You're in possession; you *know*." But truth, according to James, is less fixed than this. Similar to the theory of meaning, truth involves asking "what concrete difference will its being true make in anyone's actual life?"

As an example of the pragmatic theory of truth, James asks us to consider a clock on the wall. We consider it to be a clock not because we have a copy-view of it. The so-called "reality" of the clock consists of its internal mechanism, which we cannot see. Our idea of the clock consists mainly of its face and hands, which in no way matches "reality." Still, our limited idea of the clock passes for true because we *use* this conception as a clock and as such it *works*. Some practical consequences of this idea are that we can lecture "on time" and catch the train. We could scientifically verify aspects of our idea, such as inspecting the internal components of the clock. In point of fact, though, we rarely do this. What more would be added to the truth of our idea that the object before me is a clock than we already have in the successful regulation of our behavior? James writes, "for one truth-process completed there are a million in our lives that function in this state of nascency." Truth, then, lives "on a credit system."

Ideas become true insofar as they help us to make successful connections among various parts of our experience. Truth is therefore part of the process of living. As part of a process, successful experiences *make* truth, and this constitutes the verification process. Advocates of the correspondence theory believe that truths are absolute in the sense that there is a real clock on the wall whether anyone sees it or not. For James, though, questions about the "truth" of the clock arise only in actual life when we live "as if" that thing on the wall is a clock. Our successful behavior *makes* the truth of the clock. There is, then, no single absolute truth, but instead there are as many truths as there are concrete successful actions. James distinguished between what he called *tough-minded* and *tender-minded* approaches to truth. A tough-minded pragmatist would only look at more scientific kinds of successful behavior in the truth process. For example, my concept of the clock is true because I show up to events at the proper time, and I can check my notion of the clock against the time indicated by other clocks. A tender-minded pragmatist, though, would consider less scientific behavior in the truth process. For example, without scientifically analyzing things, my concept of the clock is true if it serves its principal function in organizing my daily routine. James believed that both the tough and tender-minded approaches to truth were valid in their own ways.

We can't all be scientists. But this does not mean that truth is whimsical. Even with the tender-minded approach a true belief must work beneficially, just as an untrue one will work destructively. For example, an imaginary clock will not do a good job of organizing my daily schedule, and will in fact adversely affect my routine.

If we ask the pragmatist why anyone *ought* to seek the truth, James answers that "our obligation to seek the truth is part of our general obligation to do what pays," just as one ought to seek health because it pays to be healthy. Above all, James thought that the pragmatic theory of truth could bring a desperately needed service to philosophy by providing a means for settling disputes. Some disputes cannot be resolved if each party simply affirms that his views are true. James would ask, which theory fits the facts of real life? One such dispute, which has exercised philosophers through the ages, is the question of freedom versus determinism.

Free Will

William James was convinced that we cannot rationally prove that human will is either free or determined. We will only find equally good arguments for each side of the dispute. He was nevertheless convinced that the pragmatic method would shed new light on the problem. The crucial practical question here is, what difference does it make in actual life to accept one or the other side of a dispute? The issue is worth investigating since it involves something important about life: either we are mechanically driven by physical forces or we have the power to shape at least some of our life events as we see fit. For James this was not simply an interesting puzzle. His whole philosophical orientation revolved around this problem of the role and status of the will. He was greatly concerned about human action and choosing those ideas and types of behavior with the highest cash value. Accordingly, he saw philosophy in terms of human striving, and this, he was convinced, indicated a certain kind of universe.

According to James, the issue of free will "relates solely to the existence of possibilities," of things that may, but need not, be. The determinist says that there are no ambiguous or uncertain possibilities, and that what will be will be. On this view, "those parts of the universe already laid down absolutely appoint and decree what the other parts shall be. The future has no ambiguous possibilities in its womb." On the other hand, the indeterminist says that there is some "loose play" in the universe, and that the present arrangement of things does not necessarily determine what the future will be. Here, then, are two contradictory points of view. What divides us into *possibility* people and *anti-possibility* people? The answer is differing claims of rationality. For some it seems more rational to say that all events are set down from eternity, whereas for others it seems more rational to assume that people can engage in genuine choice. If both of these points of view seem equally rational to their respective proponents, how can the dispute be resolved?

To solve the problem, according to James, we simply ask the pragmatic question, what does a deterministic world imply? That is, what kind of universe are we living in if all events without exception are rigorously determined from the beginning of time so that they could not have happened in any other way? We could only answer that such a universe is like a machine, where each part fits tightly and all the gears are interlocked, so that the slightest motion of one part causes a motion of every other part. There is no loose play in the machine. But James feels that we are not just mechanical parts in a huge machine. What makes us different is our consciousness. For one thing, we are capable of judgments of regret. For example, someone may regret caving into peer pressure during high school, failing to study during college, or doing a poor job at work. But how can we regret anything if events were rigidly fixed and we could not have done otherwise?

Not only do we make judgments of regret, but we make moral judgments of approval and disapproval. We persuade others to do some actions and avoid others. We also punish or reward people for their actions. All these forms of judgment imply that we constantly face genuine choices. A forced or determined act is simply not a choice. In actual practical life, we see others and ourselves as vulnerable. People are capable of lying, stealing, and killing. We judge these to be wrong, not only in retrospect, but wrong because we feel that they were not inevitable when they were done. People doing these things "could have" done otherwise. The determinist must explain away all of these judgments and instead define the world as a place where what "ought to be" is impossible. James says in conclusion that this problem is finally a "personal" one, and that he personally cannot conceive of the universe as a place where murder *must* happen. Instead, it is a place where murder *can* happen and *ought not*. For James, then, there are very practical implications to the free will issue, and, for him, the free will option is pragmatically more true because it better accommodates judgments of regret and morality. If this reflects only his "instinct" concerning the kind of universe this is, then, James says, "there are *some* instinctive reactions which I, for one, will not tamper with."

The Will to Believe

The tough-minded scientist might think that our individual hopes should have no impact on the truth that we are investigating. In fact, a scientist might argue that we should in fact abstain from belief in situations where there is no clear evidence. For example, religious questions have a way of running ahead of evidence. Thus, in the absence of any clear evidence for the existence of God, a scientist might recommend agnosticism—neither believing nor disbelieving in God. In his essay "The Will to Believe" James combats this scientific view and argues that, when reason is truly neutral on an urgent issue, we may rightfully believe based solely on our feelings. However, we cannot will to believe just anything under any and all circumstances. This right to believe as we feel applies to only special situations. Right off, according to James, our reason must be completely neutral on the issue. For example, I am not justified in believing that Abraham Lincoln is still alive, since there are quite a number of compelling reasons to believe that he is dead. With other issues, though, reason seems to be genuinely neutral, such as the question of God's existence. According to James, proofs and disproofs for God are equally shaky. Beyond the stipulation of reason's neutrality, James lists three other conditions that determine when emotionally based beliefs are justified.

First, the belief must be a *live* option—as opposed to a dead one. That is, it must be a conception that we are psychologically capable of believing. For example, if a traditional Christian was asked to believe in the Muslim savior Mahdi, he or she would not be psychologically capable of making that shift. Belief in Mahdi, then, would be a dead option for such Christian believers. Second, the choice must be *forced* in the sense that we must either accept or reject a conception, and nothing in between. For example, I must either accept or not accept the contention that the Christian God exists. Third, the issue must be *momentous*, that is, of major concern rather than trivial. Belief in God seems to be a matter of some urgency. When all of three of these conditions are fulfilled, we have what James calls a "genuine option." He then states his thesis here:

> Our passional nature not only lawfully may, but must, decide an option between propositions, whenever it is a genuine option that cannot by its nature be decided on intellectual grounds; for to say, under such circumstances, "Do not decide, but leave the question open," is itself a passional decision,—just like deciding yes or no,—and is attended with the same risk of losing the truth.

In short, James holds that, when reason is neutral in matters that are genuine options, we can decide the issue based on our hopes and feelings.

According to James, we often receive real benefits when we proactively believe things that we cannot rationally demonstrate. This involves some intellectual risk, but it is a risk worth taking. Suppose, for example, a young man wants to know whether a certain young woman loves him. Let us also suppose that objectively it is a fact that she loves him but he does not *know* it. If he assumes that she does not, then his doubt will prevent him from saying or doing what would cause her to reveal her love. In this case, he would "lose the truth." His will to believe would not necessarily create her love. That is already there. But belief has the effect of making what is already there come full circle. If the young man required evidence before he could know the truth, he would never know it, because the evidence he is looking for would become available only after he acts on his belief. Similarly, in the realm of religious experience, we might not discover religious truth until we actually become religious believers—even in the absence of evidence for our belief. Again, our proactive religious beliefs would not make our religious experiences true, but it provides us with the only means of discovering their truth.

Occasionally nonrational proactive beliefs can even *create* facts, and not just *discover* them. For example, I may get a job promotion chiefly because I believed that I could achieve it and acted resolutely on that belief. Assuming the truth of my abilities, I incorporate this into my life, and take a risk for the sake of it. My faith *creates* its own verification. Similarly, in a political campaign, a candidate's optimistic will to believe can generate enough enthusiasm among the constituents to win a majority vote. James illustrates this point with an example of a train robbery. All of the passengers on a train may be individually brave, but each one is afraid that by resisting the robbers he or she will be shot. However, if they optimistically believed that the others would arise, resistance could begin. But if one passenger actually arose, that could influence the others, and would help create a unified resistance.

DEWEY

William James's lively writing style was unsurpassable, but in the final analysis John Dewey was the most influential of the pragmatists. By the time of his death at the age of 92, Dewey brought about a reconstruction of philosophy and influenced many American institutions, particularly school systems and some political processes. His influence extended beyond the boundaries of the United States, especially into Japan and China, where his lectures made a lasting impression. Born in Burlington, Vermont, John Dewey was educated at the University of Vermont and at Johns Hopkins University, where he received his Ph.D. in philosophy in 1884. For the next 10 years, except for one year when he was at Minnesota, he taught at the University of Michigan, and for the next decade at the University of Chicago, where he gained renown for his pragmatic concepts of education. As director of the Laboratory School for children at the University of Chicago, he experimented with a more permissive and creative atmosphere for learning. He set aside the more traditional and formal method of learning—that is, listening and taking notes—and instead encouraged students to become directly involved with educational projects. From 1904 to 1929 he was a member of the faculty at Columbia University. He produced an enormous number of writings even after his retirement in 1929. His interests covered a wide range, and he wrote on logic, metaphysics, and the theory of knowledge. But as Dewey's chief expression of pragmatism was in the social rather than individual realm, his most influential works related to education, democracy, ethics, religion, and art.

The Spectator versus Experience

Dewey's chief quarrel with earlier philosophy was that it confused the true nature and function of knowledge. For the most part, he said, the empiricists assumed that thinking refers to fixed things in nature—that for each idea there is a corresponding something in reality. It is as though knowing is modeled after what is supposed to happen when we look at something. Thus, to see something is to have an idea of it. This he called "a spectator theory of knowledge." But rationalists argued that the reverse process was true, namely, that when we have a clear idea we are guaranteed that the object of our thought exists in reality. In either case, empiricists and rationalists both viewed the human

John Dewey
(Culver Pictures, Inc.)

mind as an instrument for considering what is fixed and certain in nature. Nature is one thing and the mind another, and knowing is the relatively simple activity of looking, as a spectator does, at what is there.

Dewey believed that this view of knowledge is both too static and too mechanical. Influenced by Darwin's theories, Dewey looked upon human beings as a biological organism. As such, we can best be understood in relation to our environment. As any other biological organism, human beings struggle for survival. Although Dewey gave up his early Hegelian orientation, he still believed that human beings were enmeshed in a dialectic process, specifically a conflict in the material or natural environment. Dewey's grand concept was therefore *experience,* a concept he employed for the purpose of connecting people as dynamic biological entities with our precarious environments. If I and my environment are both dynamic, it is clear that a simple spectator-type theory of knowledge will not work. My mind is not a fixed substance, and knowledge is not a set of static concepts. Human intelligence is the ability within us to cope with our environment. Thinking is not an individual act carried on in private or in isolation from practical problems. Instead, thinking, or active intelligence, arises in "problem situations"; thinking and doing are intimately related.

All thinking, Dewey says, has two aspects, namely, "a perplexed, troubled, or confused situation at the beginning and a cleared-up, unified, resolved situation at the close." He named his theory *instrumentalism*, emphasizing that thinking is always instrumental in solving problems. Whereas empiricism and rationalism separate thinking and doing, instrumentalism holds that reflective thought is always involved in transforming a practical situation. My mind does not know simply individual things, but instead mediates between me as an organism and my environment. My mind spreads itself over a range of things as these bear upon my desires, doubts, and dangers. Knowing may very well consist of a "cognitive act"—of an activity in my mind—but the full description of knowing must include the environmental origin of the problem or situation that calls forth the cognitive act. In this way, instrumentalism differs from empiricism and rationalism.

Thinking, therefore, is not a quest for the "truth," as though the truth were a static and eternal quality in things. Thinking, rather, is the act of trying to achieve an adjustment between individual people and our environments. The best test of the value of any philosophy, Dewey says, is to ask, "Does it end in conclusions which, when referred back to ordinary life-experiences and their predicaments, render them more significant, more luminous to us and make our dealings with them more fruitful?" In this way, his instrumentalism is a problem-solving theory of knowledge.

Habit, Intelligence, and Learning

Dewey built his theory of instrumentalism around a special view of human nature. Even though he believed that people are strongly influenced by education and social surroundings, he nevertheless held that we have certain instincts. These instincts are not a fixed inheritance, he argued, but instead are "highly flexible" and will work differently under different social conditions. He writes that "any impulse may become organized into almost any disposition according to the way it interacts with surroundings." For example, *fear* may become cowardice, or reverence for superiors, or the cause for accepting superstitions. Just what an impulse will result in depends upon the way an impulse is interwoven with other impulses as well as outlets supplied by our environment. Dewey thus rejected the simple mechanical stimulus-response account of behavior. Even when an impulse always reflects itself in the same way time after time, this is not a mechanical necessity but only the product of *habit*. But habit is only *one* way of responding to the stimuli of one's impulses, and there is no *necessary* connection between a person's natural impulses and any *particular* response. All responses, he argues, are learned through the interaction between human nature and culture. Habits, then, do not represent fixed forms of human behavior. We can even test them for their usefulness based on whether they support life and generally facilitate the successful adaptation of a person to the environment.

Perhaps the most important implication of Dewey's analysis concerns the nature of social and human "evil." Evil is not the product of some permanent instinct or impulse in human nature that cannot be altered. Instead, evil is the product of the special ways a culture has shaped and conditioned people's impulses. In his view, evil is the product of the "inertness of established habit." *Intelligence* itself is a habit by which we adjust our relation to its environment. Habits therefore include not only ways of reacting to certain stimuli but also ways of thinking about the environment. Since all habits are only *established* but *not necessary* types of behavior, the clue to overcoming personal and social evil is to alter a society's habits—its habits of response and its habits of thought.

Nothing is more important than *education* in remolding a society. If we are creatures of habit, then education provides the conditions for developing the most useful and creative habits. Dewey regretted that progress in the past was achieved only when some catastrophe or major social upheaval broke the spell of long-standing habits. He would prefer a more controlled approach to change, and nothing, he thought, provides us with more power to control than knowledge. Instead of revolution, therefore, we should bring about change through the skillful alteration of habits through education. He was convinced that "the chief means of continuous, graded, economical improvement and social rectification lies in utilizing the opportunities of educating the young to modify prevailing types of thought and desire." The spirit of education should be *experimental,* because our minds are fundamentally problem-solving instruments. It is therefore more important to try alternative means for successfully solving problems than to pursue neat theoretical formulations.

Dewey's instrumentalism was governed by the presuppositions of science. Like science, education should recognize the intimate connection between action and thought—between experiment and reflection. Achieving knowledge is a continuous process. It is a struggle to fashion theory in the context of experiment and thought. But if education is the key to social improvement, and if experiment is the best way to discover the instrumental *means* for solving problems, the crucial questions concern the problem of *ends.* Improvement assumes a scale of values, and means are employed toward ends. How does society discover its ends or the foundations of its values? Dewey specifically examined this difficult problem of relating facts to value, science to morality, and in the process fashioned a new theory of value.

Value in a World of Fact

Dewey's theory of value followed his general theory of knowledge. Our minds discover values the same way that we discover facts, namely, through experience. Values do not exist as eternal entities some place to be discovered by the theoretical mind. Every person experiences the problem of choosing between two or more possibilities. The question about values arises in these experiences where choices have to be made. We most often make choices about means for achieving ends. Where an end is already clear, we can pursue the means with scientific rigor. For Dewey, the act that will bring about the end most successfully is by definition the most "valuable" act. Suppose, for example, that the roof on my house leaks. This all at once raises the questions of both *ends* and *means*—the goal of stopping the leak, and the ways of accomplishing this. I quickly realize that a leaky roof calls for action. Before I begin any action, I try to intelligently sort out the various possibilities for stopping the leak, drawing on past experience or experiment. According to Dewey, to deal effectively with this problem I do not need to draw on elaborate value theories. He thus rejected any theory of values grounded in so-called "essences" of things or transcendent eternal truth. There is, Dewey says, "only relative, not absolute, impermeability and fixity of structure." Since the quest for values rests on a scientific methodology, all that we need to do is intelligently sort out the best means to achieve our aims.

Since intelligence is the agency for bridging the gap between *any* problem and its solution, he believed that this same experimental and instrumental approach could successfully resolve the problems of individual and social destiny. This is so for value theories pertaining to morality, social policy, politics and economics. His optimism rested upon the spectacular successes of the sciences. If we asked Dewey where we could discover values in the absence of traditional moral and religious standards, Dewey answered, for the most part "from the findings of the natural sciences." There is some resemblance between Dewey's theory and utilitarianism—the view that right actions are those that produce the best consequences for society. However, Dewey sought to go beyond the theory of utilitarianism. Our moral choices begin by designating what we in fact desire, such as a fixed roof or a reformed school system. We then submit these desires to the inspection of our intelligence, which in turn offers a satisfactory solution of the problem.

Unfortunately, we cannot devise a neat formula for determining how any given act will terminate, and what the best means might be for attaining an end. Life is simply too dynamic and the circumstances of behavior too diverse to permit the making of any kind of *list* of rules. The best values are those that produce satisfactory consequences, relative to the aim that we hope to achieve. It is through experience that we discover ends toward which life and behavior should move. According to Dewey, each generation should formulate its own ends in the context of democracy. Democracy itself represented Dewey's *faith* in the capacities of human intelligence. He believed that apart from "pooled and cooperative experience" there is no reliable source of knowledge, wisdom, or guidance for collective action.

PROCESS PHILOSOPHY

Just when modern science was reaching its most impressive heights of achievement, two bold speculative philosophers called into question the basic assumptions of scientific thought. Neither Bergson nor Whitehead wished to deny that the scientific method gave people considerable control over nature and to that extent was a brilliantly successful enterprise. What concerned them primarily was a philosophical question, namely, whether reality was what science assumed it to be. As late as the second half of the 19th century and the early decades of the 20th, the major assumption of science was that nature consists of material objects located in space. On this view, matter is the final irreducible stuff out of which all things are formed. The model for thinking about the contents and behavior of nature was that of a machine. All the particular things in nature were thought to be parts of a large mechanism. This meant that the behavior of each part could in time be described with mathematical exactness, since material objects moved in space in accordance with precise rules or laws. Moreover, as parts of a mechanism, things were related to each other in a tight sequence of cause and effect. Human nature was also viewed in these material and mechanical terms. As parts of a tightly organized cosmic machine, people were no longer thought of as being "free," as possessing freedom of the will.

Each of these assumptions raised serious philosophical problems for Bergson and Whitehead. They wondered whether nature really does consist of inert material objects located in space. They also wondered whether the human intellect is capable of discovering "out there" such an orderly and mechanical arrangement of things as the logical and mathematical reasoning of science portrays. How, moreover, can there be any genuine novelty in nature if the basic reality is material and its various parts organized in a tight mechanism? Can a world made of material things ever become anything more than these same objects simply rearranged from time to time? How, in short, can inert matter overcome its static status and evolve? How can we explain the concrete experience of life in terms of a lifeless nature? And how can human freedom be explained in a thoroughly mechanical universe? Science itself recently developed new concepts as, for example, the theory of evolution, which made the mechanical model of nature less and less plausible.

Whitehead pointed out that late in the 19th century, the people of science "were quite unaware that the ideas they were introducing, one after the other, were finally to accumulate into a body of thought inconsistent with the Newtonian ideas dominating their thoughts and shaping their types of expression." Whitehead moved, as it were, from within science to his metaphysics, drawing out many of the implications of the emerging new physics. Similarly, Bergson had no intention of rejecting science, but thought instead that metaphysics and science could enrich each other. What Bergson and Whitehead did challenge in science, however, was the assumption that the scientific type of thought could be the sole comprehensive source of knowledge. Accordingly, they sought to show just what the limits of science are and what unique insights could be provided by discovering the metaphysical processes that form reality.

BERGSON

Henri Bergson was born in Paris in 1859, the brilliant son of a Polish father and an English mother. This same year saw the publication of Darwin's *On the Origin of Species by Means of Natural Selection* and the birth of John Dewey. Bergson's rise in the academic world was rapid. At the age of 22 he became

Henri Bergson
(New York Public Library Picture Collection)

professor of philosophy at the Angers Lycée, and by 1900 he was appointed to the distinguished chair of modern philosophy at the Collège de France. With uncommon lucidity and a captivating style, Bergson wrote a series of works that won wide attention and stimulated considerable discussion, including *Time and Free Will* (1889), *Matter and Memory* (1897), *An Introduction to Metaphysics* (1903), *Creative Evolution* (1907), and *The Two Sources of Morality and Religion* (1932). These last three works gained particular fame and contain his most distinctive ideas. Their publication assured him of a worldwide reputation and attracted people from many countries to hear his lectures in Paris, where he lived until his death in 1941 at the age of 82.

Going Around versus Entering Into

At the center of Bergson's philosophy is his conviction that there are "two profoundly different ways of knowing a thing." The first way, he says, "implies that we move around the object," and the second, that "we enter into it." Knowledge derived in the first way depends upon the vantage point from which we observe an object, and therefore this type of knowledge will be different for each observer and, on that account, *relative.* Moreover, knowledge derived by observation is expressed in symbols, where the symbol used can refer not only to this specific object but to any and all similar objects. The second kind of knowledge, however, is *absolute,* Bergson says, because in this case, by "entering" the object, we overcome the limitations of any particular perspective and grasp the object as it really is.

Bergson illustrates these two types of knowing with several examples. First, there is the example of the movement of an object in space. My observation of this object, he says, will vary with the point of view from which I observe it, particularly whether I myself am moving or stationary. When I try to describe this motion, my expression of it will vary with the points of reference to which I relate it. Both in observing and describing the moving object, I am placed outside of it. In describing the object's motion, I think of a line that is divided into units and I express this through the symbol of a graph with its axes, a series of points through which the object is thought to move. By contrast to this attempt to plot and chart movement in terms of discrete units of space, there is, Bergson says, the true movement, a continuous flow, where there are in reality no points being crossed. Suppose, Bergson says, that you were inside the object as it moved. You would then know the object as it really is and moves and not only as translated into the symbolic language of points and units of distance. For, "what I experience will depend neither on the point of view I may take up in regard to the object, since I am inside the object itself, nor on the symbols by which I may translate the motion, since I have rejected all translations in order to possess the original." Instead of trying to grasp the movement from where I stand in my static position, I must try to grasp the object's motion from where *it* is, from within, as the motion is in the object itself. When I raise my own arm, I have a simple and single perception of the movement I have created; I have an "absolute" knowledge of this movement. But, Bergson says, for the spectator watching me raise my arm from the outside,

> your arm passes through one point, then through another, and between these points there will be still other points. . . . Viewed from the inside, then, an absolute is a simple thing; but looked at from the outside, that is to say, relatively to other things, it becomes, in relation to these signs which express it, the gold coin for which we never seem able to finish giving small change.

The case is the same when we take a character in a novel. The author labors to describe his traits and to make him engage in action and dialogue. But, Bergson says, "all this can never be equivalent to the simple and indivisible feeling which I should experience if I were able for an instant to identify myself with the person of the hero himself." The reason why descriptive traits do not help me know this particular hero is that such traits are merely symbols, "which can make him known to me only by so many comparisons with persons or things I know already." Such symbols take me outside of him, and "they give me only what he has in common with others and not what belongs to him alone." It is not possible, Bergson says, to perceive what constitutes a person's "essence" from without, because by definition his essence is internal and therefore cannot be expressed by symbols. Description and analysis require the use of symbols, but symbols are always "imperfect in comparison with the object of which a view has been taken, or which the symbols seek to express." Not all the photographs of Paris, taken from every conceivable point of view, and not even motion pictures, would ever be equivalent to the solid Paris in which we live and move. Not all translations of a poem could render the inner meaning of the original. In every example, there is, first of all, the original, which we can know absolutely only by entering into it. There is then second of all the "translation," or copy, which we know only relatively, depending upon our vantage point and the symbols we use for expression.

What, more precisely, does it mean to "go around" an object and to "enter into it"? To go around an object is what Bergson means by that special activity of the intellect that he calls *analysis*. By contrast, to enter into an object is what is implied by his use of the term *intuition*. By intuition, Bergson means "the kind of *intellectual sympathy* by which one places oneself within an object in order to coincide with what is unique in it and consequently inexpressible." The basic contrast between science and metaphysics turns upon the difference between *analysis* and *intuition*.

The Scientific Way of Analysis

Bergson believed that in the end scientific meaning, insofar as it is based upon analysis, misrepresents the nature of whatever object it analyzes. This follows, he said, from the fact that analysis "is the operation which reduces the object to elements already known, that is, to elements common both to it and other objects." Therefore, "to analyze . . . is to express a thing as a function of something other than itself." To analyze a rose is to take it apart and discover its constituents. From such an analysis we do in fact derive knowledge of the rose, but in such a state of analysis, the rose is no longer the living thing it was in the garden. Similarly, the science of medicine discovers much knowledge of human anatomy by dissecting it into parts.

In every case, Bergson says, the analytic intellect learns, ironically, by destroying the object's essence. Its essence is its dynamic, thriving, pulsing, living, continuing existence—its duration. Analysis, however, interrupts this essential duration. It stops life and movement. It separates into several independent and static parts what in true life is a unified, organic, and dynamic reality.

The language of analytic science tends, moreover, to exaggerate even further this static and disjointed conception of things through its use of symbols. Each new object is described by science as using as many symbols as there are ways of looking at a thing. And, Bergson says, the content of each such perception is abstracted, that is, drawn or lifted out from the object. Thus, the intellect forms a series of concepts about a thing, "cutting out of reality according to the lines that must be followed in order to act conveniently upon it." Since we think in terms of our language, that is, in terms of single concepts, we tend to analyze things into as many concepts as there are ways of looking at and moving around an object. This is the ordinary function of scientific analysis, namely, to work with symbols. Even the sciences concerned with life "confine themselves to the visible form of living beings, their organs and anatomical elements. They make comparisons between these forms, they reduce the more complex to the more simple; in short, they study the workings of life in what is, so to speak, only its visual symbol." There seem to be, Bergson says, a "symmetry, concord and agreement" between our intellect and matter, as though our intellect were made to analyze and utilize matter. Indeed, he says, "our intelligence is the prolongation of our senses." Even before there was either science or philosophy, "the role of intelligence was already that of manufacturing instruments and guiding the action of our body on surrounding bodies."

If, then, the intellect has been made to utilize matter, "its structure has no doubt been modeled upon that matter." But it is precisely for this reason that the intellect has a limited function. Its very structure and function fit it for analysis—for separating what is unified into its parts. Even when it comes to the study of the most concrete reality—namely, the *self*—the intellect, proceeding analytically, is never capable of discovering the true self. As all other sciences, psychology analyzes the self into separate states such as sensations, feelings, and ideas, which it studies separately. According to Bergson, to study the self by studying separately the various psychical states is like trying to know Paris by studying various sketches, all of which are labeled *Paris*. The psychologists claim to find the "ego" in the various psychical states, not realizing that "this diversity of states has itself only been obtained . . . by transporting oneself outside the ego altogether." And "however much they place the states side by side, multiplying points of contact and exploring the intervals, the ego always escapes them."

The Metaphysical Way of Intuition

But, Bergson says, there is another way of knowing the self, and that is by *intuition*. As he says, "there is one reality, at least, which we all seize from within, by intuition and not by simple analysis. It is our own personality through time—our self which endures." Just as Descartes did, Bergson also founded his philosophy upon the immediate knowledge of the self. But whereas Descartes built a system of rationalism upon his self-knowledge, Bergson set forth the method of intuition, which was in sharp contrast to rationalism. Intuition, Bergson argued, is a kind of intellectual sympathy. It enables our consciousness to become identified with an object. Intuition "signifies . . . immediate consciousness, a vision which is scarcely distinguishable from the object seen, a knowledge which is contact or even coincidence."

Most importantly, Bergson says, "to think intuitively is to think in *duration.*" This is the difference between analytic and intuitive thought. Analysis begins with the static and reconstructs movement as best it can with immobilities in juxtaposition. By contrast, "intuition starts from movement, posits it, or rather perceives it as reality itself, and sees in immobility only an abstract moment, a snapshot taken by our mind." Ordinarily, analytic thought pictures the new as a new arrangement of what already exists; although nothing is ever lost, neither is anything ever created. But "intuition, bound up to a duration which is growth, perceives in it an uninterrupted continuity of unforeseeable novelty;

it sees, it knows that the mind draws from itself more than it has, that spirituality consists in just that, and that reality, impregnated with spirit, is creation." Intuition, then, discovers that the self is an enduring and continuous flux.

Bergson compares the inner life of the self to a continually rolled up thread on a ball: "for our past follows us, it swells incessantly with the present that it picks up on its way; and consciousness means memory." An even better way of thinking about the self, he says, is to imagine an infinitely small elastic body, which is gradually drawn out in such a manner that from that original body comes a constantly lengthening line. While even this image is not satisfactory to him, Bergson does see in it an analogy to human personality. The drawing out of the elastic body is a continuous action representing the duration of the ego, which is the pure mobility of the self. But whatever images are used to describe it, "the inner life is all this at once: variety of qualities, continuity of progress, and unity of direction. It cannot be represented by images. . . . No image can replace the intuition of duration."

The Process of Duration

Bergson focused on the process in all things that he called *duration,* that is, becoming. Duration, he argued, constitutes the continuous stream of experience in which we live. His criticism of classical schools of philosophy was that they failed to take duration seriously. For the most part, philosophers such as Plato, Descartes, and Kant sought to interpret the world through fixed structures of thought. This was particularly the case with Plato, whose notion of the Forms provides us with a static structure of reality. Even the empiricists, in spite of their preoccupation with experience, analyzed experience into static components. This was so for Hume, who described knowledge in terms of individual impressions. Neither the rationalists nor the empiricists, Bergson charged, took the matter of mobility, development, becoming, and duration seriously. He was not entirely clear about how this metaphysical notion of duration could be employed in scientific knowledge. But he was certain that to "think in duration" is to have a true grasp of reality. Such thought also gives us a more accurate notion of time—real and continuous time—as compared with the "spatialized" time created by the intellect.

Only when we think of time and motion in such "spatialized" terms do we encounter the logical paradoxes that Zeno spoke of. Zeno, we will remember, said that a flying arrow really does not move, because at each instant the arrow occupies a single point in space, which would mean that at each instant the arrow is at rest. Bergson says that Zeno's argument would be irrefutable if his assumptions about space and time were correct. But he argues that Zeno was in error in assuming that there are real positions in space and discrete units of time. Bergson believes that these so-called positions are merely *suppositions* of the intellect. The units of time are only the artificial segments into which the analytic intellect slices what in reality is a continuous flow. What Zeno's paradoxes show us is that it is impossible to construct mobility out of static positions, or true time out of instants. Although our intellects are capable of comprehending static parts, we are incapable of grasping movement or duration. Only intuition can grasp duration. And reality is duration. Reality, Bergson says, does not consist of *things,* but only of "things in the making, not self-maintaining *states,* but only changing states." Rest is only apparent, for all reality "is tendency, if we agree to mean by tendency an incipient change of direction."

Evolution and the Vital Impulse

Is not the theory of evolution an example of how science can successfully understand duration and becoming? After examining the major conceptions of evolution, Bergson concludes that none of these scientific theories are adequate, and thus he offers a theory of his own. The particular inadequacy he found in the other theories was their inability to give a convincing account of how the transition is made through the gap that separates one level from a higher level. Darwin speaks of variations among members of a species, and DeVries speaks of mutations as the conditions leading some members to possess variations favorable for survival. But neither Darwin nor DeVries explained how such variations in a species could occur. Both of them said that either slowly or suddenly a change occurs, presumably in some part of the organism. This overlooks the functional unity of an organism, which requires that any variation in one part must be accompanied by variations throughout the organism. Again, though, neither Darwin nor DeVries explained just how this can occur. This leaves unanswered the question of how there can be a continuity of function in spite of successive changes of form. The neo-Lamarckian theory attributed evolution to the special "effort" employed by certain organisms, causing them to develop capacities favorable to survival. But can such acquired characteristics be transmitted from one generation to the next? Bergson insisted that although "effort" had some promising implications, it was too haphazard a notion to explain the overall process of development. Nor was Spencer's theory of the transmission of acquired characteristics satisfactory, since, again, this seemed to Bergson to be an unsuccessful attempt to construct movement or evolution out of unchanging parts.

   Evolution, Bergson concluded, is best explained in terms of a vital impulse (*élan vital*), which drives all organisms toward constantly more complicated and higher types of organization. The vital impulse is the essential interior element of all living things, and is the creative power that moves in unbroken continuity through all things. Since the intellect can grasp only static things, it is not capable of grasping the vital impulse, because this is the essence of duration and of movement, and "all change, all movement, [is] . . . absolutely indivisible." Bergson argued that knowing is a secondary activity. Living, though, is more basic, and therefore is primary. Intuition and consciousness, not analytic intellect, grasp this primary life and discover it to be a continuous and undivided process of which all things are expressions and not parts. All things are motivated by this vital impulse, and it is the fundamental reality. We discover it first through the immediate awareness of our own continuous self: we discover that we *endure.*

Here, finally, is where intuition must challenge intellect. For intellect, as we have seen, sees movement as static states. Intuition, though, discovers that movement is continuous, that it cannot be reduced to parts, and that the creative process caused by the vital impulse is irreversible. Bergson writes that "To get a notion of this irreducibility and irreversibility, we must do violence to the mind, go counter to the natural bent of the intellect. But that is just the function of philosophy."

The intellect would describe evolution as a single and steady line moving upward through measurable levels. Intuition, though, suggests differing tendencies at work. According to Bergson, the vital impulse moved in three discernible directions, producing (1) vegetative beings, (2) anthropods, and (3) vertebrates (including, finally, human beings). Distinguishing intellect and intuition, he says that the emergence of intellect and matter occurred together, and these were intended to work together. He writes, "our intellect in the narrow sense of the word, is intended to secure the perfect fitting of our body to its environment, to represent the relations of external things among themselves—in short, to think matter." Moreover, "matter is weighted with geometry." But neither matter nor geometrical figures represent ultimate reality. The vital impulse must itself resemble consciousness, from whence emerged life and all its creative possibilities. Evolution is creative precisely because the future is open. There is no preordained "final" goal; duration constantly endures, producing always genuinely novel events, like an artist who never knows precisely what he will create until he has created his work. Bergson finally refers to the creative effort of the vital impulse as being "of God, if it is not God himself."

Morality and Religion

Bergson argues that there are two sources of morality. The first is the sheer feeling of the necessity for solidarity, and to achieve such social solidarity, a society formulates certain rules of obligation. The second source lies in a deeper seat of feeling, which is sparked by the example of great moral people whose emotional appeal transcends particular cultural groups. These two sources—the pressure of social necessity and the aspiration toward higher types of life—reflect the differences between intellect and intuition. The intellect thinks in particular terms, directing specific rules to specific people to achieve specific ends. To this extent, the intellect tends to restrict morality to a closed society. Bergson was aware that the intellectually oriented Stoics believed that reason is a source of universal morality. But even when the intellect formulates laws for all people, we still need intuition to develop a genuine morality that extends to a wider group. Intuition opens up richer sources of emotional power, at once inducing aspiration and providing creative power to embrace new types of life. Such moral progress occurs only when obscure moral heroes appear. These mystics and saints raise humanity to a new destiny, and "see in their mind's eye a new social atmosphere, an environment in which life would be more worth living." In this way morality moves constantly from a consideration of the self and of one's society to the larger field of humanity.

The difference between intellect and intuition is reflected also in two types of religion, which Bergson calls *static* and *dynamic.* Since we find that all people are religious in one way or another, religion must be due to some inherent aspect of human structure. Moreover, since the intellect is formed to aid us in survival, the intellect must be the source of religion, inasmuch as religion presumes to answer certain basic demands of life. Religious concepts seek to provide security, confidence, and a defense against fear. But these concepts soon become institutionalized and are converted into belief to protect them against critical reason. They are often surrounded by ceremonies and disciplines and tend to become embedded in the social structure. This is static religion, the religion of social conformity. Dynamic religion, on the other hand, is more in the nature of mysticism. Bergson's definition of *mysticism* closely follows his notion of intuition when he says that "the ultimate end of mysticism is the establishment of a contact, consequently of a partial coincidence, with the creative effort which life itself manifests." Just as intuition grasps reality more completely than intellect does, so does dynamic religion discover God more vividly. For, Bergson says, we must consider static religion "as the crystallization, brought about by a scientific process of cooling, of what mysticism had poured, white hot, into the soul of man."

WHITEHEAD

Whitehead reacted, as Bergson did, against the analytic type of thought, which assumed that facts exist in isolation from other facts. His main theme was that "connectedness is the essence of all things." What science tends to separate, philosophy must try to see as an organic unity. Thus, "the red glow of the sunset should be as much a part of nature as are the molecules and electric waves by which men of science would explain the phenomenon." The function of natural philosophy, he thought, is "to analyze how these various elements of nature are connected." Describing Wordsworth's romantic reaction against the scientific mentality, Whitehead says that "Wordsworth was not bothered by any intellectual antagonism. What moved him was moral repulsion." He was repulsed by the fact that scientific analysis left something out, "that what had been left out comprised everything that was most important," namely, moral intuitions and life itself. Agreeing with Wordsworth, Whitehead went on to say that "neither physical nature nor life can be understood unless we fuse them together as essential factors in the composition of really real things whose interconnections and individual characters constitute the universe." And, he says, "it is important therefore to ask what Wordsworth found in nature that failed to receive expression in science. I ask this question in the interest of science itself." Whitehead was convinced that "the status of life in nature . . . is the modern problem of philosophy and science." Although he shared these same problems with Bergson, Whitehead brought a different intellectual background to their solution and produced therefore a different and novel speculative metaphysics.

Alfred North Whitehead had three careers, two in England and one in America. Born in the village of Kent in 1861, he was educated at Sherborn School and at Trinity College in Cambridge. For 25 years he taught mathematics at Trinity. It was here, too, that Whitehead collaborated with Bertrand Russell on their famed *Principia Mathematica,* which went to press in 1910. From Trinity he moved to London, eventually becoming associated with the University of London as a member of its faculty of science and later as the Dean of this faculty. During these 13 years at London, he also developed a strong interest in the problems of higher education, being concerned particularly with the impact of modern industrial civilization upon the enterprise of learning. But his major writings while at London represented an attempt to replace Isaac Newton's concept of nature with his own empirically grounded theory. These works on the philosophy of science include his *Enquiry Concerning the Principles of Natural Science* (1919), *The Concept of Nature* (1920), and *The Principle of Relativity* (1922).

When Whitehead was 63 years old and nearing retirement, he was appointed professor of philosophy at Harvard University and he embarked upon the third and, in many ways, most important of his careers. To his achievements as a logician, mathematician, and philosopher of science he added his works as a metaphysician. His major works of this period are his *Science and the Modern World* (1925), *Process and Reality* (1929), and *Adventures of Ideas* (1933). What motivated Whitehead to write these books was his conviction that scientific knowledge arrived at a point in its history that called for a new scheme of ideas to reflect more adequately the new developments in science. Since scientific thought always relies upon some scheme of ideas, he said, the importance of philosophy is to make such schemes explicit so that they can be criticized and improved. Though his chief speculative work, *Process and Reality,* is a massive and intricate statement, Whitehead acknowledges in the preface that "there remains the final reflection, how shallow, puny, and imperfect are efforts to sound the depths in the nature of things. In philosophical discussion, the merest hint of dogmatic certainty as to finality of statement is an exhibition of folly." Thus, his metaphysical writings combine bold and creative speculations tempered with a sensitive humility. In 1937, Whitehead retired but continued to live near Harvard Yard until his death in 1947 at the age of 87.

The Error of Simple Location

Whitehead was convinced that Newtonian physics was based upon a fallacy, consisting in the theory of *simple location.* He called it the *fallacy of misplaced concreteness.* Newton followed Democritus in assuming that the nature of things consists of individual bits of matter existing in space. What is fallacious about this? Whitehead says that

> to say that a bit of matter has *simple location* means that, in expressing its spatio-temporal relations, it is adequate to state that it is where it is in a definite region of space and throughout a definite duration of time, apart from any essential reference of the relations of that bit of matter to other regions of space and to other durations of time.

Against this view, Whitehead argues that "among the primary elements of nature as apprehended in our immediate experience, there is no element whatsoever which possesses this character of simple location." The concept of an isolated atom, he says, is the product of intellectual abstraction. He admits that, by a process of abstraction, we can "arrive at abstractions which are the simply-located bits of material." But these abstractions, by definition, represent the lifting out of a thing from its concrete environment. To mistake the abstraction for the concrete is the error that Whitehead calls the *fallacy of misplaced concreteness.* Such things as instants of time, points in space, or independent particles of matter are certainly helpful concepts for scientific thought. However, when we take them as descriptions of ultimate reality, they are distortions of concrete reality.

When it came to giving his own account of concrete reality, Whitehead developed a novel form of atomism. He sought to draw out the implications of the recent developments in quantum physics, the theory of relativity, and evolution. His units of reality differed from the atoms of Democritus and Newton in two ways, namely, in their *content* and in their *relations* to each other. Whitehead discarded the word *atom* because historically this term meant that the content of an atom is hard, lifeless matter and that being hard, atoms never penetrate each other. Hence their relations to each other are always external. In place of the term *atoms,* Whitehead therefore substituted the term *actual entities* or its equivalent *actual occasions.* Unlike lifeless atoms, Whitehead's actual entities are "chunks in the life of nature." As such, they never exist in isolation but are intimately related to the whole field of life that throbs around them. Whereas atomistic materialism gives us a mechanical view of nature, Whitehead's notion of actual occasions permits us to view nature as a living *organism.* Thus, whether we speak of God or "the most trivial puff of existence," there is the same principle of life in all things, for "actual entities are the final real things of which the world is made up."

Self-Consciousness

Whitehead saw in our own self-consciousness a good example of an actual occasion. He felt that the "direct evidence as to the connectedness of [my] immediate present occasion of experience with [my] immediately past occasions, can be validly used to suggest . . . the connectedness of all occasions in nature." Because an actual occasion is not a material thing, it is best understood as an experience. These occasions do not exist, they happen. The difference is that merely to exist implies no change, whereas to happen suggests a dynamic alteration. Whitehead's actual occasions represent continually changing entities, a change that comes about through the input of entities upon each other. Consider what occurs when a person has an experience. We usually think that in this case there is, on the one hand, a permanent subject and then something "out there" that the subject experiences. Whitehead argues that the subject and the object are both in a continual process of change, and that every experience the subject has affects the subject. If it is true, as Heraclitus said, that we cannot step into the same river twice, it is also true that no person can think the same way twice, because after each experience he or she is a different person. And this is true of all of nature as it consists of actual occasions or aggregates of actual occasions. Thus, if all of reality is made up of actual occasions—drops of experience—nature is a throbbing organism undergoing constant change throughout. "The universe is thus a creative advance into novelty. The alternative to this theory is a static morphological universe."

Whitehead drew on his theory of actual occasions to account for the relation of body and mind and also to account for the presence of feeling and purpose in the universe. He believed that Democritus had not satisfactorily described how it is possible to have sensation, feeling, thinking, purpose, and life in a universe consisting solely of lifeless material atoms. Nor could Descartes ever join together his two substances—thought and extension. Leibniz did recognize that from lifeless matter it was impossible to derive life, and so he described nature as consisting of monads. Though they resembled the atoms of Democritus in some ways, Leibniz thought they were individual "souls," or centers of energy. Although the Leibnizian monad was a somewhat more satisfactory concept than the atom of Democritus, Whitehead considered it inadequate. Specifically, although Leibniz believed that monads undergo change, this change did not involve any truly novel process—no evolution, no creativity—but only the running of its predetermined course. By contrast, Whitehead's actual entities have no permanent identity or history. They are always in the process of becoming. They feel the impact of other actual occasions and absorb them internally. In this process, actual occasions come into being, take on a determinate form or character, and, having become actual occasions, perish. To "perish" signifies that the creativity of the universe moves on to the next birth and that in this process an actual occasion loses its unique character but is preserved in the flow of the process. Perishing, Whitehead says, is what we mean by memory or causality—that with the passage of time something of the past is preserved in the present.

Prehension

We do not ever experience a single isolated actual entity, but only aggregates of these entities. He calls an aggregate of actual entities either a *society* or a *nexus* (plural *nexūs*) in which the entities are united by their *prehensions*. These are some of the novel words Whitehead invented to explain his novel ideas. He writes, "In the three notions—actual entity, prehension, nexus—an endeavor has been made to base philosophical thought upon the most concrete elements in our experience. . . . The final facts are, all alike, actual entities; and these actual entities are drops of experience, complex and interdependent." Whitehead visualized reality as a continual process in which actual entities are constantly becoming—a process in which *what* an actual entity becomes depends upon *how* it becomes. His emphasis is upon the notion of *creativity* as the fundamental characteristic of the process of nature. Creativity is the ultimate principle by which the many enter into complex unity. If we took each actual entity separately, we should have a disjoined universe, but the creative unity of the many constitutes the conjoined universe.

Whitehead uses the term *prehension* to describe how the elements of actual entities are related to each other and how these entities are further related to other entities. Nothing in the world is unrelated. In a sense, every actual occasion absorbs, or is related to, the whole universe. Actual entities are brought together by the creative process into sets, or societies, or nexūs. In this process of becoming, actual entities are formed through prehension. Every prehension, Whitehead says, consists of three factors: first, the "subject" that is prehending; second, the "datum which is prehended"; and third, the "subjective form," which is *how* the subject prehends the datum. There are various species of prehensions: *positive prehensions,* which are termed *feelings,* and *negative prehensions,* which "eliminate from feeling." The subjective forms, or the ways data are prehended, are of many species, including emotions, valuations, purposes, and consciousness. Thus, for Whitehead, emotional feeling is the basic characteristic of concrete experience. Even in the language of physics it is appropriate to speak of *feelings,* for *physical feelings* are the physicist's idea that energy is transferred. Both physical feelings and conceptual feelings are positive prehensions, or internal relations of the elements of actual entities.

The distinction between physical and conceptual feelings does not imply the older dualism of body and mind. It is of course still meaningful to use the terms *body* and *mind.* But Whitehead insists that to assume that these terms imply a basic metaphysical difference, as Descartes said existed between his terms *thought* and *extension,* is to commit again the fallacy of misplaced concreteness. This fallacy, we will recall, is committed when one mistakes an abstraction for the concrete. Both body and mind are, for Whitehead, societies, or nexūs—they are sets of actual entities. The only concrete reality is an actual entity, but actual entities can be organized into different kinds of societies, such as body and mind. But in each case, the actual entities possess the same characteristics, namely, the capacity for prehension, for feeling, for internal relations. Body and mind are both abstractions in the sense that their reality depends upon the peculiar organization of the actual entities. Hence, body and mind are not permanently or ultimately different. To speak of the body as an abstraction is similar to speaking of a political body as an abstraction where only the individual citizens are the concrete reality. Whitehead insisted that "The final facts are, all alike, actual entities," and all of these are capable of being interconnected in a stream of experience.

Eternal Objects

We might ask at this point just how Whitehead accounts for the underlying process of reality. That is, what is the process of creativity which brings actual entities into being and organizes them into societies and preserves what to our experience appears as the endurance of things? Here Whitehead's thought displays a strong Platonic influence. What makes an actual entity what it is, he says, is that the entity has been stamped with a definiteness of character by certain *eternal objects.* These *eternal objects,* resembling Plato's Forms, are uncreated and eternal. They are patterns and qualities, such as roundness or square-ness, greenness or blueness, courage or cowardice. An actual occasion ac-quires a definite character (and not other possible characters) because it selects *these* eternal objects and rejects *those*. Hence, an actual event is constituted by the togetherness of various eternal objects in some particular pattern.

Eternal objects, Whitehead says, are *possibilities*, which, like the Platonic Forms, retain their identity independent of the flux of things. He describes the relation between the eternal object and an actual entity as *ingression*, which means that once the actual entity has selected an eternal object, the latter *in-gresses*, that is, stamps its character upon the actual entity. Thus, "the function-ing of an eternal object in the self-creation of an actual entity is the 'ingression' of the eternal object in the actual entity." Simple eternal objects stamp their character upon actual entities, whereas complex eternal objects give definite-ness, or the status of fact, to societies or nexūs.

To speak of eternal objects as *possibilities* required that Whitehead describe how and where these possibilities exist and how they become relevant to ac-tual occasions. Since only actual occasions exist, what is the status of eternal objects? Whitehead designated one actual entity as being timeless, and this en-tity he called God. For him God is not a creator; he is "not *before* all creation, but *with* all creation." God's nature is to grasp conceptually all the possibilities that constitute the realm of eternal objects. This realm of eternal objects differs from Plato's system of Forms. For, whereas Plato visualized one perfect order for all things, Whitehead's God grasps virtually unlimited possibilities, "all possibilities of order, possibilities at once incompatible and unlimited with a fecundity beyond imagination." What makes the creative process of the world orderly and purposive is the availability of eternal objects, of possibilities. These possibilities exist in God as his primordial nature. God, moreover, is the active mediator between the eternal objects and the actual occasions. It is God who selects the relevant possibilities from the realm of eternal objects.

God does not impose the eternal objects upon actual entities. Rather, God presents these possibilities as *lures* of what might be. Persuasion, not compul-sion, characterizes God's creative activity. That God always presents relevant possibilities is no guarantee that actual entities will select them. When God's persuasive lure is accepted, the result is order, harmony, and novel advance. When it is rejected, the result is discord and evil. God is the ultimate principle striving toward actualizing all relevant possibilities. What we experience as the stable order in the world and in our intuition of the permanent rightness of things shows forth God's "consequent nature." "God's role," Whitehead says, "lies in the patient operation of the overpowering rationality of his conceptual harmonization. He does not create the world, he saves it: or, more accurately, he is the poet of the world, with tender patience leading it by his vision of truth, beauty and goodness."

CHAPTER 17

Analytic Philosophy

*D*uring a large part of the 20th century, the dominant philosophical movement in the English-speaking world was known as *analytic philosophy.* Analytic philosophers differed widely in their stands on traditional philosophical issues and also in their methods for addressing these issues. What unifies them, though, is their agreement concerning the central task of philosophy, namely, to clarify notions through an analysis of language. For example, Ludwig Wittgenstein (1889–1951) said that "the object of philosophy is the logical clarification of thoughts" so that "the result of philosophy is not a number of philosophical propositions, but to make propositions clear." There is both a negative and positive side to this new approach to philosophy.

On the negative side, to say that the philosopher does not formulate "philosophical propositions" meant for the early analysts that there must be a self-imposed limit upon the scope of philosophical activity. Practitioners of 19th-century idealism, especially Hegelians, constructed complete systems of thought regarding the whole universe. Analytic philosophers now undertook the more modest task of working upon individual problems. Not only would these problems be single and manageable, but they would all fit into a single class: they would all be problems revolving around the meanings and usages of language. For this reason, it would no longer be the task of the philosopher to investigate the nature of reality, to build complete systems that seek to explain the universe, or to fashion moral, political, and religious philosophies of behavior. Philosophy, in this new vein, "is not a doctrine but an activity" and as such it can produce "no ethical propositions," Wittgenstein said. Philosophers are no longer to consider themselves capable of discovering unique forms of information about the world and human nature. The discovery of facts is the task of the scientist. There are no facts left over for the philosophers after all the sciences have done their work.

On the positive side, the new assumption was that philosophers can render a genuine service by carefully unpacking complex problems whose origin rests in the imprecise use of language. Scientists discussed their findings in language that was often misleading and in certain ways confusing. That is, scientific language contained ambiguities of logic, which required clarification. Analytic philosophers also assumed that rigorous linguistic analysis could *prevent* the use or abuse of language in ways that would cause us "to draw false inferences, or ask spurious questions, or make nonsensical assumptions," as Alfred Jules Ayer (1910–1989) said. For example, we often use propositions about nations as though nations were people. We talk about material things as though we believed in a physical world "beneath" or "behind" visible phenomena. We use the word *is* in relation to things whose existence we could not possibly want to infer. We call upon philosophy to remove these dangers from our use of language, Ayer said. In this way, analytic philosophy is closely related to the enterprises of science. It is not a rival discipline offering propositions of what reality is like. Instead, philosophy functions as the proofreader of the scientists' expressions, checking the literature of science for its clarity and logical meaningfulness. It is not the philosopher's function to either propound vast systems of thought after the manner of Plato, Aristotle, and Hegel or to tell people how they ought to behave. Instead, the philosopher would analyze statements or propositions to discover the causes of ambiguities and the foundations of meaning in language.

BERTRAND RUSSELL

What caused this dramatic shift in the enterprise of philosophy? In the early decades of the 20th century, several Hegelian philosophers still engaged in the idealist task of system building—most notably F. H. Bradley (1846–1924), Bernard Bosanquet (1848–1923), and J. E. McTaggart (1866–1925). At Cambridge University, Bertrand Russell (1872–1970) and George Edward Moore (1873–1958) reacted against this idealist trend. They questioned the extravagance of the metaphysical language these Hegelians used, and wondered just what could be meant by these interpretations of the whole universe. Although Moore did not necessarily want to give up metaphysics, he was especially disturbed by the contrast between metaphysical language and so-called "common sense." For example, McTaggart's famous notion that "time is unreal," seemed to Moore to be "perfectly monstrous." This inspired Moore to analyze language—particularly to clarify ordinary language from a common-sense point of view. Bertrand Russell, on the other hand, was a brilliant mathematician, trained in precise thought, and in comparison with the language of mathematics, metaphysical language seemed to him loose and obscure. He did not want to reject metaphysics, any more than Moore did, but he did want to tighten up the language of metaphysics. While Moore set out to analyze common-sense language, Russell tried to analyze "facts" for the purpose of inventing a new language, namely, *logical atomism.* This would have the exactness and rigor of mathematics because this new language would be made to correspond exactly to the "facts." Neither Moore nor Russell gave up the attempt to understand reality. Nevertheless, the way

Bertrand Russell
(UPI/Corbis-Bettmann)

they went about their task emphasized the fact that philosophy is concerned not with discovery but with clarification and, therefore, in a sense, not with truth but with meaning.

Logical Atomism

Bertrand Russell's point of departure in philosophy was his admiration for the precision of mathematics. Accordingly, he announced that "the kind of philosophy that I wish to advocate, which I call logical atomism, is one which has

forced itself upon me in the course of thinking about the philosophy of mathematics." He wanted to set forth "a certain kind of logical doctrine and on the
basis of this a certain kind of metaphysics." Russell thought that it was possible to construct a logic by which the whole of mathematics could be derived
from a small number of logical axioms. He did this with Alfred North Whitehead (1861–1947) in their co-authored work *Principia Mathematica* (1910–1913).
Russell also considered that logic could also form the basis of a language that
could accurately express everything that could be clearly stated. Through his
"logical atomism," then, the world would correspond to his specially constructed logical language. The vocabulary of the new logic would, for the most
part, correspond to particular objects in the world. To accomplish this task of
creating a new language, Russell set out first of all to analyze certain "facts,"
which he differentiated from "things."

"The things in the world," Russell says, "have various properties, and
stand in various relations to each other. That they have these properties and relations are *facts*." Facts constitute the complexity of the relations of things to
each other, and therefore "it is with the analysis of *facts* that one's consideration
of the problem of complexity must begin." Russell's basic assumption was that
"facts, since they have components, must be in some sense complex, and hence
must be susceptible to analysis." The complexity of facts is matched by the
complexity of language. For this reason, the aim of analysis is to make sure that
every statement represents an adequate picture of its corresponding reality.

Language, according to Russell, consists of a unique arrangement of
words, and the meaningfulness of language is determined by the accuracy
with which these words represent facts. Words, in turn, are formulated into
propositions. "In a logically perfect language," Russell said, "the words in a
proposition would correspond one by one with the components of the corresponding facts." By analysis, certain *simple* words are discovered. These are
words that cannot be further analyzed into something more primary and can
therefore be understood only by knowing what they symbolize. The word *red*,
for example, is not capable of further analysis and is therefore understood as a
simple *predicate*. Other words, similarly simple, refer to particular things, and
as symbols of these things they are *proper names*. Language consists in part,
then, of words, which in their simplest form refer to a particular thing and its
predicate, as, for example, a *red rose*. A proposition states a fact. When a fact is
of the simplest kind, it is called an *atomic fact*. Propositions that state atomic
facts are called *atomic propositions*. If our language consisted only of such
atomic propositions, it would amount only to a series of reports regarding
atomic facts.

The underlying logical structure of language becomes more apparent when
we assign symbols to our atomic propositions. For example, I can use the letter p
to stand for the atomic proposition "I am tired," and the letter q to stand for "I
am hungry." I can then link these two atomic propositions together with logical
connectives such as *and* and *or*. The result will be a *molecular* proposition, such
as "I am tired and I am hungry," which I can symbolize with the expression p
and q. According to Russell, there is no single atomic fact corresponding to the

entire proposition "I am tired and I am hungry." How can we test the truth or falsity, then, of molecular propositions such as this? The truth of this statement rests on the truth of the component atomic propositions. For example, if it is true that I am tired and it is also true that I am hungry, then the molecular proposition is also true, that "I am tired and I am hungry." In short, we make statements about the world in molecular propositions, which in turn are composed of atomic propositions, which in turn correspond to atomic facts. This ideal language expresses all there is to say about the world.

Problems with Logical Atomism

Russell's theory has problems when we try to account for universal statements such as "All horses have hooves." It is one thing to say that "This horse has hooves," where we check truth or falsity by connecting the *words* "horse" and "hooves" with the atomic *facts* of this particular horse and these hooves. It is another thing to say that "All horses have hooves." How would we test the truth or falsity of such a statement? According to logical atomism, we should analyze this statement into its atomic propositions and test *their* truth or falsity. However, there is no atomic fact corresponding to "all horses," for this means more than just this horse and that horse, namely, all horses, and this is a *general* fact.

Another problem with logical atomism is that it cannot adequately explain its own theory. Propositions can be stated meaningfully only when they are ultimately based on some atomic fact. However, Russell did more than simply state atomic facts: he tried to say things *about* facts. That is, he attempted to describe the relation between words and facts, as though their description was somehow immune from the logical atomist theory itself. If only propositions that state facts are meaningful, then language *about* facts is meaningless. This would then make logical atomism and most of philosophy meaningless. Ludwig Wittgenstein recognized this problem in his own theory of logical atomism and concluded that "my propositions are elucidatory in this way: he who understands me finally recognizes them as senseless, when he has used them to climb out beyond them. (He must so to speak throw away the ladder, after he has climbed up on it)." What we need to throw away is the central assumption of logical atomism that there really are atomic facts, and that these facts exist in some metaphysical way. The next movement in analytic philosophy—logical positivism—attempted to rid philosophy of metaphysical entities once and for all.

LOGICAL POSITIVISM

While Russell championed the cause of analytic philosophy in England, across the English Channel a handful of mathematicians, scientists, and philosophers formed a group in Vienna in the 1920s, known as the Vienna Circle. This group included, Rudolph Carnap, Herbert Feigl, Kurt Gödel, Otto Neurath,

Moritz Schlick, and Friedrich Waismann. The Vienna Circle thought of them-selves as the 20th-century heirs of Hume's empirical tradition, and were in-spired by Hume's strict criterion of meaning that we find at the close of his *Enquiry Concerning Human Understanding* (1748):

> When we run over libraries, persuaded of these principles, what havoc we must make? If we take in our hand any volume; of divinity or school meta-physics, for instance; let us ask, Does it contain any abstract reasoning con-cerning quantity or number? No. Does it contain any experimental reasoning concerning matter of fact and existence? No. Commit it then to the flames: for it can contain nothing but sophistry and illusion.

Also inspired by Comte and other 19th-century positivists, they were disposed to reject metaphysics as outdated by science. Unlike Hume and Comte, though, the Vienna Circle had a new weapon against metaphysics: the logical character of language. Members of the Vienna Circle called themselves *logical positivists*—or sometimes *logical empiricists*—to differentiate themselves from the earlier Comtean positivists and Humean empiricism. The Vienna Circle eventually dissolved in the 1930s when its members went off to teach at British and American universities. For the English-speaking world, A. J. Ayer's book *Language, Truth, and Logic* (1936) did "something to popularize what may be called the classic position of the Vienna Circle" as Ayer later said with considerable understatement.

The Principle of Verification

Logical positivists charged that metaphysical statements are meaningless. This charge, though, required some criterion to determine whether a given sen-tence did or did not express a genuine factual proposition. Accordingly, the logical positivists formulated the verification principle. If a statement passes the stringent requirements of the verification principle, then it is meaningful, and if a statement fails to do so, then it is meaningless. Ayer describes the veri-fication principle as follows:

> The principle of verification is supposed to furnish a criterion by which it can be determined whether or not a sentence is literally meaningful. A simple way to formulate it would be to say that a sentence had literal meaning if and only if the proposition it expressed was either analytic or empirically verifiable.

The verification principle offers a two-pronged test. A statement is mean-ingful only if it is either (1) analytic—that is, true by definition or (2) empirically verifiable. Both of these points need some explanation. Many philosophers in the 18th and 19th centuries drew rigid distinctions between analytic and em-pirical statements. Analytic statements derive their meaningfulness from the definitions of their words or symbols. To say that "all bachelors are unmarried men" has literal significance because the word *bachelor* is defined in such a way as to include the idea *men.* As Kant argued, in analytic statements the subject already contains the predicate, and, if we deny the predicate then we get a contradiction, such as "bachelors are married men." The meaning of analytic statements does not depend upon experience, but only upon the consistent use of their clearly defined terms. Analytic statements, then, are necessarily true by the sheer definitions of the words in the statements. Thus, the first prong of the verification principle is that analytically true statements are meaningful. They have a *formal* meaning, since their meaning is not based on empirical facts but from the logical implications of words and ideas, as particularly in mathematics and logic.

The second prong of the verification principle designates that empirically verifiable statements are also meaningful. An empirical statement is one whose truth rests on some kind of empirical observation, such as "the sun will rise tomorrow." With this example, the notion of "rising tomorrow" is not already contained in the notion of the "sun." Further, we could in fact deny the predicate of this statement and not have a contradiction, as in "the sun will not rise tomorrow." We certainly expect the sun to rise tomorrow, but this expectation is not based on the definition of the word "sun." Throughout our lives, we see the sun rise in the morning and set in the evening, and this experience confirms or "verifies" the statement that "the sun will rise tomorrow." Logical positivists did not believe that we actually had to verify empirical statements before they would be meaningful. Instead, we only need to have a possible procedure by which we could empirically verify the truth or falsehood of a given statement. For example, the statement "there are flowers growing on Pluto" is empirically verifiable since we could in theory build a space ship to Pluto and then explore the planet for flowers. In this case, we most likely would not find any flowers, and would thus disconfirm the statement. Regardless of the statement's actual truth or falsehood, it is still meaningful because it allows for some possible empirical inspection. The problem, then, with metaphysical statements is that they are neither true by definition, nor do they allow for some possible empirical inspection.

Rudolph Carnap

Among the foremost members of the Vienna Circle was the eminent positivist Rudolph Carnap (1891–1970). Born in Germany in 1891, he taught in Vienna and Prague from 1926 to 1935. After arriving in the United States in 1936, he taught for many years at the University of Chicago, and from 1954 until his death in 1970 he was associated with the University of California at Los Angeles. "The only proper task of Philosophy," Carnap writes in his *Philosophy and Logical Syntax*, "is Logical Analysis." It is the function of logical analysis, he said, to analyze all knowledge, all assertions of science and of everyday life, in order to make clear the sense of each assertion and the connections between them. The purpose of logical analysis is to discover how we can become certain of the truth or falsehood of any proposition. One of the principal tasks of the logical analysis of a given proposition is, therefore, to discover the method of verification of that proposition.

For Carnap, the method of a proposition's verification is either direct or indirect. If a proposition asserts something about a perception I am having—for example, that I see a house—this proposition is effectively tested or verified by my present perception. On the other hand, there are propositions that cannot be verified so directly. To say, for example, that "this key is made of iron" requires an indirect method of verification. One way to verify the assertion that the key is made of iron is to place it near a magnet, which enables me to perceive that the key is attracted. It now becomes possible to arrange a series of propositions in a tight logical sequence leading to verification as follows: A verified physical law holds that "if an iron thing is placed near a magnet it is attracted"; another verified proposition asserts that "this metal bar is a magnet"; it is verified through direct observation that "the key is placed near the bar." When the magnet finally attracts the key, the verification is complete. Thus, when we cannot directly verify a proposition, we must indirectly do so by verifying propositions deduced from the original, one and linking these with more general propositions that have already been empirically verified. If a proposition is phrased as a prediction, as in the proposition "The magnet will attract the key," its verification requires observation of the completed attraction. If the magnet attracts the key, there is a considerable degree of certainty about the truth of the description of the key. Statements of predictions, however, are only *hypotheses* since there is always the possibility of finding in the future a negative instance. For this reason, even though the degree of certainty is sufficient for most practical purposes, the original proposition will never be completely verified so as to produce *absolute* certainty.

These two forms of verification—direct and indirect—are central to the scientific method. Carnap argues that in the field of science every proposition asserts something about either present perceptions or future perceptions. In both cases, verification is either through direct perception or by the logical connection of already verified propositions. Thus, if a scientist made an assertion from which no proposition verified by perception could be deduced, it would be no assertion at all. For example, we could not verify the claim that there is a levitational force just as there is a gravitational force. While propositions concerning gravity can be verified by observing its effects upon bodies, there are no observable effects or laws describing levitation. According to Carnap, assertions about levitation are no assertions at all because they do not speak about anything. They are nothing but a series of empty words—expressions with no sense.

When logical analysis is applied to metaphysics, Carnap concludes that metaphysical propositions are not verifiable, or, if an attempt at verification is made, the results are always negative. Take, for example, the proposition propounded by Thales that "the principle of the World is Water." We cannot deduce any propositions asserting any perceptions whatever that may be expected in the future. Such a proposition therefore asserts nothing at all. Metaphysicians cannot avoid making their propositions nonverifiable because if they made them verifiable they would belong to the realm of empirical science since their truth or falsehood would depend upon experience. Carnap therefore rejects metaphysics, as he writes in Chapter One of his *Philosophy and Logical Syntax:*

> Metaphysical propositions are neither true nor false, because they assert nothing, they contain neither knowledge nor error, they lie completely outside the field of knowledge, of theory, outside the discussion of truth or falsehood. But they are, like laughing, lyrics, and music, expressive. They express not so much temporary feelings as permanent emotional or volitional dispositions. . . . The danger lies in the *deceptive* character of metaphysics; it gives the illusion of knowledge without actually giving any knowledge. This is the reason why we reject it.

According to Carnap, ethics and value judgments in general belong to the realm of metaphysics. When he applies his method of logical analysis to the propositions of ethics, these propositions predictably turn out to be meaningless. There can, he argues, be a science of ethics in the form of psychological or sociological or other empirical investigations about the actions of human beings and their effects upon other people. But the philosophy of moral values does not rest upon any facts since its purpose is to state norms for human action. The value statement "Killing is evil" has the grammatical form of an assertive proposition. But, Carnap says, "a value statement is nothing else than a command in a misleading grammatical form. It may have effects upon the actions of men, and these effects may be in accordance with our wishes or not; but it is neither true nor false. It does not assert anything and can neither be proved nor disproved."

Carnap held that the propositions of psychology belong to the region of empirical science in just the same way as do the propositions of biology and chemistry. He was aware that many people would consider it an offensive presumption to place psychology, "hitherto robed in majesty as the theory of spiritual events," into the domain of the physical sciences. Yet that is what he proceeded to do. In his essay "Psychology and Physical Language" he writes that "every sentence of psychology may be formulated in physical language." What he meant by this was that "all sentences of psychology describe physical occurrences, namely, the physical behavior of humans and other animals." This is part of the general theory of physicalism, which Carnap described as the view that "physical language is a universal language, that is, a language into which every sentence may be translated." In effect, Carnap would make psychology an aspect of physics since all science would become physics and the various domains of science would become parts of a unified science. In this manner, we are to test propositions in psychology by translating them into physical language. Thus, the statement "John is in pain" is translated into a statement describing the observable state S of John's body. This process of translation requires only that there be a scientific law stating that someone is in pain if and only if his bodily condition is in a particular state S. It is then meaningful to say that "John is in pain" and "John's body is in state S" since, while not equivalent, these are interchangeable translations. Only those statements that can be directly verified or translated into verifiable statements have meaning. Neither metaphysics, some aspects of psychology, theories of "reality," nor the philosophy of normative values could satisfy the criterion of verifiability, and Carnap therefore rejected them as meaningless.

In time, there were objections to Carnap's early formulation of the criterion of verifiability. Carnap shifted his ground from verification to *confirmation*. Carnap agreed that if verification is taken to mean a complete and definitive establishment of the truth, then the laws of science could never be verified. The number of instances to which the laws of biology or physics apply is infinite. If strict verification required personal observation of every instance, then obviously there could not be verification as so defined. Though we cannot verify the universal scientific law, we can nevertheless verify its universal application—that is, single instances in the form of particular sentences derived from the law and from other sentences previously established. In this manner, *verification* in the strict sense gives way to the gradually increasing *confirmation* of scientific laws.

As a further aid to logical clarity, in his book *The Logical Syntax of Language,* Carnap distinguished between what he called the *material* and the *formal* modes of language. He argued that the *material* mode, commonly used in philosophy, frequently leads to the ambiguities and errors of metaphysicians and in general is the source of meaningless philosophical controversy. To overcome these dangers, Carnap felt it was necessary to translate sentences from the material idiom into the more accurate *formal* idiom. He gives the following example: The sentence "The moon is a thing" is in the material mode. It can be translated into the formal mode in this sentence: "The word 'moon' is a thing-designation." Every sentence which states "Such and such is a *thing*" belongs in the material mode. Carnap holds that many other words, such as *quality, relation, number,* and *event,* also function the same way as the word *thing.* As another example, the sentence "7 is not a thing but a number," is in the material mode; its formal mode translation is "The sign 7 is not a thing sign but a numerical sign." The way to avoid the "dangerous material mode," Carnap says, is to avoid the word *thing* and use instead the syntactical term *thing-designation.* Similarly, instead of using the word *number,* we should use the term *numerical-designation.* Instead of *quality, quality-designation.* Instead of *event, event-designation,* and so forth. Other examples would include "He lectured about Babylon" as is translated into "The word Babylon occurred in his lecture."

By this method of translating sentences into the formal mode, Carnap hoped that we would free "logical analysis from all reference to extra-linguistic objects themselves." Analysis would then be concerned principally with the form of linguistic expressions—with *syntax.* In spite of this emphasis on syntactical form, Carnap believed that we must not forget the objects themselves to which our words refer. He writes, "there is no question of eliminating reference to objects themselves from object-sciences. On the contrary, these sciences are really concerned with objects themselves, with things, not merely with thing-designations."

Problems with Logical Positivism

The theory of logical positivism was not warmly received by many philosophers. Some were appalled at the incredible denial of meaning to moral language. Others noted inherent defects with the verification principle, which the logical positivists themselves soon recognized. Among the difficulties encountered was, first of all, it seems that the verification principle was not itself verifiable. Consider this sentence: "meaningful statements are either analytic or empirically verifiable." But is this statement itself meaningful based on its own criteria? This sentence is neither true by definition, nor can it be verified through experience. Thus, this statement of the verification principle fails its own test, and is thus meaningless. Logical positivists recognized this problem and said that their principle was more like a recommendation than it was a meaningful scientific contention. The question still remains, though, why a metaphysician would want to adopt a recommendation like this if it rendered meaningless everything the metaphysician said.

A second problem arose in the very area where this principle was presumed to have its greatest relevance, namely, the sciences. Scientific knowledge is frequently expressed in the form of universal laws. These "laws" are the basis for scientific *prediction.* But the problem the logical positivists faced was whether to consider scientific statements meaningful. How can a statement that makes a prediction be verified? Can my present experience, or experiment, tell me anything about the future? Obviously, literal significance or meaning is one thing when we verify the statement "There is a black cow in Smith's barn." It is quite another thing when the scientist says, for example, that when a moving body is not acted upon by external forces, its direction will remain constant. The first case is specific and verifiable. The second involves an indefinite number of cases, and any single case in the future can falsify that statement. Since there is no single fact that can *now* verify the future truth of a general scientific statement, such a statement, by a rigorous application of the verification principle, would be meaningless. Logical positivists solved this problem by offering a weaker version of the verification principle. That is, that a statement need only be "verifiable in principle," or *capable* of verification, that is, confirmed in some degree by the observation of something physical.

A third problem involves the crucial question of what constituted *verification.* To answer "sense experience" raised the further question "whose experience?" The problem begins with the central assumption behind the verification principle that our empirical utterances need to be translated into more foundational statements. Scientific language would ultimately be reducible to *observational statements.* But what is the fact that an observation statement reports? Is it a subjective experience about a physical object, or is it a pure picture of that object? The technical problem concerns whether it is ever possible to translate a person's internal experience into a statement about a physical object, or vice versa. This is the problem of *solipsism,* the view that the self is the only object of real knowledge and that therefore the experiences of one person cannot be the same as those of another. Each person's experience is different, and all of our experiences are different from the objectively real world. If this is the case, what does the verification principle amount to in the end? Verification statements would mean one thing to one person and something else to others.

A fourth and more general problem with the verification principle is why it placed such a high premium on sense experience. That is, why rule out the meaningfulness of statements that are grounded only in our intuitions, hopes, or gut feelings? Logical Positivists did not answer this question in any formal way. It may be that for them empirical verification was central to the distinction between scientific procedures, on the one hand, and metaphysical speculation on the other. Being oriented chiefly toward science, the Logical Positivists assumed that only language that referred to physical objects and their interrelationships could have cognitive meaning. By coupling of all statements to physical facts, they hoped to achieve the *unity of science* and that such a unified knowledge would give sciences a common language and tell us all there is to say.

Because of all of these problems, logical positivists toned down the intensity of their views. The blanket rejection of metaphysics and morals was reversed, and analysts began to focus their attention on these traditional areas of philosophy. Ayer described this new temper by saying that "the metaphysician is treated no longer as a criminal but as a patient: there may be good reasons why he says the strange things he does." Ethics, for example, is no longer nonsense but a discipline whose language is analyzed both for its relation to fact and for its value in pointing to a problem. Although logical positivism in its classical form dissolved from the weight of its inner difficulties, its impact continues in the analytic movement, which is still concerned overwhelmingly with the usages and analysis of language.

Quine's Critique of Empiricism

By the mid-20th century, logical positivism as a movement was largely a thing of the past. Nevertheless, fears of violating the verification principle still lingered in the minds of metaphysicians and moralists, many of them avoided straying too far from empirical facts. But logical positivism was only the most recent effort to put forth an empiricist agenda. The empirical trend in philosophy is much older, going as far back as Francis Bacon, and for several centuries after has been a driving force in philosophical discussions. In 1951, Willard Van Orman Quine (b. 1908) attempted to expose a more fundamental problem with empiricism that applied not only to logical positivism, but all traditional accounts of empiricism. He addresses this in his 1951 essay "Two Dogmas of Empiricism." The first dogma of empiricism is the longstanding assumption that statements neatly divide between those which are *analytic* and those which are *synthetic* (that is, empirical). He writes, "a boundary between analytic and synthetic statements simply has not been drawn. That there is such a distinction to be drawn at all is an unempirical dogma of empiricists, a metaphysical article of faith." The other dogma is that of *reductionism,* which holds that every meaningful statement can be translated into a statement about immediate experience.

Quine was aware that to reject these dogmas would mean abandoning, or at least "blurring the supposed boundary between speculative metaphysics and natural science." Nevertheless, this is what he tries to do. As to the first dogma, he argues that the notion of "analyticity" is very difficult to clarify, apart from a few limited logical statements. Even logical statements, presumably true "no matter what," can be altered in the interests of new conceptions of physics. Quine asks, "What difference is there in principle between such a shift [in logic] and the shift whereby Kepler superseded Ptolemy, or Einstein, Newton, or Darwin, Aristotle?" Synthetic statements, he argues, do not live up to their empirical verifiability as clearly as they are supposed to. Quine scrutinizes various ways that philosophers tried to establish the truth of both analytic and synthetic statements; he then concludes that "no statement is immune to revision." This would mean that both analytic and synthetic propositions contain only contingent truth and, to that extent, do not differ.

What would science be like without the dogmas of empiricism? As an empiricist himself, Quine believed that science and logic are important conceptual schemes, and useful as tools. Indeed, the total range of our knowledge, he says, "is a man-made fabric which impinges upon experience only along the edges." Any conflict between a statement that we hold to be true and a new experience at variance with it requires an adjustment. We must alter not only our initial statement, but ultimately all of the interconnected concepts. Certainty seems greatest in the physical realm, but Quine argues that physical bodies are themselves only a convenient conceptual tool. Indeed, he says that physical objects are simply "irreducible posits," comparing them to the gods of Homer. As an empiricist he thinks that it would be erroneous to believe in Homer's gods rather than physical objects. "But," he says, "in point of epistemological footing the physical objects and the gods differ only in degree and not in kind." To argue in this manner clearly undercuts the distinction both between analytic and synthetic statements and between metaphysics and science. In the end, Quine settles for a strongly pragmatic conception of truth, saying, "Each man is given a scientific heritage plus a continuing barrage of sensory stimulation; and the considerations which guide him in warping his scientific heritage to fit his continuing sensory promptings are, where rational, pragmatic."

LUDWIG WITTGENSTEIN

Wittgenstein's Road to Philosophy

Ludwig Wittgenstein was born on April 26, 1889, the youngest of eight children of one of the wealthiest and highest placed families in the Austro-Hungarian Empire. His father, Karl Wittgenstein, built an immense fortune during the 1890s as a leader in the heavy metals industry. As he neared retire-

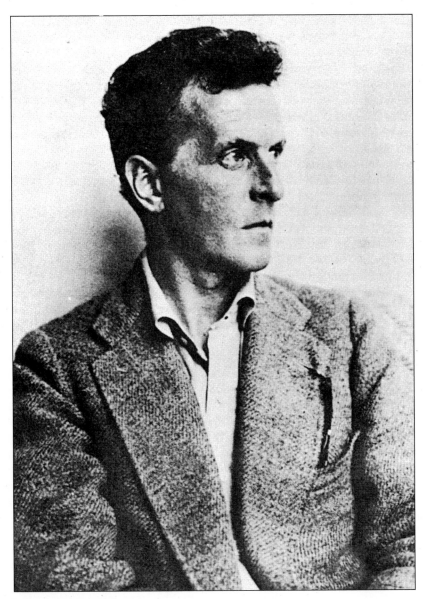

Ludwig Wittgenstein

ment, he understandably wanted his children to find their place in his vast company. But for the most part, his children followed their own interests. Under his sister Gretl's influence, Ludwig read some philosophy, but at the same time he could not altogether turn a deaf ear to his father's wishes for him to study engineering to prepare for his entry into the family's company.

Wittgenstein left Europe and went to Manchester to study aeronautics. But his decision to study engineering was simply a temporary decision, as he could not deny the powerful inner drive to pursue his interest in philosophy. Even when he was involved in the problems of engineering, his great interest lay in the philosophy of mathematics. This caused him to suffer the strains of deciding between the two professions of philosophy and engineering. But he still needed some confirmation that he had sufficient talent in philosophy to pursue it as a career. He took a sample of his work to the eminent philosopher Gottlob Frege in Jena, author of *The Foundation of Mathematics*. Wittgenstein felt that his interview went well enough, since Frege encouraged him to travel to Cambridge to study under Bertrand Russell.

After meeting Wittgenstein, Bertrand Russell said that "my German friend threatens to be an infliction, he came back with me after my lecture and argued till dinner time—obstinate and perverse, but I think not stupid." Again, "my German engineer very argumentative and tiresome. He would not admit that it was certain that there was not a rhinoceros in the room. . . . [He] came back and argued all the time I was dressing." Finally "my German engineer, I think, is a fool. He thinks nothing empirical is knowable—I asked him to admit that there was not a rhinoceros in the room, but he wouldn't." In time these conversations became more relaxed so that Russell "learned more about Wittgenstein than his all-consuming interest in philosophical problems, as for example, that he was Austrian and not German, and also that he was very literary, very musical, pleasant mannered . . . and I think really intelligent." When Wittgenstein returned to Cambridge in January 1912, he showed Russell a manuscript that he wrote during the vacation. This changed Russell's opinion of Wittgenstein to a very positive appreciation of his abilities, calling the manuscript "very good, much better than my English pupils do," adding, "I shall certainly encourage him. Perhaps he will do great things." During the next term Wittgenstein worked so hard at mathematical logic that Russell believed that Wittgenstein surpassed him, saying that he learned all he had to teach, and indeed had gone farther. "Yes, Wittgenstein has been a great event in my life—whatever may become of it." In fact, Russell now looked upon Wittgenstein as the one who could solve the problems which were raised by his own work. "I am too old" said Russell, "to solve all kinds of problems raised by my work, but want a fresh mind and the vigor of youth. He is *the* young man one hopes for." As a matter of fact, Russell was so impressed with Wittgenstein's abilities that he considered Wittgenstein his "Protégé."

In addition to the high praise of Bertrand Russell, Wittgenstein developed a bond with G. E. Moore, whose lectures he began to attend. But in spite of the praise of these philosophical leaders, Wittgenstein did not pursue a straight line in his philosophical development. There were certain peculiarities in his personality that deflected him from his course from time to time. His intense desire for solitude led him to withdraw to a rural setting in Norway where he built a cottage and where he could devote himself entirely to his analysis of the problems of logic, which he thought would be his unique philosophical contribution. But he suffered from physical and emotional isolation. In time Wittgenstein inherited considerable wealth which, without explanation, he gave away, leaving him without sufficient funds. As the military situation was developing in Europe, Wittgenstein enrolled in the Austrian army, taking with him his manuscript on which he was working. By the time he completed his military duties, he was able to return to Cambridge with a virtually finished manuscript and a position as a lecturer at the university. He was not happy in that teaching position, and strangely enough he urged the young scholars who were influenced by his teaching not to go into teaching themselves. Instead, Wittgenstein urged them to undertake some physical or manual work. Although his brilliance was recognized by his peers, Wittgenstein was not a happy scholar. He appeared to make his life difficult by making choices that undermined his clear commitment both to his work and to his friendships. In the end, he lost the friendship and support of Bertrand Russell, who gave him such strong support at the beginning of his career.

The only book of Wittgenstein's published during his lifetime is his early *Tractatus Logico-Philosophicus* (1919), which develops a theory of logical atomism similar to that of Russell's. Although Wittgenstein was not a member of Vienna Circle, he conversed with them, and Circle considered his *Tractatus* to express its philosophical point of view with great accuracy. Not only did Wittgenstein say that "whatever can be said at all can be said clearly," he concluded his book by saying that "whereof one cannot speak, thereof one must be silent." After Wittgenstein's death in 1951, a number of books by him appeared based on manuscripts and lecture notes by students. Principal among these are his *Philosophical Investigations* (1953). These works reflect a completely different turn of thought from the *Tractatus,* and it is his later views that have brought him fame within the field of philosophy.

The New Wittgenstein

Shortly after his *Tractatus* appeared, Wittgenstein repudiated much of that work. He now believed that his former views were based on the erroneous assumption that language has only one function, namely, to state facts. The *Tractatus* further assumed that sentences for the most part derive their meanings from stating facts. Finally, Wittgenstein assumed, as did Carnap, that the skeleton behind all language is a logical one. What struck Wittgenstein now was the somewhat obvious point that language has *many* functions besides simply "picturing" objects. Language always functions in a *context* and therefore has as many purposes as there are contexts. Words, he said, are like "tools in a tool-box; there is a hammer, pliers, a saw, a screwdriver, a rule, a glue-pot, glue, nails, and screws. The function of words is as diverse as the functions of these objects."

What made him think earlier that language had only one function? He says that he was held captive by the view that language gives names to things, just as Adam in the Bible gave names to animals. He writes that we are all the victims of "the bewitchment of our intelligence by means of language." Our incorrect picture of language is "produced by grammatical illusions." Analyzing grammar might lead us to discover some logical structure of language. But would that justify the conclusion that all language has essentially the same rules, functions, and meanings? It occurred to Wittgenstein that the assumption that all language states facts and contains a logical skeleton was derived not by observation but by thought. We simply assume that all language, in spite of certain superficial differences, is alike, the way all games are alike. He uncovered the flaw in this analogy by taking the case of games and asking,

> What is common to them all?—Don't say: There *must* be something common, or they would not be called 'games'—but *look and see* whether there is anything common at all.—For if you look at them you will not see something that is common to *all*, but similarities, relationships, and a whole series of them at that. To repeat: don't think, but look.

Wittgenstein therefore shifted his plan of analysis from a preoccupation with logic and the construction of a "perfect" language to the study of the ordinary usages of language. He moved away from what Russell and Carnap were doing and turned instead in the direction of G. E. Moore's earlier emphasis upon the analysis of ordinary language, testing it by the criterion of common sense.

Wittgenstein now felt that language does not contain one single pattern alone, but that it is as variable as life itself. He writes, "to imagine a language means to imagine a form of life." Analysis, then, should consist not in the definition of language or its meanings but rather in a careful description of its uses: "We must do away with an explanation, and *description alone* must take its place." We must, said Wittgenstein, "stick to the subjects of everyday thinking, and not go astray and imagine that we have to describe extreme subtleties." Confusions arise not when our language is "doing work," but only when it is "like an engine idling."

Language Games and Following Rules

A central concept in Wittgenstein's philosophy is the notion of rule-following. Throughout our daily routines we engage in a variety of tasks that involve some kind of rules. We often copy the behavior of other people when, for example, we try to learn a dance routine. We often participate in ceremonies, such as graduation, in which we wear special clothes, walk in a long line with fellow graduates, and receive a diploma in our hands. Similar rule following underlies all language. We say utter certain things in certain contexts, and we follow specific grammatical rules when we organize our words. Not just our spoken words, but our entire thinking activity involves rule following. Wittgenstein suggests that the rules of language are like rules of different games—language games—that vary in different contexts. When a student ask questions in a biology class, she follows the rules of various language games, such as, the language game of an inquiring student in a formal classroom, and the language game of discipline of biology. He writes,

> But how many kinds of sentence are there? Say assertion, question, and command?—There are *countless* kinds: countless different kinds of uses of what we call "symbols", "words", and "sentences". And this multiplicity is not something fixed, given once for all; but new types of language, new language-games, as we may say, come into existence, and others become obsolete and get forgotten. . . . Here the term "language-game" is meant to bring into prominence the fact that the *speaking* of language is part of an activity, or of a form of life.

Because philosophical problems grow out of language, it is necessary to acquire a basic familiarity with the uses of the language out of which each problem arises. As there are many kinds of games, there are many sets of rules of the games. Similarly, as there are many kinds of languages (that is, the many forms of ordinary language of work, play, worship, science, and so forth), there are many *usages.* Under these circumstances, "the work of the philosopher consists of *assembling reminders* for a particular purpose."

Clarifying Metaphysical Language

How does Wittgenstein deal with metaphysical language? Unlike the positivists, he did not reject the statements of metaphysics outright. Instead, he considered the metaphysician as a patient instead of a criminal, and the function of philosophy would be therapeutic. Metaphysical language can indeed create confusion, and the central concern of philosophy is to deal with problems that baffle and confuse us because of the lack of clarity. Philosophy is a "battle against the bewitchment of our intelligence by means of language." Bewitchment causes confusion, and so "a philosophical problem has the form: 'I don't know my way about.'" Philosophy helps us to find our way, to survey the scene; it brings "words back from their metaphysical to their everyday usage."

Philosophy does not provide us with new or more information, but instead adds clarity by a careful description of language. It is as though I can see all the parts of a jigsaw puzzle but am baffled by how to put it together. I am actually looking at everything I need to solve the problem. Philosophical puzzlement is similar and can be removed by a careful description of language as we ordinarily use it. What confuses us is when language is used in new and unordinary ways. Hence, "the results of philosophy are the uncovering of one or another piece of plain nonsense." If metaphysics displayed resistance or a prejudice that obscures the ordinary usage of words, he concedes that this is "not a *stupid* prejudice." The confusions of metaphysics is part of the human condition:

> the problems arising through a misinterpretation of our forms of language have the character of *depth.* They are deep disquietudes; their roots are as deep in us as the forms of our language and their significance is as great as the importance of our language.

True philosophy does not consist in giving crisp abstract answers to questions. A person who has lost his way wants a map of the terrain, and this is supplied by the selection and arrangement of concrete examples of the actual use of language in ordinary experience.

But it is not enough to just look at these examples of usage, any more than it is sufficient simply to look at the pieces of the jigsaw puzzle. We frequently "fail to be struck by what, once seen, is *most* striking and most powerful." The most important things are hidden "because of their simplicity and familiarity." But what does it mean to "fail to be struck?" There is no sure method according to Wittgenstein to guarantee that we will "be struck" and thereby find our way. In any case, what Wittgenstein sought to do was to shift philosophy's concern from meanings—from the assumption that words carried in them as so much freight "pictures" of objects in the world. Instead, he directed attention, through the assembling, selecting, and arranging of relevant examples, to the actual uses of words. Because most *philosophical* problems were assumed to arise from puzzlements about words, the scrupulous description of their ordinary uses would eliminate this puzzlement.

JOHN AUSTIN

Another philosopher concerned with the ordinary use of language was Oxford scholar John Austin (1911–1960). He did not publish extensively, partly because of his untimely death at age 49. He once said that he had to decide early on whether he was going to write books or teach people to do philosophy in a way that he found so useful and satisfying in his own work and life. Austin had a unique approach to philosophy. In his essay on "A Plea for Excuses," he tells the reader that philosophy provided for him what it is so often barren of, namely, "the fun of discovery, the pleasure of cooperation and the satisfaction of reaching agreement." With relief and humor, he tells how his research enabled him to consider various words and idioms, "without remembering what Kant thought" and to move by degrees to discuss "deliberation without for once remembering Aristotle or self-control without Plato." In contrast to heavy and grim philosophizing, Austin exhibited a deceptive simplicity. In the opening sentence of *How to Do Things with Words,* he writes, "What I shall have to say here is neither difficult nor contentious: the only merit I should like to claim for it is that of being true, at least in parts."

Austin was aware that the use of such phrases as "the analysis of language," or "analytic philosophy" or even "ordinary language" could lead to the misunderstanding that philosophical analysis was *only* and *solely* concerned with words. Austin was not only concerned with words, but also "the realities we use the words to talk about." "We are using a sharpened awareness of words to sharpen our perception of, though not the final arbiter of, the phenomena." He even wondered in passing whether his approach to philosophy might not more usefully be called "linguistic phenomenology," a notion he gave up as being "rather a mouthful." Austin had little interest in criticizing the methods of other philosophers or putting excessive emphasis upon his own style. He developed a technique for studying the nature of language and found it successful in dealing with various philosophical problems.

The Notion of "Excuses"

Turning to his essay on "A Plea for Excuses," we find in it some flavor of Austin's fruitful analysis of ordinary language. He elaborates in some detail just how and why he philosophizes about words. For one thing, he felt that philosophy can be "done" in a wide variety of ways. Unlike any one of the sciences, whose subject matter and methods are highly organized, philosophy functions in those spheres where no one is sure just what is the best way to resolve a particular problem. Austin thus selects some area of discourse that he thinks is of interest to philosophers. For him the word *excuses* provided a rich field for the study of language as well as human behavior. Through the analysis of this word, Austin discovers distinctions of various degrees between words closely connected with *excuses.* Moreover, his analysis uncovers interesting insights into human behavior as suggested by the distinctions among a web of interrelated words.

At the outset, the word *excuses* turns out to be a term surrounded by other significant words, such as *defiance, justification,* or *plea.* It is necessary, Austin argues, to give a complete and clear account and to consider the largest number possible of cases of the use of the chosen word. In general, excuses involve a situation where people are *accused* of having done something wrong, or "bad," or "inept," and they either try to defend their conduct or establish their innocence. They can admit that they *did* what they are accused of doing and then argue that under the prevailing circumstances it was either the right or the acceptable or at least the understandable thing to do. This would be to "justify" the action. A quite different way to proceed would be for the accused to admit that the act was a bad one but that it would be unfair to say without qualification that they *did* it. It could be that their action was unintentional, an accident, or precipitated by some other event. The word "responsibility" becomes significantly related to "they did it" and to "excuses." And the distinction between an "excuse" for an action and a "justification" of it turns out to be an important one. Moreover, if the charge happens to be murder, a plea for the accused could rest on the justification of self-defense or excused as accidental. Words with finer degrees of distinction could be employed here, including "mitigation" and "extenuation." And what about the language of a defendant who says, "I didn't do it—something in me made me do it." An act can also be the result of a "fit of anger" as distinguished from a "deliberate act."

Why go through this analysis of the word "excuses" or any other term of discourse? Apart from the fact that the fashioning of excuses has occupied such an important role in human affairs and is on that account worthy of careful study, Austin believed that moral philosophy could benefit by this analysis for two reasons. For one thing, such an analysis could facilitate in developing a more accurate and up-to-date version of human conduct. Second, as a corollary, it could contribute toward the correction of older and prematurely settled theories. Since moral philosophy is the study of the rightness and wrongness of conduct or the doing of actions, it becomes crucial to understand what it means to "do something" before we can properly say about it that it is either right or wrong.

"Doing an action," Austin says, is a very abstract expression. Do we mean by it "to think something," "to say something," or "to try to do something"? It is just as inaccurate to think that all our actions are of the same nature as it is to think that all "things" are of the same kind—that winning a war, as an action, is the same as sneezing, that a horse as a thing is equal to a bed as a thing. Do we *do* an action when we breathe or see? For what, then, is the phrase "doing an action" an appropriate substitute? What rules are there for the proper word signifying "the" action for which a person is responsible or for which he or she manufactures excuses? Can human actions be divided in order to attribute one part to the actor and the remainder to someone or something else? Moreover, is an action a simple event? Austin emphasizes rather the complex nature of a human act. This even includes the mere motion of the body, which could involve intentions, motives, responses to information, the reflection upon rules, a studied control of the motion of a limb, or a shove from someone else.

Austin believed that the questions just raised and the problems posed can be illuminated by an analysis of the word *excuses.* For one thing, an excuse implies that a certain type of behavior went wrong in some way. To determine the nature of the wrongness involves a clarification of the "right." The abnormal frequently clarifies the normal. The careful study of excuses provides the opportunity to determine when excuses are appropriate, what actions can be classified as excusable, what particular abnormalities of behavior are truly "actions," and, in a more intricate manner, determine what constitutes the very structure or mechanism of human behavior. The study of excuses can also resolve some traditional mistakes or inconclusive arguments in moral philosophy. High on the list is the problem of freedom. Here Austin compares the words *freedom* and *truth,* pointing out that just as "truth" is not a name characterizing assertions, neither is "freedom" a name characterizing actions. Freedom, Austin says, is "the name of the dimension in which action is assessed." He then says, "in examining all the ways in which each action may not be 'free', i.e., the cases in which it will not do to say simply 'X did A,' we may hope to dispose of the problem of freedom."

The Benefits of Ordinary Language

Besides throwing light on moral philosophy, the study of excuses provides Austin with a concrete application for his philosophical method. He begins with "ordinary language" through which he expects to discover "what we should say when" and therefore "why and what we should mean by it." This, he believes, can clear up the uses and misuses of words and in that manner avoid the traps in which we can be caught by imprecise language. The analysis of ordinary language also emphasizes the differences between words and things and enables us to remove the words from the realities we use words to talk about, and in that way get a fresh look at those realities. Most of all, Austin believed that "our common stock of words embodies all the distinctions men have found worth drawing, and the connections they have found worth making, in the lifetimes of many generations." This stock of words in ordinary language must, he felt, be more sound and more subtle than any we could think up for the purpose of philosophizing. For, they have stood up to the test of time and the competition of other possible words. Moreover, ordinary language provides the philosopher "a good site for fieldwork." It makes possible a different climate of philosophical discourse by disengaging individuals from frozen and rigid philosophical positions. How much easier it is to agree on the uses of words or even on how to reach agreement. Austin hoped that this method could someday be applied to the turbulent field of aesthetics, saying, "if only we could forget for awhile about the beautiful and get down to the dainty and the dumpy."

Austin was aware that ordinary language, as a basis for analysis, could present certain problems. For one thing, there is a certain "looseness" in ordinary language so that one person's usage may not be the same as another's. To this Austin replies that there is not as much disagreement in the use of words as we might think. Surface differences tend to disappear when, through analysis, we discover that it was not really the *same* situation about which different people have been speaking: "The more we imagine the situation in detail," says Austin, "the less we find we disagree about what we should say." Sometimes, however, there are disagreements in the use of words. But even here, Austin says, "we can find *why* we disagree," and "the explanation can hardly fail to be illuminating." Besides its looseness, another question about ordinary language is whether it should be construed as the "last word" on matters. While ordinary language does not claim to be the last word, it is significant that it embodies the inherited experience and insights of many generations. And although these insights have been focused particularly upon the practical affairs of people, that fact further strengthens the claim for its accuracy. For if the distinctions of words work well in ordinary life, "then there is something in it." Scholars may well have interests other than those whose language pertains to ordinary life. And there is no reason to believe that error and superstition cannot survive for long periods of time in a language. To this extent, he readily concedes that "ordinary language is *not* the last word: in principle it can everywhere be supplemented and improved upon and even superseded." But, he believes, it is the first word in his plan of analysis.

Austin recommends three resources which we can use in undertaking a full-scale analysis of the word *excuses*. Similar resources and methods would presumably be available for the analysis of other words as well. First, he advocated using the dictionary. A concise one would do, and he suggests reading through it entirely and listing all relevant words, remarking that it would not take as long as many would suppose. Or one could make a list of obviously relevant words first and consult the dictionary to discover their various meanings—a process which would then lead to other germane words until the relevant list is complete. A second source for this purpose would be the law. Here we would be provided with a vast number of cases along with a wide variety of pleas for excuses along with many analyses of the circumstances of the particular conduct in question. The third source is psychology. The use of psychology is an interesting example of how ordinary language is supplemented and even superseded. For psychology classifies some varieties of behavior or gives explanations of ways of acting which may not have been noticed by laypeople nor captured by ordinary language. Given these resources "and with the aid of imagination," Austin was confident that the meanings of a vast number of expressions would emerge and that a large number of human actions could be understood and classified, thereby achieving one of the central purposes of this whole process, namely, "explanatory definition."

CHAPTER 18

Phenomenology and Existentialism

*T*hroughout much of the 20th century, the analytic approach to philosophy launched by Bertrand Russell dominated philosophical thought in the United States, Great Britain, and other English speaking countries. However, within continental Europe—particularly Germany and France—philosophy had a different emphasis, which emerged in the movements of Phenomenology and Existentialism. Phenomenology set aside questions about the so-called objective nature of things; it recommended instead that we explore phenomena more subjectively, from within our human experience. Existentialism adopted phenomenology's subjective approach, and further developed practical issues of human experience, such as making choices and personal commitments. Phenomenology was launched by Edmund Husserl (1859–1938) and modified by Martin Heidegger (1889–1976). Shortly after there followed a group of writers often called "religious existentialists," including Karl Jaspers (1883–1969) and Gabriel Marcel (1889–1973). Existentialism received its definitive expression through Jean-Paul Sartre (1905–1980) and Maurice Merleau-Ponty (1908–1961).

EDMUND HUSSERL

Husserl's Life and Influence

Edmund Husserl was born of Jewish parents in the Moravian province of Prossnitz in 1859, the same year in which Bergson and Dewey were born. After his early education in that province, he went to the University of Leipzig, where, from 1876 to 1878, he studied physics, astronomy, and mathematics and found time to attend lectures by the philosopher Wilhelm Wundt. Husserl continued his studies at the Friederich Wilhelm University in Berlin. In 1881 he went to the University of Vienna where, in 1883, he earned his Ph.D. for his dissertation on "Contributions to the Theory of the Calculus of

Edmund Husserl

Variations." From 1884 to 1886, he attended the lectures of Franz Brentano (1838–1917), who became a most significant influence on Husserl's philosophical development, especially through his lectures on Hume and John Stuart Mill and his treatment of problems in ethics, psychology, and logic. On Brentano's advice, Husserl went to the University of Halle, where in 1886 he became an assistant under Carl Stumpf (1848–1936), the eminent psychologist under whose direction he wrote his first book, *Philosophy of Arithmetic* (1891). His *Logical Investigations* appeared in 1900, and in the same year he was invited to join the philosophy faculty at the University of Göttingen. It was here that Husserl spent 16 productive years, authoring a series of books developing his concept of phenomenology. Because of his Jewish origins, Husserl was forbidden to participate in academic activities after 1933. Although he was offered a professorship by the University of Southern California, Husserl declined the offer, and after several months of suffering, he died of pleurisy at the age of 79 in 1938 at Freiburg in Breisgau.

Husserl's philosophy evolved gradually through several phases. His early interest was in logic and mathematics. Next, he developed an early version of phenomenology which focused chiefly upon a theory of knowledge. Then, he moved on to a view of phenomenology as a universal foundation for philosophy and science. Finally he entered a phase in which the conception of the life-world (*Levenswelt*) became a more dominant theme in his phenomenology. It is no wonder, then, that Husserl's philosophy should have had a variety of influences upon different scholars at various times. For example, Martin Heidegger, who became Husserl's assistant at Freiburg in 1920, was familiar during his student days with Husserl's work in logic and his earlier writings in phenomenology. As his assistant from 1920–1923, Heidegger worked closely with Husserl. Together they prepared an article on phenomenology for the *Encyclopaedia Britannica.* Heidegger also prepared some of Husserl's earlier lectures for publication. Even after Heidegger left in 1923 to become a professor at Marburg, he continued his close association with Husserl. As time passed, however, Heidegger found it difficult to share Husserl's novel developments, especially those dealing with transcendental phenomenology. In his major work, *Being and Time,* Heidegger was critical of Husserl's method and his distinctive view of the ego. By the time Heidegger succeeded to Husserl's chair at Freiburg in the fall of 1928, their relationship began to weaken and eventually came to an end.

Similarly, although Sartre was influenced by Husserl's writings when he studied German phenomenology at Freiburg, he eventually came to believe that Heidegger's modification of Husserl's view was philosophically more significant. Nevertheless, upon his return to Paris from Germany in 1934, Sartre called Merleau-Ponty's attention to Husserl's book *The Idea of Phenomenology* (1906–1907) and urged him to study it carefully. Merleau-Ponty was impressed by several distinctive elements in Husserl's phenomenology and was inspired to work further in Husserl's writings. He was particularly influenced by Husserl's *The Crisis of European Sciences* (1936). Although Merleau-Ponty was thoroughly familiar with Husserl's ideas as interpreted by Heidegger and Sartre, he made his own extensive study of the original documents. He even went to Louvain where he had access to the Husserl archives. These archives, which contain over 40,000 pages of Husserl's manuscripts written in shorthand, are gradually becoming available through transcriptions and translations. What we find, then, without analyzing all the details, is that Husserl exerted a strong influence upon Heidegger, Merleau-Ponty, and Sartre, the leading exponents of phenomenology and existentialism. And even though they rejected many of Husserl's key ideas, their finished works bear the imprint of his phenomenology.

The Crisis of European Science

Before answering the question "What is phenomenology?" it is helpful to ask, "What prompted Husserl to develop phenomenology in the first place?" His philosophy grew out of his deep conviction that Western culture lost its true direction and purpose. His attitude is reflected in the title of his last major philosophical work, *The Crisis of European Sciences* (1936). The "crisis" consists of philosophy's departure from its true goal, which is to provide the best possible answers to human concerns, to deal rigorously with our quest for the highest values, and, in short, to develop the unique broad-range capacities of human reason. Husserl described the "crisis" as the "seeming collapse of rationalism," and he set his lifetime objective as "saving human reason." What human reason has to be saved from, according to Husserl, provides the background for his phenomenology.

The key to the crisis of modern thought is the enterprise of "natural science." Husserl was impressed by the brilliant successes of the sciences. In fact, his ultimate objective is to save human reason by developing philosophy into a rigorous science. His criticism is, therefore, not directed at science as such but rather at the assumptions and methods of the natural sciences. Husserl believes that the natural sciences have over the years developed a faulty attitude about human beings, regarding what the world is like and how best to know it. The natural sciences rest upon the fatal prejudice that nature is basically physical. On this view, the realm of spirit—that is, human culture—is causally based upon physical things, which ultimately threatens our conceptions of knowing, valuing, and judging. The natural scientist rejects the possibility of formulating a self-contained science of the spirit. This rejection, Husserl argues, is quite naive, and explains to a large degree the crisis of modern people. What makes this scientific rationalism naive is its blind reliance on *naturalism,* which is the view that physical nature envelops everything there is. It also means that knowledge and truth are "objective" in the sense that they are based upon a reality beyond our individual selves. The problem started when philosophers and scientists departed from the original philosophical attitude developed in ancient Greece.

Before the days of Socrates, Plato, and Aristotle, people had very practical lives, seeing to their basic needs for food, clothing, and shelter. They developed mythologies and early religions that supported the practical concerns of individuals and larger groups. In this condition there was no culture of ideas in the sense of concepts that reached beyond the immediate boundaries of local experience and practical interests. Greek philosophers then entered the picture with a new kind of outlook, namely, a universal critique of all life and its goals. The positive side of this critique was its aim of elevating people through universal reason toward a new humanity, rising above the limited horizons of custom, geography, and social groups. What made this possible was a new conception of truth. This truth was independent of tradition, universally valid, and capable of infinite refinement. Here, then, is the origin of the spiritual life and the culture of Europe. The systematic formulation of this attitude is what the Greeks called *philosophy.* Correctly understood, Husserl writes, this philosophy "bespeaks nothing but universal science, science of the world as a whole, of the universal unity of all being." Philosophy had a comprehensive grasp of all nature, which included the cultural as well as the physical—ideas as well as objects. In time, though, this one science—philosophy—began to splinter into the several separate sciences. The dominant step in this splintering was the discovery of how the world of perceived nature can be changed into a mathematical world. This discovery eventually led to the development of the mathematical natural sciences. Ultimately, the success of the sciences resulted in the gradual scientific rejection of the spirit.

Democritus had much earlier offered a similar view that reduced everything in the world to material stuff and physical laws. Socrates rejected this view since he felt that spiritual life existed within the context of society. Plato and Aristotle also held this Socratic view of the spiritual dimension. For, while human beings belong to the universe of objective facts, we are nevertheless people who have goals and aims. But with the later success of the mathematical natural sciences, the scientific methods soon enveloped knowledge of the spirit. A person's spirit was now conceived as an objective fact founded upon physical stuff. So, the same causal explanations that apply to the physical world also apply to the spiritual. Husserl argues that, from the attitude of natural science,

> there can be no pure self-contained search for an explanation of the spiritual, no purely inner-oriented psychology or theory of spirit beginning with the ego in psychical-self-experience and extending to the other psyche. The way that must be traveled is the external one, the path of physics and chemistry.

He concluded that we cannot improve our understanding of our true human purposes so long as naturalistic objectivism studies spirit according to the methodology of the natural sciences. He thus formulated his transcendental phenomenology as a way of grasping the essential nature of the spirit and thereby overcoming naturalistic objectivism.

Descartes and Intentionality

Having explored Husserl's motivations for developing phenomenology, it will be helpful to look at one of his key sources of inspiration for his method, namely, Descartes. Husserl says that "phenomenology must honor Descartes as its genuine patriarch." There were other influences upon Husserl's thought, notably the empiricism of Locke, the skepticism of Hume, the Copernican revolution of Kant, and the pragmatism of William James. In every case Husserl went beyond these and others whose insights shaped his own ideas. Nevertheless, Descartes's influence was decisive, for it led Husserl to begin where Descartes began, with the thinking self. However, whereas Descartes sought through systematic doubt to achieve an absolutely certain foundation for knowledge, Husserl formulated the distinctive atmosphere of phenomenology by accepting only one part of Descartes's starting point. Husserl writes, "We thus begin, everyone for himself and in himself with the decision to disregard all our present knowledge. We do not give up Descartes's guiding goal of an absolute foundation for knowledge. At the beginning, however, to presuppose even the possibility of that goal would be prejudice." Husserl thus takes an even more radical approach than Descartes did, for he tries to build a philosophy without *any* presuppositions, looking solely to "things and facts themselves, as these are given in actual experience and intuition." Husserl made it a cardinal rule "to judge only by the evidence" and not according to any preconceived notions or presuppositions. He sought to recapture humanity's prescientific life, which is filled with "immediate and mediate evidences." Thus, whereas Descartes employed systematic doubt, Husserl simply withheld any judgment about his experiences, seeking instead to describe his experiences as fully as possible in terms of the evidence of experience itself.

Experience obviously revolves around the self—the ego—and for Husserl as well as Descartes the source of all knowledge is the self. But while for Descartes the self becomes the first axiom in a logical sequence, which enables him to deduce, as one would in mathematics, a series of conclusions about reality, Husserl sees the self simply as the matrix of experience. Husserl therefore puts primary emphasis upon experience instead of logic. His concern is to discover and describe *the given* in experience as it is presented in its pure form and found as the immediate data of consciousness. Husserl criticizes Descartes for moving beyond the conscious self to the notion of extended substance, a body, which ties the subject to an objective reality producing thereby the mind-body dualism. Instead, Husserl believed that "pure subjectivity" more accurately describes the actual facts of human experience. Moreover, whereas Descartes emphasized the two terms in his famous "I think" (*ego cogito*), Husserl believed that a more accurate description of experience is expressed in the three terms "I think something" (*ego cogito cogitatum*). This is the philosophical concept of *intentionality*—consciousness is always consciousness *of* something.

The clearest fact about consciousness is that its essence is to point toward, or to intend, some object. Our perception of things consists of our projection toward intended objects. Thus Husserl believed that the essence of consciousness is intentionality. By intentionality, Husserl means that any object of my consciousness—a house, a pleasure, a number, or another person—is something meant, constructed, constituted, that is, intended by me. Pure consciousness has no segments; rather, it is a continuous stream. Our primitive perception consists of the undifferentiated world. The separate objects of perception are those parts of the stream of consciousness which we as subjects constitute by intending them. Kant described earlier how the mind organizes experience by imposing such categories as time, space, and causality upon sensory experience. Similarly, Bergson said that "in the continuity of sensible qualities we mark off the boundaries of bodies." For Husserl, too, intentionality is the active involvement of the self in creating our experience. Indeed, for Husserl, intentionality is both the structure of consciousness itself and the fundamental category of existence. This means that, in the process of discovering reality, we should look for reality in things, since things are what we intend them to be. For example, when I look at someone, I perceive him from a limited perspective, such as seeing only his profile. I also see him in a given setting, such as shopping at a store. These perceptions are only fragments of reality, and from these our consciousness "intends," *the* person in question. This process of intentionality is typically not conscious, but rather one that is automatic. The self's constitution of the world is what he calls a *passive genesis.*

Phenomena and Phenomenological Bracketing

The term *phenomenology* rests on Husserl's refusal to go beyond the only evidence available to consciousness, namely, phenomena, which is derived from appearances. Most theories of knowledge distinguish between a knowing mind, on the one hand, and the object of knowledge on the other. Husserl, though, sees virtually no distinction between consciousness and the phenomenon. In fact, he argues that phenomena are ultimately contained in the very subjective act of experiencing something. This stands in sharp contrast to the more natural attitude, which assumes that there is an objective world of phenomena irrespective of my consciousness of it. For Husserl, knowing something is not like the act of a camera taking pictures of things. By focusing on the phenomena of a thing available to our consciousness, we actually have a more enlarged description of it. For it now includes the real object, our actual perception of it, the object as we mean it, and the act of intentionality. This, he believes, moves beyond the description of the superficial aspects of a thing's appearances to the intricate activity of consciousness. Husserl writes, "consciousness makes possible and necessary the fact that such an 'existing' and 'thus determined' Object is intended in it, occurs in it as such a sense." In short, we can best understand the elements of our experience by discovering the active role of consciousness in intending and creating phenomena.

Can we say anything about the external things themselves that we are experiencing? Husserl answers that we must put aside—or bracket—any assumptions about external things. He calls this process *phenomenological epochē*—where the term *epochē* is Greek for "bracketing." He writes that this method involves "detachment from any point of view regarding the objective world." Descartes began by doubting everything, including all phenomena except his thinking self. By contrast, Husserl "brackets" all phenomena, all the elements of experience, by refusing to assert whether the world does or does not exist. He abstains from entertaining any belief about experience. Thus Husserl brackets the whole stream of experienced life, including objects, other people, and cultural situations. To bracket all these phenomena means only to look upon them without judging whether they are realities or appearances and to abstain from rendering any opinions, judgments, or valuations about the world. We stand back from the phenomena of experience and rid our minds of all prejudices, especially the presuppositions of the natural sciences. When we do this, it makes little difference whether we deny or affirm the existence of the world. For, phenomenological bracketing "discloses the greatest and most magnificent of facts: I and my life remain—in my sense of reality—untouched by whichever way we decide the issue of whether the world is or is not."

Phenomenological bracketing ultimately leads us back to the center of reality, namely, the conscious self. We discover that we ourselves are the life of consciousness through which the objective world exists in its entirety. He writes, "I have discovered my true self. I have discovered that I alone am the pure ego, with pure existence. . . . Through this ego alone does the *being of the world,* and, for that matter, any being whatsoever, make sense to me and have possible validity." Unlike Descartes, who deduced the objective world from the fact that he exists, Husserl argues that the self *contains* the world. In his *Paris Lectures,* Husserl says:

> For me the world is nothing other than what I am aware of and what appears valid in such *cogitationes* (my acts of thought). The whole meaning and reality of the world rests exclusively on such *cogitationes.* My entire worldly life takes its course within these. I cannot live, experience, think, value and act in any world which is not in some sense in me, and derives its meaning and truth from me.

Thus, the structure of thinking itself determines the appearance of all objects. He designates this immediate phenomenal world of experience as the *transcendental realm,* and rejects any philosophical theory that attempts to go beyond that realm. He thus rejects Kant's distinction between the *phenomenal* (experience) and the *noumenal* (the thing-in-itself).

The Life-World

We have seen that Husserl urges us to bracket all presuppositions and essentially go back to a prescientific view point, which he believes reflects the original form of human experience. This is the realm of our daily world—our life-world (*Lebenswelt*). The life-world consists of all those experiences in which we are typically involved, including perception, response, interpretation, and the organization of the many facets of everyday affairs. This life-world is the source from which the sciences abstract their objects. To that extent the sciences provide only a partial grasp of reality. Much of the rich and meaningful elements of experience remains after the sciences have abstracted the elements of their concern. In fact, the very nature of being a scientist is unaccounted for by science itself. Only a rigorous analysis of the way in which the life-world functions in people's unsophisticated experience as well as in science will provide an adequate basis for philosophy. In the last analysis, the basic justification or confirmation of truth is to be found in the type of evidence that derives from events of the life-world. The totality of these events of the life-world is what Husserl calls "our world-experiencing life."

Through this notion of the life-world, Husserl sought to liberate the philosopher—the phenomenologist—from a point of view which is dominated by the various natural sciences. For the purpose of an even more useful type of science, but especially in order to liberate the spirit, he fashioned a way of discovering what the world is like before it is interpreted by the scientific outlook. Through bracketing, the life-world emerges as a fresh terrain for the enterprise of description, opening a new way of experiencing, thinking, and even theorizing. Husserl thought he discovered that the "world" is what we as subjects know it to be.

MARTIN HEIDEGGER

Heidegger's Life

Even before Heidegger ever published anything, his reputation as an extraordinary thinker spread among students in the German universities. What was unusual about Heidegger as a teacher was that he did not develop a "set of ideas" or a "system" of philosophy. He produced nothing in the way of a neat structure of academic ideas that a student could quickly understand and memorize. He was not interested so much in objects of scholarship as in matters of thinking. He shifted attention away from the traditional concerns about theories and books and focused instead upon the concerns of thinking individuals. We are born in the world and respond to all of our experiences by thinking. What Heidegger set out to explore was the deepest nature of our thinking when we are thinking as existing human beings.

Born in 1889 in Germany's Black Forest region, Heidegger received his preparatory schooling in Constance and Freiburg. He was introduced to philosophy at the age of 17 when the pastor of his church gave him Franz Brentano's book entitled *On the Manifold Meaning of Being according to Aristotle*. This book, though difficult, made such an impression upon the young Heidegger that it launched him on his lifelong quest for the meaning of Being, or "the meaning that reigns in everything that is." Along the way, Heidegger was also influenced by Kierkegaard, Dostoevski, and Nietzsche, from whom he discovered that some concerns of philosophy are most creatively clarified by paying attention to concrete and historically relevant problems. At the University of Freiburg, he began his studies in theology, but after four semesters he came under the influence of Husserl and changed his major field to philosophy. Upon completing his dissertation and some further advanced studies, Heidegger became Husserl's assistant until he was appointed in 1922 as an associate professor at the University of Marburg. Here, he pursued his studies in Aristotle, formulated a fresh interpretation of phenomenology, and was hard at work on a manuscript which was to become his most famous book. In order to facilitate his promotion, his Dean at Marburg urged him to publish this manuscript, and in 1927, deliberately leaving it incomplete, Heidegger hurriedly published his book with the title *Being and Time*. One year later, in 1928, Heidigger was chosen to be Husserl's successor to the chair of philosophy at Freiburg.

He was elected Rector of the University in 1933, and for a brief period he was a member of the Nazi party. In less than a year, in 1934, he resigned as Rector and, for the next 10 years, taught courses critical of the Nazi interpretation of philosophy. He was drafted into the "People's Militia," having been declared in 1944 the "most expendable" member of the Freiburg faculty. The French occupying forces did not permit him to return to his teaching until 1951, one year before his retirement. Even after his retirement, he published several essays and interpretations of the history of philosophy, including a two-volume study on Nietzsche (1961) and, his last work, *The Matter of Thinking* (1969). Heidegger died in 1976 in Freiburg at the age of 86.

Dasein as Being-in-the-World

Husserl, we have seen, argued that we understand the phenomena of the world only as it presents itself to our conscious selves. Heidegger takes a similar approach in *Being and Time* and attempts to understand Being in general by first understanding human beings. The notion of "human being" can be deceptive. This is particularly so since, throughout the history of philosophy, definitions of "human being" have tended to resemble the definition of things. Inspired by Husserl's phenomenology, Heidegger avoids defining people in terms of properties or attributes that divide them from the world. Phenomenology focuses rather upon the full range of experienced phenomena without separating it into distinct parts. Heidegger took seriously the meaning of the Greek word "phenomenon" as "that which reveals itself." It is our human existence that reveals itself, and this is a quite different conception of "human being" than we find in traditional philosophy. To clearly separate his view of human beings from traditional theories, he coined the German term *Dasein,* meaning simply "being there." People—Dasein—are best described as a unique type of being rather than defined as an object. As Heidegger points out, "because we cannot define Dasein's essence by citing a 'what' of the kind that pertains to [an object] . . . we have chosen to designate this entity [person] as 'Dasien,' a term which is purely an expression of its being." If, then, we ask what is the essence of human nature, the answer lies not in some attributes or properties but rather in how people exist. That is, what do our basic human experiences tell us about who we are?

Our basic state of human existence is our *being-in-the-world.* Consider, first, our ordinary daily experiences, which Heidegger calls "average everydayness." To be in the world as Dasein is not the same as one thing being in another thing, as water is in a glass or as clothes are in a closet. Dasein is in the world in the sense of "dwelling upon," of "being familiar with," or "I look after something." Here the emphasis is not upon one object related in space to another object, but rather upon a type of understanding. To say, for example, that "she is *in* love" does not refer to her location but rather to her type of being. Similarly, to say that people are in the world is not only to place them in space but to describe the structure of their existence which makes it possible for them to think meaningfully about the world.

The central feature of our being-in-the-world is that we encounter things as "gear," and what they are for. That is, we see things as utensils. Take, for example, a hammer. Our first encounter with a hammer is how we use it. We use it as a utensil to accomplish some purpose. The more I hammer, the less I am aware of the hammer as an object. There seems to be no distance between me and the hammer. I also see things like hammers as part of a project, fulfilling its purpose within a context of various purposes included in the project. If the hammer breaks, we see it in a different way—as a thing or an object. According to Heidegger, we have a special kind of insight, called "circumspection," which reveals the purpose of the item. We do not choose a tool or utensil by inspecting its properties first and then inferring its purpose from those properties. Instead, we see its purpose first. This means that it is not the *properties* of a thing that determine whether it is a utensil, on the one hand, or a mere object, on the other. Rather, we *project* the context within which any item assumes its unique role that explains our different views of that item. Moreover, an item, such as a hammer, has a purpose only in relation to a task that involves several other purposes. No item possesses any properties that throw light on other purposes in the undertaking; for example, no properties in the hammer show that a ladder will also be needed to hammer nails on the roof. Any particular item has meaning only as it is related to other purposes. It is this networked relation of purposes that is revealed prior to our encounter with things as utensils and which gives us the understanding of items as being utensils. It is part of our nature to develop this network or context of purposes. There can be different worlds even composed of the same things because of the different ways individuals project "their" world.

Dasein possesses a threefold structure that makes possible the way that we project the world. First is our *understanding*, by which we project contexts and purposes to things. It is through these projected interrelationships things derives meaning. Second is our *mood* or *approach*, which impacts how we encounter our environment. In a despairing or joyful mood our task will open up as either despairing or joyful. These are not merely attitudes but instead they describe our manner of existence and the way the world exists for us. Third is our *discourse*. Only something that can be formulated in speech can be understood and become subject to our moods.

Dasein as Concern

For Heidegger, Dasein's "being-in-the-world" is our most primitive and basic view of things. But this is not the whole story. More important is the fact that we become preoccupied with things that we encounter. In a sense, we are consumed by things, tasks, and relationships. We have a practical concern for the tools and tasks in our environment. We have a personal concern for the community of people that surrounds us. This is so central to our identities that *concern* is our fundamental attribute. To understand Dasein, then, we must understand the underlying nature of this concern. Heidegger argues that there are three components of concern, each of which generates a substantial amount of anxiety within us. First, we all have simply been thrown into the world. I did not ask to be born, but here I am nonetheless. This feature of our past he calls facticity. Second, we have freedom of choice. We are responsible for transforming our lives, and we must constantly become our true selves by making appropriate decisions. This involves our future and is a feature that he calls existentiality. Third, we are fallen, in the sense that we lose our "authentic" character. My authentic existence requires me to recognize and affirm my unique self and my responsibility for my every action. As facticity and existentiality involved my past and future respectively, fallenness involves my present situation.

My drift into an inauthentic existence is subtle but in every case it involves a tendency to escape from myself by finding shelter in a public self and an impersonal identity. I become an impersonal "one," behaving as one is expected, rather than a concrete "I," behaving as I ought to. I suppress any urge to be unique and excel, and thereby bring myself down to the level of an average person. I gossip, which reflects my shallow interpretation of other people. I seek novelty for the sake of distraction, and I have an overall sense of ambiguity for failing to know my own purpose. However, I cannot indefinitely avoid confronting my true self. Anxiety intrudes. For Heidegger, anxiety is not simply a psychological state, but rather a type of human existence. Nor is anxiety similar to fear. Fear has an object, such as a snake or an enemy against which it is possible to defend ourselves. But anxiety refers to nothing, precisely to *no-thing*. Instead, anxiety reveals the presence of "nothingness" in our being. There is no way to alter the presence of nothingness in the center of our being—the inevitability that we shall die. Time itself becomes an element of anxiety for us. We know time principally because we know that we are going to die. Each moment of my life is bound up with the fact that I will die, and it is impossible to separate my life from my death. I attempt to deny my temporality and to evade the inevitability of my limited existence. In the end, I must affirm my authentic self, and thereby see transparently what and who I am. I will then discover that, in my inauthentic existence, I have been trying to do the impossible, namely, to hide the fact of my limitations and my temporality.

RELIGIOUS EXISTENTIALISM

Like Heidegger, other writers were also struck by the phenomenological method that placed human existence at the center of our investigation of reality. Several philosophical theologians saw interesting parallels between the existential descriptions of human nature and religious conceptions of our relation to divine reality. For example, several existentialist theologians saw a parallel between the fall of Adam in the Garden of Eden and Heidegger's conception of inauthentic existence. Just as divine salvation is the solution to original sin, so too is authentic life the solution to inauthenticity. It's not just that these notions parallel each other. Instead, according to some theologians, the biblical themes of sin and salvation are simply mythological ways of expressing the distinction between inauthentic and authentic life. Foremost among religious existentialist were Karl Barth (1886–1968), Emil Brunner (1889–1966), Martin Buber (1878–1965), Rudolf Bultmann (1884–1976), Gabriel Marcel (1889–1973), Karl Jaspers (1883–1969), and Paul Tillich (1886–1965). We will look at the contributions of Jaspers and Marcel.

Karl Jaspers

Karl Jaspers (1883–1969) was a professor at Heidelberg and, after World War II, at Basel. He wrote in several areas, including psychology, theology, and political thought. He was influenced by Kierkegaard, Nietzsche, and Husserl, and his philosophical works develop phenomenological and existentialist themes. His main publication in existentialist thought is the three-volume

Philosophie (1932). The human condition, he argues in this work, has deterio-
rated with the development of technology, the emergence of mass movements,
and the loosening of the bonds of religion. Each of the sciences has carved out
a special area for its subject matter, and each science has developed its own
method. Just as each science functions within strict subject-matter limits, so
too the aggregate of all the sciences is characterized by a limitation of cover-
age. Thus, each of the sciences is ill-equipped for dealing with the broader
issue of total reality. We could not explain total reality any better if we attempted to bring together all of the sciences with their various perspectives.
For, the central approach to science is to access objective data, and total reality
is not limited to objective data.

Jaspers's quest is for the reality that underlies human life—a reality that
he simply calls *Existence* (*Existenz*). We discover this component of our existence through philosophy, and not through science. There are indeed various
human sciences, such as psychology, sociology, and anthropology, but these
deal with human nature on an incomplete and superficial level, viewing us
only as objects. He writes, "Sociology, psychology and anthropology teach
that man is to be regarded as an object concerning which something can be
learnt that will make it possible to modify this object by deliberate organization." Jaspers does recognize the value and usefulness of each of these sciences
in the context of their respective narrow goals. His argument, though, is that
the task of philosophy is not the same as that of science. Thus, when studying
Existence, philosophers must not mimic the sciences by treating Existence as
an *object* of thought; this would simply turn Existence into one among many
beings. Thus, although Jaspers does not reject the technical knowledge of science, he insists that the "practice of life" requires that we bring to this knowledge some additional reality. All the principles and laws of science, he insists,
are of no avail "unless individual human beings fulfill them with an effective
and valuable reality." The piling up of knowledge cannot by itself assure any
particular outcome for us. He writes, "Decisive is a man's inward attitude, the
way in which he contemplates his world and grows aware of it, the essential
value of his satisfactions—these things are the origin of what he does." Philosophy, therefore, must be *existence philosophy.*

The main task of existence philosophy, then, is to deal with Existence, and
to do this philosophers must consider their own immediate inner and personal
experiences. Under these assumptions, philosophical thinking cannot set out
"to raise philosophy to a science," as Hegel had. Instead, philosophy must
reaffirm that "truth is subjectivity," and that philosophizing means communicating not about objects or objective knowledge, but about the content of personal awareness produced by the individual's *inner constitution.* Existential
thinking, he says, is "the philosophic practice of life."

Jaspers does not offer any systematic definition of existence philosophy.
Nevertheless he give some of its characteristics. Primarily, existence philosophy is the manner of thought through which we seek to become ourselves. It
is a way of thought that does not restrict itself to knowing objects but rather
"elucidates and makes actual the being of the thinker." It does not discover

solutions in analytic reflection but rather "becomes real" in the dialogue that proceeds from one person to another in genuine communication. Existence philosophy does not assume that human existence is a settled piece of knowledge, since that would make it not philosophy but, once again, anthropology, psychology, or sociology. There is the danger that existence philosophy may lapse into pure subjectivity, into a restrictive preoccupation with one's own ego, into a justification for shamelessness. But Jaspers considers these possibilities as aberrations. Where it remains genuine, existence philosophy is uniquely effective in promoting all that makes us genuinely human. Each person is "completely irreplaceable. We are not merely cases of universal Being." The concept of Being, for existence philosophy, arises only in the consciousness of each concrete human being.

If existence philosophy can be said to have a "function," it is to make our minds receptive to what Jaspers calls the *Transcendent.* The human situation involves three stages. First, I gain knowledge of objects. Second, I recognize in myself the foundations of existence. Third, I become conscious of striving toward my genuine self. At this last stage, I discover my finitude. There are certain "limiting situations" that I face, such the possibility of my own death. However, when I become aware of my own finitude, I simultaneously become aware of the opposite, namely, Being as the Transcendent. This awareness of the Transcendent, which traditional theology calls God, is a purely personal experience incapable of specific delineation or proof. It is simply an awareness that everything, including myself and all objects, is grounded in Being. Central to my awareness of the Transcendent is my concurrent awareness of my own freedom. In my striving to fulfill my genuine self, I am free to affirm or deny my relationship to the Transcendent. Authentic existence, however, requires that I affirm it. I stand in the presence of a choice—an either-or—without the help of any scientific proof or even knowledge, only an awareness. In the end, I must express a *philosophical faith,* which signifies a union with the depths of life.

Gabriel Marcel

Like Jaspers, Gabriel Marcel (1889–1973) centered his existentialist philosophy upon the problem of Being, particularly upon the human question "What am I?" The central notion of Marcel's thought is his distinction between a *problem* and a *mystery.* He argues that it is not possible to answer the question "What am I?" by reducing it to a problem, analyzing its parts, and then producing a solution. A problem implies that we lack some information or knowledge and that all we need to do is look for it, engage in "research," and thereby overcome our temporary ignorance. A problem usually revolves around an object or a relationship between objects. Information regarding objects and their relationships can be gathered and calculated. But the question "What am I?" cannot be reduced to a problem, because the *I* is not an object or an *it.* Although I am some sort of object, since I do have a body, my being is a combination of subject and object. Because the subjective part of myself can never be eliminated, I cannot be reduced to a mere object, and therefore the question about my existence is not merely a problem: It is a mystery. *Mysteries,* then, are certain kinds of experiences that are permanently incapable of being translated into objects "out there." These experiences *always* include the subject, and are therefore matters of mystery. Marcel believed that the element of mystery is virtually irreducible precisely because human existence is a combination of "being and having." When we *have* things and ideas, we can express these in objective terms; for example, "I have a new car." However, *being* is always a subjective matter.

In the end, human existence derives its deepest meaning from the subjective affirmation of Being through fidelity. Marcel writes that "the essence of man is to be in a situation." He means by this that a person's relation to Being is different from a stone's. For one thing, we are the only beings "who can make promises," a phrase of Nietzsche's which Marcel wanted to underscore. To be able to make a promise places us into a unique relationship with another person, a kind of relationship that could not possibly exist between two objects. This moral aspect of existence led Marcel to believe that the ultimate character of a person's relationships involves the element of fidelity. Fidelity offers a clue to the nature of our existence, since it is through fidelity that we continue to shape our lives. We discover fidelity through friendship and love, which gives us the power to overcome the "objectivity" of other people and to produce a new level of intimacy. We commit ourselves to them, such as we do with our spouses. Making commitments, though, creates a new problem. The future is always uncertain, and we do not know for sure what other people might do. Our spouses, for example, might just pack up and leave some day. Should we then just naively go into these relationships? The way out of this problem is to put a higher and more absolute faith in a divine and mysterious order. This has a kind of trickle down effect, and supports our more routine faith commitments between people. Although Marcel was in no sense a traditional theologian, he nevertheless found in the Christian faith the basic spirit of his philosophy, and converted to Roman Catholicism at the age of 39.

JEAN-PAUL SARTRE

Sartre's Life

Born in 1905, Jean-Paul Sartre was the son of Jean-Batiste, a naval officer, and Anne-Marie Schweitzer, a first cousin of the famous theologian and jungle doctor Albert Schweitzer. Sartre was educated at the École Normale Supérieure in Paris, exhibiting at an early age his precocious gift for literary expression. While at the École Normale, he was attracted to philosophy by Henri Bergson, whose *Time and Free Will* (1889) left him "bowled over" and with the feeling that "philosophy is absolutely terrific, you can learn the truth through it." He spent the year 1934–35 at the Institut Français in Berlin, where he studied Husserl's phenomenology. Sartre wrote his *Transcendental Ego* (1936) in Germany while at the Institut, and, as he says, "I wrote it actually under the direct influence of Husserl." It was in Berlin also that he worked on his novel *Nausea,*

Jean-Paul Sartre
(The Granger Collection, New York)

which he considered his best work even at the end of his career. In that novel, Sartre deals with the pathological feeling we have upon experiencing through intuition the accidental and absurd nature of existence, the feeling that human existence is "contingent" and without explicit purpose. Because he could not find words adequate to describe this philosophical insight to the reader, "I had to garb it in a more romantic form, turn it into an adventure."

During World War II, Sartre was active in the French Resistance movement and became a German prisoner of war. While in the prisoner-of-war camp, he read Heidegger and "three times a week I explained to my priest friends Heidegger's philosophy." The notes he took on Heidegger at this time influenced Sartre very strongly and were, he says, "full of observations which later found their way into *Being and Nothingness*." For a brief period, he taught at the lycée at Havre, the lycée Henry IV, and the lycée Cordorcet, afterwards resigning to devote himself exclusively to his writings, which ultimately numbered over 30 volumes. As a sequel to *Being and Nothingness* (1943), Sartre wrote another major work entitled *Critique of Dialectical Reason* (1960). His last book was the three-volume work on Flaubert (*The Idiot of the Family,* 1971–72). Although Sartre was influenced by Marxism and continued to be a political activist, he was never a member of the Communist party. While some commentators sought to moralize about Marxism, they were not very successful, Sartre says, "because it was pretty hard to find much in Marxism to moralize about." His own criticism of Marxism was that it provided no explicit role for morality and freedom. Nor should we consider, Sartre says, "that morality is a simple superstructure, but rather that it exists at the very level of what is called infrastructure." Because of his commitment as an activist, he resisted personal acclaim, and when he was awarded the Nobel Prize in Literature in 1964, he refused to accept it on the grounds that he did not want to be "transformed into an institution."

While a student at the elite École Normale Supérieure he met a fellow student, Simone de Beauvoir, with whom he enjoyed a lifelong companionship. This was no ordinary relationship. Both were brilliant students. Although she was of immense assistance to Sartre in his prolific literary work, Beauvoir herself achieved great fame as a writer. Sartre never published anything before Beauvoir had a chance to read it critically and to approve it. While Sartre was honored by the Nobel Prize Committee, Beauvoir similarly moved to first place among women of letters. At the time of Sartre's death, she was considered France's most celebrated living writer. Her novel *The Mandarins* won the Prix Goncourt. Her book *The Second Sex,* in which she wrote the often quoted words "one is not born a woman but becomes one," gave her recognition as a well-known feminist. Her literary works gave her money, fame, and independence. Although Sartre and Simone de Beauvoir never married during their 51 years together, they had a strong relationship of loyalty and love. There were, however, complications along the way. In one of her memoirs, Beauvoir says, "I was vexed with Sartre for having created the situation with Olga." This event became the theme of Beauvoir's first novel, *She Came to Stay,* a couple's intimate secret about the fictional character's relation with another woman.

Simone de Beauvoir
(Pierre Boulat/Life Magazine/Time Inc.)

This made Beauvoir say about her own situation, "From now on we will be a trio instead of a couple." Sartre said earlier that Beauvoir was his "privileged," but not his only, female companion. Sartre once said philosophically that "one can always be free"; Beauvoir asked, "What is the freedom of the women in a harem?" They were a rare couple—she was strikingly beautiful and tall while Sartre was ugly and a full head shorter. Together their fame reached around the world.

Sartre lived simply and with few possessions, finding fulfillment in political involvement and travel, and needing only a small apartment on the left bank in Paris. In declining health and virtually blind, Sartre died on April 15, 1980, at the age of 74.

Existence Precedes Essence

Sartre's name became identified with existentialism primarily because of the lucid and popular manner in which he wrote. What appeared first in the heavy language of Husserl and Heidegger now came forth from Sartre's pen in the open and captivating style of novels and short stories. His principal contribution to existentialism is undoubtedly his lengthy *Being and Nothingness.* However, for some time his views were best-known from his brief lecture *Existentialism is a Humanism,* published in 1946. Sartre later rejected this piece and defined existentialism in somewhat different terms. Nevertheless, in this lecture Sartre presents his classic formulation of the basic principle of existentialism that *existence precedes essence.*

What does it mean to say that existence precedes essence, and how does this formula bear upon our understanding of human nature? Sartre argues that we cannot explain human nature in the same way that we describe a manufactured article. When we consider, for example, a knife, we know that it has been made by someone who had in his mind a conception of it, including what it would be used for and how it would be made. Thus, even before the knife is made, the knife maker already conceives it as having a definite purpose and as being the product of a definite process. If by the *essence* of the knife we mean the procedure by which it was made and the purposes for which it was produced, we can say that the knife's essence precedes its existence. To look upon a knife is to understand exactly what its useful purpose is. When we think about human nature, we tend to describe ourselves also as the product of a maker, of a creator, of God. We think of God most of the time, Sartre says, as a heavenly artisan, implying that when God creates, he knows precisely what he is creating. This would mean that in the mind of God the conception of human nature is comparable to the conception of the knife in the mind of the artisan. Each individual, in this view, is the fulfillment of a definite conception, which resides in God's understanding.

Some philosophers of the 18th century, including Diderot, Voltaire, and Kant, were either atheists or else suppressed the idea of God. Nevertheless, they retained the notion that people possess a "human nature"—a nature that is found in every person. Each person, they say, is a particular example of the universal conception of Humanity. Whether someone is a primitive native, in the state of nature, or in a highly civilized society, we all have the same fundamental qualities and are therefore all contained in the same definition or conception of Humanity. In short, we all possess the same essence, and our essence precedes our individual concrete or historical existence.

Sartre turned all this around by taking atheism seriously. He believed that if there is no God, then there is no *given* human nature precisely because there is no God to have a conception of it. Human nature cannot be defined in advance because it is not completely thought out in advance. People as such merely exist and only later do we become our essential selves. To say that existence precedes essence means, Sartre says, that people first of all exist, confront themselves, emerge in the world, and define themselves afterward. At first, a person simply is, and then we are simply that which we make of ourselves.

Perhaps our first reaction to this formulation of Sartre's first principle of existentialism is that it is highly subjective—that we can presumably set out to make of ourselves anything we wish. However, his chief point here is that a person has a greater dignity than a stone or a table. What gives me dignity is possession of a subjective life, meaning that I am something which moves myself toward a future and am conscious that I am doing so. The most important consequence of placing existence before essence in human nature is not only that we create ourselves, but that responsibility for existence rests squarely upon each individual person. A stone cannot be responsible. And if human nature was already given and fixed, we could not be responsible for what we are.

Freedom and Responsibility

What began in Sartre's analysis as an amoral subjectivism now turns out to be an ethics of strict accountability based upon individual responsibility. If, that is, we are what we make of ourselves, we have no one to blame for what we are except ourselves. Moreover, when I *choose* in the process of making myself, I choose not only for myself but for all people. I am therefore responsible not only for my own individuality but, Sartre says, I am responsible for all people. This last point seems to contradict the line of reasoning that Sartre has so far been developing. For, before I can choose a way of action, I must ask what would happen if everyone else acted so; this assumes a general human essence that makes *my* type of action relevant to *all* people. Sartre does in fact say that even though we create our own values and thereby create ourselves, we nevertheless create at the same time an image of our human nature as we believe it ought to be. When we choose this or that way of acting, we affirm the value of what we have chosen, and nothing can be better for any one of us unless it is better for all. This all sounds very much like Kant's categorical imperative. But Sartre does not wish to invoke any universal law to guide moral choice. Instead, he is calling attention to one of the clearest experiences of human beings. That is, all people must choose and make decisions, and although we have no authoritative guide, we must still choose and at the same time ask whether we would be willing for others to choose the same action. We cannot escape the disturbing thought that I would not want others to act as I do. To say that others will not so act is a case of self-deception. The act of choice, then, is one that all people must accomplish with a deep sense of *anguish*, for in this act we are responsible not only for ourselves but also for each other. If I evade my responsibility through self-deception, I will not, Sartre argues, be at ease in my conscience.

Although Sartre's moral language sounds at times very much like traditional moral discourse, his intention is to carry out the rigorous implications of atheism. He accepts Nietzsche's announcement that "God is dead" and takes seriously Dostoevsky's notion that "if God did not exist, everything would be permitted." In a Godless world, our psychological condition is one of *abandonment,* a word Sartre takes from Heidegger. Abandonment means for Sartre that with the dismissal of God there also disappears every possibility of finding values in some sort of intelligible heaven. Again, there cannot now be any "good" prior to my choice since there is no infinite or perfect consciousness to think it. Our sense of abandonment is a curious consequence of the fact that everything is indeed permitted, and as a consequence we are forlorn, for they cannot find anything on which we can rely either within or outside ourselves. We are without any excuse. Our existence precedes our essence. Apart from our existence there is nothingness. There is only the present. In his *Nausea,* Sartre writes that the true nature of the present was revealed as what exists, that what is not present does not exist. Things are entirely what they appear to be, and apart from them there is nothing.

To say there is nothing besides the existing individual means for Sartre that there is no God, no objective system of values, no built-in essence, and, most importantly, *no determinism.* An individual, Sartre says, is free; a person is freedom. In a classic phrase, he says that people are *condemned* to be free. We are condemned because we find ourselves thrown into the world, yet free because as soon as we are conscious of ourselves, we are responsible for everything we do. Sartre rejects the notion that we are swept up by a torrent of passion and that such a passion could be regarded as an excuse for our actions. He also rejected Freud's view that human behavior is mechanically determined by unconscious and irrational desires; this provides us with an excuse to avoid responsibility. For Sartre, we are responsible even for our passions, because even our feelings are formed by our deeds. Kierkegaard said that freedom is *dizzying,* and Sartre similarly says that freedom is appalling. This is precisely because there is nothing forcing me from behind to behave in any given way, nor is there a precise pattern luring me into the future. I am the only thing that exists. We are all free, Sartre says, therefore we must choose, that is, *invent,* because no rule of general morality can show us what we ought to do. There are no guidelines guaranteed to us in this world.

Nothingness and Bad Faith

There is an element of despair in human existence, which comes, Sartre says, from the realization that we are limited to what is within the scope of our own wills. We cannot expect more from our existence than the finite probabilities it possesses. Here Sartre believes that he is touching the genuine theme of personal existence by emphasizing our finitude and our relation to nothingness. "Nothingness," he says, "lies coiled in the heart of being, like a worm." Heidegger located the cause of human anxiety in people's awareness of their finitude when, for example, we confront death—not death in general but *our own* death. It is not only people who face nothingness, Heidegger says, but all Being has this relation to nothingness. Human finitude is therefore not simply a matter of temporary ignorance or some shortcoming or even error. Finitude is the very structure of the human mind, and words such as *guilt, loneliness,* and *despair* describe the consequences of human finitude. The ultimate principle of Being, Heidegger says, is *will.* Sartre concurs by saying that only in action is there any reality. We are only a sum of our actions and purposes; besides our actual daily lives we are nothing. If I am a coward, I *make* myself a coward. It is not the result of my cowardly heart or lungs or cerebrum, or because of my physiological organism. I am a coward because I made myself into a coward by my actions.

Although there is no prior essence in all people, no human *nature*, there is nevertheless, Sartre says, a universal human *condition*. By discovering myself in the act of conscious thought, I discover the condition of all people. We are in a world of *intersubjectivity*. This is the kind of world in which I must live, choose, and decide. For this reason, no purpose that I chose is ever wholly foreign to another person. This does not mean that every purpose defines me forever but only that we all may be striving against the same limitations in the same way. For this reason, Sartre would not agree that it does not matter what we do or how we choose. I am always obliged to act in a *situation,* that is, in relation to other people, and consequently my actions must not be capricious, since I must take responsibility for all my actions. Moreover, to say that I must make my essence, invent my values, does not mean that I cannot *judge* human actions. It is still possible to say that my action was based on either error or upon self-deception, for if I hide behind the excuse of my passions, or espousing some theory of determinism, I deceive myself.

To invent values, Sartre says, means only that there is no meaning or sense in life prior to acts of will. Life cannot be anything until it is lived, but each individual must make sense of it. The value of life is nothing else but the sense each person fashions into it. To argue that we are the victims of fate, of mysterious forces within us, of some grand passion, or heredity, is to be guilty of bad faith (*mauvaise foi*) or self-deception, of *inauthenticity*. Suppose, Sartre says, that a woman who consents to go out with a particular man knows very well what the man's cherished intentions are, and she knows that sooner or later she will have to make a decision. She does not want to admit the urgency of the matter, preferring rather to interpret all his actions as discreet and respectful. She is, Sartre says, in self-deception; her actions are inauthentic. All human beings are guilty, in principle, of similar inauthenticity, of bad faith, of playing roles, and of trying to disguise their actual personality behind a facade. The conclusion of Sartre's existentialism is, therefore, that if I express my genuine humanity in all my behavior, I will never deceive myself, and honesty will then become not my ideal but rather my very being.

Human Consciousness

Underlying Sartre's popular formulation of existentialism is his technical analysis of existence. He argues that there are different ways of existing. There is first *being-in-itself (l'en-soi),* which is the way that a stone is: it merely exists. In one respect, I am no different from any other kind of existing reality. I exist, just the same way anything else *is,* as simply *being there.* Second there is *being-for-itself (le pour-soi),* which involves existing as a *conscious subject,* which is what people do, and things like rocks cannot do. As a conscious subject, I can relate to both the world of things and people in a variety of ways. At one level, I am conscious of "the world," which is everything that is beyond or other than myself and which therefore transcends me. At this level, I experience the world simply as a solid, massive, undifferentiated, single something that is not yet separated into individual things. Sartre describes this type of consciousness in *Nausea* where the character Roquentin is sitting on a park bench. He looks at all the things before him in the park and all at once he *sees* everything differently, everything as a single thing— "Suddenly existence had unveiled itself." Words vanished, and the points of reference which people use to give meaning to things also vanished. What Roquentin saw was existence as "the very paste of things": "The root [of the tree], the park gates, the bench, the sparse grass, all that had vanished: the diversity of things, their individuality, were only an appearance, a veneer. This veneer had melted, leaving soft, monstrous masses, all in disorder—naked." Only later, when we reflect, does the world become our familiar one. But, Sartre says, "The world of explanations and reasons is not the world of existence." At the level of Roquentin's experience, the world is the unity of all the objects of consciousness.

Sartre agrees with Husserl that all consciousness is consciousness of *something*, which means that there is no consciousness without affirming the existence of an object which exists beyond, that is, transcends, our consciouness. As we have seen, the object of consciousness can be "the world" as simply "being there." But in addition to the world as a single solid mass, we speak of specific objects like trees, benches, and tables. Whenever we identify a specific object, we do this by saying what it is not—we differentiate a thing from its background. When a chair appears as a chair, we give it that meaning by blacking out the background. What we call a chair is fashioned or drawn out of the solid context of the world by the activity of consciousness. The world of things appears as an intelligible system of separate and interrelated things only to consciousness. Without consciousness, the world simply is, and as such it is without meaning. Consciousness constitutes the meaning of things in the world, though it does not constitute their being.

When we view the world as being-in-itself, as simply being there, Sartre says that "the essential point is contingency. I mean that by definition existence is not necessity. To exist is simply to be there." Contingency means that when something exists, it does so by chance and not because it necessarily follows from something else: "Existences appear . . . but you cannot deduce them." The world we experience is "uncreated, without reason for being, without any relation to another being; being-in-itself is gratuitous for all eternity." The meaning anything will have in the world will depend, Sartre says, upon the choices people make. Even a table will have alternative meanings depending upon what a particular person chooses to use it for, to serve dinner or to write a letter. A mountain valley will mean one thing to a farmer and something else to a camper. Here, consciousness shifts us from being-in-itself (simply being there) to being-for-itself, where consciousness dramatically differentiates the objects of the world from the conscious self as subject.

The activity of consciousness is at this point two-fold. First, consciousness defines specific things in the world and invests them with meaning. Second, consciousness puts a distance between itself and objects and, in that way, attains freedom from those objects. Because the conscious self has this freedom from the things in the world, it is within the power of consciousness to confer different or alternative meanings on things. The activity of consciousness is what is usually called "choice." We choose to undertake this project or that project, and the meaning of things in the world will depend to a considerable extent upon what project we choose. If I choose to be a farmer, then the mountains, the valley, and the impending storm will have special meanings for me. If I choose to be a camper in that valley, the surroundings and the storm will present different meanings.

Marxism and Freedom Revisited

Although Sartre believed that Marxism is the philosophy of our time, he was aware of a striking contradiction between his existentialism and Marxist dialectical materialism. Sartre's existentialism strongly espouses human freedom. By contrast, Marxist dialectical materialism emphasized that all the structures and organizations of society and the behavior and thinking of human beings are determined by prior events. In this view, freedom of choice is an illusion and we simply are vehicles through which the forces of history realize themselves. Whereas Sartre argued that it is human consciousness that "makes history" and confers meaning upon the world, Marxism holds that the social and economic structures of history direct its own development. Rather than conferring meaning upon the world, our minds, the Marxist says, discover this meaning within the historical context as a matter of scientific knowledge. One reason why Sartre never became a member of the Communist party is, he says, because "I would have had to turn my back on *Being and Nothingness*" and its emphasis on human freedom.

In his earlier writings, Sartre focused primarily on the individual and freedom. Later, in his *Critique of Dialectical Reason,* he focused more specifically upon the historical and social context in which people find themselves and which has an effect on their behavior. He thought that Marx succeeded more than anyone else in describing how social and economic structures develop and how they bear upon human decisions. Sartre accepted increasingly the limitations upon human choice—the limitations of birth, status in society, and family background. Earlier, he sought to describe how individuals are capable of deceiving themselves by making excuses for their behavior, as if they were not free to have behaved otherwise—a form of self-deception. He never did depart from this emphasis upon the freedom of the individual. But he did adjust his thinking under the influence of Marxism by facing the fact of people's social existence, their relationship to other people, especially as a member of a group—as, for example, a labor union. Acknowledging the influence of group structures on human behavior and consciousness, resulting particularly in labor's sense of alienation, he revised his optimistic view of human freedom to some extent.

In 1945 Sartre wrote that "no matter what the situation might be, one is always free." As an example, he states that "a worker is always free to join a union or not, as he is free to choose the kind of battle he wants to join, or not." Recalling this statement some years later in 1972, Sartre says that this "all strikes me as absurd today." And he admits, "There is no question that there is some basic change in [my] concept of freedom." In his lengthy work on Flaubert, he concludes that although Flaubert was free to become uniquely Flaubert, his family background and his status in society meant that "he did not have all that many possibilities of becoming something else . . . he had the possibility of becoming a mediocre doctor . . . and the possibility of being Flaubert." This means, Sartre says, that social conditioning exists every minute of our lives. Nevertheless, he concludes that "I am still faithful to the notion of freedom." It is true, he says, that "you become what you are in the context of what others have made of you"; nevertheless, within these limitations a person is still free and responsible. This is Sartre's way of reconciling the fact that historical conditions affect human behavior with his intuitive certainty that human beings are also capable of shaping history. In doing this, Sartre sought to overcome with his existentialism what he considered the major flaw of Marxist philosophy, namely, its failure to recognize the individual as a "real person."

MAURICE MERLEAU-PONTY

Merleau-Ponty's Life

Maurice Merleau-Ponty was born in 1908 and from 1926 to 1930 he studied at the École Normale Supérieure. The philosophy curriculum at that time was steeped in both rationalism and idealism. Merleau-Ponty says of his teacher, Leon Brunschvicg, that he "passed on to us the idealist heritage. . . . This philosophy consisted largely in reflexive effort . . . [which] sought to grasp external perception or scientific constructions as a result of mental activity." Merleau-Ponty was one year behind Sartre, who also attended that school. An interesting interview between Sartre and Simone de Beauvoir describes the relation between the two at that time. Beauvoir: "You were standoffish with people you did not like. Merleau-Ponty, for example. You were on very bad terms with him, weren't you?" Sartre: "Yes, but even so I once protected him from some men who wanted to beat him up." Beauvoir: "You were singing obscene songs; and being pious, he wanted to stop you?" Sartre: "He went out. Some fellows ran after him—there were two of them—and they were going to beat him up because they were furious. So I went out, too. I had a sort of liking for Merleau-Ponty. . . . [I said] Leave him alone, and let him go. So they didn't do anything; they went off."

In 1929 Merleau-Ponty came under the influence of Gustave Rodrigues, director of the Lycée Janson-de-Sailly where Merleau-Ponty was fulfilling his student teaching assignment. Merleau-Ponty, the young Catholic, found Rodrigues, an atheist, to have an "extraordinary character," leading Merleau-Ponty to say that "an atheist resembles other men." In 1936, he departed from Catholicism as he worked through his version of phenomenology in his first work, *The Structure of Behavior*. He saw active duty during World War II, from 1939–1940. He taught at the Lycée Carnot in Paris during the German occupation, and at this time composed his greatest philosophical work, *The Phenomenology of Perception*.

Maurice Merleau-Ponty
(French Embassy, Washington, DC)

From their early days at École Normale, the lives and careers of Sartre and Merleau-Ponty unfolded as a stormy relationship during which they would be alternately friends and enemies. With the help of Merleau-Ponty, Sartre organized a resistance network in the winter of 1941, called "Socialism and Liberty." Their goal was to bring about a form of political society based upon a harmony between a socialist economy and freedom for the individual. In a collaboration that lasted from 1945 to 1952, Sartre and Merleau-Ponty together founded *Les Temps Moderne,* a journal aimed at political commentary. The principal editors of this journal were Sartre, Beauvoir, and Merleau-Ponty. While engaged in the journal, Merleau-Ponty taught at the University of Lyon and then the Sorbonne, and, in 1952 he was appointed Chair of Philosophy at the Collège de France, a position that he held until his death.

Merleau-Ponty's political views were progressively becoming less sympathetic toward the Soviet Union. In 1950, two years before he left *Les Temps Moderne,* Merleau-Ponty wrote an editorial denouncing the labor camps in the U.S.S.R. He writes,

> If there are ten million concentration camp inmates while at the other end of the Soviet hierarchy salaries and standard of living are fifteen to twenty times higher than those of the free workers—then . . . the whole system swerves and changes meaning; and in spite of the nationalization of the means of pro-

duction, and even though private exploitation of man by man and unemploy-
ment are impossible in the U.S.S.R., we wonder what reasons we still have to
speak of socialism in relation to it.

These labor camps, Merleau-Ponty said, are "still more criminal because they
betray the revolution." Around 1952, while Sartre was moving toward closer
ties with the communists, Merleau-Ponty left the editorship of *Les Temps
Moderne.*

A few years later, Merleau-Ponty wrote a book, *Adventures of the Dialectic,*
in which he included a chapter analyzing in detail Sartre's relationship with
communism. The chapter, "Sartre and Ultrabolshevism," ended with this critical sentence: "One cannot at the same time be both a free writer and a communist." Actually, both Sartre and Merleau-Ponty ultimately became disenchanted with communism. As we saw earlier, Sartre never became a member
of the Communist party because it would have forced him to give up his
strongly held position that people are free. With his philosophical work still
far from complete, and while at the height of his creativity, Merleau-Ponty
died on May 4, 1961, at the age of 53.

The Primacy of Perception

In *The Phenomenology of Perception* Merleau-Ponty offers a theory of perception
in reaction against both dualist and realist theories. Intellectualists (or dualists),
such as Descartes, argued that our minds are not only distinct from our bodies,
but that our mental concepts and processes have priority over the sensory data
that we get from our bodies. Our minds interpret sensory information, fill in
the gaps, and make it meaningful. Descartes vividly espouses this view here:

> when looking from a window and saying I see men who pass in the street, I
> really do not see them, but infer that what I see is men. . . . And yet what do
> I see from the window but hats and coats which may cover automatic ma-
> chines? Yet I judge these to be men. And similarly solely by the faculty of
> judgment which rests in my mind, I comprehend that which I believed I saw
> with my eyes.

Realists took the opposite view that we receive perceptions of the world exactly as it is, and our minds do not organize our perceptions any further.
Merleau-Ponty strikes a middle ground: the perceptual nature of our bodies
constructs and shapes sensory data; our higher mental functions play no such
role. In fact, even our higher intellectual thought processes are grounded in
the perceptual framework of our bodies. He writes, "All consciousness is perceptual, even the consciousness of ourselves." The main theme of this theory,
then, is the *primacy of perception.* He writes,

> by the words, the 'primacy of perception,' we mean that the experience of per-
> ception is our presence at the moment when things, truths, values are consti-
> tuted for us. . . . It is not a question of reducing human knowledge to sensa-
> tion, but of assisting at the birth of this knowledge, to make it as sensible as
> the sensible, to recover the consciousness of rationality.

Merleau-Ponty was particularly influenced by the early 20th-century theory of Gestalt psychology, which held that our perceptual experiences are shaped by inherent forms and structures which give sense, meaning, and value to our experiences. For Merleau-Ponty, these structures are embedded in bodily perception.

Merleau-Ponty encapsulates his position in the notion that "I am my body," thus denying that I can somehow separate myself as a mental subject from myself as a bodily object. The two components of myself are united in my lived experience through my body. By identifying the self as a body, Merleau-Ponty is not espousing the materialist views in the tradition of Democritus and the Atomists. According to traditional materialism, I am essentially a physical machine, and the mental components of my life are more or less explained away by the machinery of my body. Instead, for Merleau-Ponty, the mental aspects of me are embedded in my body; I am a body-subject, rather than a thoughtless and mechanical body.

The Relativity of Knowledge

Merleau-Ponty says that "in the final analysis every perception takes place within a certain horizon and ultimately in the 'world.'" This follows from the fact that perception results from a person's bodily presence in the world. A bodily presence already means that as a subject, a person is situated in the world at a certain time and with a unique perspective. The ideas we ultimately have reflect this partial view and our experience in time so that "the ideas to which we recur are valid for only a period of our lives." The thing we perceive is not a complete thing or ideal unity possessed by the intellect, like a geometrical notion: "It is rather a totality open to a horizon of an indefinite number of perspectival views." This means further that "the things which I see are things for me only under the condition that they always recede beyond their immediate given aspects." For example, we never see all sides of a cube or a lamp or any other thing. Similarly, other observers will see things from *their* perspectives. Moreover, my perceptions occur during the ticking away of time, even though I am not aware of this sequence of the segments of time. At this point, Merleau-Ponty asks,

> Can I seriously say that I will always hold the ideas I do at present—and mean it? Do I not know that in six months, in a year, even if I use more or less the same formulas to express my thoughts, they will have changed their meaning slightly? Do I not know that there is a life of ideas, as there is meaning of everything I experience, and that every one of my most convincing thoughts will need additions and then will be, not destroyed, but at least integrated into a new unity?

He concludes that "This is the only conception of knowledge that is scientific and not mythological." It means, moreover, that "the idea of going straight to the essence of things is an inconsistent idea if one thinks about it." The most we can get from our perception of the world is "a route, an experience which gradually clarifies itself, which gradually rectifies itself and proceeds by dialogue with itself and others."

A dialogue with "others" assumes that everyone can in some way share a similar experience of the world. But can Merleau-Ponty's theory, which concentrates on each subject's internal experience of the world, explain how two people can have a coherent conversation? Perceptions are relative to each person as a result of our unique perspectives, since "our body . . . is our *point of view of the world.*" Merleau-Ponty tries to solve this problem by using the concept of an "a priori of the species." As members of a single species, all human beings perceive certain forms in a like manner. He says that "as Gestalttheorie has shown there are for me preferred forms that are also preferred for all other persons." I will, of course, "never know how you see red and you will never know how I see it. But our first reaction to this separation of our consciousnesses is to "believe in an undivided being between us." As I perceive another person, "I find myself in relation with another 'myself,' who is, in principle, open to the same truths as I am." Even though there are two of us looking at the world, it is not the case that because of our different perspectives, there are "two numerically distinct worlds." There is, Merleau-Ponty says, a demand that "what I see be seen by [you] also."

Perception and Politics

We might think that Merleau-Ponty's account of the relativity of perceptual knowledge would not be well suited to deal with the problems of political, social, and economic order. After all, these subjects call for permanent and stable notions of "justice" and "freedom," which Plato's or Kant's theories might better explain. This would contradict the existentialist notion that there are no essential, timeless values, that there is no essential human nature to be fully realized, and that people must create their own values. Merleau-Ponty has an answer to this. Right off, he rejects the lofty claims of abstract theories of politics, justice, and morality. Although Plato and others claimed that such values were based upon "timeless" notions of the human good, these values in fact are simply reflections of the present circumstances of a particular culture. So-called universal political values were imposed on us by people who themselves had not participated in creating those systems of government; as such, such values are not a blessing but the heavy hand of oppression. Invariably, the so-called universal values turned out to be to the advantage of special groups. This was one reason why Merleau-Ponty found in Marxism a congenial type of thought. Marxism, while abstract up to a point, was nevertheless embodied in an actual system, the communism of the then Soviet Union.

Further, Merleau-Ponty argues that "things" are not all that we encounter through perception. Values are just as specifically perceived and have the same status as other aspects of the world. Values are significant, Merleau-Ponty says, "because they are apprehended with a certainty which, from the phenomenological viewpoint, is a final argument." In addition, perception provides us with the important element of *meaning.* This is particularly significant when our perceptions encounter the actual ways people live among each other. From these actual living and working arrangements, Merleau-Ponty says, we can discover certain background meanings that reveal the change and movement of specific groups of people. These changes are not simply facts, but they reveal the direction of history. This is another reason why Merleau-Ponty was attracted to communism, for here was a system and theory that could be observed concretely as the bearer of meaning located in the aspirations of the whole class of workers. Thus, in the absence of any viable abstract theories of justice, Merleau-Ponty looked to the only sure source of political knowledge, namely, the primacy of perception. Here he felt that he discovered, not the universality of an idea but the universality of the proletariat, which is the bearer of the meaning of history.

Both Sartre and Merleau-Ponty were drawn to communism after World War II for similar reasons. It represented the chief alternative to the status quo, and the turbulent events of the time called for a new philosophical basis for political action, which they felt existentialism and phenomenology could provide. But they did not always agree with Marxism nor with each other's views of Marxism. Their prolonged and heated disagreements ultimately led in 1952 to the termination of their friendship and affected their views on communism. As Sartre wrote in 1961, "Each of us was conditioned, but in opposite directions. Our slowly accumulated disgust made the one [Merleau-Ponty] discover, in an instant, the horror of Stalinism, and the other [Sartre] that of his own [bourgeois] class."

Merleau-Ponty held that it is possible to perceive in actual society the developing consciousness of the working class. He saw a relationship here between the individual, the institutions of society, a scale of values, and reality. Most importantly, he thought he perceived that the developing consciousness of this class was the bearer of a rather specific meaning, a meaning that was growing steadily stronger and was shaping the direction of history. At the center of this overall perception was the urge on the part of this class to resolve the contradictions of the workers' conditions and to organize a humane appropriation of nature. It also meant "as a universal class . . . to transcend national and social conflicts as well as the struggle between man and man." This was the heart of the communist promise, which Merleau-Ponty originally thought was corroborated by his own perceptions. But he was willing to admit that Marxism would be refuted if the proletariat could not overcome the strong structure of capitalism, if it could not eliminate violence, and if it could not bring about humane relationships among people. "It would mean," Merleau-Ponty says, "that there is no history—if history means the advent of humanity and the mutual recognition of men as men."

CHAPTER 19

Recent Philosophy

Philosophy has undergone dramatic changes since the mid-20th century. Foremost is the booming number of people writing in the field. Part of this owes to the remarkable increase in philosophy professors at college and university campuses around the world, which reflects both a spike in world population growth and a continually increasing percentage of people attending college. Not only are there more academically trained philosophers, but there also are increased expectations in universities for philosophers to write—publish or perish as the famous motto goes. Thus, perhaps five times as many philosophy books and journal articles appeared in the year 2000 as compared with the year 1950. A consequence of this literary productivity is that philosophy is now very specialized. It is impossible for a single philosopher to have a full grasp of all the innovative ideas emerging in the different areas of philosophy. When philosophical output was more manageable, we might expect a great figure like Kant to single-handedly alter the direction of metaphysics, epistemology, ethics, aesthetics, and the philosophy of religion. Now, the most creative philosophers focus on only one or two of these areas. An influential writer in one area of philosophy may be a completely unknown figure to a specialist in another area. Paralleling other academic disciplines, philosophy now is driven less by the thoughts of great individual people and more so by great issues and movements within the discipline. Some individual names certainly rise to the forefront in specific areas of philosophy, but the time may have passed which produced giants like Descartes, Hume, or Kant.

Philosophy is also more multicultural now than it ever has been before. In past centuries, leading philosophers in the Western world were white men who perpetuated a European tradition of thought. Most notable now is the presence of women in the discipline, who, in the United States, accounted for one-quarter of the academic philosophers by the beginning of the 21st century. This rising number of women philosophers sparked an interest in philosophical issues that directly address the concerns of women. Some of these discussions have a politically revolutionary tone, and draw attention to the ways that male-centered culture has oppressed women. Other discussions explore how uniquely female ways of thinking impact traditional problems of philosophy, such as theories of knowledge, ethics, and aesthetics. Philosophy is also more multicultural in that it now recognizes the philosophical contributions of non-European cultures. This is particularly so with Asian philosophy, which has a history of philosophical writings as old as the Greek tradition is in the West. As specialized and culturally diverse as philosophy is today, at best only a sample of key issues and figures can be presented here.

THE MIND–BODY PROBLEM

The mind–body problem is one of the oldest and most explored areas of philosophy. We have seen that Democritus and other Atomists attempted to reduce all human mental processes to the operations of material stuff, which strictly follow physical laws. Plato, by contrast, believed that our souls (and thereby our rational minds) were distinct from our bodies and could not be reduced to material constituents. Developing Plato's view, Descartes attempted to explain how our spiritual minds interact with our physical bodies. His solution was that messages pass between our spirits and bodies by way of the pineal gland within our brains—which acts as a type of metaphysical switchboard. Although Descartes's specific theory created more problems than it solved, the tendency in philosophy after Descartes was to nevertheless accept his radical split between our spiritual minds and physical bodies. As biologists learned more about the human brain in the 19th and 20th centuries, Descartes's mind–body dualism became more untenable—at least to a scientific way of thinking. For scientists, the original contention held by the Atomists seemed more correct, namely, that mental events are simply the result of physical brain activity. This position—most generally called *materialism*—is now the standard philosophical solution to the mind–body problem. Some philosophers within religious traditions still defend the spirit–body dualism of Descartes, but the majority of the writers on this subject are from nonreligious universities and have set Descartes's solution aside. The dominant issue is not one of how our spiritual minds interact with our physical brains. Instead, the concern is with how our mental experiences can be best explained in terms of brain activity. Even if I lack an immaterial spirit, it is difficult to see how my mental experiences are simply the result of biological machinery in my brain.

Ryle and the Ghost in the Machine

The inspiration for most discussions of the mind–body problem today is the book *Concept of Mind* (1949) by British philosopher Gilbert Ryle (1900–1976), who began teaching at Oxford University in 1924. Ryle contends that the "official doctrine" of mind is unsound and contradicts virtually everything we know about human mentality. In its simplest form, the official doctrine holds

Gilbert Ryle at Magdalen College, Oxford
(Samuel E. Stumpf)

that every human being has both a mind and a body, that these two are coordinated, but that upon the death of the body the mind may continue both to exist and exert its powers. Not only is this basic theory of mind-body incorrect, Ryle says, but it also leads to many other serious errors as we elaborate the implications of this theory. One erroneous consequence of this theory is its implied view that each person has two parallel histories, one consisting of the events of the body and the other consisting of what transpires in and to the mind. Whereas human bodies are in space and are governed by mechanical physical laws, minds do not exist in space and are not subject to such laws. A person's bodily life is publicly observable, while the activities of the mind are not accessible to external observers and are therefore private. This requires us to say that the workings of the body are external whereas the workings of the mind are internal. It is then a short step to say that the mind is *in* the body. This language describing the place of the mind may be metaphorical, since minds do not occupy space and thus could hardly be in any particular place. Nevertheless, Ryle argues, we often do take quite literally this contrast between the outer and inner realms. Psychologists, for example, assume that sensory stimuli come from *outside* and from far distances, and generating mental responses *inside* the skull. All of this suggests some type of transaction between the mind and body. However, no laboratory experiment can discover this relationship. This also suggests that what goes on inside my mind is a secret activity, which people on the outside do not have access to. For example, my mental acts of knowing, hoping, dreading, or intending are private events.

Because this traditional theory completely isolates the mind from the body, Ryle calls this view the "dogma of the Ghost in the Machine." What Ryle finds wrong with this dogma is not that some details here and there are ambiguous, but that the very principle on which the theory rests is false. It is not even a series of particular mistakes. It is, Ryle says, one big mistake of a unique kind, and this he calls a "category-mistake." The big mistake consists of representing the facts of mental life as if they belonged to one and the same logical category whereas in fact they belong to quite different and separate ones. The official theory is therefore a "myth," and it is necessary to "rectify the logic of mental-conduct concepts."

To illustrate this category-mistake, Ryle describes the imaginary visit of a foreigner to Oxford University for the first time. The visitor is shown the museums, scientific laboratories, and some of the colleges. Having seen these various places, the visitor asks, "But where is the University?" The question assumes that the University is yet another institution, or a counterpart to the colleges and laboratories, or another entity that can be seen in the same way as the others. Actually, the University is simply how all of these components are coordinated. Thus, the visitor's mistake consists of his assumption that we can correctly speak of Oxford's library, the museum, and other various components, *and* the University as if the University was the same kind of member in the class to which the others belong. In short, a visitor mistakenly placed the University into the wrong category—a category in which it does not belong. In a similar illustration, Ryle speaks of the mistake that a child makes when watching a military parade in which a division is marching by. Having been told that he was seeing battalions, batteries, and squadrons, the child wants to know when the division was going to appear. Again, the child assumed that the division is another unit similar to the others, not realizing that in seeing the battalions, batteries, and squadrons he already saw the division. The mistake was in thinking it correct to speak of battalions, batteries, squadrons, *and* a division. He placed the division in the wrong category. These category-mistakes show an inability to use certain elements in the English language correctly. What is more significant, Ryle says, is that people who are perfectly capable of applying concepts are nevertheless liable in their abstract thinking to allocate these concepts to logical categories to which they do not belong.

Ryle believes that the Ghost in the Machine dogma makes a similar error and that "a family of radical category-mistakes is the source of the double-life theory." Advocates of the dogma hold that a person's feelings, thinking, and purposive activities cannot be described solely in terms of physics; because of this they conclude that mental activity must be described in a set of counterpart idioms. Moreover, because mental conduct differs so from bodily activities, advocates of the dogma held that mind had its own metaphysical status, made of a different stuff and having a different structure, and possessing its own complex organization. And so they held that body and mind are separate fields of causes and effects, with the body being mechanical and the mind nonmechanical.

How did this category-mistake originate? Although Ryle designates Descartes as the major culprit of this error, it is obvious that the mind–body dualism has a history extending very much further back than the 17th century. Descartes's specific version was inspired by the view that scientific methods were capable of providing a mechanical theory that applied to every occupant in space. From a strictly scientific point of view, Descartes was impressed with the mechanical description of nature. However, as a religious and moral person he was reluctant to agree with the claim that human nature in its mental aspects differs only in degree of complexity from a machine. Consequently, Descartes and subsequent philosophers wrongly construed mental-conduct words to signify nonmechanical processes and concluded that nonmechanical laws must explain the nonspatial workings of minds. But what this explanation retained was the assumption that mind, though different from body, was nevertheless a member of the categories of "thing," "stuff," "state," "process," "cause," and "effect." Thus, just as the visitor expected Oxford University to be another, extra unit, so Descartes and his heirs treated minds as additional though special centers of the causal process. From these conclusions a host of theoretical difficulties arose. How are the mind and body related? How do they bring about effects in each other? If the mind is governed by strict laws analogous to the laws governing the body, does this not imply determinism, in which case such notions as responsibility, choice, merit, and freedom make no sense? Worst of all, only negative terms could be used to speak of the mind: minds are *not* in space, have *no* motions, are *not* aspects of matter, and are *not* observable. For these and other reasons Ryle concludes that the entire argument of the Ghost in the Machine is "broken-backed."

How then should we understand mental events such as acts of knowing, exercising intelligence, understanding, willing, feeling, and imagining? Ryle's alternative to the Ghost in a Machine dogma is a view now called *logical behaviorism,* the theory that talk of mental events should be translated into talk about observable behavior. Virtually every assertion about the mind involves some relevant facts about bodily behavior: "when we characterize people by mental predicates, we are not making untestable inferences to any ghostly processes occurring in streams of consciousness which we are debarred from visiting; we are describing the ways in which those people conduct parts of their predominantly public behavior." Mental terms, then, refer to the way that people do things, and not to private spiritual states. Ultimately, all of our mental states can be analyzed through our behavior, and he denies that our mental states reflect anything more than a predictable way of acting. For instance, when I speak of human emotions I do not infer the working of some interior and obscure mental forces. In favorable circumstances, Ryle says, "I find out your inclinations and your moods more directly than this. I hear and understand your conversational avowals, your interjections and your tones of voice; I see and understand your gestures and facial expressions."

Identity Theory and Functionalism

Ryle's theory of logical behaviorism had its critics. Even if we accept his critique of Cartesian dualism, there are problems with his solution that reduces mind to observable behavior. Ryle's behaviorism presumes that we can explain everything there is about mental events by looking solely at sensory input and behavioral output. For example, I see a lion (input) and I exhibit fearful behaviors, such as trembling (output). For Ryle, these inputs and outputs explain all that there is about my fear. This, however, seems too simplistic. Hoping to avoid committing a category mistake himself, Ryle ignores everything that takes place *between* the input and the output. But what about the most obvious source of my fear, namely my brain? Even Descartes recognized that the human brain plays an important role in processing sensory data. And, for the past few decades, many physicians have defined death in terms of the cessation of brain activity. Addressing this problem, *identity theory* is the view that mental states are identical to brain activity. For example, if I wish to know something about my emotions when I see a lion, I need to look at the type of activity that takes place within my brain. My experience of fear, then, is explained by a series of neurological events, which occur in different parts of my brain. Identity theory attempts to bring the whole issue of human consciousness under the umbrella of science—specifically neuroscience. Gone are the days when soothsayers, exorcists, theologians, or even metaphysicians could contribute anything meaningful to the subject by speculating about the nature of an immaterial human spirit.

The effort to identify human consciousness with brain activity is not unique. As noted, Democritus and other Atomists suggested this view, and, more recently, in the 18th and 19th centuries, some biologists offered somewhat crude theories of how brain functions elicit conscious thought. As theories of brain functions have become more sophisticated in recent decades, so too have theories of mind–brain identity. Two philosophers, J. J. C. Smart and David Armstrong, are associated with the current version of this theory. Perhaps the most common criticism of identity theory is that it fails a principle called *Leibniz's Law.* Leibniz argued that if two things are truly identical, then properties asserted about the one thing must also be asserted about the other. Thus, according to Leibniz's law, if mental events and brain activity are really identical—as Smart and Armstrong contend—then all properties about mental events apply to brain activity and vice versa. However, as the criticism goes, there are some things that we can say about mental events that do not seem to apply to brain activity, and vice versa. First, brain activities are localizable in space, and mental events do not seem to be. We can, for instance, point to a particular region of my brain in which neurons are firing. However, we cannot point to a part of my brain and say "My idea of a tree is right there." Second, brain activities are objectively observable in the sense that we can monitor them with scientific equipment, and mental events cannot be observed in that way. Finally, mental events have the distinct feature that they are directed *at* something—that is, they exhibit intentionality. I have an idea *of* a tree, I wish *for* a new car, I think *about* political turmoil around the world. By contrast, brain activities are not *about* anything. They simply are physical events.

Die-hard identity theorists are not bothered by any of these problems. In fact, they feel that the more we know about brain activity the more comfortable we will become with pointing to parts of a brain and saying "an intentional thought is occurring right there." Nevertheless, identity theory faces another and somewhat different criticism. Specifically, it presumes that mental events, such as thoughts and emotions, *must* be activities of a biological brain. Why, though, can't thoughts occur in nonbiological systems, such as silicon chips? According to a rival theory called *functionalism,* mental events depend primarily on the networks, pathways, and the interconnection of mental processes, and not on the material stuff that it is composed of. Functionalists do not deny that human mental processes are a function of human brain activity. They simply throw open the criteria of mental activity to include computers, robots, or other human-made devices that exhibit the relevant processes.

The field of *artificial intelligence* attempts to realize the functionalist theory and duplicate human cognitive mental states in computing machinery. For some time scientists have tried to replicate human thought processes in some kind of mechanical form. The 1939 New York World's Fair displayed a human-looking robot that mimicked some human activities. At the time, the visual effect was convincing, and many spectators believed that scientists produced a truly human-like creature. However, at that stage of technology, the robot was little more than a wind up toy, and it exhibited none of the internal processes that functionalists would associate with thinking. Computer technology of recent decades has provided the first viable opportunity for at least attempting to replicate human thought processes. In some ways, the goal of artificial intelligence today is modest. Rather than attempting to replicate all human mental processes in machine form—such as emotions, willful activity, and artistic sensibility—advocates of artificial intelligence focus only on the thinking process—analyzing sensory data and making judgments about it. The claims of artificial intelligence advocates are as varied as are their techniques. Two approaches, though, are commonly distinguished. A *weak* version of artificial intelligence holds that suitably programmed machines can simulate human cognition. *Strong* artificial intelligence, by contrast, holds that suitably programmed machines are actually capable of cognitive mental states. The weak claim presents no serious philosophical problem, since a machine that merely simulates human cognition does not need to actually possess conscious mental states. The strong claim, though, is more philosophically controversial since it holds that a computer can have human-like thoughts.

Searle and the Chinese Room Argument

The most well known attack on strong artificial intelligence is by John Searle, a former student of John Austin's at Oxford University, and later professor at the University of California, Berkeley. Searle was bothered by grandiose claims by computer scientists that some computer programs could interpret stories the way humans do. That is, the computers could read between the lines and draw inferences about events in the story which we as humans draw from our life experience. Proponents of strong artificial intelligence claimed that the program in question both understands stories, and explains our human ability to understand stories—that is, it provides the sufficient conditions for "understanding." Searle counters this view with a picturesque thought experiment. Suppose that I, or some other non-Chinese speaking person, am put in a room and given three sets of Chinese characters: (1) a large batch of Chinese writing constituting the structure of that language, (2) a story, and, (3) questions about the story. I also receive a set of rules in English—kind of like a computer program—that allow me to correlate the three sets of characters with each other. Although I do not know the meaning of the Chinese symbols, I may get so good at manipulating the symbols that, from the outside, I answer all the questions correctly and no one can tell if I am Chinese or not. According to Searle, it is quite obvious that "I do not understand a word of the Chinese stories. I have inputs and outputs that are indistinguishable from those of the native Chinese speaker, and I can have any formal program you like, but I still understand nothing." For Searle, this scenario goes against both of the above two claims of strong artificial intelligence. That is, I neither understand the Chinese stories, and the process I am following does not fully explain the notion of "understanding." In short, even if a computer program appears to meaningfully interpret nuances of a story, the program does not really understand the story.

Searle himself anticipated a variety of objections to his Chinese room argument. What if a computer program was imbedded within a robot that acquired data by interacting with the real world, rather than simply being supplied with that data? The robot might ably interact by means of a video camera and motorized arms and legs. However, Searle argues, this would still only produce data very much like the data already imbedded in the computer, and nothing significantly new would be changed in how the computer processes the information. What, though, if a computer program simulated a pattern neurons firing, rather than simply the interrelations between words? Searle replies that we still only have a simulation, and not the real thing. According to Searle, then, a computer program—no matter how elaborate—is not capable of cognitive mental states. This is a feature reserved for biological and organic brains. Although Searle denies the extravagant claims of functionalists and advocates of artificial intelligence, he does not want to concede victory to either the pure identity theorist or the olden day Cartesian dualists. He instead tries to forge a middle ground between the latter two theories, which he called Biological Naturalism. Like the identity theorist, he believes that mental events are really biological in nature, specifically involving higher-level brain functions. So, when we investigate the nature of the human mind, we investigate the brain, and there is no mysterious spiritual component to our mental events. Like the dualist, though, Searle is swayed by Leibniz's law and insists that our descriptions about brain activity (e.g., neurons firing) are fundamentally different from descriptions about mental events (e.g., I wish *for* a new car). Accordingly, philosophical descriptions of human thinking will never be replaced with scientific descriptions of brain activity. Each is valid within its own territory.

RORTY

Ever since Plato, traditional philosophers tried to discover the foundations of knowledge. They wanted to know exactly what is "out there"—outside the mind—to distinguish between mind and body, between appearance and reality, and to provide a grounding for absolutely certain truth. By contrast, analytic philosophers scaled down the enterprise of philosophy to the more modest objective of discovering the foundations of meaningful language. Sentences or propositions would be considered meaningful only if they corresponded to objective and verifiable facts. In this way, philosophy would resemble the rigor of scientific knowledge. But did this shift in the concerns of philosophy represent a major revolution? To be sure, linguistic analysis clarified some philosophical problems by demonstrating the frequent misuse of language. More dramatically, several traditional issues were simply eliminated from the agenda of philosophy when analytic philosophers insisted that language must

Richard Rorty
(David Burnett/Contact Press Images)

accurately represent facts. What "facts" could be "represented" by language when talking about the "good" or the "beautiful" or the "just" or "God"? If there were no such facts, philosophy could no longer speak meaningfully about ethics, aesthetics, religion, justice, and metaphysics. Surely, we might think, this represents a revolutionary departure from the traditional concerns of philosophy.

However, according to American philosopher Richard Rorty, analytic philosophy did not usher in a major change in the assumptions of philosophy. In his provocative book *Philosophy and the Mirror of Nature* (1979). Rorty argues that analytic philosophy is not something new but, rather, a variation of what Descartes and Kant did, namely, to provide a "foundation" for knowledge. What is new in analytic philosophy, Rorty says, is the conviction that knowledge is represented by what is linguistic and not by what is mental. But to say this is to leave unchanged the assumption that as human beings we possess by our very nature some framework within which the activity of inquiry takes place. We still have in analytic philosophy, (1) a "knowing subject," (2) "reality out there," and (3) a "theory of representation" which describes how reality is represented to the knowing subject. The old account of how we know is still the same, namely, that the mind is like a great mirror containing representations of nature, some accurate and some inaccurate, which we then study by pure "rational" methods. Analytic philosophy does not remove the assumption that the mind is like a mirror. It simply tries to increase the accuracy of the representations captured by the mind, as Rorty says, by "inspecting, repairing and polishing the mirror." Moreover, to engage in repairing and polishing the mirror implies the presence of another old assumption, namely, that there is some reality that is eternally "out there," but which for some reason is inaccurately represented to the mind. For these reasons, Rorty believes that a truly revolutionary move in philosophy would require the final rejection of several assumptions. We must first abandon the traditional mirror-imagery—the assumption that human beings are equipped with a structural framework which dictates how our inquiries must proceed. We must also abandon the assumption that even before there is thinking or history, there is an "essence" to reality, which to know is to know the truth.

Rorty was himself an analytic philosopher as a young professor at Princeton University. He was born in 1931 and raised in New York City as an only child whose parents were freelance journalists and whose maternal grandfather, Walter Raschenbusch, was an eminent liberal Protestant theologian. At age 14, Rorty entered the University of Chicago and later completed his graduate studies in philosophy at Yale University. After a brief teaching assignment at Wellesley College, he joined the faculty at Princeton, whose philosophy department at that time was strongly oriented toward analytic philosophy. For a few years, Rorty immersed himself in "doing" analytic philosophy but finally grew dissatisfied with the piecemeal task of unraveling linguistic and logical puzzles. After a brief period of professional crisis during the early 1970s and to the considerable surprise of his colleagues, Rorty chose a new direction for his studies, toward the pragmatism of John Dewey.

Influence of Pragmatism

In 1909, on the 50th anniversary of Darwin's *The Origin of Species* (1859), Dewey delivered a lecture titled "The Influence of Darwinism on Philosophy." The influence it had, Dewey said, was that it introduced a new type of thinking—a type that influenced Dewey himself. The theory of biological evolution, Dewey said, emphasized that change is fundamental to everything that exists. This change represents not only simple rearrangements of bits of matter, but the presence of "organic systems" and their creativity with respect to the environment. This meant that knowledge could no longer aim at realities lying behind any notion of the mathematical order of nature or any vestige of Platonic "eternality." There is no "givenness" about the world. Philosophy would no longer enquire about absolute origins and absolute final ends, as in Hegel's gradual realization of the Idea of freedom or Marx's final phase of human society. Philosophy would no longer seek to prove that our life necessarily must have certain qualities or values as a result of an earlier cause, such as creation, or a specific goal. The world, in this view, is not described as reflecting an eternal pattern, out there, abstractly.

Instead, according to Dewey, philosophical thinking should begin with our immediate concrete life experiences. We would then see human life as Aristotle did, namely, that although we are a part of nature and behave in certain mechanical ways as described by science, we are nevertheless *human.* And although we have some characteristics of other animals, we are nevertheless unique. What makes us unique is that we are aware of the processes of nature and we can know how we *function.* We know where some forms of behavior lead and what values or ends they support or frustrate. Experience tells us what things are "necessary for," or "better for" or "worse for" other things. We can evaluate things not in terms of some remote and abstract standards, but rather in terms of some more obvious "ends" built into the very natural functions of organisms. Human life in this view reveals a close relationship between the functions of human nature and the various simultaneous functions of the larger natural environment, which provides wide choices of ends and values. It is easy to see how the new Darwinian approach to knowledge influenced Dewey in the direction of pragmatism. Instead of pursuing a single ultimate truth about reality, his emphasis shifted to a pluralism of truths, many truths, and the characteristic that these ideas or notions are true because they "work."

Rorty was drawn to Dewey's pragmatism for these and several other reasons. For one thing, it gave him an avenue of escape from the severe limitations which linguistic analysis placed upon the scope of his philosophical activity. Pragmatism provided him with a basis for finally rejecting the traditional view that the mind is a reliable mirror reflecting reality, a notion that assumed that only those thoughts and language are true which faithfully represent the real world. Since there is no way to be absolutely certain that a thought or statement accurately corresponds to reality, it is, he thought, better to think that a statement is true if it leads to successful behavior, that is, if it "works." We should look upon statements as "tools" whose truth is based upon their usefulness. Since there are several types of statements, there are correspondingly several kinds of truths. To look upon truth in this manner is to bring back to philosophy the subject matter of many fields. From this point of view, science has no special claim upon truth since it is only one among many areas of practical human concern, along with politics, ethics, art, literature, history, and religion. Scientific methods cannot therefore provide the sole criterion for truth since there are several particular kinds of truth.

What especially attracted Rorty to pragmatism was that its pluralistic view of truth opened wide areas of legitimate philosophical discussion. In addition to the analysis of language, it now became philosophically useful to study novels and poetry to find insights into human problems which philosophy virtually abandoned. Moreover, Anglo-American philosophers could more comfortably engage in discourse with their counterparts in Continental Europe, where the darker themes of dread, *angst,* and solitude permeate the works of Kierkegaard, Nietzsche, and Heidegger. Rorty discovered that while analytic philosophy isolated itself from some of the deepest concerns of life, it is possible to overcome this isolation by expanding the range and type of literature considered worthy of study. Following this insight, Rorty left the department of philosophy at Princeton and, in 1983 became University Professor of Humanities at the University of Virginia. Here, his approach to philosophy relied heavily upon literary and cultural criticism and acknowledges the morally illuminating power of novelists and poets. Rorty has no interest in nor does he think it is useful to engage in "systematic" philosophy. More and more, he believes, the emphasis will be on "edifying" philosophy, whose practitioners will be concerned with culture and self-transformation.

The Contingency of Language

If there is one theme that captures the truly radical aspect of Rorty's philosophical point of view, it is his conviction that there are no eternal "essences." For example, there is no "human nature," "true nature of the self," or "universal moral law," discoverable by human reason. Instead of a timeless and stable structure in reality, what we find, Rorty says, is that everywhere we are confronted with "contingency," by the ever-presence of "chance." If everything is "contingent," how can there be any meaning to life? If there is no timeless truth, how can we know whether our lives fall short of their intended purpose or value? Rorty is aware of these consequences of his pragmatism. But instead of being intimidated by this bewildering world of chance, he sees in it wide opportunities for overcoming contingency by constant self-transformation or self-creation. Still, he insists that it is philosophically important to recognize that contingency and chance characterize such fundamental aspects of our experience as our *language,* our idea of our *selfhood,* and our conception of human society or *community.*

We normally think of language as a means by which our vocabulary represents reality to our minds. How can a vocabulary represent or be the medium of something "out there"? One way is to use the metaphor of a jigsaw puzzle. By the use of words it is assumed that we can describe various pieces of the puzzle so that as the vocabulary changes and evolves, our language will come closer and closer to what exists out there. But this assumes that out there are to be found fixed and stable realities capable of being described.

Take, for example, the language of science. Galileo created a new vocabulary when he described the behavior of the earth and the sun in relation to each other. What does this history of the change in scientific language illustrate? Does it show that Galileo's new description represents a deeper insight into the intrinsic nature of the natural world? Rorty does not think so. "We must," he says, "resist the temptation to think that the re-descriptions of reality offered by contemporary physical or biological sciences are somehow closer to 'the things themselves.' " It is not as though the new language has filled in more of the jigsaw puzzle. Rather, we should instead use the metaphor of language as a "tool" so that the new vocabulary of science will simply enable those who create the new language to accomplish new objectives. There is no necessary line of development in language any more than there is a necessary line of evolution in nature. We cannot return to the way nature and its purposes were thought about before the time of Darwin. Contingency and chance—that is, the more or less random behavior of things—explains the changes in nature and in language. Physical evolution did not have to occur precisely as it did. Was it necessary or only by chance that orchids came upon the scene? And didn't Mendel "let us see mind as something which just happened rather than as something which was the whole point of the process?" To say the opposite, namely, that the world has an intrinsic nature which the physicist or poet has glimpsed, is, he says, "a remnant of the idea that the world is a divine creation, the work of someone who had something in mind, who Himself spoke some language in which He described His own project."

Because our language is the product of random choices made by those who sought to describe the world, there is no reason now to be bound by that inherited language. The language of the past certainly has influenced the way we think. However, we should create our own new vocabulary if that would be more useful in solving our problems. "It is essential to my view," Rorty writes, "that we have no pre-linguistic consciousness to which language needs to be adequate, no deep sense of how things are which it is the duty of philosophers to spell out in language." Truth, Rorty says, is no more than what Nietzsche called "a mobile army of metaphors."

The Contingency of Selfhood

Plato gave us the metaphor of two worlds: the world of time, appearance, and change, on the one hand, and the world of enduring, changeless truth on the other. Our lives involve an attempt to escape from the distractions of the flesh and dominant opinions of a particular time and place in order to enter the real world of reason and contemplation. With this vocabulary, Plato created a language designed to describe the essence of human nature, implying that there is only one true description of our human situation. As we face the contingent events of our lives, we are to control our affections by the use and power of our reason and thereby achieve moral and intellectual virtue. Theologians offered basically this same metaphor, urging human beings to strive toward our "true nature." Similarly, Kant described the difference between our daily experiences with their local influences on our choices, on the one hand, and our internal moral consciousness which reveals for all human beings our timeless and universal moral laws on the other. These versions of the two worlds that we encounter represent the true world as compared with the deceptive world that we must try to escape.

Rorty believes that Plato, the theologians, and Kant imposed labels and descriptions of "the self" upon our consciousness as if these were absolutely true descriptions. There are, after all, alternative ways of defining the self. If, for example, Nietzsche says that "God is dead," he implies that there is nothing more to reality than the flow of events, and the flux of chance. Nor is there any universal moral law nor a "true self." This skepticism leaves the question of how to provide a meaning for human life. There is no other choice, Nietzsche says, to which Rorty agrees, than for each person to give meaning to his own life by writing his own language and describing his own objectives. In a real sense, each of us must be involved in transforming our "self," not by seeking the truth but by overcoming the old self and by choosing and willing a new self. According to Rorty, "we create ourselves by telling our own story."

Plato tried to describe human nature in some specific detail when he spoke of the tripartite aspect of the self, including the physical body, the passions and affections, and, highest of all, the mind. He assumed that our minds had a clear shot at the truth and could overcome the contingent events encountered in daily life. But Rorty finds that quite different descriptions of consciousness have been offered without assuming a realm of eternal truth. On the contrary, he finds in the writings of Freud a tripartite description of the self as nothing but the product of contingent events. The sense of guilt is explained not by an innate knowledge of the moral law. Rather, as Freud says, "a regressive degrading of the libido takes place, the super-ego becomes exceptionally severe and unkind, and the ego, in obedience to the super-ego, produces strong reaction-formations in the shape of conscientiousness, pity and cleanliness." It may be that the metaphor of the two worlds has been too powerful to overcome. But Freud replies that,

> if one considers chance to be unworthy of determining our fate, it is simply a relapse into the pious view of the universe which Leonardo himself was on the way of overcoming when he wrote that the sun does not move . . . we are all too ready to forget that in fact everything to do with our life is chance, from our origin out of the meeting of spermatozoon and ovum onwards. . . . Everyone of us human beings corresponds to one of the countless experiments in which [the countless causes] of nature force their way into experience.

The Contingency of Community

How can human beings live together, or, how can human beings achieve solidarity and community? Here, again, Plato drew a tight connection between "the essential human nature" and the social and political arrangement of the community. Plato thought that the three classes of society were necessary extensions of the three parts of the human soul or self. The artisans embody the physical element of the person, the guardians express the spirited passions, and the rulers are the incarnation of the mind, reason. Plato also argued that there must first be a harmony of the three parts of the private individual if the collective harmony of the community was to be achieved. All the elements of the self must be subject to and governed by the highest faculty, that is, by reason. Similarly, all the classes of society must be subordinate to the ruler. This whole arrangement is dictated by the structure of human nature.

Rorty disagrees with this notion that our public life must be based upon the antecedent facts of human nature. Theologians have also offered their versions of the Platonic account of the origin and justification of political authority, especially in their theory of the divine rights of kings, while Karl Marx drew from his description of history, and from the relation of human beings to the material order of nature, a theory of a classless society. These various vocabularies or languages describing the good society are contingent upon the special perspectives of each author. Each account focuses upon a different concept of "ultimate reality," and a different view of essential human nature. It is not surprising, then, Rorty says, that there can be no single concept of community which is required by some true description of human nature.

For his part, Rorty holds that since there is no absolutely true account available of human nature, there is no point in looking in that direction for some moral basis of society. The contingency of language and the contingency of the self mean that there is no reliable objective information that can lead to the *right* kind of community. There is no theory of knowledge that can guarantee the just society—neither "rationality, the love of God, or the love of truth." Instead, Rorty agrees with the insights of Dewey as reflected by John Rawls in his Dewey Lectures:

> What justifies a conception of justice is not its being true to an order antecedent and given to us, but its congruence with our deeper understanding of ourselves and our aspirations, and our realization that, given our history and the traditions embedded in our public life, it is the most reasonable theory for us.

The central value on which to build a community is the value of freedom and equality, which is the ideal of liberal democracy. It is not helpful, Rorty says, to ask at this point, "How do you *know* that freedom is the chief goal of social organization?" any more than it is to ask, "How do you *know* that Jones is worthy of your friendship?" The preference for freedom and equality and the desire to eliminate suffering are not discovered by reason but by chance. These values were not always obvious nor always chosen. They were not always options, for example, for the Egyptians, nor can they be defended rationally against those who refuse to accept them. The social glue that holds a liberal society together consists in a consensus, Rorty says, in which everybody has an opportunity at self-creation to the extent of their abilities. From the point of view of his pragmatism, Rorty says that what matters most is the widely shared conviction that "what we call 'good' or 'true' [is] whatever is the outcome of free discussion," for if we take care of political freedom, "truth and goodness will take care of themselves."

VIRTUE THEORY REVISITED

For much of the 19th and 20th centuries, moral philosophers have been waging a war between two camps. On the one side are empiricists who believe that morality is determined solely by looking at the consequences of our conduct. If an action produces a greater balance of happiness or benefit, then it is morally good. If it produces a greater balance of unhappiness or disbenefit, then it is morally bad. A representative from this camp is the utilitarian Jeremy Bentham, who argued that we can very mechanically calculate the balance of happiness and unhappiness that results from our actions. On the other side of the dispute, rationalists believe that humans are naturally implanted with moral intuitions, similar to other rational concepts, such as the principle of cause and effect. On this view, an act is morally good if we can rationally assess that it is consistent with our moral intuitions. If inconsistent, then it is morally bad. Immanuel Kant is a representative of this camp. Moral empiricists argued that we simply have no rational moral intuitions and the rationalist approach is wishful thinking aimed at discovering a universal and unchanging standard of morality. Moral rationalists, on the other hand, charge that the empirical approach ignores our truly rational nature and reduces morality to the whims of social groups. Defenders of each side have continually modified and strengthened their theories in response to attacks from their opponents. In recent decades, though, several philosophers have argued that the entire dispute between these two camps is misguided. On this view, moral philosophy went astray in the 18th century when it set aside the central notion of ethics, namely, virtue, especially as developed by Aristotle. Virtues, for Aristotle, are habits that regulate our more animalistic desires. When we cultivate these virtuous habits, our actions reflect our natural purpose as rational and social creatures. The first such recent defense of virtue theory was by British philosopher Elizabeth Anscombe (1919–2001).

Elizabeth Anscombe

Anscombe was a student of Ludwig Wittgenstein, and, inspired by her teacher's views of the philosophy of mind, she made considerable contributions to that field as well. Her conception of virtue theory appears in her essay "Modern Moral Philosophy" (1958). Anscombe notes here that we commonly use several ethically loaded words in our moral vocabulary. I say that you *ought, must,* or are *obligated* to do certain things. These terms express a kind of moral edict or command. For example, if I say that "you ought not steal," then I imply that thieves violate some universal moral law and are accordingly morally guilty and punishable for stealing. Where does this notion of moral edict come from? She argues that Christian philosophers in the middle ages introduced it. Preoccupied with the concept of divine law, medieval philosophers believed that God was the ultimate authority behind proper conduct. Some actions such as stealing are sinful, and God demands that we avoid these actions. Ultimately, for medieval philosophers, all morality involves obedience to God's laws or edicts. In more recent centuries, philosophers such as Hume and Kant offered secular accounts of the origin of morality. Hume in particular was committed to offering a theory of morality that made no reference to divine authority, but instead was grounded in feelings and other psychological features of human nature. The problem, though, is that Hume and others retained the medieval notions of *ought* and *moral law* while at the same time casting off the idea of God as moral lawgiver. Put most simply, the notion of "law" requires a lawgiver, and it makes no sense to keep talking about obligations to moral laws once we abandon the notion of God as moral lawgiver. However,—and this is Anscombe's key concern—philosophers from Hume until the present day continue discussing notions of *ought* and *moral law* anyway. Anscombe writes, "It is as if the notion 'criminal' were to remain when criminal law and criminal courts had been abolished and forgotten." Some philosophers offer questionable explanations of the foundation of moral obligation, and others concede that the concept of *ought* has no real content. Nevertheless, the concepts of *ought* and *moral law* are central to current ethical theories. In fact, such moral edicts are so imbedded in contemporary moral theories that the theories would collapse without them.

There is more at stake here than simply a theoretical dispute among academic philosophers about the notions of *ought* or *moral law,* and the groundless edicts that emerge from contemporary moral theories. According to Anscombe, some of the moral theories after Hume have contributed to a dangerous kind of moral reasoning in real life. One such theory is *consequentialism*—a revision of utilitarianism that Anscombe associates with 19th-century British moral philosopher Henry Sidgwick. On this theory, right actions are those that bring about the best consequences that we can foresee. For Anscombe, the problem with this approach is that it fails to distinguish between two completely different types of consequences. First, there are consequences that involve intrinsic goods, such as truth telling and not killing. Second, there are more indirect consequences in which we might say that the ends justify the means—such as stealing a loaf of bread to feed one's starving family. True morality, according to Anscombe, should focus on intrinsic goods, without attempting to counterbalance these against the second and more indirect type of consequences. In another essay she provides a vivid example of how people sometimes blur these two consequences with disastrous results. According to Anscombe, at the close of World War II President Harry

Truman used consequentialist reasoning when deciding to drop atomic bombs on the Japanese cities of Hiroshima and Nagasaki. On one side of the balance Truman placed the negative consequence of killing tens of thousands of innocent Japanese civilians; Anscombe contends that avoiding such killing would have been a fundamentally good thing to do. On the other side of the balance Truman considered that the bombs would bring a quick end to the war, and thus serve as a useful means to an end. Believing that the latter reasoning was more weighty, he decided to drop the bombs—a decision that Anscombe believes was murderous. Thus, consequentialism is not only flawed, but even hazardous when applied to decisions like this. And, in turn, the misguided force of consequentialism rests on the misguided conception of moral edicts embedded in concepts like *ought* and *moral law.*

What is the solution to this problem surrounding moral edicts? Anscombe herself is a secular moral theorist and would not recommend reviving medieval Christian conceptions of divine law. That is, she would not advise reinstating God as giver of the moral law. Instead, she recommends that we simply reject all talk about moral law and obligation and look to Aristotle for inspiration. Aristotle did not speak of divine legislators or moral edicts. Instead, he describes virtues—habits that regulate our behavior in response to our animalistic appetites. People are bad, not because they violate moral laws, but because they fail to acquire virtues, and instead develop vices such as cowardice, untruthfulness, unchasteness, or unjustness. If we adopt Aristotle's approach, not only will we abandon the notions of *ought* and *moral law*, but we will also abandon all the notions in moral psychology that philosophers since Hume have relied on, such as "action," "intention," "pleasure," and "wanting." This amounts to "laying aside" the whole discipline of moral philosophy until we have more adequate notions of moral psychology that are consistent with Aristotle's notion of virtue. In the decades after the appearance of her essay, several philosophers took Anscombe's challenge to heart by rejecting consequentialism and other traditional conceptions of moral obligation that involved moral edicts. These new virtue theorists also explore the psychological underpinnings of moral virtues, attempting to supplement Aristotle's discussion with more current accounts of human nature.

Nel Noddings

One recent defender of virtue theory is Nel Noddings, who in her essay "Ethics from the Standpoint Of Women" (1990) sees virtues as a way of articulating a uniquely female conception of morality. Noddings and other feminist writers argue that much of our intellectual heritage was not only formed by men but reflects a male way of looking at the world. There is some controversy surrounding possible differences between male and female ways of thinking. Male approaches, though, tend to emphasize following rules, devising strict laws, and finding subtle logical distinctions according to which we can categorize people and things. Female ways of thinking, by contrast, emphasize a capacity for nurturing and caring for others. We see this distinction when comparing vocations that tend to be male dominated—such as engineering and mathematics—with those that are female dominated—such as social work and education. Much of philosophy has been driven by male ways of thinking and, perhaps in some ways, contaminated by it. Ethics, Noddings argues, is a case in point. Kant, for example, argued that morality is grounded in cold rational duty, even to the point that "acts done out of love do not qualify as moral acts." Nietzsche model of morality is that of a warrior who casts aside traditional values and forges new ones. His theory is "overtly and proudly masculine, and much of it depends directly on the devaluation of women and all that is associated with the feminine." Some of these moral philosophers even blatantly make sexist statements, devaluing the rational capacity of women and belittle female sentimentalism.

According to Noddings, the solution to the problem caused by male-oriented ethical theories is to replace them with ones that are female-oriented. Why, though, not just make ethics gender neutral? After all, moral theories aim at universalization, that is, applying to all people. Focusing on only one gender undermines this. For Noddings, though, "To construct an ethic free of gendered views may be impossible in a thoroughly gendered society." At minimum, female-oriented theories need to be proposed to counterbalance male theories, and perhaps at some future time we can transcend them both with gender-neutral approaches. A critic might still argue that the traditional activities and attitudes of women have nothing to do with ethics, and cannot serve as a basis for developing any meaningful moral theory. Examples of tasks commonly imposed on women are child-rearing, cooking, cleaning, and homemaking. These all tend to be menial, and even exploitive when imposed on women at the expense of more meaningful and challenging life activities. Not only do men avoid these tasks and the effeminacy associated with them, but many contemporary women also denounce them as oppressive. Nevertheless, Noddings believes that even within these traditional women's activities we can find a foundation for female ethics. The theme that underlies all of these activities is *care,* or the capacity to nurture other people. Even if contemporary women abandon these tasks completely, the most oppressive of these activities still reflects an orientation towards caring for others.

Noddings believes that the ethical emphasis on care fits neatly into virtue theory. The caring attitude itself is a habit that we cultivate, similar to other virtues such as courage and temperance. Further, virtue theory and the caring attitude are both resistant to the harsh rules of traditional moral theories. There is a spontaneity to both virtuous and caring conduct that involves unique responses to unique situations. This, though, does not mean that we should simply adopt Aristotle's theory of virtue just as it is. Aristotle's account rests on an elitist and male-dominated conception of society in which the lifestyles of women and slaves were of no concern:

> Aristotle's identification of virtues depended almost entirely on the establishment of exclusive classes and the activities appropriate to each. The virtues of women and of slaves were not those of educated citizens. He made no attempt to identify virtues in one class that might be cultivated in others by

extending the range of privilege or sharing the array of common tasks. If he had made such an attempt, it would surely have moved in only one direction. One might try to inculcate the virtues of the highest class into lower classes, but one would never try to develop, say, feminine virtues in men.

We must, then, expand Aristotle's list of virtues by adding ones that reflect the lifestyles of dejected groups, particularly women.

Feminists might still question whether women should identify themselves so boldly with a caring attitude. Just as nurturing women in the past were exploited, perhaps caring women today may make themselves vulnerable to the same kind of oppression. They may find themselves "dependent on men or on welfare in order to care for their children, and are sometimes physically abused." Noddings agrees that if only women adopted the ethics of caring then, indeed, oppression toward women would continue. What, though, if the attitude of caring was instilled in men too? This would force us to recognize that all humans are interdependent on each other, regardless of gender. With the right kind of moral education, we could instill in people a virtue of care that contains proper limits and prevents people from taking advantage of nurturers.

CONTINENTAL PHILOSOPHY

By the mid 20th century, a rift existed between Anglo-American philosophers of the analytic tradition and Continental European philosophers of the phenomenological and existentialist tradition. The two groups differed in methodology, with analytic philosophers emphasizing logic and language, and Continental philosophers emphasizing ontological concerns of human nature and action. They also sought inspiration from different major philosophers—Hume, Russell, and Wittgenstein for analytic philosophers, and Nietzsche, Husserl, Heidegger, and Sartre for Continental ones. In recent decades, the gulf between the two has narrowed. Analytic philosophy is now taught in European universities, and Continental philosophy has made its way into British and American educational institutions, particularly within English and Literature departments. Recent Continental philosophy is associated with several "isms" which overlap each other: structuralism, post-structuralism, deconstructionism, and postmodernism. We will look at these.

Structuralism

Structuralism began in the early 1900s as a theory explaining the nature of language. Its champion, Swiss linguist Ferdinand de Saussure (1857–1913), was bothered by standard 19th-century linguistic theories that presumed to find some commonality between various foreign languages. As tempting as this approach might seem, Saussure believed it was fundamentally mistaken. Each language, he argued, is a closed formal system—an entity unto itself—with no significant connection to other languages or even to the physical objects to which the words presumably refer. A given language, like English, consists of an arbitrary system of words whose meanings are based solely on conventional structures or patterns of use. A single word is like the thread of a fabric, whose function is determined only in relation to the surrounding weave of threads; by itself, the thread has no function. For example, a toddler just learning how to pronounce words might be hungry and say "muck"; by itself, this word means nothing and certainly is not what an adult means by it. An astute parent, though, will understand the larger context of the toddler's language abilities and behavior, and recognize that the toddler means "milk." Language, in short, is an arbitrary social institution, and all the pieces of a language derive their meaning from that larger system of social structures.

Saussure realized that his theory had implications beyond language, and in fact could apply to other systems of social convention. Following his lead, several writers pushed the structuralist agenda into the fields of anthropology, psychology, intellectual history, and political theory. The unifying theme of this movement was that any cultural object or concept gets its meaning from its surrounding cultural structures. French anthropologist Claude Lévi-Strauss (b. 1908) argued further that the surrounding cultural structures will typically involve a pair of opposites, such as male/female, odd/even, light/dark. These paired opposites give systems a stable logical structure. For example, the Hindu caste system involves a hierarchy of social classes that are based on the paired opposites of purity and impurity: the higher castes are more pure and the lower castes are more impure. The two key components of the structuralist movement, then, are (1) the meaning of a thing is defined by its surrounding cultural structures, and (2) the system has a coherent structure that is reflected in paired opposites. Suppose, for example, that I wanted to understand the meaning of a wedding ring. It would be futile for me to investigate my own wedding ring in isolation from everything else in my culture. Instead, I should try to understand the internal structures of various wedding rings, such as whether they are flashy or modest (paired opposites), and the meanings that these features convey in our culture. I should also try to understand how wedding rings play a role in the larger system of cultural structures, such as the signals that wedding rings send to others, and how wearing a wedding ring might differ from wearing a high school ring.

Although structuralism was not initially developed as a philosophy *per se,* its philosophical implications soon became apparent, and it quickly emerged in reaction against Sartre's existentialism. Sartre believed that individual people create their own natures through free choices, and people are not predefined by their social surroundings. Lévi-Strauss and other structuralists rejected this emphasis on individual people and the subjectivism that existentialism implies. Just as wedding rings are defined by larger social structures, so too are people, and we cannot view ourselves as free independent agents stripped of our social context. We must always use other people as a basis for understanding ourselves. By the 1960s, structuralism overshadowed existentialism as France's most popular philosophy.

Post-Structuralism

Post-structuralism—which appeared in the 1970s—is both an expansion upon and refutation of structuralism. Like structuralism, post-structuralism has branched out into several disciplines, perhaps most notably in the field of literary criticism. Consider, for example, what structuralists might say about interpreting a novel such as *Gone with the Wind.* We might be tempted to see this book as a somewhat historical discussion of the U.S. Civil War. However, structuralists would argue that the meaning of particular passages in the book rests mainly on the structures within the book itself, which is a closed system. Further, the structures in the book involve paired opposites of war/peace, wealth/poverty, and love/strife. Post-structuralism pushes the matter further. First, if *Gone with the Wind* is truly a closed system, then I must exclude any fact or consideration outside of that novel, such as what I might find in a history book on the civil war. I must even set aside the author's intentions, which also rest outside of the novel, such as what I might find in a biography of the author. Whatever meaning the book has depends on what I the reader think about the book as I enter into that closed system. Since each reader will likely have a different interpretation of the book, the book will thus have *no* definitive meaning. Second, post-structuralists will argue that if we look carefully for so-called paired opposites within *Gone with the Wind,* we will find this to be an oversimplification. For example, although the book does contain elements of love and strife, we also see indifference: "Frankly, I don't give a damn," as Clark Gable expresses it in the movie. Similarly, we don't simply see wealth and poverty, but middle level income as well. Structuralists believed that paired opposites provided logical coherence to closed systems. But once we reject this notion of paired opposites—as post-structuralists recommend—then we are left without any internal logical structure of the book. Each reader, then, will play with the book, bringing his or her own meaning to it.

   In philosophy, post-structuralism is most associated with French philosopher Jacque Derrida (b. 1930). Unlike other post-structuralists who focus on literary criticism, Derrida targets philosophy books. He argues that throughout the history of Western thought philosophers have built their theories around key opposing concepts, such as appearance/reality, opinion/knowledge, spirit/matter, and truth/falsehood. On face value, these opposing concepts might support the structuralist theory that philosophical systems have a coherent structure, which is reflected in paired opposites. However, just as we should reject paired opposites in novels, Derrida believes that these philosophical concepts are also suspect. Through a technique that he calls *deconstruction,* he attempts to show that all of these paired opposites in philosophy are in fact self-refuting. For example, Husserl emphasizes a distinction between what is *present* to our consciousness (phenomena) and what is *absent* from it (whether the world exists). But when Husserl himself explores what is actually present to our consciousness, he finds that the "present" principally includes memories of what happened in the past and anticipations of what will occur in the future. The problem now is that neither the past nor the future are really "present" to our consciousness. Thus, Husserl's initial distinction between presence and absence collapses: the two concepts are in fact intertwined. Derrida believes that we can similarly deconstruct all of the standard paired opposites in philosophy. For example, with the appearance/reality dichotomy, when attempting to describe reality, my descriptions seem to be based solely on appearances, such as what appears to my senses. Similarly, with the matter/spirit dichotomy, when attempting to say something about spirits—my own spirit or a divine being—my descriptions are all grounded in some material reality. Because the internal logic of such philosophical systems is flawed, no such system offers an adequate description about the world.

According to Derrida, one of the more central dichotomies underlying philosophical discourse is that between speech and writing. French philosopher Jean Jacque Rousseau (1712–1778) drew this distinction most clearly. Speech, Rousseau argues, is our natural form of communicating feelings and as such it conveys what is real and certain. Writing, by contrast, is a degraded copy of speech. Because writing only indirectly conveys our feelings, it relies on a series of conventional devices that ultimately distort truth and are the source of illusion. However, Derrida argues, both speech and writing involve basic elements of language, such as conventional use of symbols and strict rules of grammar. In fact, we might argue that writing is a better vehicle of language than speech because established conventions are so central to language, and, on Rousseau's reasoning, writing relies on conventions more than speech.

Postmodernism

Post-structuralism and the specific technique of deconstruction make quite skeptical pronouncements about the success of traditional philosophical systems. Post-structuralists also cast doubt on finding any meaning to the world beyond what we as individual observers impose on things. It seems that the whole historical enterprise of finding a unified meaning of things is fatally flawed. In Western civilization, the problem started during the Renaissance and Enlightenment periods—the 16th through 18th centuries—when scientists and philosophers ushered in a new and modern way of viewing the world. Scientists hoped to find a unified system of physical laws that govern the natural world around us. As an addendum to this scientific plan, philosophers described the mechanisms of human thought, thereby explaining how human beings and human culture fits into the larger natural machinery. The philosophical theories of humanism, rationalism, empiricism, and idealism all reflect the basic assumption that the world is one, and there is a single explanatory system that governs everything. All beliefs and values that we form are grounded in this unifying system. This modern conception of things was passed on through the 19th and 20th centuries, right down to the present times. The modern notion of a unified world system is a nice fairytale, but a fairytale nonetheless. We need to step beyond this modern conception of things into a *postmodern* frame of mind.

Postmodernism is not a single philosophical theory; to be so would be self-defeating. Instead, it is an umbrella movement that covers a variety of critiques of the modern conception of things. Post-structuralism is perhaps the most dominant of these, and, for this reason the terms "postmodern" and "post-structural" are often used interchangeably. However, much of recent philosophy targets modernism and thus would also count postmodern. Rorty rejects the standard conception that there are "essences" to things, such as human nature. Anscombe challenged the "lawgiver" assumption behind modern moral theories. Feminist philosophers reject the largely male-oriented manner of imposing rigid schemes on things. We even find hints of postmodernist attitudes in earlier times, such as with Nietzsche who rejected traditional value structures of the masses. Even American pragmatists such as Dewey rejected fixed solutions to standard philosophical issues and argued that there is no "givenness" about the world. Much of postmodernist discussion extends well beyond the discipline of philosophy, which is only one manifestation of modern culture. Literature, music, art, theater, film, and architecture are also under the sway of modernist attitudes of unified order, symmetry and harmony. Postmodernist writers, musicians, and artists thus attempt to break the traditional molds of their respective genres.

Glossary of Key Concepts

Aesthetics The branch of philosophy concerned with the analysis of concepts such as beauty or beautiful as standards for judging works of art.

Agnostic One who neither believes nor disbelieves that God exists since there is no conclusive evidence either way.

Analytic statement An analytic statement is necessarily true because the predicate is already in the subject, e.g., "all dogs are animals" where the word *dogs* already contains the concept "animal."

A posteriori Literally, after experience; *a posteriori* knowledge is that derived from experience. This is in contrast with *a priori* knowledge (see below).

Appearance How something presents itself to our senses as compared with its true reality. For example, the oar appears bent in the water, but it really is not bent.

A priori Literally, before experience; *a priori* knowledge is before or independent of experience. For example, according to some philosophers, we know that "every event has a cause" even though we have not experienced every event.

Artificial intelligence Contemporary theory that attempts to duplicate human cognitive mental states in computing machinery.

Authority A source of our theological knowledge, specifically for philosophers and theologians who hold that the mysteries of faith surpass the reach of human reason.

Autonomy Literally, self-rule; independence from external authority. Kant, freedom of the will to make its own law or rule of conduct in contrast with *heteronomy* (being subject to someone else's rules).

Becoming In Hegelian thought, the world of becoming is the world in which everything in our daily experience, persons and things, comes into being and passes away.

Behaviorism, logical Contemporary theory of the mind–body problem associated with Gilbert Ryle that reduces mental events to sensory input and behavioral output.

Being A general term in metaphysics referring to ultimate reality or existence. True being, for Plato, is the realm of the eternal Forms.

Categorical imperative In Kant's moral theory, the categorical imperative is the absolute moral law understood as a duty by any rational creature. This is compared with *hypothetical imperatives,* which permit exceptions.

Categories Term used by Aristotle and Kant, meaning the concepts that the human mind brings to knowing, e.g., cause and effect, space and time.

Causality The relation of cause and effect, in which one event necessarily follows another.

Cause Something that has the power to produce a change, motion, or action in another thing; this change *(effect)* can be explained in terms of the behavior of the cause.

Change The alteration of anything, the rearrangement of something's parts, the coming into being of something that did not exist before, and the decline and dissolution of something.

Chinese Room Argument Thought experiment offered by John Searle aimed to refute the claims of strong artificial intelligence advocates that suitably programmed machines are capable of cognitive mental states.

Cogitatum The content of what is thought; hence, to think *(cogito)* is to think something *(cogitatum).*

Cogito Literally in Latin, "I think." Used by Descartes to describe the self as a thinking thing.

Cognition In the broadest sense, knowledge, or the act of knowing.

Cognitive meaning A term used by logical positivists and analytical philosophers in reference to statements that are either true by definition or empirically verifiable (see *verification principle*).

Contingent An event that is not necessary, i.e., it may or may not be, depending upon other events which also may or may not be.

Cosmological argument A proof for the existence of God based upon the idea that there had to be a first cause for the existence of the universe.

Deconstruction Post-structuralist theory associated with Jacque Derrida which attempts to show that all pairs of opposite concepts in philosophical systems are in fact self-refuting.

Deduction A process of reasoning by which the mind relates the truth of one proposition to the truth of another by inferring that the truth of the second proposition is involved in and therefore derived from the first *(see induction).*

Determinism The theory that every fact, or even the universe, is determined or caused by previous facts or events; human behavior and the events of history follow strict laws of causation or necessary connection. Accordingly, in this view, human beings do not possess freedom of the will or the power to originate independent or genuine choices.

Dialectic   As in dialogue (Socrates) or debate over opposites (Hegel) and clash of material forces (Marx) producing dynamic change. Or, a process of reasoning based upon the analysis of opposing propositions. Socrates used the dialectic method of teaching by distinguishing between opinion and knowledge. Hegel and Marx developed dialectic conceptions of history in which for Hegel, opposing ideas were the key, while for Marx history was explained as the conflict of material forces.

Dionysian   Concept in Nietzsche's philosophy referring to the forces of life. For Nietzsche, true culture is a unity of the Dionysian and Appolonian elements, the latter of which is the love of form and beauty.

Dogmatism   The act of making a positive assertion without demonstration by either rational argument or experience.

Dualism   A theory which holds that there are two independent and irreducible substances, such as mind and body, the intelligible world of ideas and the visible world of things, or the forces of good and evil. Dualism is in contrast to monism and pluralism.

Empiricism   The theory that experience is the source of all knowledge, which thereby denies that human beings possess inborn knowledge or that they can derive knowledge through the exercise of reason alone.

Epistemology   The branch of philosophy which studies the nature, origin, scope, and validity of knowledge.

Essence   The chief characteristic, quality, or necessary function which makes a thing what it uniquely is.

Ethics   (1) A set of rules for human behavior; (2) a study of judgments of value, of good and evil, right and wrong, desirable and undesirable; and (3) theories of obligation or duty or why we "ought" to behave in certain way.

Existentialism   A movement in 20th-century philosophy, the leading exponents of which were Sartre and Merleau-Ponty. For Sartre, the central thesis of existentialism is that *existence* precedes *essence*, i.e., people have no given identity until they have made specific decisions and have chosen their work and have thereby defined themselves.

Extension   In Descartes, the character of physical things as having dimension in space and time.

Finitude   Having definable limits.

Form, theory of   Plato's view that ultimate reality is located in a spirit-realm containing archetypes of things, such as *triangularity*, *humanity*, or *justice*.

Free will   The theory that in some cases the will makes decisions or choices independent of prior physiological or psychological causes.

Functionalism   Contemporary theory of the mind-body problem that mental events depend on networks, pathways, and the interconnection of mental processes, but not on any specific material stuff that it is composed of, such as neurons. Functionalism holds open the possibility that mental events can occur in nonbiological systems, such as silicon ships.

Gestalt theory   20th century psychological theory that our perceptual experience consists of a full range of characteristics—form, structure, sense, meaning, and value—all simultaneously.

Herd-mentality   A view in Nietzsche's philosophy that people are often reduced to a common level of mediocrity.

Idealism   The view that mind is the ultimate reality in the world. Idealism is opposed to *materialism,* the view that all reality is composed of material things

Identity theory   Contemporary theory of the mind-body problem associated with David Armstrong and J. J. C. Smart that reduces mental events to brain activity.

Illusion   An erroneous impression, such as an optical illusion, or, for Freud, a false belief growing out of a deep wish.

Impression   Hume's term for experience consisting of sensations and mental reflections.

Indeterminism   The theory that in some cases the will makes decisions or choices independent of prior physiological or psychological causes.

Induction   Proceeding from the observation of some particular facts to a generalization (or conclusion) concerning all such facts *(see deduction).*

Innate Ideas   Inborn notions that we know without requiring proof from experience.

Instrumental   A thing, quality or act is instrumental when it is a means for achieving something else, versus *intrinsic,* which describes a thing, quality or act as existing for its own sake.

Instrumentalism   Dewey's theory that thought is instrumental insofar as it produces practical consequences.

Intrinsic   A thing, quality, or act is intrinsic if it exists for its own sake, versus *instrumental,* which describes a thing, quality, or act as a means to some other end.

Intuition   Direct and immediate knowledge of the self, the external world, values, or other metaphysical truths, without the need to define the notions, to justify a conclusion, or to build up inferences.

Logical positivism   The 20th-century movement in the analytical tradition that rests on the verification principle.

Materialism   The view that matter constitutes the basis of all that exists in the universe. Hence combinations of matter and material forces account for every aspect of reality, including the nature of thought, the process of historical and economic events, and the standard of values based upon sensuous bodily pleasures and the abundance of things; the notion of the primacy of spirit or mind and rational purpose in nature is rejected.

Metaphysics   The branch of philosophy concerned with the question of the ultimate nature of reality. Unlike the sciences, which focus on various aspects of nature, metaphysics goes beyond particular things to inquire about more general questions, such as what lies beyond nature, how things come into being, what it means for something to be, and whether there is a realm of being which is not subject to change and which is therefore the basis of certainty in knowledge.

Monism   The view that there is only one substance in the universe; idealism and materialism are monistic theories. Monism is in contrast to dualism and pluralism.

Nihilism   The view that there are no values. According to Nietzsche, "death of God" will be followed by the rejection of absolute values and the rejection of the idea of an objective and universal moral law.

Noumenal world   The real world as opposed to the world of appearance. According to Kant, the noumenal world cannot be known.

Ontological argument   A proof for God's existence devised by Anslem, that God is defined as the greatest possible being, which necessarily entails existence.

Ontology   The study of being, from the Greek *ontos,* "being," and *logos,* "science"; related to the field of metaphysics.

Participation   A central notion in Plato's theory that things in this world are modeled after ideal archetypes in the realm of the forms.

Perception   The sensory vehicle by which we obtain knowledge about the world.

Phenomenal world   In Kant's theory, the world of appearance versus the noumenal world beyond our knowledge.

Phenomenology   A 20th-century philosophical movement founded by Husserl, that, in accounting for knowledge, we should not go beyond the data available to consciousness derived from appearances.

Pluralism   The view that there are more than one or two separate substances making up the world. This stands in contrast with both *monism* and *dualism.*

Positivism   A 19th-century philosophical movement founded by Comte that we should reject any investigation that does not rest on direct observation.

Postmodernism   Theory in contemporary Continental philosophy which rejects the Renaissance and Enlightenment assumption that the world can be explained in a unified system.

Post-structuralism   Radical extension of the structuralist position contending that novels and philosophical texts are completely closed systems and their meanings derive from what individual readers bring to the texts.

Postulate   In Kant's theory, a practical or moral principle which cannot be proved, such as the existence of God, the freedom of the will, or immortality, which must be believed to make possible our moral duty.

Pragmatism   A 20th-century movement associated with Peirce, James, and Dewey contending that there is little value in philosophical theories that do not somehow make a difference in daily life.

Prime mover   A view in Aristotelian thought that there is a first cause of everything and does not itself require a cause.

Rationalism   The philosophical view that emphasizes the ability of human reason to grasp fundamental truths about the world without the aid of sense impressions.

Relativism   The view that there is no absolute knowledge, that truth is different for each individual, social group, or historic period and is therefore relative to the circumstances of the knowing subject.

Scholasticism   The theological and philosophical method of learning in the medieval schools which emphasized deductive logic and the authority of key figures such as Plato, Aristotle, and Augustine.

Sense-data   The elements of information that we receive through our senses.

Skepticism   The tendency to doubt some fundamental component of knowledge. Also, the ancient Greek school of thought associated with Plato's later Academy, Pyrrho, and Sextus Empiricus.

Solipsism   From the Latin *solus*, "alone" and *ipse*, "self", the view that the self alone is the source of all knowledge of existence, which sometimes leads to the conclusion that the self is the only reality.

Sophists   Wandering teachers in fifth-century Athens who especially prepared young men for political careers, who hence emphasized rhetoric and the ability to persuade audiences and win debates, and who were less concerned with pursuing truth.

Sovereign   A person or state independent of any other authority or jurisdiction.

Structuralism   Theory in contemporary Continental philosophy associated with Ferdinand de Saussure and Claude Lévi-Strauss that the meaning of a thing is defined by its surrounding cultural structures, which in turn rely on pairs of opposite concepts such as light and dark.

Substance   A separate and distinct thing; that which underlies phenomena; the essence of a thing which underlies the other qualities of a thing.

Syllogism   A form of reasoning. *Example:* All humans are mortal (major premise); Socrates is a human (minor premise); therefore, Socrates is mortal (conclusion).

Synthetic   In Kant's theory, a synthetic sentence adds an idea to the subject which the subject does not already contain, e.g., "a dog will help catch foxes," but that is not true of all dogs. This is in contrast with analytic sentences, in which the subject contains the predicate.

Teleology   From the Greek word *telos* for "purpose", the study of purpose in human nature and in the events of history.

Utilitarianism   An ethical theory associated with Bentham and Mill that an action is morally good if it produces as much or more good than any alternative behavior.

Verification   Demonstrating or proving something to be true either by means of evidence or by formal rules of reasoning.

Verification principle A principle in logical positivism contending that a statement is meaningful if (a) it asserts something that is true simply because the words used necessarily and always require the statement to be true (as in mathematics) or (b) it asserts something that can be judged as true or false by verifying it in experience.

Wager, Pascal's A contention by Pascal that, when reason is neutral on the issue of God's existence, we should be psychologically compelled to believe based on the benefits of such belief.

A Selected Bibliography

CHAPTER 1: SOCRATES' PREDECESSORS

Original Writings:

Barnes, Jonathan, *Early Greek Philosophy* (Harmondsworth: Penguin, 1987).

Freeman, Kathleen, *Ancilla to the Presocratic Philosophers: A Complete Translation of The Fragments in Diels' Fragmente der Vorsokratiker* (Oxford: Basil Blackwell, 1956).

McKirahan, Richard D. Jr., *Philosophy Before Socrates* (Indianapolis: Hackett Publishing Company, 1994).

Critical Studies:

Guthrie, W. K. C., *The Greek Philosophers: from Thales to Aristotle* (New York: Harper and Row, 1960).

Kirk, G. S., and Raven, J. E., *The Presocratic Philosophers* (New York: Cambridge University Press, 1960).

Long, A. A., *The Cambridge Companion to Early Greek Philosophy* (Cambridge: Cambridge University Press, 1995).

Mourelatos, A. P. D., ed., *The Presocratics* (Princeton: Princeton University Press, 1993).

CHAPTER 2: THE SOPHISTS AND SOCRATES

Original Writings:

See Chapter 1 bibliography for primary sources on the Sophists and Chapter 2 bibliography for primary sources on Socrates

Critical Studies:

Benson, Hugh H., ed., *Essays on the Philosophy of Socrates* (New York: Oxford University Press, 1992).

Reeve, C. D. C., *Socrates in the Apology* (Indianapolis: Hackett Publishing Company, 1989).

Santas, G. X., *Socrates: Philosophy in Plato's Early Dialogues* (London: Routledge & Kegan Paul, Ltd., London, 1979).

Vlastos, Gregory, *Socrates: Ironist and Moral Philosopher* (Ithaca: Cornell University Press, 1991).

Vlastos, Gregory, *Socratic Studies* (Cambridge: Cambridge University Press, 1994).

CHAPTER 3: PLATO

Original Writings:

Cooper, John M., ed., *Plato: Complete Works* (Indianapolis: Hackett Publishing Company, 1997).

Hamilton, Edith, ed., *The Collected Dialogues of Plato, Including the Letters* (New York: Pantheon Books, 1961).

Critical Studies:

Annas, Julia, *An Introduction to Plato's Republic* (Oxford: Clarendon Press, 1981).

Grube, G. M. A., *Plato's Thought* (Indianapolis: Hackett Publishing Company, 1980).

Irwin, T. H., *Classical Thought* (Oxford: Oxford University Press, 1989).

Kraut, Richard, *The Cambridge Companion to Plato* (Cambridge: Cambridge University Press, 1992).

Vlastos, Gregory, *Platonic Studies* (Princeton: Princeton University Press, 1981).

Vlastos, Gregory, *Plato's Universe* (Seattle: University of Washington Press, 1975).

CHAPTER 4: ARISTOTLE

Original Writings:

Barnes, Jonathan, ed., *The Complete Works of Aristotle* (Princeton, N.J.: Princeton University Press, 1984).

Cohen, S. M., Curd, P. and Reeve, C. D. C., eds., *Readings in Ancient Greek Philosophy* (Indianapolis: Hackett Publishing Company, 1995).

McKeon, Richard, ed., *The Basic Works of Aristotle* (New York: Random House, 1941).

Critical Studies:

Ackrill, J. L., *Aristotle the Philosopher* (Oxford: Oxford University Press, 1981).

Barnes, Jonathan, *Aristotle* (Oxford: Oxford University Press, 1982).

Barnes, Jonathan, ed., *The Cambridge Companion to Aristotle* (Cambridge: Cambridge University Press, 1995).

Cooper, John, *Reason and Human Good in Aristotle* (Cambridge, Mass.: Harvard University Press, 1975).

Kraut, Richard, *Aristotle on the Human Good* (Princeton: Princeton University Press, 1989).

Rorty, A. O., ed., *Essays on Aristotle's Ethics* (Berkeley: University of California Press, 1980).

Ross, W. D., *Aristotle* (New York: Barnes and Noble, 1949).

Sherman, N., *Aristotle's Ethics: Critical Essays* (London: Rowman and Littlefield, 1999).

CHAPTER 5: CLASSICAL PHILOSOPHY
AFTER ARISTOTLE

Original Writings:

Bailey, C., *Epicurus: The Extant Remains* (Oxford: Clarendon, 1926).

Epictetus, *The Handbook of Epictetus* (Indianapolis: Hackett Publishing Company, 1983).

Inwood, B. and Gerson, L. P., *Hellenistic Philosophy, Introductory Readings* (Indianapolis: Hackett Publishing Company, 1988).

Inwood, B., *Hellenistic Philosophy: Introductory Readings* (Indianapolis: Hackett Publishing Company, 1988).

Long, A. A. and Sedley, D. N., *The Hellenistic Philosophers* (Cambridge: Cambridge University Press, 1987).

Lucretius, *On the Nature of Things,* trans. W. H. D. Rouse (Cambridge, MA: Harvard University Press, 1975).

Marcus Aurelius, *The Meditations,* trans. G. M. A. Grube (Indianapolis: Hackett Publishing Company, 1985).

Plotinus, *Enneads,* tr. A. H. Armstrong (Cambridge: Harvard University Press, 1966–1988).

Sextus Empiricus, *Against the Professors,* trs. R. G. Bury, (Cambridge, MA: Harvard University Press, 1935–1949), 3 vol.

Sextus Empiricus, *Outlines of Pyrrhonism,* trs. J. Annas and J. Barnes, *Outlines of Scepticism* (Cambridge: Cambridge University Press, 1994).

Sextus Empiricus, *Selections from the major writings on scepticism, man, & God,* ed., Philip P. Hallie (Indianapolis: Hackett Publishing Company, 1985).

Critical Studies:

Graeser, A., *Plotinus and the Stoics* (Leiden, Netherlands: E. J. Brill, NV, 1972).

Inwood, B., *Ethics and Human Action in Early Stoicism* (Oxford: Oxford University Press, 1985).

Long, A. A., *Hellenistic Philosophy* (London: Duckworth, 1974).

Long, A. A., *Stoic Studies* (Cambridge: Cambridge University Press. 1996).

Mitsis, P., *Epicurus' Ethical Theory* (Ithaca, NY: Cornell University Press, 1988).

Rist, J. M., *Plotinus: The Road to Reality* (Cambridge: Cambridge University Press, 1967).

Schroeder, F. M. *Form and Transformation: A study in the Philosophy of Plotinus* (Montreal: McGill University Press, 1992).

CHAPTER 6: AUGUSTINE

Original Writings:

Augustine, *Concerning the Teacher* and *On the Immortality of the Soul* (New York: Appleton-Century-Crofts, Inc., 1938).

Augustine, *Confessions* (Baltimore: Penguin Books, 1961).

Augustine, *Enchiridion on Faith, Hope and Love* (Chicago: Henry Regnery Company, 1961).

Augustine, *The City of God* (Garden City, N.Y.: Doubleday & Company, Inc., 1958).

Oates, Whitney J., ed., *Basic Writings of St. Augustine* (New York: Random House, 1948).

Critical Studies:

Brown, Peter, *Augustine of Hippo* (Berkeley, CA: University of California Press, 1967).

Chadwick, H., *Augustine* (New York: Oxford University Press. 1986).

Dihle, A., *The Theory of Will in Classical Antiquity* (Berkeley, CA: University of California Press, 1982).

Gilson, Etienne, *The Christian Philosophy of Saint Augustine* (New York: Random House, 1961).

Kirwin, Christopher, *Augustine* (London: Routledge, 1989).

Meagher, R. E., *An Introduction to Augustine* (New York: New York University Press, 1978).

CHAPTER 7: PHILOSOPHY IN THE EARLY MIDDLE AGES

Original Writings:

Anselm, *Anselm's Basic Writings* (La Salle, Ill.: Open Court Publishing Company, 1962).

Averroes, *Averroes on theHarmony of Religion and Philosophy*, ed. G. Hourani (London: Luzac, 1961).

Averroes, *Averroes' Tahafut al-Tahafut (The Incoherence of the Incoherence)*, ed. S. Vanden Bergh (London: Luzac, 1954).

Averroes, *Averroes' Three Short Commentaries on Aristotle's 'Topics', 'Rhetoric' and 'Poetics,'* ed. C. Butterworth (Albany, NY: State University of New York Press, 1977).

Boethius, *Consolation of Philosophy* (New York: Frederick Ungar Publishing Co., 1957).

Fremantle, Anne, ed., *Age of Belief: The Medieval Philosophers* (New York: New American Library of World Literature, 1955).

Hyman, A., and Walsh, J. J., ed., *Philosophy in the Middle Ages: the Christian, Islamic, and Jewish Traditions* (Indianapolis: Hackett Publishing Co., 1973).

Maimonides, *Guide of the Perplexed* (Chicago: The University of Chicago Press, 1963).

Maimonides, Moses, *The Guide for the Perplexed*, trans. M. Friedlander (New York: Dover Publications, 1956).

McKeon, Richard, ed., *Medieval Philosophers* (New York: Charles Scribner's Sons, 1959).

Critical Studies:

Bett, Henry, *Johannes Scotus Erigena* (New York: Russell & Russell, 1964).

Carré, M. H., *Realists and Nominalists* (Oxford: Oxford University Press, 1946).

Church, R. W., *Saint Anselm* (London: Macmillan & Co., 1937).

Hick, John and McGill, Arthur C., eds., *The Many-Faced Argument* (New York: Macmillan, 1967).

Katz, S., ed., *Maimonides: Selected Essays* (New York: Arno Press, 1980).

Kraemer, J., ed., *Perspectives on Maimonides: Philosophical and Historical Studies* (Oxford: Oxford University Press, 1991).

Marenbon, J., *The Philosophy of Peter Abelard* (Cambridge: Cambridge University Press, 1997).

Rand, E. K., *Founders of the Middle Ages* (Cambridge, Mass.: Harvard University Press, 1941).

Sikes, J. G., *Peter Abailard*, The University Press, 1932.

Wahba, M., and Abousenna, M., eds., *Averroes and the Enlightenment* (New York: Prometheus, 1995).

CHAPTER 8: AQUINAS AND HIS LATE MEDIEVAL SUCCESSORS

Original Writings:

Aquinas, *Basic Writings of St. Thomas Aquinas,* ed. Anton Pegis (New York: Random House, 1945).
Aquinas, *Philosophical Texts* (Oxford: Oxford University Press, 1960).
Aquinas, *Summa Theologiciae,* ed., Thomas Gilby (London, 1963–75), 60 vols.
Aquinas, *Treatise on Happiness* (Englewood Cliffs, N.J. Prentice-Hall, 1964).
Blakney, R. B. ed., *Meister Eckhart: A Modern Translation* (New York: Harper & Row, Publishers, 1941).
Duns Scotus, *Philosophical Writings* (New York: The Liberal Arts Press, 1964).
Fremantle, Anne, ed., *Age of Belief: The Medieval Philosophers* (New York: New American Library of World Literature, 1955).
McKeon, Richard, ed., *Medieval Philosophers* (New York: Charles Scribner's Sons, 1959).
Ockham, *Philosophical Writings* (New York: The Liberal Arts Press, 1964).

Critical Studies:

Copleston, F. C., *Aquinas* (London: Penguin Books, 1955).
Gilson, Etienne, *The Christian Philosophy of St. Thomas Aquinas* (New York: Random House, 1956).
Ingham, M. E., *Ethics And Freedom: An Historical-Critical Investigation Of Scotist Ethical Thought* (Washington, DC: University Press of America, 1989).
Kenny, Anthony, ed., *Aquinas: A Collection of Critical Essays* (New York: Anchor Doubleday, 1969).
Kenny, Anthony, *The Five Ways. St. Thomas Aquinas' Proofs of God's Existence* (London: Routledge & Kegan Paul, 1969).
Kent, B., *Virtues of Will: The Transformation of Ethics in the Late Thirteenth Century* (Washington, DC: Catholic University of America Press, 1996).
Kretzman, Norman and Eleonore Stump, eds., *The Cambridge Companion to Aquinas* (Cambridge: Cambridge University Press, 1993).
Marenbon, J., *Later Medieval Philosophy (1150–1350)* (London: Routledge, 1987).
Wolter, A. B., *The Philosophical Theology of John Duns Scotus,* ed. M. Adams (Ithaca, NY: Cornell University Press, 1990).

CHAPTER 9: PHILOSOPHY DURING THE RENAISSANCE

Original Writings:

Bacon, Francis, *The Oxford Francis Bacon* (Oxford: Clarendon Press, 1996).
Bacon, Francis, *The Works of Francis Bacon,* edited by J. Spedding (London: Longmans, 1857–1874).

Galileo, *Dialogue Concerning the Two Chief World Systems,* tr. S. Drake (Berkeley: University of California Press, 1953).

Galileo, *Letter to the Grand Duchess Christina,* in *Discoveries and Opinions of Galileo,* tr. S. Drake (New York: Doubleday, 1957).

Hobbes, Thomas, *Leviathan, or the Matter, Form and Power of Commonwealth, Ecclesiastical and Civil,* ed., E. Curley, (Chicago, IL: Hackett Publishing Company, 1994).

Hobbes, Thomas, *The English Works of Thomas Hobbes,* ed., W. Molesworth (London: John Bohn, 1839), 11 vols.

Kraye, Jill, ed., *Cambridge translations of Renaissance philosophical texts* (Cambridge: Cambridge University Press, 1997).

Pascal, Blaise, *Pensées,* tr. A. J. Krailsheimer (London: Penguin Books, 1995).

Pico della Mirandola, Giovanni, *On the Dignity of Man* (Indianapolis: Hackett Publishing Company, 1998).

Critical Studies:

Bouwsma, W. J., *The Culture of Renaissance Humanism* (Washington: American Historical Association, 1973).

Butterfield, H., *Origins of Modern Science* (New York: Collier Books, 1962).

David Boonin-Vail, *Thomas Hobbes and the Science of Moral Virtue* (Cambridge: Cambridge University Press, 1994).

Davies, S., *Renaissance Views of Man* (New York: Barnes & Noble, 1979).

Krailsheimer, A. J., *Pascal* (New York: Oxford University Press, 1980).

Kraye, Jill, ed., *The Cambridge Companion to Renaissance Humanism* (Cambridge: Cambridge University Press, 1996).

Machamer, Peter, ed. *The Cambridge Companion to Galileo* (Cambridge: Cambridge University Press, 1998).

Pater, Walter, *The Renaissance* (Cleveland: The World Publishing Company, 1961).

Peltonen, Markku, ed., *The Cambridge Companion to Bacon* (Cambridge: Cambridge University Press, 1996).

Sorell, T., ed., *The Cambridge Companion to Hobbes* (Cambridge: Cambridge University Press, 1995).

Symonds, J. A., *The Renaissance in Italy* (London: John Murray, 1937), six vols.

Taylor, Henry Osborn, *Philosophy of Science in the Renaissance* (New York: Collier Books, 1962).

CHAPTER 10: RATIONALISM ON THE CONTINENT

Original Writings:

Descartes, Rene, *The Philosophical Writings of Descartes,* tr. J. Cottingham, R. Stoothoff, D. Murdoch and A. Kenny (Cambridge: Cambridge University Press, 1984).

Leibniz, *Leibniz: Philosophical Essays,* edited by and trans. R. Ariew and D. Garber (Indianapolis: Hackett Publishing Company, 1989).

Spinoza, Benedict, *The Chief Works of Benedict de Spinoza,* tr. R. H. M. Elwes (New York: Dover, 1951).

Critical Studies:

Cottingham, John, ed., *Descartes* (New York: Oxford University Press, 1998).

Cottingham, John, ed., *The Cambridge Companion to Descartes* (Cambridge: Cambridge University Press, 1992).

Donagan, A., *Spinoza* (Chicago: University of Chicago Press, 1989).

Grene, M., *Spinoza, A Collection of Critical Essays* (Garden City, N.Y.: Anchor Books, 1973).

Jolley, Nicholas, ed., *The Cambridge Companion to Leibniz* (Cambridge: Cambridge University Press, 1995).

Kashap, S. P., *Studies in Spinoza* (Berkeley: University of California Press, 1972).

Kenny, Anthony, *Descartes: A Study of His Philosophy* (New York: Random House, 1968).

McRae, R., *Leibniz: Perception, Apperception, and Thought* (Toronto: University of Toronto Press, 1976).

Mercer, C., *Leibniz's Metaphysics: Its Origins and Development* (Cambridge: Cambridge University Press, 1998).

CHAPTER 11: EMPIRICISM IN BRITAIN

Original Writings:

Berkeley, George, *The Works of George Berkeley, Bishop of Cloyne,* edited by A. A. Luce and T. E. Jessop (Edinburgh: Thomas Nelson, 1948–57). 9 vols.

Hume, David, *A Treatise of Human Nature,* edited by David Fate Norton, Mary J. Norton (Oxford; New York: Oxford University Press, 2000).

Hume, David, *An Enquiry Concerning Human Understanding,* edited by Tom L. Beauchamp (New York: Oxford University Press, 1999).

Hume, David, *The Philosophical Works of David Hume,* edited by T. H. Green and T. H. Grose (London: Longman, Green, 1875), 4 vols.

Locke, John, *An Essay Concerning Human Understanding,* edited by P. H. Nidditch, Clarendon Edition (Oxford: Oxford University Press, 1975).

Locke, John, *The Works of John Locke* (London: T. Tegg, 1823), 10 vols.

Locke, John. *Two Treatises of Government,* edited by P. Laslett (Cambridge: Cambridge University Press, Oxford: Oxford University Press, 1967).

Critical Studies:

Ashcraft, R., ed., *John Locke: Critical Assessments* (London: Routledge, 1991), 4 vols.

Ayers, M., *Locke* (London: Routledge, 1991), 2 vols.

Berman, David, ed., *George Berkeley: Eighteenth-Century Responses* (New York: Garland Publishing, 1989).

Chappell, Vere, ed., *The Cambridge Companion to Locke* (Cambridge: Cambridge University Press, 1994).

Fieser, James, ed., *Early Responses to Hume* (Bristol, England: Thoemmes Press, 1999–2003), 10 vol.

Grayling, A. C., *Berkeley: The Central Arguments* (London: Duckworth, 1986).

Norton, David Fate, ed., *The Cambridge Companion to Hume* (Cambridge: Cambridge University Press, 1993).

Tweyman, Stanley, ed. *David Hume: Critical Assessments* (London: Routledge, 1991), 4 vols.

Winkler, K. P., *Berkeley: An Interpretation* (Oxford: Clarendon Press, 1989).

CHAPTER 12: KANT

Original Writings:

Kant, Immanuel, *Critique of Judgment: Including the First Introduction,* tr. W. S. Pluhar (Indianapolis, IN: Hackett Publishing Company, 1987).

Kant, Immanuel, *Critique of Pure Reason,* tr. Werner S. Pluhar and Patricia Kitcher (Indianapolis: Hackett Publishing Company, 1996).

Kant, Immanuel, *Grounding for the Metaphysics of Morals,* tr, James W. Ellington (Indianapolis: Hackett Publishing Company, 1985).

Kant, Immanuel, *Kant's Critique of Judgement,* tr. J. C. Meredith (Oxford: Clarendon Press, 1952).

Kant, Immanuel, *Lectures on Ethics,* tr. P. Heath (Cambridge: Cambridge University Press, 1997).

Kant, Immanuel, *Prolegomena to any future metaphysics that will be able to come forward as science,* tr. James W. Ellington (Indianapolis: Hackett Publishing Company, 1977).

Critical Studies:

Aune, B., *Kant's Theory of Morals* (Princeton, NJ.: Princeton University Press, 1979).

Broad, O. D., *Kant: An Introduction* (Cambridge: Cambridge University Press, 1978).

Chadwick, R., ed., *Immanuel Kant: Critical Assessments* (London: Routledge, 1992), 4 vols.

Ewing, A. C., *Short Commentary on Kant's "Critique of Pure Reason,"* (Chicago: University of Chicago Press, 1987).

Guyer, Paul, ed., *Kant's Groundwork of the Metaphysics of Morals: Critical Essays* (New York: Rowman & Littlefield, 1998).

Guyer, Paul, ed., *The Cambridge Companion to Kant* (Cambridge: Cambridge University Press, 1992).

Höffe, O., *Immanuel Kant* (Albany: State University of New York Press, 1994).

Strawson, P. F., *The Bounds of Sense: An Essay on Kant's Critique of Pure Reason* (London: Methuen, 1975).

Walker, R. C. S., *Kant* (London: Routledge & Kegan Paul, 1978).

Wolff, R. P., ed., *Kant: A Collection of Critical Essays* (Garden City: Doubleday Anchor, 1967).

CHAPTER 13: GERMAN IDEALISM

Original Writings:

Hegel, G. W. F., *Elements of the Philosophy of Right,* trans. H. B. Nisbet, ed. A. Wood (Cambridge: Cambridge University Press. 1991).

Hegel, G. W. F., *Introduction to the Philosophy of History,* trans. L. Rauch (Indianapolis: Hackett Publishing Company, 1988).

Hegel, G. W. F., *Lectures on the Philosophy of Religion,* trans. C. P. Hodgson and R. F. Brown (Los Angeles, CA: University of California Press, 1984–7) 3 vols.

Hegel, G. W. F., *Phenomenology of Spirit,* trans. A. V. Miller (Oxford: Clarendon Press. 1970).

Hegel, G. W. F., *Philosophy of Nature,* trans. and ed. M. J. Petry (London: Allen & Unwin, 1970) 3 vols.

Schopenhauer, Arthur, *Manuscript Remains,* tr. E. F. J. Payne (Oxford, New York and Hamburg: Berg, Schopenhauer, Arthur, 1988–90), vols 1–4.

Schopenhauer, Arthur, *On the Basis of Morality,* tr. E. F. J. Payne (Providence, RI and Oxford: Berhahn Books, 1995).

Schopenhauer, Arthur, *On the Will in Nature,* tr. E. F. J. Payne (New York and Oxford: Berg, 1992).

Schopenhauer, Arthur, *Schopenhauer's Early Fourfold Root,* tr., F. J. White (Aldershot: Avebury, 1997).

Schopenhauer, Arthur, *The World as Will and Representation,* tr. E. F. J. Payne (New York: Dover, 1969), 2 vols.

Critical Studies:

Atwell, J. E., *Schopenhauer: The Human Character* (Philadelphia, PA: Temple University Press, 1990).

Beiser, Frederick C., ed., *The Cambridge Companion to Hegel,* edited by (Cambridge University Press, 1993).

Fox, M., ed., *Schopenhauer: His Philosophical Achievement* (Brighton: Harvester, 1980).

Hardimon, M., *The Project of Reconciliation: Hegel's Social Philosophy* (Cambridge: Cambridge University Press. 1994).

Inwood, M., *Hegel* (London: Routledge & Kegan Paul. 1983).

Jacquette, D., ed., *Schopenhauer, Philosophy and the Arts* (Cambridge: Cambridge University Press, 1996).

Janaway, C., *Schopenhauer* (Oxford: Oxford University Press, 1994).

Pippin, R. B., *Hegel's Idealism: The Satisfactions of Self-Consciousness* (Cambridge: Cambridge University Press, 1989).

Stern, R. ed., *G. W. F. Hegel: Critical Assessments* (London: Routledge & Kegan Paul, 1993) 4 vols.

Taylor, C., *Hegel* (Cambridge: Cambridge University Press, 1975).

White, F. C., *On Schopenhauer's Fourfold Root of the Principle of Sufficient Reason* (Leiden: E. J. Brill, 1992).

CHAPTER 14: UTILITARIANISM AND POSITIVISM

Original Writings:

Bentham, Jeremy and Mill, John Stuart, *The Utilitarians: Jeremy Bentham and John Stuart Mill* (Garden City, N.Y.: Dolphin Books, 1961).

Bentham, Jeremy, *A Fragment on Government* (Cambridge: Cambridge University Press, 1988).

Bentham, Jeremy, *Introduction to the Principles of Morals and Legislation* (New York, Hafner Publishing Company, 1948).

Bentham, Jeremy, *The Works of Jeremy Bentham,* ed., J. Bowring (Edinburgh, 1843), 10 vols.

Comte, Auguste, *System of Positive Polity,* tr. J. H. Bridges, F. Harrison (New York: Burt & Franklin, 1966), 4 vols.

Comte, Auguste, *The Positive Philosophy,* tr. H. Martineau (London: G. Bell, 1896), 3 vols.

Mill, John Stuart, *Autobiography* (New York: The Liberal Arts Press, 1958).

Mill, John Stuart, *Collected Works of John Stuart Mill,* ed., J. M. Robson (London: Routledge and Toronto, Ont.: University of Toronto Press, 1991).

Mill, John Stuart, *Six Great Humanistic Essays of John Stuart Mill* (New York: Washington Square Press, 1963).

Critical Studies:

Albee, Ernest, *History of English Utilitarianism* (New York: Collier Books, a division of Crowell-Collier, 1962).
Crisp, R., Mill on Utilitarianism (London: Routledge, 1997).
Gray, J., *Mill on Liberty: a Defence* (London: Routledge, 1996).
Harrison, R., *Bentham* (London: Routledge, 1983).
Lévy-Bruhl, L., *The Philosophy of Auguste Comte* (New York: G. P. Putnam's Sons, 1903).
Long D., *Bentham on Liberty* (Toronto Ont.: University of Toronto Press, 1977).
Mill, John Stuart, *Auguste Comte and Positivism* (Ann Arbor: University of Michigan Press, 1961).
Pickering, M., *Auguste Comte: An Intellectual Biography* (Cambridge: Cambridge University Press, 1993).
Scharff, R., *Comte after Positivism,* (Cambridge, Cambridge University Press, 1995).
Skorupski, John, *John Stuart Mill* (London: Routledge, 1989).
Skorupski, John, ed. *The Cambridge Companion to Mill* (Cambridge: Cambridge University Press, 1998).
Ten, C. L., *Mill on Liberty* (Oxford: Oxford University Press, 1980).

CHAPTER 15: KIERKEGAARD, MARX, AND NIETZSCHE

Original Writings:

Kierkegaard, Søren, *Concluding Unscientific Postscript,* trans. D. F. Swenson, L. M. Swenson and W. Lowrie (Princeton, NJ: Princeton University Press, 1941).
Kierkegaard, Søren, *Either/Or,* trans. H. V. Hong and E. H. Hong (Princeton, NJ: Princeton University Press, 1987), 2 vols.
Kierkegaard, Søren, *Fear and Trembling and Repetition,* trans. H. V. Hong and E. H. Hong (Princeton, NJ: Princeton University Press, 1983).
Kierkegaard, Søren, *Philosophical Fragments,* trans. H. V. Hong and E. H. Hong (Princeton, NJ: Princeton University Press, 1985).
Marx, Karl, and Engels, Friedrich, *Collected Works* (London: Lawrence & Wishart, 1975-).
Marx, Karl, *Basic Writings on Politics and Philosophy: Karl Marx and Friedrich Engels,* ed., Lewis Feuer (Garden City, NY: Doubleday & Company, 1959).
Marx, Karl, *Economic and Philosophic Manuscripts of 1844* (New York: International Publishers Company, 1964).
Marx, Karl, *Selected Writings,* ed. D. McLellan (Oxford: Oxford University Press, 1977).
Marx, Karl, *The Pelican Marx Library* (Harmondsworth: Penguin, 1975-).
Nietzsche, Friedrich, *Beyond Good and Evil* (Chicago: Henry Regnery Company, 1959).
Nietzsche, Friedrich, *Joyful Wisdom* (New York: Frederich Ungar Publishing Co., 1960).
Nietzsche, Friedrich, *Philosophy in the Tragic Age of the Greeks* (Chicago: Henry Regnery Company, 1962).
Nietzsche, Friedrich, *The Birth of Tragedy and the Genealogy of Morals* (Garden City, N.Y.: Doubleday & Company, Inc., 1956).

Nietzsche, Friedrich, *The Portable Nietzsche* (New York: Viking Press, 1954).
Nietzsche, Friedrich, *Thus Spoke Zarathustra* (Baltimore: Penguin Books, 1961).

Critical Studies:

Callinicos, A., *Marxism and Philosophy* (Oxford: Oxford University Press, 1985).
Elster, J., *Making Sense of Marx* (Cambridge: Cambridge University Press, 1985).
Gardiner, Patrick, *Kierkegaard* (Oxford: Oxford University Press, 1988).
Hannay, Alastair, *The Cambridge Companion to Kierkegaard* (Cambridge: Cambridge University Press, 1998).
Krimse, Bruce, *Kierkegaard in Golden Age Denmark* (University of Indiana Press, 1990).
Lowrie, Walter, *A Short Life of Kierkegaard* (Princeton University Press, 1942).
Magnus, Bernd, ed., *The Cambridge Companion to Nietzsche* (Cambridge: Cambridge University Press, 1996).
Nehamas, A., *Nietzsche: Life as Literature* (Cambridge, MA: Harvard University Press, 1985).
Rosen, M., *On Voluntary Servitude: False Consciousness and the Theory of Ideology* (Cambridge: Polity Press, 1996).
Rudd, A., *Kierkegaard and the Limits of the Ethical* (Oxford: Oxford University Press, 1993).
Schacht, R., *Nietzsche* (London: Routledge & Kegan Paul, 1983).
Torrance, J., *Karl Marx's Theory of Ideas* (Cambridge: Cambridge University Press, 1995).
Weston, M., *Kierkegaard and Modern Continental Philosophy* (London and New York: Routledge, 1994).
Young, J., *Nietzsche's Philosophy of Art* (Cambridge: Cambridge University Press, 1992).

CHAPTER 16: PRAGMATISM
AND PROCESS PHILOSOPHY

Original Writings:

Bergson, Henri, *Creative Mind* (New York: Philosophical Library, 1956).
Bergson, Henri, *Introduction to Metaphysics* (New York: The Liberal Arts Press, 1949).
Bergson, Henri, *Selections from Bergson* (New York: Appleton-Century-Crofts, 1949).
Bergson, Henri, *The Two Sources of Morality and Religion* (Garden City, NY.: Doubleday & Company, 1954).
Bergson, Henri, *Time and Free Will* (New York: Harper & Row, Publishers, 1960).
Dewey, John, *A Common Faith* (New Haven, Conn.: Yale University Press, 1960).
Dewey, John, *Experience and Nature* (New York: Dover Publications, 1929).
Dewey, John, *On Experience, Nature and Freedom* (New York: The Liberal Arts Press, 1960).
Dewey, John, *Philosophy of Education* (Paterson, N.J.: Littlefield, Adams & Company, 1956).
Dewey, John, *Quest for Certainty* (New York: Capricorn Books, G. P. Putnam's Sons, 1960).
Dewey, John, *Reconstruction in Philosophy* (Boston: Beacon Press, 1957).
Dewey, John, *The Early Works of John Dewey, 1882–1898; The Middle Works of John Dewey, 1899–1924; The Later Works of John Dewey, 1925–1953,* ed. J. A. Boydston, (Carbondale, IL: Southern Illinois University Press, 1969–1990), 37 vols.
Dewey, John, *Theory of Moral Life* (New York: Holt, Rinehart and Winston, 1960).
James, William, *Essays in Pragmatism* (New York: Hafner Publishing Company, 1940.

James, William, *Essays on Faith and Morals* (Cleveland: The World Publishing Company, 1962).

James, William, *The Will to Believe* and *Human Immortality* (New York: Dover Publications, Inc., 1956).

James, William, *The Works of William James* (Cambridge, MA, and London: Harvard University Press, 1975–1988), 17 vols.

James, William, *Varieties of Religious Experience* (New York: New American Library of World Literature, 1958).

Northrop, F. S. C., and Mason W. Gross eds., *A.N. Whitehead: An Anthology* (New York: The Macmillan Company, 1961).

Peirce, Charles Sanders, *Collected Papers of Charles Sanders Peirce,* eds. C. Hartshorne, P. Weiss, and A. Burks (Cambridge, MA: Harvard University Press, 1931–1958), 8 vols.

Peirce, Charles Sanders, *The Essential Peirce,* ed. N. Houser, and C. Kloesel (Bloomington, IN: Indiana University Press, 1992–1994).

Peirce, Charles Sanders, *The Writings of Charles S. Peirce: A Chronological Edition,* eds. M. Fisch, C. Kloesel, E. Moore, N. Houser (Bloomington, IN: Indiana University Press, 1982-).

Whitehead, Alfred North, *Adventures of Ideas* (New York: New American Library of World Literature, 1955).

Whitehead, Alfred North, *Modes of Thought* (New York: Capricorn Books, G. P. Putnam's Sons, 1959).

Whitehead, Alfred North, *Process and Reality* (New York: Harper & Row, Publishers, 1960).

Whitehead, Alfred North, *Religion in the Making* (Cleveland: The World Publishing Company, 1960).

Whitehead, Alfred North, *Science and the Modern World* (New York: New American Library of World Literature, 1949).

Whitehead, Alfred North, *The Function of Reason* (Beacon Press, Boston, 1958).

Critical Studies:

Alexander, I. W., *Bergson, Philosopher of Reflection,* (Bowes & Bowes, Ltd., London, 1957).

Bird, G., *William James* (London and New York: Routledge, 1987).

Boisvert, R., *Dewey's Metaphysics* (New York: Fordham University Press, 1988).

Brent, J., *Charles Sanders Peirce: A Life* (Bloomington, IN: & Kegan Paul, 1987).

Campbell, J., *Understanding John Dewey* (Chicago, IL: Open Court, 1995).

Colapietro, V., *Peirce's Approach to the Self* (Buffalo, NY: State University of New York Press, 1989).

Hausman, C., *Charles S. Peirce's Evolutionary Philosophy* (Cambridge: Cambridge University Press, 1993).

Hookway, C., *Peirce* (London: Routledge & Kegan Paul, 1985).

Indiana University Press, 1993).

Johnson, A. H., *Whitehead's Philosophy of Civilization* (New York: Dover Publications, 1962).

Kline, George, ed., *Whitehead's Theory of Reality* (New York: Dover Publications, 1952).

Leclerc, Ivor, *Whitehead's Metaphysics* (New York: The Macmillan Company, 1958).

Lowe, V., *Alfred North Whitehead: The Man and His Work* (Baltimore, MD: The Johns Hopkins University Press, 1990), 2 vols.

Mays, W., *Whitehead's Philosophy of Science and Metaphysics, and Introduction to His Thought* (The Hague, Netherlands: Martinus Nijhoff, 1977).

Myers, G. E., *William James: His Life and Thought* (New Haven, CT, and London: Yale University Press, 1986).

Putnam, R. A., eds., *Cambridge Companion to William James* (Cambridge: Cambridge University Press, 1997).

CHAPTER 17: ANALYTIC PHILOSOPHY

Original Writings:

Austin, John L., *How to Do Things with Words* (New York: Oxford University Press, 1965).
Austin, John L., *Philosophical Papers* (Oxford: Clarendon Press, 1970).
Austin, John L., *Sense and Sensibilia* (Fair Lawn, N.J.: Oxford University Press, 1962).
Ayer, A. J., *Language, Truth and Logic* (New York: Dover Publications, 1946).
Ayer, A. J., *Logical Positivism* (New York: The Free Press of Glencoe, 1958).
Carnap, Rudolf, *Logical Syntax and Language,* (New York: Harcourt, Brace & World, 1937).
Carnap, Rudolf, *Philosophy and Logical Syntax* (London: Kegal Paul, 1935).
Carnap, Rudolf, *The Logical Structure of the World* (Berkeley: University of California Press, 1967).
Carnap, Rudolf, *The Unity of Science* (London: Kegan Paul, 1934).
Moore, G. E., *Philosophical Papers* (New York: Collier Books, a division of Crowell-Collier Publishing Co., 1962).
Moore, G. E.: *Philosophical Studies,* (Paterson, N.J.: Littlefield, Adams & Company, 1951).
Moore, G. E.: *Some Main Problems of Philosophy* (New York: Collier Books, a division of Crowell-Collier Publishing Co., 1962).
Quine, W. V., and Ullian, J. S., *The Web of Belief* (New York: Random House, 1970).
Quine, W. V., *From a Logical Point of View,* (Cambridge, Mass.: Harvard University Press, 1953).
Quine, W. V., *Word and Object,* (Cambridge, Mass.: the M.I.T. Press, 1960).
Russell, Bertrand, *Analysis of Matter* (New York: Dover Publications, 1954).
Russell, Bertrand, *Human Knowledge* (New York: Simon and Schuster, 1962).
Russell, Bertrand, *Inquiry into Meaning and Truth* (Baltimore: Penguin Books, 1963).
Russell, Bertrand, *Our Knowledge of the External World* (New York: New American Library of World Literature, 1960).
Russell, Bertrand, *Sceptical Essays* (New York: Barnes & Noble, 1961).
Russell, Bertrand, *The Problems of Philosophy* (Fair Lawn, N.J.: Oxford University Press, 1912).
White, Morton, ed., *Age of Analysis: 20th Century Philosophers* (New York: New American Library of World Literature, 1955).
Wittgenstein, Ludwig, *On Certainty,* (Oxford: Basil Blackwell & Mott, 1967).
Wittgenstein, Ludwig, *Philosophical Investigations,* (Oxford: Basil Blackwell & Mott, 1968).
Wittgenstein, Ludwig, *Tractatus Logico-Philosophicus* (New York: Humanities Press, 1961).

Critical Studies:

Ayer, A. J., *Wittgenstein* (Chicago: University of Chicago, 1986).
Baker, G. P. and Hacker, P. M. S., *An Analytical Commentary on the Philosophical Investigations* (Oxford: Blackwell, 1990), 3 vols.
Barrett, R. B. and Gibson, R., eds., *Perspectives on Quine* (Oxford: Blackwell, 1990).
Canfield, J. V., ed., *The Philosophy of Wittgenstein* (New York and London: Garland Publishing Company, 1986–1988), 15 vol.

Clark, R. W., *The Life of Bertrand Russell* (London: Cape and Weidenfeld & Nicolson. 1975).

Gibson, R., *The Philosophy of W.V. Quine* (Gainesville, FL: University Presses of Florida, 1982).

Grayling, A. C., *Russell* (Oxford: Oxford University Press. 1996).

Hacker, P. M. S., *Wittgenstein's Position in Twentieth Century Analytic Philosophy* (Oxford: Oxford University Press, 1996).

Hahn, L. E. and Schilpp, P. A., eds., *The Philosophy of W.V. Quine* (La Salle, IL: Open Court, 1986).

Johnston, P., *Wittgenstein: Rethinking the Inner* (London: Routledge, 1993).

Kripke, Saul, *Wittgenstein on Rules and Private Language* (Oxford: Blackwell, 1982).

McGinn, M., *Sense and Certainty: A Dissolution of Scepticism* (Oxford: Blackwell, 1989).

Monk, R., *Bertrand Russell* (London: Jonathan Cape, 1996), 2 vols.

Monk, R., *Ludwig Wittgenstein* (London: Jonathan Cape, 1990).

Orenstein, A. and Kotatko, P., eds., *Knowledge, Language and Logic: Questions for Quine*, Boston Studies in the Philosophy of Science (Dordrecht: Kluwer, 1998).

Savage, C. W. and Anderson, C. A., eds., *Rereading Russell: Essays in Bertrand Russell's Metaphysics and Epistemology* (Minneapolis, MN: University of Minnesota Press, 1989).

Schilpp, Paul A., ed., *Philosophy of Bertrand Russell* (New York: Harper & Row, Publishers, Incorporated, 1963), 2 vols.

CHAPTER 18: PHENOMENOLOGY AND EXISTENTIALISM

Original Writings:

Heidegger, Martin, *Basic Writings* (New York: Harper & Row, Publishers, 1977).

Heidegger, Martin, *Being and Time* (London: SCM Press, 1962).

Heidegger, Martin, *Poetry, Language, Thought*, tr., A. Hofstadter (New York: Harper & Row, Publishers, 1971).

Husserl, Edmund, *Ideas: A General Introduction to Pure Phenomenology* (New York: The Macmillan Company, 1937).

Husserl, Edmund, *Phenomenology and the Crisis of Philosophy* (New York: Harper & Row, Publishers, Incorporated, 1965).

Husserl, Edmund, *The Paris Lectures* (The Hague, Netherlands: Nartinus Nijhoff, 1964).

Jaspers, Karl, *Man in the Modern Age* (New York: Doubleday & Company, Inc., Garden City, 1957).

Jaspers, Karl, *Philosophy and the World* (Chicago: Henry Regnery Company, 1963).

Jaspers, Karl, *Reason and Existenz* (New York: Noonday Books, Farrar, Straus & Cudahy, 1957).

Jaspers, Karl, *Truth and Symbol* (New Haven, Conn.: College and University Press, 1962).

Kaufmann, Walter, ed., *Existentialism* (Cleveland: The World Publishing Company, 1956).

Kern, Edith, ed., *Sartre* (Englewood Cliffs, N.J.: Prentice-Hall, 1963.

Marcel, Gabriel, *Man Against Mass Society* (Chicago: Henry Rignery Company, 1962).

Marcel, Gabriel, *Mystery of Being* (Chicago: Henry Rignery Company, 1960) 2 vols.

Marcel, Gabriel, *Philosophy of Existentialism* (New York: The Citadel Press, 1961).

Merleau-Ponty, Maurice, *Primacy of Perception*, tr., William Cobb (Evanston, IL: Northwestern University Press, 1964).

Merleau-Ponty, Maurice, *The Phenomenology of Perception*, tr., Colon Smith (London: Routledge & Kegan Paul, 1962).

Merleau-Ponty, Maurice, *Visible and the Invisible,* tr., Alphonso Lingis (Evanston, Ill.: Northwestern University Press, 1968).

Sartre, Jean-Paul, *Being and Nothingness* (New York: Philosophical Library, 1956).

Sartre, Jean-Paul, *Existentialism and Human Emotions* (New York: Philosophical Library, 1947).

Sartre, Jean-Paul, *Sartre By Himself* (New York: Urizen Books, Incorporated, 1978).

Sartre, Jean-Paul, *The Critique of Dialectical Reason* (London: NLB, 1976).

Critical Studies:

Beauvoir, Simone de, *Adieux: A Farewell to Sartre,* tr. Patrick O'Brian (New York: Pantheon Books, 1984).

Caws, P., *Sartre* (London: Routledge & Kegan Paul. 1979).

Caws, Peter, *Sartre* (Routledge, Chapman and Hall, 1984).

Cohen-Solal, A., *Sartre: A Life* (New York: Pantheon, and London: Heinemann. 1987).

Howells, C., ed., *The Cambridge Companion to Sartre* (Cambridge: Cambridge University Press, 1992).

Howells, C., *Sartre: The Necessity of Freedom* (Cambridge: Cambridge University Press, 1988).

Kockelmans, J. L., *Phenomenology: The Philosophy of Edmund Husserl and Its Interpretation* (Garden City, NY: Doubleday and Company, 1967).

Mehta, J. L., *Martin Heidegger: The Way and the Vision* (Honolulu: University of Hawaii Press, 1976).

Murdoch, Iris, *Sartre. Romantic Rationalist* (New York: Viking, 1987).

Pietersma, Henry, ed., *Merleau-Ponty: Critical Essays* (Washington, DC: University Press of America, 1990).

Sallis, J., *Delimitations: Phenomenology and the End of Metaphysics* (Bloomington, IN: Indiana University Press, 1995).

Schilpp, P. A., *The Philosophy of Jean-Paul Sartre* (La Salle, Ill.: Open Court Publishing Company, 1981).

Schmidt, James, *Maurice Merleau-Ponty: Between Phenomenology and Structuralism* (New York: St. Martin's Press, 1985).

Schürmann, R., *Heidegger on Being and Acting: From Principles to Anarchy* (Bloomington, IN: Indiana University Press, 1987).

Smith, B. and Woodruff Smith, D., eds., *The Cambridge Companion to Husserl* (Cambridge: Cambridge University Press, 1995).

Smith, B. and Woodruff Smith, D., eds, *The Cambridge Companion to Husserl* (Cambridge: Cambridge University Press, 1995).

Whiteside, Kerry H., *Merleau-Ponty and the Foundation of an Existential Politics* (Princeton, N.J.: Princeton University Press, 1988).

Wilcocks, R., ed., *Critical Essays on Jean-Paul Sartre* (Boston: G. K. Hall. 1988).

CHAPTER 19: RECENT PHILOSOPHY

Original Writings:

Anscombe, G. E. M., *Collected Philosophical Papers* (Minneapolis, MN: University of Minnesota, Press, 1981) 3 vols.

Armstrong, D. M., *A Materialist Theory of the Mind* (London: Routledge & Kegan Paul, 1968).

Derrida, Jacque, *Of Grammatology,* tr. G. Spivak (Chicago, IL: University of Chicago Press, 1974).

Derrida, Jacque, *Speech and Phenomena and Other Essays on Husserl's Theory of Signs,* tr., D. Allison (Evanston, IL: Northwestern University Press, 1973).

Derrida, Jacque, *Writing and Difference,* tr. A. Bass (Chicago, IL: University of Chicago Press, 1978).

Lévi-Strauss, Claude, *Structural Anthropology* (New York: Basic Books, 1963).

Noddings, Nel, "Ethics from the Stand Point Of Women", in Deborah L. Rhode, ed., *Theoretical Perspectives on Sexual Difference* (New Haven, CT: Yale University Press, 1990).

Noddings, Nel, *Caring: A Feminine Approach to Ethics and Moral Education* (Berkeley, CA: University of California Press, 1984).

Rorty, Richard, *Consequences of Pragmatism* (Minneapolis: University of Minnesota Press, 1982).

Rorty, Richard, *Contingency, Irony, and Solidarity* (Cambridge: Cambridge University Press, 1989).

Rorty, Richard, *Linguistic Turn* (Chicago: The University of Chicago Press, 1988).

Rorty, Richard, *Philosophy and the Mirror of Nature* (Princeton, N.J.: Princeton University Press, 1979).

Ryle, Gilbert, *Dilemmas* (Cambridge: Cambridge University Press, 1960).

Ryle, Gilbert, *The Concept of Mind* (New York: Barnes & Noble, 1950).

Saussure, Ferdinand de, *Course in General Linguistics,* tr. W. Baskin (Glasgow: Fontana/Collins, 1977).

Searle, John R., "Minds, Brains, and Programs," *Behavioral and Brain Sciences* (1980), 3: 417–24.

Searle, John R., *Minds, Brains, and Science* (Cambridge, Mass.: Harvard University Press, 1984).

Smart, J. J. C., "Sensations and Brain Processes," *Philosophical Review* (1959), 68: 141–56.

Critical Studies:

Culler, J., *Saussure* (Glasgow: Fontana/Collins, 1976).

Descombes, V., *Modern French Philosophy,* tr. L. Scott-Fox and J. M. Harding (Cambridge: Cambridge University Press, 1980).

Held, Virginia, *Feminist Morality: Transforming Culture, Society, and Politics* (Chicago, IL: University of Chicago Press, 1993).

Leach, E., *Lévi-Strauss,* Modern Masters Series (London: Fontana, 1970).

Lepore, E. and van Gulick, R., eds., *John Searle and his Critics* (Oxford: Blackwell, 1991).

Lyons, W., *Gilbert Ryle: An Introduction to His Philosophy* (Brighton: Harvester Press, and Atlantic Highlands, NJ: Humanities Press, 1980).

Merquior, J. G., *From Prague to Paris. A Critique of Structuralist and Post-structuralist Thought* (London: Verso, 1986).

Norris, C., *Derrida* (London: Fontana, 1987).

Rosenthal, D. M., ed., *The Nature of Mind* (London: Oxford University Press, 1991).

Saatkamp, H. J., Jr., ed., *Rorty & Pragmatism: The Philosopher Responds to His Critics* (Nashville, TN, and London: Vanderbilt University Press, 1995).

Tong, Rosemarie, *Feminine and Feminist Ethics* (Belmont, CA: Wadsworth, 1993).

Index

624–546 B.C.	Thales
active ca. 525–500 B.C.	Pythagoras
500–428 B.C.	Anaxagoras
ca. 490–421 B.C.	Protagoras
ca. 490–430 B.C.	Leucippus
ca. 490–430 B.C.	Empedocles
b. ca. 489 B.C.	Zeno
ca. 470–399 B.C.	Socrates
ca. 460–360 B.C.	Democritus
ca. 428–ca. 348 B.C.	Plato
384–322 B.C.	Aristotle
ca. 361–ca. 270 B.C.	Pyrrho
341–271 B.C.	Epicurus
ca. 96–55 B.C.	Lucritius
ca. 60–117	Epictetus
ca. 200	Sextus Empiricus
354–430	Saint Augustine
1033–1109	Saint Anselm
1221–1274	Saint Bonaventura
1225–1274	Saint Thomas Aquinas
1533–1592	Michel de Montaigne
1564–1642	Galileo
1588–1679	Thomas Hobbes
1596–1650	René Descartes
1623–1662	Blaise Pascal
1632–1677	Baruch Spinoza
1632–1704	John Locke
1642–1727	Sir Isaac Newton
1646–1716	Gottfried Leibniz
1685–1753	George Berkeley
1711–1776	David Hume
1712–1778	J. J. Rousseau